KU-690-967

FRED TERMAN AT STANFORD

Fred Terman at Stanford

Building a Discipline,

a University,

and Silicon Valley

C. STEWART GILLMOR

Stanford University Press   Stanford, California 2004

Stanford University Press
Stanford, California

Printed in the United States of America on acid-free, archival-quality paper

Assistance for publication of this book was provided by The School of Engineering, Stanford University.

Library of Congress Cataloging-in-Publication Data

Gillmor, C. Stewart
Fred Terman at Stanford : building a discipline, a university, and Silicon Valley / C. Stewart Gillmor.
p. cm.
ISBN 0-8047-4914-0 (alk. paper)
1. Terman, Frederick Emmons, 1900–1982. 2. Radio engineers—California—Stanford—Biography. 3. Stanford University. Dept. of Electrical Engineering. I. Title.

TK6545.T47 G55 2004
621.384'092—dc22

2003025166

Original Printing 2004
Last figure below indicates year of this printing:
13 12 11 10 09 08 07 06 05 04

Typeset by Alan Noyes in 10/14 Janson

Contents

Foreword

Richard Atkinson

"Father of Silicon Valley": these words seem to leap from the page. Invariably this is the only description now applied to Fred Terman in newspaper and magazine articles. It is not an inaccurate title, but it hardly begins to do justice to the genius that was Frederick Emmons Terman. It is difficult to know where to begin when describing him. He was without a doubt a brilliant electrical engineer, a learned scholar who authored groundbreaking textbooks on radio engineering and electronics, an inspiring teacher who kindled the spirit of discovery in his students, and an academic administrator whose devotion to excellence and visionary leadership firmly set a university on the path toward greatness. It was the latter, coupled with the extraordinary depth of his vision that I find the most compelling and enduring of Fred's many accomplishments. When all is said and done, one cannot separate Fred Terman from Stanford University, for their stories are inextricably intertwined.

Fred Terman set a standard of excellence for the Stanford campus that has endured to this day. He was a driving force in the development of university policy, and his vision for Stanford and the surrounding community is still the envy of universities throughout the world. He ranks among the finest academic administrators in the history of American higher education. His theories on the development of a modern research university and his implementation of those theories have stood the test of time. I would strongly encourage any twenty-first-century administrator interested in developing a campus and its curriculum to study closely Fred Terman's work at Stanford.

It seems strange that a man who would alter the course of a university would spend the better part of his life in one place, only occasionally venturing away from that university and from academic life. Fred Terman grew up at Stanford and his entire career, except for the war years, was essentially spent at the university. His devotion to Stanford was total, and his love for that institution led him to work ceaselessly on its behalf. He and Stanford's legendary president, Wallace Sterling, took what was considered a respected university and transformed it into one of the truly great universities in the world.

That transformation seems to have had its beginning during Fred Terman's tenure in the Department of Electrical Engineering. As the department grew in stature, so did Fred as an academic administrator. He recruited the most talented students in the field. He encouraged those students to stay in the area, as he himself had done, and to use their knowledge to create what we now refer to as start-up companies. From there it was a natural progression for him to develop close ties with local industries begun by his students. I have always felt that the cross-fertilization between academic and industrial research, encouraged by Terman more than a half century ago, is one reason why university scientific discoveries are so rapidly translated into new industries, companies, products, and services. It is also one of the reasons the United States generates new companies, new jobs, new products and services at a much faster pace than the rest of the world.

But, once again, the creation of the Silicon Valley is only a portion of Fred Terman's work that is worthy of examination. As an academic, he not only recognized the necessity of providing a broad curriculum for engineering students, but he was also, as Stewart Gillmor points out, "especially interested in the multifaceted interdepartmental approaches to academic planning and research." For instance, under Provost Terman, although I was a professor of psychology, I also held appointments in the School of Engineering, the School of Education, the Applied Mathematics and Statistics Laboratories, and the Institute for Mathematical Studies in the Social Sciences. Terman understood the value to students and faculty of cross-disciplinary work and encouraged its development to the greatest extent possible.

Terman knew that for Stanford to mature, it would have to focus on what it could do best—what he commonly referred to as "steeples of excellence." He had a tremendous sense of quality and encouraged the establishment of departments and growth in areas where Stanford could be truly superlative—engineering, physics, chemistry, mathematics, and computer science, to name but a few. "Mediocrity" was not in Terman's vocabulary, and he constantly strove for excellence in every aspect of his own life and in the life of Stanford and its students. He was extremely adept at acquiring government funding to support activities that had the potential to attract faculty of the highest order. Although controversial, his solicitation and use of government money served to, as Gillmor points out, "dramatically improve Stanford's financial base," thus making it possible to recruit some of the finest faculty in the country. By the end of Terman's career, Stanford had become an institution of higher education known throughout the world for adhering to the highest standards of excellence. And academics clamored to gain appointment at the university.

If there is a model for me in academic life, it is Fred Terman. I was a member of the Stanford faculty for almost twenty-five years. During much of that time, Fred was provost of the campus, working closely with President Sterling on the vitalization of the institution. We were brought together by Albert Bowker, who was one of Fred's closest associates and an exceptional academic administrator in his own right; he would later become chancellor of the University of California, Berkeley. I was able to apply the knowledge I gained from Fred's work at Stanford years later when I became chancellor of the University of California, San Diego (UCSD). I sought to use the "Terman Model" as a roadmap for UCSD's partnerships with the telecommunications and biotechnology industries that were beginning to spring up in the region, and as I encouraged the development of UCSD's own peaks of excellence. We were successful in San Diego, and I owe a debt of gratitude to Fred Terman for providing me with a perspective on the evolving role of the research university.

Fred Terman was a brilliant, complex, and unassuming man. He never sought recognition, but preferred to remain in the background, to bask in the reflected glow of Stanford's newfound glory. When I think of Fred, I am often reminded of a quote from the Chinese philosopher Lao Tzu:

> Therefore the sage holds in his embrace the one thing (of humility), and manifests it to all the world. He is free from self-display, and therefore he shines; from self-assertion, and therefore he is distinguished; from self-boasting, and therefore his merit is acknowledged; from self-complacency, and therefore he acquires superiority. It is because he is thus free from striving that therefore no one in the world is able to strive with him.*

The time has come for an in-depth examination of the remarkable growth and development of Stanford University and the role Fred Terman played in its post–World War II transformation. I am pleased that Stewart Gillmor is giving the world an opportunity to know Fred Terman not simply as the creative force behind the development of Silicon Valley, but also as a superlative engineer and researcher and as an academic administrator of uncommon vision.

Richard C. Atkinson
President Emeritus
University of California

* Lao Tzu, *Tao Te Ching*, trans. James Legge (Oxford: Oxford University Press, 1891; reprint, Mineola, NY: Dover Publications, 1997), 19.

Preface

Fred Terman was the first faculty member I met when I entered Stanford in the fall of 1956. I had chosen Stanford partly because of its outstanding electrical and radio engineering programs. I carefully read several university catalogs, but applied only to Stanford, resisting the pressure to attend either a fine technical institution in Southern California or a fine old Ivy League university. Respected engineers in Kansas City had told me that Terman was *the* outstanding radio engineering educator.

It was not an unusual meeting. Fred had begun his tenure as provost of the university the year before, and perhaps was filling in for President Wallace Sterling as official greeter when some thirteen hundred of us frosh trooped up to the President's House for a social gathering on our first weekend on campus. I remember standing in line, walking uphill and across the lawn to the receiving line under the trees and coming to Provost Terman. He greeted me, asked where I was from, and in what subject I hoped to major. I responded simply, "Kansas City, and Radio Engineering." "Good Man!" said Terman, adding a few remarks I don't remember, shaking my hand and passing me along to a dean or to the refreshment table.

I never had any further conversations with Fred Terman, although I saw him numerous times coming and going from his office in the campus Quad's old Engineering Corner. He was a kindly looking, somewhat rumpled man with glasses and tousled hair, of medium height and weight, dressed in a suit and vest. He always walked with a purpose, carrying files of paper. He never ambled. Once he became provost, Terman no longer had time to teach radio engineering courses, and although I heard him lecture on occasion, I never had the opportunity to take a class with him. Although I knew Fred Terman more by reputation than experience, I did come to know his youngest son, Lew, an electrical engineering graduate student and a member of the Stanford student radio station, KZSU, where

Lew and I served as part-time jazz disk jockeys and fellow cornet players. I also came to know and study with perhaps a dozen Stanford faculty members who had been Fred Terman's students in their undergraduate or graduate days, and I studied with others who had worked with him during World War II or who had taught with him for years. I dedicate this book to two such longtime students and associates of Fred Terman—to Robert A. "Bob" Helliwell and to the memory of Oswald G. "Mike" Villard Jr. Mike Villard came to Stanford from Yale as a graduate student in 1938, and Bob Helliwell was a homegrown Palo Alto product, entering Stanford as a freshman in the fall of 1938. (Villard and Helliwell became Terman's first students to be elected to the National Academy of Sciences.) Their stories, along with many others, are woven into this volume.

I am also deeply grateful to two other Terman students, William R. Hewlett and David Packard. Grants from the William R. Hewlett Revocable Trust and the David and Lucile Packard Foundation have provided the financial support to make this biography possible. William Hewlett and David Packard were among the earliest and certainly rank as the most generous of the successful entrepreneurs in the twentieth century's high-tech world. Their pride in Fred Terman's achievements and in Stanford was perhaps only exceeded by Fred Terman's continued delight in the success of Bill and Dave and of their company, Hewlett-Packard. In the spirit of their helpfulness to Stanford—a spirit fostered by Fred Terman—all royalties gained from the publication of this volume go to the Hewlett-Packard Graduate Engineering Fellowships at Stanford University.

My participation in this project also was facilitated by John Hennessy and Joseph Goodman (then Stanford's dean and senior associate dean of engineering, respectively) and by Laura Breyfogle, the Engineering School's senior associate dean for external relations. Later in the project I was assisted by the new dean of engineering, James Plummer. I am grateful for the hospitality shown to me by the Department of Electrical Engineering at Stanford and by Professor Umran Inan and the StarLab Group. I am also indebted to the generous sabbatical policy of Wesleyan University, my academic home for more than thirty years.

This project has fully occupied me for seven years, although of course I have been writing about the history of physics and engineering for many more years than that. I owe thanks for courteous professional assistance to the Harvard University Archives; to the Bancroft Library at the University of California, Berkeley; to the staff of the Archives at the Massachusetts Institute of Technology; to the archival staff and members of the Association of Old Crows, Alexandria, Virginia; to the Palo Alto (California) City Library and Palo Alto High School; to the Princeton University Archives; to the U.S. National Archives; to the Hewlett-Packard Company Archives; and to the archival center of the Institute of Electrical and Electronic Engineers for electronic transcripts of interviews. I am immensely grateful to Stanford University, particularly to the Department of Special Collections of the Green Library, and additional libraries at Stanford for help of all kinds in locating and providing materials. Patricia E. White of the Stanford University Archives and Jean Deken of the Stanford Linear Accelerator Center were very helpful. I especially wish to thank Karen Bartholomew. Her great store of knowledge of Stanford and its history frequently led me to important documents; she has shown me invaluable passageways through the archives, for which I am deeply indebted.

I wish to thank members of the Terman family for interviews, correspondence, and photographic materials, and especially Fred's sons Lewis Madison Terman II and Terence Christopher Terman, his granddaughter Patricia Terman, niece Doris Tucker, and Sibyl Terman's nieces Coralie Somers and Myrilla Sparhawk. I have personally interviewed or corresponded with many people in connection with this biography, and I cite more than ninety of them in endnotes. I thank them all.

It is sometimes fun and often times trying to read a manuscript in progress, and particularly to be honest in comments to the author. A number of readers have assisted me. For their helpful criticism, I wish to acknowledge Bob Beyers, Albert Bowker, Gene Franklin, Joseph Goodman, Bob Helliwell, Margaret Kimball, Cassius L. Kirk Jr., Cecilia Miller, Stephen W. Miller, William F. Miller, Alan Nathanson, and Oswald G. Villard Jr. Other, helpful readers read parts of chapters in draft. I thank an outside reader for the Stanford University Press for his honest and helpful comments, and I thank also editor Norris Pope and Press staff for their extended assistance.

A very special note of thanks goes to Dr. Roxanne Nilan, historian, author, and former university archivist at Stanford, who has greatly assisted me in editing and improving the manuscript. "Rocky" has gone beyond the expected and even the hoped-for in bringing to my use her writing skills and her extensive knowledge of Stanford and the Stanford community.

In looking back as an undergraduate student at Stanford, I have memories of so many faculty as teachers or advisors: Harry Rosenberg in history; Edwin Goode, religion; Tom Arp and Thom Gunn, English; Ken Clark, Sandy Huntley, and Stanley Donner, speech and drama; Jack Herriot, math; Quinn McNemar, psychology; Langdon White, geography; Felix Keesing, anthropology; Isabel Schevill, Spanish; George Parks and Fred Koenig, chemistry; John Vennard, civil engineering; Felix Bloch, Pief Panofsky, Marvin Chodorow, Nina Byers, Walter Meyerhof, Robert Hofstadter, and Charles Schwartz, physics; and Hugh Skilling, Von Eshleman, Ron Bracewell, Bob Helliwell, Allen Peterson, Mike Villard, Alan Waterman, Rudy Panholzer, Milton Hare, Willis Harman, Phil Gallagher, and Ralph Smith, electrical engineering. In writing of Fred Terman's life and career, I see these faculty members as if it were yesterday.

C. Stewart Gillmor
Higganum, Connecticut

FRED TERMAN AT STANFORD

INTRODUCTION

Building a Discipline, a University, and Silicon Valley

This biography is about a very unusual man, about his dedication to engineering, and about his pride and loyalty to his university and its surroundings. It is not a kiss-and-tell story of romance and skullduggery in Silicon Valley, nor is it a lives-of-the-saints tale of institution building—there are enough self-congratulatory volumes on the bookshelves.

Fred Terman was an outstanding American engineer, entrepreneur, and manager, but the scene here is the American university during the four decades surrounding World War II. The setting, more often than not, is Stanford University, for Terman spent nearly his entire life at Stanford, from his arrival as a faculty child at the age of ten until his death, at eighty-two, in his campus home. This book, therefore, is not just a biography but also an examination of university life and of the web of interactions he fostered among academia, government, and industry where the "product," at least for Fred Terman, was people.

During the past several decades, scholars have turned from more traditional institutional histories to analyze the influence on American higher education of governmental and industry funding, particularly in engineering and the sciences.[1] Initially, these writings had focused on American reactions to the threat by nuclear war, but the rise of "Big Science," backed by extensive federal funding, has come to occupy center stage.[2] This in turn has given rise to a historiography of university science and the cold war.[3] Such studies brought greater attention to the entwined, and at times controversial, relations between funding agencies and university educational policies, and they have emphasized the role played by senior university academic administrators in the emergence of major American research universities backed by large federal grants.[4]

Academic science enjoyed a huge rise in political influence and public prestige after World War II. Federal funds flowed into American universities in the postwar years, as Terman predicted, but did not arrive without constraints applied by the federal, often military, sponsors. Stanford and MIT make especially attractive subjects, and Fred Terman, as dean and provost, an attractive focal point.[5]

According to several authors, the rise of certain fields—among them nuclear and chemical weapons research, aeronautical research, electronic communications, countermeasures and radar, electronic computation, cryptography and associated mathematical techniques, geophysics, space physics, and biomedical fields—developed with the outbreak of war in Korea out of proportion to the natural balance of traditional university fields. Several additional fields outside of the sciences and engineering—psychology, political science, and foreign-language study—similarly developed only insofar as they could benefit the military-industrial complex. Some scholars go on to suggest, however, that other *non*governmental sources of support, notably from industry, also "altered the content" of university research, so much so that research agendas were no longer driven by faculty interests or student needs, but rather by more prosaic needs of administrators hungry for money.[6]

There is no such thing as a free lunch, even at a university. For the past two centuries, all American universities have reflected in their educational offerings, philosophies, and research agendas, the direct or indirect wishes of their funding sources. Ivy League endowments, rising in the nineteenth century, gathered in funds with strings attached by wealthy donors. Large state universities contend with governors and politically appointed boards of regents with their own thoughts on the appropriate goals for university teaching and research; private colleges founded by Gilded-Age industrialists reflect the personal and religious values of their founders. The increasing role of the federal government in American higher education after World War II is simply one of degree.

Fred Terman's formula for success, both in life and for his university, was fairly simple: hard work and persistence, systematic dedication to clearly articulated goals, accountability, not settling for mediocre work in yourself or in others. Such a strategy succeeded for him, and for Stanford, regardless of whether funding came from governmental agencies, industry support, idealistic benefactors, or devoted alumni. He firmly believed, and as an administrator maintained the policy, that sponsored research was taken on only if driven by individual faculty interest and if it benefited and involved students at a high level. He was not willing to let Stanford become a contract or job-shop factory; he envisioned a university where learning and research were intimately tied together as part of the teaching process.

He did not "network" for personal gain or to hook a juicy funding agency, but rather saw his own job as expediting a circle of relationships: professors and students, students into employees and managers, teachers and researchers; alumni into employers, inventors, builders, philanthropists. He was immensely proud of those students who followed full circle, becoming influential teachers and productive researchers, or creating viable products and companies, and coming back to Stanford not simply as donors but as supportive advisors and university trustees.

This book is not, therefore, an examination of the rise of electronics. Nor will it attempt to answer the mysteries behind the creation of that industrial research community later known as "Silicon Valley." Fred was not devoted to the electronics industry, or to research parks, or to the rise of Big Science and High-Tech. He was not even interested in earning great wealth. To an almost unimaginable degree, Fred Terman was devoted to his students, to engineering, and to Stanford University. This biography necessarily focuses on the weave of personality and place across time—as a faculty child growing up at an ambitious little regional university; as a young professor in the heady 1920s and the doldrums of the Depression; as an engineering manager and educator in the midst of large-scale wartime research projects and the postwar rise of Big Science and Big Engineering; as a university administrator on the razor's edge of great expectations and fragile budgets; and finally, as a senior statesman of engineering education.

Admittedly, Fred Terman looked at life as an engineer, and this story is thus also one of broadening horizons. As dean of engineering, Terman almost reveled in the opportunity to energize the many engineering and science fields he saw as interrelated, within electrical engineering, across the realms of electrical, mechanical, and civil engineering, and ultimately touching on chemistry, physics, geology, statistics and mathematics, and computer science. As provost, he was asked to put his management style and methods, and his assumptions about faculty and student quality, to the task of building Stanford's other undergraduate and graduate programs in the sciences, social sciences, and humanities. He did not intend to build "Terman Tech," as some feared, but agreed with President Wallace Sterling that Stanford, as a great university, had to be broad in its greatness. Faculty in the humanities did not always appreciate Terman's penchant for measurable results, and some thought he lacked empathy with their own goals and methods. Yet while Fred may not have understood the manners of humanists, he considered Stanford's social science and humanities departments to be important parts of the university and he firmly believed that they should be encouraged to be as strong as other campus departments.

At the height of his power as provost, there were plenty on campus who were in awe of Fred Terman, some who were unnerved and fearful, and some who despised and resented him. Throughout his life, Fred Terman was uncompromising in his expectations of himself, of his students, and of his fellow faculty. He was unflinching in his belief that quality could be quantified, and he was adamant that a university's success must, in the end, be measured by the success of its students.

To move ahead with confidence, to build on departmental strengths (and eliminate weaknesses), he looked for means to judge "quality" and methods to assure accountability. A full examination of his influence on his discipline, his university, and the evolving industrial research community that surrounds Stanford, requires both a wider and deeper examination of Provost Terman's work than has thus far been offered.

This book unfolds, as biographies are wont to do, chronologically, but this is especially important in the examination of the career of Fred Terman. He was not, as some want to portray him, a cold-hearted automaton, but a boy strongly influenced by his family and his hometown. Choosing the life of an academic, he straddled the world of engineering and that of the educator at a time of great changes in the professions, in higher education, in the country at large.

Fred was the son of the eminent Stanford psychologist Lewis M. Terman, whose reputation (and income) devolved from his studies of the "gifted" and from his development of quantitative testing methods of human intelligence. As a youth, he absorbed his father's belief that one can measure and quantify human effort, that even "quality" itself can be quantified, just as he absorbed family values of an almost obsessive industriousness, persistence, and personal ambition. Growing up in the household of an influential campus figure, he watched and absorbed the internal politics of university life. Although he would be offered many opportunities to go elsewhere, and would take advantage of several, Fred would always return home to Stanford—as the center of his career, but also as the center of three generations of Terman family life.

Like most Stanford faculty kids, Fred matriculated at his father's university, first going into mechanical engineering (electrical engineering was only a graduate program in 1916) but graduating in 1920 with a bachelor's degree in chemistry. His boyhood enthusiasm for the new field of radio, however, brought him to electrical engineering as a graduate student. Stanford was a good place to study electrical engineering in 1920. Power transmission expert Harris J. Ryan was at the helm of the Electrical Engineering Department, and Federal Telegraph Company, a world provider of the newest radio technology in those days, was located next door in Palo Alto. Radio was "hot" as stations popped up across the Santa Clara Valley. However, even Ryan understood that Stanford was limited in its potential for further study, and he encouraged Fred, determined to have an academic rather than an industry career, to attend MIT, the country's best technical institute, for his doctorate in electrical engineering.

As at Stanford, Fred continued his comparatively broad technical education, getting a thorough grounding in advanced chemistry and mathematics, as well as electrical engineering. As an excellent and industrious student, he made a strong impression, just as MIT and the associations he made there would have a strong influence on his career.

Although he had worked with Harris Ryan and subsequently with Vannevar Bush at MIT on power transmission studies, he returned to his first engineering love, radio, when he came back to Stanford. Radio was challenging electrical power for dominance in the field of electrical engineering, and Terman would play a major role, both nationally and internationally in developing the field of radio engineering (renamed "electronics" by the mid-1930s). With Fred's notable contributions as a teacher, text writer, and engineering society administrator, electrical engineering turned from an emphasis on power lines and illumination to one of electronics, communications, and information flow. The electron itself became the symbol of communication of information rather than that of production of heat and light.

Terman was an immensely popular professor of communications and radio engineering at Stanford, but he was also a catalyst. As a young professor and department head, he led the transformation of the Department of Electrical Engineering by attracting more and better-qualified students, by finding better fellowship and salary support, and by working hard at the grueling task of finding jobs for his students during the Depression. Although later mistaken as rigidly specialized, Fred sought to broaden his students' education, first by strengthening physics and mathematics instruction, and by improving their writing skills through better English instruction. By the end of the 1930s, his department faculty had become increasingly productive as teachers as well as scholars.

His skills honed by the challenges of Depression-era budgets, Terman was vigorous in attracting attention to his department in Stanford's alumni publications and popular journals, through an extensive correspondence with alumni and other engineers, through talks at universities and professional associations. He made a name for himself and for his department not only as an educator but also as *the* man in radio engineering. He set out to topple the leading text in radio engineering, and did so by producing several leading texts before he reached the age of forty. His texts, used throughout industry, government agencies, and the military services, as well as academia, also changed the atmosphere of graduate work at Stanford, for Terman not only kept problems and case studies in his texts relevant and up-to-date, but fully acknowledged and detailed the work of his own students.

Terman's impact on Stanford's Electrical Engineering Department was clear. In 1940, Stanford physicist William Hansen nominated Terman as a candidate for Stanford's presidency, pointing out that Stanford's radio engineering program was the best in the country; Terman knew how to attract the best. Retiring President Ray Lyman Wilbur also suggested Fred's name, but young Fred was a dark horse, and a reluctant candidate. Wartime agendas and Fred's own plans pointed elsewhere.

American intervention into the war in Europe and the Pacific was on the horizon. By December 1941, Fred had initiated three separate lines of research in communication and radio engineering at Stanford: electronic circuits, radio wave propagation studies, and electron tube design and construction. Stanford would become a world leader in each of these in the years following the war, but Fred's wide experience, his knowledge of the pool of young trained radio engineers, and his recent national presidency of the Institute of Radio Engineers (IRE) made him the logical choice to head a secret government effort to develop radar countermeasures: the Radio Research Laboratory at Harvard (RRL), a counterpart to MIT's Radiation Laboratory for radar. Terman's sojourn east, what he later called his "Harvard seasoning," would again shape his thinking and his career.

Fred built RRL from a group of six in early 1942 to a staff of more than eight hundred by summer 1943. By that summer, RRL's budget was larger than that of Stanford University. Working at a number of U.S. and foreign war-zone sites, RRL staff developed more than 150 radar countermeasures devices and saved an estimated 800 Allied bomber aircraft and their crews. (More than half of Germany's electronic research from late 1943 onward would be devoted to saving German radar systems from countermeasures efforts.) More than thirty Stanford graduates and faculty were on his technical staff of some two hundred twenty-five at the Radio Research Laboratory. Many of these people, joined by others from the MIT Radiation Lab, followed Terman, newly appointed dean of engineering, back to Stanford and to the fledgling Stanford Research Institute.

Terman's RRL experience of managing, planning, expediting, and working with a wide array of engineers and scientists, military officers and government officials, industry advisors and contractors, provided him with administrative skills that would come in handy over the next two decades. It also gave him the opportunity to think, and to absorb the advice of men like Harvard University treasurer Bill Claflin. For the next thirty years, he would mention his debt to Claflin, his Cambridge neighbor. Literally over the garden fence, Claflin talked to Terman about university strategies to recruit and support the best students and faculty. Stanford, Fred quickly realized, was a very minor player in government research, yet he also saw that after the war, government funds would flow into universities. He was determined that Stanford's Engineering School would be poised to excel in those fields bound to grow with the injection of major federal grants. Fields such as the electronics of circuits, radio wave propagation and electron tubes, thermodynamics and mechanical structures would become his first lines of department building in the years to come. He saw potential in the field of engineering economics, or industrial engineering, in the Civil Engineering Department, and possibilities for the development of engineering mechanics and aeronautics within mechanical engineering.

Fred Terman looked more broadly at Stanford's future even while back east during the war. In 1943, his twenty-year plan for Stanford's development, supported by the university's fledgling development office, captured the attention of Stanford President Donald Tresidder and Vice President Alvin Eurich. Terman was always able to see beyond strict boundaries. Fred's influence with Tresidder and the university's board of trustees helped firmly establish Bill Hansen's Microwave Laboratory at Stanford—the forerunner of Stanford's series of linear accelerators and the famous Stanford Linear Accelerator Center (SLAC). Fred's graduate students assisted in microwave projects nearly from day one, testing and developing the klystron tube. Dean Terman continued to encourage curriculum development in related fields, especially in chemistry, physics, geology, mathematics, statistics, and computer science.

As Fred expanded and strengthened the School of Engineering, his young faculty leaders attracted the interest of U.S. military research branches, and especially the Office of Naval Research (ONR). ONR contracts were supplemented by significant alumni support to build and expand Stanford's Electronics Research Laboratory (ERL) between 1951 and 1956. An Applied Electronics Laboratory (AEL) was added next door. Terman continued to seek innovative ways to work the circle of students, faculty, alumni, and employers for mutual benefit. In the early 1950s, he conceived of the Honors Cooperative program as a means to allow individuals in electrical engineering to enroll as part-time graduate students while working for local companies. Sponsoring firms paid double tuition to Stanford. This program, formalized in 1954, became so successful for both companies and Stanford that similar programs were created in other engineering departments and the School of Humanities and Sciences.

As electronics and aeronautical research and development took root in the towns surrounding Stanford during the 1950s, Stanford was ready to be the creative center. By the end of the decade, Terman was hailed as the magnet that drew talent together. Terman played a key role not only in attracting faculty, graduate students, and funding to Stanford, but also through his continued interest in Stanford land use and development. Generally supporting the university's policy of planned income-generating use of select portions of university property, his eye was on the commingling of university and industry research. Thus, in 1951, he helped Varian Associates become the university's first tenant in the Stanford Industrial (later, Research) Park, and he helped university officials line up other valued tenants.

Terman was not blindly pro-development, however. An influential member of the faculty Advisory Committee on Land and Building Development, he spoke against nonuniversity-related development of Stanford's foothills and favored preservation of an "academic reserve" of at least thirty-seven hundred acres. As Stanford trustees debated plans for nonuniversity residential housing developments, yet prohibitively high land lease costs for SLAC, the provost is remembered to have stated the case bluntly: it was time to decide whether Stanford was a research institution or a real estate operation. Terman not only saved the SLAC project but also insured the permanence of Jasper Ridge Biological Preserve.

In the early 1950s, Stanford President Wallace Sterling struggled with many of the same problems as his predecessors: locating new sources of funding to improve faculty salaries, student fellowship, buildings and facilities; to upgrading the university's undergraduate and graduate academic programs; revitalizing and relocating the medical school; and accommodating and balancing the many changes going on within academic fields. Sterling had created the post of university provost in 1952 to help with academic affairs, but the responsibilities of the post remained flexible. Sterling preferred picking the individual rather than the job description, but the times required great energy, creativity, and risk-taking, as well as a clear sense of direction. In 1955, he picked Fred Terman.

Sterling "struck it rich," he later recalled, when Terman joined him in 1955. Terman had enjoyed building a better engineering school, he told the president, and he now thought it would be fun to help build a stronger university. The two worked well together for the next ten years, a decade of unprecedented campus growth and rise in prestige for Stanford University in social sciences, fine arts, and humanities as well as science and engineering. No other university made such a remarkable rise in national ranking surveys during the 1950s and 1960s.

Terman transformed the office of provost into a powerful force on campus. Never particularly interested in popularity or campus politics, he was interested in building and in results. Fred loved numbers, tables, and charts, and he had a passion for full documentation. Much to the annoyance of some department heads and deans, he often knew a department's budget details far better than department chairs themselves. He expected department faculty search committees to compile detailed documentation on the individuals they wished to hire and expected them to know at least as much about the individual's career and the future potential of the field, as he did through his own inquiries. He was not averse to saying "no."

As he always had done, Terman left productive people alone so that they could get on with the job and he promoted those who, regardless of age or status, showed results. "Productivity" and "results" were not, in his view, amorphous concepts. He disliked whining, inefficiency, sloppy or incomplete work, but he was open to debate, to discussion of the ways in which fields he was less familiar with were changing, and to new fields of scholarship, new faces, and new methods. Fred was especially proud of overseeing the rebuilding of the Chemistry Department, the home of his BA degree, but he also spoke of his joy in bringing major scholars in history, for example, and in English, psychology, and political science to the Stanford faculty.

An incorrigible workaholic, Terman's intensity and directness could appear harsh and humorless. He could be very tough, but he was not as heartless as some would like to think. He was, in fact, a shy man, inclined to be kindly to students, staff, and colleagues alike. He is remembered fondly, even protectively, by those who worked closely with him.

After his retirement in 1965, Terman continued to speak out on the value of faculty quality and graduate student excellence and on the strategy that favored targeted "steeples of excellence" (and eliminated troughs of weakness) rather than broad-based mediocrity as the key to university success. Determined not to interfere with his successors (particularly when university campuses like Stanford erupted in antiwar protest), he directed his time to government and corporate boards, consulting and service to his professional organizations. He undertook rigorous studies of higher technical education for private, state, and national organizations in some twenty U.S. states and foreign countries. Of his many consultancies carried out after retirement, two efforts in particular would stand out in his mind. As president of the Southern Methodist University Foundation for Science and Engineering (1965–73), he played an important role in the rebuilding of engineering and the physical sciences at SMU. As an extension of earlier consulting in Asia, he assisted in the creation of the Korean Advanced Institute of Science (KAIS), an important contribution to Korea's economy as well as to the evolution of the Korean Advanced Institute of Science and Technology (KAIST).

It is difficult to exaggerate Fred Terman's devotion to Stanford, but he was also an ardent westerner. He sought not only to build Stanford but the San Francisco Bay Area, and to protect the West Coast from the cultural and industrial domination by the Eastern seaboard. This theme resonates throughout Fred's career. In the 1930s and 1940s Fred regretted the loss of his best students to colleges and jobs in the East. He sought, therefore, not only to provide more opportunities for advanced study at Stanford, but also to attract industry—and therefore employment—for his students back home in the West. Throughout his career but especially as president of the Institute of Radio Engineers, he sought for recognition of western engineers in national professional societies. (He was the first IRE president from west of Rochester, and later as vice president of the American Society for Engineering Education, he fought for greater western presence in that association and in the discipline.)

Shortly after his retirement, Terman told a graduate student group at Stanford that above the awards and prizes and promotions, his greatest personal reward had come from the opportunity granted to him to build things—the Electrical

Engineering Department, the Harvard Radio Research Lab, the School of Engineering, and finally, Stanford University itself. He had been given the chance, he said, to help students build their careers, to help the companies and institutions in which his students became involved. Years later, he wrote simply, "Stanford has been good to me. . . . If I had my life to live over again, I would play the same record."[7]

CHAPTER ONE

California Boy

1900–1924

Fred Terman was born in Indiana in the first year of the twentieth century, but until he was ten, his childhood associations were more with family than with place. The Terman family would move many times, around Indiana, to Massachusetts, and on to California, as Fred's father's academic career rose in higher education and the emergent field of psychology. By 1910, however, the Termans had taken root, settling down on the Stanford University campus. Lewis Terman's experience as an increasingly influential campus figure, as well as his academic interest in the quantification of human intelligence and potential, would strongly influence his son's perspective of the academic world.

Young Terman was gifted at his studies, both at Palo Alto High School and as a Stanford undergraduate during the turbulent years surrounding World War I. Fred completed a difficult and unusually broad undergraduate curriculum in engineering and chemistry, and he filled his summers with study or related technical work. Ambitious and driven as he was as a student, however, he also participated in sports and other activities, and he long treasured friendships and associations that he made at this time.

Fred's graduate work in electrical engineering at Stanford was a means rather than an end, for he would not go straight into industry like most of his classmates but was determined to follow his father into academia. His engineering mentor, Harris J. Ryan, like his father, encouraged Fred to study for his doctoral degree at MIT, the premier technical institution in the country. The influence of three MIT men—Arthur Kennelly, Norbert Wiener, and especially Vannevar Bush (who would play a key role in wartime and postwar scientific research)—would be long lasting.

Returning home to California in 1924, Fred was stricken with a bout of tuberculosis, a Terman family shadow. The months spent recuperating, however, would allow him to think about his future and where he could best make his mark. Balancing offers from both Stanford and MIT, he chose to return to his alma mater. He also chose to return to his first technical love, the rapidly growing field of radio and electronics.

Out of Indiana

Frederick Emmons Terman was born in Indiana in 1900, the first child and only son of Indiana-born schoolteachers. Both sides of Fred Terman's family fell squarely into the pioneering milieu of early nineteenth-century America—a distinctly protestant mix of Scots, northern Irish, Welsh, "Pennsylvania Dutch" (German), and French Huguenots, who, along with rural English families, had immigrated to the middle and southern colonies in the eighteenth century. Working the land, Terman's ancestors had farmed, married, and moved ever further west, into Kentucky, Ohio, and on to Indiana.

Fred's father, Lewis Terman, would have a particularly strong influence on his only son, not simply as a father but as an intellectual immersed in the study and encouragement of gifted children, and as a career academic. Young Fred Terman's own memories of Indiana would be few, but those of life as a faculty child were enduring. Before he was four, Fred was off on a family adventure, following his father's academic career briefly to Massachusetts, then on to California. By the time he was six, he was in the midst of Southern California's land boom; at ten, he was a part of Stanford University's campus community. Aside from several sojourns to Massachusetts, Stanford would be his home for the remainder of Fred's life.

Fred's father, Lewis Terman, had made a concerted effort to move beyond the confining influences of rural Midwestern life. Lewis was, in fact, somewhat astonished that what he saw as his own unremarkable, almost bleakly ordinary ancestry could produce a child like himself, that is, a bookish and unathletic boy, who craved intellectual companionship rather than the robust life of a farm child. Yet Lewis Terman's own family clearly represented many of the values he would impress on his son: an ambitious, industrious, and solidly prosperous family, they had been willing to confront the challenges of new territory and new lives. While promoting self-sufficiency among their children, they also respected intellectual curiosity and allowed Lewis, the eleventh of fourteen children, to find his own sense of accomplishment.[1]

Lewis Madison Terman had been born on January 15, 1877, the first son to survive in twelve years, into the large family of James William Terman, a prosperous farmer, and Martha Parthenia Cutsinger, the well-educated daughter of an equally comfortable farming family. The Terman's farm, near Franklin, in Johnson

County, Indiana, was located about seventeen miles southeast of Indianapolis. James Terman was an avid reader. His library of some two hundred books, including an *Encyclopedia Britannica*, was comparatively large for such a farming community, and he subscribed to numerous newspapers and periodicals.

A lively, affectionate, and industrious family, the Terman's older children played an important role in minding the younger ones. Lewis was especially attached to his eldest brother John, fourteen years his senior. John shared with Lewis his love of reading, his interest in music, and his ambition to move away from farming to teach.[2]

Post–Civil War America placed a new emphasis on self-improvement, but most Americans still associated success with character—a matter of industry, skill, and determination—rather than the product of academic attainment. For a family like the Termans, there had been little need to pursue more than an eighth-grade education, acquired over winters in a one-room schoolhouse. Lewis and his siblings, however, came of age as American higher education was expanding to meet the occupational needs of its pragmatic middling classes and emerging professions.

Lewis was especially good at his studies and loved schoolwork, completing the eighth grade by the time he was twelve. Nonetheless, young Lewis was sensitive about always being the youngest, the smallest, the least robust of his schoolmates; the world of scholarship provided him a path to success. At fifteen, he followed his brother John into teaching, matriculating at John's alma mater, Central Normal College, in Danville, Indiana, a few miles west of Indianapolis. He later considered his years at Danville to be among the happiest of his life.[3] Alternating his studies with stints at teaching, he earned two degrees (including a bachelor's degree in pedagogy) from the college by 1898. Along the way he also took charge of his first schoolroom at age seventeen, and eventually returned to Johnson County as teacher and principal of the high school.

While at Danville, eighteen-year-old Lewis met Anna Belle Minton, who was teaching school nearby. Born in Pulaski County, Indiana, on December 6, 1876, Anna was the daughter of Reuben B. Minton, farmer, merchant, and banker of Star City, and his wife, Sarah Jane Murray. Like the Termans, the self-made Minton traced his ancestry to Virginia by way of Kentucky. Lewis and Anna were married three years later, on September 18, 1899.[4]

The newlyweds settled into a farmhouse near the small village of English, Indiana, just north of the Indiana-Kentucky border and about forty miles west of Louisville, near his work at the high school. Less than a year later, on June 7, 1900, their first child, Frederick Emmons Arthur, was born. Fred's names were taken from those of three of Lewis's college friends: Frederick N. Duncan, who would later become a college professor of biology; Purley C. Emmons, who became a high school principal; and Arthur M. Banta, later a distinguished geneticist.[5] Fred Terman used all three prenames on official forms until he dropped

"Arthur" in high school, but throughout his life he preferred to be called simply "Fred."

Shortly after his son's birth, Lewis recovered from a brief but severe attack of tuberculosis. Tuberculosis had long plagued the Terman family—most of James Terman's nine siblings had died of "consumption" before the age of fifty, and Lewis's oldest sister died of the disease when he was three. Young Lewis may have been infected at that time. At the very least, he assumed, he had inherited a particular susceptibility to the disease, a condition apparently passed on to his own son, Fred. TB remained a serious health concern for Lewis throughout his adulthood. In 1900, his doctor told him to quit work and move to a more temperate climate, but he refused, worried about supporting his new family. Instead, he began a self-regimen that he would successfully employ later in life, combining bed rest, open-air walks, wide-open windows, and separate quarters to protect his wife and children.[6]

At Danville, Lewis had learned that teaching was a means, not simply an end. His teachers at Danville recognized his ambition and encouraged him to move on to Indiana University, close by and not too expensive, to work toward a university degree in educational psychology. Lewis allotted himself two years at Indiana University. The Termans moved to Bloomington in 1901, backed by family loans and a modest income earned by Anna, who took in student boarders. He was granted two years' university credit for his work at Central Normal College, and on schedule he graduated with both a bachelor's and a master's degree in 1903.

Although Lewis later viewed his master's thesis as unscientific, it foreshadowed his lifelong interest in distinguishing characteristics of gifted children. Using some of the ideas and techniques of the French psychologist Alfred Binet (who had developed a test to identify "slow children"), Lewis determined to measure leadership among children, defined as the tendency of an individual to rise to a position of influence within a group. He designed a test to measure a child's quickness in speaking up before others.[7]

Lewis Terman's university studies only whetted his academic appetite, however, and kindled his desire to become a college professor of psychology. He had read widely in philosophy, education, and psychology. Intellectually inspired and back in good health, Terman was again encouraged by professors to continue for a doctorate. He had two children now—daughter Helen Claire was born in Bloomington in 1903—an empty purse and growing school debts, but he turned down a faculty position at Central Normal School when he received a fellowship to Clark University. With yet further loans from his family, Terman moved his family to Worcester, Massachusetts.[8]

Founded in 1889, Clark University was small, and after Johns Hopkins, the second American campus devoted solely to graduate study. At the time Lewis attended (1903–5), it offered coursework only in biology, chemistry, mathematics, physics, and psychology. Clark's founding president was the noted psychologist G. Stanley Hall, a dominant figure in the child-study movement of the 1890s whose work had greatly influenced Lewis and his professors at Indiana. In the growing debate over the influence of environment versus the influence of heredity in the formation of a child's character, Hall came down squarely in favor of heredity. Yet he also believed that gifted children should be given special treatment and their capacities fostered—opinions that paralleled Terman's.

Hall, however, distrusted both mental testing and giftedness as fields of study, and felt quantitative methods were misleading.[9] Terman, in turn, became disillusioned by Hall as a scientist, but he found him an inspiring teacher. Hall's depth of reading, his intensity, and his Monday-night seminars given at his home were models for Terman's own university teaching.[10]

When Terman became interested in the processes involved in intelligence (the capacity to learn), he turned from Hall to Clark's model of a methodical empiricist, Edmund C. Sanford. Terman's dissertation, completed in 1905 under Sanford, compared two groups of boys—one group chosen as "bright," the other as "dull"—in their performance on a number of tests.[11] He worked for five months with a group of students with similar backgrounds and opportunities who had been selected by Worcester school principals and teachers as representing the extreme 2 percent at each hypothetical end. His statistical evaluation of data from a battery of eight tests was crude, but suggested a methodology worth continued study and reinforced Terman's belief that innate capacity to learn was more important than training.

Terman's experience at Clark shaped his career as an educator and psychologist as well as some of his firmest friendships. Three of Terman's closest friends—Edwin G. Boring, Arnold Gesell, and Robert M. Yerkes—were products of Clark University and Hall's teaching. Their scholarly interests—the psychology of genius, the measurement of intelligence and of differences among individuals, and the implications of school hygiene—echoed each other's and those of Hall.[12]

From East Coast to Far West

While at Clark, Lewis Terman's tuberculosis had flared up again. Finishing his doctorate, he decided to seek a position in a more congenial climate. He turned down university positions in Florida and Texas, and he chose a post as high school principal in San Bernardino, California. In 1905, the Termans moved west to a semiarid desert land that during Southern California's land boom of the 1880s had been turned into hundreds of square miles of orange groves.

Fred Terman's first view of California came as the train carrying his family sped across the Mojave Desert. "As our train coasted down the Cajon Pass," his father later wrote, "and the San Bernardino Valley opened up before us almost encircled by mountains of 4,000 to 11,000 feet, the Valley seemed to be truly the paradise that the chamber of commerce literature had depicted it." Although he told none of his new colleagues of his anxiety about his health, Lewis listened eagerly to their pride in their restorative climate. The townspeople, he remembered, were "as friendly and kind as the climate itself."

Within weeks of taking up his new position, Lewis had a more serious outbreak of hemorrhaging. Keeping his illness to himself, he went on daily walks and slept in a room with the windows open and was back at work in less than two weeks. That summer, Fred and his family spent several months camping high in the San Bernardino mountains, where he shared with his father a love of the outdoors while learning from Lewis's determination and self-sufficiency in dealing with his bouts of tuberculosis.[13]

Although the year had gone well—Lewis found his work interesting, his colleagues competent and cooperative, and his neighbors friendly—he moved ahead on an opportunity at college-level teaching when he was offered the position of professor of child study and pedagogy at the Los Angeles State Normal School, located downtown.[14] In the fall of 1906, the Termans moved to Hollywood, a pretty, upscale suburb of about four thousand to the northeast of Los Angeles. Before leaving on yet another summer in the mountains, the Termans bought an acre north of Glendale in the San Fernando Valley at the foot of the Verdugo Mountains along Valley View Road.[15]

Fred Terman had fond memories of the house in Glendale, where the family lived for the next three years. Despite the distance, the commute to Los Angeles was easy on the new "Red Line," the interurban trolley system that linked hundreds of small towns throughout five Southern California counties. Fred's father could leave at 8:30 AM, and be home in time to work in the garden before dinner. In 1908, the four Termans posed for a family photograph, proudly working in their vegetable garden.

When Lewis Terman's friend and colleague Arnold Gesell, arrived in January 1908 to take a new position in psychology at the Normal School, Gesell and his brother Robert built a bungalow in an orange grove across the road from the Termans. The brothers appointed Fred "chief-assistant builder," claiming later to have seen early signs of his engineering talent.[16]

Like his father, Fred was allowed to develop his own interests without parental pressure and enjoyed introspective play and wandering the outdoors on his own. Lewis believed his own children—or at least his son—should develop talents at their own pace. Fred was taught reading and arithmetic at home by his mother and was not placed into school until he was nine, when he entered third grade in Glendale. Although a year behind when he began, like his father he enjoyed school and soon caught up. He would graduate at twelve years old from the eighth grade.[17]

Fred's stay at the Glendale school, however, was short-lived. Lewis's health and confidence were now fully restored, and he was restless for a more stimulating intellectual environment. In 1910, he was offered a position in the Department of Education at Stanford University. John Howard Bergstrom, Terman's former professor at Indiana, had moved to Stanford in 1909 to fill a newly created position in educational psychology but had died shortly after. Terman was highly recommended as a replacement. While speaking in Los Angeles at a teachers' institute, Professor Elwood P. Cubberley, head of Stanford's Education Department, was introduced to Terman, and the two got along famously.[18] Terman accepted the position, even though Stanford's salary offer was below his Normal School salary. "I found myself," Lewis later wrote with joyous hindsight, "a member of the faculty of Stanford University, the university that I would have chosen before any other in the world."[19]

Stanford and the Valley of Heart's Delight

In the summer of 1910, the Termans moved four hundred fifty miles north to Palo Alto, a university town on the northerly reaches of the Santa Clara Valley, the "Valley of Heart's Delight," some forty miles south of San Francisco.

Lewis's search for a gratifying intellectual environment was fulfilled. His career soon blossomed at Stanford, and the Terman family took deep root in Stanford soil. But if one journey came to an end, another began. Lewis and especially his son Fred would pursue careers devoted not only to their individual fields of study but to the university itself. Fred Terman's identification with and devotion to Stanford was grounded in far more than alumni sentimentality. His life had already been shaped by his father's personality, beliefs in child rearing, and bouts with tuberculosis. His experiences as a faculty child, his close association with a young and ambitious university, and his youth spent near a burgeoning electronics industry would now direct his path into engineering and academia.

Although not yet twenty years old in 1910, Stanford University had evolved considerably from its first years as a struggling campus on a California rail baron's ranch. Lewis Terman had no doubt learned something of the Stanford legend while still in Indiana, for Stanford's first president, David Starr Jordan, had been stolen away from Indiana University. Jordan, in turn, had drawn among his friends and colleagues at Indiana and other Midwestern universities as well as his own alma mater, Cornell, to build Stanford's first faculty in the early 1890s.[20]

The founding of Stanford University in 1885 had created something of a sensation in the insular world of American higher education. Leland Stanford, railroad president and land baron, former California governor and soon to be elected to the U.S. Senate, envisioned an educational complex from kindergarten through graduate study in memory of his son, Leland Jr. Opening its doors in October 1891, Leland Stanford Junior University was much-pared down in structure, but not in philosophical substance: as promised, it offered its students a tuition-free, nonsectarian, coeducational university education, with courses in engineering and the sciences, humanities and social sciences. Although equipped at the outset with only fifteen professors, barely adequate student housing, inconvenient community services, and only a dozen buildings yet completed from its grandiose quadrangle architectural plan, the new California campus attracted more than 400 students on opening day, the first day of registration; by spring 1892 the student body numbered 555, including 116 upperclassmen and 37 graduate students.[21]

Stanford's student body came from across the country (many upperclassmen, like the graduate students, had followed their faculty from the Midwest and upstate New York), although some two-thirds came from California. Many came from families like the Termans—farm families sending their children to college for the first time. Indeed, Stanford University was intended for the upwardly mobile middling classes, not to serve as "educational millinery," as Leland Stanford himself put it, for the urban elite. Its founding grant articulated Senator Stanford's firm belief in individualism and the work ethic, and the fundamental assumption that through education, the public can best govern itself and promote the general welfare.

Stanford's commitment to coeducation was controversial, but its first efforts at affirmative action—accepting as "special" students those who did not meet minimum entrance requirements (nearly 25 percent of its first year's student body were "specials")—brought fierce criticism from competing campuses alleging lowered academic standards. The policy was aimed at older, working students who had not had the opportunity to attend an accredited high school and could not afford tutoring. Many of these young men had their eyes on engineering jobs. Just as he had done in Indiana, President Jordan stumped the rural communities of California during summers to encourage young people to further their education and improve their lives. Since no "direct assistance" (scholarships or fellowships) yet existed, however, the distinctive presence of working students—those who had to earn enough for living expenses, books, lab fees, and travel fare—remained a prominent factor in Stanford's college life. The university remained committed to their cause for decades.[22]

The university's purpose was simple: "to qualify its students for personal success, and direct usefulness in life." Its curriculum lent itself toward engineering, field sciences, and teaching. Aside from the undeniable attractions of the climate, the absence of tuition, and the sense of adventure offered by Stanford, many students (and their parents) were drawn by the practicality and flexibility of the curriculum. Most male students majored in the sciences, engineering, and preprofessional majors such as education and law. Some 25 percent of women students (as compared to 4 percent nationally) majored in the sciences. Students, male and female, who chose humanities and social sciences often took additional coursework to qualify for a California teacher's certificate.[23]

While students were continually reminded to keep practical career goals in mind, they were encouraged to select electives widely. The concept of a broadly educated Stanford student was taken seriously among the engineering and science faculty as it was among the humanists. Soon after opening, Stanford could boast of twenty-five departments (though some were staffed by only one faculty member), offering a wide range of electives. For many years, the only subject required to graduate was English, the only major requirements were those determined by each student with a "major professor" or mentor.

The university's bright hopes had been sidetracked by financial problems brought about by Senator Stanford's death in 1893 and the country's severe economic depression, but it had recovered by the end of the century. The university library had taken shape, as did several campus laboratories. Hopkins Seaside Laboratory (today's Hopkins Marine Laboratory) opened on Monterey Bay in the summer of 1892. The Geology Department's first field trip in 1892 had evolved into a regular series of summer surveys by 1902, sponsored by the U.S. Geological Survey. In 1903, a new chemistry building opened, lauded as one of the best-designed and -equipped chemistry laboratories and teaching facilities in the United States.

By the time Lewis Terman arrived at Stanford, the newness had worn off. Its current student body, now numbering 1,442 undergraduates and 157 graduate students, had no memory of Leland Stanford and of Jane Stanford, who passed away in 1905. The 1906 San Francisco earthquake left serious scars. Ornamental portions of the memorial campus completed by that spring—the massive Memorial Arch, Memorial Church's steeple, and sections of the outer quadrangle and museum—had been lost, along with the grandiose new library and gymnasium buildings, but reconstruction began quickly. A new sense of confidence and promise had reasserted itself by 1910. A major expansion of the academic program occurred in 1908 when Stanford acquired the facilities and property of the Cooper Medical College of San Francisco. Stanford had established a reputation in the biological sciences, geology, and engineering. It had shown that it could compete academically with older, more established campuses, although its eyes were always on the competitive strengths of the University of California across the bay at Berkeley, and on Cornell.

Lewis Terman's arrival was, in itself, part of a gradual academic restructuring process that had begun with faculty turnovers and departmental readjustments as early faculty left—or were encouraged to leave.[24] Earl Barnes, Stanford's first professor of education and an alumnus of Cornell and Indiana Universities, had been among the pioneer faculty appointments at Stanford in 1891. Barnes, like Lewis Terman, believed that children should learn in freedom.

Barnes left the university under a cloud of personal, not professional, misconduct in 1898. After an interim appointment of ethics professor Edward H. Griggs, Barnes's place was filled by yet another Indiana alumnus, Elwood P. Cubberley. The department was "in disrepute," said President Jordan, and he told Cubberley to clean it up. Cubberley guided the department's expansion, becoming its first dean when the department became the School of Education in 1917.[25] By Lewis Terman's appointment in 1910 and that of Jesse Sears a year later, Elwood Cubberley had significantly strengthened the department to five faculty members.[26]

The campus that became Fred Terman's home, however, was just as much "the home of a large, busy, and enthusiastic family" as it had been in the 1890s, and just as introverted and self-satisfied. "We were parochial," wrote journalist Bruce Bliven, class of 1911. "Of the many world events during that decade, few reverberated more than faintly along the sandstone corridors beneath the red-tiled roofs."[27] Its pioneer classes and faculty had quickly organized clubs, fraternal organizations, literary and news publications, athletic teams, dramatic and musical events, so that the full fair of student life was available without going far from the university. Classes, laboratories, departmental offices, and the library were housed in the Quad or buildings next door; faculty houses, Encina and Roble dormitories, fraternities and sororities, rooming houses, the Stanford Inn, a post office, and a bookstore were close by.

This center of campus, however, was set within more than eight thousand acres of grain fields, oak and eucalyptus groves, and wooded foothills. "The Farm," as Stanford's campus was fondly called, provided an intoxicating sense of space and freedom of movement, a special ambiance of its own between San Francisco's bustle and the thriving farm towns and rich vineyards, orchards, and gardens of the "Valley of Heart's Delight," one of the most fertile agricultural regions in the West.

Automobiles were still a rarity, and the community relied on bicycles, livery stable "buses," and walking until the trolley line from Palo Alto to the campus was completed late in 1908. Although an early ban on cars on campus had been lifted, they were still restricted to a handful of peripheral roads. Automotive access to the main artery from Palo Alto to the Quadrangle—University Avenue (later renamed Palm Drive)—was absolutely forbidden until 1917.[28] Unlike pioneer faculty families of the 1890s, the Termans had the "Toonerville Trolley" at hand, which took passengers and freight to and from campus cheaply and regularly. Running from Panama Street and Engineering Corner past Encina Hall and along Galvez Street to Palo Alto, the trolley line down University Avenue provided a junction going southeast onto Waverley, passing near Palo Alto High School.

Travel to San Jose, twenty miles to the south, as well as to the watering holes at Saratoga or extended trips to Santa Cruz and Capitola beaches had become more practical with extension of the interurban transit line in 1907. For more rare and costly trips to San Francisco, "The City," and its restaurants, dances, opera, shops, and bookstores, there was the Southern Pacific train depot in Palo Alto.

Everyday life for the Terman family centered on the campus and nearby towns. The town of Palo Alto, where the Termans lived their first two years at Stanford, had wedged itself in between the established towns of Menlo Park to the north and Mayfield to the south. Consisting of a few buildings near the rail station when the university first opened, the town of Palo Alto began serious development in 1893. Faculty and other families were attracted by Palo Alto's prohibition of the manufacture and sale of alcohol—a prominent feature of Mayfield's saloon-ridden main street. (When Mayfield went dry, at the instigation of its professor-mayor, saloon business picked up in Menlo Park.[29]) Student drinking on campus remained a problem, despite a 1909 state law banning the sale of alcohol within a mile and a half of Stanford (as well as the University of California). "Whiskey Gulch," just beyond Palo Alto at the far end of University Avenue, continued to be a thorn to prohibitionists, as did the "blind pigs" in the south end of Mayfield and beer joints like "Rossotti's" up in the foothills along Alpine Road.

Families were also attracted to Palo Alto's schools. Palo Alto residents had put up a fight to separate from the Mayfield School District in 1893, whose grammar school was two miles away. Faculty families living on campus, however, faced makeshift arrangements until Mrs. Stanford provided a small school building after the turn of the century. Fred attended both Palo Alto and Stanford's elementary schools with other faculty children.[30]

The Termans first rented a spacious cottage with a large sleeping porch about a mile and a half from the campus, an easy bicycle ride for Lewis. In 1912, Lewis was promoted to associate professor. The sale of their Glendale house, along with a university loan and a recent inheritance, allowed the Termans to build their own house on campus. The three-bedroom house at 7 Dolores Street (later renumbered 761 Dolores) was situated on more than an acre on the side of San Juan Hill, an easy walk to the university's Quadrangle past faculty houses and the fraternities and sororities along Mayfield Road. Lewis and Anna Terman spent the rest of their lives in this house, and with the exception for an undergraduate year or so when they lived in their respective fraternity or sorority houses, Fred and Helen both lived at the house on Dolores until they graduated from Stanford. The house, Fred believed, was an important symbol to his parents of their stability and success, but it also provided room for Fred's growing interest in ham radio, a hobby he could now share with other faculty kids. Radio amateurs were rare in those days. As Fred later recalled, "After all, people who knew anything about electronics were scarce, very scarce. If you saw a 90-foot pole sticking up somewhere, you'd go and knock on the door and get acquainted with him."[31]

The year before the Terman family arrived in Palo Alto, a recent Stanford electrical engineering graduate named Cyril Elwell ('07) broadcast a wobbly version of *The Blue Danube* from Palo Alto to radio receivers in Los Altos and Mountain View, some five miles away. Not long after Elwell's *Blue Danube* broadcast, another Stanford alumnus, Charles David "Doc" Herrold, began "San Jose Calling," a regular broadcast of voice and music (which he identified with the call letters FN, but later known as KQW, then KCBS). Elwell's two 75-foot wooden masts at 1431 Cowper Street and later, the giant radio tower of Federal Telegraph on the corner of Emerson and Channing Street would become important geographical landmarks in young Terman's life.[32] Sometime Stanford student Douglas Perham set up a radio spark transmitter in 1906 in his house/machine shop at 913 Emerson, and Cyril Elwell took over his bungalow in 1910. Young Francis McCarty, son of one of Leland Stanford's coachmen, had been at work improving a damped wave transmitting method when he was tragically killed; his financial backers turned to Stanford professor Harris J. Ryan to suggest a successor. Ryan recommended Cyril Elwell. To improve reliability of continuous wave transmissions, Elwell went to Denmark in 1909 to purchase American licensing rights for Valdemar Poulsen's electric arc radio transmitting method. It was an expensive proposition, and after New York possibilities fell through, Elwell approached President David Starr Jordan at Stanford. Jordan gave him five hundred dollars, and Professors Charles D. Marx and John Casper Branner (fathers of avid young radio hams) joined in contributing. Soon after, Elwell established the Poulsen Wireless Telephone and Telegraph Company (renamed Federal Telegraph in 1911) in neighboring Palo Alto.

Elwell's first transmission demonstrations used the Palo Alto amateur station of Roland Marx. By 1911, Federal demonstrated a 50-mile long, two-way continuous wave communication between Sacramento and Stockton, and soon after, a 2,100-mile transmission to Honolulu, using 300-foot masts designed by Stanford engineering professor C. B. Wing. By 1912, Federal had a San Francisco to Honolulu commercial wireless route in operation. When Lee de Forest, already at work on his three-element vacuum or "audion" tube by 1906, went looking for a job, he became research director at Federal Telegraph in 1911. With an expert team that included Charles Logwood and Herbert Van Etten, they continued to develop the audion, as well as the first amplifier, and experimented with the problems caused by feedback. The triode vacuum tube would remain the fundamental component of radio, television, and computer operation until the invention of the transistor in 1947 and fuel the rapid growth of the radio industry in the 1920s.[33] De Forest and Leonard Fuller (Stanford's first PhD in engineering) published articles in 1913 and 1915 interpreting empirical data concerning differential radio frequency propagation effects between Federal's transmitters in San Francisco and Honolulu as supporting the idea of a Kennelly-Heaviside Layer (or ionosphere as it would later be called).[34] These interpretations of radio wave refractions in the Earth's ionized upper atmosphere were ten years before the similar but more thorough work of Edward Appleton, who was later to win the Nobel Prize in 1947 for his contributions to ionospheric physics.

Fred Terman, drawn to the magic of the emerging radio industry, was an avid amateur radio operator by age fourteen. He had constructed a crystal set receiver in 1913, and in the autumn of 1914 Fred checked out from the Stanford Library the book *Wireless Telegraph Construction for Amateurs*, by a popular writer of the time who wrote on electricity and wireless for *Boys Magazine*. The book told how to make the spark wireless gear of the day, including construction of tuners, antennas, high-voltage spark coils, and crystal detectors; all that one would need to get on the air.[35] Teenagers all over America were fooling around with radios, but perhaps no small town in the country hosted such a concentration of spectacular radio transmitting devices and research as Palo Alto. As with Roland Marx, George Branner (son of John Casper Branner of geology) had set up his radio gear in Palo Alto as early as 1907.[36]

Like a number of his friends, Fred hung around Federal Telegraph as a kid and worked there during one of his college summers. Norman Scofield was very interested in ham radio and first became acquainted with Fred as a ham operator. Similarly, Norman's younger brother Phil became interested in ham radio through Fred. Both Scofields went to Stanford, and Fred joined Norman's fraternity, Theta Xi.[37] Federal Telegraph would quickly go through many of the changes typical of high-technology companies later in the century. It began with an outstanding chief engineer and research director, developing new technology in a fast-growing industry and attracting the best of Stanford's graduating engineers.[38] In its future were defections, spin-offs, financial problems, and ultimately, in 1931 corporate takeover.[39] In 1916, however, as Fred Terman looked to his own future as a Stanford engineer, Federal Telegraph was—literally—a looming presence. Four 50-foot poles strung with twelve miles of aluminum wire for "secret" experiments now graced the company's new site along El Camino.

Having been persuaded by the Palo Alto City Council not to move to cheaper land in Redwood City, Federal Telegraph expanded its facilities while concentrating on production of equipment for commercial and governmental radio-transmitting stations. By June 1916, it was announced that "the parent factory is now in direct wireless communication with the stations at Arlington, VA, near Washington DC, Tuckerton, NJ, San Diego, Englewood, Los Angeles, Honolulu, Portland, OR, South San Francisco, and the beach station at San Francisco." The *Palo Alto Times* initially assured citizens they need not be afraid of the ungainly mess of mysterious wires in the air, but people were now warned to stay clear of the new Federal Telegraph building where the transmitting arcs were being tested. Danger signs were posted around the factory, and an electric safety fence extended around the grounds. What an invitation for a teen-aged boy interested in science and engineering.[40]

High School Days

In 1913, thirteen-year-old Fred Terman entered Palo Alto High School, a square, two-story structure with nine classrooms, an assembly hall, and a large basement, built in 1901 on Channing Avenue. He did well in ancient history, American history, and economics (straight As throughout) and took three years of German (averaging an A-). Freshman "general science" did not inspire him (a B), but math and physics did (straight As in geometry, algebra, trigonometry, and physics).

English was Fred's most difficult subject during his three and a half years of high school, although he worked his grade up gradually from a B to an A. Fred made his first literary appearance in the December 1915 issue of *Madrono*, the school literary magazine, as the author of a poem in his junior year:[41]

A Reporter's Vindication of Himself

Eugene McCall had a reporter been
Who died at the young age of two score ten.
And when Saint Peter asked him of his life,
McCall replied, "I was with honor rife,
No statement that I ever made was right;
When possible a man's career to blight.
I always quoted that which was not said;
The truth the paper's readers never read,
For I and my good colleagues swore that we
A constant enemy of truth would be.
And as I carried out this oath so well
That from my pen no justice ever fell,
I rose 'til I became an editor
With greatly increased powers, on truth to war.

And as I never from my oath did swerve,
I feel that I in heav'n a place deserve.

A number of Fred's high school friends, including Winifred Johnston who was his later girlfriend at Stanford, were children of Stanford faculty. In the 1915–16 year, the school established a debating forum. It is not known whether Fred was in the forum that first year but for the 1916–17 year he was elected vice president of the forum. The club met each Tuesday, alternating practice on parliamentary law and debating. An appeal went out—more students were needed to "put the required 'jazz' into the organization."[42] Fred also was elected vice president of his class that year, and Winifred Johnston was elected auditor of the student body government.

Slight like his father, Fred nonetheless went out for both track and rugby. Sports were popular in this campus community and encouraged at Palo Alto High School. Superintendent Walter H. Nichols and teacher G. E. Mercer, each weighing in at more than 200 lbs, were among several of the teachers who had participated in college or semiprofessional sports. (The energetic Nichols also directed school plays.[43])

Fred maintained a lifelong interest in both sports and made lifelong friends. At Palo Alto High, brothers Robert ("Dink") and Ruric ("Ric") Templeton were avid trackmen, and Norman and Phil Scofield were good at both track sprints and at rugby.[44] Norman Scofield, in Fred's class, broke the school record in the quarter mile with a 53.1 seconds in the spring of 1917. Fred made the school's second-string rugby team as a senior and played in several games, but his interest centered on track. In his junior year (spring 1916), Fred ran the mile and half-mile in a respectable, if not excellent, time. The Palo Alto team did well that year in the Peninsula Track Championships, where Fred took third place in the mile. Competition was stiff. At least three times that spring Fred ran the mile against champion runner Arthur Forward of San Jose, who broke the local mile record each time he ran. When Fred ran the half-mile, Forward again broke records.[45]

By the end of fall term of 1916, Fred had received the fifteen units of credit suitable for entrance to Stanford University. Superintendent Nichols added a fine recommendation: he deemed Fred, who had finished among the top three of his group of sixteen seniors, "prepared to undertake college studies with good prospect of success" both by adequate preparation and "by reason of character, maturity and seriousness of purpose." Terman, Nichols wrote on his Stanford application form, "is a fortunate acquisition for any school. He is far above the average in scholarship and is alive to all School interests."[46]

In December 1916, Fred was an early or "midyear" graduate, along with fifteen colleagues. The year before, a move had been made to create a union high school district including Palo Alto, Stanford, and Mayfield. The new district would not become reality until shortly after he graduated, but planning was underway for a new building at a site closer to the Stanford campus along El Camino Real. Nevertheless, his half-year class of 1916 was the first class to receive new diplomas engraved with "Palo Alto Union High School—Mayfield, Stanford, Palo Alto," the same phrase that would later be carved in stone above the new Spanish-revival school building when it opened on December 24, 1918 (its present site).[47]

In the *Madrono*, each graduate's formal portrait photo (the boys wore high collar shirts and dark jackets, the girls wore white) was accompanied by a clever caricature drawn by classmate Kenneth Crowninshield. Fred Terman is depicted as a bespectacled academic wearing a threadbare, patched robe and high-button shoes. A philosophy text is tucked under one arm as he walks, a magnifying lens in his hand while he reads a book entitled obliquely "-ology." Fred was not the only boy to be portrayed with already old-fashioned high-button boots, but he continued to wear such boots as a young professor and was fondly remembered by friends as Fred "Boots" Terman.[48]

For Fred, moving from Palo Alto High School across El Camino Real to the Stanford campus was a natural progression. Many of Palo Alto High's graduating seniors went on to Stanford, including Terman's friends "Dink" and "Ric" Templeton, and the Scofield brothers, Norman and Phil.[49] Birge Clark, who graduated from the high school in 1910, recollected that thirty-eight of forty-two in his own graduating class went on to Stanford. The high ratio was the result both of Stanford's attractions—it charged no tuition, and the sons and daughters of faculty knew the campus and felt at home there—and of an earlier winnowing—compulsory attendance ended at age sixteen in California, and most non-college-bound students had already left the school.[50]

The Stanford Undergraduate

Frederick Emmons Terman (Fred had dropped the "Arthur") entered Stanford in the spring semester, January 1917. Stanford would change to quarters the following fall, but switching from semesters to quarters was only one of many "efficiency" moves brought about by Stanford's new president. Fred's years as an undergraduate were shadowed by the First World War but dominated by the personality, philosophy, and agenda of President Ray Lyman Wilbur. By 1920, few alumni and "old-guard" faculty would recognize Stanford's academic program.

Wilbur, who took office in January 1916, believed Stanford to be on a threshold. The university had just celebrated its twenty-fifth anniversary. Behind were its "pioneer years," including the administration of founding President David Starr Jordan and interim president John Casper Branner (the noted geologist was the first man asked to join the new university faculty in 1891). Wilbur was a Stanford alumnus ('96, AM '97, Cooper Medical College MD '99) and influential faculty member (professor of medicine, head of the Medical Department, and the Stanford Medical School's first dean). He was also a man of action. He was ready to bring in the "dynamite squad" to transform Stanford's academic organization, upgrade its facilities and salaries, jump-start fund-raising, and civilize student life. During his first decade in office, Wilbur also put Stanford back on course to becoming a full-fledged university by expanding graduate study and professional education, promoting faculty research and outside consulting, and stressing scholarship over extracurricular activities.[51]

Entering midyear and living at home, Fred missed the usual fall quarter madness for incoming freshmen boys—the hazing and "tubbing" at Encina, fraternity rush, and the general harassment of freshmen by upperclassmen, especially by the new sophomores. By temperament, he also was not among those targeted by the president for improvement: students "content to do the minimum amount of work and a maximum amount of play." Wilbur later wrote, "Stanford's inviting climate for outdoor activities may have had something to do with it, but there was a general trend over the whole country to overemphasize the social aspects, the side shows, of college life." In the fall of 1916, Wilbur wrote Stanford parents and prospective students alike: "A student's principal business is his study. . . . The student who is not content to lead the simple, clean, industrious life expected on the Stanford campus should go elsewhere." No doubt the Terman family agreed.

Fred Terman entered Stanford as a mechanical engineering major. Engineering was considered one of Stanford's strengths, in part due to the highly respected men who headed each department: Charles D. Marx (who founded the Civil Engineering Department in 1891), William Durand (mechanical), and Harris J. Ryan (electrical), each of whom had served as president of their respective national engineering societies. Each set high standards for their students, encouraged initiative and resourcefulness, and they worked with each student to plan coursework adjustable to individual needs and talents.

Established in 1891, the Mechanical Engineering Department was among the oldest, largest, and strongest departments on campus and was the most prominent of its engineering departments. Young Fred admired the distinguished, dour, and formal Durand, a nationally known expert in airplane propeller design who was always referred to as "Dr. Durand" by students and colleagues alike.[52] A graduate of the U.S. Naval Academy with a PhD from Lafayette, Durand had spent much of his career at Cornell where he had specialized in marine engineering and screw design. He also invented logarithm paper. Moving to Stanford in 1903, he extended this interest in fluid dynamics to work on water power problems in western states, and then, in 1915 at age fifty-six, to the design of airplane propellers.[53] That year, Durand was appointed by President Wilson as one of the five founding members of the National Advisory Committee on Aeronautics (NACA), charged with coordinating national efforts in aeronautical research and a model for the later establishment of the National Air and Space Administration (NASA). Durand was named chair of the committee in 1917. The following year, Durand and Assistant Professor E. P. Lesley founded Stanford's new Aeronautical Experimentation Laboratory to conduct several joint investigations with NACA installations.

The department's longest-serving professor was Guido Hugo Marx, an expert in machine design and gears, who had followed his older brother Charles Marx to Stanford in 1894 after receiving his degree of "civil engineer" from Cornell.[54] Highly adept at both design and fabrication, Marx had pieced together from virtually nonexistent budgets a respectable university machine shop, while carrying a heavy load of teaching and serving as acting department head of the department during long absences of Durand and his predecessor, Albert W. Smith. Marx, an outspoken critic of President Jordan's sometimes haphazard faculty relations, had been instrumental in the formal organization of Stanford's Academic Council and in clarifying tenure and promotion policies. His studies of faculty conditions helped prompt Stanford's reassessment of faculty salaries.[55]

Stanford had drawn heavily from Cornell for its engineering professors. In addition to Professors Durand and Marx were Professor of Experimental Engineering William Rankine Eckert (who studied pipe-line flow and heat transmission losses), Assistant Professor Charles N. Cross, and Assistant Professor Everett Parker Lesley (an aeronautical engineer who had studied for his Stanford AB with Durand), each with Cornell degrees of "engineer." Rounding out the department's faculty were Assistant Professors Lawrence E. Cutter (AB, Stanford) and Instructor Horatio Ward Stebbins (AB, California, BS, MIT).[56]

Given its curriculum need for work in foundry, forging, machine shop, patternmaking, and other applications, the Mechanical Engineering Department relied on a staff of master tradesmen, who were given titles as "instructors" who had entered engineering the old-fashioned way. Drawn from industry rather than from a college or university, they were experienced as skilled master tradesmen who rarely held advanced academic degrees. Although their inclusion in the faculty ranks would later cause some friction in faculty hiring and salary setting, the Mechanical Engineering Department continued to rely on their experience and skill not only for teaching but to design and fabricate research apparatus and parts for faculty research projects, presaging the large, specially funded research projects that would later come to Stanford.

Why would Fred Terman enroll as a prospective major in mechanical engineering, when his main hobby was radio? During Fred's years as an undergraduate, electrical engineering at Stanford was a graduate program and entrance was obtained with a Bachelor's degree in mechanical engineering. Entering midyear (January 1917), Fred jumped right into his work, taking seventeen units and subsequently earning the lowest semester grades he would receive at Stanford. He chose a five-unit condensed elementary economics course (earning an A), and a trigonometry course (an A+). Since his three years of high school German allowed him to satisfy the language requirement with a single semester of reading German scientific literature, he also tried a course recommended for sophomores and upperclassmen, and earned a B. The rest of his time was spent in the required course, "Forge and Drawing." (The lecture proved easy [an A] but drawing [a B] and working in the forge itself [a C] more frustrating.) Like any mechanical engineering student of the era, however, much of Fred's time as a mechanical engineering undergraduate would be spent in the shop or in mechanical drawing classes.

After a summer at home working on a military surveying crew at nearby Camp Fremont, Fred spent his sophomore year taking a number of civil as well as mechanical engineering courses on machine design, thermodynamics, hydraulics, descriptive geometry, and courses in mechanical drawing. He continued the mathematics series begun in his first year through the next two years, adding calculus, analysis, and intermediate theoretical mechanics, and he began his required three terms of physics.

Although the broader requirements of the lower-division curriculum had yet to be implemented at Stanford (1920), undergraduates were encouraged by world events to look beyond the confines of their major course of study. Fred developed a keen interest in political history and political economy, and in spring 1918, took World Politics with Edward Benjamin Krehbiel, an engaging professor of history. Fred especially enjoyed economics, moving on from a required engineering economics course his sophomore year to two courses in economics and political economy during the summer quarter of 1918: Labor Problems with Frederick Garver, and Combinations and Trusts with Albert Whitaker. Many of Stanford's engineering faculty, including Charles Marx and C. D. Wing, had actively participated in local Progressive politics and negotiations regarding utility regulation.

Stanford and World War I

Looking back over his first two years in office, President Wilbur wrote proudly in the student yearbook of the significant improvement he saw in student responsibility and of "the increasing efficiency of the student groups." While his administration continued to encourage improvement in scholarship standards and social behavior, particularly in Encina and among the fraternities, his plans were soon sidetracked by America's entry into the war in Europe.

Since his retirement in 1912 as Stanford's president, David Starr Jordan had served at the forefront of the World Peace movement. In London when war broke out in August 1914, a chagrined Jordan wrote back to Stanford, "Most of us who have worked for peace, in common with the businessmen of Germany, must confess our mistake." Many Americans, caught without funds when hostilities broke out, were helped by Stanford's most prestigious alumnus, Herbert Hoover ('95). Bert Hoover, an extremely successful mining engineer, and his wife, Lou Henry Hoover, had already turned their London home into a meeting place for visiting Stanford people. "Hoover organized the finances of the Stanford student body in the early days," Jordan added in his note from London, "and any man who could conduct financial operations at Stanford in those times is able to handle anything."[57] It was Hoover's Commission for the Relief of Belgium, however, that caught Stanford's, and the country's attention. At the behest of U.S. Ambassador

Walter H. Page, Hoover organized an extensive fund-raising, shipping, and distribution network of food and clothing for Belgium's civilians following the invasion by Germany in the final months of 1914. At its peak, the Belgian Relief Commission provided supplies worth $25 million per month. Ambassador Page, writing to President Wilson in January 1916, concluded that Hoover had saved Belgium.[58]

Hoover's Belgian Relief efforts were more personalized for Stanford than for other American communities. Beyond the obvious name association, Hoover called on Stanford alumni and faculty to work, both at home and in Europe, for the commission. Alumni clubs were organized and more than one "European Market" was held in the Palo Alto Circle (complete with visits by Lou Henry Hoover and May Hopkins, wife of Stanford trustees' president Timothy Hopkins) to gather clothing and raise money for European relief efforts in 1915 and 1916. The August 1916 deaths of Professor Robert Edouard Pellisier and James Grant Ferguson ('08), who had both returned home to enlist, prompted fund-raising for Stanford's first of five Ambulance Corp units.

As Fred marked his first full month as a Stanford undergraduate in 1917, the U.S. government severed diplomatic relations with Germany. Stanford's first ambulance unit left for France early in February. The emotional appeal of Dr. Jordan's pacifism still appealed to many on campus, however. A campus meeting of some five hundred faculty and other Stanford community members was held on February 5 in the Stanford Union (the student "union" so recently brought into being by Bert and Lou Henry Hoover). While Jordan emphasized the need for "understanding" and Edward Krehbiel, a history professor, spoke abstractly about balance of power, it was President Wilbur who "created some unrest among the pacifically inclined by emphasizing the idea of 'force' for the maintenance of international order." In his autobiography, Wilbur wrote of the meeting, "It seemed to me inevitable that we were going into the war, and I was convinced that we had better prepare for it as rapidly as possible." Wilbur and his faculty began to study Stanford's manpower resource "so that we could respond quickly and effectively if war were declared."[59]

Throughout 1917, German U-boats sunk Allied shipping at twice the rate at which ships were being built worldwide. By late April 1917, Britain appeared to have only a two-month food supply. The psychological toll of both U-boat and zeppelin aerial bombing was compelling.[60] A year earlier, Fred had published a short story in his high school literary magazine showing the impression made by these new weapons and foreshadowing his own contributions in the next world war. His story featured an English prisoner forced to fly in a new German zeppelin and ordered to point out English munitions factories from the air. By a technical trick, the Englishman manages to cause the hydrogen gas in the zeppelin to explode, crashing the zeppelin over the sea. The factories are saved, with the loss of all on board the zeppelin including "The Unnamed Hero."[61]

Imagine the turmoil of Fred's first full year at Stanford as war came home. A multilingual waitress, complete with red wig, was arrested as a spy not long after arriving in Menlo Park from Los Angeles. Army Intelligence arrested another alleged spy, a cavalry soldier arriving at Camp Fremont from the Philippines who turned out to be a German citizen. The influx of soldiers for training at nearby Camp Fremont caused a stir. Alcohol was not only illegal on base, but the towns of Menlo Park and Palo Alto were officially dry, and the sale of liquor within a mile and a half of university boundaries forbidden by state law. Reports of drunken soldiers, the rise in the number of traffic accidents, and other incidents hit the newspapers, along with news of local contributions to the war effort: the largest concrete ship in the world, the 5,000-ton *Faith*, was launched at Redwood City. California's wartime economy boomed. As the United States sharply increased its shipbuilding (completing 533 ships totaling 3 million tons in 1918), new shipyards sprang up around San Francisco Bay.[62]

Proud of the spirit of the hundreds of students who lined up at his office door that April to discuss enlistment, Wilbur nonetheless worried about their preparation and their exposure on the front lines. "It is the duty of every man to find out where he can do his nation the most good. Anybody can enlist. It is easy to learn to fight. We admired the sacrifice a man is willing to make, but it is intelligence that will win the war." For every man at the front, Wilbur reminded the students, there had to be eight more behind him. The university's ROTC course (first organized in the 1890s but so unpopular that it was discontinued soon after) had been reinstated by Wilbur in September 1916. Enrollment jumped from 250 to 850 by spring 1917.[63]

By commencement that May, it was obvious that pacifism had given way to preparedness. The graduating "War Class of 1917" was filled with young men in uniform. So many seniors of the class of 1918 were gone that intercollegiate sports that fall were in disarray. Stanford's rugby and track teams lost more than one team captain, the track team its coach, as star athletes like Dink and Ric Templeton left to serve in the military. Stanford women could not enroll in military service, but volunteered for active duty in other ways. In August 1917, Professor Edith Mirrielees of the English Department organized eighteen Stanford women into a Women's Ambulance Service Unit in France and served with the Red Cross. Professor Clelia Mosher surveyed conditions for relief of war orphans and refugee children. Other Stanford women enlisted to work in army, navy, and Red Cross hospital units.[64] On campus, women students outnumbered men and they enthusiastically filled in as student body officers and publications editors.

Commencement in June 1918 was a sad affair. Honor certificates were given to parents of 68 Stanford men and women known to have died in service, and certificates were awarded to 722 others who had left to enter the U.S. armed services (and 18 others who joined the other Allied forces).[65]

Stanford's athletic program for 1918–19 was managed by the army's Students' Army Training Corps (SATC) program, and intercollegiate competition was discontinued for the year. SATC sponsored an American-rules football game against Cal's military students, helping to ease the way back to a more traditional "Big Game" with Cal.

By January 1918, there were only 800 nonmilitary male students at Stanford, but more than 8,000 men training at Camp Fremont. Fred, employed on a surveying team, was among the 2,500-man workforce that quickly constructed the camp in the summer of 1917, the hottest in the area's recorded history, in the quiet town of Menlo Park along the university's border. The camp (named for the famous explorer, Civil War general, and California's first U.S. Senator, John C. Fremont) had some one thousand buildings used for warehouses, mess halls, and recreational facilities, a tent city of six thousand canvas tents for trainees, and facilities for ten thousand horses.[66]

Stanford administrators initially protested that the camp was too close to campus boundaries; in fact, it overflowed onto some 200 acres of Stanford land. Patriotism, and possible economic advantages, prevailed, however. Eight regiments, including cavalry, began arriving in mid-October 1917. (At its peak, Camp Fremont housed 42,000 soldiers.) Professor Oliver Johnston of Stanford and other volunteers began teaching math, English, typing, and French to the soldiers, and Chancellor David Starr Jordan lectured on cleanliness. Camp Fremont athletic teams were coached by Stanford people and engaged in sporting events with Stanford students.

Fred had taken military drill during the 1917–18 academic year and the following summer quarter. His least favorite subject was required of all Stanford male students. Even so, he had the opportunity to experience the rigorous standards of Major Jens Bugge, the army reservist in charge of Stanford's Reserve Officers' Training Corps (ROTC). Bugge was sent to France to serve on General Pershing's staff, however, and the disorganized program was dropped into the lap of Harry Maloney, the popular athletic trainer, for the remainder of the quarter. Maloney and his cadet officers no doubt felt the pressure to make a good showing—Stanford needed to stay on the War Department's list of ten distinguished institutions in order to be entitled to ten commissions directly into the regular army. Maloney was happily relieved of duty by Captain Sam M. Parker, and the visit of the government inspector early in spring quarter "found Stanford in tiptop shape."

The first major American engagement had occurred in April 1918. The first wave of 245,000 American draftees had shipped out to France in May, to be joined by a second group of more than 300,000 in July. Having turned eighteen on June 7, 1918, Fred registered for the draft on Registration Day, September 12, 1918. (The Draft Act had been amended in August to include all men aged eighteen to forty-five years.) Soon, as with Irving Berlin's current popular song of 1917, he would find that "Oh! How I hate to get up in the morning." Except for a two-unit Mechanical Forge class Fred took in his first semester, the only C grades he received during four years as an undergraduate and two as a graduate were the Cs he was given in Military Drill.[67] Nevertheless, that year Fred was certainly not alone in deciding to pose proudly in his uniform for his yearbook picture.[68]

President Wilbur's major concern, shared with President Maclaurin of MIT, was to protect students like Fred Terman, students "of high ability in technical fields," from being drafted as privates for combat duty. (The draft in 1917 had registered students twenty-one and older, but the age was dropped to eighteen in June 1918.) This was to be an ongoing battle with what Stanford's president called military men "of the established type." College administrators were worried not only about preparing their students, but about keeping their institutions open. (Not only were enrollments dropping, but word was out that President Woodrow Wilson was considering shutting down colleges altogether.) Ray Lyman Wilbur and other college presidents worked with the War Department to find ways to more effectively use college personnel and facilities to assist the government in training men, especially officers and technical experts. The Students' Army Training Corps was put into effective operation in 1918—Stanford was among the first to apply for a SATC unit and was accepted August 14, 1918. "These units acted not only as valuable training centers of officer material," Wilbur noted, "but saved from destruction many of our educational institutions whose student bodies had been drained off almost to the vanishing point by the war." Stanford was assigned army, navy, and marine corps units (the latter composed of high school students with good preparation for technical training). Encina and Sequoia halls were turned into army barracks, and a large temporary mess hall for twelve hundred was set up.

Seventeen military officers superintended by Captain Sam Parker, the campus ROTC commander, ran the units. Wake-up call was about 6 AM, and taps was sounded at 10 each night, except that the technical students were allowed an additional hour for homework. Students did eleven hours of drill a week, except only six hours for the technical students. Full-dress drill and parade formations occurred on Saturday mornings. Students were at liberty from noon Saturday until Sunday evening and were paid thirty dollars per month. Technical students like Terman enrolled in most of the same courses they would normally have taken.[69] SATC officers were hardly older than the students. Most had received their lieutenant's commission after completing the first Officer's Training Camp at the Presidio in San Francisco earlier that year.

By fall 1918, national enrollment had reached 185,000 men, most of them registered as privates and chosen by normal means of college admissions. Five hundred twenty-five units mustered into service just in time for the influenza epidemic sweeping across the country at army bases.[70] The Spanish influenza pandemic first struck the East Coast of the United States in September 1918, and reached the West Coast in October. Fully one-quarter of the U.S. population contracted the disease, and nearly five hundred thousand persons died in the United States alone. Breaking out first at Camp Fremont, it quickly spread to Menlo Park, Palo Alto, and Stanford. County schools were closed, while students on campus wore gauze masks to class. Stanford was fortunate that alert medical staff hospitalized and isolated victims quickly, and only 6 of 260 campus cases proved fatal. However, the epidemic highlighted the university's inadequate student medical services. These would be upgraded by 1921 with new facilities managed for the first time by the university. In addition to Stanford's Isolation Hospital, the university requisitioned a fraternity house and two local residences as infirmaries. By Thanksgiving, the epidemic appeared to be over (cases continued, however, through January 1919).[71] With the end of the war in November 1918, Stanford's SATC soldiers, including Fred, were mustered out at the end of the fall quarter.

War also brought about a new attention to fitness, and suggested to Lewis M. Terman the possibility of evaluating "intelligence" by applying IQ tests. Fred's father left Stanford for Washington DC to serve on the Committee on the Psychological Examination of Recruits (a National Research Council subcommittee for the Surgeon General's Department) and the Committee on Classification of Personnel for the Army. Professor Terman helped work out a new intelligence scale, which was used in the psychological testing of one hundred thousand recruits, on examination of aviation candidates, and on methods of rating students in the officers' training camps.[72]

By the time the latest record-setting American concrete ship, the 435-foot tanker *Palo Alto*, was launched from Oakland in May 1919, Camp Fremont was being dismantled. With the camp's closure that fall, local businesses that had flourished with military contracts had a last chance to buy and sell war surplus materials. Even road gravel was dug up, rescreened, and sold for road and building needs in the vicinity. When rumors circulated that Henry Ford was considering the Camp Fremont property for a Ford automobile factory, members of Menlo Park's Chamber of Commerce sent Mr. Ford effusive welcoming telegrams but nothing came of the plan. That fall, Herbert Hoover spoke on campus in support of the League of Nations and many faculty, including Lewis M. Terman, signed a petition supporting the League.[73]

During the war, Wilbur was inclined to believe that an important step had been made in government acknowledgment of the role of American higher education, particularly in technical fields. At the very least, Stanford's faculty had felt a revitalization of the university's philosophy of direct usefulness and service while providing an important opportunity to build and test their technical expertise. Mathematician Hans Blichfeldt had worked at the Aberdeen Proving Ground, while G. H. Clevenger conducted research on precious metals for the U.S. Bureau of Mines and served as head of the metallurgy section of the National Research Council. Norris F. Hall, Tenney L. Davis, Norris W. Rakestraw, and Edward C. Franklin worked in the Chemical Warfare Service. Harris J. Ryan, in charge of the Pasadena Special Laboratory of the NRC, also chaired a committee investigating use of supersonics in antisubmarine warfare. Ryan later commented that he "netted an experience in mechanical radio that has been highly valuable because of the many uses I have found for the same in my work with students."[74] Meanwhile, his friend William Durand, as chairman of the National Advisory Committee for Aeronautics, encouraged joint investigations at Langley Aeronautical Laboratory and Stanford's new campus aeronautics laboratory.

Years of Change on the Farm

During much of Fred's undergraduate years, class work and the rhythm of campus life had been subsumed by the war effort, but by his senior year, the university had returned to "normal" with a new sense of vitality. "So much of our academic life has come down to us from the past without rhyme or reason that we can now look forward to some fresh thinking both by faculty and students," President Wilbur concluded in 1918.[75] Wilbur was all for rethinking. When students and alumni came back to campus over the next few years, it would present a fresh new look and some significant changes in the academic program. Interestingly, in looking back at these years, President Wilbur would remember the end of rugby in 1919 as the most difficult problem, aside from war-related issues, of his early administration.

With its year-round temperate climate and rural setting, Stanford's college life had always meant all levels of sport and outdoor recreation for both men and women students. The color and drama of intercollegiate athletics, particularly football, had caught the public eye, however, and Stanford's "Big Game" competition with the University of California (a competition that included debate and women's basketball as well as the expected football, baseball, and track events) had been serious business since 1892. Reflecting the growing commercialization of football, educators across the country increasingly called attention to the role of athletics in college life. Critics pointed to the growing professionalism of athletes, to coaches who willfully ignored scholarship requirements, to betting and payoff scandals, to the growing number of injuries and violent, warlike atmosphere on the field. In 1906, both Stanford and California, along with a number of other West Coast colleges, turned to rugby as the best alternative to American-rules football. Exhibition games by Australian and New Zealand teams had highlighted rugby's open play, fast passing, and emphasis on individual skill rather than on coaching strategy and "gladiatorial combat." Popular local star athletes like Ric and Dink Templeton spoke at public gatherings on rugby's behalf. Although not widely popular at first (the decision to switch was made by a faculty committee), Stanford students, along with local high schools like Palo Alto, were soon hooked.

Despite this reform, disagreements between Stanford and Cal over rules infringements, freshmen eligibility, and scholarship requirements brought relations between the two to an all-time low by 1915. Cal returned to American-rules football in protest that year, but after a noisy public debate, a student demonstration, and a closely decided referendum, Stanford chose to continue with rugby. Three years of disappointing alternative "Big Games" (with the University of Santa Clara and, in 1918, against a local army team) followed. During Fred's senior year, Stanford returned to American-rules football and the spirited, and lucrative, competition with Cal. Stanford's return to football was aided by changes nationally to the sport, especially in refereeing and harsher penalties, and important campus changes in coaching, training, and financial management. While some modest facilities were maintained by the university, intercollegiate teams and events like the Big Game had been traditionally organized and managed by the Associated Students (ASSU). Although gate receipts from the fall Big Game football game with Cal were substantial, ASSU managers also faced increasing travel expenses, coaching salaries, and facilities maintenance, often nearly bankrupting the organization. In 1917, Wilbur created the independent Board of Athletic Control, which served as a de facto athletics department from 1917 to 1943. It maintained athletic buildings, equipment and fields, appointed coaches and trainers, and controlled funding for and from events. The board proved to be exceptionally efficient and profitable. It financed not only construction of a large new football stadium (1921), but several other major sports projects and buildings in the following decade.[76] A number of other major buildings were constructed during Fred's student days at Stanford, among them a new art gallery (1917) and buildings at Hopkins Marine Station (1918), a large presidential "residence" on the Knoll; and a new general library (1919). In order to provide more non-"Row" housing, a much larger women's dormitory, the new Roble Hall (1918), housed women not living in sororities, while old Roble Hall, renamed Sequoia Hall, was used to house men (including an inaugural year of housing soldier-students). Yet another new men's dorm, Toyon, was constructed in 1923.

Track and Field and Theta Xi

Fred had always liked running. In his college days the student newspaper gave a lot of attention to the men going out for track and published articles about who was trying out for each event. *Intra*mural competition was relatively more important in those days and great emphasis was put on how each class did against the others in all-campus events. Fred went out for track in the winter-spring of 1918, his sophomore year. The training track was a quarter-mile cinder oval behind Encina Hall. The varsity track was not too far from its present-day location. The year 1918 was really difficult for sports, with students going off to war, and most meets were cancelled. Ric and Dink Templeton each helped coach the track team. Fred ran against Cal at home in the Big Meet, which Stanford won 70–52, but he didn't place in the mile. The next year Fred again was a distance runner on the team. He was probably the third or fourth best miler on the team but, as with his sophomore year, the team captain was several years older than Fred and a splendid miler! Fred's best finish for the year was a third place against USC in the mile, which saw first place run in 4:45.1. Fred's friend Lloyd Dinkelspiel was a very good sprinter and quarter-mile athlete and was a leader in about every activity on the campus. In the Big Meet on May 3, 1919, Dinkelspiel anchored the mile relay to a win in the last event and gained a Stanford victory over Cal by a score of 73½ to 66½.[77] Fred's friendship with Lloyd continued many years, through the time when Dinkelspiel served as President of the Stanford Board of Trustees.[78]

There is a photo in the 1919 *Quad* yearbook of all the track members in their tracksuits. Eighteen-year-old Fred is sitting in the front row, second from left in the photo, looking handsome, young, and rather thin. He was ill at the time of the photo and soon after dropped out of school for the quarter. On his second left in the photo is young Lloyd Dinkelspiel. Fred was proud of his track efforts, as in his *Quad* senior class photo and activities entry he noted "varsity track 2, 3, also interclass meet, 2."

Some of Fred's track friends also were members of his fraternity, Theta Xi, a group favored by engineering and science students. The frat house was on Dolores Street, only a short distance from Fred's home and was caricatured in the *Quad* as the "Engineer's bunk house," depicting the brothers having track races across their lawn. Fred served as a faculty representative to his fraternity in his early teaching years and even through the 1940s he assisted with their financial matters.

Fred Terman was not a star athlete but a star student at Stanford. He enjoyed sport and perfectly represented the Stanford student athlete in a day when professionalism was frowned on and even some of the university coaches were students. He prized his time in sports and often recalled track and football scores years later. Former Stanford track coach Payton Jordon remembered Terman as provost in the 1950s quietly visiting the track team at practice and Terman's fantastic memory of former meets, runners, and scores. Robert Helliwell recalled that Terman asked him one day whether Ben A. Wambsganss, a student electrical engineering lab paper-grader in 1946, was related to the major league baseball player Bill Wambsganss.[79]

Administrative Changes at Stanford

Many administrative changes at Stanford were nearly invisible to most students, although Fred no doubt heard more than most of his classmates about their impact at faculty discussions in his parents' campus home. Fred later stated that around the family dinner table as a youth, he learned more about faculty life and university operations than did almost any of the junior faculty members.[80] Four changes had a greater impact on student academics, however: the elimination of the major professor system, the establishment of lower- and upper-division courses of undergraduate study, the institution of university-wide course requirements, and most grueling of all—the introduction of undergraduate tuition.

Wilbur had considered jettisoning freshmen and sophomore courses altogether into a junior college system, but instead organized new lower and upper divisions in 1920. The new lower division, described as a "frank reincarnation" of liberal education, required students, regardless of majors, to take courses in English, history, science, foreign language, and citizenship. Although this system did not go into full effect until Fred's senior year (1919–20), the reorientation of the undergraduate curriculum would significantly impact Stanford's engineering departments during his years as a graduate student and young professor. This concept of a broader, university education was closely related to the disappearance of Stanford's traditional professor-student mentoring system, whereby the individual student could, under the direction of one's "major" professor, formulate individualized, if need be idiosyncratic, selection of courses. Critics of the original system, however, including the faculty committee undertaking review of the university's curriculum in 1919, contended that Stanford's twenty-six independent departments, each of which set major requirements and granted degrees, forced early specialization and discouraged coursework outside the department.[81]

Most students, while blissfully unaware of the many financial challenges faced by Stanford's administrators, could not avoid the most significant policy change of the era. Even Leland Stanford had predicted the need for tuition in the university's future. Various fees had been charged during the financial crisis of the mid-1890s—registration, laboratory and book fees, fees for special student status—and tuition fees for graduate study in law and medicine had been charged since 1908. Wilbur's ambitions for Stanford needed firmer support than the university's stagnant endowment could offer, however. To make necessary improvements in faculty salaries and benefits, teaching and research facilities, scholarships, library and scientific collections, student housing, and even the water supply, the university turned first to tuition. After a brief discussion at their October 1919 meeting, the board of trustees, led by alumnus Herbert Hoover (elected to the board in 1912), took up Mrs. Stanford's 1903 suggestion and instituted undergraduate tuition fees of forty dollars a quarter to begin the following quarter, January 1920. Wilbur did not hesitate to confront student and parental complaints about the abrupt change by pointing out that it was difficult to tell a faculty member who could only afford a bicycle that he must teach for free a student who arrived on campus in his own automobile. Hoover pointedly countered a student editorial by noting that "the receipts of the ice cream parlors in the neighborhood would go a long way toward the needed increase in income."[82]

The institution of tuition, along with significant changes made in the way the university's endowment was invested, made it easier to attract increased outside funding for Stanford. In a series of fund-raising efforts, Wilbur initiated the first development campaign in the history of Stanford in 1922 with a "First Million for Stanford" campaign to raise endowment funds for faculty salaries. The campaign involved not only trustees, students, and alumni but an important matching grant provided by the General Education Board, founded by John D. Rockefeller. (A "Second Million" campaign aimed at funding new construction, a "Third" partially endowed the medical school.) As the 1920s progressed, outside funding would also play an increasingly important role in academic research.[83]

Many of Stanford's male students were still at least partially self-supporting, and even before the institution of tuition, had to turn to the YMCA employment bureau, to faculty, and to neighborhood businessmen, farmers, and housekeepers to find jobs. During Fred's undergraduate years, overall expenses were estimated at about $125 to $200 per quarter for those living in student housing. (At Encina, Sequoia, and Roble halls, students roomed for $5.50 to $7.50 per week for a double, or $7.50 to $9.00 for a single. Room and board in a university-approved local boarding house or private home ranged from $20 to $35 per month.) Students also paid a quarterly student health fee of $2 to the "Student Guild" health plan, and a gymnasium fee of $3.50. According to the *Stanford Register* for 1916–17, room and board could be earned by working about four hours per day (typically domestic or manual labor), although student assistants could earn about $75 per quarter.

Except for one year while his parents were in Washington DC, Fred lived at his parents' home on Dolores Street, but he still faced the expenses of buying books and paying quarterly lab fees. Even so, as both an undergraduate and graduate student, Fred was in a comparatively good financial position for the average Stanford student of the era.

From Mechanical Engineer to Chemist

In April 1918, Fred had a change of heart about majoring in mechanical engineering. That spring, he petitioned to change to the Department of Chemistry, stating succinctly: "I, F. E. Terman, wish to change my major subject from mechanical engineering to chemistry. Reason: I wish to become a chemical engineer." His request was approved by Guido Marx of mechanical engineering and Robert Swain of chemistry. He plunged into chemistry that summer: Swain's course in Principles of Inorganic Chemistry, and Qualitative Analysis, a lab course, with William Sloan.

Why Fred made the switch is unclear. A mechanical engineering degree could be applied to further graduate work in either electrical engineering or chemical engineering. Both electrical engineering and chemical engineering required a couple of years of mechanical engineering training. Most Stanford chemical engineers first worked toward a chemistry degree, following an option designed for chemical engineers dominated by mechanical engineering courses. Clearly, Fred simply enjoyed chemistry and may have found the heavy dose of machine shop during his first two years boring. Whatever the reason, the transition was easy.

Fred again used his summer to take courses. Beginning with a semester chemistry course during the summer between his sophomore and junior years, most of Fred's courses in his last two years would be in chemistry, along with associated courses in applied mathematics, electricity and electrical machines, and mechanical engineering.

Fred Terman entered Stanford's Chemistry Department in the midst of the "Swain era." Robert Eckles Swain, a biochemist, had presided over construction of Stanford's large chemistry building, constructed in 1903 near the main Quadrangle and reputed to be the largest and best-equipped chemistry laboratory on an American campus. (The old metallurgical assay building next door housed chemical engineering classes.) Swain also was active in local town politics, serving as Palo Alto's mayor from 1914–16, and then on the Palo Alto City Council during Fred's years in the department.[84]

While busy with American Chemical Society affairs, Chairman Swain relied on the advice of E. C. Franklin, one of the most unusual and broadly talented of the department's faculty. Franklin had played cornet in a brass band and had worked as a pharmacist's assistant and a printer. He had come to Stanford after working in Central America and for several years as a professor of chemistry at the University of Kansas. Elected president of the American Chemical Society in 1923,

Franklin was a master of the chemistry of ammonia and trained a number of distinguished chemists.[85] Until the 1960s, Franklin was the only Stanford chemist in the National Academy of Sciences. Fred Terman knew Franklin, a neighbor, well before he enrolled at Stanford and he and Franklin's son Jack were radio pals. A few years later Terman coauthored a text with Franklin's brother. Perhaps here is part of the reason Fred Terman turned to chemistry as a major.

Chemistry Department faculty had long been influential in the relatively small circle of university political power. Its first professor and department head, John Maxson Stillman, the only faculty member recommended by Leland Stanford, had been a close friend and advisor to President Jordan and had served as university vice president under both Jordan and his successors, John Casper Branner and Ray Lyman Wilbur (he resigned his post in 1917 once Wilbur was settled in office). Swain, in turn, had the ear of President Wilbur (he would serve as acting university president during the four years Wilbur served in Washington in the Hoover cabinet). Similarly, E. C. Franklin served as Stanford's first dean of graduate studies from 1917–27, while Professor John Pearce Mitchell (BA '03, MA '04, PhD '09, Stanford) moved from chemistry in 1925 to the post of registrar as well as the force behind the Board of Athletic Control, and was an important figure within President Wilbur's circle of advisors.

Terman took one notable course with Franklin, and another from Richard Curtiss, then visiting from the Throop Institute (Caltech), but he was not much impressed by some of his other chemistry professors. Stewart Woodford Young, whom Terman remembered as uninspiring, taught general physical chemistry, while William Henry Sloan, who taught quantitative and qualitative analysis, was better remembered for his acumen in real estate transactions.[86]

Late in spring quarter 1919, his junior year, Fred temporarily dropped out of school on the grounds of "recent illness," on the advice of Dr. George de Forest Barnett, a physician at the student health service.[87] His unnamed "recent illness" was most likely a bout with tuberculosis, subsequently treated at home. Fred had completed enough of the organic preparations laboratory course under Franklin to earn an A, but had to withdraw from courses in machine design, theoretical mechanics, and Swain's chemical principles, some thirteen units of credit. Nevertheless, following his father's pattern, Fred bounced back that fall, now free of military drill and the heat-forging lab to complete his entire fourth year of work with a straight-A average. He graduated June 21, 1920, with his bachelor's degree in chemistry, and was elected to Phi Beta Kappa.[88]

Fred Terman greatly enjoyed his undergraduate years at Stanford. He long remembered the congenial environment, and the respect and reverence with which students held their professors. As a senior, Fred was one of seven students inducted into Phi Lambda Upsilon, the chemistry honor fraternity. That spring, they organized an "All-Engineers" smoker, honoring the Chemistry Department's first faculty member, the recently retired professor John Maxson Stillman. Free to all engineering, mining, geology, and chemistry majors, the outdoor evening featured speeches by Professors Ryan, Durand, Wing, and Stillman—but equally important were the vocal and instrumental quartets, novelty singer, wrestling and boxing matches, free tobacco for all, ice cream, "eats," and punch.[89]

While social formality and distance between students and faculty remained the rule, students were better acquainted with their own individual professors, he felt, and knew each other better than students and faculty of the post–World War II campus.[90] Of course, Stanford University of 1920 was a smaller and different place than the campus after 1945.

Early Days of Electrical Engineering

In the spring of 1920, Fred decided to continue graduate study, not in chemistry, but in electrical engineering. His early interest in ham radio and experience with the rapidly developing state of commercial radio in nearby Palo Alto, combined with a nationwide boom in developing telephone networks and long-distance power transmission systems, proved too attractive to resist. Electrical engineering, and especially communications, would not only change the direction of Terman's academic career but take him away from Stanford for the first time in his adult life.

Unlike Stanford's other two engineering departments, the electrical engineering program had gone through a number of ups and downs in its thirty years. By the time Fred entered the department, its curriculum had been narrowed to that of a graduate program, with its courses and research largely driven by the interests of Harris J. Ryan in high-voltage power transmission.[91]

Stanford's Electrical Engineering Department, like similar departments across the country, had its roots in physics. Among the first professors to be appointed at the new university was the physicist Fernando Sanford, a former high school teacher and superintendent and professor of physical science at small colleges, who led the Physics Department until 1919. Sanford wrote one of the university's first research publications, "Some Observations upon the Conductivity of a Copper Wire in Various Dielectrics," published in 1892.[92] (Research in physics departments in the 1890s often involved the generation of energetic electrical particles and beams under vacuum conditions, generally developing the electromagnetism of James Clerk Maxwell. Sanford's publication, however, also showed the connection between American physics and industry in the late nineteenth century.)

The early Mechanical Engineering Department also claimed the field of electricity, promising such courses during its first years—but listing no relevant faculty. "Details will be announced later," stated the second year's *Register* of courses for 1892–93. As at MIT, it was the Stanford Physics Department, however, that first moved to build a faculty interested in electricity. In 1892, Fernando Sanford was joined by Albert Pruden Carmen, a Princeton-trained physicist, as professor of electricity, in the Physics Department. His title a year later became professor of theoretical physics.[93] Carmen had been professor of physics and applied electricity at Purdue, and during his first year at Stanford taught mathematical physics and electrical currents.[94] Two years later, in 1894, Frederic Auten Combs Perrine, a Princeton classmate of Carmen, joined the faculty as Stanford's first professor of electrical engineering. Until about 1923, courses in the physics of electrical telegraphy, telephony, and wireless were taught in the Physics Department as well as in the Department of Electrical Engineering. Thus Stanford's Department of Electrical Engineering started in 1894 with a physicist, Perrine, whose physicist friend Carmen had begun the teaching of electricity at Stanford in 1892. Both Carmen and Perrine entered electricity from the side of physics rather than that of mechanical engineering.

Perrine had spent three years with the U.S. Electric Lighting Company in Newark, New Jersey, then four years more as manager of the insulated wire department of Roebling's wire works in Trenton, New Jersey. The year before he came to Stanford, he was treasurer of the Germania Electric Company in Boston.

Carmen and Perrine were among the first science and engineering faculty at Stanford to bring "earned" (rather than honorary) doctorates, but like many of Stanford's pioneer faculty they completed research on campus while carrying a heavy teaching load. Perrine and his students field-tested a locally developed oil switch, facilitating later construction of a 40,000-volt line across the state to harness water power. Both Perrine and Carmen left Stanford by 1899. Perrine, however, published several works on municipal electrical power monopolies, electrical conductors, and power plants soon after leaving Stanford.[95] Most likely, his views had been worked out during his six years as professor of electrical engineering, perhaps influenced by fellow Stanford faculty keenly interested in local issues involving reform of municipal utilities and services.

During his first few years at Stanford, Perrine taught all electrical engineering courses with the aid of one lab assistant. Among Perrine's assistants were several promising graduate students: Camillo Olivetti (of the typewriter firm) from Turin, Italy, and Frank George Baum (AB '98, EE '99, Stanford), who subsequently became a nationally known electrical consultant. In 1898, Clement Copeland (ME, Cornell '86, EE, Stanford '97), came back north after a year at the Edison Electric Company in Los Angeles to join the faculty as assistant professor of electrical engineering. During Perrine's first year, 1892–93, there were twenty-five undergraduates, eight "specials" (including the Electrical Engineering Department's first foreign student, Joie Hisayaro Miyahara from Hiroshima,

Japan), but, reflecting the university's newness, there were no graduate students studying electrical engineering at Stanford. The first bachelor's degree in electrical engineering was conferred in 1894. In May 1895, Stanford's fourth commencement—the pioneer class of 1895, Stanford's first four-year class—would see seventeen bachelor's degrees awarded in electrical engineering. In May 1896, two students were awarded the first Stanford graduate degrees of "Engineer in electrical engineering."[96] Electrical engineering's first doctorate, indeed the first doctorate in engineering at Stanford, would not be granted until 1919.[97]

When Perrine left Stanford in 1899 the Electrical Engineering Department went into receivership under the direction of the Department of Mechanical Engineering, although the bachelor's degree in electrical engineering was still awarded. Stanford needed to find a senior faculty replacement for Perrine.

In the interim, electrical engineering was taught as one of six options within the Mechanical Engineering Department: steam, electricity, mills, marine, railways, and hydraulics. The Mechanical Engineering Department offered courses in motors, electric power, electric railroads, and instruments, all of which were related to the engineer's interest in power generation and transmission. Some courses covered the actual placing of power poles, installation of electric railways, and other pragmatic matters. The electrical engineering courses included those on constructive materials and machinery (which studied methods and materials for constructing electric lighting, railways, power lines, and telegraph and telephone lines, and the elements of dynamo machine design); application and design; central power station design and management; and engineering construction. Students were advised to be thoroughly grounded in mathematics, mechanics, physics, and chemistry before taking the electrical courses. Some knowledge of French or German was also recommended, since much of the literature in the field was European.[98]

Harris J. Ryan and the Ryan Era, 1905–1926

In August 1905, Harris Joseph Ryan (ME 1887, Cornell) took over Perrine's long-vacant position as professor of electrical engineering. Ryan's arrival marked the strengthening and growth of the Electrical Engineering Department at Stanford. He served as the department's executive head (chair) until his retirement in 1931 and led Stanford to a prominent position in the field of long-distance transmission of high-voltage electrical power.

After a year in business in Nebraska working with Cornell colleague Dugald C. Jackson, Ryan returned to Ithaca to serve on Cornell's engineering faculty, moving through the ranks to professor of electrical engineering. He spent much of his career at Cornell, but was drawn west by his friend and colleague, William Durand.

Durand had joined Stanford's mechanical engineering faculty in 1903 and was subsequently asked by President Jordan to recruit a senior electrical engineer.

Ryan brought to Stanford an outstanding reputation among academic and industrial colleagues alike. His special interest was high-voltage electric breakdown in transmission systems and the design of transmission lines. In 1904, Ryan was the first to suggest that corona, or ionization of air around a transmission line and its subsequent breakdown and discharge to the ground, could be used to measure the voltage at breakdown.[99] Over several years, Ryan and his Stanford students conducted a series of investigations regarding dielectric stress of components, design of electrical insulators and transmission cables, and measurement of parameters—peak voltages, transient surges, load imbalances—on long, high-voltage electrical lines.

The transmission of electricity across long distances was of special interest in the American West. In 1916, major California power companies (including Pacific Gas and Electric Co. (PG and E) and Southern California Edison) began contributing equipment to Ryan's laboratory at Stanford, enlisting Ryan and Assistant Professor James Cameron Clark as consultants on the problem of bringing hydroelectric power from the Sierras to California's population centers on the coast. "All the ordinary transmission lines that run up and down the inland valleys of California," Ryan's student Hugh Skilling later remarked, "are based on Ryan's work."[100] Ryan's laboratory became the West Coast center for research on high-voltage, long-distance power transmission. The lab's work bolstered the coast's power companies, and in turn the California economy, making possible, for example, the 270-mile-long 287,000-volt line from Hoover Dam on the Colorado River to Los Angeles, the world's largest line when it opened in the mid-1930s.

Ryan began his work at Stanford with two instructors, Kenneth Livermore Curtis and Samuel Barclay Charters Jr. Curtis assisted Ryan, while Charters initiated an optional fourth-year course in electrical transmission of intelligence, the first course within engineering to teach radio, or "wireless." Charters died in 1912, however, and he was replaced by James Cameron Clark. In addition to his high-voltage lab work, Clark, with Henry Harrison Henline (who joined the department in 1917 as an instructor), introduced Stanford's first course in radio communications in 1918 at the request of the U.S. Army Signal Corps. The course was initially aimed at engineers planning to enter the Signal Corps School for radio specialists. Henline later initiated Stanford's Communication Laboratory, made possible by a gift of equipment from the Bell Telephone System.

Harris Ryan's reputation remained high, but after 1916 he devoted most of his time to research and consulting. By 1920, his courses related largely to his work on High-Voltage Laboratory Practice and Research. His Advanced Electrotechnics was heavily oriented toward power transmission over long distances. Despite Ryan's impressive research agenda—or perhaps because of his distractions—the number of electrical engineering degrees awarded had again fallen dramatically. The department had discontinued registering entering undergraduate students in electrical engineering altogether in August 1912. This in some ways was a reversion in policy that saw the initial BA degree in engineering to be a preparation for the graduate degree of "Engineer." Thus, mechanical engineering at the BA level would be followed by (depending on the university) one or two years' work for the professional graduate degree of Engineer, whether in electrical engineering or another field. Undergraduate students planning for the professional degree of Engineer would major in mechanical engineering at the BA level, or if aiming toward chemical engineering, would do an undergraduate major in chemistry, with considerable preparatory studies in mechanical engineering. Because Stanford graduate electrical engineering now required a BA in mechanical engineering, by 1916 the number of electrical engineering students dropped to a handful.

When Terman entered Stanford as a freshman in 1917, interested electrical students were expected to take the four-year bachelor's degree curriculum in mechanical engineering and then continue, if they wished, for a fifth-year professional degree of Engineer in electrical engineering. The Electrical Engineering Department continued to offer its introductory electrical course for all prospective engineering students and its more advanced courses for graduates. The return of students to the university following the war, however, brought renewed interest in the field, along with men returning with some experience with radio use. The Department of Electrical Engineering's course enrollments jumped accordingly: a 38 percent increase in autumn 1920 over 1919, another 25 percent increase in the autumn of 1921. The number of graduate electrical engineering students in 1921 was double that of the year before (from six to twelve). Equally important were renewed industry connections between the department and the Federal Telegraph Company of Palo Alto. The boom in interest in radio transmission and radio as a new consumer market influenced enrollments and course offerings in electrical engineering departments around the country during and just following the war.

Stanford science and engineering faculty had encouraged young engineering graduates to enter the radio field, and watched with pleasure as the Federal Telegraph Company of Palo Alto not only grew to worldwide reputation and, in turn, hired yet more Stanford graduates.[101] In 1914 Cyril F. Elwell gave Stanford a 5-kilowatt Poulsen arc generator, and later the company provided a 12-kilowatt arc generator set with accompanying equipment. Elwell and Stanford graduate student Leonard Fuller, then working at Federal, helped install the equipment themselves.[102] This equipment proved especially helpful as Ryan extended his own coronal studies to higher radio frequencies. Soon after, he was publishing the results of this research with his former Stanford student and now Federal Telegraph Engineer Roland G. Marx. In 1919, Ryan awarded Fuller Stanford's first PhD in electrical engineering, full credit for his dissertation research done at Federal. In fact Fuller's work was done under a U.S. Navy contract to Federal Telegraph; his dissertation was classified and the degree withheld for a few months until the end of hostilities in World War I. In 1920, alumnus Elwell endowed a Stanford graduate scholarship in electrical engineering.[103]

Federal Telegraph developed new technology in arc transmitters and continued to support important research in vacuum tubes and radio propagation studies. Lee de Forest (who left Federal Telegraph in 1913), and Fuller separately published papers in 1913 and 1915 in radio and electrical engineering journals that interpreted empirical radio transmission data as revealing a conducting layer in the upper atmosphere.[104]

Terman's Graduate Study at Stanford

As an undergraduate, Terman would have noted that students interested in electrical engineering could follow one of three programs of courses of study. The first was a general electricity sequence for fourth-year students in all engineering fields.[105] The second option, dubbed the "dynamic group," was for third- and fourth-year students (drawn largely from mechanical engineering) intending to go further in electrical engineering. They would take courses on electrical energy, electrical machinery, and "general practice." Introductory physics was a prerequisite. The third option was for graduate students. This "electrotechnical group" was intended for graduates who had completed Stanford's bachelor's degree in engineering and who had taken the three courses in the "dynamic group," along with a course in electric and magnetic circuits. This option, with the addition of other advanced electrical engineering courses and several courses cotaught with physics and applied mathematics faculty, led to Stanford's Engineer's degree in electrical engineering.[106]

The "electrotechnical group" was Fred Terman's path to his graduate Engineer degree in 1920–22. Some forty-five to fifty-four quarter hours of credit were required for the degree, which could be done in one year by using all four quarters. (However, beginning in fall 1926, the Engineer's master's degree would require ninety to one hundred eight quarter hours of credit, or two years, beyond the bachelor's degree.)

As usual, Fred Terman threw himself into his work with gusto. Rather than rush to complete the minimum forty-five units required for the advanced degree of Engineer, Fred in fact accumulated eighty-two units in six quarters taking a range of related courses in electrical and mechanical engineering, mathematics, and physics.

Fred's application for candidacy for the degree of Engineer, filed on February

1, 1922, listed fifty-one units of credit "and numerous other less-advanced courses." Among these "unlisted" courses were Alternating Current Electrical Machinery (with Henline); Electrical Engineering—Economics, Reliability, and Safety (with Ryan); Ions and Electrons in Physics (with Fred J. Rogers), Machine Shop (with a shop machinist); and an elementary French class.

Ryan, Clark, and Henline made up the Electrical Engineering Department faculty during Terman's first graduate year. Ward B. Kindy, who joined the faculty in 1921 as instructor, taught only the less-advanced courses. Terman took his graduate machinery courses with Clark, Electric Circuits with Henline, and a course in electrical engineering practice with Ryan. He also enrolled in applied mathematics with H. C. Moreno. Fred's outstanding record in his math courses subsequently led to a request by the applied math faculty that he teach a section of introductory mathematics (algebra and analytical geometry) aimed at engineering students. He also took three courses in mechanical engineering: Machine Design with Guido Marx; Design and Operation of Pumping Machinery with Durand; and Hydraulic Machines and Power Stations with Eckart. Fred continued to struggle with hands-on machine work, earning Bs in his hydraulic machines course and a machine shop course. But with the exception of these two courses and his French class (something of a whim in which he received a B+), he received all As in his coursework his first year.

Fred didn't really need to take an additional foreign-language course while studying for his Engineer's degree. Perhaps he enrolled in elementary French in the fall of 1921 because of his fondness for Winifred Johnston, another Stanford faculty child; her father, Oliver Martin Johnston was professor of Romanic languages (French and Italian). Although Winifred was two years older than Fred, they were in the same class at Palo Alto High School. Like Fred, Winifred lived with her family at their campus home (4 Alvarado Row), and like Fred and his father, she confronted a serious illness that had forced her to drop out of Stanford for a time.

Fred and Winifred dated while at Stanford, but drifted apart in 1922. That summer, Lewis, Anna, Helen, and Fred Terman took a family vacation to Lake Tahoe, Yosemite, and the Mariposa Big Trees, and at summer's end Fred left California for Massachusetts. That fall, in Fred's absence Winifred met another Stanford electrical engineering graduate student, Charles Benjamin Carpenter (whose father, Hubert V. Carpenter, was professor of electrical engineering and dean of engineering at Washington State College). Carpenter, who would receive his engineer's degree in electrical engineering in June 1923, had earned a BSEE from Washington State College, a school with its own radio station. In her senior year (she received her degree in January 1923), Winifred asked her younger brother whom he preferred—Charles or Fred? Whatever her brother's answer, Winifred didn't wait. She married Charles at the end of the academic year.[107]

The Transient Crest Meter

In his second graduate year at Stanford, Fred took the course in physics (ions and electrons) but his remaining technical courses were all with Harris Ryan: weekly seminars, and high-voltage laboratory work. At this time, Ryan was especially interested in the breakdown of high-voltage insulators and cables under differing weather conditions (including lightning), and the conductivity and breakdown of insulating oils. Terman also assisted Ryan and Clark for several weeks on a study of possible corona losses from 220,000-volt power lines that the Pacific Gas and Electric Company (PG&E) intended to use on its Pitt River Project.

He began to help with the development of a "transient crest meter," a device to detect and measure voltage and current "crests" (peaks) as brief as two-tenths of a microsecond. This meter was intended to aid the study of the origin and character of unaccounted flash-over voltages on long transmission lines in large power networks.[108] The problem was to measure accurately very high voltages of unknown magnitude, while drawing as little current as possible, that is, dissipating minimal energy while measuring the voltage. This project became the subject of Fred Terman's Engineer degree thesis, "Transient Crest Voltmeter," and the basis for his first professional paper, delivered at the regional AIEE meeting.

Ryan was especially proud of Terman's work on the transient crest meter. In his department report to President Wilbur for 1922, Ryan cited six graduate student projects. Terman's was not only listed first, but further described as a study of the integrity characteristics of the transient crest meter. "A paper by Mr. Terman based on the results of this work," Ryan added, "was read before the San Francisco Section of the American Institute of Electrical Engineers in May, 1922." Ryan added that Terman's work was "a determination by the transient crest meter of the voltage-distance relation in transient oscillating flash-over discharges through long (300 centimeter) air columns"; and "a field study of the crest values of transient voltages present in long distance power transmission lines in sections where unaccounted for flash-overs occur."[109]

Having received his Engineer's degree June 19, 1922, Fred continued to develop a workable peak-voltage reading instrument or "crest" meter. During that summer of 1922, he worked with Pacific Gas and Electric company engineers in the field, studying transients on their transmission lines using his newly built instrument. After field-testing the device on a 110,000-volt PG&E line, Fred revised his paper and read it at the national midwinter meeting of the AIEE in New York City, in February 1923.

Fred's paper, discussing principles, applications, and details of construction and use of the crest meter, was published soon after as "The Measurement of Transients," in the *Transactions, American Institute of Electrical Engineers*.[110] The paper, his first publication, is a good early example of Terman's ability to write clear, technical prose.

Before Fred's work, a number of methods had been devised to measure peak voltages of high value. One involved a contact apparatus driven by an electrostatic motor, which momentarily connects an electrostatic voltmeter to the high-voltage circuit. In another scheme, a large air condenser is put on the high-voltage circuit, and a galvanometer is used, short-circuited during each half-cycle of the AC voltage. Other schemes used mercury arc rectifiers in series with condensers and an ammeter; or an oscillograph, with photography of the light trace. Yet another used Irving Langmuir's new "Kenotron" vacuum tube as the rectifier, while still others used inductive transformers with a voltmeter tied to a low-voltage tap of the transformer, or measurement of the width of the spark gap obtained during discharge.[111]

The concept behind Fred's transient crest meter was suggested by Professor Ryan. As Fred designed it, the meter consisted of a gold leaf electroscope in series with a rectifying device, an electron tube, which enabled the electroscope to charge, but prohibited discharge. The charge captured is proportional to the maximum impressed voltage. When sufficiently insulated, such an electroscope, with its gold leaves separated by some angle, will hold its charge for several minutes and the separation of the electroscope leaves can be read and then the value of the maximum voltage obtained. Fred's meter was essentially a maximum-voltage reading device, but with proper use of inductance, resistance, and capacitance the meter could be made to read the maximum slope of the wave form (or rise time), or the maximum area of the voltage or current waves (roughly, the pulse shape).

Fred had several critical parameters: the need for a small capacitance led to the adoption of a gold leaf electroscope. One hundredth of an ampere flowing for 0.1 microseconds can charge the electroscope to 500 volts. Thus the device stores minute energy yet at very high voltage. And, extremely good insulation is necessary to keep the electroscope from discharging quickly to ground. Fred used a block of cast sulfur to isolate the electroscope and estimated the sulfur block's resistance as "several trillion ohms." He surrounded the electroscope on four sides by soldered tin sheet (thus, four sides of a cube were covered). On the fifth and sixth sides he soldered a wire screen. The cage containing the electroscope was now shielded, yet Fred could read the electroscope angle of separation through the sides with the wire screening and measured against a protractor. Glass covers were placed over the screened sides to stop air currents. The electroscope was supported by the sulfur block and inserted on a rod extending through a hole in the tin top. Fred estimated he could read the separation of the gold leaves with an accuracy of plus or minus a half degree. (This seems to be a slight exaggeration.) The rectifier vacuum tube provided special problems. Glass accumulates moisture and surface contamination, leading to increased leakage of charge. To lessen these problems, Fred had the Moorhead laboratories in San Francisco build special rectifier tubes having the leads exit opposite ends of the tube. During operation, he covered the tube with a celluloid hood to keep the walls of the glass tube warm and minimize the moisture film on the glass.

The equivalent circuit of Fred's meter is a pure capacitance (the electroscope) in series with the electron tube, acting as a capacitance shunted by a variable resistance. He described how to calibrate the instrument, and the need for frequent calibration, and suggested additional circuitry and uses of the meter. In particular, a second electroscope leaf inside the meter could be used to trip a small current relay to disconnect the device from the voltage line and simultaneously ring a bell to alert the investigator. Since the meter captured only one polarity of the wave, two meters connected in opposite polarities could be used to study both positive and negative half of the pulse. Field testing of the meter in the summer of 1922 included use of a water-filled hose acting as a potentiometer and operation of the meter for two weeks' continuous duty, with a 110,000-volt line source. (At Stanford, the water supply yielded a resistance of about 1,400 ohms per cc at 15 degrees C. In this way, the 110,000-volt line voltage could be led to ground through an extremely high-resistance water line.[112])

In the discussion of his paper at the AIEE meeting, Fred was asked about problems of measuring short transients, those of about one millionth of a second, and dielectric spark lag. Fred replied that the vacuum tube rectifier responds to transients of one ten-millionth of a second, and thus there was no problem. MIT Professor F. S. Dellenbaugh Jr. applauded the work (by this time, Fred was a new graduate student at MIT) and suggested that the transient crest meter would become a valuable instrument. Measuring peak voltage, he noted, was of great interest since the transient peak voltage often resulted in ruptured cable and transformer insulation. The comments of C. L. Fortescue of Westinghouse, however, revealed the ongoing skepticism of industry for academic research. Simply measuring peak voltage, he rose to say, was not particularly important to men, like those employed by Westinghouse, out working in the real world.[113]

Moving on for the Doctorate

Lewis Terman was convinced that his son's cumulative grade point average was the highest at Stanford. Whether it was true, Professor Terman was also convinced that his son should continue on for a doctorate. Fred had graduated with his Engineer's degree in June with an exceptionally good record. A week later, his transcript was in the mail to "Boston Tech" (MIT).

Unlike his father's field of psychology, however, engineering provided different pathways for advancement. The greatest rewards in the engineering profession went to the good student who earned a bachelor's degree or perhaps the degree of Engineer, and then took a position with a company or as an industry consultant. This was the advice Fred's professors gave to young Terman, and the example he had among Stanford alumni like Cyril Elwell.

On both the West and East Coast, industry led academia in the new technology of radio and vacuum tubes. There was little to gain in the early 1920s in specializing in graduate work in radio communications or vacuum tubes at Stanford. The most learned and accomplished people in these fields worked nearby at Federal Telegraph in Palo Alto.

In the fall quarter of his senior year, Fred later recalled, Civil Engineering Professor Charles Moser had congratulated Lewis Terman on Fred's success. "Now the thing for him to do," Moser added, "as soon as he gets through is to go out and get some experience." Lewis, however, encouraged Fred not only to continue on for a doctorate but to do so at another university—he had, after all, taken all the electrical engineering courses that Stanford offered. A psychologist friend recommended Columbia University, but Harris Ryan's advice held more sway: "MIT is far better."[114]

Fred Terman was an attractive candidate for MIT, and especially for its energetic young professor of electrical engineering, Vannevar Bush. Fred had completed his bachelor's degree in chemistry with extra work in mechanical engineering, in three and a half years with outstanding grades and then completed his graduate degree of electrical engineer. Fred also was prepared for the mathematical challenges presented at MIT by Bush, Norbert Wiener, and Arthur Kennelly, who applied hyperbolic functions, differential equations, vector analysis, and Fourier Series to transmission line and network problems in electrical engineering. Supplementing his advanced electrical engineering courses with further work in mechanical engineering and physics, Fred was prepared for further graduate work in chemistry, mechanical engineering, or electrical engineering. Elected to Phi Beta Kappa, the chemistry honor society Phi Lambda Upsilon (1920) and to Stanford's chapter of the science honor society Sigma Xi (1922), Fred also had acquired valuable work experience during his summers—on a survey team in 1917, working on arc radio transmitters at Federal Telegraph in 1920, and in 1922 testing transient conditions on PG&E transmission lines, and had worked for a month in 1921 making corona measurements at Stanford's High-Voltage Laboratory for PG&E's Pitt River installation. All his additional preparation would prove important: Stanford's engineering bachelor's degree was one year behind the equivalent technical preparation of the bachelor's degree at MIT.

MIT

"Fred flew the nest a couple of weeks ago," Lewis Terman wrote his friend Truman Kelley in September 1922. "He is now getting acquainted with his cousins in

Indiana, and will land at Boston Tech about the 25th. His leaving gave the old man quite a wrench."[115] Fred's departure may have been a blow to his father, but young Terman moved ahead as usual at full steam, paying little attention to the significant differences between his parents' suburban campus home at Stanford and its still largely rural surroundings and the urban environment of Boston and Cambridge.[116]

He quickly found rooms at 426 Newbury Street, a three-story brick building located near the subway line and just across the street from the Massachusetts College of Osteopathy. Living four blocks south of the Charles River, Fred could walk to the new MIT campus across the river in Cambridge by going up Massachusetts Avenue and across the Harvard Bridge. The building was also just a block north of the railroad tracks of the Boston and Albany, and the New York Central.[117] Fred soon reported to his father that he was enjoying his work at "Tech" and the new experience offered by the "effete" environment of Cambridge and Boston.[118]

Electrical engineering at MIT was in flux when Fred Terman arrived in September 1922 with his freshly awarded Stanford Engineer's degree. Still called "Boston Tech," though not for much longer, MIT had thrived in the late nineteenth century and was undergoing a new surge of growth in the 1920s.

Chartered in 1861 at its original location in downtown Boston, the Massachusetts Institute of Technology had moved across the Charles River to Cambridge in 1916. Student enrollment, which had jumped significantly at the turn of the century, jumped once again at the end of the war. The year Terman arrived, there were 3,180 students, including 739 in electrical engineering, or Division VI. Fred was among the 44 regular graduate students enrolled in electrical engineering (there were 37 more in the electrical engineering "Co-op" or VIa master's program, for a total of 81 electrical engineering graduate students). Terman was particularly impressed that less than half of his fellow electrical engineering graduate students had a previous degree from MIT—a situation much unlike Stanford. Fred's tuition bill was slightly less than he had paid the year before: $100 per term or $300 for the year, compared to Stanford's $120 per quarter. (The cost of thirty-eight weeks of study at MIT, including tuition, fees, lodging, clothes and books, was estimated at $980.[119]) MIT, however, provided some financial assistance for graduate students, unlike Stanford, the University of California, and Caltech at this time, another difference Terman would long remember.[120]

Harvard University, which had formed its Lawrence Scientific School in 1847 for both applied science and engineering, had eyed "Boston Tech" since it opened its doors to students in 1865. Charles William Eliot, Harvard's dynamic president for four decades and a former MIT chemistry professor, attempted unsuccessfully to merge MIT with Harvard, but ran headlong into MIT's equally forceful president, Francis A. Walker.

Although first split off from the Physics Department in 1902, MIT's Electrical Engineering Department flourished with the arrival of Dugald C. Jackson in 1907, who served as its head for twenty-seven years. (In 1891, the Cornell-trained Jackson had organized the Department of Electrical Engineering at the University of Wisconsin.) In 1913, MIT set up the Division of Electrical Engineering Research, which received regular contributions from General Electric, American Telephone and Telegraph (AT and T) and other firms. MIT had benefited particularly from its close relationship with General Electric; many GE executives had been trained at MIT.

In 1903, the estate of industrialist, inventor, and great Harvard benefactor Gordon McKay provided a large bequest to Harvard to support applied science. Harvard and MIT arranged to share the McKay funds in 1914, providing for jointly offered engineering and mining courses and joint professorial titles. Skeptics could claim that this was proof that Harvard did not really want engineering to gain much of a foothold in Cambridge. As a result, Harvard Professors Arthur E. Kennelly, Comfort A. Adams, and Harry E. Clifford joined MIT's Division of Electrical Engineering Research. (Kennelly would later serve as the division's head.) The following year, an advisory committee led by MIT Trustee Gerard Swope of Westinghouse Electric, examined the MIT curricula and urged more research emphasis.[121] The curriculum was changed somewhat, although it remained centered on electrical power systems, with some courses in illumination and telephony. When MIT moved to its new Cambridge home in 1916, the Electrical Engineering Department took Buildings 4 and 10. The basement of Building 10 held the showpiece of the department, the Dynamo Electric Machinery Laboratory, a complete electrical substation with electrical machines and transformers. But just as at Stanford, one of the major research problems was "transient phenomena." Other research problems included insulation, corona, skin effect, radiation resistance, telephone apparatus and telephone interference, application of power, and generators and motors.[122]

The research interests of Chairman Dugald Jackson still served as a department focal point. While at Cornell and Wisconsin, Jackson had taught alternating-current theory and alternating-current machinery. At MIT, he turned to engineering management, the study of executive and administrative aspects of industrial concerns, an interest he shared with his friend and former colleague, Harris J. Ryan of Stanford. Jackson also retained his active role in Jackson and Moreland Co., which consulted on long-distance power transmission problems. Jackson was not an inventor, but rather a master at organizing ideas, materials, and personnel. Engineering, he believed, served as the bridge between the physical sciences and the social sciences, particularly sociology and economics, and he felt strongly that research be included at all levels of engineering education.

Like many American universities, MIT had been shaken from its complacency by American intervention in Europe in the spring of 1917. Many of its students had been involved in military training or left prematurely for active service, while many of its faculty were preoccupied with service on or off campus. MIT also had been hard hit by the Spanish Influenza epidemic in 1918. With the war's end, however, Jackson decided to rebuild the department. He began with MIT's cooperative program with General Electric, established in 1917 to allow students to alternate work at GE with their MIT studies. William H. Timbie reorganized the program and Terman remembered it years later when a somewhat similar program was inaugurated at Stanford.

In 1919, a court action restricting the Gordon McKay funds to Harvard proved to be a different sort of catalyst. Harvard's engineering faculty, with the exception of Kennelly, resigned their dual positions (Kennelly remained half-time at MIT until his retirement in 1925). The loss of McKay funds led MIT's president, Richard Maclaurin, to devise a "Technology Plan": in return for financial support, American companies were offered library and laboratory facilities at MIT and some faculty assistance in problem solving. Shortly after, in January 1920, Maclaurin died, but his plan was continued under interim president Elihu P. Thompson, a noted engineer and MIT graduate, and by Samuel W. Stratton, who subsequently took the president's office in January 1923.

In spite of the loss of the McKay funds, the Electrical Engineering Department's faculty ranks grew significantly. In 1920, the department's faculty numbered twenty-one (including nine with the rank of associate or full professor). By 1929, the faculty had grown to forty-four. Among the new arrivals was Vannevar Bush as associate professor.[123] Bush initially taught an introductory electrical engineering course and helped Kennelly with the Electrical Engineering Research Division; he would soon have a dramatic impact on the department, the institute, and on the career of Frederick Terman.

The MIT Student

Fred Terman registered as an applicant for the degree of Doctor of Science in Electrical Engineering at MIT on October 2, 1922.[124] As a student with a baccalaureate degree from a recognized university, Fred was required to spend at least three years in graduate work at the institute, although this time could be reduced with credit granted for previous graduate work. In Fred's case his Engineer's degree served as equivalent to a master's degree, but he quickly noticed that MIT's undergraduate curriculum was particularly rigorous—its first three years covered the material taught at Stanford over four years. The fourth year at MIT was much like the fifth year coursework undertaken for Stanford's Engineer degree.[125]

Fred's first year at MIT thus was taken up with six graduate courses in chemistry to complete his minor requirements (MIT's doctoral students had to prepare both "major" and "minor" fields). Ordinarily, work in the minor subject was completed one year before submitting the doctoral dissertation. Fred readily chose chemistry as his minor field. In 1922, the Chemistry Department, second in size only to the Electrical Engineering Department, had a faculty of twenty-three professors, plus thirteen instructors and three postdoctoral research associates.[126] Fred received the "honors" grade in all three terms of the year-long graduate series in Chemical Principles, a course in physical chemistry taught by Miles Standish Sherrill, associate professor of theoretical chemistry. He also took a course with Sherrill in colloidal chemistry, and a one-term course in thermodynamics taught by Frederick George Keyes, professor of physico-chemical research (as well as director of the Research Laboratory of Physical Chemistry and acting head of the Chemistry Department). His sixth course, Chemical Physics–Atomic Structure, taught by Arthur Alphonzo Blanchard, associate professor of inorganic chemistry, studied modern views of the atom, radiation, radioactivity, and allied fields. Although Fred enrolled in the thermo and colloids courses on what would be called today a credit–no-credit basis, he braved the Atomic Structure course on a graded basis and received the honors mark. His chemistry minor was promptly completed by opening day of fall term, October 1923.

He filled out his years' coursework with a year-long sequence of electrodynamics, taught in the Physics Department by Newell Caldwell Page, associate professor of electricity. This upper-level undergraduate course required proficiency in intermediate electricity and electromagnetic theory for entrance (Fred received the grade of honors for the three terms).

Even during his summer, Fred stayed busy. Although he may have visited relatives in Indiana, he did not go back to California, but instead worked for the Western Electric Company. There he studied a problem on the effects of gas in vacuum tubes for Dr. Mervin J. Kelly. (Kelly later directed research for Bell Laboratories, organized from Western Electric's research arm in 1925.[127]) It was not until a year and a half after Fred's arrival in Boston that he had a chance to visit an old friend of his father's, Harvard psychologist E. G. Boring. Boring reported to Lewis that the Boring family enjoyed a pleasant afternoon with Fred, who was "certainly an exceedingly unusual chap and one of broad interests."[128] Fred apparently made occasional visits to relatives around Indianapolis, Greenwood, and Star City, Indiana, several times in the period 1922–24.[129]

Fred's second year at MIT was equally busy. He passed his general doctoral qualifying exam in November 1923 and a month later was accepted as a candidate for the degree of Doctor of Science. His coursework, however, was not yet over. In 1923–24, he took four courses in the fall term and three each in the winter and spring terms, in addition to his thesis studies. The one-term course he took that fall was Electric Railways, a series of advanced lectures regarding the application of electricity to the propulsion of railway trains taught by Theodore Harwood Dillon, professor of electric power transmission and electric transportation. Why Terman took the railway course is unclear, but it is likely that it was suggested by Jackson or Bush, since Dillon soon after joined the two professors on Terman's dissertation committee. (Dillon was professor of electric power transmission at the time, and Bush the associate professor of electric power transmission.)

Terman's remaining three courses—three year-long course sequences—were taught by Arthur Kennelly (electrical communication of intelligence), Norbert Wiener (Fourier Series), and Vannevar Bush (advanced alternating currents). These three men would have enduring effects on Fred's career.

Arthur Kennelly

Fred was able to study radio with Arthur Kennelly in the professor's last year or two of instruction in that subject at MIT and received the grade of honors.[130] Kennelly was the author of ten books (he coauthored eighteen others) and, by his retirement in 1930, of more than 350 technical papers.[131] The recipient of many academic and professional honors, Kennelly was self-taught in both electrical engineering and higher mathematics. Born in 1861 of British parents near Bombay, India, Kennelly was one of the true telegraph and wireless pioneers, who served as Thomas Edison's chief lab assistant for six years. An able and prolific writer and lecturer, he was, in Dugald Jackson's words, a "natural philosopher" rather than an electrical experimenter, and he worked easily with others and communicated well both in small and large groups.[132] In March 1902, Kennelly published a suggestion that the long-distance propagation of radio waves might be due to reflection from a conducting layer at an elevation of about 80 km above the earth's surface. This preceded by eight months a similar posit by Oliver Heaviside and led to the early naming of the ionosphere as the "Kennelly-Heaviside Layer." Kennelly had not only been a pioneer in early radio propagation but became an important author, and interpreter, of texts concerning applied mathematics, hyperbolic functions, and vector calculus, specialties that would later influence the work of both Vannevar Bush and Frederick Terman. Kennelly was among the first in electrical engineering to use complex numbers. Kennelly's year-long lecture and lab course, Electrical Communication of Intelligence, covered the theory of telegraphy, wire telephone, and radio communications (including problems of wave transmission of sinusoidal and nonsinusoidal impulses and wavetrains, line loading, repeating vacuum tube effects, and radio transmission). Terman was particularly influenced by Kennelly's work introducing complex numbers and vector impedances, and his numerous articles on the equivalence of star and delta networks in transmission line theory.[133]

Norbert Wiener

Fred Terman was fortunate to spend a year studying mathematics with one of the greats of the twentieth century. His year-long course series with Norbert Wiener treated Fourier Series, Laplace's Coefficients, Bessel Functions, zonal and spherical harmonics, "and their applications to the solution of such problems in physics as can be expressed by certain partial differential equations." Future MIT president Julius Stratton later recalled being nearly blown away by the intensity of Wiener's courses. Wiener, a mathematics prodigy (he had completed his Harvard doctoral work as a teenager), was also a gifted linguist and philosopher. He had come to MIT in 1919 after government and army service during the war. Wiener's interest in nonlinear systems began while teaching applications of mathematics to electrical engineering. As he later wrote, the general way of studying nonlinear problems around 1920 was to look for a direct extension of the notion of impedance that could cover nonlinear as well as linear systems. Wiener regarded this situation as comparable to the late stages of Ptolemaic astronomy during the Middle Ages where epicycle was piled on epicycle, hoping to account correctly for planetary motions. The vast Ptolemaic patchwork of theoretical additions and corrections ultimately came down of its own weight. Just as Copernicus brought a new perspective to planetary astronomy, Wiener worked to bring a new approach to nonlinear problems in electrical engineering, and indeed to much of science.[134] Wiener was pondering these new approaches in his first years of teaching and in the very courses he taught Fred Terman.[135] Terman did well in the class, appreciating Wiener's approach (he received an honors grade in these courses as well). This work was well ahead of anything Fred had seen at Stanford but it suited his overall approach to electrical engineering as a discipline in need of buttressing by mathematics, chemistry, and physics.

Terman and Bush

At the end of his career, Terman wondered whether he should have spent more time with Arthur Kennelly, but when the moment came in 1923 for Fred to choose a research topic, Kennelly was nearly sixty-two years old and spent at least half of his time on the Harvard campus.[136] Instead, Fred cast his lot with Vannevar Bush. Fred Terman's past training with Harris Ryan, combined with Bush's interest in transients and long transmission line systems, made Fred an excellent fit with Bush.

Edward L. Bowles, who had received his master's degree under Bush in 1922, was appointed instructor for the fall of 1922 and assisted both Bush and Kennelly. Bowles helped set up the laboratory for communications courses. Although he never completed his doctorate, Bowles remained at MIT to build the Communication Laboratory during the 1920s and 1930s, much as Terman would do at Stanford. Terman and Bowles became friends and, in later years, sometime rivals.

Vannevar Bush, then thirty-three and the Electrical Engineering Department's first faculty appointment with a doctorate, was a fireball. He had earned his bachelor's and master's degrees in engineering at Tufts University. After working briefly at General Electric, he entered Clark University but soon after transferred to MIT. He had astonished his advisor Arthur Kennelly by completing his dissertation at MIT in one year.[137] His first teaching post was at Tufts (1916–19), simultaneously working for American Radio and Research Corporation (which later evolved into the Raytheon Corporation). He joined the MIT faculty in 1919.

In his first four years on the faculty as associate professor of electric power transmission, he had energized the Electrical Engineering Department. Working to build up the research division, he helped William Timbie increase the number of master's degree candidates by an order of magnitude. (There had been four master's degrees awarded in electrical engineering in 1921; by 1923 there were forty-five.) This effort continued through the 1920s such that by the decade's end, the department averaged fifty electrical engineering master's degrees throughout the period. Bush was named MIT's dean of engineering and vice president in 1932, and in 1938, became president of the Carnegie Institution of Washington. His influence now nationwide, Bush headed the National Defense Research Committee beginning in June 1940, and later the Office of Scientific Research and Development when it was established in 1941. Much of Bush's progress through American science was still in the future when Terman picked him as a thesis advisor, but Bush's influence on young Terman was profound, and their relationship one of mutual respect.

Bush would have a special influence throughout Terman's life. Although ten years his senior, Bush had much in common with Terman. Both were strongly influenced by their fathers. As boys, both had liked mechanical things and ham radio (Terman built his first receiver at thirteen, Bush at nineteen). Although Bush continued his numerous hobbies such as "tinkering," inventing, and shop work throughout his life, Terman set aside his boyhood hobbies of fishing, running, and hunting rabbits when he became a college professor and turned his hobby of radio into his career.[138] As young men, each had to contend with serious illness: Bush suffered an appendicitis at age twenty-one, and Terman had both TB and an appendicitis at twenty-four. Each ran the mile in track in college—Bush was not much good, Terman somewhat better—and each tended to work with endless energy. They both were members of engineering fraternities, both had first taught while in college (Bush tutored fellow students, Terman was a teaching assistant while getting his engineering degree).

There would be similarities in their careers as well: Bush's first patent was awarded when he was twenty-two years old, Terman's first patent application when he was twenty-six, and neither made money from these first efforts. More successful in later patent effort, Bush generally gave his patent rights to MIT while Terman gave most of his patent earnings, small as they were, and a good deal of his considerable book royalties to Stanford. As young professors, both were influenced by the success of university-industry cooperative arrangements at their alma maters, and both greatly stepped-up their departments' master's degree programs. As their careers progressed, both would have a dramatic influence on their departments long before becoming department chairs. Each viewed the ideal engineer as versatile and capable in physics, chemistry, and mathematics. Interestingly, Bush would be dean of engineering (and vice president) at MIT at the age of forty-two, and Terman, at forty-four, was named dean of engineering at Stanford. As managers, they believed in choosing good young men to work with and then delegating authority.

There were, of course, significant differences, particularly in their personalities. Terman was a private man, little concerned for his appearance, dressing "rough" in engineering boots while a student and proper but "rumpled" as a young professor. Bush was a public man, dapper, self-conscious of his appearance and bearing, and he enjoyed the life of high political circles and glamour of Washington DC that Terman found tedious.[139] Bush clashed frequently with Dugald Jackson and later bullied the aged Arthur Kennelly in a manner Terman would never use. Bush said he disliked historians and wanted no biography written, but instead worked with two professional writers to produce in 1970 his semi-autobiographical *Pieces of the Action*.[140] Rather than write his own memoirs, in retirement Terman wrote shorter pieces about the rise of the electronics industry, granted several long oral-history interviews, and spent considerable time during his final retirement arranging and describing his large archive of professional and personal papers, which he had donated to Stanford University.

Terman's Doctoral Dissertation

Terman's year-long course with Bush, Advanced Alternating Current, chiefly concerned the transmission and control of electrical power, including networks and transmission lines in the steady state, unbalanced polyphase systems, transients in circuits with lumped constants, and waves on transmission lines. Much of the work was treated mathematically. MIT's graduate students were encouraged to study transmission line problems, extremely important considerations in both electrical engineering and applied physics in the early 1920s. (Arthur Kennelly had directed Charles Lambert Manneback's 1922 ScD dissertation on "Radiation from Transmission Lines," the only ScD given at MIT that year, while MIT's two math master's theses that year were both on partial differential equations applied to transmission lines.)

As at Stanford, MIT's electrical engineering faculty were deeply interested in "superpower" electric power transmission systems. Moving from his own dissertation work on artificial transmission lines, Bush continued his research on transmission line problems, giving several papers on transmission line transients at AIEE meetings between 1923 and 1925.[141] Arthur Kennelly had published two books and numerous papers on mathematical methods of studying transmission lines, while Norbert Wiener worked on general mathematical approaches applied to relevant electrical engineering problems.

And like Harris J. Ryan's close association with western power companies, the pragmatic needs of regional power companies came into play at MIT. In the fall of 1922, Terman's first year at MIT, the Boston firm of Jackson and Moreland worked with a client to analyze the mechanical and electrical feasibility of transmitting a large block of electrical power from Canada to New England over a distance of five hundred miles. In October 1922, the company's preliminary report concluded that such a "super" system was feasible. R. D. Booth of Jackson and Moreland, chief design engineer on the project, had as his major consultant Vannevar Bush. Who better to assist Bush with his consulting than his new graduate student, Fred Terman, a man with experience in high-voltage transmission line analysis.[142] Fred, in turn, was assisted in his dissertation work by both Bush and Booth. (The company also furnished Terman with assistance and empirical data.)

Analysis of long electrical lines had begun in the late nineteenth century when problems of insufficient signal strength and distorted signals led Oliver Heaviside, Michael Pupin, and others to discuss inductive loading coils and other devices to "balance" undersea telegraph lines. At this early point, transmission of information through telegraph and telephone lines rather than electrical power was the primary goal. As large, centralized electric power stations began to deliver electric power to increasingly larger groups of customers in the 1880s and 1890s, problems arose such as the choice of direct or alternating current, how to synchronize generating sets, and how to adjust the line load when demand went up or down. By 1915, American electrical engineers faced new problems with the use of long-distance power transmission line lengths and more complicated operating networks. (If an electrical line is half a wavelength long, or multiples of this length, then the electrical impedance seen at each end is the same; but if the line is an electrical quarter-wave in length or odd-numbered multiples of this, then the impedance at each end can be radically different. With a transmission line not well matched to source or load, voltage and current can vary to extremes along the line. More current may flow into an open line than into one shorted at the far end.)

Voltage surges on unmatched lines or transient pulses can cause other major problems, and in the case of electrical high-voltage power lines, could lead to disastrous events such as the line blowing out, destroying equipment, and causing fires. (At a frequency of 60 cycles, an electrical wavelength is about three thousand miles, but with loading conditions of a practical electrical power line, it might be two thousand miles. A quarter-wavelength electrical power transmission line at 60 cycles was about the length of the "superpower" system lines considered practical in 1920.) Analysis of lines operated at so-called steady-state still did not account for problems of sudden load changes, partial breakdowns, or transients caused by lightning or other factors. When a transmission line is electrically long enough to see great changes in voltage, current, and impedance along the line length, for example, corona flashover may occur at high-voltage points, or thermal breakdown may occur with current overload.

Fred studied several aspects of these problems of transmission in "superpower" systems in his ScD dissertation. "The long distance transmission of power," he wrote, "is gradually bringing to light features regarding the properties of transmission lines that had not been previously appreciated. This is a necessary consequence of the fact that the maximum power limit of a line diminishes with increasing length, bringing the operating range of these 'Superpower' systems to a place never touched by the ordinary lines." The pragmatic old questions remained: "Will it pay to transmit power this distance?" If the power line is increased to 250 miles, "can an appreciable amount of power be transmitted the necessary distance with the conventional type of line?" The answers, he concluded, involved "the characteristics of transmission lines over practically the entire possible range of operation."[143]

Frank G. Baum (one of Stanford's early electrical engineering graduates and a longtime consultant to the electrical power industry) thought that a long line, supplied with voltage at one end, results in increased charging current near the station end, which, in turn, raises the voltage. Intermediate condensing stations along the line, he believed, would solve the problem and keep the voltage regulated along the line. Terman showed this not to be the case. Condenser loading had negligible effect since it leaves the maximum power limit of the line practically unaffected and increases the power current limits only at low voltage. (Charging current grows in importance with the square of the line length because the charging current and the inductance it flows through are both proportional to the line length.) Lowering the operating frequency would also lessen the problems for a given length of line less than one-quarter wavelength, of course, since the electrical line length would then be shorter.

According to Terman's analysis, the most serious factor was voltage fluctuation, and during transient conditions, voltage fluctuated considerably. In a transmission system, all component parts must be considered, and inductance is the most critical component. This includes generator leakage inductance, transformer reactance, reactors, and transmission line reactance. Since the inductance of the transmission part of a system is mostly fixed, Terman concluded that the place for improvement was in the terminal apparatus and that the generator leakage reactance, transformer reactance, and reactor reactance should be, at the very minimum, consistent with safety and cost. Such lowering of inductance would both raise the limits of power transmittable, he suggested, and improve the regulation of the voltage.

In reaching his conclusions, Terman worked through two hundred pages of calculations using the conception of network constants recently developed by R. D. Evans of Westinghouse and H. K. Sels of Public Service of New Jersey, as well as the devices of the geometric plots or circle diagrams worked out by Evans and Sels, and by L. Thielemans in France. (The circle diagram plot of transmission line performance gives the relation between real and reactive powers that must be maintained at the receiving end to obtain the assumed voltage conditions at the generating and the receiving ends.) Terman would elaborate on these latter techniques in a paper published in 1926, soon after he began teaching at Stanford, and in the textbook, *Transmission Line Theory* that he would publish that same year with W. S. Franklin of MIT.[144]

Terman and the "Superpower" Transmission Systems Debate

Terman finished his dissertation just as an important session on "Superpower Transmission" systems was held in Philadelphia at the February 1924 national midwinter convention of the AIEE.[145] Nearly all the session papers, which would take up seventy large-print pages of the meeting's proceedings, were given by Westinghouse engineers, including C. L. Fortescue, who had seen little importance in Fred Terman's transient crest meter the year before. The session was chaired by Frank G. Baum, proponent of condenser-loaded transmission lines. Some discussion followed (much of it took the form of papers), but the major attack on the Westinghouse presentations came from Vannevar Bush and the Jackson and Moreland firm. A sense of competition was clearly in the air when Robert L. Moreland described his firm's consultation on the proposed five-hundred-mile Canadian Superpower line and their discussions with research engineers at General Electric. Moreland suggested that the Westinghouse analyses were flawed because they based their conclusions regarding stability of operation and limitations of power on steady-state conditions. (The GE analysis was similarly flawed, but Moreland did not discuss it.) Bush and R. D. Booth also offered criticisms, backing up Moreland's comments with charts and plots. They would reply more fully a year later at the February 1925 convention in New York City.[146]

Others took shots. For several years, engineers had been building mechanical machines with wheels, cogs, rollers, disks, and the like to simulate electrical network or transmission line operations, using weights to imitate inductors, springs to imitate condensers, and dashpots to imitate resistance. Professor V. Karapetoff of Cornell and Arthur Kennelly discussed progress on such simulation machines. With his dissertation specifically covering this "Superpower Transmission" topic but still three months from submission, Fred Terman entered the fray cautiously. He noted how the circle diagram methods of R. D. Evans and H. K. Sels could be improved and illustrated some mathematical simplifications and improvements. He also illustrated a chart showing the effects of conductor spacing and diameter, crediting Bush for the suggestion.[147]

Ironically, the five-hundred-mile "superpower" system that the Jackson and Moreland company (and Fred Terman) had studied was soon abandoned. The analyses of Bush, Booth, Terman, Moreland, and others were probably correct, but in the end economics ruled the day. The amount of power that could be brought in dependably from Canada over that five-hundred-mile distance was not sufficient to justify the expense of construction and maintenance of transmission lines and purchase of right-of-ways.[148]

Fred Terman submitted his doctoral dissertation to MIT on May 15, 1924. Having completed his final exam on May 26, he was awarded the degree of Doctor of Science in the field of electrical engineering on June 10, 1924. The graduation ceremonies, on a Tuesday morning, featured a procession, a concert by the Coast Artillery Band, and the awarding of degrees by President Samuel Wesley Stratton. Frank Edward Shepard, director of the Denver Mint, gave the address. Fred was one of six to earn the ScD degree (awarded for pure or applied science) that year—his was the eighth doctoral degree to be awarded in electrical engineering by MIT—while eleven others earned the PhD degree, awarded for pure science.[149]

Returning to Stanford

Fred had made a name for himself at MIT. Department chair Dugald Jackson offered him an instructorship in electrical engineering for the coming year. Back at Stanford, Harris Ryan also offered Fred an instructorship in his Electrical Engineering Department to fill the vacancy left by the recent resignation of James Cameron Clark. "In my judgment, the best man available in the nation today is Fred E. Terman," Ryan wrote Stanford president Ray Lyman Wilbur in August 1924. "If appointed, the good work that he will do should, in my judgment, be one of the outstanding achievements of his generation of Stanford faculty men."[150]

Fred had returned to California that summer to visit his family but only three weeks later suffered an attack diagnosed as tuberculosis. His condition quickly worsened, with severe hemorrhaging and weight loss. Under the care of Russel V. Lee, later a noted physician and cofounder of the Palo Alto Medical Clinic, Fred began a regimen of total bed rest, with weights on his chest, that would last some nine months. Fred later credited Lee with saving his life, but his mother also devoted her attention to his health, and her nursing skills contributed much to his progress.[151]

Throughout Fred's year-long recuperation, both Stanford and MIT held their offers open. If Fred had gone back to MIT, he could have assisted Vannevar Bush, whom he admired greatly. "I had been one of his handymen, and it was good to be tied to the tail of his kite, a good man," he later recounted modestly. "I've always wondered what would have happened if I [had]."[152]

Stanford, however, had the edge. Like Lewis Terman's physicians had done, Dr. Lee encouraged Fred to stay in a warm climate. In the interim, Ryan had offered Joseph S. Carroll, a promising Stanford graduate student, an instructorship for the 1924–25 fall and winter quarters, but Carroll expected to resume his graduate work the following spring. Ryan continued to urge Terman to stay. He got advice from Fred's physicians that Fred could support a part-time teaching load while recuperating. Ryan proposed that Fred teach a half-time course load for a year, beginning in the fall of 1925. Fred, making marvelous progress that winter, accepted.

"His progress has been extraordinarily fine in every respect," Lewis wrote Arnold Gesell in February 1925, eight months after the attack. "At present he is sitting up two hours a day and will begin mild exercise in a few days. Within a couple of months he will be up and around all the time, and the doctors think he will be ready for light work next fall." Lewis received welcome messages of support from his own colleagues about "Dear old, brilliant Fred," his health, and the Stanford job offer.[153]

While Fred Terman's 1924 struggle with tuberculosis is well known, few knew that as he neared recovery in May 1925, he nearly died from a ruptured appendix and was bedridden yet again for several months. Due to the precarious state of his lungs, doctors had advised against a general anesthetic for the appendectomy, and thus Fred had been operated on with only localized anesthesia.[154]

His long months recuperating in bed were not idle ones, however. Fred was restless about his work. In his last months at MIT, he had begun a collaboration with W. S. Franklin, an MIT professor of physics and author of mathematics texts, on a book on transmission line theory and practice. The book featured transmission line results from Fred's own doctoral dissertation, along with work he had done with Kennelly and Bush on hyperbolic functions and information about mechanical differential analyzers as computers to solve differential equations. Fred took up the work while recovering, although it would be another year before the book was published.

Fred's love of radio also occupied his time. Fred had found useful the 1920 book of Hendrik J. Van der Bijl's *The Thermionic Vacuum Tube and Its Applications*, which had covered recent work at Western Electric and General Electric on vacuum tubes and associated circuits and the use of vacuum tubes as amplifiers and oscillators. Van der Bijl "was one of the men who pulled together, in a very readable book, the whole set of principles that had been worked out," he later remembered.[155] Vacuum tubes had become readily available to the average radio ham after World War I, and the design of circuits for their use was very new. During his convalescence, Terman built a homemade broadcast receiver and listened to the radio.

> Then I discovered that this circuit theory that I learned from Kennelly, telephone things and so on, could be tied with what I knew about vacuum tubes. Bush had taught me circuit theory, too, and all this tied together. I could put the vacuum tube circuits and the non-vacuum tube circuit theory that I'd learned there at MIT all together for a nice understanding of amplifiers and tuned amplifiers, and things like that. I worked this out for fun, just recreational reading, and worked out some equations for how much amplification you could get from vacuum tubes.[156]

As his health improved, Fred also taught a "research tutorial," Electrical Engineering 243, an outlet for student research offered by Professors Ryan and Henline. His student was Herbert Hoover Jr., then an undergraduate, whom he had become friends with around 1913. Fred and Herbert Hoover Jr. developed a friendship "that lasted for life."[157] A few months before the beginning of World War I, Herbert Hoover Sr. rented a house directly across the street from the Terman campus home on Dolores Street. In 1919 the Hoovers built their own home about a block and a half from the Terman home. As youths, Fred, Herb Hoover Jr., and Jack Franklin (son of chemistry professor E. C. Franklin) had built numerous radio devices. As Hoover later recalled, "I get a big kick to think back to the time when all three of us were neighbors and upon pushing the key of one of our imposing contraptions, would holler out of the window to see if it had been received on the other side of the street."[158]

During his tutorial with Terman in winter quarter 1925, Hoover tested several radio receivers and in the spring quarter built a radio transmitter and altered its circuits. Hoover installed the ham radio set in his undergraduate room in Toyon Hall, the newest of Stanford's dormitories, stringing an antenna from his room out across the roof and a deck. He used an experimental radio station call 6XH for transmitting. Hoover saw radio's newest frontier to be the study of how waves spread around the world, and the factors which impeded or propelled them, a specialty called radio wave propagation.[159]

No doubt Terman enjoyed the tutorial. Four years later, he would apply for funds to build a radio propagation building in Stanford's foothills and would begin work on his most successful text, *Radio Engineering*. Terman certainly was aware of the truly gigantic radio "boom" in broadcasting. The fledgling radio industry was outstripping in growth even the celebrity electric power and automotive industries. Sales of radios had grown from $2 million in 1920 to $120 million in 1923. While Fred was in bed recovering, radio sales topped $325 million![160] During America's intervention in Europe in 1917–18, the government clamped down on amateur broadcasting in the United States, but at the end of the war, commercial broadcasting blossomed. By 1921, thousands of government, commercial, and amateur radio sets were in operation. Most broadcast stations operated on a wavelength of about 500 KHz frequency or 600 meters wavelength (although ship-to-shore signals could be found at from 125 to 1,000 KHz). Older stations, like "Doc" Herrold's in San Jose, replaced old arc transmission equipment with improved tubes, at considerable expense, as stations across the country applied for the new U.S. broadcasting licenses (authorizing operation at powers from 5 to 3,000 watts). During September and October 1921, a number of licenses were issued on the East Coast (including Lee de Forest's station in the Bronx), but the first granted to a California station went to Arno Kluge for KQL in Los Angeles. A flood of California licenses soon followed.[161]

Federal Telegraph was now constructing transmitting stations around the world. In addition to huge arc transmitters in Hawaii, along the Pacific Coast and across the Southwest, it equipped U.S. Naval stations abroad and for foreign customers as far flung as the Eiffel Tower in Paris and in Bordeaux, Lyon, and Toulon; in London, Rome, and Corfu. The Bordeaux 1,000,000-watt arc transmitter installed in 1919 for the U.S. government was sold to the French government for four million dollars. At the time, it was the most powerful radio station in the world.[162] In 1921, Federal won a five-million-dollar contract with the Chinese government to build the most powerful station in the world at Shanghai with six 1,000-foot steel antenna towers. At home, Federal Telegraph built a new Marsh Station out on the bay lands at the end of Embarcadero Road. Its 626-foot tower (the highest on the Pacific Coast) was again designed by C. B. Wing and remained standing until 1960. Federal's Palo Alto station had perfected "quadruplex" transmission, the ability to send four radio signals simultaneously, at the time the only station that could do so.

Federal Telegraph was booming. The company had its own baseball team, the "Radios," said to be one of the "fastest teams on the Peninsula." Faces at the top were changing, however. By this time, both Elwell and de Forest were gone (de Forest left for the East Coast in 1913, after selling his audion tube improvements to AT&T; Elwell left the company soon after, joining an English company after he lost financial control of Federal to a team of investors and promoters). Frederick A. Kolster, a celebrated designer was then chief research director from 1921 until Federal left Palo Alto in 1931.[163] In the early 1920s, Palo Alto's local newspaper was full of radio news and inventions—a radio facsimile service could send photos over wireless, radio services were available for farmers, and radio sets for the police; radio could connect isolated Alaskan villages. Emile Portal had a radio set at the Colin B. Kennedy radio plant in Los Altos. With his transmitter—two 50-watt Cunningham tubes, one acting as self-oscillator and the other as modulator—Portal reported that he was exchanging voice and musical messages with someone from Great Bend, Kansas. The first national wireless convention was hosted in Chicago in August 1921 by the American Radio Relay League (ARRL), the first national amateur radio association with more than three hundred clubs and 6,500 licensed members with Commerce Secretary Herbert Hoover as a featured speaker.[164]

By 1922, everybody seemed to be making radios. Like the software boom of the late twentieth century, teenagers were solving problems for adult technology users. Youthful ham operators were assembling and selling radio receivers to adults. The *Palo Alto Times* began a "Radio" column. It was front-page news when Leonard Fuller (who had moved from Stanford and Federal to join nearby Colin B. Kennedy radio company) donated to Stanford University a radio set "with record range . . . the finest apparatus of the kind ever made."[165] The receiver covered the range from 180 to 26,000 meters (1.66 MHz down to 11 KHz), "the whole radio spectrum." The newspaper went on to report that Professor Ryan, the "chief authority in problems of transmission with wires, is beginning a series of extensive experiments on wireless communication," and would use the receiver.

"Radio" listings in the newspaper advertised several San Francisco stations (KSL, the Emporium Store; KDN, the Fairmont Hotel; KLS, Warner Brothers; KCO, San Francisco *Examiner*), and two in Oakland across the bay (KZY, Rockridge, and KZM Oakland Hotel). In neighboring Los Altos there was KLP (the Colin B. Kennedy Company) and further south in Sunnyvale KJJ (the Radio Shop). A significant early agreement had been reached: only one station could broadcast locally at a time. Typically, between 9 AM to 9 PM each Bay Area station would be on the air for about one hour at a time, when another would take its place. The lack of selectivity and dynamic range of receivers—a typical radio receiver could not "tune out" offending stations—would soon change. By spring 1923, with the evolution of radio receiver design, several local stations would be on the air simultaneously, competing for the listener's attention, although the stations agreed to a designated "quiet" night, when all local stations stayed off the air so that listeners could operate "DX," that is, could listen for distant stations from the Midwest and East Coast. Nevertheless, while most hams now used new vacuum tube and continuous wave telegraphy or telephony, there were those amateur ham operators operating the old-fashioned (and now illegal) "spark gap" transmitters who still could foul up listening within several miles of their sets.[166]

As Fred Terman recuperated in his Stanford campus home in 1924, spending hours in bed each day with sandbags on his chest, he probably weighed carefully his career. He had been critically ill. For one reason at least, the California climate would be better for a recovering tubercular. Two jobs were being held open for him—one in electrical engineering at Stanford and one at MIT.

At MIT Fred would be in the largest department in the institute, in numbers both of faculty and students. Dugald Jackson, the MIT electrical engineering chairman, liked Fred a lot, but Jackson was mostly interested in engineering management, not the scientific aspects of engineering research. Fred would be the protégé of MIT's fastest-rising engineer, Van Bush. Yet under Bush, Fred might be constrained to be the assistant to Bush as Joe Carroll would be at Stanford under Harris Ryan. As one under Bush's wing, Fred might be expected to continue in electric power methods or analog computation devices. Edward Bowles at MIT was hardly, if any, more experienced than Fred in radio and Bowles had no doctorate. Yet Arthur Kennelly was retiring, Bush wasn't interested, and Bowles more or less had a head start in radio at MIT.

At Stanford, by contrast, Fred could be a big fish in a smaller pond. Joe Carroll would be tied to Harris Ryan and the high-voltage electric transmission work for years. Henry Henline, who had just started some experimental work in radio in 1924 was much less able theoretically than Fred and in any case Henline may have indicated that he would leave Stanford if a financially more rewarding engineering administrative position opened for him elsewhere. As the only one in the Electrical Engineering Department with a doctorate and with advanced training in mathematics and physics, Fred was assured of and would be expected to teach the advanced courses in the department.

As he lay in bed, as Fred explained later, he saw how he could apply the network theory and mathematics he had learned at MIT from Kennelly, Wiener, and Bush to radio circuit and vacuum-tube design.[167] The leading radio transmitting firm on the West Coast was Federal Telegraph on the El Camino highway, only two miles from his family's campus home. From his own experience at Federal as a student summer employee and his personal knowledge of the numerous Stanford engineers working there, Fred surely saw the potential for cooperation in university research. As a young faculty member, Fred would foster cooperation between Stanford and Federal Telegraph, as well as with other smaller western electronics firms.

Later in life, Fred would reminisce about what might have happened if he had studied with Kennelly instead of Bush, or if he had stayed at MIT, tied to the tail of Vannevar Bush's kite. A rising kite may pull its tail upward, Terman acknowledged, but the tail always follows the kite. By early 1925, Fred Terman was determined to fly his own kite through life.

CHAPTER TWO

The Stanford Professor

1925–1937

The years between Fred Terman's return to Stanford to begin teaching in 1925 and his promotion to executive head of the Electrical Engineering Department in 1937 would be formative ones for both his life and career. Fred established his teaching and research interests and made a place among his academic colleagues. He also met Sibyl Walcutt, a vivacious psychology graduate student at Stanford. Married in 1928, Fred and Sibyl Terman settled down in a campus home of their own and started a family.

Young Professor Terman saw his teaching, his research, and his textbooks as closely intermingled. It was during this initial period on the Stanford faculty that Fred significantly strengthened the Electrical Engineering Department's Communication Laboratory while furthering his own research in vacuum tube circuits and design and, later, in antennas, radio wave propagation, very-high frequency techniques, and vacuum tube construction. He subsequently spent much of the 1930s writing textbooks, and very popular ones, while applying successfully for numerous patents for his work and consulting for a number of engineering companies on the West Coast.

Equally important, Terman would become an outstanding teacher of Stanford engineering students. While experimenting with ways to recruit graduate students and enhancing their fellowship support and research opportunities, he also took a strong interest in the undergraduate curriculum. In addition to extending the Electrical Engineering Department beyond its traditional strength in power transmission, he supported Stanford's commitment to a broad, rather than a highly specialized, engineering curriculum, and he encouraged better instruction for engineers in English. He did not forget his students after their graduation, but worked especially hard to find them employment during the economic downturn of the 1930s.

As part of this process, he developed and maintained a growing network of alumni friends through correspondence and personal visits. Students later considered to be among Terman's "stars"—William Hewlett, David Packard, Bernard Oliver, Edward Ginzton, and Joseph Pettit—would be success stories not only because of their career accomplishments but for their strong commitment to Stanford University and its students, a commitment instilled in them by Fred Terman.

Getting Back to Work

While recuperating in bed in the fall and winter of 1924–25, and while coaching Herbert Hoover Jr. on his research tutorials, Fred Terman took up again Hendrik Van der Bijl, *The Thermionic Vacuum Tube and Its Applications*, the best early book on vacuum tubes.[1] Despite his illness, he began thinking about patent ideas concerning electronic circuits, particularly radio circuits, while working on a book project with a senior physicist at MIT.

Terman's coauthor, William Suddards Franklin (1863–1930), was a professor of physics at MIT and brother of Stanford chemist E. C. Franklin, with whom Fred had studied.[2] Since 1896, Franklin had published, with coauthors, more than a dozen textbooks on physics, electrical engineering, and calculus. Franklin saw an opportunity in working with young Fred Terman, an up-and-coming electrical engineer who had ambitions of his own. As Fred was finishing his doctoral dissertation and preparing for the AIEE 1924 winter convention session on "Superpower Transmission Systems," Franklin asked Fred to assist with three new textbooks: a revision of an introductory textbook on the elements of electrical engineering; a new dynamo machinery laboratory manual; and a book on transmission lines. As junior author on each of the three books, Franklin added, Fred was expected to pay a quarter of the costs of publishing and accept a quarter of any profits.[3]

Fred saw the opportunity to quickly publish his Stanford and MIT graduate work on transmission lines, but it is clear that he had little interest in reworking two elementary textbooks for a minor author and publisher. Even so, he began his collaboration with Franklin while still at MIT and continued during the summer of 1924.[4] From his sickbed, Terman corresponded about publishing costs and publishers and began contributing manuscript text.[5] In spite of his illness, he was able to contribute a fair amount of material. The manuscript was nearly finished by December 1925 when Fred mailed off an excellent chapter on artificial lines and wave filters. Two months later, Franklin sent most of the completed manuscript to the printers in England. The book was published in the late summer of 1926 as *Transmission Line Theory, and Some Related Topics* by William Suddards Franklin, ScD, and Frederick Emmons Terman, ScD.[6]

The book opens with presentation of nonperiodic waves along lines and proceeds to harmonic waves. Overall, the first part of the book was designed to help the practicing engineer by providing information ordinarily used by physicists. The alternating-current long-line in steady state is developed, followed by the three-phase line and the circle diagram. The first part closes with the topic of artificial lines and wave filters. To Fred, this was one of the most important portions of the book, since it was the first textbook explanation of the filter properties of *practical* use to engineers. Similarly, Fred thought the description of the use of hyperbolic functions provided concrete meaning for transmission line engineers.[7]

The second part of the book is devoted to Fourier Series and nonharmonic waves, a revision of Franklin's own earlier coauthored book *Calculus* (by Franklin, MacNutt, and Charles, 1913). The third part follows with appendices, including an introduction to vectors and complex quantities and their use in solving transient problems on long transmission lines, on coronal loss, and on the use of A. E. Kennelly's hyperbolic function charts.

The book received a few friendly, although otherwise uninfluential, reviews that echoed Fred's own opinions about the practical value of such material presented clearly and at a sophisticated level. The book was not a financial success. Fred's share of the costs was about $550, and it appears that by 1933 he had received about $200 in royalties. (About four hundred copies were sold in the United States in the first two years.) Nevertheless, Fred had his name on a textbook. He used it in his transmission line courses at Stanford, writing Franklin that it was quite a help to him in his lectures, but helping Franklin in his further projects was a different matter. When Franklin wrote, concerned about Fred's health, he replied that his eyes had been giving him a great deal of trouble and limited his reading time. Fred thanked Franklin for his patience in the transmission line book project and excused himself from further collaboration on books due to his eye problems. (Ten months later, Fred reported that his eyes had improved so that he could read three hours a day.[8])

If not a financial success, Fred Terman's first project was nonetheless a professional success. Fred learned much from this project. He had completed his portion of the work in eighteen months, even though stricken with tuberculosis and later appendicitis. He had maximized his recent research and his graduate work at MIT by publishing his work on long transmission lines and the circle diagram, and his Stanford work on coronal loss (while referencing the work of his professors, including Vannevar Bush's work on transients and the harmonic wave analyzer, and Kennelly's hyperbolic charts). These same topics also figured in his first AIEE published papers. Henceforth, however, Terman would use his own carefully thought-out plans for publishing and would work with influential publishers who could properly market his product. Meanwhile, Fred settled into life as a young professor in a brand-new School of Engineering.

Stanford's School of Engineering

In developing graduate education at Stanford, President Wilbur felt he was carrying on "where Dr. Jordan left off."[9] The junior-college movement had been growing in popularity in the United States, and especially in California. Wilbur believed that this meant that major universities such as Stanford could then concentrate their efforts on students above the junior-college level, and encouraged the reorganization of the undergraduate curriculum at Stanford into a lower division and an upper division, while fostering increased emphasis on postgraduate studies. As Wilbur wrote, the "emphasis at Stanford must be upon advanced work if we are to serve our real purpose in the training of students who may take places of leadership in every phase of the life about us."[10] Stanford's graduate work already was reasonably well respected. In a 1925 survey of academic department heads, Stanford's graduate programs were ranked fourteenth nationally, with the University of Chicago in the lead.[11]

On May 15, 1925, the Stanford trustees approved the School of Engineering and discontinued the Department of Applied Mathematics, which was absorbed within the Engineering School. A month later, Theodore Jesse Hoover, brother of Herbert Hoover and head of the Department of Mining and Metallurgy since 1919, was appointed dean of the new School.[12] The establishment of the School of Engineering was part of a larger reorganization of academic departments carried out by President Wilbur over the course of his first decade in office, beginning with the School of Education in 1916. As Wilbur moved forward with his reforms in Stanford's academic program, fund-raising, and student conduct, he turned to reorganizing departments and creating a more sophisticated administration. Key to Wilbur's taking control was his gradual gathering of Stanford's various independent departments, each led by department "heads" used to great influence under Stanford's earlier presidents, into schools. (Stanford was the first American university to coordinate related departments into schools in this manner.)

The engineering department heads in 1923—C. B. Wing, W. F. Durand, H. J. Ryan, and T. J. Hoover—had submitted a report to the president, in which they concluded that their ideal of the six-year engineering curriculum could *not* be advanced by the establishment of a School of Engineering.[13] In the view of Theodore Hoover, head of the Mining Engineering Department, there had been enough faculty dislike for the six-year plan, but weakening the departments by additionally superimposing a School of Engineering was out of the question. Wing, who following Charles Marx as head of civil engineering, especially disliked the idea of the School of Engineering, fearing that it lowered the standard for the degree of Engineer, required red tape for all actions, took power away from the departments, and made a mess of the curriculum.[14]

Stanford's engineering professors were not the only faculty members who had their doubts about the new school system, but despite their concerns and disagreements, they managed to successfully create a workable unit.[15] The plan was for the four-year BA engineering course, to be followed by a one- or two-year course leading to the advanced degree of Engineer. This had already been the case in electrical engineering since 1913—the degree of electrical engineer being pursuable only after a BA in mechanical engineering.

Wilbur persisted, however, and Hoover gave his "loyal support."[16] In spite of his ambivalence about the idea of a school, Hoover had accepted Wilbur's offer of the deanship. Hoover privately commented to Wilbur on observations about engineering at Stanford, its weaknesses and its opportunities: in the two years of Wilbur's pressure since 1923, however, more of the "old guard" had retired, and some of the younger men had had time to "think things over." Hoover personally felt that there was a distressing lack of professional pride—the "superabundance of dirty cords, lack of collars, and general slouchiness" was a reflection of this lack of pride in his view.

Similarly, the employment of "teaching specialists" without appropriate university credentials and the excessive use of manual training shops belonged in a trade school, not a university. Hoover advised that the teaching specialists, whom he alleged had little understanding of fundamental principles of technology and showed contempt for all scientific control of industry, should be phased out. Research should be granted more status, and engineers should strive to open new, "unexplored territory well worth attention."

Lest this sound like a 1960 prescription for the modern engineering research school, Hoover went on to assert that the proper place to seek faculty was in industry, rather than in the universities. The ideal engineering instructor, in his view, should have years of industrial experience, particularly since industry had left academia "hopelessly behind" in some research areas. Hoover felt that current faculty members were not putting in enough hours each day. "A professor's job should not be considered an easy graft," he commented.

Hoover's views were his own, and not necessarily those of the engineering faculty, either in his criticism of student attire or his description of faculty activity. Two decades of Stanford tradition among the students dictated that rough dress symbolized Stanford's "democratic spirit" and lack of snobbery, and as such it became a style especially well-suited to its young engineers and geologists.[17]

Hoover believed that the major purpose of the six-year engineering program was to permit the broadening of the bachelor's degree student, not to narrowly specialize him. Stanford should turn out engineer-executives with a thorough grounding in mathematics, physics, chemistry, and geology and knowledge of the use of precision apparatus, he argued, as well as knowledge of a modern foreign language and a background in history, English, and economics.[18]

On becoming the first dean of the new School of Engineering in the fall of

1925, Theodore Hoover set to with a will. He requested all departments to report on personnel, department needs, research aims, and curricular plans. The former department head now moved to increase the power of the dean's office through centralization, for example, requiring instructors who used university facilities for their own consulting practice to pay overhead to the university. All proposals for research that involved the use of university equipment were to be submitted to the dean for approval.[19] He was adamantly against Stanford, or any university, capitalizing on its researches through patents. Interestingly, Hoover felt strongly that faculty, not the university, should be rewarded with the proceeds of patents. Years later, just before his retirement in 1936, Dean Hoover reaffirmed his view that a major portion of the patent profits should go to the researcher while the university "should donate its equity, if any, to the public free."[20]

Whatever Hoover's private feelings and those of his colleagues about the Engineering School, the *Stanford Illustrated Review* published in May 1926 Hoover's contention that the idea of a School of Engineering "met with considerable favor from the first."[21] In the article, Hoover outlined the school's prospects and its philosophy of a broad education in the first four years with courses in citizenship, English, history, foreign languages, economics, psychology, and business law, as well as courses in math, science, and engineering. Students entering after May 1926 would then study for the bachelor of arts degree in engineering, no matter what their subspecialty. This four-year course of study, requiring 180 (quarter) units for graduation, would be allotted as follows:

Humanistic studies	60 units
Science	54 units
Engineering fundamentals	25 units
Engineering	21 units
Electives	20 units
Total	180 units

Following the establishment of the School of Engineering in 1925, and the institution of the reorganized four-year BA program, Hoover set out in the spring of 1926 to determine the structure of the new graduate program, which would not come into place until 1928. He wrote to each faculty member and asked for their opinions concerning graduate planning and policy.[22] T. H. Morgan, Ward B. Kindy, Henry H. Henline, and Fred Terman from electrical engineering were among those who responded. Morgan opted for the status quo except that the two-year graduate program should require courses more broadly across the various departments in the School of Engineering. Kindy, too, voiced the opinion that things should go along as usual, but added that it was very important to select the best students for graduate training.

Henline, whose major interests included engineering pedagogy, submitted a lengthy and detailed proposal. He suggested the need for extending both research and instruction in the fields of power, high-voltage transmission, and communication. Henline proposed dividing the department into three "Divisions—Electric Power, Communication, and High-Voltage," adding that "Dr. Terman's courses covering the advanced theory of electric circuits would run thru all of them." It is clear that, already in his first year of full-time teaching, Fred Terman was central to the Electrical Engineering Department. A list of the Electrical Engineering Department graduate courses as planned for 1926–27 clearly indicated that Fred Terman was taking the theoretical load for the department, teaching the courses in electric and magnetic circuits, advanced electrotechnics, advanced electric circuits, as well as coteaching the Communication Laboratory and communication research work with Henline. Even so, because of Ryan's fear for Fred's health, Terman was listed for that coming year as "not quite" full-time.[23]

None of these suggestions of his colleagues compared to Terman's in frankness and audacity. Terman's ideas to Dean Hoover stressed the need for engineering faculty to have a solid grasp of mathematics, physics, and chemistry and to have invested in a graduate education, preferably the PhD, so that they would not be the blind leading the blind. A curriculum alone was not the solution, Terman wrote, but the real test would be in the "excellence of the *training*" that would be offered as judged by the best standards. The Electrical Engineering Department at MIT offered superior and exciting work in at least five electrical fields that Stanford did not offer—electrical machinery, electrical circuits, telephone and radio communication, mathematical methods of handling electrical problems, and engineering mathematics. Terman wrote that although his report stressed electrical engineering, he had done work at Stanford equivalent to an AB in chemical engineering and something more than an AB in mechanical engineering. Thus, he was able to compare Stanford's engineering work overall with that at MIT.

Terman admitted that his statements might appear extreme, but he noted that in the past fourteen years, no one on the entire Stanford engineering faculty had experienced contact with an institution such as MIT, either as a graduate student or as a professor, and that electrical engineering at Stanford had published practically nothing outside the high-voltage field for the past fifteen years. Stanford was isolated geographically, with local academic competition of the "most mediocre kind" and had fallen unknowingly below the very best. As to curriculum, MIT's curriculum also was out of date, and the Stanford student worked just as hard as the one at MIT. The great difference, Terman felt, was that the MIT faculty had a much greater knowledge of the subjects they taught and that a large proportion of the MIT staff were as expert in their own fields as Professor Ryan was in high voltage. It was a fatally wrong strategy that Stanford hired a young man, who, with loyalty, industry, and patience, "advances in salary and rank and finally reaches a position for which his training is totally inadequate." The result of this was that *practically all* of the younger members of Stanford's engineering faculty would find the regular first-year graduate work at MIT to consist of subject matter largely unfamiliar to them, he wrote.

As an example of teaching inefficiency, Terman recounted that when he was a student in James Clark's transmission lines course at Stanford in 1922, it consisted of forty lectures. When Terman himself began teaching the course in the winter quarter just past (1926), he reorganized and consolidated the course, made it more universally applicable, and reduced it to twelve lectures. Terman also commented on a Stanford undergraduate course in mechanical engineering that he himself had taken several years before "in which for years the equivalent of an entire week's study time for a four unit course was spent in drawing hundreds of rivet holes in a boiler plate layout and in drawing hundreds of individual bricks in a boiler foundation!"[24]

Theodore Hoover actually agreed with Fred on a number of these points, particularly the importance of research in engineering, the excess of manual shop training, and the need for reorganizing coursework. But Hoover greatly valued industrial experience and thought it the solution to finding adequate faculty. For all their pride in young Terman and his abilities, both Hoover and Harris Ryan thought industrial experience to be an appropriate prerequisite for engineering faculty leadership, and this perspective would keep Fred Terman from the position of head of the Electrical Engineering Department for a decade.

At the time of his report to Dean Hoover, however, Fred was collecting information for Professor Ryan on the amount of productive research in electrical engineering carried on at American colleges. The conclusions Terman voiced to Hoover, backed by the results of his literature search, would be published a year later in an audacious article, "The Electrical Engineering Research Situation in the American Universities," in *Science* magazine.

Life in the Electrical Engineering Department

It was mere coincidence but perhaps fortuitous that Fred Terman's first fall quarter part-time teaching at Stanford in 1925 saw the organization of an engineering school. Fred was the only member of the Electrical Engineering Department with a doctorate and he had joined a department that resembled a one-legged milking stool, no matter that the one-leg (high voltage) was a very stable one.

As Terman began his first year as a (nearly) full-time teacher in fall 1926, the biggest event locally was the opening of the Ryan High-Voltage Laboratory on September 17, 1926, with an initial public demonstration of its 2,100,000-volt test station, the largest in existence anywhere. The lab was a steel-frame asbestos-covered building, 173 feet long, 60 feet wide, and 65 feet high. Three doors, "the largest ever built," each 47 by 40 feet, allowed one side of the building to be opened along a 120-foot length.[25] It was the crowning event of Ryan's career, but his major work was already behind him, and within a half-dozen years the High-Voltage Lab would stand as a temple to the electrical past.

Dean Hoover favored the enlargement of the electrical engineering staff in 1925, but positions on the department's faculty mostly opened up only through attrition. The resignation of James Cameron Clark in the spring of 1924 had opened the slot that Harris Ryan offered to Terman. In recommending Terman to President Wilbur, Ryan wrote that he considered Terman "the best man available in the nation today."[26] Terman's serious illness delayed his appointment for a year, and in the interim Ryan filled a temporary, part-time replacement position with his favorite student, Joseph S. Carroll, who assisted Ryan in the High-Voltage Lab. When Terman joined the faculty in fall 1925 as a part-time instructor he was a salary notch behind Carroll, even though Carroll was still a graduate student working on his PhD dissertation. Ryan had been genuinely worried about Terman's health and did not want him to overdo it, but the salary discrepancy continued well after 1927.[27] (Carroll's salary would remain 20 percent higher than Terman's for nearly a decade.) By contrast, Joe Carroll had resigned an instructorship in electrical engineering at the University of Utah to become a graduate student at Stanford and he badly needed the financial support.[28]

Terman had been offered a position as instructor at MIT for the 1924–25 year by Dugald C. Jackson, with a promise of promotion to assistant professor after one year. Vannevar Bush and Jackson talked again in 1926 about recruiting Terman for MIT and held the door open for him.[29] But when Henry Henline resigned in late 1926 to take a much better paid administrative position with the AIEE, Terman fully took over both his faculty slot and the Communication Lab at Stanford, while an instructor was hired to take over Henline's other courses and to fill-in generally as leave replacement. When that young instructor died in 1931, Leland Brown and William George Hoover were added to the department. When Harris Ryan retired, and then T. H. Morgan resigned in June 1931 to become head of the Electrical Engineering Department at Worcester Polytechnic in Massachusetts, Hugh Hildreth Skilling was hired as instructor to replace Morgan.[30]

By this kind of ratcheting upward in size a half position or so at a time, the Electrical Engineering Department faculty grew from a full-time equivalent staff of four in 1924 to a staff of six by 1927 and this size remained through 1934. Though Terman was the only member with a PhD degree in 1925, others earned them along the way; first Joe Carroll, then Leland Brown, Hugh Skilling, and William "Bill" Hoover. Of the six faculty members on salary after Ryan's retirement in 1931, only Ward Kindy did not earn a PhD or ScD.

Teaching in Electrical Engineering

From the beginning of his service, Fred Terman taught mostly graduate courses. His teaching schedule included one or two courses per quarter, plus labs and thesis tutorials. Even though the department was predominantly aimed at training graduate students, he taught some undergraduate courses and directed undergraduate research.

Ward Kindy's courses were nearly all for undergraduates, while others in the department taught that part of the curricula that was in their special area. Morgan and Kindy handled the machinery courses in 1926, for example, while Joe Carroll assisted Ryan with the high-voltage courses (and took these over at Ryan's retirement). As they entered the department, Hugh Skilling gradually took over the circuit theory courses, and Leland Brown and Bill Hoover assisted with machinery and high-voltage courses. Former graduates Ezra Scattergood and Leo G. Gianini, as visiting lecturers, taught courses on hydroelectric power and on illumination.

The major change in the Electrical Engineering Department curricula during Fred Terman's first decade was his development of communication and electronic courses. In his first full year, 1926–27, Terman added the graduate course Radio Communication (EE 220), to the existing Communication Lab course (EE 221), and Communication Research seminar (EE 230). In 1926–27, Terman also taught the Electric and Magnetic Circuits courses (fall, 3 units), Advanced Electrotechnics (winter, 5 units), and Advanced Electric Circuits courses (spring, 3 units). He later commented that while Clark and Henline had been teaching these in the mid-1920s, they had not been doing a first-rate job, particularly Clark.[31] In addition, Terman taught the demanding 5-unit winter lab course, Communication Engineering Lab (cotaught with Henline for one year, then by Terman alone after 1926). He taught advanced tutorials and thesis courses such as Communication Research.

In September 1927, Terman submitted a proposal for increased support for the Communication Laboratory. The lab courses were a large drain on faculty time and energy, since lab equipment was almost nonexistent and there was little staff support. Terman supplied the lab with much of his own apparatus. He had devised safeguard circuits to protect the instruments from overload, and with his students, he also designed and built a number of the lab instruments, since there was little money to order them from outside suppliers. Other jobs that nowadays would be assigned to lab assistants required Terman's personal time. Little additional funding was forthcoming.

Several of the faculty advised theses, but by the time Terman began teaching full time in 1926–27 about half of the graduate degrees in electrical engineering were in the fields of radio and electronics (including vacuum tube circuits, measurements, and audio and radio frequency research). With so many undergraduate and graduate students choosing radio and electronics, Terman did manage to get an assistant, instructor James M. Sharp, in 1934 to ease the load. (In 1937, as incoming department head, he was also able to add Karl Spangenberg to the faculty.)

Enrollment of students in engineering at Stanford actually increased in the first several years of the Depression, until 1932. Professor H. C. Moreno attributed this to the return of old students who had lost their jobs and of recent graduates who were unable to find work.[32] But the middle years of the Depression, 1933–37, saw a distinct drop in graduate students in electrical engineering.[33]

As a beginning professor, Terman's strategy was to get his research going, to educate his students (particularly those who were candidates for the Engineer degree), and to write an up-to-date textbook for radio engineering. And these things he promptly did. Fred's area of teaching was laid out on his arrival: teach the advanced and theoretical courses, and during the period 1928–36, he directed forty-six electrical engineering engineer theses, more than half the Electrical Engineering Department's total and more than the total from the entire Civil Engineering Department.

Fred's research choices were his to make, and he focused on the Communication Lab. From 1920 through 1927, the lab had received an average of only $150 per year on equipment, in addition to equipment donated by the army signal corps in World War I and by the Bell System.[34] Over the next decade, Fred would put together for the lab financial support from his father, some increased funding from Stanford, and occasional funds or equipment derived from his own patent royalties. His carefully laid plans would be side-tracked by both internal and external factors: the lukewarm support of Dean Hoover and emeritus professor Harris J. Ryan, and the serious financial downturn in the country's economy in 1930.

Paying the Stanford Faculty

To place these figures in perspective, Stanford's 153 faculty salaries in 1924 ranged from the top salary given President Wilbur of $15,000 down through such senior faculty members and administrators as Food Research Institute Director A. E. Taylor's at $8,000; Medical School Dean William Ophüls, Professors Elwood Cubberley (dean of education), P. J. Hanzlik (head of pharmacology), C. D. Marx (head of civil engineering), and L. M. Terman (head of the new department of psychology) at $7,500; not far behind was the esteemed W. F. Durand (engineering) at $7,250. Most faculty members fell well below these, at $4–5,000 or less. At the low end of the scale were younger engineering professors like Ward Kindy and T. H. Morgan and assistant professors in English, Edith R. Mirrielees and Elizabeth Buckingham at around $2,600.[35]

Improving and balancing faculty salaries had been an ongoing battle at Stanford. Even before the Depression, faculty salaries remained comparatively low. The university salary scale in 1930 was:

Instructor	$1,800 to $2,400
Assistant Prof.	$2,500 to $3,000
Associate Prof.	$3,250 to $4,000
Professor	$4,500 to $7,500 (with "a few at $10,000")

Only full professors had tenure and were members of the Academic Council. Nor had much changed since reorganization of the faculty just after the turn of the century, when professors' hold on tenure was strengthened but that of assistant and associate professors made more tenuous. According to Stanford's faculty contract and salary policy in 1930, instructors were appointed on a one-year basis, assistant professors for three years, and associate professors on a five-year basis. As for retirement policy, Stanford generally followed the rules of the Carnegie Foundation for the Advancement of Teaching, but firmly kept to the policy that was sixty-five years instead of seventy. Retirement was generally at one-half of the average of the last five years of salaried work, plus $400; or, for those who were first employed after November 17, 1915, Stanford paid 10 percent of the individual's salary into an annuity managed by the Teachers Insurance and Annuity Association.[36] Another useful benefit was undergraduate tuition remission for faculty children.

Fred Terman started out with a half-time salary of $1,250 in 1925–26. (Fred's salary during his entire working career [1925–65] up to retirement is listed in Appendix A.) Eighteen months after Terman replaced Henline as head of the Communication Lab, his salary was increased from $2,500 to $2,750. Ryan wrote that Terman "is bound to be an outstanding figure in his generation."[37] When he was promoted to professor and head of the department on March 25, 1937, Terman's salary was raised to $4,050. Several years into the Depression, Stanford had chosen to cut all salaries 10 percent rather than lay off staff. On December 20, 1937, salaries were restored by 10 percent, and Terman's salary was improved to $4,275.

One of Terman's first acts as head of the department was to secure Carroll's promotion to full professor and improve his salary ($4,011) to $4,275, to equal his own.[38] Nevertheless, salaries at Stanford were still weighted heavily toward years of service, and in the Electrical Engineering Department there was a special aura around those who worked with Ryan and the High-Voltage Lab. Dean Hoover had advanced Ward Kindy to associate professor in 1934. Kindy had completed his Engineer degree in 1929 and served as acting head of the department after Ryan's retirement, but his publications list consisted of one paper (published December 1930).[39] Hoover's recommendation that Kindy's salary for 1935–36 be $3,250 and Terman's salary $3,350 clearly indicates some tribute paid toward Kindy's longevity and loyalty.[40]

The table provides a snapshot of Electrical Engineering Department salaries in the years surrounding Ryan's retirement:[41]

Stanford Department of Electrical Engineering Salaries for Selected Years

	1925–26	1929–30	1930–31	1932–33	1934–35#	1935–36
Ryan	$6,500	$6,500	$7,000	na	na	na
Henline	$3,500	na	na	na	na	na
Carroll	$1,250*	$4,000	$4,000	$4,000	$3,600	$3,700
Morgan	$2,300	$3,000	$3,150	na	na	na
Kindy	$2,500	$2,800	$2,900	$2,900	$2,800	$3,250
Duncan	na	$2,500	$2,550	na	na	na
Terman	$1,250*	$3,000	$3,250	$3,350	$3,015	$3,350
Skilling	na	na	na	$2,400	$2,160	$2,250
Brown	na	na	na	$2,250	$2,000	$2,200
Hoover	na	na	na	$1,620	$1,800	$2,000
Sharp	na	na	na	na	$1,800	$1,900

*=part-time
#=reflects facultywide salary cuts of May 1933
na=not applicable

Challenging the Profession

In the spring of 1927, only a year after Fred had sent Dean Hoover his views on the proper structure and organization of a graduate school of engineering, Fred Terman published an article in *Science* magazine concerning electrical engineering research in American universities.[42] Terman's short article caused a commotion, later reprinted in the Sunday *New York Times*, embarrassed Harris Ryan and delighted others.[43] The article illuminated the split between those older engineers who saw the academic engineer as "consultant" to industry, and engineers like Terman who called for an increase in the educational level of engineering faculty, a raised appreciation for the role of research in the university, better teaching conditions for faculty, and an increase in research output.

Fred was not writing in a vacuum. In 1925 the AIEE sponsored several sessions on engineering education and research and published the papers. But Fred Terman opened old wounds, first, by ranking only a very small number of electrical engineering schools as those that did significant research, and second, by taking his argument *outside* of the engineering profession to scientists, business readers, and the general public.

Fred's article was intemperate and youthful but his philosophy is important. He took a small sample of the literature and drew numerous conclusions. He took as his database the six years 1920–25 of the AIEE *Transactions*, where "practically all researches of permanent value which American electrical engineers perform are reported." He found that only an average of 12 percent of 442 technical articles published in the journal were contributed by teachers of electrical engineering and their thesis students (for a total of only nine articles per year). He added to his data the same six years from the *Proceedings* of the IRE for the new field of radio and found only five articles a year from universities, with over half of these contributions coming from physics departments. (He admitted that from time to time, electrical engineers might publish in national physical or mathematical journals, but concluded that these would not materially affect his results.) Eighty percent of the university-produced articles for AIEE, he noted, came from just five universities: MIT, Johns Hopkins, Stanford, Cornell, and Purdue. From the IRE article list, only one university, Columbia, produced more than two articles. Terman called these universities the "productive electrical engineering departments." In addition, he noted that more than half of the university-produced articles came from just eight men and their students, three from MIT and one each at the other five colleges. Apparently, Terman concluded, not more than a dozen technical schools in electrical engineering were "making much if any effort in the way of research," with more than half the published output the work of only eight men.

Terman went on to comment that the large industry laboratories made progress in research largely without the contributions of university faculty, yet the country's supply of technically trained young men could come only from the university environment. The electrical industry was so new and progressing so rapidly that an electrical engineering teacher who stood aside, without doing research himself, would see the rest of the technical world pass him by. This situation existed, Terman said, not due to the lack of expensive equipment (for "pencil and paper constitute the main essentials") but was caused by heavy teaching schedules that left little time for research, the lack of adequate training for the engineering teachers, and the lack of personal reward for research. As a result, the students received out-of-date ideas and did out-of-date thesis work.

By inadequate training, Terman meant that many engineering faculty still had only a bachelor's degree, and very few engineers expected to work for a doctorate. Compare this to physics and chemistry, Terman wrote, where the best schools require a PhD for permanent appointments. Engineering schools, by contrast, leave the overworked instructor to educate himself while two years of solid graduate work could do the job much better. Ironically, most engineering schools valued the practice of consulting, which requires only that the consultant knows more than his client, rather than new knowledge through research. But poorly trained teachers write poor textbooks, and thus inadequately train future teachers to write even worse textbooks. All this, he bluntly concluded, creates "a self-perpetuating system in which a second-rate technical education is considered first-class because of general ignorance that there might be something better."

Revealing the influence of his father, Terman discounted the weight the AIEE placed on the opinions of the general members regarding what was needed for engineering education. Ordinary engineers, he believed, did not appreciate many aspects of engineering curriculum and research. It "will take more than questionnaires and symposiums on curricula," he wrote, "to get us far enough out of the rut." Terman signed the article simply, "Frederick Emmons Terman, Stanford University." (By signing it thusly, Fred did what academics normally do, give one's affiliation, without implying that it represents Stanford policy.)

Wow! What had he done? Publishing his article in *Science*, rather than through the AIEE, young Fred went outside of his profession, seeking an arena where he would be heard but not dismissed. He openly criticized the activities of his seniors and of the AIEE, and in turn dismissed the opinions of the rank-and-file engineer. He had compared engineering to science and found the former sadly wanting in its level of preparation and in its expectations.

Initial responses to the article were largely positive. Fred's old chemistry professor, Robert E. Swain (soon to be appointed Wilbur's acting president of Stanford while Wilbur served as President Hoover's secretary of the interior), wrote on May 2 of his "very hearty appreciation . . . that is precisely the point of view which engineering education must ultimately reflect in this country. We are all indebted to you."[44] But storm clouds were gathering. A month later, Fred's old MIT department head Dugald Jackson wrote to tell Fred that the *New York Times* had reprinted the article in its Sunday edition.[45] Jackson remarked that, even though "gossip in college circles" found it superficial, he thought Fred's study was correct and that if Fred had included physics journals and other scientific journals where electrical engineers sometimes published, the results would probably remain about the same. He encouraged Fred to continue this study.

University of Washington Engineering Dean C. E. Magnusson, however, was outraged. Magnusson apparently did not know who was this upstart Terman of Stanford, and communicated directly with Ryan instead. Ryan responded with a brief biography of Terman in his reply, assuring Magnusson that Fred was one of the ablest and best-balanced young men he had ever known, as well as the son of Lewis M. Terman. Ryan, clearly embarrassed, denied prior knowledge of the paper and stated that he was "sorry for the whole thing." In listing "Stanford University," he even suggested, Fred was simply giving his home address (where "he lives with his parents") and was not invoking the backing of Stanford University.[46]

Ryan thought Terman would regret any injustice to his colleagues but Fred had no regrets. In his first reply to Dean Magnusson, he accepted the dean's offer to submit a contrary analysis. "My own personal viewpoint on these matters is not the traditional one of engineers," he admitted unapologetically. "I have spent practically my entire life in a university atmosphere, and growing up in contact with the physical and biological sciences has made me appreciate how radically different from the viewpoint of the electrical engineer toward research and extensive graduate study is that of the chemist, for example." Terman went on to quote Magnusson's own remarks in a 1925 AIEE paper, where Magnusson said that in the majority of engineering colleges and technical schools very little, if any, research was in progress, and that even at leading institutions, very few academic engineers were actively engaged in worthwhile investigations. Magnusson also had been very clear in his own 1925 speech that technological institutions did not value research.[47] "I have to soothe an irate gentleman from Univ. of Washington," Fred wrote his fiancée Sibyl Walcutt on September 3, "who seemed to think that my article in *Science* on Engineering Research was a personal attack on him and his school."[48]

In responding to Magnusson, Fred maintained that he was quite constructive in his article, and that existing conditions were *not* well known but could well be changed for the better. He felt that *Science* was an especially suitable medium for publication of discussions about technical education. After all, Fred wrote, Magnusson himself had made most of the same charges in his own speech at Seattle in 1925.[49] Terman and Magnusson became fairly good friends within several years.

This lengthy interchange was not merely one between a wise elder engineering dean and a young whippersnapper. Fred Terman had been expressing his opinion on this matter for at least two years. In his view, major changes were needed in engineering education, especially in expectations of faculty. Science, particularly physics, chemistry, and mathematics, had to be built more into engineering curricula and the role of research had to be strengthened. Stanford's dean of engineering had heard from Fred on this more than once, and it is reasonable to think that he did not like hearing some of it. In years ahead, when Stanford searched for a successor to Harris Ryan, Dean Hoover made it very clear that he did not want a scientist-engineer as head of the Electrical Engineering Department. Hoover ignored outside suggestions of Fred Terman as a good local choice to replace Ryan. Yet Terman's views would be heard again and again in future, both at Stanford and in other organizations in which he played a role: Be especially good in at least one area; get a top-grade technical education instead of individually trying to reinvent the wheel; unify the research-teaching activity; and incorporate the student's research work as a vital part of the university research organization.

Getting Back into Radio

There were tremendous achievements in radio and early electronics during the period of Fred Terman's college years. They emerged from a foundation of work in the previous half-century by James Clerk Maxwell, Heinrich Hertz, H. A. Lorentz, J. J. Thomson, O. W. Richardson, and others. These men benefited little from the commercial fortunes that had been made, and would continue to be made, in radio and electronic communications.

Development of electromagnetic theory and the theory of the electron allowed the development of the vacuum tube. About 1905, John A. Fleming and, independently, Arthur R. B. Wehnelt, developed the two-electrode vacuum tube as a rectifier of current, a device with a unilateral conductivity. But in 1907, Lee de Forest inserted a "grid" between filament and plate and named the device the "Audion." This tube (or audion, valve, pliotron, triode, or thermionic valve, as it was variously called in the early days) consisted of the filament, plate, and a third electrode, called a grid, made in the form of a wire screen placed between the filament and the plate. By applying varying voltages to the grid, the electron current flowing between filament and plate could be varied. A small current flowing through the grid could control a much larger current from filament to plate. The relationship between the grid voltage applied and the plate current obtained is usually nonlinear at the extremes and linear in the middle ranges. Depending on the ranges utilized, the tube now could be used not only as a detector, but also as an amplifier of alternating current, and as an oscillator.

This great innovation was further developed as early as 1914 by commercial laboratories in the United States and in Europe. Perhaps the major commercial driving force was the need for improving long-distance telephone circuits. The Western Electric Company and General Electric research labs made numerous studies of the characteristics of vacuum tubes. By 1915, American Telephone and Telegraph Company and the Western Electric Company demonstrated the use of the vacuum tube in transmitting voice by radio from Arlington, Virginia, to Paris and to Honolulu. Vacuum tubes developed for the Allies in World War I became readily available to amateurs by 1919 or 1920, and ham operators began exploring new wavelengths of the radio spectrum. The vacuum tube could operate over much greater wavelength bands than could the Poulsen arc and Alexanderson alternators then in use by the commercial radio installations.

A few years after this, in the early and mid-1920s, the use of thin slices of quartz crystals allowed the vacuum tube circuits to operate on precise, narrow frequencies. This work evolved from crystals employed in acoustic "sonar" devices developed for submarine warfare in World War I.

In 1900, the year Fred Terman was born, huge buildings housing many banks of large condensers and coils and employing thousands and thousands of watts of electric power and using antenna towers hundreds of feet tall were needed to send wireless telegraph messages at a speed of perhaps twenty words per minute across a distance of several hundred miles. When Fred graduated from high school in December 1916, the vacuum tube was beginning its first commercial use in long-distance telephone repeater circuits and in experiments with long-distance radio. By the time Fred began teaching at Stanford in 1925, the vacuum tube was everywhere, amateur radio operators were communicating around the world with wireless telegraph and with voice, and using 5, or 50, or 100 watts of power instead of 200,000 or 1,000,000 watts as had the commercial spark or arc installations a few years before. Their selectivity and tuning circuits were now much narrower in bandwidth so that power needs for most radio communications *decreased* by at least a factor of one hundred. And the effective number of operating channels had risen by perhaps a factor of one thousand, due to use of narrow-band crystal circuits and to the new use of the medium- and short-wavelength radio bands.

In addition, the consumer public had been buying radio broadcast receiving sets by leaps and bounds since 1920. The national industrial research labs, especially Western Electric and General Electric, had a big lead over nearly all university research work in vacuum tubes and early electronics. And, as Fred Terman would learn, they locked down control of many basic patents broadly covering areas of vacuum tube and electronic circuit design. It was Hendrik Van der Bijl, research physicist at Western Electric and AT&T, who wrote the best early book on vacuum tubes.[50] Van der Bijl's book had the latest story on vacuum tubes (but not yet on crystal control), and Fred discovered the new book as he was working with Harris Ryan on his Engineer degree at Stanford. It is from this book, written by an industrial research physicist, that Fred grasped the vacuum tube fundamentals that he married to the transmission line and power circuit theory he had learned from Ryan, and from Bush and Kennelly at MIT.[51] While recuperating in bed in the fall and winter of 1924–25, and while coaching Herbert Hoover Jr. on his research tutorials, Fred took up again the Van der Bijl book and began thinking about patent ideas concerning electronic circuits, particularly radio circuits, while also working on the book project with Professor Franklin at MIT. But Fred was going to leave power lines as a research subject and go back to radio.

The Communication Lab and the Short Life of Radio Station KFGH

The Stanford Communication Lab was started in October 1924 as a result of a gift of more than $1,000 worth of equipment from the Bell System, but it has an interesting earlier history. One of the peculiarities of radio at Stanford was that some professors wanted Stanford to get into the radio broadcasting and public culture business. These faculty included Theodore Jesse Hoover and other mining engineering professors, but notably excluded the electrical engineering faculty. Dean Hoover's enthusiasm for the School of Engineering appears less than his enthusiasm over the years for Stanford to own and operate a cultural radio station and moving-picture school. He advised, urged, and cajoled Wilbur on this from as early as 1922 until his last years as dean.[52] He was encouraged in this by his brother. Herbert Hoover himself was also interested in Stanford having a radio station, not so much for cultural broadcasting as for part of an interuniversity radio system across the country. As secretary of commerce, Bert Hoover envisioned an electronic communications system linking U.S. universities and colleges and set aside the 1,290-meter wave band (230–235 KHz) for U.S. educational institutions.[53] (A half-century later saw the beginnings of such a network with the development of the ARPANet.)

On November 22, 1922, Stanford University received a federal radio license for a 100-watt experimental radio transmitter and during the next two years (1923 and 1924) various athletic events and talks by faculty were broadcast on an irregular basis. The call sign of Stanford's station was KFGH, operating at 830 KHz frequency. On May 7, 1924, the university was granted a license for a 500-watt broadcast station to operate on 1,110-KHz frequency, but due to lack of funds the larger station did not operate and the license was surrendered on December 20, 1925.[54] Nevertheless, Theodore Hoover asked President Wilbur to purchase a 1,000-watt radio transmitter for $50,000, estimating that operating costs of the station would be about $10,000 per year. One of the station's main purposes, Hoover now wrote, would be to counteract the "lurid press," for the "newspaper men as a class are hostile to radio." A world news service interpreted by "sound men in university faculties" could serve as an antidote to "the biased, untrue, and in many cases, vicious news service."

Theodore Hoover constructed for Wilbur a sample program day for KFGH, which opened at 8:10 AM with a biology class lecture by President Wilbur, followed by other regular lectures until noon by Ralph H. Lutz on history, Leon B. Reynolds on hydraulics and sanitary engineering, and Alonzo E. Taylor on food resources. Chimes at noon would precede a Memorial Chapel service and an organ concert. Following at 2 PM would be a lecture by Rennie W. Doane on insects in the garden and orchard. The rest of the afternoon would provide book reviews by the library staff, news commentaries by faculty, talks on health, and performances of cheerleading practice, Glee Club singing, and the English Department faculty reading aloud. The evening would enlighten the audience with dance music from the Women's Club House, followed by an organ recital and chimes, more news, and finally a closing by Chaplain D. Charles Gardner reading the Bible.[55] Support for the scheme was mixed. Several alumni and influential faculty, including historian Edgar E. Robinson, advised President Wilbur that there were numerous difficulties presented in Theodore Hoover's vision of radio broadcasting at Stanford.[56] The Stanford Electrical Engineering Department had other ideas for station KFGH. In the spring of 1924, representatives of AT&T, Western Electric, and the Pacific Telephone companies met with Stanford faculty about beginning a communication engineering program at Stanford. AT&T representatives were on a tour of fifteen leading American universities to encourage the institution of communication engineering studies. While at Stanford, they visited with Professors Ryan and Henline of the Electrical Engineering Department and D. L. Webster and F. J. Rogers of the Physics Department.[57]

The AT&T Bell System promised to loan some instruments and assist the university, including sending Professor Henline to New York for a conference on the subject. Stanford accepted the offer, and Henline began to build a communication program. Henline converted the fledgling KFGH broadcast operation to experimental station 6XBM in the autumn of 1924 and transmitted continuous wave test signals at intervals for the Bureau of Standards.[58] The Stanford experimental station commenced by using two 250-watt tubes belonging to Stanford undergraduate student Herbert Hoover Jr. The university later replaced the tubes with ones loaned by the Bureau of Standards and other tubes purchased through C. F. Elwell, then in England. Even though quite ill, Fred Terman must have been aware of, perhaps even involved in these doings, since he was at that time tutoring Herbert Hoover Jr. For a time, Stanford's 6XBM functioned as the West Coast operating station of the Bureau of Standards' WWV standard frequency signals service.[59]

Henline's standard transmission tests in cooperation with the Bureau of Standards ended for a time the fear that Stanford would drown the Bay Area in radio culture. Radio at Stanford would instead develop along Fred Terman's lines of radio and electronics research, and popular radio culture would be left to others in San Francisco and Los Angeles, better able to blend radio with Theda Bara and Art Hickman's Dance Orchestra and the selling of flakes, both of soap and of corn.

Dean Hoover continued to hope that Stanford would play a dominant part in broadcasting. In 1929, he asked President Wilbur to raise more than one million dollars to put Stanford into the movie and radio business; but this idea perished with the Depression. He again petitioned President Wilbur in 1934 to have Stanford purchase radio station KQW, and thus "double or triple the influence of the University as a moral force." He assured the president that the station would broadcast advertising of an inoffensive character and would provide university courses as a source for community uplift, and this time he suggested that a new department staffed with three or four people be established to run the operation.[60] Wilbur declined to pursue the offer.

When Henline left Stanford, Terman took over the Communication Lab in January 1927. He immediately added a two-unit course in the principles of power and telephone lines to the course in the principles of radio communication that he had taught since the spring of 1926. Terman then submitted a proposal for support for the Communication Lab in September 1927, describing its history and its needs. Terman described the lab's rapid growth in the proportion of students who were choosing at least some work in communication. In fall 1927, the total inventory of the lab's communication equipment, excluding that given by Terman, was valued at between $3,000 and $3,500. Most of the purchases, he added, had been made for classroom instruction or for the now discontinued standard frequency transmissions Henline had been doing for the Bureau of Standards. None of the research projects undertaken, he more than hinted, would have been possible if he had not personally loaned or given pieces of apparatus from his own collection. In sum, Terman wrote, "It is desired that Stanford be equipped to conduct communication research worthy of being published. Stanford can become a center for research in this field if the faculty and student power now devoted to communication can be efficiently utilized." Terman was planning to add five units of laboratory and four units of lecture courses to the curriculum, and with such training, "students in this field should not be required to putter away their research energies on inconsequential problems as a result of lack of ordinary equipment." Terman could not help noting that a first-class communication lab could be equipped for 10 percent of the cost of a high-voltage lab. He requested that the Communication Lab be granted $1,000, spread over three years, which would go at least part of the way toward establishing instruments of a good lab.[61] He received part of the funds he requested, and the number of his students continued to increase.

Fred Terman was very busy during his first years of teaching and research. However, in 1927 romance came into the life of the young professor in the form of a young Stanford graduate student in psychology, Miss Sibyl Walcutt.

Sibyl

In 1927, Fred Terman met the woman who was to be his wife for forty-seven years. Their personalities were very different. Young Sibyl Walcutt was something of a cutup, very interested in boys and socializing but clearly smarter and more ambitious than her school grades would imply. Sibyl came to Stanford for graduate work in psychology and education, where she studied with Professor Lewis Terman. Various anecdotes exist as to exactly how Fred and Sibyl met, but she liked to say years later that after she and Fred had gone out on more than a half-dozen dates, the young professor went over to the Psychology Department and looked up her I.Q. scores—then, according to Sibyl, things heated up.[62]

Sibyl L. Walcutt was born in Montclair, New Jersey, on January 19, 1902, the fifth of eight children. By high school, Sibyl dropped the "L" and for the rest of her life was simply "Sibyl." The Walcutt children, three boys and five girls, nearly all had nicknames: Lowell, Gifford (Gif), and Charles (Bill), and Alice, Myrilla (Winkie), Sibyl ("Sib" and sometimes "Slivers" or "Swivel"), Constance (Connie), and Winifred (Winnie). On her father's side, Sibyl Walcutt was descended from early New England settlers. Sibyl's father, Henry Leeds Walcutt, born in New York in 1865, became a bookbinder in New York City. He and his brothers later founded the "Walcutt Brothers Company," a book embossing firm on East 25th Street in Manhattan. Henry married Clara J. Child, one year younger than himself. The Childs also descended from old New England stock, most notably from Richard Warren, who arrived on the *Mayflower*, and from the Lowells of Massachusetts.[63]

By the time Sibyl was a teenager her father had asthma or bronchial problems, and he and her mother Clara spent winter vacations in Florida or in the uplands of North Carolina. This health problem led the Walcutts to move to Tucson, Arizona, in 1922.[64] Sibyl attended Montclair High School from September 1916 to June 1920. Her grades were fair. Several years later, the petite, brown-haired Sibyl humorously characterized herself as a "flapper."

Sibyl persuaded her family to allow her to journey to Europe for a year to study art, languages, and history. In the fall of 1920, following her high school graduation, she set off across the Atlantic by steamship. She was escorted, in a sense, by the family of John Van Sickle, assistant secretary to the American Reparation Committee, assigned to Vienna. The late fall was spent visiting the sights and art galleries of Paris, and just after Christmas 1920, Sibyl took the Orient Express to Vienna. There she enrolled in courses at the university in art, languages, and literature, music history, and horseback riding. At first, she stayed with the Van Sickles in an old but luxurious apartment, but later moved into rooms by herself, much to her family's distress.[65] Her father was particularly fond of Sibyl and sent her money each month; he expected Sibyl to return to the States in August 1921, but Sibyl was in no hurry to return. "My dear," Henry Walcutt wrote to his daughter, "you'll drive your poor old father to vote the prohibition ticket and also into an early grave. Why will you so seldom put the name of the town on your letters, to say nothing of the year in which you did it? In later days you may like to read over these letters and a few particulars would be agreeable."[66]

On the trip over to Europe, Sibyl had met a young Canadian, John A. Weir, who was on his way to study at Oxford. Young Mr. Weir evidently fell hard for Sibyl, and by the spring of 1921, he and Sibyl were engaged to be married. The Walcutt family took the news well. Her father had already counseled her, "Do not say no too often. Many women have said no when they meant yes and spent their lives regretting it."[67] The sisters were thrilled, and rather titillated, and some "secret" letters from Sibyl were burned by her sisters after reading.[68] When a high school chum "learned of your engagement," Winnie wrote, "Priscilla simply shrieked. You were always such a man-hater that she couldn't get over it."[69] Evidently John was more smitten than Sibyl, for she broke off the engagement within six months.[70] He did not forget Sibyl easily, going to Vienna at least once more to visit her. "I wonder what you will do with J. W.," Winkie wrote Sibyl in June 1922. "Walk around the block or take him to the movies? This much I state old dear, I shall not urge you into the arms of a man you care not for and I think the family will not hector you too much."[71]

Sibyl was having a good time in Vienna, making friends and visiting Switzerland and various cities in Austria. Money was not all that plentiful in the Walcutt household, although the parents continued to winter in the South and had a tennis court on their property in Montclair. Winkie and Alice wrote several times about how it would be great if some or all of the sisters could visit Sibyl, perhaps in Italy, but that there was not enough money available. Money eventually became a serious problem, for the Walcutt Brothers almost went broke in the summer of 1921 in the postwar recession, but the situation improved in the spring of 1922. Health problems led Henry and Clara Walcutt to finally move the family to Arizona that year.

Sibyl, meanwhile, went on to Lausanne, where she took spring- and summer-term courses in languages and literature. In late July, she returned to the United States on the *President Garfield* from Cherbourg, a confident twenty-year-old who had traveled Europe more or less on her own.

A year later, she entered the University of Arizona in Tucson as a sophomore, having been granted credit for forty-two semester hours of study for her work at Vienna and Lausanne in German and French. Sibyl majored in languages, psychology, and education at Arizona and graduated with honors from Arizona on June 3, 1925. That fall, she enrolled in fifteen units of graduate work in education and psychology, but she was hoping to go into further graduate work at Stanford.[72]

Sibyl's father died in 1926, however, which put a strain on the family finances. Winkie got a job as secretary in the administration offices of the University of Arizona (she served as secretary to two university presidents over the next twelve years). Others in the family moved around, getting married one by one. Older brother Bill went off to study English at Northwestern, where he got to know speech and drama Professor Hubert Heffner (Heffner left Northwestern for Stanford in 1939). Sibyl enrolled at Stanford in October 1926 as a graduate student in psychology. She was not very happy with her initial housing arrangements, but finally settled down at 252 Kingsley Street, Palo Alto, to stay with Lydia Mitchell (the mother of Professor L. Pearce Mitchell) in exchange for performing light housekeeping chores.[73] Her time with Mrs. Mitchell was pleasant, and Sibyl even accompanied her on a trip to the East Coast in the summer of 1927.

At Stanford, Sibyl studied with four psychologists as she worked toward her master's degree: Walter Richard Miles, Calvin Perry Stone, Maud Amanda Merrill, and Lewis Madison Terman. Lewis Terman had taken over the Psychology Department five years previously and was in the midst of molding it to his designs. In addition to his teaching, he continued his interest in the measurement of intelligence with further studies of gifted children. A popular guest lecturer, he could now ask $150 per day for lecturing fees. With his publications, the Stanford-Binet test royalties and lecture fees, Lewis Terman's income had risen with his scholarly reputation and a public presence.[74]

Sibyl studied the psychology of endowment (intelligence, mental inheritance, and the psychology of genius) with Terman, but most of her work was with Miles, who taught the psychology of memory, the history of psychology, and experimental problems in psychology. Miles supervised her thesis on color blindness.[75] Sibyl also continued her interest in English, studying verse form from Samuel Swayze Seward Jr., her neighbor on 262 Kingsley Street, and English and Scottish popular ballads with Margery Bailey. Sibyl completed the required forty-five quarter hours of credit in the course of a year, finished her thesis during fall quarter, and received her MA in psychology in January 1928.

Sibyl intended to continue on for the doctoral degree and completed a further thirty-three quarter hours in the 1927–28 academic year, with an additional thirteen hours in the summer of 1929. She continued to work with Miles, Stone, and Terman, but also studied social psychology with Paul Randolph Farnsworth, statistics with Truman Lee Kelley, and educational administration and history of education with Elwood Patterson Cubberley.

As lively as ever, Sibyl had continued her busy social life on moving to Stanford. John Weir had attempted a reconciliation while Sibyl was attending Berkeley summer session during 1924, but he had arrived to find that another gentleman, by the name of Sellman, was there to visit her. Weir wrote from Canada some months later, "The last four years of my life have been *hell!*", referring to her effect on him.[76] By summer 1925, there are no further references to John in her letters, but "Doc" and Harry entered the scene. Sibyl met "Doc" in Arizona sometime in 1925 or 1926 (he was known to her sisters), while Harry was apparently a graduate student in psychology. Harry jestingly wrote Sibyl that Mrs. Mitchell must have wondered what was going on when Sibyl came in so late one night, signing off as her synthetic husband.[77] Sibyl was taking men much too seriously, her sister Connie wrote her in the fall of 1926, only two months after Sibyl had arrived at Stanford. Connie counseled her not to worry about men, they will get over things; Harry has undoubtedly been in love before. "And why in hell take all the fun out of kissing Harry by worrying about what Doc will do?" she asked. "Anyway, you're not more than half in love with Doc so why not give somebody else a fair chance?"[78]

Even so, Sibyl buckled down to studying at Stanford and won a scholarship. She was busy carrying a full-time school load, maintaining high grades, and housekeeping for Mrs. Mitchell. "You never mention Doc anymore," Connie wrote her, "Is he out of the scene? We still think you should annex a Ph.D. husband who could help support you."[79] That summer Louise, a friend, wrote to Sibyl to say, "That's too bad about the men—I supposed mobs of lonely school superintendents would be flocking about so you'd be well fixed."[80]

Little did they know. Sibyl seemed prone to whirlwinds. Less than a month after Louise's letter, Sibyl again became engaged, this time secretly, to Professor Terman's twenty-seven-year old son, Professor Fred Terman.

Wedding Bells and a New House

The Walcutt-Terman engagement occurred on August 6, 1927, when Fred gave Sibyl an engagement pin. Two weeks later, Sibyl left to visit her mother and sisters in New Jersey, where they were putting the Walcutt house on the market. Fred sent her off with candy, books (from Lewis Terman, including a book of 100 famous love poems), and a set of luncheon napkins to be embroidered (most likely the idea of Anna Terman). Sibyl wrote effusively from the train:

> Fred darling, I can't say on paper the things I want to, but you know that I am thinking of you every minute. The last two weeks were the most wonderful and happiest of my life, and I know our future is going to be even more glorious. Few girls, I am sure, look forward to their marriage with as perfect trust in their mate and as perfect assurance of happiness as I do. You are the prince charming of my dreams come true and since I was lucky enough to find you, I have a feeling we are going to get all our other wishes.[81]

The "secret" of their engagement was let out by dribs and drabs. Fred had told his parents almost immediately and several weeks later his mother told Fred's sister Helen Terman Mosher. Sibyl's graduate advisor, Dr. Walter Miles, "nearly fell over" when he learned Sibyl was engaged to Fred. (Miles's son Kirk, then in high school, had been helping Fred taking circuit measurements in the Electrical Engineering Communication Lab.) Fred asked Sibyl: "Is your family used to the idea of your getting married . . . with it coming out of a clear sky?"[82] Walking on air, Fred's letters were addressed to "Dearest Sweetheart" and "Fairy Princess," and return letters from Sibyl were addressed to "My Dearest" and "Darling Boy."

Fred was still recovering his strength from the tuberculosis and the appendix crises of 1924–25, and his eyes were still bothering him, but he remained busy as always, working in the lab, working on patent applications, and preparing his Stanford courses. He was excited, he wrote her, about the new "research center" that Federal Telegraph Company was adding in Palo Alto since their work was "exactly along my line."[83] Sibyl was president of the Palo Alto Unitarian Young People's Society and, joking about the need for more equipment for his lab, Fred wrote that maybe Sibyl could influence the Almighty. "As for myself, I believe it best to go along without directing his attention in my direction."[84] A few days later Sibyl warned Fred that "If we lived in Montclair, you'd have to go to church with me twice a year instead of the once I promised to let you off with in Palo Alto."[85]

By mid-September, the word was out. Sibyl had wanted to make it a grand surprise to her family in New Jersey, and she had urged Fred to have a new photo taken. She did not like the center-parted hairstyle Fred had adopted while in graduate school and, according with her wishes, he went back to parting his hair on the side. She casually placed frames with his pictures on her bureau so that her sisters and friends could hear, one by one, "Oh, that's just a picture of my fiancé."

She was open with Fred about her previous boyfriends, telling him that when her mother told a sister-in-law of the engagement, she responded brightly, "What, again?" Sibyl told one of her cousins that she was marrying a Stanford professor, "Dr. Terman." "Not *the* Dr. Terman!" "That's what they all say," Sibyl wrote Fred, "and you might as well warn your father that it will probably be all over the U.S. pretty soon that he has lost/killed/divorced his wife and is marrying a flapper."[86]

One of the first things newly engaged Fred did was to spruce up his Buick. In late August, he had "Old Faithful" in for body work and new upholstery. Two weeks later, a wiser Lewis Terman sold "Old Faithful" and gave Fred his own coupe, a better and quieter car.

Sibyl began to look for furniture and silver patterns and wrote him that she had particularly liked a Spanish-medieval bedroom set "*made* for us and for a Spanish house."[87] Besides window-shopping, Sibyl kept busy helping the family move books and other family items from the Montclair home, embroidering that set of napkins, and giving I.Q. tests to her nephews. In the meantime, Fred successfully approached Stanford comptroller Almon Roth about a mortgage to build a house on campus.

Fred and Sibyl had discussed Fallen Leaf Lake in the Sierras, a mountain resort near Lake Tahoe popular among Stanford faculty, as a nice place for their honeymoon. Fred thought it a good idea, since they could see Stanford friends there. Ten days of thought and a letter from Sibyl caused Fred to change his mind about Fallen Leaf Lake. "We had better try a more remote and solitary spot for the first two or three weeks," she commented.[88] Fred agreed, "I think we don't want to go there the first week or so. Too many bridge afternoons and social luncheons. I like bridge, but we don't want to have to do this for a few weeks."[89]

Fred was, after all, an engineer, and now made a true romantic faux pas in suggesting a sort of working honeymoon. While at a Pacific Coast AIEE convention in mid-September at the Del Monte Lodge Hotel near Monterey, California, Fred marveled at its size. Sibyl had been there before and remarked, "That joint is famous chiefly for booze."[90] Mulling over the convention, a recent photo of Sibyl in her new bobbed hair, and a possible honeymoon site, Fred offered a disastrous alternative. "The big convention of the electrical engineers is to be held in Denver," he wrote her. "It takes place in the last of June. . . . We might take it in on our honeymoon. We would have plenty of time to take the trip leisurely. There are some drawbacks, for during the four days of the convention it would be necessary to neglect either the new bride or the convention at least a little. They always plan things to keep the ladies busy during the session. Fallen Leaf Lake is almost on the main road leading back home from Denver."[91] Sibyl's response has not been preserved in the Terman papers. Fred never mentioned this crazy idea again, and their honeymoon took place, according to Sibyl's wishes, in March 1928 in the much quieter seaside town of Carmel.

Fred planned to visit the Walcutts in Tucson over Christmas break 1927. Clara Walcutt wrote to Fred to welcome him and to warn him that he would be quite overwhelmed by sisters during his visit. Clara also commented on how fortunate the couple was to be able to start building their own house the next summer. Sibyl enjoyed planning a house more than anything.[92]

Originally, Fred and Sibyl planned to marry in June 1928, but Sibyl rushed to finish her MA thesis and received her degree in January 1928. The wedding was rescheduled for March.[93] Sibyl and Fred were married on March 22, 1928, a Thursday, in Stanford's Memorial Church.[94] The Walcutt family financial resources were still thin, and none of the family was able to attend the wedding.[95] By May, Sibyl was negotiating with architects and decorators about the new home under construction on Salvatierra Street, only a few streets away from the senior Terman home on Dolores.[96]

The house at 659 Salvatierra Street was built in a short time. With gables and a shingled roof but stucco exterior, it resembles an English cottage as much as a Spanish-style home. It was a very comfortable home, with a study for Fred on the ground floor, and three bedrooms upstairs. The house was soon filled with children: Frederick Walcutt Terman was born in 1929, followed by Terence Christopher Terman in 1931 and Lewis Madison Terman II in 1935. In 1937, the house was enlarged when a handsome new living room and fireplace were added at one end, and a master bedroom above. At the back of the property was a two-room cottage with bath, and a garage. For many years the Termans rented the cottage to graduate students or student married couples. Former tenants from the 1940s recall that Sibyl Terman was very kind to them and invited the student tenants from time to time to have dinner with the Terman family.[97]

Fred was literally back in the middle of the campus community in which he had been raised. Alf Brandin, former Stanford football star and later university business manager, lived across the street in the later 1940s and 1950s. Brandin recalls Fred playing ball with children in the street, chatting with neighbors, and helping everyone look for the first artificial space satellite. (After his retirement, Fred and Sibyl donated the house to Stanford University, and moved to another home on campus further up the hill at 445 El Escarpado Way.)

Sibyl continued to take courses in psychology and education and received a California State Secondary School Teaching Credential on October 16, 1929. She taught part-time at Menlo College and in the Psychology Department at San Jose State College.[98] By 1931, with a growing family, she decided not to actively pursue a career in education, but she maintained an interest in education, and particularly in methods of teaching reading to children. More than two decades later, she and her brother Charles would write a controversial book on the subject.[99]

Building Communications—Electronics and Radio Wave Propagation

After Henry Henline left the department in January 1927, Fred fully took over not only the teaching of radio and electronics theory but also the working of the Communication Lab. It was a rather poor haul of gear, the Communication Lab. Housed on the second floor of Building 500 under the attic, the list of meters and tubes was pretty meager. Fred began by donating much of his own gear and instruments for the use of his students. He also requested from Harris Ryan financial support to purchase more instruments.

Fred decided to get a start in the field of radio wave propagation and the effects of the ionized layers above the earth (later called the "ionosphere").[100] The ionosphere had been exploited at least since 1902, and Lee de Forest and Leonard Fuller had basically demonstrated its existence in the period 1913–15. The field was established in 1924–25 by Edward Appleton in England and by Gregory Breit, Merle Tuve, and A. Hoyt Taylor in the United States with persuasive experimental demonstrations of the height of the ionosphere. With the development in 1927 by AT&T and RCA of Trans-Atlantic ionospherically propagated radio traffic, medium- and short-wave radio propagation was a hot field with much commercial interest. Fred hoped to do experimental radio transmitting once again, and he wrote his friend Herbert Hoover Jr., to see whether Hoover had kept up the registration for their old experimental call 6XH, suggesting that it might be good to reassign it to Stanford because his research was once again getting into radio transmission studies.[101]

In the summer of 1929, Fred Terman approached Harris Ryan, Stanford Comptroller Almon Roth, and Acting President Swain to request funds to build a small building for radio propagation studies to be located near the newly constructed Ryan High-Voltage Lab in the back of the campus. Terman showed Ryan that the total sum spent by Stanford for communications from 1920 through 1927 was only $1,245.62. Added to this were gifts from the army signal corps in World War I, from the Bell System, and from miscellaneous donors, for a total of only $3,060.60. Terman also carefully itemized a large quantity of instruments and parts loaned by himself: meters, condensers, coils, resistors, transformers, switches, insulators, buzzers, and more than thirty vacuum tubes.[102]

Terman's proposed radio propagation building would house equipment to monitor long-distance radio broadcasts, measure the down-coming angle and polarization of radio waves, study radio echo signals, and, most importantly, send radio pulses up into the ionosphere and receive the reflected pulses back on the ground. The pulse equipment could give an idea of the heights of the various ionospheric regions or layers, and the maximum density of electrons in the ionosphere as a function of height. It was known at that time that the electron concentration varied in number and height as a function of time of day, and probably by season and geomagnetic location. Depending on the frequency of the radio wave, it would be absorbed in the ionosphere and disappear, or pass right through the ionosphere and be lost in space. Or, the signal might be fully refracted by the ionosphere and carried directly back to earth or be sent obliquely for hundreds or thousands of miles before returning to earth.

Fred prepared a proposal, including site plans, and submitted it to the university administration.[103] For location of the radio antennas, Fred proposed a site of several acres between Palo Alto reservoir and the Ryan Lab, with an indication of where future expansion might occur. He explained that the radio wave propagation "buildings" would be down the hillside toward the Ryan Lab, both for esthetic purposes and convenience, out of the way of the antenna fields. There was an advantage that the towers of the Ryan Lab could be used to support radio antennas; power and water would be available there, along with equipment that could be loaned back and forth. As to his radio wave lab building, it would be more or less hidden from general view. It would be 25 by 40 feet, not more than 10 feet high, and located 200 feet from the Ryan Lab building. Fred's building could be corrugated sheet iron, he suggested, and like the Ryan Lab, weather-tight "and reasonably burglar proof. I suggest some form of grating in the window construction, and ground glass panes which would prevent boys looking inside and getting their desires aroused by the equipment there." Initially, the roof of the Ryan Lab could support a short tower, and a single 60-foot wooden pole could probably be donated by the telephone or power company. He hoped to build four wooden poles 60 feet or more in height to serve as additional antenna supports.

Fred was anxious to get a building, he wrote, however modest, since several individuals had intimated to him that if he began some wave propagation work, they might find it desirable to help with finances, and perhaps even personnel. At present, one-third to one-half of the electrical engineering graduate students specialized in communication, he pointed out. His research program had thus far dealt primarily with vacuum tubes, and within the past eighteen months he had published six technical articles and presented four technical papers at IRE meetings. "The construction of this building will make it possible to extend this research into the phenomena involved in wave propagation which is a very active field at the present time. We are very favorably located for such work, and by going into it now would be one of the very first universities in the country to undertake a program of systematic research on the propagation of radio waves."[104]

A week later Terman wrote a long letter to Acting President Robert Swain, describing the history of the Communication Lab, listing published papers emanating from work there, and explaining his plans to expand from vacuum tube studies to include radio wave propagation. Radio wave propagation was a very active field at the present, he reiterated, but had been entered by only a few universities, and none west of Chicago. With plenty of free open space and no university competitors within 1500 miles, "Stanford is ideally situated to become the western terminal of experimental work on radio waves."

Terman went on to tell Swain how he also hoped to expand his studies of vacuum tube circuits to include research on vacuum tube construction. "This is a field that is now completely monopolized by a group of large manufacturing organizations, and offers tremendous opportunities to some university which goes into this work with a few ideas and complete freedom from commercial requirements." The radio wave propagation studies could go forward, he suggested, with about $2,000 for the simple building, $2,000 to $3,000 for equipment and with an annual operating cost of about $1,500, including the cost of a research assistant. Stanford could then attract further financial assistance from industry and from research foundations.

The vacuum tube construction facility would require a vacuum pump, one or two furnaces, a spot welder, and some glass-blowing equipment and laboratory space. Costs, he estimated, would initially be several thousand dollars, with operating expenses of $400 per year. Fred anticipated further cooperation in future with the Chemistry, Physics and Mathematics departments on certain problems.[105]

Fred received encouragement.[106] Almon Roth agreed to fund the Radio Wave Propagation Lab building from the Stanford building fund. Fred pinned down offers of equipment and of cooperation from the telephone company and from General Electric. At the fall AIEE Pacific Coast convention, he found several other professors eager to cooperate with Stanford in radio wave studies. In November, Fred wrote to Harris Ryan, Dean Hoover, and Acting President Swain to tell them of his progress and to remind them that Stanford would profit from the project by attracting more and better-qualified graduate students.[107]

At Swain's request, Terman outlined a definite plan and submitted it to Swain through Ryan and Hoover for consideration within the 1930–31 university budget plans. In some survey work for the Carnegie Institution, he had learned that of thirty papers published in radio wave propagation in the ionized regions of the upper atmosphere (ionosphere), only four papers originated from U.S. universities (one each from Cornell, Pennsylvania, MIT, and Chicago). He reiterated Stanford's almost unique position on the West Coast, its availability of land, and its opportunity to become a leader in radio wave propagation studies. He had already gotten a very good communication lab going in the last two years, and he could leverage his work with the proximity of the Ryan High-Voltage Lab. Radio wave propagation was so popular with radio amateurs and with college students that numerous high school and undergraduate students would become interested, he added. The work would be of interest to the Physics Department, and even to those in humanities who had approached him about establishing a phonetics laboratory in connection with communications. It was certainly a rosy future for radio wave propagation studies at Stanford that Fred described. In December 1929, Harris Ryan endorsed Terman's proposal, recommending that Terman be given $2,500 in the 1930–31 budget to equip the radio wave propagation site in addition to the building.[108]

In January 1930, Swain wrote to Roth that he had consulted with President Wilbur and now authorized the construction of a building near the Ryan Lab. Ray Lyman Wilbur gave his long-distance approval, but had written a cautionary note across the letter: "This seems to be a good project. In setting up area put in a clause which makes use of the land temporary."[109]

In May 1930, Terman brought Harris Ryan up-to-date on Roth's agreement to build the radio wave propagation building near the Ryan Lab. The cost of the research assistant would be paid that year by his father's donation, Fred mentioned, and in future he himself expected to personally finance some of the personnel costs from his consulting work and his patent licenses. However, "to keep the proposition from dying," he wrote ominously, he still needed $1,500 in the dean's budget to purchase the necessary equipment.[110] Not one but two clouds were on the horizon: the full impact of the Depression and Dean Hoover's new plan to recreate Hollywood at Stanford.

For Stanford, the year 1929 had opened with great optimism, with respected alumnus Herbert Hoover serving as president and university president Ray Lyman Wilbur as secretary of the interior. Stanford football was in the limelight with the coaching of Glenn "Pop" Warner, while Stanford athletes brought home four gold medals from the 1928 Olympics, and a new 18-hole golf course had been opened in the Stanford foothills. But by 1930, breadlines were forming in San Francisco and the homeless slept along San Francisquito Creek. Family farms, once the backbone of the fertile Santa Clara County, were falling into debt. Stanford students, facing rising tuition and room and board costs, competed with the local unemployed for fewer and fewer jobs.[111]

Stanford's faculty also felt the impact. Salaries would not be cut for another three years, but departmental budgets were shrinking.[112] Equally diverting, Dean Hoover presented a proposal to the president regarding the establishment and equipping of a moving-picture program at Stanford to train film directors, sound and lighting engineers, and movie camera operators. In 1929, Hoover had proposed a program costing $310,000, plus operating costs of $40,000 annually. These costs, plus the necessary endowment of salaries for several new faculty members, would require the raising of a departmental endowment of $1.25 million dollars.[113]

Hollywood mogul Louis B. Mayer, then vice president of MGM studios, had visited Stanford in May 1929 and expressed his interest in funding movie work at Stanford. Hoover then visited Hollywood studios in 1930 to discuss the possibilities. No support, however, came through for Stanford.[114] Hollywood was already doing well training its own in the movie industry. And, as Stanford alumnus J. N. A. Hawkins, chief sound engineer at Disney Studios, later told Terman, Hollywood had little regard for university-trained men.[115] Nevertheless, in 1930, Dean Hoover asked Terman to prepare a memo on the costs of equipping a sound laboratory as part of the movie proposal and to suggest how such a sound laboratory could benefit the movie industry and other radio and phonograph companies. Terman estimated that Stanford would have to add at least one faculty member and construct a new laboratory, measuring rooms, an office, an anechoic chamber, and so on. Terman estimated an initial outlay of about $45,000, plus annual operating costs of $2,500, exclusive of construction costs and the cost of a permanent faculty member's salary.[116]

In the end, Fred received none of the financial support he had been promised for the Communication Lab in 1930. He put his hope on hold until 1936, when he would expand his radio circuits and vacuum tube investigations into radio wave propagation studies, and then into vacuum tube construction research.

In the spring and fall of 1931, Terman again asked Dean Hoover for funds for lab instruments and he received some support. Fred had actually accomplished a good deal with few tools and aging instruments. By late 1931, the lab had no standard signal generator or cathode ray oscillograph, no equipment suitable for measuring radio frequency voltages, and no beat frequency oscillator (BFO). Research for three theses for the Engineer degree had been carried out using a borrowed BFO. Terman wrote to Acting Head Ward Kindy in December 1931 that four of his courses (two in circuit theory and two in radio communication) were nominal requirements for all candidates for the degree of Engineer in electrical engineering. With this greatly increased student load, Terman asked for $50 to $100 per academic quarter to pay a student to help out with charging batteries and repairing instruments and test equipment, things that Terman had been doing himself (along with acting as occasional janitor). His time, he suggested, would be better spent working with the students.[117]

In late 1932, Terman asked Kindy for a teaching assistant. In addition to teaching twenty-five units of organized class instruction that year, Terman was directing nine theses. Kindy forwarded the request to Acting President Swain who wrote on it, "Worth considering. Terman is maturing rapidly and attracting advanced students in larger numbers every year. His recent book on Communications which I have read is admirably done and will bring him much recognition."[118] Funds were not forthcoming. The following year, Fred's father Lewis Terman began an annual contribution of $450 toward part of the cost of a research assistant. Former student James M. Sharp, the research assistant, was promoted to instructor in 1934, paid partly by Lewis Terman's funds. Fred had even proposed paying $250 of Sharp's salary from his own pocket, but President

Wilbur declined the offer.[119] Terman also arranged for Harold F. Elliott ('16) and Charles V. Litton ('24, Engineer '25) to give communication lectures at no charge, and a Telephone Company specialist from San Francisco to give a series of lectures for $10 per visit, including transportation costs.

Despite the Depression's discouraging impact on his plans, Terman continued to make high marks with his dean and president. In January 1935, Hoover commended Terman's outstanding work to Wilbur, remarking:

> He is a teacher of unusual ability. . . . He has a high appreciation of the relation of his students to the future welfare of the country. . . . The fine type of work given in his courses has attracted many graduate students to the Electrical Engineering Department. . . . His output has already been remarkable for his age and he shows ever increasing powers. . . . His personality is entirely acceptable to his associates and students.[120]

Even so, Hoover did not support Fred's promotion to full professor, and did not favor appointing Terman as head of the Electrical Engineering Department. Until Hoover's retirement in 1936, the department languished. No successor had been found to head the department since the 1931 retirement of Harris J. Ryan (the dynamic Ryan, who remained a strong presence in the department, died in 1934).

In 1936, Samuel Brooks Morris, professor of civil engineering, became Stanford's new dean of engineering. A Stanford-trained engineer and an expert in seismology and dam construction, Morris had spent most of his career in industry, working his way up the ranks of the Pasadena Water Department between 1913 and 1935. Morris was just the sort of engineer that Ryan and Hoover had touted, yet it was Morris who would fully support Fred Terman and the kind of advanced academic engineering training and research that Terman represented in the years to come. Fred would get into full stride with his promotion in 1937, and the chance to hire a gifted teaching associate, Karl Spangenberg.

Improving Teaching

While most of his teaching responsibility was aimed at fourth-year and graduate students in electrical engineering, Fred Terman was interested in broader questions of curriculum planning and policy. He was actively involved in undergraduate curricula and teaching through the late 1920s and 1930s. In 1931, he advised Dean of Engineering Hoover that plans to schedule a new undergraduate mechanics course in the Physics Department for the fall quarter would seriously derail sophomore students in electrical engineering. He suggested moving the mechanics course to the winter quarter and the heat physics course to the spring quarter.[121] Terman and Joseph Carroll drafted recommendations from the Electrical Engineering Department to the Physics Department on what the course should cover.[122] The Physics Department was accommodating, no minor matter since the large majority of students taking physics courses in the first year, and some in the second year, were engineering students. As had been true since the beginning years of the century, most university physics teachers earned their salaries by teaching physics to engineering and premed students. Just as it paid instructors' salaries in the Department of English for the teaching of English to engineering students, the Engineering School paid part of the costs of the lab expenses of the Physics Department.[123]

The Physics Department had scolded the Engineering School for letting its students take the less-demanding courses. Physicist Paul Kirkpatrick, a conscientious and popular teacher, revealed his feelings about the problems of engineering students taking Physics 25 (the noncalculus-based course for premeds and liberal arts students) instead of the more demanding Physics 101:

> Last year quite a number of engineers took 25, getting the same amount of credit for much less work than 101 would involve. The enrollment in 25 has grown to ungainly dimensions, and these students not only swell the numbers but since they are uniformly better able to handle the work than the general run of the enrollment, they walk away with the A grades and spoil the morale of the pre-meds and other also-rans.[124]

Terman was very concerned that engineering students learn more chemistry and mathematics than the engineer of 1915. By 1933 or 1934, largely due to Terman's initiative, the Mathematics Department altered the mathematics course sequences so that nonmathematics majors could take various analysis courses with fewer prerequisites than previously required. By the mid- to late-1930s, Stanford added several analysts to the mathematics faculty, that is, mathematicians who were expert in and comfortable in teaching differential equations, complex variables, and matrices. The Hungarian Gabor "George" Szego arrived to take over the chairmanship of the Mathematics Department. Terman and several others interested in mathematics for physicists and engineers, arranged for Stanford's physical theorist Felix Bloch, recently arrived from Switzerland, to meet Szego at the local railroad station on his arrival to assure him of the high esteem in which mathematics was held by Stanford's chemists, physicists, and engineers. (Others involved in the move to make math more available to engineering and science students were Philip A. Leighton of chemistry, and Lydik S. Jacobsen and Stephen P. Timoshenko of engineering mechanics.) Szego liked the idea, as Terman recalled, and "taught one of the courses—a critical course in the sequence—himself, because he wanted to see that it was done right. George Pólya [who arrived in

1942] taught another one, and he was a superb teacher and also a great mathematician. All at once we got a sequence of math courses that, for our better engineering students, were just great."[125]

Getting good, realistic problems for his courses, and in turn into his textbooks, was important for Terman. Even though Terman's own Engineer thesis and ScD dissertation concerned high-voltage power lines and he had coauthored a book on the subject, he wanted to keep his lab course current. He wrote to the Water Power Department of the City of Los Angeles that he'd like to "make up a good up-to-date problem" for his transmission-line course. At his request, they sent him information on the new Boulder Canyon line as to the specifications of transformers, condensers, and generators used on the project.[126]

Engineering education became more and more of a concern for Terman as the 1930s progressed. In 1931, he was made chair of the Special Committee on English for Engineers at Stanford. Serving with him on this committee were E. P. Lesley, professor of mechanical engineering, and L. B. Reynolds, professor of hydraulic and sanitary engineering. Perhaps Fred was made chair because of his known interest in writing and communicating, or, as often happens on committees, perhaps it was because he was the youngest of the three and was expected to do most of the committee work. After a study lasting two years, the committee noted that the Stanford engineering student was required to take nine required credit hours of English composition and exposition, equivalent to the required units of calculus. In the case of the calculus, it was easy to determine which students had had calculus and which had not. From their writing and expository performances before and after taking the nine units of English, however, the committee found that it was nearly impossible to determine which engineering students had benefited. Their ultimate aim was to encourage the engineer to be "English conscious" in all his or her written work. They suggested several schemes for improvement: requiring more English coursework by those who did not improve; concentrate on those who held promise of being the best students; hire tutors to examine constantly the writing of all the engineering students in all classroom assignments and reports; finally, perhaps a "professor of engineering reports" could be appointed (paid out of the Engineering School budget) to teach engineering students to write persuasive and accurate reports.[127]

The English Department had its doubts. Professor of English Samuel Swayze Seward Jr. (on the faculty since 1900, he would pass away only a few months after commenting on the committee's report) felt that the English Department was not qualified to teach technical writing. By contrast, a trained engineering writer would not "find the teaching of good English to his taste." Seward, tossing the ball back to the engineers, suggested that the engineering faculty type up and mimeograph samples of good engineering reports. He agreed that a tutor in English, however, made available to engineering students, would be valuable.[128]

The English Department left the problem with a "Mr. Day" (perhaps a graduate student since he is not listed in faculty registers). Terman wrote to Dean Hoover that there was still the likelihood that there was no way to measure the success of courses proposed by Day, that is, no way to guarantee that they improved students' abilities at English.[129] Terman's committee proposed that before further efforts were made, some sort of measurement plan be constructed to determine whether taking of six units of English 2 and three units of English 131 had any effect on the student.[130]

Terman's call (or threat) to measure the success of English Department instruction led to some unexpected changes in English teaching on campus. Professors of English George Hinkle, John McClelland, and William Dinsmore Briggs agreed to a plan to measure learning; Professor Reginald Bell of the Education Department was eager to supervise the measurements, and L. Pearce Mitchell and the lower-division faculty committee were "extremely sympathetic." Work on this project began in the early spring of 1933, but before they got very far, a new factor entered into the picture. The English Department itself formed a committee to examine the teaching of English A, 2, and 131. The general policy of the past had been to parcel out sections to instructors of English without any real supervision and instruction. The teaching personnel, largely graduate students, changed often and their performance was mixed. The English Department "committee quickly came to the conclusion that much more supervision of these courses was desirable to ensure that uniform standards, uniform subject matter, and uniform methods were used by the instructors handling different sections of the same course," Terman's committee reported. The English Department requested that the Engineering School postpone their measurement experiment until they themselves reorganized their English courses A, 2, and 131. Professor Hinkle wrote to Terman, "I am convinced that the traditional method of instruction has been wasteful and ineffective." Hinkle outlined his ideas for improvement, including more stress on literary skill and measurement by exams given in the courses. Terman then reported to the dean of engineering that his committee had clarified the problem and probably had been an important factor "in causing the English Department to become aware that more careful supervision of the English composition work by the permanent members of the staff is essential if the best results are to be obtained."[131]

In later years, Terman continued to be involved in undergraduate education, especially the question of the nature and extent of nonengineering courses in the undergraduate engineering curriculum. In the 1940s, Stanford would come under severe pressure from a national engineering accreditation committee to limit the humanities and social sciences courses taken by the engineering undergraduate, but Terman would help deflect this pressure and keep Stanford's tradition of the broadly educated engineer.

Patents and Consulting

Side-tracked into power transmission while at MIT, Fred Terman returned to radio when he came back to Stanford. Not only was radio booming when Terman was a university student and beginning instructor, but radio inventors were celebrities. Most of the other engineering faculty at Stanford still centered their off-campus activities on consulting for companies on particular projects. The radio inventor, by contrast, sought patent protection for his own invention, while the radio manufacturer tried to obtain use of such patents, or better yet, to find ways to get around patents and manufacture the items without having to pay big licensing fees. In his first years of inventing, Fred experienced little financial success but gained useful knowledge of the patent game.

Beginning in 1919, the Radio Corporation of America (RCA) was formed from four great companies (American Telephone and Telegraph, General Electric, Westinghouse, and Western Electric, who shared their patents). RCA held nearly a monopoly on patents in the radio communications field. As a result, it was very difficult to find something that did not fall under the broad patent ownership of RCA. In addition, the consortium RCA along with big companies like General Electric and Bell Labs bought up patents while their staffs busily plugged holes in the patent fabric. Within this environment, Fred and other small-scale inventors fought an uphill battle for recognition. The strategy of an individual worker like Fred Terman, competing against the likes of RCA's labs, would be to either get a small piece of the action, or devise something valuable enough that one of the big companies would buy the patent, or perhaps a slight novelty would allow a small company to build a radio, not as cleverly designed but designed well enough to avoid the necessity of paying a large licensing fee to RCA.

Fred's initial radio ideas in 1925 were admittedly naïve. The first manuscripts Fred sent to patent attorneys were not very sophisticated and suggest that Fred did not thoroughly research comparable patents before submitting his ideas. As he progressed, he became much more knowledgeable about patent strategies.

In 1924–25, while recovering from his illnesses and tutoring Herbert Hoover Jr., Fred had taken up Van der Bijl's book and the subject of vacuum tubes and radio. Fred constructed a radio receiver and began taking notes on ideas for invention in late 1924. Several times during 1925, Fred collected his notes and had them notarized, including ideas, however elemental, regarding ways to improve radio reception, reduce static interference, and make a radio with wider tuning range. Soon after, he began to act on these ideas.

Several of the Lyon brothers, Stanford alumni from Los Angeles, were patent lawyers. All three Lyon brothers were approximately Fred's age and attended Stanford at roughly the same time. Leonard Saxton Lyon graduated BA in prelaw in 1918, married a classmate, and for a few years served for a time as a lecturer at the Stanford Law School. His brother, Richard Forbes Lyon, attended Stanford for two years and then transferred to MIT, as did a brother Lewis Estes Lyon. Richard Lyon, whom Fred knew also at MIT, was the Lyon and Lyon firm's radio specialist. In early 1926, after hearing Leonard Lyon lecture at Stanford, Fred approached him for help in patenting his ideas. Soon after, Fred began a six-year relationship with the firm.[132]

Lyon and Lyon attended to Fred's first few ideas about radio inventions. They advised him, for example, that his ideas of a superheterodyne circuit with the local oscillator frequency *higher* than the received frequency, and other ways to get around the superheterodyne patent, were probably already covered, yet Fred persisted and filed one idea on November 15, 1926 (for which Lyon and Lyon charged $175 for their work plus $20 for the U.S. Patent filing fee). By 1931, Fred had been allowed only one of twelve claims in his patent application, and he abandoned the idea of "Method and Apparatus for Frequency Changing and Amplifying."[133] Fred made a similar attempt on the "neutrodyne" method of neutralizing an amplifier so that it not break into oscillation. The key patent had already been awarded to Hazeltine Radio Company, and other patents covered approaches to neutralization. In 1926 Fred wrote to Richard Lyon about this idea, "The main value of this circuit is a commercial one for, of course, scientifically it does not amount to very much."[134] Nearly a year later Fred hoped that "if it is possible to convince the examiner that there is a difference between my idea and the Hazeltine patent, I have something that is worth immediate money almost without doubt. Otherwise there is nothing to patent."[135] In 1929, this idea too was abandoned.

Fred received his first patent in 1930 for an "Electrical Measuring Instrument."[136] Beginning in 1930, Fred began to use the patent law firm of Lippincott and Metcalf in San Francisco for his patent affairs, although he continued for two more years with Lyon and Lyon for patent work in progress. Fred's main contact was Donald K. Lippincott, a radio engineer and lawyer. Though Lippincott was not a Stanford alumnus, his wife had graduated in the class of 1912. Lippincott had an advanced knowledge of radio and electronic circuitry and regretted he had not more time for his own radio research. Fred and Don Lippincott saw each other not only at Lippincott and Metcalf in San Francisco, but also at AIEE and IRE section meetings, nearly always held in the City.

The patent situation began to look up for Fred as his reputation expanded. For example, following an article Fred published in the spring of 1928, the chief engineer of the Wired Radio Company in New York City wrote to Fred to ask whether his ideas had been filed for patent. Fred began a correspondence with C. W. Hough, president of Wired Radio. Hough proposed that Fred sign their "Standard Inventor's Contract" wherein *all* of Fred's ideas would be given first to Wired Radio, which would pay him a fee for any ideas accepted, then a larger sum if the ideas were patented. Fred declined after talking with a friend "in the East who is a patent attorney," and responded that he would send what he saw fit. After some hesitation, Hough sent Fred a "Special Option Agreement," which let Fred do as he wished. Fred was learning the ropes. By mentioning that he had spoken with the anonymous patent attorney friend "in the East," he had invoked some of that East Coast aura that he was to spend his career redistributing westward. Fred immediately sent off five of his ideas to Wired Radio. After searching the literature, Wired Radio accepted only one idea, however, that of a "Transmitting System Involving a Thermal Relay for Temperature Control," and even that idea was later found to have been previously covered.[137] Nevertheless, Fred sold several patents to Wired Radio over the next few years, including one for driving a galvanometer with a vacuum tube (No. 1,784,119), and one for design of inductance coils (No. 1,816,448). He was paid $550 for the two. Another concerned his "Inverted Vacuum Tube" (No. 1,846,043) that could serve as a voltage-reducing power amplifier, oscillograph, or power transformer. He received $400 for this patent. Wired Radio had stepped into Fred's sphere, however, and he contacted them later in the 1930s in an attempt to get business for his friend Cyril Elwell.

Simultaneous with his first negotiations with Wired Radio in 1928, Fred tried closer to home—Federal Telegraph in Palo Alto. By then, Federal was one of five subsidiaries of Kolster Radio Corporation in San Francisco. In spite of a hearty welcome, Kolster declined to sign Fred as a consultant and wrote that they might look at something Fred submitted from time to time.[138] Fred got other consulting jobs: $78 for analyzing a radio position indicator for geophysical prospecting, and $38 for analyzing a radio frequency device for measuring the moisture content of lumber.[139] (Radio consultants normally earned $25 to $35 a day at that time.) In 1932 Fred analyzed an oddball rectifier tube with double cathode for a local inventor, measured the tube's characteristics, and sent him a typed eight-page report on the measurements; he charged $25.[140]

Fred entered into what he hoped would be a long-term arrangement in 1930 with his Stanford classmate in chemistry, Ralph Heintz, then a partner in the San Francisco radio design firm of Heintz and Kaufman (H and K). The H and K sales office was at 311 California Street in the City, but their plant and design shop was in South San Francisco. H and K made tubes and sold completed radio stations for the Dollar Steamship Line. In May 1930, they happily signed Fred as a consultant with an annual contract at $1,000 per annum (almost one-third of Fred's Stanford salary), plus $25 per day for extra consulting. By agreement, they periodically presented problems to Fred for his consideration. Any ideas or devices emerging from the consultation became property of H and K. Fred was thrilled with this agreement, which lasted for four years.[141]

Fred fed H and K several good ideas. For example, in February 1931 he pointed out that Harris Ryan was seriously concerned with the need for a nationally marketed electronic hearing aid device. Western Electric had made several and had given one to Ryan for trial, but Fred guessed that RCA patent limitations prevented Western Electric from marketing a hearing aid. He noted that several million customers in the United States could use such an aid, and he advised H and K that they could produce one without needing any specially designed tubes or miniature microphones. A year later, he learned that Mackay Radio was installing long, directional "Vee" wire antennas at their East Palo Alto marshland radio site. Fred pointed out that RCA communications had been doing a lot of work on these antennas, but that he knew that C. P. Steinmetz of GE had basically covered the idea years before and thus it would be out of patent protection. The design of Vee antennas was covered, Fred noted, on pages 531–32 of his *Radio Engineering* text. Fred's old Stanford chum Phil Scofield of H and K was extremely interested in this idea.[142]

Fred made another sort of patent arrangement in 1930. He signed an agreement with Dr. Russel V. A. Lee and his father Lewis M. Terman, to form a sort of patent corporation. In return for their each paying half of all expenses and fees for patent attorneys and filing fees, Dr. Lee and Lewis Terman would each receive one-sixth of the revenues coming from Fred Terman's patents, and Fred would receive two-thirds.[143] This agreement remained in force for almost nine years.

When Fred wrote to Dr. Lee to terminate the contract in 1939, he noted that with his receipts from Heintz and Kaufman, Elwell (for British patents), British Marconi, the Swedish patent rights, and Gilfillan Brothers, they had taken in $2,812.42. Russel Lee and Lewis Terman each had contributed $1,067, and Fred had put in $865.25 (which was not part of the contract). Thus, the corporation had not been so successful. Fred calculated that his father and Dr. Lee each needed to be paid $248.76 if they were to be returned their initial investment. Fred paid them back, and after other costs were included, Fred was left $444.23 in the hole. As he wrote Dr. Lee, it was too bad that the partnership returned no profits, but "developments in recent years have been such that a new venture launched in 1930–31 has had more difficulties to encounter than could have possibly been anticipated, and I imagine that most money invested at that time has failed during the last eight or nine years even to preserve its capital."[144]

Fred kept up his patent interests all through the 1930s, but he made accelerated runs during several different periods, one being in 1932 when he had finished the text for his highly successful textbook *Radio Engineering* with McGraw-Hill. At this time, he made efforts to get patent agreements with the Wired Radio Company, the Hickok Instrument Company, Federal Telegraph, and International Telephone and Telegraph (IT and T), among others. Also in 1932 Fred entered into a partnership patent agreement with Cyril Elwell, then in Europe. Fred knew that his patent applications were sometimes blocked by earlier patents awarded in Britain or on the Continent, so he sought to gain protection for those patents he had been awarded by filing in Britain. His contact for this was Cyril

Franklin Elwell. Elwell had been an acquaintance of Fred's since World War I, when Fred hung around Elwell's Federal Telegraph Company in Palo Alto. Elwell later became a friend, patent partner, and lecturer in electrical engineering at Stanford.[145] After he lost Federal Telegraph to outside interests (including the Spreckels family of San Francisco and Hawaii), Elwell went to England and started a radio consulting company, specializing in the building of very tall radio towers. He visited Palo Alto on occasion, however, and during the 1930s he and Fred tried to get consulting and other work for each other.

In fall 1932, Elwell returned to England after a six-month visit to Palo Alto. With an agreement in hand, Terman and Elwell filed jointly for patents in Britain, with the applications that Fred had already filed in the United States. In return for sharing half of any patent rights, Elwell engaged the London patent firm of Frank B. Dehn and Company, and paid the costs of filing and pursuing the British patents. All the applications listed both Elwell and Terman as residing at Stanford University. At least seven of Terman's patents had been awarded in Britain to Elwell and Terman by May 1934.[146] Unfortunately for the duo, companies were wary of putting out cash for patent rights. Elwell wrote to Terman that after paying the attorney fees for preparing and arguing the patent cases, and the filing and registration fees, he made very little profit for the two men.[147]

In letters beginning in early 1936, while discussing their patent applications, Elwell revealed to Terman that since December 1935 he had been designing and building eleven wooden radio towers, each 247 feet high, for the British to protect themselves against Hitler's bombers. They were a very difficult design, and no other firm wished to undertake the task. He was also building 250-foot-tall steel towers for the BBC.[148] (Sometime during a visit to Palo Alto in 1939, it was revealed publicly in Palo Alto that Elwell had built eleven towers along the southern English coast to guard against German air attack.) Fred Terman asked Elwell in 1937 to submit a short piece describing his tower-building activities, which was published in the *Stanford Illustrated Review* in February 1938, to demonstrate the electrical engineering activities of Stanford's graduates.[149] Even though Elwell's published material spoke about direction finding and did not actually mention radar, experts in British radar and its history have speculated that Elwell's revelations to Terman are certainly curious, and if known to the British at the time, would have landed Elwell in jail.[150] The public in England during the late 1930s had been told that the radio towers (which were part of the secret British "Chain Home" radar system), were put up for research in ionospheric physics. Elwell's letter to Fred Terman in January 1936 reveals that Terman knew about England's radar defense plans even before Edward Appleton, the famed British ionospheric physicist. Appleton and others were kept from radar knowledge because of secrecy regulations. The knowledge that these towers were a vital part of the world's first successful defensive radar network was supposed to be highly classified knowledge.

Fred didn't fail as a patenter by any means. Appendix B lists thirty-six of Fred's U.S. patents issued between the years 1930 and 1947. Work on all save the last was completed before Terman left Stanford in early 1942 to direct the Radio Research Laboratory for Radar Countermeasures at Harvard. The list does not include the numerous cross-filings for Terman's patents in Argentina, Britain, Brazil, Canada, and Switzerland. Fred Terman could have received more patents than in fact were awarded to him, if time and money were no object. In some cases, his patent idea would appear so obscure as to have no market, or so indefensible that it could not be protected against infringement. In other cases, Fred abandoned the claim by neglecting to file within a certain period. In several instances, Fred clearly carried the ideas of a rejected or abandoned claim to a new, related device he worked on subsequently.

Yet, Fred was philosophical about the experience, feeling that his patent activities had helped him build up important contacts and establish himself as a potential consultant in patent litigations. He established contacts with numerous important firms, including RCA and IT&T, and these experiences helped him *and* Stanford in the agreements with IT&T and Sperry Gyroscope that were signed in the late 1930s. Earlier in the 1930s, Stanford University was still inexperienced about patent rights and agreements. (Only the Medical School had any significant experience in patents for university-related research work.) In addition, Terman's patent and consulting contacts proved useful when he looked for jobs for his graduating students during the Depression. Terman built up a thick file of data on salaries and wages paid by various firms (Gilfillan, Bell Labs, Westinghouse, GE, Galvin, RCA) and names of personal contacts and Stanford alumni whom he could approach to help a student gain employment.

Planning a Publishing Career

By the time of his retirement in 1965, the total of Fred Terman's textbooks in their various English-language editions, amounted to 6,439 pages. Some of his books were translated into Russian, Chinese, Korean, and other languages. Fred later noted that if one added together all the various editions of his works, including the foreign-language versions and pirated editions, the different volumes filled a shelf 7 feet, 4 inches in length. His book royalties over the years, including his royalties as consulting editor of the McGraw-Hill technical series, which consisted of more than 108 titles, earned him more income as a writer and editor than he received in his forty years as a professor, dean, and provost at Stanford.[151]

Soon after beginning his teaching career, Fred Terman decided to write a radio engineering text to cover the rapidly increasing market with students of communication and radio engineering. In the first half of the twentieth century several electrical engineering authors had three or four different texts in print at the same time. Around 1910, such might have included a text on "magnetic circuits" and one on "electric circuits" (what the British call "electrical applied physics," and indeed, some of these texts were written by physics professors). The books were intended to give the electrical engineering student the theory necessary for calculation of dynamo-electrical machinery and for transmission lines. In addition, there was a market for an accompanying book for laboratory measurements, and another for laboratory experiments. There was a market for specialty texts on motors or transmission lines, on mathematics applied to electrical problems, or simplified texts for technical high schools and trade schools.

Fred Terman's model in writing his own texts was the work of Vladimir Karapetoff (1876–1948), a Russian who published numerous English- and German-language technical books, along with his own poetry. Karapetoff taught for many years at Sibley College, the engineering school at Cornell University. A major figure in the AIEE by World War I, Karapetoff took part in AIEE meetings, served on national committees, and commented frequently in print on things electric. In 1929, Terman served as a member of the AIEE's eighteen-member Electrophysics Committee, chaired by Karapetoff, which also included Vannevar Bush and R. A. Millikan. Terman later said that he admired Karapetoff because he had a clear writing style and yet wrote his texts at a high level.[152]

The first American textbook author to establish himself at the top of the growing field of radio was Columbia University professor John Harold Morecroft (1881–1934).[153] Morecroft had started just before World War I with a short volume on electrical machinery, a lab manual for alternating-current study, and an elementary electrical engineering text for technical high schools. In 1923, he engaged a collaborator and produced an electrical circuits and machinery treatise in three volumes that went through three editions by 1933. But Morecroft's most significant production was his *Principles of Radio Communication*. He was assisted in this by two assistants. The book was a daunting 935 pages long in 1921, and 1,084 pages in the thoroughly revised third edition of 1933. (Morecroft also brought out a shorter and simplified version of the book.) In 1931, he produced a laboratory exercises book, *Experimental Radio Engineering*. Just before his death in 1934, Morecroft brought out a text on vacuum tubes, *Electron Tubes and Their Application*. By 1933, Morecroft had single-handedly covered the new field of radio-communications-electronics.

All of Morecroft's main works were published by John Wiley and Sons, along with McGraw-Hill one of the most influential American engineering publishers. Morecroft's radio communication text dominated the market in the 1920s to the extent that radio people simply called it "Morecroft," as in "You can check that out in Morecroft."

Reading Terman's correspondence, one is struck by the twenty-nine-year-old engineer's coherent long-range plans. Fred Terman aimed his sights at replacing "Morecroft"—not simply the big book but the shorter elementary version and the book on laboratory experiments. Terman even planned a handbook. Within fourteen years from his initiation of the plan, Terman would have in print five books, two of them great technical best-sellers, and he would become McGraw-Hill's star technical author. Terman considered Wiley and Sons but chose McGraw-Hill and stayed with them throughout his text-publishing career that ended in 1955 with the fourth edition of his radio engineering volume (Fred also edited a very successful technical series for McGraw-Hill). By the late 1930s, "Terman" had replaced "Morecroft" as the place to go to "check that out."

Terman's *Radio Engineering*

Curtis G. Benjamin, a McGraw-Hill salesman in San Francisco, was Terman's original contact when he proposed writing a radio engineering textbook. Fred met Curtis Benjamin through his wife Sibyl, for Benjamin had begun his book-selling career in Arizona and had known Sibyl at the University of Arizona. One day when Benjamin was crossing the Stanford campus he ran into Sibyl, who told him to visit her new husband.[154] Fred's meeting with Benjamin would quickly ripen into a life-long friendship. Benjamin and McGraw-Hill's senior vice president James S. Thompson became Terman's links to his long and very successful publishing career with that firm. Promoted to manager of McGraw-Hill's College Department, Benjamin moved to New York City before Fred's first book appeared in 1932. When Fred was in the East attending IRE meetings, he always left his contact address as c/o Curtis G. Benjamin at McGraw-Hill.

Since 1927, his first full year of teaching, Fred Terman had planned to write a text book on radio communication suitable for the senior electrical engineering student. As he came closer to building the product, he estimated that the book would have about the same level of mathematical requirements as Morecroft's and be about the same length as Van der Bijl's.[155] McGraw-Hill was extremely interested to learn that Fred might produce "a more simplified and teachable text than Morecroft," the radio flagship of their major competitor, Wiley Publishing.[156]

The aim of *Radio Engineering*, Terman wrote, was to present a comprehensive engineering treatment of the more important vacuum tube and radio phenomena. He designed the book so that it could be used in the senior-year undergraduate electrical engineering curriculum, yet from the beginning he insisted that he would not fill it with the usual mass of formulas and derivations, nor with the customary review of the same material in the standardized manner. He would organize the material in his own way. He would avoid the mistake, he wrote, that

Morecroft and others made "of writing other peoples' ideas into my own book without having subjected them to very [close] thought, and without organizing them to fit logically with the rest of the material."

Writing a successful book would get his research publications increased recognition, he felt, and at the same time, his steady output of research articles would strengthen the future of the book. Fred concluded that he was young enough, with most of his career ahead of him, to be able to keep the book updated and revised for at least twenty or thirty years. Fred concluded that McGraw-Hill was the logical publisher of his manuscript, and that he could have a finished manuscript to them within eighteen months.[157]

This was just what McGraw-Hill wanted to hear. James S. Thompson responded, "Your conception of the problem and your record of experience seem to be all that is necessary for a perfect book."[158] Thompson advised Terman to look at Morecroft's abridged version, and to send McGraw-Hill two or three chapters and a detailed plan. Thompson stated that McGraw-Hill hoped to consider Terman's book a permanently valuable addition to a most important area of electrical engineering, and he offered royalties of 10 percent of list price on the first 2,500 copies, 12.5 percent on the next 2,500, and 15 percent thereafter.

Fred was ill with thyroid problems for three months in the fall of 1929, but was able to report to Thompson in February 1930 that he had drafted thirty-five thousand words and had employed a graduate student part-time to do drafting, computing, and data collecting. He planned to employ an assistant full-time during the summer of 1930.[159]

This was an auspicious beginning. That summer, Fred dangled his prospective book not only before McGraw-Hill but also before their main rival John Wiley and Sons. Rudolf M. Triest of Wiley wrote in June 1930, asking the status of the manuscript. Couldn't Wiley see at least a few chapters? Things were coming along well, Fred responded, and if Wiley was still interested, they could see it in the fall.[160] (By November 1930 he had ninety thousand words drafted and had begun actively collecting illustrations and data from GE, RCA, General Radio, and other companies.) By March 1931, Terman decided to go with McGraw and sent them 515 typed pages, the first nine chapters of the book. Although Fred requested a sentence by sentence review, McGraw responded simply that their outside reviewer liked the manuscript a lot, and they felt that Fred was as good as anyone they had on their list of reviewers. "This may amuse you," wrote Thompson, "but frankly this is a rather curious field," and it was simply too difficult to get really good reviewers.[161]

In a letter to McGraw-Hill, Fred stressed the importance of his manuscript and criticized Morecroft's *Principles of Radio Communication*. (Fred asked that his comments to McGraw-Hill be kept confidential, but they reveal Terman's strong feelings about Morecroft's text.) The first part of his own *Radio Engineering*, Fred wrote, is devoted to the theory of tuned circuits and the fundamental properties of vacuum tubes and vacuum tube applications. This material was important to *all* electrical engineers and was presented in the first eleven chapters. Fred felt that most texts, including Morecroft, wasted the introductory chapter in trying to skim over all of introductory electromagnetism and DC and AC circuits: if the reader was unfamiliar with such introductory matter, then one chapter would not suffice; if he was already familiar, then the chapter was a waste.

Fred's second chapter had a special feature in that he emphasized the importance of the quantity Q, the ratio of reactance (L) to resistance (R) in a coil or resonant circuit. He felt Morecroft had made a mess of this. For the same reason, Fred felt his own treatment of resonant circuits in chapter three was a great improvement, given the importance he gave to extensive use of the quantity Q. Fred's chapters five and six, on voltage and power amplifiers, he felt were a great improvement over Morecroft, who gave a treatment that is "incomplete, contains many errors, and is full of mathematics." Fred's discussion of transformer-coupled amplifiers and of power amplifiers was available in no other textbooks at the time. Morecroft did not mention the linear amplifier, even though it was used in practically all radio telephone transmitters then being built. Regarding chapter seven, on vacuum tube oscillators, Fred claimed again that Morecroft was full of errors, omitted important topics, and included page after page of special cases with no general instructions to help the student to understand the design of oscillator circuits. Morecroft barely mentioned quartz-crystal oscillators, very important in radio since about 1926. In his own book, Fred included also the latest material on screen-grid tubes and other newer tubes such as the magnetron, the pentode, and the space-charge grid tube. [162]

As Fred set up his book, the general material in the first eleven chapters could be covered in a one-semester course, if desired. The following seven chapters cover more specialized topics—radio transmitters and receivers, antennas and the propagation of radio waves, radio navigational aids, measurements, and audio equipment. Terman specifically noted that his aim was to exclude unnecessary mathematical equations and use words as far as possible, yet he felt that the book carried the analysis much deeper than customary approaches and that, therefore, the key mathematical relations stood out in greater relief. It was most important, he believed, to get the student really interested in the material and able to understand the physical concepts, free of "attention-diverting trivial equations." This was Terman's policy through the four editions of his immensely popular text.

As it turned out, *Radio Engineering* was of interest to more than the undergraduate student. A number of original research features of the time were included. Fred's chapters on triode amplifiers illustrated results of his own work and that of his students, particularly the transformer-coupled amplifier, the analysis of the so-called Class A and Class B amplifiers, the analysis of rectifier-filters, and screen-grid tubes. As a particular example: the universal resonance curve, a Terman innovation, became a standard radio engineering analysis tool. The universal resonance curve is related to the idea of "Q." In a radio coil, as mentioned, this is the ratio of the coil reactance $X = \omega L$, to the coil resistance R. $Q = \omega L/R = (2\pi f)L/R$. "$\omega$" is defined as the radian frequency, or 2π times the frequency f. If something is broadly tuned, the Q is low, if narrowly tuned, the Q is high. To give an audio analogue: if one were to bow a violin near to a drum head and the head vibrated over a wide range of violin pitches, then the Q would be low. If one bowed the violin over a wide range and the drum head vibrated noticeably at only one violin pitch, the resonance or Q would be very high. In a radio series resonant circuit (a capacitance C, an inductance L, and some resistance R in series) the characteristics depend primarily on the ratio of $\omega L/R$, or Q. The radio current flowing through the circuit increases as one approaches the resonant frequency and then decreases as one passes through that frequency. If the series resonant circuit has truly negligible resistance, at resonance the current tends to infinity, or to very large values. Terman rearranged the analysis of the current flowing in the circuit at any frequency compared to the current at resonance and derived a quantity δ. δ represents the ratio of the number of cycles by which the actual frequency is off resonance to the resonant frequency, or the fractional deviation of the frequency from resonance. Furthermore, δ is positive or negative as the actual frequency is greater than or less than resonance respectively. It is then possible to plot the universal resonance curve, from which the exact resonance curve and phase angle of any series circuit may be obtained without calculation when Q is known. Terman's curve can also be applied to the *parallel* resonant circuit.

Terman's curves, for series and parallel circuits, were very useful because they are independent of the resonant frequency and of the ratio of inductance to capacity in the circuit. In nearly all practical cases, Terman's curve could give answers with less than 1 percent error, aside from measurement errors, if the Q was higher than about ten. Most effective radio circuit constants were not known within errors of several or more percent, and calculations using the full formulas would require five-place logarithm tables to best an error of 1 percent. In short, here was a real addition to the helpful tools used by the radio engineers before the existence of electronic calculators and sophisticated electronic measuring devices.[163]

Fred had all 950 typed pages of the manuscript to McGraw-Hill by Thanksgiving 1931, and the publisher spent the spring of 1932 getting the type and illustrations set. McGraw was prepared to omit the last chapter (on sound) but Fred insisted on its inclusion. During the summer, Fred argued to keep the price of his book down to $5 and McGraw finally agreed, since the final product would come in at a few pages under 700, rather than the estimated 750 pages. The price of $5 was an important consideration for at least two reasons: the Depression economy and Morecroft's price of $7.50.[164]

The book came out in time for delivery for the fall 1932 classes, and McGraw was delighted with the sales. Within several weeks, eleven schools adopted the book and several more were good prospects. Fred was aggressive about promoting the book, advising them to push the advertising for *Radio Engineering*.

Fred wrote to Benjamin that he was thinking about producing an elementary abridged version, about 300 to 350 printed pages, which could be used to teach radio at liberal arts colleges. It was too soon yet to consider an abridgement, Benjamin responded, since some instructors were reporting Fred's text looked too difficult, others that it was too easy. Benjamin worried about Fred's overworking. "I had begun to wonder what manner of man was this who needed nor wanted any rest, after having turned out a complete textbook within two years." Nevertheless, McGraw's editor, Hugh J. Kelly, wrote soon after to state that McGraw was probably going to go to a second printing in anticipation of second-semester book sales. By January 1933, James Thompson agreed that Fred should issue an elementary abridged version to come out about 1936.

Twenty-one institutions ordered *Radio Engineering* by early January 1933, and another fifteen by February, selling 1,685 copies, a "splendid record for these lean times."[165] Fred noted happily that, according to Wiley's advertisements promoting the latest edition of Morecroft's *Principles of Radio Communication*, of the fifty-nine institutions that had used Morecroft's book, twenty-two had switched to Fred's *Radio Engineering*, including many state universities, Caltech, MIT, Harvard, Carnegie, Columbia, and Tufts.[166] By spring 1934 the book was selling steadily about two hundred copies per month, "really a remarkable record in the face of the Depression," wrote Thompson.[167]

Terman did not put down his text-writing pen for the next two decades. His energy and enthusiasm, and McGraw's successful marketing and sales, led them by spring 1934 to agree to a string of four books: (1) *Radio Engineering* (which they expected to revise in five to six years; new editions subsequently came out in 1937, 1947, and 1955); (2) a laboratory measurements volume; (3) an abridged version of *Radio Engineering*; and (4) a radio handbook. All this came to pass by 1943.

The measurements volume was published as *Measurements in Radio Engineering* by McGraw in 1935 and also was a financial success; years later it was revised as *Electronic Measurements* (1952) by Terman and Joseph Mayo Pettit. Fred thought his measurements book differed from other such manuals, and yet complemented his *Radio Engineering*, since his was written to emphasize laboratory techniques rather than primarily to illustrate principles.[168] While the main text covered the fundamentals, the measurements book covered laboratory and measuring techniques. Terman emphasized to Curtis Benjamin that the main use of his book was to learn fundamental principles of measuring and measuring equipment.

Since each university would have different laboratory apparatus and each instructor would have his or her own preferences of the specific experiments to use in the laboratory exercises, Terman made the appendix on experiments an outline in more or less skeleton form.[169]

The abridged version of *Radio Engineering* appeared in January 1938 as *Fundamentals of Radio*, with the collaboration of U.S. Navy Lieutenant F. W. MacDonald. The handbook, delayed some by World War II, appeared in August 1943 as *Radio Engineer's Handbook* and was a worldwide success.

By 1941, seventy-five universities had adopted *Radio Engineering* and fifty-four had adopted *Fundamentals of Radio*.[170] *Radio Engineering* became *Electronic and Radio Engineering*, assisted by Robert Helliwell and others, in its fourth edition in 1955. All of these were published by McGraw-Hill. Two became "classics," and "Terman" in the 1940s and 1950s now meant either Terman's *Radio Engineering*, or Terman's *Radio Engineer's Handbook*.

Textbooks and Teaching

Research, teaching, and textbook writing were intimately related in Terman's work. He not only utilized the research of his graduate students in his book *Radio Engineering*, but also mentioned them by name in print, either in the preface, or in the text of the book, indicating whether the work reported had been published.[171] His literature reviews led to other research and teaching ideas in the next several years. For example, while writing the antenna chapter of *Radio Engineering*, Fred became interested in antenna arrays. He consulted with broadcast radio stations about design problems, advised his clients Heintz and Kaufman about antenna usage, thought about possible patent applications, and entered into antenna research with William Hansen, his colleague in the Stanford Physics Department.

Hansen began work in 1935 on radiation fields from antennas, and he and his graduate student J. G. Beckerley submitted a paper on antenna radiation resistance to the IRE in 1936.[172] Fred Terman encouraged Hansen and interested him in wave propagation in the ionosphere. By the spring of 1937, Hansen had prepared a manuscript on the time of reflection of a radio pulse from the ground to the ionosphere and back and termed this "Terman's Problem on Reflections from the Ionosphere." Hansen and Terman filed for a patent on an antenna array in 1938, "Directional Radiating System," which was granted October 15, 1940, as US Patent 2,218,487. About the same time, 1936, Hansen developed his "rhumbatron" tube. He went on to collaborate with Russell and Sigurd Varian in Russ Varian's spectacular invention of the "klystron" tube in 1937, and designed the first klystron, built by Sig Varian.[173]

Another example of the teaching-research connection is Terman's research in the late 1920s in transformer coupling of triode amplifiers, which pointed Fred and student Ira E. Wood to further studies of audio transformers. This appeared as a significant section of his chapters (five and six) on triode amplifiers in *Radio Engineering* and reappeared in revised form in chapter eight of his 1935 book *Measurements in Radio Engineering.*

Undergraduate research by his student Herbert Hoover Jr. in 1925 awakened Fred to the promise of radio wave propagation research. Terman's preliminary literature research on this subject surfaced in *Radio Engineering* as Fred's chapter fifteen on propagation of radio waves. A rather complete outline of methods of measuring ionospheric and radio wave propagation appears in Fred's 1935 measurements text. Fred collaborated with Norris Bradbury of Stanford's Physics Department, who was interested in upper atmosphere physics.[174] Bradbury, in his postdoctoral work at MIT, had taken laboratory measurements of electron attachment in oxygen and published results in 1933. In 1936 he discussed with Terman about extending his work to the ionized gases in the ionosphere. Between 1937 and 1940, Bradbury published four papers concerning ionization and recombination in the ionosphere, especially in the E-region.[175] One of Bradbury's papers was coauthored with Terman's electrical engineering graduate student William T. Sumerlin.[176] From Fred's research into ionospheric propagation, he learned that a graduate student experienced in radio wave propagation, Nathan Hall, was interested in coming to Stanford. Nathan Hall then initiated radio wave propagation research at Stanford in 1936 under Fred's direction and built at Stanford the first ionospheric pulse transmitter-sounder on the West Coast. Hall's work was continued by Sumerlin, O. G. Villard Jr., Lowell Hollingsworth, Millett Morgan, and Robert Helliwell and became one of Stanford's most productive and celebrated activities.

Yet another example of Fred's commingling of teaching, text writing, and research is Fred's interest in vacuum tube characteristics, cathode-ray tubes, and special very-high-frequency tubes in his texts. He begged and borrowed such tubes for his communication lab students. He asked Charles Litton to assist Stanford in establishing a vacuum tube facility. With Litton's volunteer help, a graduate student, Henry P. Blanchard, began to set up a tube construction facility in 1936. Year after year, due to lack of finances, Terman and his students designed and built much of their laboratory and measurement gear, which compared, he wrote, "quite favorably with the best commercial equipment available."[177] By 1937 Terman, recently appointed head of the Electrical Engineering Department, was able to search for the best available young vacuum tube expert for Stanford's faculty. He hired Karl Spangenberg, and at about the same time, offered Edward Ginzton, Joseph Pettit, and David Packard graduate fellowships. He assisted William Hansen and the Varian brothers with their microwave research. He arranged for Laszlo Marton, an expert who had worked with Vladimir Zworykin at RCA, to come to Stanford to work in electron optics, shared between electrical engineering and physics. In 1934 Terman published an influential paper on the use of tuned transmission lines as elements in very-high-frequency and microwave circuits.[178] He had already by 1937 received twenty U.S. patents and published numerous articles on vacuum tube design and circuits.

The examples given above offer clear evidence that in preparing his textbooks, Terman expanded his research horizons through his literature surveys and visits and correspondence with research companies. He fed his own research articles and patents into these texts, and in turn, ideas from these texts became material for further investigation by his students. New areas of research that Terman initiated or assisted at Stanford, such as antenna and radio wave propagation, microwave techniques and vacuum tube design, arose from his determination to keep his texts up-to-date as well as from the interests and talents of his students. The catholicity of his interests (as, for example, in insisting on including sound and sound equipment as part of radio engineering) was reflected later in his support for sound engineers within the IRE and, indirectly, in Hewlett and Packard selling their first instruments to the Walt Disney Studios for sound editing.

Local Resources

Fred volunteered his time, and that of his lab, both to his campus and town communities. This not only promoted good will for his laboratory, but connected his graduate students with the outside world of sample problems and possible employment. Early in the 1920s, the Electrical Engineering Department had been reluctant participants in proposals for a Stanford cultural radio broadcasting station, but department faculty and students also arranged to install audio amplification equipment for the university in various halls. Fred continued this tradition during the 1930s.

Terman and his graduate student William Sumerlin designed and installed the audio public address system for the new Stanford Memorial Auditorium in the summer and fall of 1937. This required so much time and effort that Sumerlin's graduate research on improving the ionospheric sounding transmitter and receiver was delayed.[179] Thus, further ionospheric experiments were postponed until the arrival of Oswald Villard Jr. the next year. When the Stanford Medical School in San Francisco experienced problems with its electronics equipment in 1936, Terman personally fixed an audio amplifier for them.[180]

In 1933–34, he made a thorough analysis of the most cost-efficient mobile radio system for Chief H. A. Zink and the Palo Alto Police Department. After corresponding with the Federal Radio Commission about police and public-service radio regulations and with industrial suppliers of mobile radios, Terman had his graduate students install radio equipment for the Police Department and instruct officers and staff in operations. While Terman's assistance was gratis, his graduate students, such as John Kaar, got a boost in their careers.[181] Terman also advised the Stanford Theatre on University Avenue in Palo Alto in 1936 on the electrical design of their lighting and audio system.[182]

Fred contributed freely to several different universities' astronomy observatories on the use of one of his control circuit inventions applied to telescope guidance. After advising the nearby Lick Observatory over a period of four years about their electronic problems, he recommended David Packard in 1939 as someone who could solve their latest problems.[183]

Indeed, perhaps the best example of Terman's interweaving of teaching, research, publishing, and entrepreneurship is his relationship with two special Stanford students, William Hewlett and David Packard.

Encouraging Students: Terman, Hewlett, and Packard

Looming in the background of the careers of William Hewlett and David Packard are Fred Terman's wide-ranging interests in electrical engineering, particularly in radio and communications, and in teaching, and in Stanford. It was in Terman's graduate seminar on feedback electronics and measuring instruments that William Hewlett constructed the prototype of the audio oscillator that would become the initial product of the Hewlett-Packard Company. Terman had suggested that Hewlett spend a first graduate year with him before leaving for the rigorous graduate work at MIT. Hewlett returned to Stanford to study further with Terman. After Dave Packard left Stanford to work at General Electric, Terman encouraged him to return to graduate studies at Stanford. Watching the two as graduate students, Terman suggested that Hewlett and Packard go into business together, and he was exceptionally proud of HP's success. Hewlett and Packard became Terman's lifelong friends and lifelong benefactors of Stanford University.

Terman's earliest research interests had been in radio circuits, vacuum tubes, and instruments. His own 1922 Engineer's thesis was on instrumentation: the design and use of a high-voltage peak reading meter. One of his most successful patents was an instrument patent (No. 1,782,588, issued Nov. 25, 1930) that he signed over to Hickok Instrument Company in 1933 in exchange for $1,000 of Hickok instruments for his Stanford Communication Lab.[184] By the mid-1930s, most of the Communication Lab's instruments and test equipment were either gifts from Terman's own collection, purchases made possible by the sale of his patents, built by his students, or donations in kind from companies, usually where former Stanford students were employed or where Fred had consulted.

Terman's major textbooks illustrate his encyclopedic interest in radio and communication engineering. Since the late 1920s, he had consulted widely with local companies Federal Telegraph Company, Heintz and Kaufman, C. V. Litton, and Eimac, and with Gilfillan Brothers in Los Angeles; he visited and consulted with national companies such as Western Electric, Raytheon, Sylvania, and AT&T. By 1933 he became increasingly interested in resistance stabilized oscillators, antennas, radio propagation, ultra-high-frequency devices, and network theory. Breakthroughs in feedback designs, begun at Bell Telephone Labs about 1934, encouraged Terman to increase his own research in feedback circuits, and he began teaching these in graduate electrical engineering lab courses. Feedback would link Terman to two of his best students, Bill Hewlett and Dave Packard.[185]

William Hewlett was the son of a Stanford Medical School professor. Dave Packard came from Pueblo, Colorado. Both graduated from Stanford with bachelor's degrees in engineering in 1934.[186] Packard, who graduated with great distinction, Stanford's equivalent to summa cum laude, went East to General Electric where he became something of an expert at mercury thyratron tubes. Hewlett spent the year 1934–35 in graduate studies at Stanford in electrical engineering with Terman, preparing himself for further work at MIT. (Terman remembered how relatively advanced was the BA degree from MIT, and advised him to take a year to prepare.) Hewlett wrote a touching letter to Terman in the summer of 1935, telling how much he appreciated all Terman had done for him as a teacher:

> Dear Sir
>
> I am sorry that I was unable to see you before I left for the East. My application to MIT was accepted with the requirements that I take some Economics and obtain a reading knowledge of French or German.
>
> I would like to tell you how much I enjoyed my year in the lab under your direction. It was for that express purpose that I took the first graduate year at Stanford. I hope that I shall enjoy my year at MIT as much.
>
> I am going to stop at GE for a week or so with Dave [Packard]. He is going to show me through and in this way I hope to get some idea of research and large scale production.
>
> Of the three keys I am enclosing, only two belong to the lab, but I don't know which they are. The odd one is no use to me, so if it does not fit anything you may throw it away.
>
> Sincerely,
>
> William R. Hewlett[187]

Hewlett earned his MS in electrical engineering from MIT in 1936. Soon after getting to MIT, Hewlett wrote to say he'd found a mistake in Terman's new (1935) lab book on measurements:

> Dear Dr. Terman,
>
> Several weeks ago I bought your new book on Measurements and although I had read parts of it before I have found it very useful. There are several mistakes in it that I have found and although most of them are mistakes in printing, there is one that seems to be fundamental.
>
> On page 164, fig. (C), there is a set up for measuring G of a tube in a bridge.[188]

After a full explanation, Hewlett goes on to write:

> My probable thesis subject is the use of a resonant line as a filter to permit the transmission and reception on the same antenna at the same time on frequencies very close to each other. . . . In my spare time I am building up a universal ohmeter-voltmeter-ammeter for a repair checking instrument.

Terman had just published an article on such a "Multirange Rectifier Instrument."[189] Terman replied to Hewlett:

> Dear Bill:
>
> I enjoyed your letter very much and also wish to thank you for the errors that you have discovered in the measurements book.
>
> You are absolutely right with regard to the circuit. . . . It is a rather bad and embarrassing mistake to have.[190]

Jobs were very hard to find in 1936. A small electronic company in Philadelphia wrote about possible job openings and their interest in former Terman students. Terman replied, recommending two in particular:

> I would suggest the consideration of David Packard. Mr. Packard has been with the General Electric Company for one and a half years.[191] He is a Stanford graduate, Phi Beta Kappa, a varsity football and baseball player, campus politician, etc.[192] He is a big, attractive fellow with unusual energy, very brilliant in theory, and extremely competent in a laboratory. He has had considerable amateur experience in radio, has taken my course at Stanford and is now working in the research division of the General Electric Company and is taking the Advanced Course.[193] Another possibility is a former Stanford student, William Hewlett who did one year of graduate work with us and has just completed a second year at Massachusetts Tech . . . a good substantial young man with an excellent personality and social poise. His chief characteristic is tremendous energy. He always has to have several irons going simultaneously and whenever he is around things happen. Hewlett needs a little finishing from the commercial point of view but is going to go places wherever he is.

Terman assured the company, "I have not mentioned the possibility of employment with your concern to either Hewlett or Packard." But went on to nudge, "The employment situation has improved sufficiently during the last year so that you will not now find the very best men wandering around at loose ends looking for a job."

Hewlett returned to Stanford as a research assistant in electrical engineering and as a graduate student with Terman in the fall of 1936, just as Terman began to build up the number and quality of the graduate students admitted. In July 1937, Terman wrote to Bernard M. Oliver (then on a study fellowship in Germany), with lab news that "Hewlett has been developing communication techniques for medical research during the past year and has spent most of his time in our laboratory although the work is being done for a doctor in San Francisco."[194]

When Terman became head of the Electrical Engineering Department in 1937, his first hire was Karl Spangenberg to assist in the electronics and vacuum tube part of the department. Terman wished to move forward quickly in tube circuitry *and* in tube design and development. He began to set up a tube construction facility so that students could gain experience in all phases of vacuum tubes, beginning with graduate student Henry P. Blanchard in late 1935.[195] Here, he thought, David Packard could be a very useful graduate student and researcher. Terman kept up correspondence with several who would one day be HP executives (besides Oliver, Noel Eldred, and Noel Porter, all his former students). In June 1938 Terman wrote to Oliver to say:

> You will be interested in knowing that the research assistantship for the investigation of the special tube has been offered to Dave Packard. He heard about it through Hewlett and has been interested in making a break at GE and applied for this as a means of doing so gradually. He would naturally be almost ideal because of his industrial experience in tube development and so we felt he should have first call on the place if he wished it.[196]

In January 1937, Terman had published an article in *Electronics* on "Feedback Amplifier Design," that discussed resistance networks and amplification independent of frequency. Then in 1937–38, Terman compiled his own earlier work and the group work of several of his graduate students and completed a beautifully written, comprehensive article on feedback amplifiers and oscillators. Hewlett was so pleased that he wrote Packard that Terman had included his work in the paper, and that he was proud to have his name on a paper with Terman. Hewlett urged Packard to apply for the fellowship in Terman's lab and suggested that the two could work together on electronic devices. The letter is well worth reproducing here.

> Dear Dave, May 21 [1938]
>
> This is a letter that I should have written long ago, but you know how I am and it seemed that the longer I waited the more I seem to have to say to you.
>
> In the first place, my heartiest congratulations to both you and Lucille [*sic*]. Everybody knows that it is an idea [*sic*] match. I saw Lucille just before she went east, and was she excited. She was showing her presents and parading around in the dress she was to be married in—happy as a clam at high tide. At that time I told her that I had some good news for you, and so I have.

The first thing is that I have got my name on a paper with Terman as one of the collaborators. The paper is on feedback as applied to laboratory equipment, and refers to linear amplifiers, tuned amplifiers, oscillators, and wave analyzers. Terman is going to read it at the convention in New York June 16–18. Terman actually did all the writing, we [R. R. Buss, Hewlett, and F. C. Cahill] just did some of the experimental and theoretical work. Nevertheless the paper will have our names on it.

I have been working on a new type of oscillator that have [*sic*] no inductances. The oscillator operates by a combination of positive and negative feedback. [Hewlett goes on to describe the circuit in some detail.] . . . It may be seen that the resonant frequency is proportional to R and 1/C, whereas in the conventional oscillator the frequency is proportional to $\sqrt{1/C}$. This means then that with the ordinary variable condenser with a capacity range of 10:1, a frequency range of 10:1 may be obtained instead of $\sqrt{10:1}$. The oscillator would then cover the audio frequency range in three steps 20–200, 200–2,000, and 2,000–20,000 [Hertz]. This means that the same frequency may be used with multiplying factors of 1, 10, and 100.

Actually the balance of + and − feedback would be very critical unless some means of amplitude control was introduced. This is achieved by a diode amplitude control in the + feedback. In this way good wave shape is obtained as well as constant amplitude in all bands. It is not necessary to have special layout and very careful constructions as in the case of a beat-frequency osc. and yet it is just as good in most respects and better in some. We should be able to sell them at quite a low figure.

I am going to give a paper on this osc. at the Pacific Coast convention of the IRE this August at Terman's suggestion. I will then try to get the paper in *Electronics*.

I am also including a diagram of the 6 watt amplifier. [Hewlett describes the amplifier and indicates that John Kaar ('33, EE '35), founder of a radio manufacturing plant in Palo Alto, had quoted him a price of $24 to build it including all parts in lots of five or more.] . . . [Noel] Porter is now drumming up trade for this in the valley. Put one together, and see how you like it.

There is one more important thing and that is a possibility of a job out here. It seems that there will be a job open here next year as a research assistant in the radio lab. The pay is very small, $500 for nine months at half time, on top of that you will probably have to register for a few units and that will reduce the net to about $400. It however would be a guarantee of some salary plus whatever you could make on the side. You would have a lab to work in, and I could work down here with you. It might be just the thing. If you are interested in the slightest get in touch with Terman at once. . . . In all events, get in touch with him by airmail.

Bill[197]

Terman gave the feedback paper as a talk at IRE conventions in June and August of 1938 and submitted the manuscript for publication in November 1938. It was published in October 1939.[198] The IRE was on a cost-cutting move and tried in that year to cut down the number of papers accepted and the length of each paper. Terman fought to keep the published version of the paper from being too condensed and successfully argued against the editor's cutting the section that most closely covered Hewlett's contributions, the "Oscillator with Resistance-Capacitance Tuning" (pages 654–55 and figure 10 in the published version). This section included the clever linearity device of inserting a small light bulb as cathode resistor to control feedback and increase linearity of output over a wide audio frequency range. The oscillator used inexpensive ganged tuning condensers employed in ordinary broadcast receivers. This audio oscillator later was the basis for the initial Hewlett-Packard Company product. News of this linearity innovation by Hewlett had been sent to Terman in a letter from graduate student Bob Sink the previous July. On July 27, 1938, Sink wrote that Hewlett had made the innovation of inserting a small bulb in the circuit of the audio oscillator he was developing, and produced a device with nearly perfect output voltage linearity as a function of frequency:

> Dear Dr. Terman,
>
> Bill Hewlett and I are the only ones working in the lab now. Bill finally eliminated the bugs from his oscillator. As you know the cheif [*sic*] difficulty was in the amplitude control. He finally hit upon the scheme of using a fifteen cent light bulb in the negative feedback portion of his circuit. The result was unbeliveably [*sic*] remarkable. His total distortion is better than one fourth of one percent![199]

The best vacuum tube constructing magician on the entire Pacific Coast was probably Charles V. Litton. After an IRE meeting, Terman wrote from New York City to Litton about Dave Packard, "you will no doubt be interested and pleased to learn that Dave Packard has accepted the assistantship in connection with the ultra-high-frequency tube investigation and will be with us beginning some time in September. I think he is the best qualified man that one could conceivably hope to find, so I am highly pleased."[200] Litton was an important friend of Terman and of Stanford electrical engineering. A Stanford engineer himself, Litton learned of vacuum tube making at the little Moorhead Company in San Francisco. By 1932, after working for Federal Telegraph, and then Heintz and Kaufman, Litton set up his own lab in San Carlos to do special glass blowing and high vacuum work. Terman visited him and wrote to Herbert Hoover Jr. at Caltech about Litton's impressive setup.[201] Litton would help Terman and Stanford over the years and donate equipment and services as an unpaid lecturer. Some of Litton's work on the klystron project was patented by Sperry Gyroscope, and Litton's share of payment had been put into the Sperry pool of funds at Stanford and given to the Electrical Engineering Department. This was the financial source of the fellowship that Terman offered to David Packard.

Hewlett and Packard each received their degrees of Engineer in 1939. On July 5, 1939, Terman wrote to President Wilbur noting the gift of a "Model 200–A resistance capacity oscillator," donated by Hewlett-Packard, from William Hewlett, '34 and David Packard, '34 with a value of $54.50 [*sic*]. "It was presented in appreciation of the help that these two young men had received from the (E.E.) Department in getting their company established as a going concern."[202]

Terman was conscientious about helping his students get jobs. He advised students on job possibilities and salary offers and wrote frank letters to prospective employers. Terman had urged Hewlett and Packard to get the audio oscillator out as a commercial product. He gave the young entrepreneurs a list of about twenty-five potential customers for their oscillator. Terman had kept up correspondence in the 1930s with audio engineers in the Los Angeles area, especially with former Stanford students. One of these was J. N. A. "Bud" Hawkins, who by 1938 was chief sound engineer for Walt Disney Studios. It was through Hawkins that Disney Studios purchased eight copies of the improved "Model 200-B" oscillator at a price of $71.50 each.[203]

Terman had chosen Hewlett as a research associate in the Electrical Engineering Department for 1938–39, and Hewlett continued as an unpaid research associate from 1939 until he went to war in 1942. Packard's $500 fellowship was renewed in 1939 for a second year. Packard, too, continued as unpaid research associate or visiting lecturer throughout World War II. (Hewlett returned as visiting lecturer in 1945 after serving in the U.S. Army.)

In January 1940, Terman wrote to a former student then at General Electric, "Packard and Hewlett are getting along fine, their chief difficulty being that they are too busy. Bob Sink who is leaving in a day or two (for GE) has been working for them for the last few months."[204]

Years later, Terman recalled that he almost let Hewlett's talent slip by. "I was slow in realizing that Bill not only solved problems but looked beyond them for their implications. He could see that one good creative problem solved always led to two more unsolved."[205] Bill Hewlett and Dave Packard, in turn, were always grateful to Terman and to Stanford. When Stanford was preparing for its fiftieth anniversary celebrations in 1941, Hewlett was already active in alumni affairs, getting electrical engineering graduates in communication to donate to Communication Scholarships and Fellowships.[206]

Terman continued to help his two students beyond their graduation from Stanford. Early in Hewlett and Packard's business career, Terman introduced them to Melville Eastham, founder of General Radio, and potentially their greatest competitor. Eastham was in Palo Alto, and Terman telephoned HP to ask if Eastham could come over for a visit. Terman left them alone for half a day. Later, Eastham told Terman what fine young men they were and how much he had enjoyed his visit. Hewlett and Packard reported to Terman that Eastham had been an extremely interesting guest and had given them helpful information about business.[207]

Terman and Ham Radio

For someone who is remembered around the world as a great radio engineering teacher, Fred Terman had an ambivalent relationship with amateur "ham" radio. He made his first crystal radio set at age thirteen, and in high school and college, his pals included other young ham radio guys in high school. He had operated spark transmitter 6FT (in those days you could choose your own call letters), and operated another spark transmitter, station 6AE, as a college student. He also knew other older established ham operators of his neighborhood, such as Cyril Elwell, as well as Roland Marx and George Branner, faculty kids like Fred. As a graduate student at Stanford, then in his earliest years of teaching, he and Herbert Hoover Jr. and Jack Franklin had maintained experimental radio station 6XH on the campus for research and for hamming purposes.[208] In July 1936, when Terman recommended David Packard for a job, he mentioned many positive things but among them he noted that "he has had considerable amateur experience in radio."[209]

In effect, Terman started the Stanford amateur radio club.[210] During his time as director of the Radio Research Laboratory in World War II, about one hundred staff members were current or former licensed ham radio operators. At the conclusion of the war in 1945, Terman hoped that the major ham radio society magazine *QST* would write about the innovations in radio at the Radio Research Laboratory. And in his retirement, Terman enjoyed corresponding about the history of radio with other retired radio engineers who were hams and members of ham radio and wireless pioneer clubs. Beyond all this, Terman's outstanding radio engineering career could be said to have started from his boyhood love of ham radio.

Yet, in 1935, Terman was already revealing his growing disdain of the amateur, describing a laboratory text of one of his competitors as being "too radio amateurish."[211] Former student Bernard M. Oliver, corresponding with Terman about a prospective graduate student assistant, noted carefully that "while he is a 'radio nut' as you feared, and the holder of an amateur license, etc., I don't think this will make him incorrigible in any sense, for he apparently has a serious interest in radio as a science and a profession as well as an avocation."[212]

Even so, at about that same time, Terman visited the home of Oswald G. Villard Jr. in New York City, in part to assure Villard's father that a Yale honors graduate in English literature could profitably enroll as a graduate student in electrical engineering at Stanford.[213] In addition to being very bright, Villard was perhaps the biggest radio ham at Yale. Soon after his arrival at Stanford in the autumn of 1938, Villard and his undergraduate student friend Cameron Pierce, '39, installed ham radio stations in more than one location around the Stanford campus and Palo Alto. They also constructed, at Villard's expense and with Terman's approval, a modest ham radio "shack" behind the campus near the Ryan High-Voltage Lab. Besides using the small building for radio hamming with the Stanford radio club station W6YX, Villard became involved there with recording foreign broadcasts for the Hoover Institution, and later with conducting ionospheric radio research. Patented devices emerged from research performed at the radio ham shack. Terman was proud of this shack and for several years he listed it in the Stanford catalog under the research laboratories of the Electrical Engineering Department. Yet he also spoke to Villard and to student Robert Helliwell and others about the wariness with which one must regard amateur hams.[214]

Perhaps Terman's ambivalence toward ham radio can be better understood if one realizes that Terman expected his students to regard radio engineering as a science and a serious profession, as Bernard Oliver wrote, and not merely as an avocation. Terman felt that hams often did not understand the fundamentals of what they were doing or had merely a frivolous interest. And, unlike many hams, Terman never had the temptation to wile away the hours chatting over the radio waves to other hams.

Fred Terman returned in 1924 to a campus bustling with new construction and new approaches to teaching, administration, and fund-raising. The university was in the midst of experimenting with restructuring its undergraduate and graduate curriculum into schools, and the new School of Engineering would be among the most successful.

Yet, while the school appeared solid (it was certainly more homogeneous than the others), little changed in the curriculum or in its expectations of students. While Harris J. Ryan had retired from his official leadership of the Electrical Engineering Department, he remained an especially strong influence until his death in 1934. The department made little progress in improving aging classrooms and research facilities, and in recruiting and supporting graduate students. A fond, if paternalistic, mentor to young Terman, Ryan looked to industry, not academia, for leadership in engineering education. And like Engineering Dean T. J. Hoover, Ryan distrusted the gaining influence of younger engineers with doctorates and Ivy League ideas. Nevertheless, Fred Terman continued to carry the department's graduate program on his shoulders throughout this period, advising the work of half the graduate students in electrical engineering (one-fifth of the entire School of Engineering).

Ironically, the arrival of a new dean of engineering, Samuel Morris, who had been trained in the school of hard knocks and construction just as Ryan and

Hoover preferred, set the school in motion in a new direction. Morris, like Terman, saw no need to differentiate between "men of engineering" and "men of science," between teaching and research. Morris had no intention of losing Terman to Cornell or to other competitors. Promoted by Morris to executive head of electrical engineering in 1937, Fred could now not only strengthen but also greatly broaden the Electrical Engineering Department, fostering ties to other departments, especially to the Department of Physics.

CHAPTER THREE

Building Radio and Electronics

1937–1941

In 1937, Fred Terman was appointed executive head of Stanford's Department of Electrical Engineering. After nearly six years in the doldrums, the department would jump forward over the following four and one-half years as Terman worked to find more and better-qualified students, to build up funding for student support and engineering facilities, and to open new lines of research in ionospheric physics, electron-tube optics, and ultra-high-frequency design. Attracting funding through company contracts, Terman and his faculty became research partners with colleagues in the Physics Department in development of the new devices, the Rhumbatron and the Klystron. This interdepartmental effort, reinforced by mutual research interests and personal friendship, became a prototype for similar efforts initiated or encouraged at Stanford by Terman in later years.

Although the Depression continued to take its toll on Stanford, on faculty salaries and promotions as well as construction and maintenance, the Electrical Engineering Department had new momentum by the end of the decade. Keen on advancing the status as well as the opportunities for engineers in the West, Terman would take a special interest in the possibilities presented by the Institute of Radio Engineers. He was elected president of IRE (the first president to hail from west of Rochester).

As war clouds loomed, Terman and his faculty faced not only the probable military mobilization but the uncertain future of a new Stanford president. Replacing Ray Lyman Wilbur, in office since Fred was an undergraduate, would not be easy, however.

Finding a Leader for Electrical Engineering

After twenty-six years on the Stanford faculty, Harris J. Ryan retired in 1931. Ryan had been a superb electrical engineer and had built Stanford's Electrical Engineering Department into one of the best in the United States—at least in the field of high-voltage power engineering. In 1925, Ryan had been awarded the Edison Medal, the highest award of the American Institute of Electrical Engineers, for meritorious achievement in electrical science, electrical engineering, or the electrical arts.[1] Ryan, now an emeritus professor, remained as honorary director of the Ryan High-Voltage Laboratory and influential advisor to Dean Hoover and continued his work at the laboratory until his death in 1934. The search for his replacement as head of the department would prompt a six-year debate between Dean Hoover and Ryan, on one hand, and President Ray Lyman Wilbur and Acting-President Robert Swain, on the other, regarding the best sort of man to head electrical engineering at Stanford—indeed, about the best sort of engineer to attract to Stanford's faculty—made all the more difficult by the economic problems brought on by the deepening Depression.[2]

Their quest for a new head boiled down to faculty differences of opinion regarding the relative merits of the theoretical man versus the practical man, what Harris Ryan would call the "spirit of science" versus the "spirit of engineering." Both President Wilbur (in Washington DC since 1929 as Herbert Hoover's secretary of the interior) and his friend Swain, who carried on his administrative duties as acting president in frequent correspondence with Wilbur, felt strongly that Stanford should choose faculty with excellent reputations in research. Swain, a chemist, had been delighted with Fred Terman's 1927 article in *Science* magazine in which the young professor had excoriated American electrical engineering faculty for their low level of education and the relative lack of research output of department faculties, and Swain, like Wilbur, knew that this could be applied to any department at the university. Concerning recruits for a faculty position in biology, Swain emphasized in a letter to Wilbur, "that we want primarily to secure men of outstanding achievement or promise in biology rather than to fill two or three departmental niches." (To this, Wilbur noted simply "OK."[3]) Similarly, Swain happily reported to Wilbur that chemistry faculty J. W. McBain, E. C. Franklin, and C. L. Alsberg were urging him to entice Linus C. Pauling, an obvious prospect for a Nobel Prize, from Caltech. David Webster hoped to get the rising star F. K. Richtmyer of Cornell for the Physics Department, although if they failed, they could offer an acting associate position to Paul Kirkpatrick of the University of Hawaii.[4] (Wilbur favored Richtmyer for Stanford, while Kirkpatrick would be acceptable for "a short time."[5]) Swain and Wilbur were also trying to build the Economics Department faculty. As 1931 opened, they added the Electrical Engineering Department to their list of searches.

Dean Theodore J. Hoover, backed by Ryan, was more comfortable with a man with a record in industry and was content to search no further than the San Francisco Bay area. As Hoover had written President Wilbur in 1925 on learning of the plans for the establishment of the Stanford School of Engineering, "My idea of recruiting an engineering faculty would be to study the men in the industry and not the men in the schools."[6] In response to a list of names for Ryan's replacement given him by Swain in February 1931, Hoover championed the candidacy of A. W. Copley, a San Francisco engineer then living in Palo Alto. Copley had earned his bachelor's degree from Kansas in 1903 and then went to work for Westinghouse. He had been in the San Francisco office of Westinghouse since 1921. Although he had no record of published research, Copley shared eighteen Westinghouse patents. Copley very much wanted the position and was willing to take a significant cut in salary to come to Stanford (which could only offer, Hoover felt, $6,000 a year). Hoover informed Swain that Copley's nomination had the unanimous approval of his executive committee of the School of Engineering.[7]

Unimpressed, Wilbur responded that he would rather offer $7,500 to $8,000—presumably to someone other than Copley—to obtain the best research man in the business. E. C. Franklin, who had taught Copley in a couple of chemistry classes years before at Kansas, also had informed Swain that he thought little of Copley as an original thinker. Swain subsequently met with Ryan and Hoover, and Hoover again argued for a man with industrial experience, "a technical man, strictly of the engineering type," as Swain characterized Hoover's remarks later to Wilbur. Swain, in turn, argued for a "productive scholar" and came away with the feeling that Ryan was sympathetic to this. To counter the Copley candidacy, Swain suggested Ernest Adolph Guillemin, a Princeton alumnus who had earned his PhD with the renowned physicist Arnold Sommerfeld in Munich. Guillemin, a specialist in electrical network theory, was then thirty-seven years old and an assistant professor at MIT. Swain reported also that Caltech was interested in Guillemin, according to Linus Pauling.[8]

Whatever Swain's impression of Ryan's supportive views, Ryan responded quite differently to the April 29 meeting in some three thousand words of spirited rhetoric written to Dean Hoover.[9] In Ryan's view the spirit of science was much different from the spirit of engineering. He was concerned that Guillemin, however capable he might be in applied physics and mathematics, would be utterly lost at the High-Voltage Laboratory at Stanford. "The man with the spirit of science and without the spirit of engineering is only bored and accomplishes nothing worth while in engineering of his own initiative." Ryan purposefully recalled Swain's comparison as that of "a young PhD man strongly actuated by the spirit of science with that of a mature BS man experienced in executive electrical engineering, replete with the spirit of engineering [but] with no faculty experience." Ryan saw the rise of engineering *science* as an encroachment on the practice of engineering and believed firmly that science and engineering could not coexist equally at a university unless definite income was set aside expressly for engineering as distinct from science faculty and coursework, as was now the case at Stanford. His best example of the dangers in letting science into engineering departments was the rise to power of Robert A. Millikan at Caltech, and the subsequent "dissolving" of control by engineering there. In short, the Throop School of Engineering, once it became Caltech, gave over pride of place to science, and engineering took a back seat. Ryan thought it improbable that a school could have both science and engineering in controlling positions; one would rise at the cost of the other. As Ryan saw it, "Stanford sooner or later will face the parting of the ways as has happened at California Institute of Technology, Johns Hopkins, Columbia, Yale, and Harvard, direct, and in the reverse at Rensselaer Polytechnic, Stephens [*sic*, Stevens], and Worcester Polytechnic Institutes."[10] (Science had become preeminent at the first named schools.)

Ryan and Hoover were both whole-heartedly set against turning Stanford's engineering departments over to faculty (suspiciously like young Terman) who represented the "spirit of science." However proud of, and friendly toward their own man, Fred Terman, they viewed Leonard Fuller, the new electrical engineering head at Berkeley, as a more promising sort of man to put in such a potentially influential position at Stanford. Fuller, Ryan said, manifested the spirit of engineering.

To get around the problems with the Copley candidacy, Ryan offered the name of Frank William Peek Jr.[11] Peek had received his bachelor's degree in electrical engineering from Stanford in 1905 and had then gone to work for General Electric in Schenectady, New York. He earned his master's in electrical engineering from Union College in 1911. Peek rose quickly at GE and gained an international reputation in industrial research, authored a book and numerous papers, won national prizes, and was a fellow in the American Institute of Electrical Engineers and the American Physical Society. Peek seemed an excellent compromise. While Copley had been described as merely competent when Swain contacted industrial engineers in San Francisco, Peek was viewed as the absolute top of the profession and a "wonder."[12] Wilbur telegrammed Swain on May 4, "Your ideas regarding type of man needed coincide exactly with mine. Think effort should be made to secure Peek or someone his grade. Productive scholar essential."[13]

Swain again met with Hoover and again suggested that Copley was not a strong selection, but he agreed with Ryan's recommendation of Peek as a superb candidate. Hoover called his executive committee together on May 11, 1931, to review the situation, and once again Harris Ryan threw a wrench into Swain's strategy. In a lengthy and somewhat illogical oral and written presentation (Dean Hoover termed the presentation "highly eulogistic"), Ryan switched his support back to Copley. Peek, he argued was a wonderful fellow, a brilliant engineer with a superb reputation, but if he were to leave General Electric, the loss to the industrial and scholarly world would be too severe. There would be no such loss if Copley were to take the job at Stanford. Hoover once again received a unanimous vote from his five-man committee for his candidate, and the dean resubmitted Copley's name to the president's office.[14]

This move was too much for Swain, who angrily wrote to Wilbur that he would hold up any appointment for electrical engineering until the June meeting of the board of trustees. All the more annoying, Swain learned soon after from E. C. Franklin that Mrs. Copley had remarked that her husband was so sure of getting the appointment that he was already in the process of resigning from Westinghouse, and that Westinghouse had agreed to add a generous stipend to Copley's Stanford salary, indefinitely, to make up the shortfall.[15]

Swain and Wilbur decided to ignore Hoover and his Engineering School executive committee. The board of trustees offered the chairmanship to Peek in June 1931. Unknown at Stanford, Peek had been offered the top engineering job at GE, however, and was about to accept the promotion. He turned down the Stanford offer.[16]

The search continued. Assistant Professor Fred Terman put his thoughts on the process in a confidential letter to Swain (which he expected to be shared only with Wilbur). Fred called for a candidate with a demonstrated ability to carry on research of a nationally recognized caliber, combined with a thorough theoretical background and interest in practical engineering problems. The successful candidate should have the ability to meet with the public, of course, and should possess some amount of administrative skill. Above all else, however, he "should have the vision that sees an Electrical Engineering Department as something more than an organization for putting standardized facts before young men in the traditional manner."

Unlike Ryan, however, Terman emphasized that there was no need to make a choice between "theorist" and "practical engineer," for in the United States there surely were several candidates who combined both of those qualifications. The thing to be avoided, he wrote, was the appointment of a so-called practical man who possessed no advanced training whatever, who had no background of scientific achievement, and who was without any real conception of the role a university could play in advancing knowledge. Yale's Department of Electrical Engineering, he noted by way of example, had recently hired as its chairman Robert Doherty, a top GE engineer who possessed all the appropriate qualifications of scholarship, reputation, and achievement.[17]

In the summer of 1931, the next candidate to emerge was Leonard F. Fuller, holder of the first PhD in engineering awarded at Stanford and known widely around campus for his work with Ryan, Cyril Elwell, and Federal Telegraph Company. Ryan had always admired Fuller, but he had not recommended Fuller for the Stanford position. Two years before, Ryan, Durand, and other Stanford faculty had helped Fuller to get the position of chair of electrical engineering at Berkeley. Ryan now felt that he would "be lacking in integrity and a proper sense of the ethics involved" if he were to attempt to pull Fuller away from Berkeley after just one year in his new position. Nevertheless, Ryan wrote to Dean Hoover that a McGraw-Hill publishing executive and engineer told him recently that Fuller's greatest hope was to teach at one of his alma maters—Cornell or Stanford. Fuller had taken the Berkeley job because he and his family preferred to stay in the area, rather than move back east when Federal Telegraph moved its operations to New Jersey.[18] Fuller's scholarly achievements were considerable. He had published a dozen papers and had won the highly regarded Morris Liebman Prize from the Institute of Radio Engineers. Much of his recent research was confidential pending the settlement of patent conflicts with RCA, but as former chief engineer at Federal Telegraph, Fuller's reputation was international.

There were, however, two significant problems yet to be surmounted. Fuller had taken a stiff reduction in his salary to leave Federal for the University of California (from $15,000 to $8,000), but his new salary at Cal was still above the top of the Stanford professorial pay scale. Fuller told Ryan that perhaps he would come if he were promised $7,500 per year in the near future.[19] Campus relations between Stanford and the University of California were, in the end, a more problematic issue. Dean Hoover immediately tipped Swain to the need for sounding out University of California President Robert Sproul as to Berkeley's reaction to a Stanford raid on their faculty.[20] At lunch with Swain several weeks later, Sproul said that the president's office at University of California had no *official* objections but that the Engineering School would be outraged. Sproul reminded Swain that when Fuller was one of three or four on the final list for chair of electrical engineering at Berkeley, he had been selected in part because of the strong representation by Stanford's professors. In addition, the University of California had given Fuller very generous support in reorganizing the Electrical Engineering Department. In short, his colleagues would be furious if he left after only one year. Swain wrote to Wilbur that he would let the matter ride for a couple of months, and that maybe Peek might reconsider in the future.[21] Letting it ride meant, for the time being, acquiescing to Hoover's selection of an acting head.

In the fall of 1931, Hoover appointed Assistant Professor Ward Kindy as acting executive head of the Electrical Engineering Department. By early 1932, Swain felt that Kindy was giving attention to "ordinary routine matters" but little else, and that Kindy's administrative appointment ought to be ended. Perhaps, Swain and Wilbur discussed, it was time to look for a younger man rather than seek a senior appointment.[22] Swain remembered that Hoover had mentioned to him some time previously that Fred Terman represented "a much more constructive point of view as well as being in a stronger position professionally outside of the University."[23] Terman, Swain noted, had recently been elected to serve on the Academic Council's graduate study committee, receiving the second-highest number of votes out of eleven on the ballot for election from the Engineering School (he was the only person nominated from the Electrical Engineering Department).[24] Wilbur responded, "I suggest Terman as Acting [Head] in Electrical Engineering, rather than Kindy."[25] Yet, for whatever reasons, neither Swain nor Wilbur forced the change, perhaps still hoping that Peek would change his mind. Unfortunately, Peek was tragically killed in a railroad-crossing accident in 1933. Kindy remained as acting chair for six years.

The Electrical Engineering Department, like much of the rest of Stanford University, slumped into a holding position. With Ryan's retirement, all remaining members of the department faculty were now assistant and associate professors helped by a few instructors. Fred Terman and Joe Carroll remained associate professors through much of the decade, while Kindy, who would serve as acting executive head from 1931 to 1937, remained an assistant professor until 1934. No new faculty appointments would be made after 1931 until Karl Spangenberg arrived in 1937.

The economic depression began to affect Stanford's Electrical Engineering Department, as elsewhere on campus. The Communication Lab was in the second-floor attic of Building 500 (today the Terman Engineering Labs, Building 500) in a 2,000-square-foot area. Terman's office was in that building from 1925 until he went to Harvard during World War II. Radio work had been going on in the attic for many years. Cyril Elwell had used the same attic for his radio experiments from 1906 to 1908, experiments that led trustee Timothy Hopkins in 1908 to order Elwell to remove his radio antennas from university buildings.[26] The students were lively up in the attic, where heavy equipment was stored, and the floors had dry rot. Department secretary Burnice Bourquin worried about the weight on the floor above, given the dry rot.[27] The floors were eventually patched up, but the roof continued to leak badly. Instead of an expensive roof repair job, the university maintenance staff strategically deployed wooden troughs lined with tarpaper and caulked with tar around the upper laboratory floor to catch the dripping rainwater. Terman recalled that the trays were always partially filled with water during the rainy season and the students (and Terman) simply worked around them. One winter, Bill Hewlett added a homelike touch by stocking the tarpaper trays with live goldfish.

The boys often did chin ups and calisthenics in the lab, using the metal tie-rods running across the attic eaves. This caused significant vibration and noise. One day Terman came upstairs to see what the racket was about and one of the boys, surprised, fell from the tie-rods. Terman simply laughed at their antics.[28] Despite the economic difficulties, Fred later stated that he loved those days and loved his students, and regretted that as an administrator after World War II he did not have the time to maintain such student contact in the laboratory.[29]

There were problems on campus other than faculty promotions and roof leaks. Fred Terman's 1929 proposal for a radio propagation laboratory blew away like dry leaves. On a larger scale, the university's endowment, once among the highest in the country, dropped to seventy-fifth by 1933. In May 1933, faculty and senior staff salaries were cut by 10 percent, a cut not to be fully restored until 1940. New construction and maintenance on campus was cut to a minimum. University library purchases dwindled. Students found it more difficult to get local part-time jobs to finance their education. Economic hard times narrowed the diversity of the student body.[30]

In 1936, his last year as dean of engineering, Theodore Jesse Hoover attempted once more to secure Leonard Fuller for the position of executive head of the Electrical Engineering Department.[31] He was unsuccessful, and the position remained vacant until 1937. Two factors would finally bring the search to a close. In the fall of 1936, Hoover was replaced by Samuel B. Morris, a prominent civil (hydrological) engineer from Los Angeles.[32] And in early 1937, Fred Terman, whose accomplishments as a researcher, author, and prolific mentor to graduate students had gained him a nationwide reputation, was offered a better position by one of Stanford's rivals.

Taking Charge of Electrical Engineering

Fred was planning a trip east for winter 1937. James M. Sharp, who had occupied a temporary position helping Terman as instructor in electronics, had left and Terman planned to "canvass the situation" at the upcoming AIEE winter meeting. But he also planned to visit Cornell University. Correspondence between Fred and colleagues at Cornell had increased during the fall of 1936 where their directorship (head) of the Department of Electrical Engineering came open. Given the likelihood that Cornell would offer him the job, Terman kept his new dean informed of his plans. (In early 1937 Cornell did offer the post to Terman. As it turned out, the offer of department head even carried with it the strong possibility that Terman would have soon thereafter been offered the deanship of the Cornell School of Engineering, as Terman was to learn a year later.)[33]

Dean Morris knew a good thing when he saw it, and early in January 1937, he proposed that Terman become executive head of the Electrical Engineering Department at Stanford instead.[34] Terman liked the idea and decided to decline the Cornell offer, withdrawing his name formally from consideration.[35] (When Cornell approached him again a year later, Terman recommended his Stanford colleague, Hugh Skilling [AB '26, EE '27, PhD '31, Stanford], although Skilling did not receive an offer from Cornell.[36])

Fred was formally promoted to full professor and appointed to the position of executive head of the Department of Electrical Engineering on May 20, 1937, by the board of trustees, to take effect that fall quarter.[37] Terman's national position as textbook author, his outstanding record in research and direction of student theses, and then his wooing by Cornell University made it an easy decision to offer Terman the post. (From his first paper published as a graduate student in 1923 until he ended his active technical career in 1945, Terman published at least seventy-two technical papers or technical comments; forty-nine papers if one excludes comments and columns published as president of the IRE. Thirty-eight of the forty-nine technical papers were published or submitted for publication before Fred was appointed head of the department in 1937, as were twenty of his thirty-six patents.)

He was known nationally, and in 1930 had been offered the post of chief engineer of the Federal Radio Commission (later the FCC) at more than triple his Stanford salary. Fred also had been on the short list in 1930 for a professorship at the Polytechnic Institute of Brooklyn and at the University of Minnesota. Dugald C. Jackson told Harris Ryan in 1929 that if Fred had stayed at MIT he would have been a full professor by that year.[38]

In return for refusing Cornell and accepting Stanford, Terman clearly won from Morris the right to select an additional permanent post for a faculty member near to his own specialties: radio engineering and vacuum tube electronics. While still department head designate, Terman moved ahead with his plan to fill Sharp's temporary slot with a permanent position. Hiring the best candidate in this field was of major importance to Terman and his departmental colleagues. Terman wrote Morris, "If we are to build up a department of the greatest possible strength, the appointments to the lower ranks must be guarded just as carefully and given just as much consideration as appointments to the higher positions."[39] (This was a phrase Terman would use genuinely and often in his years as provost at Stanford.) In soliciting candidates, Terman had written to all the electrical engineering departments listed by the American Council on Education as having outstanding programs, and then wrote to others he knew of, including physics departments that were strong in radio communications.[40] No more just trying to hire somebody from the Bay Area, but a nationwide search. While back east for the electrical engineering meetings, Terman talked with eleven faculty members about various candidates and personally interviewed seven of the top candidates.

On April 10, 1937, he wrote Dean Morris that, after an intensive investigation to find the man of greatest promise in the field of communication, he recommended the appointment of Karl Spangenberg, who would receive his PhD in June from Ohio State (where he was a star student of Fred's friend, Bill Everitt). In Spangenberg's case, Terman had collected letters of reference from his undergraduate school (Case), from his graduate school (Ohio State), and from Rose Polytechnic Institute, where Spangenberg was teaching while finishing his dissertation.[41] Terman asked for comments on his scholarship in courses, his research ability, his record as an instructor in laboratory and lectures, his ability to work with others, and his ranking on intelligence tests. Because Spangenberg had already received another offer, Dean Morris wired Spangenberg Stanford's offer of an instructorship at a salary of $2,000. Spangenberg promptly accepted, and the Stanford board of trustees confirmed the appointment one week later.[42]

Dean Morris became a strong supporter of Terman. "It was most gratifying to me," Morris wrote in 1939, "to be able to recommend the appointment of Dr. Frederick E. Terman as Professor of Electrical Engineering and Executive Head of that Department. . . . His energy and leadership are already being felt in the University and in the Electrical Industry. The Department of Electrical Engineering has responded with increased activity, gifts, research and enrollment."[43] By late 1941, Morris's estimates of Terman's abilities and achievements had only grown. When he wrote President Wilbur to strongly recommend an increase in Terman's salary from $5,000 to $6,000, Morris admitted that Terman was the youngest of the engineering department heads, but pointed out that he was receiving substantially less compensation than the other heads and had been offered higher salaries at other institutions.[44] Although he had not asked Morris for a raise in 1941, Terman had let the dean know that he had just been offered the deanship of the School of Engineering at Washington State.[45]

Building Support for Students and Faculty

Fred Terman had always believed that to build a great graduate student body, the university had to have funds to help support the students. His purpose was, in fact, twofold: to recruit better graduate students to Stanford, and to encourage engineering graduate students to advance beyond the master's degree level. He considered this strategy essential to the building of any great research and teaching university. Terman also believed Stanford should never engage in mere job-shop contracts, but should maximize the student research experience. That is, graduate students should have meaningful research projects as well as earn wages as research assistants.

But Terman also believed that most people at Stanford during the 1920s and 1930s, and certainly faculty in the Engineering School, remained sadly unaware of the need to better actively recruit graduate students with attraction of fellowship funding. The situation had improved little since 1900 when Registrar Orrin Leslie Elliott complained that good graduate students would not come to Stanford unless provided some sort of financial aid. (Leland Stanford had discouraged fellowships for graduate students, and the faculty continued to fight over the value of graduate degrees and the uniformity of qualifications for doctorates, much less importance of providing fellowship support.[46])

From a study he conducted himself, Fred had learned that at MIT, Caltech, and Harvard, two-thirds to nine-tenths of the graduate engineering students came from other schools. Most of Stanford's graduate students, by contrast, finished their undergraduate work and had simply stayed on campus. Equally important, the better students at other major institutions received financial aid. Corresponding with Dean Morris about his conclusions in April 1937, Terman stressed the importance of organizing a national recruitment campaign of the best graduate students and finding adequate funding.[47] It was not just that Caltech had Robert Millikan and a famous telescope to attract students, Terman argued, but that Caltech gave students financial aid. Morris agreed. "We are in dire need of fellowships and scholarships for engineering students at Stanford," he responded.[48]

Stanford was not without some funds for students, even at this economic low point. Some university money was provided for laboratory assistants, but this was usually requested in the fall, just as classes were starting, and was intended to help out those who happened to make themselves available. There was little effort to plan ahead or assemble ongoing funding from outside sources to use in recruiting particular people for department fellowships and assistantships. Years before, Fred had persuaded Ward Kindy to let him do just that. During the 1920s, Terman's father, Professor Lewis Terman, had provided some funds to help out in electrical engineering. Later, the family of one of Terman's deceased students gave a memorial loan fund, and Terman was given additional funds from an engineering alumnus in San Francisco, and more from another colleague and friend, alumnus Sennett W. Gilfillan of Los Angeles. As the Depression hit hard in 1931, Terman corresponded much on the subject. By 1936, he felt he had enough funds at hand to write some fifty schools to parade Stanford to potential students.

Shortly after officially taking office as head of his department, Terman looked broadly at the future of engineering and wrote his conclusions in a report entitled "Stanford and the Training of the Future Leaders in Engineering" and submitted to Morris in December 1937. In order to provide the most effective training of leaders in any field, Terman argued, a university needs two things: the necessary staff, organization, and facilities; and suitable student material. In the past, Stanford had concentrated on the former, he wrote, but gave little or no attention to the second requirement. In the case of engineering, a four-year engineering education would no longer suffice in an increasingly complex world but now required a five- or six-year course. Stanford's limited undergraduate student numbers, however, would not supply a large enough number from which to select the best students to do this additional graduate work. Of the sixty-five graduating from Stanford's four engineering departments each year, he reasoned, perhaps ten had both the ability and inclination to stay on and take full advantage of the opportunities at Stanford. Therefore, Stanford should first obtain adequate funding and then advertise widely the availability of graduate fellowships, as did Caltech, Harvard, and MIT. (Both MIT and Harvard gave on average about $600 per year to one-half of their graduate engineering students, whereas in 1937, Terman calculated,

Stanford had only one engineering fellowship worth $600 or more per year, and shared in less than one additional university-wide fellowship per year.) An additional fellowship or fellowships of $600 to $750 per year for the two-year Engineer's degree course would give Stanford the pick of the outstanding graduates of the western engineering schools. "There is no better way in which an equivalent sum placed at the disposal of the Engineering School could produce as important a result, or could have as much influence upon the future of engineering," he concluded. "Money for fellowships therefore gets directly to the basic function of the university, i.e., the training of leaders, and actually makes leaders by providing men of real promise with an opportunity for full development."

Morris thought highly of Terman's report and immediately sent it to Paul Davis, director of Stanford Associates, Stanford's corps of influential fund-raising volunteers, with the idea that the Associates could help promote Terman's plan.[49] The result was the first Engineering School fund campaign, which Terman not only generated but also effectively headed.[50] Davis developed a number of funding sources and brought possibilities to the attention of the appropriate departments, in engineering as well as in related fields. In 1938, for example, Davis urged Swain of chemistry and Webster of physics along with Terman, and Morris to approach the Charles A. Coffin Foundation of General Electric Company for possible fellowships.[51]

Graduate students could, in fact, transform tasks formerly left to a janitor or skilled laborer into a valuable experience for students and faculty members alike. Fred set out to prove this by transforming the Ryan High-Voltage Lab's full-time position of mechanic-janitor into two half-time graduate research assistant positions. The department's full-time technician, Terman later commented, had formerly been a mediocre student whose major value was in knowing where to find the tools needed around the lab. As soon as he became department head, Terman insisted that Joe Carroll give the fellow a year's notice and ease him out of the job.[52] The man's salary for 1936–37 had been $1,242.[53] For the academic year 1938–39, Terman hired instead two outstanding graduate students as research assistants: Otto Joe Smith and William Johnson.[54] (Smith went on to join the Berkeley faculty in electrical engineering and Johnson became a prominent engineer with Pacific Gas and Electric.) The department's research assistantship provided a total stipend of $600 to $700, allowing each to pay tuition (around $300), room, and board.

As Fred saw it, this transformation accomplished three purposes. First, of the approximately $1,380 that the technician would have received in 1938–39, $600 went back to Stanford in the form of two students' tuition. Second, the High-Voltage Lab provided high-quality training to two more students than otherwise would be possible. Third, the High-Voltage Lab's research work, its main purpose for existence, would be carried out more effectively by placing at Carroll's disposal two very capable men as research assistants rather than one rather ordinary mechanic-janitor.[55]

By 1938, Terman could boast of a grant from IT&T, and additional funding from Sperry Gyroscope Company for klystron research shared with the Physics Department. Graduate students John Woodyard, Ed Ginzton, David Packard, and others in electrical engineering worked on the Sperry-sponsored klystron developments with Terman's colleagues on the physics faculty.[56] Other faculty outside of engineering noticed the trend. In the summer of 1938, E. R. "Jack" Hilgard of Stanford's Psychology Department asked Terman for information on how the Electrical Engineering Department's system functioned for the employment of teaching and research assistants.[57]

A year and a half later, Terman proudly wrote President Wilbur that outside support for his department now amounted to more than $25,000 per year, compared to about $2,000 six years before. The major differences in 1940 were an increase of $5,000 in fellowships (including $800 from the China Foundation); $7,500 in Patent Agreement and Research Project funds from International Standard Electric Corporation (ISEC), IT&T, and Sperry; and $10,000 from Sperry for the department to continue klystron research during Bill Hansen's planned sabbatical for 1941. Terman noted that these funds made possible the significant increase of the graduate student numbers from twenty-three to thirty-eight from the 1934–35 academic year to that of 1940–41. Among these electrical engineering students, the number of grad students in communications had grown from nine to twenty-five. These added students, he wrote, were also on average better students than those from earlier years, since now "only the very outstanding students are successful in obtaining fellowships and research assistantships."[58]

Finding a good fit between students and possible research projects was as much a part of the mix as building fellowship funds. Terman kept penciled note sheets of "Research Problems" for his students. Sometimes these were undated sheets of ideas in process of solution. For example, about 1937–38 Fred laid out the following topics:[59]

Detection:	(Lindsay M.) Applegate
Analysis of input impedance	(John R.) Woodyard
Experimental check of analysis	(Chung-Kwei) Chang
Plate detection (triodes) & Pentodes	(William T.) Sumerlin
Special uses of diodes	(Edward L.) Ginzton
	(Wilton R.) Abbott
Feedback:	
In tuned amplifier	(H. Myrl) Stearns
Analysis & principle of design	(Leonard M., Jr.) Jeffers
Experimental check	(Robert L.) Sink
Practical uses	(Robert R.) Buss
	(F. Clark) Cahill

All of the above students received Engineer and/or PhD degrees in electrical engineering between 1937 and 1941.

Other research ideas jotted down during those years included linear amplifiers, the radio compass (Joe Pettit was assigned this) and direction-finding systems, wave analyzers, field strength equipment, distortion correction in audio amplifiers, generation of very short pulses, current distribution in long-wire and non-resonant wire antennas, ground effects on antennas, free-running oscillators, resistance-tuned oscillators, oscillators with particular wave shapes, low-Q tank circuits, beam tubes, UHF tubes and ideas, and wave-propagation studies involving the ionosphere.

Some of Terman's students published with other Stanford faculty. John R. Woodyard (PhD '40) and Lowell M. Hollingsworth (EE '35, PhD '40) worked on antenna problems with Terman and Bill Hansen for several years. Their studies aimed at developing directional antenna systems for broadcasting, taking into account ionospheric layer effects of fading and interference. (Hansen had become interested in antenna radiation when he was doing a postdoctoral year with George Harrison at MIT, and Terman was a consultant to several broadcasting stations on methods of improving their antenna systems.) Hansen and Woodyard, and Hansen and Hollingsworth published on this subject in the *Proceedings* of the IRE in 1938 and 1939. (Woodyard had previously published with Terman.[60])

Terman's advanced graduate students helped the newer ones. O. G. Villard Jr. received a great deal of assistance from Hollingsworth, he later recalled, and from Stanford Visiting Lecturer Harold Elliott in transmitter coil and mechanical cam design. Villard was also grateful for Terman's help and remembered that Terman publicly gave Villard full credit for design details that were, in fact, partly conceived by Terman.[61]

Terman approached student recruiting as methodically as he did faculty searches. He personally rated each graduate student applicant and made charts of such things as previous degree (BS, BA, or MS), discipline (usually electrical engineering, sometimes physics), financial need, age, position desired (High-Voltage Lab, Communications, and so on), and overall grade average. He then ranked the candidates in groups from 1 (high) to 4 (low). In normalizing the individual grade averages from the various schools, Terman referred to studies of grades, checked how transfer students to Stanford had done at other schools, and then made his own calculations: a 1.62 average at MIT in electrical engineering, he reckoned, and a 1.89 at either Caltech or Harvard, would earn a 2.0 at Stanford. Stanford and Berkeley evened out, he estimated, while at the other schools he studied (Pennsylvania, Dartmouth, Michigan, Utah, etc.), grade averages from 2.12 to 2.7 would earn a 2.0 at Stanford.[62]

Terman's new recruiting methods paid off as early as the incoming class in fall 1938. By the 1939–40 academic year, there were thirty-three graduate students, an all-time high. Another new record was reached the next year, 1940–41, with thirty-eight students. Students from thirteen universities chose in that year to come to Stanford for their engineering degree, including those from Yale, MIT, Caltech, Berkeley, Purdue, from China and from Chile.[63] Fred was especially proud of his incoming graduate students. For the 1939–40 year, in addition to reappointments of four of them as teaching or research assistants, there were nine new appointments, three from Stanford, and six from Caltech, MIT, Purdue, Oregon State, and Berkeley. Among those new grad students were Lester M. Field, in the top percent of the senior electrical engineering class at Purdue; A. P. Green, with the highest grade average in the Caltech graduating class; and W. J. Barclay with the highest grade average in the entire Oregon State engineering school.

By 1939, the total disbursement of funds necessary for the thirteen teaching and research assistants was up to $5,875 ($1,550 of this was from Stanford budgeted funds; $750 came from Fred's own gifts to Stanford; and $3,575 came from IT&T and ISEC funds received from project and patent fund agreements). Fred added that there were additional IT&T and ISEC funds above those needed to fund the assistantships, and that these funds made it possible to significantly increase the research efforts of the department.[64] In his letter to President Wilbur recommending the appointments, Dean Morris wrote, "The appointment of such a large list of able graduate students as teaching and research assistants is made possible by the contracts which have been made with the electrical industries and by Dr. Terman's initiative and generosity."[65]

Hansen later commented that Terman's students were "unbelievably good." Bill Hansen felt that Terman was a superb judge of potential students. In supporting Terman's possible candidacy for university president in 1940, Hansen wrote that in the past three years, he had worked on klystron research with three of Terman's students who were "much better than even the better of our physics students. It seems that all of his graduates are good. Now these students don't just accidentally come to Stanford, he goes out and gets them—and he never brings back a bad one."[66] And Terman kept track of them. "He seems to know where every student he ever had is, what he's doing, how he's getting along, and how he likes his job." The radio-engineering course at Stanford, Hansen continued, "started at zero and has risen to be one of the top two or three in the country. I would say it is the top one. Partly this has been due to Dr. Terman's researches but even more, it seems to me, has it been due to the students he gets."[67]

It was all work of a piece: Terman's teaching and research, and the research emerging from an excellent pool of graduate students were melded together in papers delivered and published collegially by Terman, his students and his colleagues, and all was synthesized into new problems and solutions appearing in editions of his textbooks.

Thus, improving faculty research was as much the issue as attracting and adequately supporting a strong corps of graduate students. As late as 1940, however, university funding for faculty research had yet to get out of the Depression. From 1937 through 1941, the university's annual research fund, allocated by the trustees from general funds, totaled a mere $4,000. Of the $4,000 received in 1937 (the faculty had requested $6,000), the funds were divided among seven faculty categories: the biological sciences (five grants for $680); the Engineering School (six grants for $902 to four departments—electrical engineering got $77 for a recording ammeter for Hugh Skilling); the School of Letters got $1,615 (H. F. Fraenkel and Hazel D. Hansen of classics received, respectively, $100 and $45 for maps and photostats, while Margery Bailey and V. K. Whitaker of English received $200 and $100 for assistance in a concordance and for facsimiles); and physics (Felix Bloch, Norris Bradbury, and Paul Kirkpatrick got $455 for a Wilson Cloud Chamber and related equipment).[68]

The picture remained roughly the same over the next three years. The Electrical Engineering Department averaged less than $150 per year in research funds to cover the work of six full-time-equivalent faculty members. Other poachable funds were included in the departmental budgets, of course, but these were small and intended for teaching needs, and what little maintenance could be done. When Bill Hansen wrote to Physics Executive Head David Webster about the upcoming budget request for 1940–41, he noted that in 1928–29, the departmental research budget had been $6,300. (It once got as high as $7,500, but then shrank to $4,550 and now lost $200 each year.) In the "old days," he said, the money had been divided among three faculty but now, six physics faculty would have only two-thirds of what used to go to the three. Hansen complained that it would be difficult to keep faculty with no research support.[69] Not a man given to complaining, he nevertheless noted elsewhere that a Stanford physicist had, perhaps, one-fifth of a machinist's time and no money to buy new equipment or supplies. As a result, Hansen himself literally welded, machined, cast, and work-hardened the pumps and other equipment he needed, and once estimated that he put in twelve- to fourteen-hour days, seven days a week to get the work done.[70]

Tackling the Depression-Era Job Market

Getting jobs for his students when they graduated, much on Terman's mind, was not an easy task during the 1930s. During the ten-year period between 1928 and 1937, Fred directed fifty of the ninety-two electrical engineering engineer theses. Of these fifty, forty-seven were in communications and electronics. Due to the economic slump between 1930 and 1937, however, large employers like GE and the Bell System hired only five of Fred's graduates. Most of the rest, as late as 1937, were employed in smaller radio firms like Heintz and Kaufman, Mackay,

Hazeltine, Jensen, and Zenith.[71] Several students established their own businesses—such as Bill Hewlett and David Packard, and John Kaar. In 1939, Terman arranged for three of his best students—Myrl Stearns, Bob Buss, and Ed Ginzton—to visit Gilfillan radio, the Jensen loudspeaker company, radio station KFI, and Disney Studios in Southern California. Only Stearns got a job (at Gilfillan).[72]

The job market for physics majors before World War II was never bright, so physics undergraduates came into electrical engineering. It was therefore not uncommon for Terman's graduate students to have minors in physics. (Bill Hansen noted, for example, that electrical engineering major John Woodyard performed better on his PhD qualifying exams than any of the physics graduate students that Hansen had seen in his faculty years at Stanford. Hansen directed Woodyard's PhD dissertation.)

In searching for jobs for his graduating students, Fred kept up with fields related to electrical engineering that appeared to be changing or modernizing, such as geophysics. Herbert Hoover Jr., Terman's boyhood chum and later student, had moved from the aircraft radio field into geophysical instrumentation, and he advised Fred that the oil and energy industries had jobs for men with geophysical training. Electrical courses relating to geophysics and seismology would also be well worthwhile both for geology and for some electrical engineering students.[73] A year later, in the summer of 1938, Dean Morris and Fred Terman talked with W. W. Wetzel, professor of geophysics at Minnesota, about visiting Stanford for a quarter to initiate courses in geophysics for the benefit of appropriate students in "mining, petroleum, electrical engineering, geology, and physics."[74] The evolution of geophysics and materials research at Stanford, and its usefulness to future employment of engineers, would have to wait, however, until Terman took on the job of dean of engineering after World War II.

Judging from written records, Terman remained devoted to principles of quality of both thinking and performance when it came to recommending his students, and he was somewhat annoyed when asked questions about a student or colleague's questionable race or religion. In Terman's penciled sheets listing possible graduate student prospects in 1939, one finds such names as Weedman, Joseph, Tao, Ku, Breitweiser, Allison, Schuman, Gilardo—there is no notation or category pertaining to race or religion among this array of names.[75] When it came to job-hunting for his students and other promising young engineers in the late 1930s, however, he could not always avoid such questions.

Employers, particularly on the East Coast, looked into such backgrounds. When asked if a candidate with a Jewish-sounding name was known to be Jewish, Terman was usually forthright, if he knew the answer. Yes, Earl Schoenfeld was Jewish, he responded when recommending Schoenfeld to the General Electric Company in 1937, adding that Schoenfeld was doing an Engineer's thesis under his own direction, was chairman of the student branch of the AIEE, and that "he is a first class man in every respect and stands out even among our group of graduate students. He was the outstanding man in our senior classes in electrical engineering . . . and I can recommend him very highly both as to his intellectual ability and as to his general personality and ability to get along with other people."[76] With Terman's help, Schoenfeld instead took a job in radio engineering with the U.S. Forest Service.[77]

In 1938, Terman wrote his former Stanford colleague, T. H. Morgan at Worcester Polytechnic Institute, to highly recommend the appointment of Dale Pollack to their electrical engineering faculty. Among more than twenty candidates for the Stanford job offered Karl Spangenberg the year before, he commented that Dale Pollack had been second on their list, behind only Spangenberg. He had the best mathematical background of any candidate except Spangenberg and had done outstanding work as a student at Columbia and MIT. Pollack had taken a job at RCA when, according to a rumor heard by Terman, MIT turned him down for a teaching position because he was Jewish.[78]

In 1937, Terman wanted Berkeley student Ed Ginzton for Stanford. He encouraged him to give his paper on feedback amplifiers at the 1937 AIEE and IRE West Coast meeting in Spokane, Washington, a session Terman was organizing.[79] Ginzton not only gave his paper but won the AIEE Pacific Division student paper prize. He subsequently enrolled at Stanford in electrical engineering, where he did exceptional work with Bill Hansen and the Varians.[80] Two years later, Terman highly recommended Ginzton for a job at Bell Labs. Ginzton, he wrote, had an unusual amount of initiation and originality, and plenty of physical and intellectual drive; he was sociable and a leader among the students. Terman went on to describe in some detail Ginzton's coursework and his research. Ginzton, in short, would make good at Bell Labs. But, they asked Terman, did Ginzton have Slavic or Jewish origins? (He had, in fact, been born in the Ukraine, but had emigrated with his family while a child.) Terman didn't actually know the answer, but apparently did not feel he should ask Ginzton directly. Instead he asked Ginzton's MA thesis adviser at Berkeley, who was Jewish, who answered that he thought not. Two months later, he wrote to Bell to mention that Ginzton had, in the meantime, accepted a position at Stanford to work on the rhumbatron-klystron with Bill Hansen's team.[81]

Stanford Fights for its Broad Engineering Curricula

For decades, Stanford's engineering faculty had defended the position of making the bachelor's degree engineer the recipient of at least introductory courses in economics, writing, ethics, history, civics, and foreign languages. A product of this environment, Terman agreed with this conception of a broad and full education throughout his career. In the early thirties, Fred chaired the Engineering School's committee on English for engineers, to ensure that engineering students were getting serious attention in their writing skills.[82]

In 1936, Terman backed Dean Morris in a running conflict with the Engineer's Council for Professional Development (ECPD). Several national engineering societies had joined together to recommend standards of practice for the engineering schools so that trade schools or inadequately prepared and staffed schools could be judged by certain criteria and brought up in their level of instruction. Most university deans approved this move.[83] Since 1925, however, Stanford had divided its engineering education into two basic parts: a four-year, rather broad introduction to engineering that culminated in the BA in engineering, and a further two-year course specializing in a particular field of engineering, earning the degree of Engineer in the field (for example, in electrical engineering).[84] Although Stanford's undergraduates shared the common goal of a bachelor's in engineering, course requirements differed according to the individual student's civil, mechanical, or electrical engineering major.

An investigational committee from the ECPD visited Stanford that fall, headed by Engineering Dean G. M. Butler of the University of Arizona, regional committee chairman of the ECPD. Stanford did not fare well. Butler wrote that Stanford's BA in engineering would not pass muster unless the total credit hours were raised from 120 to 140, and the "humanities" were lessened. Stanford needed more nuts and bolts. MIT had barely passed, he added in his comments to Morris, and Yale should not have been allowed to pass.[85]

Morris negotiated with the ECPD over the winter of 1936–37. Required to make a presentation before the ECPD committee at Berkeley in June 1937, he had Fred Terman make a special presentation concerning electrical engineering. Fred demonstrated, among other things, that Stanford required more electrical engineering credits for its majors than Caltech for its major.[86]

Fred Terman compared, course-by-course, the Stanford and Caltech electrical engineering curriculum, and noted that according to Butler's ECPD standards, Caltech had far too few of the necessary electrical engineering courses. If Butler's group accredited Caltech, then certainly Stanford would have to be (although, as Fred himself pointed out, Caltech required numerous additional courses in their math and physics departments that were central to electrical engineering).[87]

Ward Kindy, serving as acting head, also joined the effort. Content counted for more than hours of credits. Stanford's plan, he wrote, was intended so that the well-balanced four-year engineering graduate would have a background in humanistic courses that "progressive authorities on engineering education are demanding with increasing insistence." In addition, the electrical engineering graduate would have a broad foundation in mathematics, physics, chemistry, and the fundamentals of engineering sufficient to practice either the profession of electrical engineering or to enter graduate study.[88]

In the end, departmental requirements were changed only slightly. Four credit hours of humanities were dropped and substituted with four units of major electrical engineering courses. Electrical Measurements, a Physics Department lab course, was added as a two-hour requirement, and it was clarified that Civil Engineering 117 was, in fact, a course in complex variables, Fourier analysis, and differential equations. Applied mathematician Halcott C. Moreno had taught the course for many years and chose the course number CE 117 when his own position was melded into the Civil Engineering Department in 1925.

The ECPD visit stimulated Fred to examine course bulletins and presidents' reports from Caltech, MIT, and Harvard; these readings helped his thinking on the importance of funding for fellowships. The 1936 ECPD controversy caused considerable concern and much corresponding for Dean Morris. Stanford was reaccredited only provisionally, as a "border-line" case, for electrical, civil, and mechanical engineering alike. Only because the Stanford department curricula were "new" were they granted the provisional three-year accreditation. Butler (a geologist) granted regular accreditation to Stanford's mining, metallurgy, and petroleum, while Stanford's general engineering B.A. degree was not accredited at all.[89] President Karl T. Compton of MIT wrote to Morris to say that the ECPD committee on engineering schools had voted *unanimously* to deny accreditation to the general engineering course, and echoed Butler's criticism that it lacked the necessary credits in technical engineering. (Only five schools up to that point had passed the standards for accreditation in general engineering.[90])

Fred Terman truly believed, as had Harris Ryan and Dugald C. Jackson of MIT before him, that professional engineers needed training and experience in "nontechnical" subjects, as one of his correspondents termed them—the ability to express oneself properly and efficiently, verbally and in writing, and knowledge of social and industrial relations, business law, and accounting.[91]

Dean Butler was back at Stanford three years later. In spring 1940, he visited the campus with Professor B. M. Woods of Berkeley, having warned Morris before arriving that he thought Stanford's curricula "too light" and that it still contained too large a proportion of humanities. Butler strongly recommended that Morris have on hand written evidence from employers of recent Stanford graduates' performance, records from Stanford graduates then in other graduate schools, and a "good many copies . . . quite a number" of quizzes, final examinations, and papers written by Stanford senior undergraduate engineering majors.[92]

Fred Terman composed an eighteen-page report for Morris stating that the undergraduate electrical engineering courses had been extensively rearranged and that the students were better prepared technically.[93] The circuits and machinery courses were more evenly divided between junior and senior years. In addition to mathematics, physics, and chemistry courses taken, undergraduates in electrical engineering were required to take courses EE 100, 101, and 102, and labs 101a and 102a in their junior year. (These courses covered AC circuits, AC and DC machinery and equipment, use of vector and complex quantity methods, and the study of nonsinusoidal waves.) Sixteen lab sessions were on generators, motors, transformers, and control mechanisms. In their senior year, students took EE 104, 105, and 106, including lab, and studied magnetic circuits, coupled circuits, impedances, transmission lines, the skin effect, hyperbolic solutions, protective devices, and transients. In addition, they took EE 124, 125, and 126, lectures and lab, on advanced AC machinery, generators, motors, rectifiers, and transformers.

Terman pointed out that additional courses were often taken by the undergraduates, including EE 110 and perhaps 111 and 112. This course series, Radio Communications, utilized Terman's new text, *Fundamentals of Radio*. They also usually took EE 108, Illumination. Some undergraduates took the advanced seminar, EE 200, and EE 215 and 216, Electric Power Systems and Distribution.

As he continued to advise Dean Morris, Terman began to argue for a movement to alter the charter of the ECPD, saying "our experiences with ECPD indicate that there is considerable danger that they will set up criteria for engineering curricula that will ensure the stoppage of all progress and experimentation in engineering curricula."[94] Once again, Stanford engineering slipped by, in part because the faculty was better prepared.

Interestingly, after his visit to Stanford with Butler, Woods wrote to Dean A. A. Potter of Purdue, another member of the ECPD committee, to complain about a trend toward overspecialization. Potter, too, feared this trend, and at Purdue they had decided to reduce undergraduate specialization.[95] Woods passed Potter's letter confidentially on to Dean Morris, who in turn wrote President Wilbur. Justifying Stanford's stand on a broadly educated BA engineer, Morris stated to Wilbur that while the ECPD accrediting process was good for the profession generally, the undue fostering of undergraduate specialization was a backward step.[96]

By the time Stanford was visited again in 1949 by an engineering accreditation committee, Fred Terman was the school's experienced dean of engineering. This time, Terman invited the ECPD to visit, as did Dean A. I. Levorsen of Stanford's School of Mineral Sciences.[97] Since the previous ECPD visit, Terman had worked to move mining, metallurgy, and petroleum into the new School of Mineral Sciences and had established a new major in engineering sciences. This latter program was aimed at the promising advanced student who hoped to go on to an academic career teaching engineering science and to have an academic research career. The major involved even more study of mathematics, physics, and chemistry than the other engineering majors.[98]

As it turned out, the ECPD asked G. M. Butler again to oversee the accrediting process. Butler first engaged in a lengthy correspondence with Terman, asserting that "engineering science" was not engineering at all, and vowing to vote against it. Terman, who was particularly proud of the new engineering science major, insisted that it was for the very best students and tied engineering more firmly with the sciences—high praise, in Terman's view, for any discipline in engineering. Nevertheless, Butler asked Terman not to include engineering science among the programs to be evaluated. Butler's ECPD superior, Curtis L. Wilson, however, insisted that Butler examine the program. Wilson wrote Terman himself to say that he agreed that engineering science was indeed a part of engineering. However, their letters apparently passed in the mail, and at the last moment, Terman withdrew his request to include the program, probably since Butler had made it so clear he would vote against it.

A seven-man group visited Stanford on April 19, 1949. Their visit to the School of Engineering went well, but not for mineral sciences. A month later, S. L. Tyler, secretary of ECPD, wrote to President Sterling to inform him that electrical engineering, mechanical engineering, and civil engineering, and the new industrial engineering program (IE) were each voted accreditation. Metallurgy, mining, and petroleum engineering, however, now in mineral sciences, were each denied accreditation.[99]

The ECPD continued to have differences with Stanford regarding evaluation of engineering curricula, standards, and practices, especially in the quickly changing field of electrical/electronic engineering. By the 1950s, the professional certification Professional Engineer (PE), which requires the passing of national exams, had little relevance to most practicing electronic and radio engineers, although it continued to apply to those engineers whose work required governmental approval or liability certification (for example, for design and construction of public utilities).

Stanford's Patent Policy

Stanford's policy toward patenting faculty, staff, and student inventions had evolved slowly over the years. President Wilbur noted in 1933 that the university had been content to deal with "each individual case as it arose." There had been few cases to consider before 1937. The only real precedent up to this point was a patent for the use of a bismuth compound, Iodobismitol, awarded to two medical school professors and administered by a faculty committee. Since 1929, it had generated a small income for the Department of Pharmacology and Division of Neuropsychology.

In the fall of 1937, however, the board of trustees adopted a patent policy in which all patents related to a faculty member's "line of research or teaching" belonged to the university, and those on "unrelated lines" belonged to the inventor.[100] The impetus for this new policy was the new Sperry-funded research in the Physics and Electrical Engineering departments, and from the contract agreements, set up in 1936, between the Electrical Engineering Department and ISEC and IT&T.[101]

The board's new policy was immediately criticized by a number of influential faculty members. Some older faculty, such as former Engineering Dean T. J. Hoover, had long articulated the concept that any compensation for inventions conceived by faculty should go to the individual faculty member, or the sponsoring outside corporation, or to the public at large—but not the university. David Webster of physics complained that if "inventions" belonged to Stanford, then so should the copyright on books, or fees for consultations, expert witnessing, and medical service. He also complained that in terms of faculty recognition and promotion, the difference should be noted between those individuals who do commercially saleable work versus those who make discoveries in "pure science," or those who merely write textbooks versus those who write review articles on advanced subjects.[102] (Obviously, Webster favored "pure science" and "review articles on advanced subjects" over his given alternatives.)

But the klystron work had raised important issues. The Varian brothers and assisting graduate students were not on the faculty, but the university provided them with space and supplies. Professors Hansen, and to a lesser extent Terman and Webster, were involved. Both future industrial collaborations and research funding were at stake (as was, possibly, Sperry's manufacturing future). A workable arrangement was formulated for President Wilbur by Business Professor J. Hugh Jackson and other faculty advisors that allowed Stanford to collaborate with the Varians and Sperry Gyroscope. Sperry, and later other companies, contributed funds for research in return for licenses, and this arrangement would set an important precedent for postwar research.[103]

In December 1937, President Wilbur appointed a committee of five faculty—Dean of Engineering Morris, chairman, with members D. L. Webster of physics, R. E. Swain of chemistry, P. J. Hanzlik of the Medical School, and Fred Terman—to develop a more concise university patent policy.[104]

A visit to campus by MIT's Edward L. Bowles in fall 1937 coincided with Stanford faculty concerns about patenting. Bowles was interested in the use of the klystron tube in an aircraft-landing system being developed in the Boston area that was of great interest to the U.S. government. (During the war, Bowles would become a major figure in the nation's radar programs, and key problem solver and consultant to the U.S. Army Air Force.) During his visit, Bowles was quizzed about MIT's patent policies, especially those with the Research Corporation. Terman described Stanford's patents as falling into four classes: medical; engineering; chemistry; and physics and other sciences. The medical patent policies were pretty much set in place, he noted (Stanford was receiving royalties from several drug companies), but the president's patent committee, Terman felt, still needed advice on the remaining three categories.[105]

Terman remained on the university patent committee (interrupted only by his war service at the Radio Research Lab) until he became provost in 1955. By then, the committee had evolved into four panels, with Edward Ginzton or W. K. H. Panofsky representing physics and the Hansen Labs; Karl Spangenberg or Donald Dunn, electrical engineering and the Electronics Research Laboratory (ERL); George Parks, chemistry and chemical engineering; and Windsor Cutting, the Medical School.[106] It was the university's intent "that a faculty member be prepared to make inventions to which he holds patent rights available to the public on a nonexclusive basis." In 1962, Stanford affirmed its policy to retain patent rights either for the inventor or for the university itself, except where government or industrial grants and contracts might specify differently. (In certain instances, as in AEC contracts, the government required transfer of the entire title.)

As historian Henry Lowood has noted, from the 1950s, research in the sciences and engineering at Stanford generated both tangible products and intangible ideas, from integrated circuits to biological materials. Stanford's patent policy in those decades differed markedly from industry and even from many peer universities in that it placed the rights, when possible, in the hands of faculty, staff, and students. Terman brought Leonard Fuller to Stanford's electronics research in 1946 to deal with patent questions as well as coordinate research contracts.[107]

Following Terman's retirement, administrator Niels J. Riemers (later, director of Stanford's Office of Technology Licensing) developed these policies further. Stanford's board of trustees adopted and enlarged patent policy in April 1970, still stressing that, except where other arrangements were specifically agreed on in writing, it was the university's policy that faculty, staff, and students retain all rights to inventions made by them.[108] Riemer credits Fred Terman and Wallace Sterling as the architects of the policy to formalize patent policy. This policy was a definite plus in the recruitment of science, engineering, and other faculty who appreciated Stanford's support for individual patent and creative rights. The policy was changed in the mid-1990s, however, to mandatory ownership by Stanford University.[109]

Reaching out for New Lines of Research

During the 1930s, Terman's research lay heavily in radio circuits and devices, at all frequencies then possible to utilize in radio. He had attempted to develop work in tube design and construction, and in radio wave propagation research, but his efforts in 1929 and 1930 had died for lack of funding. Following his promotion, he determined to expand his department's lines of research for the benefit of both department faculty and students.

The Ionosphere: Prospects brightened for radio wave propagation studies in

1936 when Terman invited Nathan Hall as a graduate student to begin a small program in ionospheric research. Hall built a manually tuned ionospheric recorder (transmitter and receiver) in the basement of the Ryan High-Voltage Lab, and Terman arranged for a special experimental radio station license from the Federal Communications Commission.[110] Hall finished construction of the equipment by spring 1937 and produced some successful records of ionospheric layer reflection of pulses sent vertically from the antennas installed next to the Ryan Lab. Hall hoped to install a second, receiving, set with antennas at Berkeley, but Leonard Fuller responded that he had started too late in the year to get through the red tape required to install equipment at Berkeley.

Based on Hall's first year's results, however, Terman determined to extend the studies in correlation of ionospheric conditions between the U.S. Atlantic and Pacific coasts, studying the nighttime "E" layer of the ionosphere, investigating ionospheric fine structure, and searching for possible low-lying layers, such as the then hypothesized "C" layer. He believed outside funding would be available in the coming year.[111] This work, he knew, would be of interest to Norris Bradbury of Stanford's Physics Department, who was studying the constitution of gases in the upper atmosphere.

Back in 1929, Fred had asked for funding for a similar project. The radio wave propagation field was rich for future discoveries, he reasoned, and there was no such work being done west of Chicago. This field of probing of the ionized upper regions above the earth was begun by E. V. Appleton in England and G. Breit and M. Tuve in the United States in 1924–26. By the mid-1930s, the National Bureau of Standards in Washington had developed an automatic, multifrequency ionospheric recorder (also called sounder, later an ionosonde). This device was improved on by Lloyd Berkner at the Carnegie Institution of Washington's Department of Terrestrial Magnetism, and Berkner then installed sets on the magnetic equator in Huancayo, Peru, and in Western Australia. During a visit to Stanford in 1939, Berkner met with Fred Terman and Norris Bradbury to discuss mutual ionospheric interests.[112] By 1940, Berkner was busy extending a network soon to include College, Alaska; Cambridge, Massachusetts (Harvard); Puerto Rico; Baton Rouge, Louisiana; and Stanford. Several other countries were building such equipment, particularly the British, who had had one or two ionospheric recorders operating regularly since the mid-1930s. The ionospheric recorder produced exciting results about the location and constitution of ionized gases in the regions from about 60 to 500 km above the earth. In addition to the knowledge about upper atmospheric physics gained from this research, the experiments reaped information valuable to the radio broadcasting industry, especially the major broadcasting and radio traffic companies and the military.

Terman's ionospheric station joined Berkner's network, and would soon be sponsored by the National Defense Research Committee (NDRC). For financial reasons, Nathan Hall left after a year at Stanford when he secured a good-paying job at Bell Labs, but his work was continued and improved on by a new graduate student, O. G. "Mike" Villard Jr. Villard was, in turn, succeeded by Robert A. Helliwell during World War II. Ionospheric and radio wave propagation work would be one of the earliest and most important areas of engineering research continued at Stanford after the war.

Tube Electronics: Terman had long wished for a faculty coworker in electronics. James M. Sharp, a Stanford graduate with an Engineer degree, had assisted him for several years, but his real chance for faculty-level collaboration came when he hired Karl Spangenberg in April 1937, almost as soon as Terman was promoted to head the department.

For Stanford in the 1930s, Terman's exceptionally thorough search for the appointment was unusual. Spangenberg opened up many possibilities for research and advanced teaching in electronics at Stanford. Terman's hopes for really significant work in tube construction and electron optics had begun with graduate student Henry Blanchard in 1936. Spangenberg's arrival a year later led Terman to use outside research funds to obtain a leading RCA expert in electron optics, Laszlo Marton, for a joint appointment between Electrical Engineering and the Physics departments. Terman then lured David Packard back to Stanford from GE as a means not only to get Packard and Bill Hewlett together as partners, but because Packard had become a top-notch man in the tube design techniques of very-high- and ultra-high-frequency tubes. While Packard worked for his Engineer degree, he served as a research assistant in electrical engineering and indirectly helped Russell Varian and Bill Hansen with klystron development, while Terman's PhD students John Woodyard and Ed Ginzton were of direct and major assistance on the klystron work.

Packard's return to Stanford from the East Coast was aided by Charles V. Litton. Litton had thought of a device, a wide-grid tube structure, which was indirectly connected with the klystron. He assigned the patent rights to this device to Stanford University, which put them into the klystron pool. Sperry Gyroscope paid $1,000 for those rights. By agreement with Litton, the $1,000 was then given to the Electrical Engineering Department to develop Litton's idea. "This $1,000 was what ultimately financed Packard to come back to Stanford," said Fred Terman. Packard and Litton then collaborated on research into wide-grid tubes.[113] Packard took classes part-time and worked with Litton afternoons and evenings at Litton's shop in Redwood City.[114]

Lester Field became a tube expert during his graduate student days in the late 1930s at Stanford. Later a world expert in traveling wave tubes at Bell Labs, he returned to direct traveling wave tube research as a professor at Stanford after World War II. Thus, not only did radio wave propagation and ionosphere studies "take-off" at Stanford beginning in 1936–37, but so did electron tube research. The electron tube research was especially aimed at the "ultra-high-frequency" spectrum, wavelengths of less than a meter, from 40 cm down to 10 cm or as short as could be obtained. Terman's own studies had turned in this direction by about 1935.

Broadcasting and Audio: Terman had always been interested in a wide spectrum of uses of radio electronics, from low-frequency audio sound to ultra-high frequency. He directed graduate research theses and published in all these areas. While his department had not been very interested in Stanford becoming a radio-broadcasting center during the 1920s; both Henry Henline and, later, Terman preferred radio research with Stanford's experimental transmitters to more general efforts at broadcasting to uplift the cultural level of the Bay Area. Dean Hoover's ambitious plan to build a Stanford motion-picture training center in 1930 was dutifully supported by Terman, at Hoover's request, but the sum of the funds required in those Depression years made Hoover's amorphous idea dead in the water at the start.

Terman supported the idea of audio engineering, however, being well within the scope of radio engineering, and he criticized the Institute of Radio Engineers when it tended to deny Hollywood motion-picture engineers promotion within the IRE. Indeed, he corresponded often with former Stanford student J. N. A. "Bud" Hawkins, a noted author for radio and broadcasting magazines and, by 1939, chief sound engineer for Disney Studios. Thus, it is not surprising to find that Terman supported technical cooperation in 1938 with Hubert Heffner's Speech and Drama Department. With Waldemar W. A. Johansen, technical director of dramatics, Terman proposed a program for studying the use of sound amplification in connection with speech and drama productions, although not much came out of this particular proposal.[115]

Earlier in his career, Terman had advised the Stanford Theater in downtown Palo Alto on its sound system, and he and one of his graduate students worked on the design and implementation of the sound system in Stanford's new Memorial Auditorium, completed in 1937. Graduate student Skipwith W. Athey worked on sound at Stanford before World War II, worked with Terman during the war, and then returned to complete his electrical engineering PhD dissertation in 1947, partly based on sound research in Memorial Auditorium. Retaining his soft spot for ham radio and young radio operators, Terman supported the founding of the student radio broadcast station KSU (later KZSU) in 1947 and promoted opportunities for electrical engineering students to gain technical experience in radio broadcasting.[116]

High Voltages and Network Analysis: In contrast to the illumination and machinery aspects of the department, which attracted few graduate students, Joseph Carroll kept fairly busy with tests at the Ryan High-Voltage Laboratory in spite of the fact that high-voltage electrical work for electrical utility companies was a declining field.

Terman got along well with Carroll and thought him a productive colleague. In 1939, Terman assisted Carroll in gaining support for the construction of a 2,000,000-volt impulse generator. Drawing $3,000 from Ryan Lab funds, Terman raised an additional $4,000 from industry. The generator, built by Stanford faculty and graduate students, was provided with a cathode-ray oscilloscope recording system to study the impulse and breakdown wave shapes. The entire project was under the charge of Assistant Professor William "Bill" Hoover, and thus helped extend a research area to younger faculty.[117]

Fred Terman learned early on that he could rely on Hugh Skilling. With Terman's support, Skilling was promoted to associate professor in 1939. Skilling had become an excellent lecturer and a skillful writer. In some ways, just as Karl Spangenberg was a younger version of Terman as an electronics researcher, Skilling was his protégé as a text writer and administrator. Skilling was, it turns out, a better lecturer than Terman. Skilling now generally taught the power circuits courses, and he gradually took over the transmission line courses as well from Terman. Skilling wanted a "network analyzer" or "network calculating board" for the Electrical Engineering Department. In those years, a "network analyzer" was basically a very large switchboard on which the important units of an electrical power distribution system were represented in miniature in a laboratory simulation. Large electrical generators were represented by miniature sources of power, while electrical loads and transmission lines were represented by resistors and reactors. The electrical power designer could set up the board to correspond to desired or experienced conditions in a system. By the 1930s, network power analyzer boards employed alternating currents and numerous transient conditions could be simulated. The manual time once required for such studies was greatly decreased if a network analyzer was used. These boards were very expensive, however, and Stanford would never be able to obtain one without outside funding.

In his 1938 proposal, Skilling noted that there were five network analyzers in the United States (there were actually six). The first had been built at MIT for Vannevar Bush. Others were at Westinghouse (two), at GE in Schenectady, at Commonwealth-Edison in Chicago, and at the Tennessee Valley Authority. Skilling and the department argued that since no such analyzer existed west of Chicago, one would be of great interest and use to electrical utilities on the Pacific Coast. Skilling suggested that if the West Coast power companies financed the building of an analyzer at Stanford, they could use it part-time, while other companies could lease time. The analyzer would primarily be used, however, for research and teaching at Stanford.

Fred Terman and Dean Morris pushed this idea with several power companies in Los Angeles, San Francisco, Portland, and Seattle. Skilling's initial estimate in November 1938 of the cost of a suitable analyzer was somewhere between ten and twenty-five thousand dollars. By July 1939, Dean Morris estimated the capital cost of the analyzer to be closer to $34,500, with annual operating costs of $3,500. Westinghouse would perhaps make a deal with Stanford.

Two more years passed. Dean Morris supported a proposal for a used analyzer that could be supplied by Westinghouse at a cost of $50,000, paid over a three-year period. Westinghouse rejected the deal but was willing to negotiate. Terman recommended in November 1941 that Stanford continue to pursue the Westinghouse deal, and Dean Morris backed up Terman and Skilling.

On November 27, 1941, President Wilbur notified Terman that the Stanford board of trustees had agreed to negotiate with Westinghouse for the network analyzer board. The entrance of the United States into World War II a few days later ended the hopes for Stanford's Electrical Engineering Department obtaining the board, which ended up going to Purdue University.[118] After the war, it was no longer needed at Stanford since network analysis could be done on a much smaller-scale using more sophisticated devices.

Hansen, Terman, and the Klystron

The most significant invention coming from the Stanford Physics Department in the first half of the twentieth century was the klystron tube. Most central to this were physics professor William Hansen and the Varian brothers, Russell and Sigurd. David Webster, head of the department, also contributed to theoretical modeling of the klystron operation, while Fred Terman played a central role in the evolution of the klystron through his graduate students who developed the tube, analyzed it, and originated circuitry for it. Terman and his Electrical Engineering Department took over Stanford's further development of the klystron once wartime preparation took most of the klystron workers east to Sperry Corporation in New York.[119]

Terman and Hansen's friendship, little discussed today, was an important factor in this development. Terman greatly admired Hansen, and judging from their correspondence, the admiration was mutual. Hansen would nominate Fred for Stanford's presidency in 1940. Just as several of Fred's students (Bill Hewlett, Dave Packard, Bernard Oliver, Noel Eldred, Noel Porter) were key to the founding and growth of the Hewlett-Packard firm, a number of other Terman students (John Woodyard, Edward Ginzton, Lowell Hollingsworth, Myrl Stearns) performed similar foundational work in the development of the klystron and later, several contributed to the establishment of Stanford's Microwave Laboratory, the Varian Associates Company, and the Stanford Linear Accelerators.

William Webster Hansen, fondly called Bill, was Stanford's most-gifted and hardest-working physicist during its first half-century, equaling in ability the theorist, and later Stanford's first Nobel recipient, Felix Bloch, who arrived at Stanford in 1934.[120] Hansen began his studies at Stanford as an electrical engineering undergraduate then changed to physics, receiving his BA in 1929, and in 1933, his PhD in physics. When Stanford alumnus and very promising physicist George R. Harrison left for MIT in the early 1930s, Hansen joined him in 1933 and spent a year and a half on a National Research Council Fellowship working at MIT with Harrison and with Julius Stratton on electromagnetic (EM) wave theory and also at Michigan. Hansen later wrote that his work on electromagnetism at MIT was central to his career.

Hansen stood out as an unusual as well as very gifted student, and his first five publications were coauthored with his advisor, David Locke Webster, executive head of the Physics Department.[121] Coming to Stanford to lead the Physics Department in 1920, Webster had reoriented physics instruction to fit in more closely with the needs of engineering students. His own research was in the field of X-rays, and his X-Ray laboratory was open to faculty of other departments. (During the 1920s, this included experiments with botanists, geologists, and crystallographers, and a cancer therapy project by W. W. Nicholas in cooperation with St. Luke's Hospital in San Francisco.)

Webster was an ambitious, and often frustrated, man. He wanted to make a mark at Stanford, like Robert Millikan, then busy building physics at Caltech. He had already lobbied hard to add a theorist to the faculty to balance the domination of experimentalists, winning Felix Bloch as an acting assistant professor with funds put together from the Rockefeller Foundation and the Emergency Committee in Aid of Displaced Foreign Scholars.

When Hansen returned to the Stanford campus as an assistant professor of physics in late 1934, Webster corralled him for his supervoltage X-ray committee, then developing a giant X-ray tube.[122] Webster hoped to use the Electrical Engineering Department's Ryan High-Voltage Lab and its 3,000,000-volt power source.

Bill Hansen's thoughts about electromagnetic waves led him in two directions. Norris Bradbury had become interested in upper atmospheric gas composition and interactions, and Fred Terman was interested in antenna arrays for broadcasting and in ionospheric physics. Hansen wrote to each of them regarding the ionosphere work and on EM antenna arrays. More important, however, was his thinking about applying rapidly varying EM fields to Webster's problem of producing very high voltages for X-ray studies. Instead of achieving strong X-rays using large static voltages, he speculated, perhaps electrons could be accelerated as radio waves at ultrahigh frequencies. Hansen's MIT work with expanding Green's Functions could be used to prove that one could have nonradiating oscillations within a sphere. He developed the idea of a hollow conductor used as a resonator to develop fields to accelerate electrons and presented these ideas to the Stanford Physics Department in a talk on January 10, 1935. Most of his colleagues, including David Webster, did not think Hansen was correct.

Webster wanted the department to concentrate on his own latest plan for X-ray tube construction, but in late 1935 his proposal was finally rejected by the Carnegie Foundation. Hansen now raised his idea of a resonating cavity. By February 1936, he had a working model, using vacuum tubes as drivers. He found that the vector wave equations he had first published in papers on antennas worked also on cavity resonators.[123] Similar work appeared in the paper Hansen coauthored with John Woodyard in 1938.[124]

Hansen was brilliant not only as a theorist but as an experimentalist. Hansen had outstanding spatial visualization powers. He was an experienced and skilled machinist, welder, and toolmaker, who built (and rebuilt) his car engine and made all sorts of tools and instruments in the physics laboratory and shop.[125] His own pace was grueling—he worked twelve- to fourteen-hour days, seven days a week and was oblivious to his own health. He was critical of most Stanford undergraduates, who he felt came to Stanford to play rather than work. He expressed the same general feelings about the liberal arts faculty at Stanford, who he believed worked only forty hours a week and then relaxed, doing little research. He mourned Stanford's reputation as a country club. As a result, he worked best with strongly motivated graduate students, and equally industrious friends like Fred Terman.[126]

Hansen's resonator implementation began with designing low-loss ("High Q") cavity resonators, and he powered these with high-frequency electron tubes. He called his successful design the "rhumbatron," and it brought some celebrity to Stanford's Physics Department in the press. The original rhumbatron was a closed copper cylinder that contained a number of three-electrode radio tubes. As Hansen wrote to a manufacturing company representative in late 1936: "If power is correctly applied to the copper cylinder, an oscillating EM field is set up in the interior with a wavelength about 1.3 times the diameter of the container." The efficiency of this rhumbatron tube proved to be extremely high and the radio frequency power generated could be "drawn off" and used for other applications. Hansen was always interested in possible commercial applications of his ideas. Hansen's original illustrations of use were for radio purposes, for medical heating and, most importantly, as a high-voltage X-ray tube.[127] In January 1937, Hansen wrote a memo to himself listing four of his ideas in the chronological order of their emergence: first was the rhumbatron and associated uses in radio and television, medicine, and X-ray research. Next was his scheme for a new type of photographic enlarger, which would always remain in focus. Third was a greatly improved form of micromanipulator, such as used by biologists. Fourth was a design for a nonchattering reamer, immensely superior to existing types.[128]

Around this time, Hansen was reunited with two pals, brothers Russell and Sigurd Varian. Their friendship would result in great physics. Russell Varian (BA '25, MA '27, physics, Stanford) had met Hansen while a Stanford physics student in the 1920s (he was, for a time, his roommate.)[129] Russ worked for Philo Farnsworth, then in the East for a while, until Sig talked him into coming home to California to set up a lab to work on an aircraft navigation and detection system to guide pilots in bad weather and at night.

Russ was dyslexic and had great difficulty in keeping up with reading materials in his classes, and he was not able to handle mathematics in a normal manner. But like the great nineteenth-century self-taught physicist Michael Faraday, Russ had a rare ability to think up problems and then propose solutions, often many solutions, to those problems. Russ's younger brother Sig was a pilot, first as a barnstormer and flying in Latin America for Pan American Airways. Sig and Russ already had discussed the possibilities of using radio waves to make an airplane warning and guidance system, which could be especially important with the likely arrival of war in Europe.

Russ had been deeply disappointed when he had been prevented by Webster from becoming a PhD candidate in physics at Stanford (he had worked in Webster's X-ray lab). Nevertheless, rather than work at home (in cattle country to the south near San Luis Obispo) the brothers managed to persuade Webster, with Hansen's assistance, to name the brothers "research associates" in the department, giving them lab space and $100 for materials and supplies to support a collaborative project with Hansen to produce microwaves. In exchange, the Varian brothers signed over to Stanford any patent rights and one-half of royalties from devices that might emerge from their work on aircraft radio warning systems.[130]

Hansen's rhumbatron fit the Varians' needs, and an extraordinary collaboration began. The rhumbatron looked to be a success, but the largest obstacle was that resonant cavities at high frequency were extremely large physically. Smaller dimensional cavities required even higher frequencies. How could one develop sufficient high-power devices with small physical dimensions? This problem of small physical dimension had thus far limited ultra-high-frequency tubes to outputs of only a watt or two. Russ Varian's creative solution, conceived in June 1937, was of velocity modulation or the "bunching" of electrons. At very high frequencies, electrons have difficulty passing the space charge barrier in a tube, but if the electrons are slowed down or accelerated, Varian thought, the electrons passing the control girds of the tube will have variable velocities. A uniform beam of electrons will be changed into a series of electron waves.

Russ showed the idea to Bill Hansen and Sig, and the trio began working immediately. John Woodyard's calculations and test model for the rhumbatron were used to begin trials.[131] Sig Varian transformed the idea into a physically working model by August 1937, utilizing two of Hansen's resonant cavities.[132] Fred Terman was among the small group who observed the output of this first prototype on August 19, 1937, but the thing was not really working well until October.[133] Electrons in the first cavity passed through a transmission line, bunching in the process, and on to a second cavity. The bunched electrons induced oscillations, and these oscillations with proper feedback could be amplified in the device. Webster joined in, and began work on a theory to explain "bunching." Russ Varian's bunching principle combined with Hansen's rhumbatron became the klystron. (With linguistic help from a professor of classics, they had named the thing the "klystron," meaning waves breaking on a beach.)[134]

It was clear that the klystron could be of great help in developing aircraft landing systems, and perhaps much more. The klystron work tied in with Hansen's work with Fred Terman on phased antenna array systems with special beam patterns, also of use to landing and detection systems. As soon as the klystron was working well, Hansen wrote to an acquaintance at the U.S. Naval Academy, saying "A fellow here by the name of Varian, with some help from myself, has conceived a device which we believe will be valuable to the Navy."[135]

The Sperry Gyroscope Company, Bell Labs, GE, Westinghouse, and other companies were seeking to develop such systems. Edward Bowles of MIT, in contact with Sperry, was already aware of the klystron's potential and flew out to Stanford in mid-December 1937 to talk about its possible connection with an aircraft blind-landing radar scheme.[136] Sperry approached Stanford in late 1937, and in early 1938 the company signed patent and financial arrangements with Stanford's Physics Department faculty. In preparation for this, thirty-three Stanford physics faculty and graduate students signed a patent agreement with Stanford University.[137] Webster was the director of Stanford's end of this patent arrangement. Later in 1938, Fred Terman and the full-time faculty of the Electrical Engineering Department, and Bill Hansen, signed similar patent agreements with ISEC, a subsidiary of IT&T, for any radio and electrical ideas, excluding any of Hansen's klystron work for Sperry.[138]

Terman and the Electrical Engineering Department became more directly involved in the klystron work because the Physics Department needed men able to make measurements of what the klystron was actually doing: What was the power output bandwidth? What was its stability? And how might it be utilized in circuits? This is how electrical engineering student John Woodyard joined the klystron project in 1937. By 1938, Woodyard was in charge of measurements, designing the equipment for measuring klystron output and characteristics. Woodyard later recalled that, even before the rhumbatron was invented, Hansen would constantly run over to Terman to ask about transmission lines or transmission line resonators. Charlie Litton was consulted for help on high-vacuum problems.[139] In the summer of 1939, Ed Ginzton joined the group to design and build circuits for use of the klystron as a receiver, as a transmitter, as a modulator, and so on. Several more Terman electrical engineering graduate students, including David Packard and Lowell Hollingsworth, plus mechanical engineering graduate student Walter Vincenti, also worked on the klystron projects in 1938 and 1939.[140]

Ed Ginzton and Walter Vincenti later recalled that Sig Varian was ill with tuberculosis in 1939, and now rarely came to the laboratory.[141] According to Ginzton, Russ Varian was busy working with patent problems while Professor Webster worked on the administrative problems. "There was only Bill Hansen to provide technical assistance to the staff—John Woodyard, myself, and two machinists."[142]

In early 1939, the Stanford klystron, with an output of 300 watts on a wavelength of 40 centimeters, was made a key part of a military blind-landing radar demonstration, both at East Boston Airport and at Wright Field in Dayton, Ohio. A microwave horn antenna, developed at MIT by W. L. Barrow, was coupled with a Stanford klystron by Professor E. L. Bowles. John Woodyard, who had completed building the klystron tube intended for the test, was in charge of transporting the klystron and troubleshooting it during the demonstration. The tests, sponsored by the Civil Aeronautics Authority, the army air corps, and the army signal corps, were a grand success. The one in Boston made national headlines.[143]

The infusion of real money into Stanford's Physics Department made a tremendous change in the campus climate for research. The Sperry money bought more shop lathes and equipment in physics, more funding in three years than the Physics Department had received for research in a half century. But there personnel—and personal—problems accompanied the money. David Webster was popular with students, but could be heavy-handed in running the Department. When Sperry engineers began to overstep their authority at Stanford, Webster boiled over. He complained effectively enough that Sperry removed eight or ten employees to a new shop to the north in San Carlos. Webster was not, as has been suggested in some accounts, totally against the intrusion of outside commercial forces into the pure world of physics research. Although partly correct, Webster was a far more complicated man. As the klystron work developed, he became paranoid about losing control of his department and left typed memoranda in his files justifying to himself his reasons for his actions. Webster detested certain Sperry engineers, especially Sperry Chief Engineer Hugh Willis and on-site engineer William T. "Bill" Cooke. In the summer of 1939, Webster and Russ Varian visited Sperry headquarters in New York to complain about Willis's alleged aggressive and unethical activities aimed at taking over the Physics Department for Sperry projects. Sperry top executives agreed to rein in Willis, according to Webster. (Webster also argued that Sperry should remove Fred Terman and his electrical engineers from the Stanford-Sperry klystron project and put them into a separate organization with Sperry.) Hansen thought it was good to put "little Hughie" Willis in his place, but did not wish to get Bill Cooke, as on-site Sperry engineering chief, into trouble because he worked well. Sperry had machinists that Stanford needed. Russ Varian wrote to the same effect. They wanted to give trouble for Willis while keeping Bill Cooke so that the two labs, Stanford and Sperry-San Carlos, could cooperate.[144]

Unlike the pharmaceutical industry in the 1930s, the radio devices industry was extremely aggressive, and Sperry had to protect the klystron ideas during patent application periods. Much to Webster's frustration, the company thus asked Stanford researchers to delay publication for a time. The klystron was one of the few major electronic patents not controlled by RCA. Sperry, breaking into the business, had to protect against possible litigation.[145] It was a classic case of the technologist's "papyrophobia" in conflict with the scientist's "papyrophilia," as described by Derek Price: science gains its currency and value from passing ideas to others; technology earns its rewards through patent or other protection of applicable ideas.[146]

Webster had other complaints. L. M. Applegate, an electrical engineering graduate student, joined the klystron project and was put to work writing patent applications. Webster couldn't stand Applegate. He called him a liar and fired him. Hansen, however, liked Applegate and hired him to do patent work for two more years. According to Hansen, Russ Varian wanted Applegate back on the job.[147]

Webster also spoke to the Varians about his difficulties of working with Hansen and of his fears that Hansen wanted to take over the operation. In a lengthy typed memo to himself, Webster detailed the acts of hostility and opposition he believed directed at him by Hansen.[148] Webster knew that Hansen felt his former mentor was trying to take credit for klystron ideas that Hansen believed to be his own. Yet, in spite of his earlier statements on behalf of pure physics research and his desire to seem in control of the research effort, Webster now spent more and more of his time with the Stanford student flying club and with local civil aviation efforts.[149] That summer of 1939, he spent much of his time arranging schedules and displays for a Stanford meeting of the American Physical Society.

Webster thought of himself as something of an amateur lawyer, and he worried greatly about contracts and patent agreements.[150] On April 27, 1938, a day after the Stanford physicists signed an agreement with the university concerning klystron physics, Webster typed himself another memo. He rehearsed his actions of the preceding weeks when he personally rewrote contracts for himself and Hansen. When he presented these to President Wilbur, he recorded, Wilbur looked them over and said, "Who wrote this, you or a lawyer?"[151] Bill Hansen later wrote, "During this period we were all business men, amateur lawyers and patent attorneys in addition to doing our research."[152]

Webster spent several months in Boston during the summer and fall of 1938 dealing with his family estate and problems with his teeth. The stress and pace of the work, however, finally led Webster to seek medical advice when he returned to Palo Alto. Dr. Russel Lee suspected Webster of hypochondria. Webster sought an eye specialist who gave him some drops for his eyes and told him to lessen his work load, including giving up the management of the Sperry project if that was what was worrying him so much. Finally, citing his eye problems, overwork, and his distaste for the Sperry applied work, Webster resigned these responsibilities in December 1939.[153]

Webster did not want to tell Sperry personally that he was resigning and asked Stanford authorities to do this for him. He had neglected to submit financial accounting of cross-country travel to Sperry for some ten months, in spite of several Sperry inquiries. His excuse for ignoring the accounting was the important matters he had to deal with involving the Stanford Civilian Pilot Training Program, the klystron work, and his eye condition.[154] Years later, Fred Terman recalled Webster's reactions: "Webster tended to get emotionally upset with all the negotiations and questions and so on. He was a temperamental person . . . the feelings of management responsibility got Webster emotionally upset." Fred believed, as did Hansen, that Webster wanted a part of the klystron invention patents, even though the invention was solely due to Hansen and the Varians.[155]

Despite his fears about Terman's participation in the klystron project, Webster now wanted to push more of the Sperry work out of physics and into engineering. For the first two years of the Sperry patent agreement, Terman had received about 10 percent of the funds for electrical engineering work related to klystron implementation, but with Bill Hansen hoping to spend either the academic year of 1940–41, or the calendar year 1941, on sabbatical leave back east, Hansen arranged for Terman to take over complete management of the klystron work during his absence. Sperry had also decided to scale back their funding of "pure" research on the klystron as of 1940 and to invite other outside firms to participate.[156] Whatever Webster's feeling about the low-grade status of klystronics to the pure physicist, other noted physicists at Columbia and MIT were very enthused. I. I. Rabi wrote to Hansen that "a tremendous field of nuclear and molecular research would be possible if we could get the short wavelengths. We need it [klystron] very badly!!" Philip M. Morse of MIT wrote Hansen that "interest in Rhumbatrons, Klystrons and other short-wave work has been getting quite hot here recently," and mentioned that Julius Stratton and a number of other members of the Physics Department were quite interested.[157]

In October and November 1940, the Stanford Associates feted Stanford's three klystron inventors—Hansen, and Russ and Sig Varian—at luncheons at the Bohemian Club in San Francisco and at the California Club in Los Angeles. Fred Terman (who was described as current director of the klystron effort) and Bill Hansen were the invited speakers.[158] The honorees brought a rhumbatron and klystron for illustration to the audiences. Though not on the original printed invitation list of Stanford Associates honorees, Webster showed up at the San Francisco luncheon and was included in remarks there.[159]

Looking back on the remarkable effort, Fred Terman felt that "Sperry was a fine company; we didn't have any trouble with Sperry."[160] Although at times

Hansen and the Varians had their arguments and disagreements with Sperry, Hansen wrote to the Stanford comptroller in fall 1938, "Sperry has done their share and a lot more, too, that the University has already profited greatly [from] without any expenditure."[161] Hansen thought highly of Sperry engineer Bill Cooke and cited Cooke's work in his own papers. And when Hugh Willis arranged for a Sperry fellowship for Hansen in the Electrical Engineering Department at MIT, Hansen responded graciously, "I am tickled to death and feel deeply grateful to Sperry, and to you, for making this possible."[162]

Ed Ginzton said of those heady days of 1937–40, "Fred Terman was a fascinating person, enthusiastic about everything he said or did. His enthusiasm permeated his laboratory and spilled over into the work of his students. At the end of each working day, he appeared in the laboratory, sat on the laboratory bench with his legs dangling, and asked questions or made suggestions or just chatted about life in general."[163] Hansen, Ginzton recalled, "was a wonderful teacher and a first-rate scientist."[164] Terman's close relationship with Hansen, and the key efforts of his electrical engineering graduate students, in turn contributed to two important postwar developments: the establishment of Stanford's Microwave Laboratory, and the founding of the Varian Associates Company.

By the fall of 1940, Sperry moved the klystron project east to an old and vacant Curtiss-Wright plant in Garden City, Long Island, New York.[165] Most of the Stanford team went along: Hansen, the Varians, Woodyard, Ginzton, Don Snow, Fred Salisbury, and two or three others. Electrical engineer Myrl Stearns, Ginzton's former graduate roommate at Stanford, was brought east from Gilfillan Brothers in Los Angeles, where he had been making the first television sets on the West Coast.[166] They would stick together, and come back five years later to Stanford and Palo Alto.

From Committee Member to IRE President

Fred Terman worked hard to bring up the status and level of activity of engineering on the West Coast and to lessen the domination of electrical and radio engineering by the large East Coast companies. Throughout the 1930s, he organized West Coast sessions at meetings and urged his students to publish in association journals. By the end of the 1930s, as chairman of a department and with his textbooks as national best-sellers, Fred was the choice of West Coast radio engineers to have a run for the presidency of a national electrical engineering society.

Fred Terman had been active in the American Institute of Electrical Engineers (AIEE) from his first days as a graduate student, and he became active in the Institute of Radio Engineers (IRE) several years later when his research turned from power transmission to radio and electronics.[167] The AIEE was formed in 1884, in the midst of dramatic growth in American industrialization and in the organization of professional societies. Early members of AIEE included pioneer telegraph operators, but the AIEE came to be dominated by interests of central power stations, electrical supply, electrical machinery, and electrical transportation. Early radio innovators also belonged to the AIEE, but the society did not want to stress the interests of those whom the Europeans termed "light current electricians."

The growth of the radio industry in the years just before World War I brought small groups together at Columbia University in New York in 1912 to form the Institute of Radio Engineers. The IRE had a more international slant. Many pioneer AIEE members joined IRE but others were from a distinct social and technical group. Until the 1960s, the AIEE remained dominated by electrical power and manufacturing industries and the IRE directed more toward technology and applied science.[168]

Even within the IRE, divisions of interest grew. For example, innovators and theorists like Edwin Armstrong, Lee de Forest, and Arthur Kennelly were faced by men like David Sarnoff, whose interests were mostly commercial. In 1930, IRE President Lee de Forest protested the domination of radio by commercial powers, as the country glorified radio and the vacuum tube. (Witness the construction of "Radio City, a temple of electronics" in New York, and the Chicago World Fair described as an "all-electronic exposition.") As the "decade of the tube" continued, IRE members continued within themselves to debate over engineering creativity versus business utility, an argument harkening back to Thorstein Veblen's classic "The Instinct of Workmanship," the belief that a craftsman did something because of the inherent goodness and design-worthiness of the product.[169] Issues surrounding this question would again surface in 1940 during Fred Terman's bid for the IRE presidency.

Terman had published his first AIEE paper in 1924 in connection with his Stanford Engineer's thesis. He continued to publish in AIEE journals over the next fifteen years, but found that by the early 1930s the organization did not have much interest in radio and electronics authors. In 1934, the AIEE had tried to interest the more technical authors, especially in communications, by organizing a Symposium in Electronics. Fred Terman became a member of the national AIEE communications committee, and soon after was asked to organize a West Coast subcommittee. His early efforts here produced mixed results, and he felt AIEE attendees still preferred the "practical" papers.[170]

Terman subsequently helped with conventions in Pasadena, Los Angeles, and Spokane. He worked hard to organize sessions and encourage attendance of radio engineers. Terman made a success of an innovative joint Pacific Coast AIEE–IRE session in Spokane in 1937, writing more than one hundred letters urging people from both industry and academia to give papers.[171] In planning for a successor Pacific Coast convention in Portland, Oregon, Terman managed to get the joint sessions made a permanent feature. His friend, Bill Everitt, chairman of the AIEE communications committee, strongly agreed.[172] But not all felt that the joint AIEE–IRE sessions would be good for either organization, and the awkward suspicion remained a potential split between university research people and industry people.[173]

By the late 1930s, Terman's major efforts turned more toward the IRE. His technical articles now went mostly to the IRE's *Proceedings* ("Prock-Eye-Are-E" as they were called in those days) and his semipopular radio and electronics articles were published in journals such as *Electronics*. He sent his more technical papers, coauthored with graduate students, to the IRE as did William Hansen with the papers he coauthored with Terman's students. All was not completely right at IRE headquarters, however—the IRE rejected an ionospheric theory paper submitted by Hansen on a topic suggested by Terman, and which Hansen called "Terman's Problem." Even more curious, IRE rejected Hansen's original paper on the rhumbatron (which was then published in the *Journal of Applied Physics*) and became the first in a series of klystron papers published by Stanford physicists from 1938–39.[174]

Terman's administrative rise in the IRE occurred in three steps. He was active in the local San Francisco section of IRE. Meetings were held once a month, usually in the City, and topics nearly always were on technical subjects: Jack McCullough on the design and construction of transmitting tubes, Don Lippincott on television developments in Europe, or Ralph Heintz on the electron multiplier.[175] Whenever he was on a trip to a regional or national AIEE or IRE meeting, Terman gave such talks himself, usually to IRE section meetings. For example, he offered to speak to the IRE Los Angeles section in 1936 on ionosphere studies and their relation to radio wave propagation (using the first data from Stanford's new ionosphere recorder), or on high-efficiency linear amplifiers and grid modulation (also based on work at Stanford).[176] Although Fred had fortunately not succeeded in his foolish plan to spend his honeymoon at a Denver AIEE meeting in 1928, he did manage to take Sibyl Terman along on one or two regional or national meetings a year, even after the three children were born.[177]

Terman was appointed to two IRE national committees—education and communications—by 1936. He had been active in the Society for Promotion of Engineering Education since the early 1930s, so the education committee appointment was no surprise. The communications committee appointment was also an obvious move, since Terman's *Radio Engineering* text (1932) and his laboratory text *Measurements in Radio Engineering* (1935) were widely known and used.

Fred was especially conscious of the needs of academic members in the IRE. He wrote to all the national board members to complain that proposed meeting dates (May) for the summer meeting made it extremely difficult for university people to attend. He suggested that meetings be held after the end of exams, and that they occur adjacent in time to the AIEE meetings.[178] He then learned that the board had agreed to make the meetings in June, but that other IRE groups (especially those in the Radio Manufacturers' Association) found that an unsuitable date.[179] Terman pushed also for keeping the summer meetings in June for the benefit of graduate students. He noted that at the Pacific Coast AIEE meetings, there were always one or two sessions for student papers and at least one student delegate from each university. Student attendance, he contended, was very important for the universities and for the profession.[180]

Terman was also behind a movement to get a summer national IRE meeting in San Francisco. His former student Noel Eldred, as chairman of the San Francisco section, and others lobbied the IRE board. Eldred cited successful Pacific Coast meetings in the recent past and mentioned that he had already reserved blocks of rooms at the Mark Hopkins Hotel for late June 1939, to link with the AIEE Pacific Coast meeting to be there.[181] The efforts succeeded, for the IRE board agreed to hold a special national IRE convention in San Francisco, June 27–30, 1939. It was not only timed with the AIEE, but with the National Association of Broadcasters' meeting, with the great added attraction of the Golden Gate International Exposition. Terman was proud to say that the meeting drew the largest gathering of radio engineers ever held in the West. He wrote to about twenty prominent radio engineers and physicists on the East Coast, including RCA, Bell Labs, Harvard, MIT, and Yale, inviting them to attend and to give papers.[182]

Radio was a favorite topic also at the American Physical Society in those days. An IRE electronics conference meeting in New York City in January 1939 showed noted physicists such as W. B. Shockley and Lee DuBridge participating.[183] For an IRE conference on ultrahigh frequency (UHF) scheduled for New York in October 1939, Fred pushed Californians from Berkeley, Heintz and Kaufman Radio, and from the klystron group at Stanford to attend and give papers. Travel budgets turned out to be too slim: Heintz and Kaufman could not afford to send anyone to the East Coast at that time, the Varians could not go, David Webster had to teach. Finally, Fred managed to persuade Bill Hansen to give a talk on resonant cavities, but the West Coast work was nonetheless written up in a review article submitted to the IRE subcommittee on UHF.[184]

In his view of the compass of radio engineering, Terman argued for a broad interpretation and maintained that sound and motion-picture engineers, dealing with electronic transmission of information, were eligible for membership and promotion within IRE. W. W. Lindsay Jr., of General Service Studio in Hollywood, had been informed by IRE Secretary Harold Westman that there was constitutional objection to his promotion to the grade of Fellow in the IRE due to Lindsay's employment in the motion-picture industry. Lindsay had previously been chief engineer at Sennett Gilfillan's large radio receiver manufactory in Los Angeles and continued to consult on radio and audio problems after he entered engineering in the motion-picture industry. Gilfillan and Terman both wrote in protest to Westman, and Terman urged the IRE membership committee and the IRE board to make a more "reasonable interpretation," stating that audio circuits in motion-picture projection, television tubes, and electron optics were all part of radio engineering.[185]

In the same year, Terman advised Westman that undergraduate students majoring in sciences such as physics certainly ought to be allowed to join IRE as student members and not be penalized because there was no engineering major at their college. "My own feeling is," he wrote, "that the connection between radio and physics is just as close as between radio and engineering."[186]

Terman's successful efforts to arrange joint AIEE–IRE sessions at Pacific Coast meetings and his enrollment of student members attracted so much notice that he was nominated in 1939 for the position of vice president of IRE for 1940 and elected in November 1939.[187] This was the second step in his ascendancy within IRE. Outgoing IRE President R. A. Heising of Bell Labs congratulated Fred on his outstanding work in raising student membership in IRE.[188] President Lawrence Horle appointed Vice President Terman to four IRE national committees: admissions, awards, membership, and standards.

Fred took membership to be his major task.[189] With his customary energy, he continued his efforts to increase overall membership, and especially to increase student membership. Student members of the IRE had tended to constitute about 5 percent of the total IRE membership. Terman's years as active membership organizer raised student membership from 314 in 1938, to 399 in 1939, to 596 in 1940, and 950 in 1941, a rise in percentage of total membership from 5.8 to 13.6.[190] As was his style, he sent out many letters, collected data, and wrote reports explaining his plans for increasing membership among students and university faculty.[191] He agreed also with faculty that it might be best to have one overall student electrical engineers' club at a given university, and let the students choose at graduation whether to join AIEE or IRE.[192] This, in fact, occurred at Stanford University where student electrical engineering majors enjoyed a "joint AIEE–IRE Student Chapter" until the AIEE and IRE joined to form the Institute of Electrical and Electronics Engineers (IEEE) in 1963. Fred also went after broadcast radio engineers and others who were technically identical to IRE members. He engineered a survey of IRE members during his vice presidency, asking for the technical field preferences of members and for interest in practical, technical, and theoretical articles.

All members of the board, with the exception of Fred, were located within three hundred miles from the New York City offices of IRE. Fred could only attend two or three of the ten meetings of the twenty-one-member IRE board during 1940, but he energetically worked on membership and arranging meeting sessions.

Not surprisingly, IRE Vice President Terman expected to climb the third step, to president of IRE. That had been a common path, with the exception that some vice presidents elected from foreign countries were viewed more as honorary officers. In preparing for this step, Terman thought ahead about asking for a sabbatical leave from Stanford for part of the year 1941 so that he could attend the IRE board meetings more frequently. (The difficulty of attending the monthly board meetings had long been one of the excuses for not having elected previously any IRE president from beyond the East Coast.) Normally, the IRE board discussed and chose the annual slate of nominees for officers in the spring, with ballots sent out to members in late summer and the results tallied and announced at a board meeting in November. Those elected took office during the winter IRE meetings in January. The IRE board consisted of seven officers: president, vice president, treasurer, secretary, editor, and the two immediate past presidents. Normally, only the president and vice president were elected for one-year terms. The board also appointed five directors for two-year terms, and the membership elected another nine directors also for two-year terms. The director's terms were staggered.

Terman was surprised and disappointed when he learned that the nominations committee presented not his name but that of GE executive W. R. G. Baker as their nominee for president for 1941. Walter Baker had been comparatively inactive as an IRE member, had done little with the Connecticut section when he was chairman there, and had no previous experience on the IRE board. He had been appointed a director for 1940, but seldom attended the meetings even though he lived in nearby Connecticut. Baker had begun work at GE, after earning his BA ('16) and MA ('18) in electrical engineering from Tufts College; from 1929 to 1935, Baker was a production manager and then vice president at RCA. When he returned to GE in 1935, he rose in management, in charge of radio and television manufacturing at both GE's Bridgeport and Schenectady plants.[193] Baker was known mainly for his efforts with the Radio Manufacturers' Association (RMA) and was seen as an industrial engineering manager and manufacturer's agent by the more technical IRE types.

Thinking about his chances, Terman wrote to his friend Melville Eastham, president of General Radio and treasurer of IRE, on April 1, 1940. Since it was common for the vice president to advance to the nomination of president, he could tell the board that if elected he would attend five to six of the ten board meetings and would visit all of the IRE sections and many universities during the year. He would apply for a long-overdue sabbatical from Stanford for the months from December through March. (The IRE board didn't normally meet during the summer.) Since no one west of Rochester, New York, had ever been president of the IRE, Terman asked Eastham if would it be presumptuous of him to ask Eastham to mention to the nominating committee that he would very seriously serve IRE if nominated and elected.

Terman had guessed that the nominating committee would meet in late April, but Terman's letter to Eastham arrived the day of the nominations committee meeting and Eastham had no opportunity to speak with committee members.[194] He heard, however, that Terman's name was second on the list and felt that if the committee had known of Fred's intentions to be in New York part of the year, things might have been different.[195] Harold Westman then wrote Terman, announcing that Fred had been nominated to the slate of six candidates for director.[196] IRE board member and former IRE president Haraden Pratt, the vice president and chief engineer of Mackay Radio, also wrote Fred. He had known Terman for years, since the days when Pratt was with Mackay out in the San Francisco Bay Area. He was outraged, he said, and saw the Baker nomination as part of a move by the Radio Manufacturers' Association to get further power within the IRE. The fall IRE meeting in Rochester, New York, had been a troublesome thing to plan with the RMA, and Baker had been point man for the RMA. Some members, particularly academics, continued to complain about the domination of the Rochester meeting by the "manufacturing group."[197] Baker's actions with the RMA continued to be a sticking point with some board members in later years.[198]

Pratt revealed to Terman that some board members told him the nomination committee was packed for Baker and the nomination was made only a couple of hours before the board's vote later the same day. Pratt, and some board members for whom he spoke, felt that Baker joined organizations primarily for what he could make of it for himself, and secondarily for his company, GE. In Pratt's view, Baker had previously done no service for the IRE (perhaps a harsh judgment) and had done no service on the board. Pratt felt the minority on the IRE board who favored the RMA positions "rather than the side of the IRE" had been more vocal, and he therefore proposed that Terman agree to have his name placed as a petition candidate. There evidently *were* divisions on the board, as Pratt suggested, for H. M. Turner of Yale wrote Terman later that year about hoping to keep Eastham on the board since he was "entirely acceptable to both groups."[199]

Terman had not been in recent correspondence with Pratt, for Pratt had just learned from Westman that Terman would have been able to spend several months in New York if elected. Pratt suspected that Terman's name was going to appear on several petitions arising from disgruntled members. It would be better, he suggested, if Terman as vice president, from the West Coast, were to be put forward by a West Coast petition, and the movement could then spread eastward. Finally, Pratt felt that Terman would represent the high standards of the IRE, still held by those such as A. N. Goldsmith, founding member and editor of the IRE *Proceedings*. He strongly urged Terman to accept the strategy.[200]

After discussing the idea with friends, Terman accepted. He chose Noel Eldred, IRE San Francisco section head, to run the show out west. Eldred, too, had said it would be best for the move to start out west but to end back east, so that

Terman would seem not to be merely a California native son. Terman asked Eldred to work with Pratt to make sure the petition, or petitions, having at least thirty-five signatures arrived at IRE headquarters before August 15, as called for by the IRE constitution. Terman then reiterated to Pratt his plans to attend more than half the board meetings and to visit nearly all of the sections and many university groups during his elected year.[201]

Terman's supporters worked hard to get the petitions signed and sent to IRE headquarters in time. Secretary Westman said nothing about their receipt in early August and kept them in a safe until near the deadline. He then presented them to the board. There was some unhappiness on the part of Virgil M. Graham of Sylvania and several other supporters of Baker, but everything was legal.[202] Pratt reported to Fred that at the board meeting, Graham, Horle, Baker, and H. A. Wheeler were on one side, while Fred's supporters appeared to be Pratt, Heising, L. P. Wheeler, F. R. Llewellyn, B. J. Thompson, F. R. Lack, A. F. Van Dyck, and H. M. Turner.[203] A ballot was mailed to members in mid-August, and when the votes were tallied on October 29, 1940, Fred Terman was the winner with 65 percent of the votes cast, winning 1,179 votes to Baker's 623.[204] Fred won by a three to two margin in the Fellows and Members grades of membership, and by a more than two to one margin in the (younger) Associates grade.[205]

Fred received the usual letters and telegrams of congratulations. He arrived in New York in early 1941 and moved into a hotel a couple of blocks from the IRE offices at 330 West 42th Street. His first meeting with IRE staff as president went well, but he had misgivings about the staff, especially about Harold Westman.[206] Fred had been tipped by Pratt that some of the directors were unhappy with the way the office was run. Fred had had his own worries several years earlier when, for example, Bill Hansen's rhumbatron cavity resonator paper was rejected by a referee, a process overseen by Westman. Soon after Fred entered into the office routine, he encountered what he considered a sarcastic or hostile attitude from Westman. He discovered correspondence that had been unanswered for months, and that IRE revenues from advertising were dropping.[207] Low advertising income was a reason Westman had given him back in 1938 when Westman wanted Fred to cut drastically the length of his important paper with Bob Buss, Bill Hewlett, and Clark Cahill.[208] Terman also remembered the sting in his western pride when Westman had told him that the IRE often had foreigners as vice presidents, and a Californian was about the same thing.[209] As Fred would find out, it would be difficult to remove Westman from his position.

Terman worked hard and attended six of the eleven board meetings held during his presidency.[210] He continued to push for membership increase and tried to increase the efficiency of the office work. Fred's efforts paid off in significantly increased memberships and in an increase among important groups, such as college faculty. He also introduced the device of waiving "entrance fees" for faculty applying for membership.[211] An interested faculty member, he believed, was worth a lot in attracting students to the IRE.

Fred worked to increase revenues to IRE. One way was to reduce the number of those dropping from membership rolls due to nonpayment of dues. Fred found that previously, only one dues notice was sent. He increased this to four notices, and the number of exiting members lessened noticeably. Fred also composed a report to prove that the IRE was not losing money by having student members. Another problem was the small and decreasing revenue from advertising in the *Proceedings* and in meeting programs. For this, he turned to Melville Eastham and General Radio for help. Eastham managed quietly to loan one of his employees, John M. Clayton, to IRE for eight months for advertising management. Eastham and Fred did this quietly because they were afraid other companies would be upset if they knew the IRE advertising was being directed by a rival's advertising man. Clayton worked part-time without charge to IRE and completely rearranged things. Clayton stirred up operations, wrote to many companies and individuals thanking them for their work, and opened new avenues for the IRE.[212] After a few months, he recommended a new advertising man, William C. Copp, to become IRE's advertising manager and predicted that revenues from ads should increase by 100 percent.[213] Copp was more conservative in his estimates of the potential increase than Clayton, but in Copp's first months on the job, ad revenues went up by 65 percent.[214] Overall, the IRE's total assets at the start of Fred's term were $95,698. A year later, on December 31, 1941, they were $108,797.[215]

Early in his term of office, Fred's friend R. A. Heising, a past president and longtime IRE board member, presented a report on things wrong with IRE in terms of leadership and management. Having consulted with Alfred Goldsmith and Terman, Heising compared the management practices of other scientific organizations with that of IRE. Heising stated that at this time, the IRE leadership "is haphazard, difficult, and poorly planned. . . . The President has no duties or powers in management according to our Constitution; and the Board as a whole is incapable of proper management." Changes recommended by Heising, including an increase in the power of the president and establishment of a six-man executive committee, were passed unanimously by the IRE board in April 1941.[216] Heising's actions were a victory for Fred's attempt to improve management of the IRE.

Another introduction by Fred was a President's State of the IRE speech, giving the members a full report on events of the year and changes planned for the future. Fred's successor as IRE president, RCA executive Arthur F. Van Dyck, agreed fully with him on this innovation.[217]

Fred and others noted that IRE seemed to avoid appointing or electing non-East Coast residents to the board. In his search through the records, Fred found that only two directors in the history of IRE had come from the Midwest

(Chicago, Wisconsin) with one from Toronto while the only "western" vice president before himself had come from Pittsburgh. In comparing IRE to other technical organizations such as AIEE, ASME (mechanical), AIME (mining), ACS (chemistry), APS (physics), and several other societies, Fred learned that in all cases, some directors were chosen for regional balance.[218] He argued for this during the year of his presidency and while he barely lost on getting the 75 percent vote needed to pass such a constitutional amendment, a similar proposal passed the IRE several years later.[219]

Another proposal Fred lost temporarily was the move to replace Harold Westman as secretary. He had amassed plenty of reasons for a change. In addition to the lack of response to members' correspondence, Westman seemed to have driven away some clerical help and, as Fred attested, delivered false or inaccurate reports to the board.[220] For example, Westman reported that the eight or ten IRE meetings held in New York during a year produced more articles for the *Proceedings* than all the 175 or so meetings held in other sections around the country. This was part of a repulse to Terman's idea to have regional directors. By searching through four years of issues of the *Proceedings*, Terman revealed that Westman's report was totally wrong. Westman, he noted, was nearly ignorant of goings-on in the sections, had not visited them, and had soured relations with numerous sections, especially with the Chicago section, second largest in the IRE.[221] Terman had been unable to ease Westman out during his year as president but achieved his goal a year later. Haraden Pratt wrote to Terman in June 1942, "The funeral chimes have definitely started to toll for our present secretary's job," and that reforming problems in the office with Westman was "like killing flies with your thumb."[222] Terman's successor as president, Arthur Van Dyck, aided by Pratt and other board members, managed to get Westman fully occupied helping with the war effort in the American Standards Association, at a $500 raise over his IRE salary. He was out of the IRE office by December 1942.[223] Haraden Pratt then took over as secretary in 1943, with a new understanding that the board secretary would be a nonpaying job, directing other, paid employees.

Fred did not hold a grudge against Walter Baker, the defeated candidate for IRE president. Six years later, Fred was approached to support Baker for presidency of the IRE for 1947. The RCA executive writing to Fred explained carefully that he had talked with Haraden Pratt and Alfred N. Goldsmith about Baker's work with the RMA and had discussed the same with Baker. Baker had been made chairman of a Radio Technical Planning Board (RTPB) in wartime 1943 in conjunction with the IRE and RMA, but then Baker had the RMA pull out of the deal, much to the disgust of the IRE.[224] In 1946, Baker admitted that he had been at fault in previous IRE–RMA matters and hoped that his nomination for IRE president would be an opportunity to rebuild relations between the two groups. After consulting with Pratt and learning of Baker's efforts on behalf of the IRE Building

Fund, Fred wrote back that he was delighted to find that the cleavages had been healed and he would wholeheartedly support Baker's nomination.[225]

Fred Terman spoke out to the membership on institute matters during his presidency and shared with his IRE brethren the feeling of the amazing expansion of the radio and electronic arts since the early 1920s. At the 1941 summer national meeting in Detroit, he gave a powerful address concerning the outstanding problems for the IRE and opportunities for service to the profession and to the country.[226] Speaking from the "hometown" of the internal combustion engine, Fred stated that the ultimate effect of radio techniques on national defense would be fully as important as that of the internal combustion engine. Frequency Modulation (FM) radio had its commercial beginning in broadcasting in 1941, and television would start commercial broadcasting before year's end. Either of these two developments alone would present a heavy load on the technical forces of the industry in normal times. Given the needs of national defense and the diversion of technical personnel, the IRE would be called on for great service.

Terman proceeded to outline the many ways in which radio and electronics would be involved in the armed forces. Developments are being applied, he said, which were closed books to all but a dozen men a year ago. (Here he was primarily referring to radar.) Another great challenge was the need now to substitute materials, find new materials, and reduce the use of other materials, to "make bricks without straw," as the Bible said. Referring to the RMA, Fred stated that "there is a feeling of regret abroad throughout the radio engineering field that a squabble should have developed involving the government and industry in the midst of our country's defense effort." Finally, Fred supported the technical standards necessary to serve the public with radio and suggested that just as the Radio Act of 1927 had been succeeded by the Communications Act of 1934, perhaps recent U.S. Senate hearings indicated that Congress would consider drafting a new act. He chided the writers of the Communications Act of 1934, for example, for meddling in specifications about the internal aspects of radio station design and control. It was evident to engineers that regulation of station performance should be restricted to specifications of external performance of the station. It should be the freedom of the engineer to design *how* the station achieved the performance standards required.

In his retirement speech as president at the IRE convention in New York in January 1942, Terman proudly noted that he had spent the equivalence of three to four months of full-time effort; he had traveled forty thousand miles on IRE business, at no charge to the institute, and had met with the executive committees of more than half of the institute's sections.[227] A year previously, the IRE *Proceedings* were two and a half months behind schedule and short of manuscript contributions. (Terman ascribed this to the fact that the journal's reputation for letting manuscripts sit unattended for months or more than a year had led to the decline of the journal in pages published.) The drop in size was compounded by a drop in advertising revenues. A. N. Goldsmith formed two special committees, increased the length of each issue, and got the issues in 1941 out on time. The journal also reached out its arms to the broadcast engineer, to include a wider range of articles, and increased the number of tutorial, summary, and review papers. The questionnaire received from IRE members concerning their journal preferences had aided the editorial committee to know, rather than guess, the needs and interests of members. Terman reviewed for the membership the history of the advertising management changes at IRE and reported that projected revenues for 1942 were 100 percent higher than revenues for 1940.

Terman also praised R. A. Heising's management and executive board changes to the IRE Constitution. Membership had risen by more than 15 percent, and for the first time in five years, a new *Membership Directory* would appear in spring 1942. Strong attention was being paid to students, while efforts were being made to improve relations with sections and to increase the members' satisfaction with their institute.

Terman briefly, yet somewhat frankly, addressed the problems previously existing with the IRE office staff and outlined changes made or planned. He noted that his effort to secure a system of regional directors had very narrowly failed (needing only eight more votes out of 1,600) in a constitutional amendment vote requiring a three-fourths majority. Finally, he praised his executive committee and the board of directors, and stated that never during his year as president had he been in disagreement with the majority of the board on any issue.

Fred Terman would serve the IRE and its successor, the IEEE, again in the future, and he would be rewarded with prizes and acclaim. One of the finest statements to Fred's energy and effectiveness is in a letter from Alfred N. Goldsmith, former student of Michael Pupin at Columbia before World War I, founding member of the IRE, and founding editor of the *Proceedings* in 1912. Goldsmith's life had been dedicated to efforts for the IRE. He wrote to Terman that among all the presidents of the IRE, "it is my conviction that you were one of the most outstanding. I regarded your energy, determination, willingness to work to the limit, and constructive analytical ability as among the finest contributions that have been made to the Institute during its history."[228]

The Search for a New President of Stanford

When Ray Lyman Wilbur told the Stanford trustees in mid-1939 that he hoped to retire soon, he had been Stanford's president for nearly a quarter of a century and a member of the Stanford community since his arrival as an undergraduate in 1892. Due to Stanford's ongoing problems in finding a successor, he agreed to stay on through the time of the half-century birthday of the university in fall 1941.[229]

Leland W. Cutler, president of the board, asked Wilbur to choose a five-person faculty committee to search for his successor. Selected were Lewis M. Terman of psychology, Eliot Blackwelder of mining, Edwin A. Cottrell of political science, with zoologist Charles V. Taylor as chairman and registrar J. Pearce Mitchell as secretary. Cutler chose a similar committee of trustees: businessmen W. Parmer Fuller Jr., C. O. G. Miller, and Stuart L. Rawlings, with attorney and judge M. C. Sloss, as vice chairman, Cutler as ex-officio member. As chair, he named Herbert C. Hoover.[230] Their first joint meeting was held on August 3, 1939.[231]

Soon after organizing, the trustees' committee requested the faculty committee to specify their desired qualifications of the next president of Stanford. Lewis Terman was perhaps the most outspoken in his draft, arguing for the scholarly brilliance of the successful candidate, for his ability to pick absolutely the best faculty members, and for Stanford to give pride of place to qualifications of graduate scholarship and research. The group as a whole, however, maintained a high and demanding vision. Speaking for the faculty group, Secretary Mitchell wrote to the trustees that the faculty committee recommended that the candidate be a man of the very highest scholarly attainments, preferably in one of "the basic fields," able to lead a university whose major emphasis should be placed on graduate instruction and basic research. In addition, the candidate should have sterling character, a healthy vigorous physique, be between the ages of thirty-five to fifty years, and have university administrative experience. The man should also be keenly alive to the social issues of his time and fully sympathetic with the place and purposes of a privately endowed American university.[232]

Letters went out in the fall of 1939 and names of nominees were received, along with comments about the obstacles to obtaining a good president. Edwin B. Wilson of Harvard's School of Public Health, for example, wrote to Lewis Terman and gave the details of presidents recently chosen for Harvard, Dartmouth, Yale, MIT, Brown, and Michigan. Wilson suggested that the grass is often greener inside one's own yard, and that one would do well to look within Stanford itself for an able man of about forty. If Harvard had kept on looking for an outside superman, they never would have found James B. Conant, he commented, one of a "dozen or twenty persons," very able men, and right under their noses.[233] By spring 1940, at least 254 candidates had been nominated, representing twenty-eight different universities and three foundations. Twenty-four of those names were from Stanford.[234]

Faculty committee members continued to write individually to inquire further about the nominations. The committees divided the more likely candidates into two lists: a First List of fifteen, and a Second List of twenty-three names.[235] This time, no name on the top two lists was a Stanford faculty member, trustee, or administrator. Herbert Hoover had introduced several names, including Warren Weaver, director of natural sciences at the Rockefeller Foundation, and E. S. Furniss, dean of the Graduate School at Yale. Blackwelder supported the candidacies of Arthur H. Compton, then physicist at the University of Chicago, and Robert Redfield, dean of the social sciences at Chicago. Cottrell supported Robert D. Calkins, chairman of the Economics Department at Berkeley, and M. M. Willey, dean and assistant to the president at Minnesota, among others.

In May 1940, Cottrell conducted a number of confidential interviews in New York, Pennsylvania, and Washington DC to inquire about the qualities of those who seemed to be among the leading candidates.[236] He sought advice from some forty people, many of them considered nominees themselves, including Vannevar Bush; Conant; Weaver; Detlev Bronk of Cornell; George R. Harrison of MIT; Archibald McLeish, the librarian of Congress; Karl T. Compton of MIT; and Robert M. Hutchins of Chicago. Cottrell returned with consensus opinions regarding the names of those on both lists. Names shifted: one or two had been added to the lists in the interim, while Cottrell's interviews suggested eliminating several names and adding another eight for consideration. Fifteen persons on the top lists stated that they would not consider a university presidency (including Vannevar Bush and Robert Redfield among the very top names, although Redfield did not absolutely close the door for a number of months;[237] Bush and Redfield had been scored by the committees as number one and two overall among the candidates). Others who eventually took themselves out of the running included Arthur Compton, Conant, and Hutchins.

Cottrell's East Coast interviews produced five items now viewed as "obstacles" to securing a good president for Stanford "at this time": wartime emergency positions would attract and hold the most outstanding scientists; Stanford's finances were well known as being too uncertain; Stanford's "overemphasis" on the scientific side would make it difficult to interest a social scientist; many of the men in the age group under consideration (about thirty-five to fifty years of age) were relatively inexperienced in higher administration; and finally, bringing a man from an eastern institution might be thought best for the trustees and the faculty but would not be very acceptable to the alumni of Stanford.[238]

A full year after beginning its search, Stanford's board still had no likely appointee for the presidency and was still compiling a solid short-list for president. Some who had been on the initial lists had changed locations—Bronk had moved to Pennsylvania, Calkins had been promoted to dean of business at Berkeley. Armed with a new active list of twelve candidates, the faculty committee asked Herbert Hoover on August 20, 1940, for a meeting of the combined committees in late September.[239]

In October 1940, William W. Hansen wrote letters to Chairman Herbert Hoover and to the faculty committee, very strongly nominating Fred Terman for president of Stanford.[240] Several days after, Felix Bloch and Charles V. Litton sent letters similarly nominating Fred Terman, as later did Harold F. Elliott.[241] Committee Secretary J. Pearce Mitchell notified Fred's father, Lewis, of the letters. Without as yet mentioning this correspondence to Fred, Lewis responded to Mitchell (and by letter also to all trustee and faculty committee members) that his son should not be considered for the presidency at this time in his career. He felt sure that Fred would agree.[242] Herbert Hoover was not enthused over any of the Stanford faculty men, Leland Cutler wrote Trustee Ira Lillick on April 1, 1941. Lillick responded that in a joint trustee-faculty committee discussion held on April 4, the Stanford faculty committee present unanimously considered Fred Terman as the top Stanford candidate over George Beadle, John Dodds, and "two others" from Stanford. Lewis Terman was the only faculty committee member absent from this meeting, but Edwin Cottrell passed on Lewis Terman's observation that perhaps Fred's strength was not able to stand up to the pressure.[243] A few days later, after some twenty months of searching and yet still no mutually satisfactory short list, Ray Lyman Wilbur wrote to Herbert Hoover: "Dear Bert: The more I study over that question the more I am inclined to think that we may have the answer in young Fred Terman, who is just forty-one years old. . . . There is no question about the fine quality of his brain, his unusual capacity, and his administrative ability." Wilbur added a note: "Bush can give you a recent impression of him from interviews. [Trustee] C. O. G. Miller asked me about him last night."[244] Nothing further came of Fred Terman's candidacy, however, except that Terman was mentioned in the local press as being spoken about as a candidate for the Stanford presidency.

It is difficult to explain the actions of Lewis Terman in presuming to speak for his son in declining a nomination for the presidency. In spite of the fact that Fred Terman did indeed have remaining eye problems, he had demonstrated the ability to work prodigiously and continuously for the fifteen years since his serious tubercular attack. Perhaps father Lewis knew of Herbert Hoover's lack of enthusiasm for any Stanford faculty member as candidate and wished to save Fred any embarrassment. From his letter of November 7, 1940, to J. Pearce Mitchell and the trustee and faculty committee members, it seems clear that Lewis had spoken for Fred without asking permission or informing Fred. Nevertheless, the statements from the faculty committee and letters of nomination reveal the strong reputation Fred Terman had made at Stanford and the support shown by senior faculty for Fred's leadership skills.

In the fall of 1941, Leland Cutler stepped down from the board presidency and was followed by Donald B. Tresidder (AB '19, MD '27, Stanford), currently president of the Yosemite Park and Curry Company and an active member of the board since 1939. Tresidder knew his most important task was to find a university president.

Tresidder interviewed advisors and potential candidates throughout 1942, while the two committees kept at their work. For example, Fred reported to his father with a very favorable assessment of Lee DuBridge, the former physicist and dean of liberal arts at Rochester, who had recently taken charge of "a large group of research physicists working at MIT on the radio short wave project."[245] But the five "obstacles" originally compiled by Cottrell would simply get worse as the year 1942 ended. In January 1943, the board came up with a creative solution and asked Tresidder to resign the board presidency to become president of Stanford.

Don Tresidder took office on September 1, 1943, but with no formal inauguration due to the war. Early in what would turn out to be an unexpectedly short-lived term in office, Tresidder adopted some of the advice he got from Stanford's faculty and from outside advisors. He altered the composition of the board of trustees, repositioned the university's treasurer, and looked to the Faculty Advisory Board for their advice.[246] But first, he had to deal with the impact of World War II on his campus.

The War Comes to Stanford

In August 1941, Stanford's faculty debated the question of intervention in Europe. In response, 176 professors signed a circulating petition that called for support of President Roosevelt's foreign policy and urging a strong defense against "the totalitarian menace." Stanford's favorite son, Herbert Hoover, as pacifist and isolationist as ever, was truly peeved. Hoover had been lobbying extensively for the creation of a new European relief program, patterned after his World War I Committee for the Relief of Belgium, to help countries already invaded by Germany. He was particularly embarrassed that opposition to his efforts had been voiced by faculty at Stanford's Food Research Institute, whose founding he himself had instigated. Hoover now responded to the faculty petition with his own survey of "the whole faculty," which proved, he announced, that the majority of Stanford's faculty disapproved of the petition and that their sentiment was to stay out of the war in Europe.[247]

Hoover's response offended a good number of influential members of the Stanford community, among them Lewis M. Terman and David L. Webster. A Stanford trustee had canvassed faculty about their personal opinions, using polling methods that were, at best, flawed and data that was misleading. (Hoover's questionnaire had been sent to eight hundred individuals at Stanford, including instructors, visiting and temporary faculty, secretaries, and librarians—Hoover did not disclose how many actually responded.) Privately, some asserted that Hoover's figures were deliberately falsified. Lewis Terman and his colleagues responded with a carefully designed poll, sent only to 483 members of the Academic Council and all others of full professorial rank. Of the 341 faculty responding, more than 80 percent approved the foreign policies of the Roosevelt administration.[248]

Mr. Hoover was not amused, but Lewis Terman was not easily shaken. Fred Terman stayed out of this debate. It was not his way of doing things. Instead, Fred paid close attention to the role his university and his profession could play in war preparedness.

The National Research Committee (NRC), the research arm of the National Academy of Sciences, was trying to arrange collaboration between university researchers and the military, but not doing an effective job of it. Terman's mentor, Vannevar Bush, now president of the Carnegie Institution and chair of the National Advisory Committee for Aeronautics (NACA), wanted to see the army and the navy involved in the process. The navy's efforts with radar had not drawn much support from Congress as yet; President Roosevelt sent a bill to Congress early in 1939 to build a second NACA research site at Moffett Field in Sunnyvale, California (built in 1931 for navy dirigibles), a few miles southeast of Palo Alto. Congress had passed over the plan until, after months of fighting in Europe, it was passed in the fall of 1939. Completed in the spring of 1940, the Ames Research Center adjoining Moffett Field would include several wind tunnels.

Bush, who also had chaired the NRC's engineering research committee, went to Franklin Roosevelt in June 1940 and persuaded the president to authorize a new research organization, the National Defense Research Committee. On June 14, 1940, Roosevelt announced that Vannevar Bush would head the new NDRC (Bush would also keep his job as chairman of NACA).[249] The NDRC would play a key role in organizing American scientists and engineers for the war effort, supervising such efforts as the Radiation Laboratory at MIT and the Harvard Radio Research Lab and projects to develop the proximity fuze (Johns Hopkins University), solid fuel rockets (Caltech), and the atomic bomb (the Manhattan Project).

Changes came quickly to the Stanford campus. It was clear that klystrons were going to be centrally involved in military radar devices. In the fall of 1940, Stanford's klystron research on campus and with Sperry Gyroscope was linked to similar efforts by Alfred Loomis and others at MIT and at GE, AT&T, and other industry manufacturers to form a Radiation Laboratory at MIT, essentially a lab to develop ultra-high-frequency radar for air defense. Several of Fred Terman's electrical engineering graduate students, including Ed Ginzton, Matt Lebenbaum, Myrl Stearns, and John Woodyard, already had left California with Sigurd and Russell Varian to go to Sperry's main labs in Long Island, New York.

Bill Hansen, planning a sabbatical year at MIT, was asked in early November 1940 if he, too, could come east as soon as possible. Hansen's Sperry colleagues, especially Hugh Willis, arranged for a Sperry fellowship for him at MIT, but the NDRC Radiation Lab overseers (including Willis, Alfred Loomis, E. O. Lawrence, and Ed Bowles) concluded that Hansen was too valuable for the war effort to allow him more than half-time at MIT. As a result, Hansen worked at Sperry on Long Island, while commuting to Cambridge to advise and give his celebrated series of lectures on the theory and practice of microwaves.

Terman, too, was already back east. With his administrative duties as president of the IRE, Fred Terman was in New York throughout much of 1941. He had also become affiliated with the NDRC that year and attended radar meetings at the Radiation Lab at MIT.

Also that fall, Terman's old friend W. L. Everitt of Ohio State headed up the NDRC new section on communications. He wrote Fred in confidence, listing all areas of communications of greatest interest to NDRC: aircraft warning and direction finding, mobile and aircraft antennas for low- to high-frequency use, speech encryption equipment for radio, and just about everything involving ultra-high-frequency receivers, transmitters, and measuring instruments. He asked for Stanford's help. Fred responded with the suggestion that the most applicable work was their klystron research, already underway with Sperry. In addition, his student Millett G. Morgan had invented a 3-MHz mobile antenna that might be of use.[250] Soon after, Everitt and the NDRC provided Stanford with $4,000, which Terman applied to Joseph Pettit's research on a radio compass/direction-finding antenna device (the subject of Pettit's Engineer's thesis and of his 1941 PhD dissertation).[251]

In the competition for U.S. defense research contracts, Stanford did not compete well with other top universities. In 1939, Vannevar Bush and James B. Conant of the NRC had sent an "urgent" request to Stanford for all kinds of data about research and manpower possibilities. As chairman of the Stanford National Emergency Committee, Dean Morris had fully and quickly complied, but almost a year passed with no word from Washington DC. The Electrical Engineering and Chemistry departments, and the Guggenheim Aeronautical Laboratory set up several contracts, but no other major work was offered to Stanford. The Physics Department in particular felt slighted. In March 1941, Morris wrote Terman for his advice. "What can I do," he asked, to increase Stanford's defense research activities?[252] Fred would try to see Bush in Washington, he responded, but he encouraged Morris to write to Bush and ask him directly whether the NRC had made any use of the data sent by Stanford. Perhaps it was wishful thinking, but Fred assured Morris that he did not think the situation was intentional, but rather the result of things not yet being very well organized. "The fellows close to Washington, and those on the inside," he told Morris, "are being overloaded on defense and the rest are under loaded or having no chance *at all*."[253]

Back on the Stanford campus, the Engineering and Physical Science departments began preparing for a wartime curriculum by planning a summer-quarter course schedule (to begin summer quarter 1941) that allowed entering freshmen and transfer juniors to accelerate their coursework so that they could graduate with the BA in three years.[254] Courses given during summer quarter were those required of most engineering or science majors, such as the introductory engineering courses and general math courses like calculus, advanced calculus, and differential equations, and advanced graduate research seminars.[255]

On December 11, 1941, four days after Pearl Harbor, Dean Morris (with Wilbur's support) announced to all engineering students that students could now substitute specialized technical courses in place of nonengineering electives formerly required in letters, social sciences, and sciences. For example, an undergraduate planning to specialize in electrical engineering communications might drop an introductory geology course and replace it with an advanced radio engineering one.[256]

By the fall of 1941, Fred Terman had enjoyed four busy years as executive head of the Electrical Engineering Department. He had extended the department's research arms to include ionospheric and radio wave propagation, electron tube design and construction, and applications of the klystron. He had added an important colleague to the department, Karl Spangenberg, who joined him in electronics research, and he had greatly increased the number of electrical engineering graduate student fellowships, the quality of the department's corps of students, and the number of students specializing in the field of communications. Terman's interest and success in seeking outside funding for the department led Dean Morris to place Fred at the front of a fund-raising program for the School of Engineering.

Terman's continually growing participation in professional activities, in both the American Institute of Electrical Engineers and the Institute of Radio Engineers, had led to his being named to the national board of directors of the IRE as vice president for 1940. In an exciting write-in campaign, Terman was elected IRE president for 1941. This experience not only gave him the opportunity to promote western engineers and engineering, but to spend the year making new contacts beyond Stanford and California.

With the coming of war, Terman knew that Stanford's engineers, especially those in radio and electronics, would be heavily involved both in instruction and directing of special courses and, if possible, in research projects. He also knew that Stanford University faced significant challenges in the search for a replacement for President Ray Lyman Wilbur. Although Terman himself was briefly talked about as a native-son candidate for the university presidency, his next job would be elsewhere: directing the government's important radar countermeasures program at Harvard.

As the year 1941 closed, Fred Terman, his father Lewis Terman, and a small group of influential faculty and trustees, were asked by Donald B. Tresidder, Stanford's young president of the board of trustees, to meet with him for a weekend of discussion about Stanford's plans for the future. What a weekend it would be.

CHAPTER FOUR

The Radio War

1941–1946

Fred Terman would long remember his four years as director of the Radio Research Laboratory as very special ones. His selection to head this secret government effort to develop radar countermeasures was hardly surprising. Serving as national president of the Institute of Radio Engineers in 1941, he had both a wide knowledge of radio engineering technology and of the pool of engineers and physicists available for the war effort. Planning, managing, and expediting the work of more than eight hundred employees, as well as overseeing a budget larger than Stanford's, did not completely divert his attention from Stanford, however. In 1946, he would bring back to the campus new management skills, valuable advice, new contacts across the country, and plans to revitalize Stanford's School of Engineering.

In fall 1941, however, Stanford faced another sort of predicament: how to fill the vacant presidency, follow Ray Lyman Wilbur's strong hand (but perhaps too long a hold), and move the Depression-wracked campus into a better frame of mind and body.

A Weekend at the Ahwahnee

On December 5, 1941, a Friday afternoon, Fred Terman, his father Lewis Terman, and a small group of senior faculty, alumni, and administrators from Stanford drove up in four autos to the Ahwahnee Hotel, the massive log resort in the Sierras managed by Donald B. Tresidder. Tresidder, president of the Yosemite Park and Curry Company, was incoming president of Stanford's board of trustees and had invited the group and several trustees up to the Ahwahnee for a weekend to talk about the university's future.

The Ahwahnee, with its forty-foot-high-ceilinged dining room, was an impressive place. The building of Ahwahnee in 1927 was a keynote of Tresidder's management of the company's Yosemite facilities. In addition to its camping and entertainment facilities, the Curry family's holdings now included a miniature golf course, an ice-skating rink, and a toboggan slide. The first ski school in the West had been established near the Ahwahnee, moving later to nearby Badger Pass. Prominent West Coast families, including those of Herbert Hoover and Stanford president Ray Lyman Wilbur, vacationed there, and California's prestigious Bohemian Club (Tresidder had been a member for some years) entertained at the Ahwahnee and had held encampments in the valley.

Like his friend Fred Terman, Tresidder was an Indiana native and Stanford alumnus (BA '19, MD '27). Six years older than Fred, Tresidder had spent time in the army air corps in flight training during the First World War before finishing his undergraduate degree. He had met Mary Curry at Stanford and had worked for "Pop" Curry while finishing medical school. After their marriage, Tresidder decided to stay with the family company rather than practice medicine.

Tresidder, aged forty-seven in 1941, was the board's youngest and one of its most energetic members. His fourteen colleagues were elderly men, few of them under sixty-five when Tresidder joined the board in 1939. Ten of the fifteen had served for more than fifteen years. One, Joseph D. Grant, had been appointed by Leland Stanford in 1891. When San Francisco businessman Frank P. Deering passed away in May 1939, Tresidder was elected. (Between 1939 and 1941, few members proved to be as committed to the university's welfare.) Both President Wilbur and Herbert Hoover, a member of the board since 1912, admired Tresidder, and when the board's presidency came open in 1941, they recruited the young man for the position. Before accepting nomination, Tresidder presented several conditions: the board must be reorganized with term limits of ten years for the board's president, and required retirement of members at age seventy; he also insisted that a woman be elected to the board. Elected unanimously in the fall of 1941, Tresidder's term of office was scheduled to begin January 22, 1942, but his number-one task could not wait. Stanford needed to find a new president. President Wilbur, reaching the required retirement age of sixty-five, had announced his intention in 1940 to retire during Stanford's golden anniversary year, 1941. The anniversary celebrations were over, and as the year ended, the board of trustees had yet to appoint a suitable successor.

Tresidder hoped his weekend getaway session at the Ahwahnee that December would draw out opinions of key faculty, trustees, and alumni about Stanford's prospects. Attorney George A. Ditz ('11, JD '13) drove up from Stockton. A second car came from Los Angeles, bringing Stanford's general secretary, Paul R. Davis ('22, EE, '23) and Louis H. Roseberry ('03), a prominent Southern California banker and state senator. Professors Fred Terman and Lewis Terman drove over from the Bay Area with speech and drama professor Hubert C. Heffner and Morgan A. Gunst ('09), a prominent San Francisco realtor. Yet another car from Stanford brought Davis's assistant, David M. Jacobson ('30, LLB '34), and Paul C. Edwards ('06), associate editor of the *San Francisco News*, George F. Morell ('30), publisher of the *Palo Alto Times*, and Alvin C. Eurich, professor of education.

Except for Lewis Terman, clearly the senior in rank and experience among the attending faculty, the group consisted of men who, with two exceptions, had long been associated with the university but whom Tresidder now wished to more fully involve in university planning as well as fund-raising. Just as he hoped to reorganize and revitalize the trustees, Tresidder looked ahead to a new manner of university.

Tresidder hoped to further encourage volunteer fund-raising efforts while integrating fund-raising more fully into university management. Davis and Jacobson had been active as alumni volunteers before joining the administration. Davis, appointed in 1937 as Stanford's first professional development officer as director of the Stanford Fund, had been promoted to general secretary earlier in 1941 and had energetically and successfully reorganized the Stanford Associates, the highly influential group of alumni brought together in 1934 by Wilbur and Dr. Harry B. Reynolds to bring Stanford out of the Depression's financial doldrums. Jacobson served as Davis's assistant at the Stanford Fund. Gunst and Roseberry, key leaders of the Special Gifts Committee, were credited with pinning down $22 million in gifts and promised bequests. Late in 1941, Edwards had succeeded Ditz as president of the Stanford Associates.[1]

These were men of influence with a future in Stanford affairs. Three of the alumni would soon join the ranks of the trustees: Ditz in August 1942, Morell in June 1944, and Edwards in October 1943. In 1942, Gunst and Roseberry would chair the Stanford Fund's Committee on Special Gifts, Trusts, and Bequests. Eurich had been at Stanford only since 1939, but along with Fred Terman, had been mentioned as possible candidates for Wilbur's successor.[2] Tresidder would appoint Eurich university vice president and Fred Terman dean of engineering, both in 1944. Heffner, although only in his third year of service at Stanford, was to head an exceptional-student program, inspired by Lewis Terman. For his part in these discussions, Lewis Terman already had queried more than a dozen senior faculty at Stanford in law, history, education, psychology, physics, and biology for their suggestions about Stanford's needs. (Most asked for better faculty and better students, stressing quality over quantity.[3])

Dress was ordered as "informal, sport type indicated. Include your red flannels and change of shoes." Afternoons were free, and dinner was served in the elegant dining room. Any light-hearted frolicking was secondary, however, to discussions that began Saturday morning, 9 AM, presided over by Paul Edwards, and continued after dinner. Topics included the nature of the exceptional student and the progress of competing universities, to a plan for Stanford's future. A spirited discussion after dinner turned to the topic: "The ideal gift-supported university at Palo Alto."[4]

Sunday's planned small-group discussions were canceled, however, when the participants learned of events in the Hawaiian Islands. While the group met in the Tresidders' apartment for breakfast, a member of the Janss family, friends of the Tresidders, telephoned from Los Angeles to tell them to turn on the radio "right away." As Al Eurich later recalled, "We turned it on—and of course it was Pearl Harbor. And we all silently walked out of the meeting to our cars and drove home."[5] Tresidder's discussions about the university's future would continue on a later day.

Pearl Harbor changed not only Fred Terman's plans for the weekend, but his plans for the next four years. In an initial search for a successor to President Wilbur, both Terman and Eurich had been suggested by colleagues. Fred was mentioned in the press as an "unwilling dark horse" for the presidency.[6] Terman, like many of his colleagues, favored his PhD advisor, Vannevar Bush, who had subsequently become dean of engineering and vice president of MIT.[7] As president of the Carnegie Institution of Washington since January 1939, Bush was well known at Stanford because he had visited the Carnegie's Division of Plant Biology, headquartered on the Stanford campus since 1928. In 1941, he became the nation's most influential scientist. As head of the federal government's Office of Scientific Research and Development (OSRD), he was the technical head of all the nation's scientific efforts in military applications.

Bush declined Tresidder's invitation to be considered for the Stanford presidency, however. In his opinion, both Herbert Hoover and Ray Lyman Wilbur continued to have too much influence. Stanford, he regretted, was a university drifting without much vision. Tresidder would continue through much of 1942 to develop a list of candidates for Stanford's presidency. By January 1943, the board was frustrated in its search—those who suited Stanford's newly ambitious plans were, like Bush, unavailable due to war efforts—and turned to the man who had shown both vision and commitment: Donald B. Tresidder stepped down from the board and was inaugurated Stanford's fourth president September 1, 1943.[8]

Meanwhile, within a few days following the initial Ahwahnee conference, Lloyd Berkner, an influential advisor to the navy on radio and electronics and a friend of Fred Terman, met with Rear Admiral Julius A. Furer, the navy's head of research and development. They discussed the urgent need for the U.S. military, especially the navy, to establish a major effort in radio and radar countermeasures (RCM), that is, identification of frequencies used by the enemy for radio and radar; to develop methods to defeat or eliminate enemy usage of radar; and to consider ways to protect Allied radar free from enemy countermeasures. Soon after, Furer asked the National Defense Research Committee (NDRC) to set up a unit for RCM, with the backing of Berkner's bureau.[9] Before the month was out, the navy and NDRC had agreed that NDRC would establish a countermeasures research and development group.[10]

Fall-quarter exams had just ended at Stanford, and Fred Terman planned to head east after Christmas for the annual winter meeting of the Institute of Radio Engineers (IRE) in New York City, scheduled for January 12–14, 1942, where he would deliver his address as the society's retiring president.[11] It had been an eventful year for the society. As IRE president, Fred had spent a considerable amount of time in the Washington–New York–Boston corridor, including at least six trips to New York for IRE board meetings.[12] While on the East Coast in September and again in November, he had also taken the opportunity to discuss Stanford's NDRC radio research contracts and to meet with colleagues at the Sperry Gyroscope Company.[13] Little did he know that he would soon be moving to the East Coast to direct the U.S. effort in radar countermeasures.

The Radio Background to Radar

Radar is said to be the invention that won World War II. The name *radar* is an acronym for *ra*dio *d*etection *a*nd *r*anging. This name was adopted in 1940 by the U.S. Navy and by the U.S. Army in 1942. The British began using the term in 1943 in place of RDF, or radio direction finding.[14] Used as early as 1939 during the German air strikes over Britain, radar was continually used until the last days of American bombing raids over Japan in mid-1945. Radar was used as offense and defense, night and day. In the air, it proved vital in bombing raids and air reconnaissance missions to locate and attack land sites as well as submarines and other enemy naval vessels. On the ground, it was used to defend against air attack as a warning device, and to aim anti-aircraft guns, searchlights, and coastal artillery batteries. At sea, radar could be used against airplanes, surface ships, submarines, and shore targets.

Since the beginning of radio transmissions in the late nineteenth century, "countermeasures" had been explored for use in both military and commercial operations. In a general sense, radar was used by Heinrich Hertz in 1887–88 to confirm experimentally the electromagnetic theory of James Clerk Maxwell. Hertz sent ultrashort radio waves, generated by a spark gap, reflecting them off a metal target back to his source. Radio's possibilities were quickly grasped by military and commercial interest. So, too, was "jamming," or interfering with others' use of radio transmission. Newsmen used jamming to stop the transmission of competing news reporters covering an important 1901 yacht race and, more significantly, in the Russo-Japanese War in 1904–5. Initially, one could simply turn on a transmitter to block out another's reception through the airwaves, but countermeasures became more sophisticated during World War I when they were used to listen in on enemy radio communications and telephone conversations.

Following the widespread adoption of the vacuum tube and crystal oscillator in the early 1920s, commercial radio expanded dramatically when broadcasting was established in the United States and Europe. Most broadcasting stations operated in frequency ranges around 1 MHz or less. Broadcasting journals appeared, radio companies were formed to supply the public, and the radio boom was on. Even French perfumes were sold in bottles made to resemble vacuum tubes. As radio use grew, more users experienced interesting and often bothersome phenomena: atmospherics (also called "strays" or X's); fading (also called "swinging" and "deviating"); and "skip" distance and "dead" zones within which some radio stations could not be received. The study of these phenomena became of great importance to both amateurs and professionals, commercial and governmental. The astonishing long distances obtained in radio communication, plus these three types of phenomena, led some to think again about the postulated Kennelly-Heaviside reflecting layer and the possibility of its role in radio wave propagation. The search to verify the existence of this layer (an early name for the "ionosphere") was one of the precursors to methods of radar.

Between 1913 and 1915, Leonard Fuller (who became Stanford's first PhD in electrical engineering in 1919) and Lee de Forest of Palo Alto noted that radio transmissions between San Francisco and Hawaii seemed to suffer fading differences depending on slight changes in frequency. They suggested that these might be explained by destructive and constructive interference between the earth's surface and an ionized layer in the upper atmosphere.[15] In 1925, an Englishman, Edward Appleton, and Miles Barnett, Appleton's student, performed the same type of tests at Cambridge University as Fuller and de Forest, except at a higher frequency and over a shorter distance, slowly varying the frequency of the transmitter and recording its strength as received at a distance about one hundred miles away. They argued that the results could be accounted for if there were an ionized layer somewhere about sixty miles above the earth that bent the waves back down to earth.[16]

A few months later, Gregory Breit at the Carnegie Institution of Washington and his PhD student Merle Tuve, independently demonstrated the same thing by using techniques of what would later become pulsed radar. Assisted by A. Hoyt Taylor and others at the Naval Research Laboratory, they pulsed a navy transmitter at 4.2 MHz, and received the direct pulse propagated over the ground; about a millisecond later, the pulse reflected off the ionosphere.[17] Thus, they both *detected*, and *ranged* by *radio*, the definition of radar even though the target detected was huge and the ranging crude. Breit and Tuve viewed their results on a mechanical oscillograph and photographed the data. Their pulse-echo method was to be greatly improved in the next fifteen years and radar would go to much higher frequencies, with much greater power and resultant marvelously better target discrimination.

Henry Guerlac, MIT Radiation Laboratory historian, writes that "radar was developed by men who were familiar with the ionospheric work and the methods involved. It was a relatively straightforward adaptation for military purposes of a widely known scientific technique."[18] Perhaps things were not as straightforward as Guerlac thought. Many others had the idea of using radio waves reflected off of airplanes to help in air navigation.[19] Interfering reflections when river boats or airplanes passed through the radio beam suggested this idea to researchers at the Naval Research Laboratory in Washington as early as 1922 and to other investigators in Germany, England, Italy, Japan, France, the USSR, and the Netherlands. Work seriously began on radar in the early to mid-1930s in several countries, when numerous problems were encountered. For example, the power returned from a radar target decreases as the 4th power of the distance, thus tremendous power was needed in terms of what was then possible. The radar pulses were not very short, thus higher average powers were used, and the long pulse length limited the distance discrimination. Whereas the ionospheric regions above the earth are a nearly continuous target, a single airplane could not be detected more than a few miles away. The early attempts at radar were on wavelengths of the orders of five to forty meters and antennas functioning well at these wavelengths themselves had to be very large. Moving the antenna to track a target only worsened the problem. When frequency was increased, thereby decreasing the radio wavelength to the order of centimeters, rather than meters, antennas could be made much smaller, but now the problem became the limitation of frequency and power output of the transmitting vacuum tubes used and the noise sensitivity of the receiving tubes. A magnetron tube invented in 1921 by A. W. Hull of General Electric promised to work at extremely high frequencies, but early magnetrons put out very little power and were not tunable in frequency. Glass triode or tetrode vacuum tubes also failed to work well at very high frequencies because the actual length of the leads and wires within the tubes became of critical significance in tube operation.

In the 1930s, Eitel and McCullough (EIMAC) in San Bruno, California, built special-purpose high-power vacuum tubes that worked well to wavelengths of about one meter. General Electric and Westinghouse developed tiny tubes with very short internal leads. Similar efforts in Germany, the Netherlands, and elsewhere produced tubes and equipment that allowed a number of nations to develop radars working from about 30 MHz (ten meters wavelength) up to more than 1,000 MHz (some centimeters wavelength) but these were effective only at the lower frequencies because the equipment operating at the higher frequencies put out powers of only about a watt. By the mid-1930s, new circuits were designed that could produce short pulses of a few microseconds. The shorter the pulse, the wider the frequency band of the emission. Thus radio and radar receivers had to be designed that could accept wide-band, short pulses. Early ionosphere sets and some early radar separated the transmitter and receivers, using separate antennas to keep the transmitted pulses from overloading the receivers. Devices, "duplexers" or "TR" switches, were needed to allow sharing of the same antenna, while blocking the transmitted pulse from overloading the receiver.

The klystron tube, invented at Stanford by a team led by William W. Hansen and Russell and Sigurd Varian, promised to work extremely well at very short (microwave) wavelengths. The klystron was tunable in frequency but, as yet, could not produce much power. The klystron was the first tube actually to make use of electron transit time. In earlier tube designs, transit time was a nuisance that was minimized but had to be endured. It was Russell Varian's genius that conceived of the "bunching" principle to exploit electron transit time.

By 1939, the British clearly had taken the lead in radar development. It was a matter of survival. Until the Battle of Britain in the summer and fall of 1940, the existence of British radar was almost completely unknown to researchers in other countries. Early British radar used tubes developed by the British Broadcasting Company for high-power short-wave broadcasting, good up to frequencies of about 50 MHz. This early British radar operated at frequencies of about 30 MHz and although rather crude, the British were far ahead of others in completing a radar *system*. That system went into full force against German air attacks over Britain and discouraged further German plans for invasion.

As with the Americans, early British ideas about radar came from radio men who had backgrounds in ionosphere research. Edward Appleton became interested in radio as a young military officer in World War I. He returned to Cambridge University eager to develop the physics of vacuum tubes. As a faculty member, he joined with Robert Watson Watt in 1922 in a research project at the National Physical Laboratory. Their aim was to determine the source and causes of radio static. This work boosted the careers of both Appleton and Watt and led them into ionospheric research. They continued with circuit and electronic work as part of their research into the ionosphere. For example, Appleton and his student Geoffrey Builder developed a "squegger" circuit for the ionospheric pulsing transmitter that was later used in producing short radar pulses. Appleton later directed the British Department of Scientific and Industrial Research during World War II. He was knighted in 1941 and received the Nobel Prize in Physics in 1947 for his ionospheric research.[20] Appleton was less involved in early British radar efforts than Watt. Watt (he chose the hyphenated surname Watson-Watt only on receiving his British knighthood in 1942) early realized the usefulness of the electronic oscillograph, the "oscilloscope," and improved it for use in ionospheric data presentation. This early work led to the adoption of the oscilloscope in numerous physical data displays, including radar.

Growing fear of enemy attack led the British to strengthen their air force in the mid-1930s, although they did not do this very quickly or effectively. W. Wimperis, then director of Scientific Research for the British Air Ministry, suggested a committee be formed to study air defense. A secret committee was formed in January 1935, chaired by Henry Tizard, rector of the Imperial College of Science and Technology in London; its members included P. M. S. Blackett (future Nobel Prize winner for physics) from University of London, and A. V. Hill, Nobel Prize winner in physiology and secretary of the Royal Society, along with Wimperis and his deputy, A. P. Rowe. Before the committee's first meeting, Wimperis queried Robert Watson Watt about the possibility of a "death ray" that could be aimed at an approaching airplane. Watt had been superintendent of all radio work at the National Physical Laboratory since 1922. Watt, with his colleague A. F. Wilkins, calculated that no such death ray was possible, but suggested that a radio-detecting system might be developed. At the committee's request, Watt and Wilkins calculated in more detail the possibilities and estimated that a bomber with a wingspan of twenty-five meters could be detected at ranges of ten miles and altitude of twenty thousand feet using the present state of radio technology. Watt proposed taking over intact "the present technique of echo-sounding of the ionosphere." He suggested using a cathode ray tube to present the data, as presently used on the ionospheric measurements, but warned that the pulse lengths would have to be very considerably shortened from the 200 microsecond pulses he was then using. The calculations turned out so favorably, Watt wrote, that he was nervous he had dropped a decimal point (though this would not pose insurmountable difficulties).[21]

The first "Chain Home" (CH) British radar station was demonstrated in 1937, and by September 1939, the British had seventeen stations along the east and south coasts. The number increased to fifty by the end of World War II. These CH stations operated in the frequency range 20–30 MHz, with one main frequency and a second back-up frequency as an aid against countermeasures jamming. Each station had three or four 360-foot steel transmitting towers and four 240-foot wooden receiving towers. The transmitters pulsed at 25 or 12.5 pulses per second with a 20-microsecond pulse length and radiated a peak power of 350 or more kilowatts. The pulse rate was chosen to be a subharmonic of the 50-cycle mains power supply. Each CH station had its own specific frequency of operation. The receiving antennas could be switched in and out to determine direction and height. Antenna patterns were calibrated for each station by flying aircraft through the beam patterns. Several antijamming techniques could be utilized, including randomly changing the pulse rate frequency, putting narrow band and "notch" filtering into the receivers, and using special zinc cadmium sulphide "long afterglow" cathode ray tubes in the oscilloscopes. In the early years of the war, the information at each CH station was manually plotted and tracked locally on a grid-referenced plotting board. This information was then telephoned into a central filter room where the information was collated, analyzed, and fed to the fighter control networks for the British defending aircraft. During the war, the system was enlarged and numerous improvements and automation were added. Women operators played a major part in the information gathering and analyzing in this system.[22]

Preparing for U.S. Radar Countermeasures

Merle Tuve, E. O. Hulburt, E. O. Lawrence, and Lloyd Berkner (all about Terman's age) grew up on the Minnesota and Dakota plains, and just like young Fred Terman, they each had constructed ham radio spark sets. These men all were to play important roles in U.S. scientific research during World War II.

Lloyd Berkner grew up in Perth, North Dakota, and Sleepy Eye, Minnesota, and received his bachelor's degree in electrical engineering from the University of Minnesota in 1927.[23] Commissioned an ensign in naval aviation in 1927, Berkner put his boyhood interest in radio and airplanes to work for a year at the navy's Bureau of Ships installing aviation radio equipment. Between 1928 and 1930, he accompanied Admiral Richard Byrd as radio engineer on Byrd's first Antarctic Expedition. Berkner subsequently joined the National Bureau of Standards in Washington DC and began developing sounding pulse ionospheric equipment to study upper-atmosphere ionization and radio propagation conditions. The economic woes of the Depression forced the Bureau of Standards to lay off a number of its technical employees, Berkner among them, and Berkner moved to the Department of Terrestrial Magnetism (DTM) of the Carnegie Institution of Washington in 1933 where he continued his work on the ionosphere. When T. R. Gilliland at the Bureau of Standards developed the world's first automatic frequency-scanning ionospheric recorder in 1934, Berkner improved this equipment. In the next several years, in an important series of experiments and installations, Berkner installed ionospheric-sounding equipment on the magnetic equator at Huancayo, Peru, in the Australian desert at Watheroo, and on the Arctic Circle near Fairbanks, Alaska.[24]

Berkner's connections with Stanford had been established when E. R. Bramhall, a 1926 Stanford graduate in electrical engineering and a professor of physics at the University of Alaska, took over operation of Berkner's ionospheric equipment in Alaska. Berkner then came to learn of Terman's interests in ionospheric research. Terman began ionospheric experiments in 1937, in connection with the theoretical work of Norris Bradbury of Stanford's Physics Department.[25] Subsequently, Terman was asked by the National Bureau of Standards to construct and operate a more elaborate ionospheric sounder at Stanford. Fred had tried to establish a radio propagation laboratory at Stanford as early as 1929, but due to the budget constraints brought on by the first years of the Depression, his plans for building a field station remained on paper.[26] Work began again on ideas for a radio propagation field site when Terman became chair of the Electrical Engineering Department in 1937. That spring, Terman began preliminary ionospheric radio sounding experiments from a room in the basement of the Ryan High-Voltage Lab where he installed a wide-band antenna system. O. G. "Mike" Villard Jr., assisted by another student, R. A. "Bob" Helliwell, would take over construction and operation of the ionospheric recorder in 1941 and manage an NDRC research contract arranged through Berkner.

Berkner subsequently arranged this research contract with Stanford to provide multifrequency recordings of the ionospheric electron density distribution as a function of height and to record these data several times a day and send the results to Washington.[27]

Between the DTM-Carnegie and the Bureau of Standards, the United States had a network of seven cooperating ionospheric stations at various latitudes and longitudes by 1941, including the set at Stanford. This network would prove most useful to planning radio communications usage during World War II, as it had already been valuable to the National Broadcasting System in issuing regular public "radio weather maps" worldwide to assist radio users in choosing appropriate times and frequencies for operation.[28]

These several years of Terman and Berkner's friendship, along with Terman's national reputation in radio engineering, brought Terman's name into play in plans for U.S. countermeasures. At Berkner's suggestion, Admiral Furer arranged a meeting on December 27, 1941, with NDRC to discuss the necessity of establishing a radar countermeasures unit. The committee recommended the immediate establishment of such a unit, initially to be within the organization of the Radiation Laboratory at the Massachusetts Institute of Technology. Led by Lee DuBridge, formerly head of the University of Rochester's Physics Department, the secret radar laboratory was called simply the Radiation Laboratory (or Rad Lab) in part to camouflage its real activities. The Rad Lab, set up in October 1940, had already grown to nearly five hundred employees by Christmas 1941 (it would reach nearly four thousand at its peak later in the war).

There already had been some activity within the lab concerning countermeasures, mostly involving the development of a search receiver, that is, a receiver with a broad frequency range of reception and a bandwidth wide enough to pass the radar pulses to be received. Since the Rad Lab centered its work on microwaves, their preliminary work on a search receiver also was aimed at the microwave region. This early Rad Lab work was the charge of Luis Alvarez, already a noted physicist. At the University of California, Alvarez had worked with Stanford's Felix Bloch and Bill Hansen on both microwave matters and cyclotron physics. At the Rad Lab, Alvarez worked on a ground-controlled landing system and on microwave antennas before transferring in 1943 to the atomic bomb project at Los Alamos. (Alvarez later won the Nobel Prize in Physics, as did two other future physics Nobel laureates who worked with Terman's Radio Research Laboratory, Felix Bloch and John Van Vleck.)

Another influential figure at the Rad Lab was Melville Eastham, president of General Radio (GR). One of Fred Terman's strong supporters at the IRE, Eastham was treasurer of the IRE board and a member of the board for several years both before and during Terman's terms as vice president and president. During Terman's presidency, Eastham had donated the efforts of John Clayton, a GR advertising manager, to help Terman improve advertising at IRE. Eastham contributed his efforts to the Rad Lab, and his organizational and strategic advice was much valued. Born in Oregon in 1885, Eastham had begun in business in 1905 making X-ray machines and radio components in New York and Boston. Moving to Cambridge, he expanded his business, making high-voltage coils, capacitors, crystal detectors, and other radio components. The U.S. Bureau of Standards and similar laboratories in Europe had been organized around 1900 to bring order to the maze of varying standards in electrical apparatus, and within a few years excellent and precise instruments were available for the direct-current and alternating-current power industries. By 1915, Eastham realized the need for measuring instruments in the radio field and established the General Radio Company. (The word "radio," rather new then, meant essentially what "electronics" would come to mean twenty years later.) As radio broadcasting grew rapidly in the 1920s, radio manufacturers were among GR's best customers. Some of GR's best-known instruments were the first commercial vacuum tube voltmeter (1928), the first commercial primary frequency standard (1929), the famous GR 650-A impedance bridge (1933), and the first complete oscilloscope commercially marketed (1934). A patent for an R-C oscillator, issued to GR in 1939, was licensed in 1940 to Hewlett-Packard (HP), a new firm in Palo Alto, California, and became a basis for their first instrument, the HP 200 Audio Oscillator. (With a few neat tricks, HP's resultant design produced an oscillator that sold for about one-sixth of the price of GR's audio oscillator.) Several of GR's field-strength and signal-generating instruments in modified form would become central equipment in products developed by the new Radio Research Laboratory, placed in thousands of aircraft and ships. In addition to bringing new instruments to the market, Eastham brought a new employment philosophy, somewhat like the firm of Carl Zeiss in Jena, Germany. As far as possible, there would be no layoffs or shutdowns at GR, and profits would be shared among stockholders, management, *and* employees. Melville Eastham was awarded the IRE Medal of Honor in 1937. Although he had little formal schooling, his main philanthropic interest was MIT. For his immense role in helping the Rad Lab and RRL during World War II, he was awarded the United States Medal for Merit in 1948.[29]

Terman's last IRE meeting as president was set for the end of the second week in January 1942 in New York. On December 28, the day after the NDRC meeting, DuBridge telephoned Terman in California, then preparing for his trip east, to tell him about a new secret project and Terman's candidacy for the post of director.[30] Fred wanted a few days to think it over, but planned his trip east to include several days at the Rad Lab and a day in New York to consult with Bill Hansen, then on leave to develop the klystron tube at Sperry Gyroscope in Garden City, New York, who delayed his own return to Stanford to talk with Terman.[31]

Bill Hansen and Fred Terman had been friends since Hansen, like Fred, had returned to Stanford from graduate work at MIT as a young faculty member to teach at his alma mater. The two had collaborated on research on radio antennas and had a joint patent-filing agreement. They worked together to provide Stanford with increased funds and equipment for physics and engineering. They shared both a friendship and an intense loyalty to Stanford.

If there was anyone with whom Fred Terman would want to talk about the proposed job of heading radar countermeasures it would be Bill Hansen. Hansen had hoped to spend the 1940–41 sabbatical year with I. I. Rabi at Columbia University, but when Rabi couldn't come up with the needed funds, Edward L. Bowles enthusiastically offered Hansen a visiting position in electrical engineering at MIT where he would teach one course each semester during the 1940–41 academic year (a course on klystrons and an advanced course on cavity resonators and boundary value problems). The organization of the Rad Lab at MIT in October 1940, however, changed all these plans. Alfred Loomis had first set up his microwave committee (which would in turn become the Rad Lab, then Division 14 of NDRC) in July 1940 with three associates: Ralph Bown, assistant director of research at Bell Telephone Labs; Edward Bowles of MIT; and Hugh H. Willis of the Sperry Gyroscope Company. Willis was Hansen's boss at Sperry. There was no question in their minds about the value of Bill Hansen to the U.S. effort in microwaves. Hansen had designed for Loomis some of the first microwave equipment to function at Loomis's research quarters at Tuxedo Park, New York, and had been a key advisor to Loomis on microwave transmitters, receivers, and antennas. (Luis Alvarez later claimed that Loomis was the first customer for Sperry's version of the Varian-Hansen klystron, arriving at Sperry's San Carlos, California, shop with checkbook in hand.[32])

It was then decided that Hansen would stay at Sperry instead of going to MIT; Sperry, however, gave MIT a fellowship so that Hansen could travel to Cambridge frequently to consult and to give what would become his famous series of lectures on the theory and practice of electromagnetic phenomena and microwaves. Hansen's lectures, given from November 1940 through December 1945 and compiled into three unpublished mimeographed volumes, were dubbed a veritable bible. "Hansen created the role of microwave electronics."[33]

After talking with Hansen and DuBridge, Fred telegrammed Stanford Engineering Dean Samuel Morris, who was then in Washington DC, from New York on January 5: "Acceptance war job probable but would like to discuss with you before becoming finally committed."[34] Morris responded positively and also noted that Vannevar Bush had written to President Wilbur to ask that Terman be granted leave from Stanford. There were too many physicists at the Rad Lab, Bush told Morris, and a few more engineers would be good for it. Bush also hoped to bring university men from around the country so that research would be stimulated at their various universities on their return.[35]

Fred was, in fact, already committed to the job. The navy and NDRC meeting on December 27, 1941, produced a proposal, effective January 1942, listing Dr. Frederick E. Terman of Stanford as the official investigator. (He had been a consultant to NDRC since June 1941.) Fred had started making notes in his room at the Statler Hotel in Boston with advice from Melville Eastham and continued the notes during his ten days in New York at the IRE meetings.[36] He also conferred with Ralph Bown, who had just returned from a fact-finding mission in England in December. Although his official appointment letters would arrive in the months to come, Fred Terman returned briefly to Stanford to arrange his transition but took over as radar countermeasures boss for NDRC in the first week of January 1942.[37]

The proposal (No. 030642-B of the National Defense Research Committee, Microwave Section D-1) recommended that the NDRC contract with MIT for the "Establishment of a Radar-Countermeasure Laboratory."

> Recently, at the insistence of the Navy, a program on Radar Countermeasures has been started under the leadership of Professor F. E. Terman of Stanford University. In order to get this project underway and to take advantage of the organizational background of the Radiation Laboratory, this project has been started at the Massachusetts Institute of Technology. Since it is desirable to separate from the Radiation Laboratory as many related activities as can be advantageously carried out in other places, and also, since the Radar Counter-Measures program is substantially different in character and in the interest of secrecy should be separate from the Radiation Laboratory, the Radar Counter-Measure project should be set up as a separate and distinct organization and its early removal from the framework of the Radiation Laboratory is to be encouraged.

Although Terman was listed as principal investigator, the project originated through the U.S. Navy and the office of Admiral J. A. Furer. The original project, slated to begin January 1, 1942, would terminate June 20, 1942. Those listed as being in on the discussion of the project were: K. T. Compton (head of NDRC and president of MIT), A. L. Loomis (head of NDRC's Division D), and E. L. Bowles, representing the NDRC; Admiral Furer and Commander Lloyd V. Berkner on the navy's behalf, and for the Rad Lab, Terman and the lab's head, L. A. DuBridge. Terman's lab orders were straightforward: "To establish a laboratory for research and development in the field of radar counter-measures, to supply apparatus to the Services, to assist in operational studies, and to report from time to time as requested. Amount $300,000. Classification: SECRET."[38]

Terman long believed it was Eastham who first suggested his name for the directorship, but Eastham denied this, perhaps facetiously. Luis Alvarez later claimed that it was he who had recommended Fred. Although he had not known Terman personally at that time, Alvarez knew of him as "the most distinguished academic radio engineer" in the country.[39] But since Lloyd Berkner knew Fred well (Terman's first pencil notes about whom to seek for advice on setting up the lab included Berkner) and had pushed Admiral Furer to establish a radio countermeasures lab, it is more likely that Berkner, Eastham, Alvarez, individually or in some combination, advocated Terman for the directorship. As the outgoing, and popular, president of the Institute of Radio Engineers, Terman was well known nationally as an engineer and educator, and author of the best-selling textbook on radio engineering. In addition, Fred had been Vannevar Bush's first PhD student at MIT, and Bush now was the overall head of the Office of Scientific Research and Development (OSRD) in charge of the entire U.S. civilian research effort, including what would become its two largest units, the Manhattan Project and the Radiation Laboratory. In an oral history interview late in life, Terman stated Lee DuBridge told him he was chosen because "you were well known among the electronics people; all the physicists knew you."[40] It was not true that all the physicists knew him, Terman then added, but it is likely that among his colleagues, Fred Terman seemed a logical selection.

In Terman's mind, his IRE experience proved especially important. He later wrote, "I feel confident that it was the exposure I received while president of the IRE, and the approval of my actions therewith was what pointed the finger in my direction when it came to selecting the leadership of this new laboratory." Before 1940, he wrote, his efforts had been in teaching, supervising student research, and writing books. "The IRE experience demonstrated that I also had a good administrative and management sense, and could handle difficult situations and personalities with considerable finesse."[41] Terman's first task was to recruit the best men and in sufficient quantity to run the RCM work, and as IRE president he had traveled some forty thousand miles (at his own expense) during 1941, visiting and talking with IRE chapters and universities across the country.[42]

With a well-received retiring president's speech at IRE behind him, Terman returned to Stanford. On the plane, he compiled notes about initial advice given him by Wheeler Loomis (no relation to Alfred Loomis), associate director of the Rad Lab and the former head of the Physics Department at the University of Illinois, by Berkner and others. He penciled in his own ideas for organizing the Radio Research Lab. And he got on with the job of recruiting. On the flight to Chicago, he sat next to a broadcast engineer he knew slightly. In chatting, Fred learned that a young engineer, John F. Byrne, might be interested in his new project. He knew that Byrne had taught with one of his best friends, Bill Everitt, head of electrical engineering at Ohio State where he had been a promising young faculty member. Byrne had since gone to Collins Radio Company in Cedar Rapids, Iowa, in broadcasting engineering but now was interested in changing his position. As soon as Fred returned to Stanford, he telephoned Byrne and offered him a position. Years later, Fred recalled his newfound ability to make expensive long-distance phone calls: He spent, he remembered, "about $40 or so on a long-distance call—of course, I could now charge it to these people, one of the things they'd said to do, you know, go right ahead, incur expenses, you'd get reimbursed for these." Byrne accepted and "was one of the first ones to turn up; he got back there in early February."[43] Even before leaving New York, Fred had talked with friends at the IRE meeting, among them Don Sinclair, a key figure at General Radio. (Back in 1934, Sinclair had written to Terman to ask whether a job was available at Stanford and had sent his résumé.[44]) Sinclair, then helping the Rad Lab with search receiver problems, would soon join Fred at RRL.

When she first heard the news of his new appointment from Fred in his January 5 telegram, Sibyl Terman was excited. "I'm dizzy. . . . I am sure you will be a great success."[45] At a faculty dinner party at Professor C. V. Taylor's, Dr. Russel Lee had said the war would be over within a year; others disagreed, Sibyl wrote. Already planning the family's move east, she added, "Maybe we will be back there till Frederick is through high school?" Young Fred was almost ready for high school, while Terence and little Lewis were in grade school. Terry was timid about changing schools, but all three boys looked forward to skis, skates, mittens, sleds, and snowshoes—everything one who lived in the snowy east might have. "Everything was topsy-turvy in those first weeks of the War," she wrote a week later, and went on to report that their friend Bill Hewlett had been over to the house to adjust a diathermy machine used in those days for treating illness. He had been called into the army, Bill told her, and was blue about being separated from his wife Flora. In less than two months, Hewlett was in the army. An avid skier, he had tried to join the U.S. Army Mountain Division ski troops but ended up instead as a first lieutenant in the signal corps stationed on the East Coast as an expediter.[46]

Once back at Stanford, Fred had only three weeks to prepare for his return to Cambridge. Fred began to line up current or former students. He talked by telephone with contacts on the West Coast and spent a half-day in Portland, Oregon, interviewing students from Oregon State and other Northwest campuses.[47] He placed his most valuable aide, Professor Hugh H. Skilling, in charge as acting head of the Electrical Engineering Department, a position Skilling would retain until 1946. Fred hurried back to Cambridge alone, with Sibyl and the children to follow a few weeks afterward.

The First Days for RCM

Terman spent much of his first months at RRL consulting with his many contacts. At his appointment, he had stressed to Alfred Loomis that the location of RRL should be very close to the Rad Lab so that he could consult with men such as W. W. Hansen and Donald Sinclair. Terman had telegrammed to Karl Compton suggesting that if Harvard refused to be the sole contractor for RRL, then perhaps Harvard would cosponsor. Loomis and Compton replied to Terman that they were working to ensure that James B. Conant would accept Harvard as the sponsor of RRL.[48]

Terman had already conferred with Ralph Bown of Bell at the New York IRE meetings about how to set up RRL. Bown suggested that RRL personnel ought to include a "sprinkling—10 to 20%—of smart hams" (amateur radio operators) engineers, plus a few physicists. (Ultimately, of approximately 225 technical staff at RRL at its full size, 102 were known to be current or former "hams."[49]) (See Appendix C.) Bown recommended that Fred choose two assistants, a right-hand man to get the lab and personnel organized and a technical collaborator. Fred soon after chose Roger Hickman and John Byrne for these initial positions. Bown also recommended that Fred and his yet-to-be-hired technical collaborator go to England for a three-week visit to study British RCM actions and needs.[50]

Terman was constantly traveling back and forth from the Rad Lab at Cambridge to Washington and cities in between. When he first arrived in Cambridge, he dined at the Commander Hotel where he would talk with Lee DuBridge, Luis Alvarez, and other Rad Lab people about projects. Very early on Fred asked both Wheeler Loomis, the Rad Lab manager, and Lloyd Berkner, "What do we need to do? What sorts of apparatus should we develop?" And each replied, "That's what we hired YOU for."[51]

As quickly as possible, Terman hoped to set up his new secret laboratory, recruit technical staff, meet with and learn to work with military and NDRC contacts, get his small staff moving full speed on interim countermeasures equipment design, and learn the most up-to-date information on radio, radar, and jamming. Finally, he had to find out exactly what his country's defense researchers needed to know about these techniques and "dark sciences," and how best to learn these things during his upcoming trip to England.

It also was decided by higher authorities that RRL work would generally be kept secret from Rad Lab staff, as well as outsiders, but RRL would have access to Rad Lab; that is, the radar people would not know what countermeasures might be doing, but the Rad Lab was expected to help if consulted and lend facilities, especially in the beginning months.

To determine programmatic needs, Terman sought advice from Lloyd Berkner, Wheeler Loomis, contacts at the navy's Bureau of Ships, Major James W. McRae of the signal corps, and Major George Haller of the army air force. McRae had earned a PhD from Caltech, had been at Bell Labs in managerial positions, and would return to Bell after World War II. Haller had a bachelor's degree in electrical engineering and a PhD in physics, both from Penn State. (After the war, he would return to Penn State as dean of the College of Chemistry and Physics, and later would become an executive with General Electric.) Terman explored ways to get things done with Lt. Col. George Metcalf of the Office of the Army Chief Signal Officer, Ralph Clark of the navy's Bureau of Aeronautics, and Brigadier General Harold M. McClelland, chief of Army Air Corps Communications.[52]

During February and March 1942, Fred Terman was drinking information from a fire hose. Frank D. Lewis of NDRC (and scientific assistant to Secretary of War Henry Stimson) told Fred that by the end of summer 1942, search receivers for all frequencies would be needed—one thousand receivers for use in the Pacific and two hundred in the Atlantic.[53] In April 1941, the NDRC Section C had met to consider work on communications jamming. This group included representatives from the navy, Bell Labs, and RCA. Three months later, British military intelligence inquired about Bell Labs' study of selective versus "barrage" (wide-band) jamming of communications. Fred Terman was brought up-to-date on these matters in his first days at RRL as well as at the meetings of the Microwave Committee of Alfred Loomis, Lee DuBridge, Ed Bowles, and Ralph Bown—the committee that had spawned the Rad Lab. He got an overview on radar, radio beacons, blind-landing work, and new vacuum tubes. At the January committee meeting, chaired by Loomis, Fred learned that an equivalent of only one to two men at Rad Lab had been studying countermeasures, but that Fred was to get an entire floor of a new building to take over for the Rad Lab. In the meantime, Fred visited the army signal corps at Fort Monmouth, New Jersey, and the Naval Research Lab and the British military mission officers in Washington DC. British countermeasures work had been disclosed in a navy meeting in Washington on February 4, just two days before Fred arrived back east, and Fred was fully briefed on this as well. Lloyd Berkner impressed on Fred the impossibility of building RCM sets "from the ground up" in time to do any good. Equipment must be cabled together and modified from the existing state of the art, felt Berkner, in order to provide the ten RCM (radio countermeasures) sets needed to be installed on naval ships in less than a month (before late March).[54] Visiting Bell Labs in early March, Terman was told of the latest work in centimeter wave receivers and signal generators, and the pioneer antenna designer Harold Beverage coached him on new findings in centimeter wave propagation.[55]

Terman was also briefed by French radar expert E. Maurice Deloraine, who had recently escaped from the Germans. Deloraine had continued his radar research work in the United States for International Telegraph and Telephone (IT and T). On March 19, Terman received a briefing of Deloraine's research, including his contracts with IT&T for radar, search receivers, and radio-jamming techniques. Most interesting for Fred was Deloraine's observation that "there were no evidences of German radar in the 1940 campaign as evidenced by the fact that the Germans asked nothing about French radar while they made many inquiries about direction finders."[56] This somewhat misleading information about German radar would soon be corrected when Fred learned of the 53cm German Wurzburg radar captured by British commandos on February 27–28.

In spite of the intense activities at RRL, little was known specifically of the British radar and RCM work. While it was clear that the British were probably using some kind of electronic countermeasures themselves, it was not clear what they were. Nor did they know what the British had discovered about German radar. Terman knew that someone from RRL would have to find out firsthand what the British knew. Two events in February 1942 were to make this visit to Britain a certainty: the capture by British commandos of critical portions of a German radar during a daring and highly successful raid at Bruneval on the coast of France on February 27–28; and the use by the Germans of radar countermeasures in the successful escape up the English Channel by the German cruisers *Gneisenau* and *Scharnhorst* on February 11–12. The Bruneval raid took close-up photographs of and captured the important frequency-determining elements of a 560 MHz Wurzburg fire-control and tracking radar and also brought back a radar operator as prisoner. The *Gneisenau* and *Scharnhorst* escaped through cover of heavy German offensive radar jamming of British systems, shocking the British military authorities and forcing a reevaluation of British RCM tactics and equipment. The *Gneisenau* and *Scharnhorst* escape was termed by Sir Robert Cockburn as "perhaps the most important single incident in the early history of countermeasures."[57]

The RRL was expected to grow quickly. As ground rules for recruiting, he learned that he could not divert to RRL someone already at the Rad Lab or someone already promised for such work. Instead, he would use his contacts at universities and at companies. The majority of his research people would be engineers, although there would be some physicists (and, as it turned out, mathematicians, astronomers, and psychologists). Nearly all those Terman would end up recruiting were young (within three years of the lab's expansion, about 60 percent of his technical people were younger than thirty years of age).

RRL was initially a small group of people, however. Fred's notes for February 27, 1942, record his immediate plans for personnel: in addition to Fred, six persons on or before March 5—Roger W. Hickman, a Harvard University physicist (who had been a candidate for the Stanford electrical engineering position offered to Karl Spangenberg in 1937), would be Fred's RRL laboratory manager; N. Preston Breed, a Harvard administrator would be RRL business manager; John F. Byrne; Harold Elliott; Donald R. MacQuivey (BA '35, EE '39, MBA '42, Stanford); and, part-time, Donald Sinclair. Three more would arrive by April 5—Robert A. Soderman, recent electrical engineering graduate from Stanford (BA '40, EE '42); Roger Pierce; and George Hulstede (BA '26, EE '37, Stanford). Five more were expected in May or June, all graduate students—Wallace Caufield ('41), O. G. Villard Jr. (EE '43), and Donald Reynolds ('41), all from Stanford, plus Gordon McCouch and William Huggins. Fred had commitments from six to eight more, subject to release by their employers—Robert B. Barnes (Stanford '33) from NBC broadcasting; Paul Reedy from Purdue University; Joseph Pettit (EE '40, PhD '42, Stanford) from the University of California; William Edson from Illinois Tech; and several men from Philco Radio Corporation. He hoped also to grab some engineers from the noted engineering consulting firm Jansky and Bailey. Finally, to add to this crew of engineers, Fred needed physicists and a few men with Rad Lab experience. He had been promised the aid of Luis Alvarez, but his first hires also included two men seconded from the Rad Lab, Winfield W. "Win" Salisbury and Richard C. Raymond, both originally from Berkeley.[58] All of these early hires would become key people at RRL.

Win Salisbury had done his graduate work in physics at the University of Iowa and at the University of California at Berkeley. From 1928 until 1936 he worked as a consulting engineer in Hollywood for sound movies and audio recordings, but in 1937 he returned to Berkeley to work on the cyclotron projects, designing high-power, high-frequency amplifiers. In 1941, he went to the Rad Lab and a year later Lee DuBridge asked him to consider joining Fred Terman. Win became one of the group leaders at RRL. He contributed to countermeasures against glide bombs and to "chaff," but mainly developed the extremely high-power jamming transmitters known as "TUBA" and "Ground Cigar." Following the war, Salisbury had a varied and productive career both in industry and as a professor of electrical engineering at Berkeley.[59]

Dick Raymond had earned his PhD in physics at Berkeley in 1941 for cyclotron research. His friend Win Salisbury suggested he apply to the Rad Lab, and Raymond moved there in August 1941. As with Salisbury, Lee DuBridge asked Raymond if he would like to move to RRL, which he did on April 1, 1942. During his time at RRL, Raymond developed high-frequency and microwave wave meters and radar receivers for aircraft. He outfitted, and then participated in, missions with the electronic eavesdropping B-17 aircraft termed "Ferrets" flying out of North Africa.[60]

Canadian-born Don Sinclair had done his graduate work in electrical engineering at MIT. He joined General Radio while working on his PhD dissertation, and by 1940 Melville Eastham put Sinclair, still a Canadian citizen, in charge of General Radio's war effort. Eastham felt that GR might as well develop measuring instruments for ultra-high frequencies and microwaves, since there was, as yet, no equipment available commercially. Sinclair decided on a field-strength-measuring device that would go as high in frequency as could be done using available vacuum tubes. This field-strength meter basically consisted of a signal generator and a receiver. GR produced both, using the new Western Electric "doorknob" tubes that would work up to 3,000 MHz. The military became interested in the receiver, and it went into production just before Christmas 1941. Soon after, Don and Fred Terman talked at the January IRE meeting about Sinclair joining RRL. Don began as a halftime employee at RRL in charge of receiver development, with GR paying all of his salary as a contribution to the war effort. Later, he went on the first Ferret missions. Fred's first recruits for Don Sinclair's receiver group were two of his Stanford students, Bob Soderman and Wally Caufield. Two more of Fred's former students, Joseph Pettit and Matthew Lebenbaum, joined the receiver group soon after. Interestingly, Don Sinclair later became president of GR, and Joe Pettit would succeed Fred Terman as dean of engineering at Stanford (he later became president of the Georgia Institute of Technology).[61]

Among the forty or so Stanford students and faculty who ended up working for Fred Terman at RRL, Terman had an especially close personal relationship with Mike Villard. Although Earl Cullum, Clark Cahill, and Joe Pettit, among others, were more experienced, Villard was Terman's man for filling holes in dikes. Terman was especially skillful at evaluating students and colleagues alike. Villard became, in some ways, an extra set of eyes and ears at RRL for Terman in finding and fixing trouble spots; in some cases this made him an annoyance—or worse—to those in the trouble spot.

Villard was among the more junior staff, an English literature graduate of Yale who had gone to Stanford in 1938 as a graduate student and was still working on his Engineer degree when he joined the RRL in the summer of 1942. A Yale BA with honors in English literature might seem an odd entrance to a segue into radio engineering, but Villard—son of the noted New York publisher—had humored his father and kept his Yale radio activities to running a radio club there. Always looking for excellent students, Terman had visited Villard's family in New York City and at their rural Connecticut home to persuade Villard's father of the wisdom of allowing young Mike to come west to Stanford and take up a career in radio engineering. Villard senior relented, although Mike Villard later recalled that his father, extremely liberal politically, had worried, "You'll go west and get mixed up with those conservative engineers." In his first year at Stanford, 1938–39, Villard and a fellow student Cameron Pierce, as a gift to Stanford, built the radio-operating shack near the Ryan High-Voltage Lab in the Stanford hills. (This "ham" radio shack was in fact used for radio research as well as student activities for more than twenty years.) With the arrival of wartime and redeployment of Stanford faculty, Villard was made an instructor in electrical engineering at Stanford for the year 1941–42, even though he was still transforming himself into an engineer by piling undergraduate courses on top of graduate work.

When Villard joined RRL he was assigned to the group concerned with evaluating Allied radar and its vulnerability to enemy countermeasures, and he was soon made a project leader. He made the first complete analysis of vulnerability of a U.S.-made radar and discovered measures to minimize those weaknesses. Early in 1944, the Germans suddenly began to use "glide bombs" in the Mediterranean. Although defense against these was not really the responsibility of RRL, the laboratory urgently adapted for the navy thirty-five jamming units designed for Air Corps use. For several weeks, five to ten destroyers and destroyer escorts at a time were ordered into the Boston Navy Yard for installation of the jamming units and training of navy electronic ratings in their use. Villard took over this truly "crash" program. In July 1944, he was sent to England to investigate and correct the misplacement of quantities of countermeasures units that were not reaching the U.S. Air Corps bombing units. This, too, was a great achievement in Terman's eyes because Villard "was working largely on his own, in a foreign country without the resources of the Laboratory in Cambridge, Massachusetts, at his elbow." In 1946, Villard returned to Stanford and completed work toward his PhD in electrical engineering. He developed the first practical high-level system of single sideband radio and began a program of research on meteors and radio wave propagation. Villard would be Terman's first former student to be elected to the National Academy of Sciences.

What did these early RRL recruits see as the *immediate* task of countermeasures research? As they learned in extensive briefings with Terman at RRL, they had to develop suitable receivers capable of listening over a very broad range of frequencies to search for any enemy radar. They had to develop or modify these receivers for operation in aircraft and ships. They had to develop broadband antenna systems, including systems adaptable to different aircraft. They had to develop methods of recording the results of the receiver searches so that the information could be brought back to analysis centers. Finally, when they located enemy radar, they needed to design jamming transmitters or other countermeasures gear to disable the enemy equipment. This was the task in the first months of RRL, all the while living with intense security measures, moving from one building to another, and managing a quickly growing organization.

As Terman had hoped, Harvard took over RRL on March 21, 1942, though it was several months before RRL actually moved to Harvard.[62] Initially, Harvard was not particularly happy about getting RRL. There was some suggestion of other locations, including Tufts University, and even Stanford. Dr. Roger Hickman of Harvard's Physics Department claimed to have exerted considerable influence on Compton and Conant to choose Harvard.[63] Fred Terman wrote to his father that it took Compton a lot of arm-twisting to convince Conant to put RRL at Harvard.

Luis Alvarez had been overseeing the small RCM program at Rad Lab and served as a sort of consultant to Fred in that early period when RRL was physically located on the Rad Lab premises. And Bill Hansen came up from Sperry almost weekly to give that memorable series of lectures to Rad Lab staff. An example of Fred's use of these intellectual resources is in his notes of discussions with Alvarez and with Hansen in March 1942, concerning cavity resonators, oscilloscope data presentations, and ideas for receivers.[64]

It was clear to Berkner, DuBridge, and others that some senior RCM person would have to visit Britain for a closer look. But, at the same time that Fred was putting in sixteen-hour days setting up RRL and considering the probability of a Transatlantic trip, he had to get his family moved across the country and settled in the Cambridge area.

Getting Settled in Cambridge

On arriving in Cambridge February 6, 1942, Fred Terman moved temporarily into the Commander Hotel. Along with his RRL responsibilities, he located a possible rental home for his family. Dr. Arthur Paul Wakefield and his wife Olive Lindsay Wakefield resided at 75 Richardson Road in Belmont, Massachusetts, only about three miles from Harvard Square. Belmont, a community adjacent to Cambridge, was popular with Harvard's faculty. Dr. Wakefield was the physician in charge of Massachusetts state clinics for children and Olive Lindsay Wakefield, a sister of the famous American poet Vachel Lindsay, was a lecturer. Both Dr. and Mrs. Wakefield were the children of missionaries in China. Dr. Wakefield had died recently, however, and Olive, scheduled to go on a college poetry reading tour in April, was desperate to find tenants for the house. Friends quickly circulated letters, and thus Terman learned of the availability of the Wakefield house.[65] Mrs. Wakefield stipulated a six-month lease at $115 per month, with an option for another six months. The house had significant attractions: five bedrooms, a large 24-foot by 24-foot basement suitable for a playroom, an oil furnace, and a good backyard, although only smallish living and dining rooms and a small kitchen. It was next to a primary school, and not far from the junior high school. And, for the time being without a car, Fred could take a ten-minute bus ride to the campus, with a bus stop only two blocks away from the house.[66] Fred arranged for Sibyl, expected to arrive by March 11 by train, to examine the house on Richardson Road before signing a lease, however. (Sibyl had rented their Stanford house to three military officers and, with the children in tow, had left California.)

Fred Terman's family had had a comfortable trip east by comparison to many families attached to the military. Instead of heading directly east, Sibyl and the boys traveled to Boston by way of Los Angeles and Tucson. Heading south from Palo Alto, she found the drawing room on the *Daylight* was luxurious; their journey across the Southwest to Tucson, Arizona, on the *Argonaut*, was nice but cramped.

While stopping briefly in Tucson (a mere fifteen minutes), she visited with her sister Winnie. The food and drink were great all the way to New Orleans—young Lewis, she reported, ate lamb chops and ice cream twice a day. They stayed over a day in New Orleans, taking a long taxi ride around town and a boat ride on the Mississippi River. Reboarding, they had twin bedrooms to Washington DC. This was deluxe treatment. Officers' families traveling by train in early 1942 often failed to get sleeping accommodations, or found themselves bumped to lesser quarters, or were detoured with little warning.

On the train out of New Orleans, Lewis lectured an army lieutenant for one and a half hours on various military matters and described *in detail* the working of radio locators. A minor bump in the itinerary occurred when they missed getting off the train in time in Washington and rode on to the rail switchyard, but they took a taxi back to Washington where the boys enjoyed a day of sightseeing. In New York City, they stayed at the Taft Hotel and visited Sibyl's relatives in the New York area with time for more sightseeing. Sibyl did not arrive in time to view the house on Richardson Road, so Fred signed the lease, and when his family arrived in Boston several days later, he moved them to the Commander Hotel.

By the time Sibyl first viewed the Wakefield house on Richardson Road, the Termans expected the house to be cleaned and ready for them to move in. But Mrs. Wakefield "had hardly begun to pack," Sibyl complained, leaving "fifty years of accumulated junk." When Mrs. Wakefield left five days later, the attic, a closet, and the basement were jammed with her things. Sibyl, her first impressions already negative, found the kitchen too small, the dining room not to her liking, and the furniture old and dirty. Mrs. Wakefield continued to pose problems throughout the Termans' stay on Richardson Road. Arriving at the house, she would claim that Sibyl had taken a set of glasses, or towels, or a casserole dish. This continued for several months and was probably a result of Mrs. Wakefield's age and forgetfulness. Typically, Mrs. Wakefield would call after a few weeks to say that she had remembered having given the glasses, or towels, or whatnot to her daughter.[67]

Within two weeks, Sibyl was looking for a more suitable house. Shortly after her arrival, Sibyl and Fred were often entertained together. Sibyl was invited to tea by presidential wives Mrs. Karl Compton of MIT and Mrs. James Conant of Harvard.[68] She quickly realized her social responsibilities would be many. Fortunately, the Terman family belongings had arrived promptly from California, nearly all unbroken. However, her responsibilities as wife of the director of the RRL were more complex than her social obligations as the wife of the head of Stanford's relatively small Department of Electrical Engineering. Expecting to entertain all RRL personnel, by June 1942 numbering more than sixty, she determined to give coffees and tea parties. That fall, she was desperate to find coffee, she wrote her mother-in law, Anna Terman. Could Anna send her coffee in 3 or

10 lb. bags?[69] Early in their residence in Belmont, Fred and Sibyl found that cocktail parties "are the thing here," as Sibyl reported. She wrote to Anna that she did not have the vaguest idea what one bought to make cocktails, or how to prepare them.[70] As Mike Villard later noted:

> the Stanford campus prewar was completely dry and even use of alcohol by faculty in their homes was discouraged. When faculty entertained for graduate students it was at coffee and dessert parties. RRL grew so fast that parties to enable people to get to know people were essential. Terman, although initially a bit ill at ease, mastered the art of the cocktail party and these gatherings were a great success.[71]

"Winifred Elliott and I agree we have gone out more since we came here than in all the rest of our lives together," Sibyl commented. "Luckily I have a maid now." The Termans were both fortunate to have old friends at hand. For example, Winifred and her husband, Harold F. Elliott were among the first from Stanford to join Fred at RRL. Early in 1944, when Donald Tresidder visited Boston soon after taking office as president of Stanford, Terman gave him a tour of RRL and at a reception for Stanford RRL'ers, he introduced Tresidder to thirty-three Stanford people (including two women on the staff):[72]

Dr. F. E. Terman	Mr. W. R. Rambo	Mr. W. B. Wholey
Lt. E. M. Fryer	Mr. J. G. Stephenson	Mr. F. C. Cahill
Lt. R. E. Lyon	Mr. R. M. Heintz	Mr. R. S. O'Brien
Mr. H. F. Elliott	Mr. R. R. Buss	Mr. W. Y. Pan
Mr. O. G. Villard	Mr. P. P. Robbiano	Dr. E. A. Yunker
Mr. R. L. Hammett	Dr. Frances Wright Wrightson	Mr. D. K. Reynolds
Mr. D. R. MacQuivey	Dr. J. M. Pettit	Dr. F. Bloch
Mr. M. D. Hare	Dr. H. E. Overacker	Mr. R. B. Barnes
Mr. C. F. Otis	Mr. W. B. Caufield	Mr. R. L. Kirkwood
Mrs. C. F. Otis	Mr. M. T. Lebenbaum	Mr. W. E. Farrell
Mr. G. E. Hulstede	Mr. R. A. Soderman	Mr. P. L. Harbury

Sibyl tried to work out a series of teas, but by the spring of 1944, RRL had some eight hundred employees, living in more than twenty different towns in Massachusetts. Winifred Elliott helped her sort out address cards gathered for her by Fred's executive secretary at RRL, Miss Elizabeth Mudge.[73] That July she wrote to Anna, "I'm exhausted giving teas for Fred's RRL wives. Tomorrow they're going to elect a committee to run themselves."[74]

"Everything is just ducky here," Sibyl wrote her sister soon after arriving. "Fred is so busy, I don't see how he lives. . . . He is late to dinner all the time, has been in Washington twice since last Friday." Sibyl's first months in Cambridge were worrisome as well as busy. Fred expected to go to England on an intelligence mission to visit British research labs and military commands working on countermeasures. He would travel on an Allied convoy sailing from Montreal unless the two naval officers accompanying him could arrange passage on a bomber. This worried Sibyl since bomber passage was strenuous and uncomfortable in a high-flying, unpressurized, unheated compartment. She got Fred a set of long woolen underwear, but a few days before he was to leave, word came that someone else from the lab would make the mission in Fred's place. Shortly after, Bo (Terence), aged 11, came down with appendicitis. Rushed to Children's Hospital in Boston, Bo had his appendix removed but was given an anesthetic during the operation that made him sick all night. While Bo was still in the hospital, Fred learned he would go to England via Pan-American clipper. Two hours later he received a call that he would instead go by bomber and was to be in Washington by Monday morning. Sibyl rushed out before the stores closed to get Fred a warm hat (she equipped him with a fur coonskin cap without a tail, while the navy issued him a "tin" helmet.) By Sunday evening, Fred was on the train to Washington and on Monday morning Sibyl brought Bo home from the hospital.[75] Fred in fact left from Montreal, where he called Sibyl Tuesday night to report, through their own secret code, that he would be traveling on a luxury liner and would make stopovers. Fred cabled from Iceland a few days later, but a worried Sibyl would not hear from him for several days.[76]

The Atlantic Diary

Although out of communication with his family, Terman busily recorded the details of his trip in a diary.[77] He had left Washington at noon on Monday, flew to New York and then on to Montreal by late Tuesday afternoon. He was fortunate to be able to make the Atlantic crossing in a Boeing Stratoliner, not a bomber, with a senior TWA crew of nine instead of the usual six. The extra three were military: two radio men and an extra navigator. The five passengers included Terman, two navy countermeasures officers (Commander A. J. Detzer Jr. and Lt. Commander W. G. H. Finch), an airfield expert, and a Lockheed aviation consultant. Navy Commander Malcolm P. Hanson, a radio expert, had strongly advised Terman to travel as a civilian but under military auspices and suggested that he have at least a commander or army colonel accompany him because of information developed from previous U.S. civilian–British meetings. Commander Detzer and Lt. Commander Finch were not mere tinsel dressing on this trip; they would have important roles in RCM throughout the war.

The plane landed first at a large brand-new field at Presque Isle, Maine, which had been a potato field six months earlier, then at Goose Bay, Labrador, where Fred took note of yet another huge airfield under construction. Both fields were part of the new effort to ferry aircraft and supplies by air to Europe. On Wednesday morning, with the temperature at -4F, they left for Greenland and arrived at "West Blouie No. 8," a field on Sondvestrom Fjord, Greenland. They disembarked on the snow-packed Arctic Circle runway and met the local base commander, the famous pilot Captain Bernt Balchen, who had been Richard Byrd's command pilot on flights to both the North and South Poles back in the 1920s. They had to stay over because Iceland was socked in with bad weather. Fred had long since donned his long underwear, coonskin cap, and gloves and an insulated flying suit. While waiting, Fred met the U.S. consul for Greenland, James Kedzie Penfield, Stanford '29. On Friday morning, they left in -10F weather bound for Reykjavik. Reaching fifteen thousand feet, Fred carefully noted that some of the passengers felt woozy in the unpressurized cabin but that he was feeling fine. The flight arrived at Reykjavik in time for Fred to send a short cable to Sibyl, and he marveled at the size of the military contingent there: twenty thousand U.S. troops, sixty merchant vessels in the harbor, naval vessels outside, a twenty-ship convoy due into port. He met a Norwegian officer, he noted, who owned a copy of his *Radio Engineering*. By Saturday, April 18, they were on their way to Prestwick, Scotland, where they had to clear customs. He was surprised when the customs agent asked him if he was related to the "intelligence Terman." On the way to London, they came down with engine trouble and landed at the RAF base at Shrewsbury, about 125 miles from London. Fred and the other passengers continued on in two British Hudson transports (baggage in one plane, passengers in the other) but the pilot of Fred's plane brought it down near Oxford due to darkness. Fred continued to London by car and caught up with his baggage in London about 1 AM on Sunday April 19. He telegrammed to Sibyl that day: "Arrived London Today. Trip without excitement but unusually interesting. Inform my office. Love."[78]

Fred was prepared to report to the British the Americans' plans for radio countermeasures. The week before his trip, Fred had met with Roger Hickman, his associate director, and his group heads at RRL, and he had relayed the meeting's results to a group of Columbia Broadcasting System engineers who were planning to join RRL efforts. Terman's laboratory plans were coming together.

At Fred's staff meeting just before leaving for England, U.S. RCM plans were:[79]

1. Development of sources of information, including gathering all U.S. and British intelligence reports and analyzing them, although it was suspected that information gathered would be slight. As part of this process, one or two men should be sent to England as soon as possible.
2. Work would continue on developing the General Radio search receiver and redesigning it for single-dial control, giving it a motor-driven sweep frequency, extend its frequency range beyond 3,000 MHz, and make it lighter and more compact. They would develop also a tunable centimeter wavelength receiver and develop methods of quickly and simply analyzing radar signals, including pulse length, pulse character, and a way of presenting or automatically recording these data.

3. Explore theoretically and practically the design of antennas for search receivers, including wide-band systems, and directional and nondirectional systems.
4. Develop monitoring and early-warning systems to provide continuous visual detection of wide bands. The Naval Research Lab was working on frequencies below 600 MHz and RRL would concentrate on higher frequencies. This would require research on crystal detectors and wide-band video amplifiers.
5. Jamming transmitters, frequency modulating and noise generating. Both conventional tubes and Litton Company high-power tubes to be used for frequencies up to 600 MHz, and above this, Sloan-Marshall or klystron tubes should be applied. In addition, systems for confusing enemy radars (re-radiation of pulses, and so on) and protection of our own equipment against countermeasures should be developed.
6. Finally, various measures for jamming long-range navigation systems, communication systems, and IFF (identification-friend-or-foe) systems should be studied and theoretical problems of noise theory, sensitivity of entire systems, and so on should be undertaken.

The report noted that neither the U.S. Army nor the Navy seemed as yet to have evolved a complete program for gathering information, analyzing, and utilizing it. With great foresight, the report concluded, "It is apparent that one of the most important functions that the RCM group can serve is to assist in devising an operational program that will give full information regarding enemy radio activities, and insure that this information properly interpreted reaches those planning military operations."[80] With this preparation, Terman, Detzer, and Finch began their visits to British radar and RCM centers.

Fred's first site visit was to the Dover area on April 22. Here he observed several CH and CHL radar stations (CHL, for "Chain Home Low," was the 200 MHz supplemental radar that provided better coverage at low-elevation angles, thus detecting planes at further distance or planes coming in at very low altitudes). He took careful and extensive notes regarding each type of receiver and jamming transmitter setup and details of antennas, recording equipment, and the like. The first "search" receiver used by the British, a regular Hallicrafters S-27 "ham" radio receiver purchased in the United States, was observed in use as backup. Search receivers were in use from very low frequencies up to 3,000 MHz. He noted that jamming transmitters at the Dover Straits sites would soon be increased to twenty for each of the four stations. The Germans were already changing their radar transmission frequencies 3 to 5 percent when "jammed" by the British, thus the British would utilize "barrage" jamming, blocking out an entire band to disable the German anti-aircraft radars. He also noted American troops installing new American 50-centimeter radars.

The various stations he visited differed somewhat, indicating the British scramble to enlarge and update their radar protection network. The following week, on April 30, Fred visited Haslemere, the radar research station for the British Admiralty, where the navy worked both on jamming and search receivers. He found the Haslemere site the second most rewarding of his dozen or so visits, from the standpoint of radar countermeasures information. The jamming transmitters used at Dover, British Type 91 at 300–600 MHz, had been developed here. Fred took extremely detailed notes concerning British receiver design, circuit peculiarities, antenna feeds, hand-filed ganged camshafts for tuning, motor-driven swept frequency receivers, balloon-borne receivers, and direction finders.

On May 7, Sir Frank Gill hosted a luncheon for Fred with Britain's most distinguished scientist-military advisors, including Charles G. Darwin (Charles Darwin's grandson and a mathematical physicist), director of the National Physical Laboratory; Sir Edward Appleton, director of the Department of Scientific and Industrial Research; Sir Robert Watson-Watt; Charles S. Wright, director of Scientific Research, the Admiralty; Sir Frank Smith, director of Telecommunications, Ministry of Aircraft Production; Sir Henry Tizard; and several others.[81]

He also visited the British General Electric Company and the Marconi Wireless Research Center at Great Baddow, where the brilliant Thomas L. Eckersley (a grandson of Thomas Henry Huxley, the ardent defender of Charles Darwin) was devising long-distance radar location techniques using what would later be called ionospheric backscatter propagation models. Terman found Eckersley's methods in practice not very convincing. (In what could perhaps only happen in Britain, Thomas Eckersley's brother, Captain P. P. Eckersley, was formerly chief engineer for the BBC, while their sister had made propaganda broadcasts for the Nazis.) Fred also visited the Admiralty Signal School at Portsmouth, where he saw Dr. John D. Cockcroft (later to win the Nobel Prize in Physics in 1951), and had special sessions with others on such topics as British Window ("chaff"), radar jamming in use in the North African campaign, details of the Bruneval commando raid, and design of wide-band amplifiers.

Terman found most valuable, however, his visit on May 10 and 11 to the Telecommunications Research Establishment (TRE) at Malvern, in the Severn Valley in Worcestershire. (RRL's British laboratory would be sited here when it was established in the fall of 1943.) Fred spent most of May 10 talking with Dr. Robert Cockburn, "who is by far the best technically informed man on counter measures that we have encountered." Cockburn related details of several jamming and antijamming measures and felt that if an enemy's range of effectiveness is limited to 25 percent of normal, then jamming is adequate. Jamming by noise modulation was thought to be the best means, superior to jamming with a sine wave or tone modulation. Airborne jammers need only 1 watt of jamming power per target, but this required one transmitter for each channel to be jammed. Early results suggested that centimeter wave equipment was the hardest to jam since it is such a directive beam and also because it scans in direction and therefore only looks at each target for a very short time. Another type of jamming with potential, Cockburn said, was to jam with modulation at the intermediate frequency (IF) of the radar. Since the IF of the Wurzburg was known from the Bruneval raid, this could be a valuable technique. Cockburn also advised Terman that RCM equipment should be simple in construction and operation on the assumption that the military personnel in the field would have only limited comprehension of radar and RCM equipment.

Cockburn reported that the British were not satisfied with the General Radio P540 search receiver, just recently received from the United States. The receiver was noisy, not very sensitive, had too narrow a bandwidth, and the conventional vacuum tubes were pushed beyond their high-frequency limits. He revealed that the Germans were first known to have used radar in 1939, and he suspected they were using radar for searchlight control. He knew for certain that the Germans had four hundred gun-laying radar sets (gunfire laid down on targets) in operation, but he suspected that they had thousands. Cockburn then outlined British knowledge of the German aerial radio navigation systems and possible methods of jamming them. He thought that German submarines were not listening to aircraft radar signals as a method for detecting attacking planes and then escaping by submerging. Airborne radar would thus be important in antisubmarine measures. TRE was also worried about the extent to which the Germans might be able to use centimeter wave radar, and whether the Germans actually had any effective 10-centimeter radar.

Cockburn also told Fred the whole story of the escape of the *Scharnhorst* and *Gneisenau* with the aid of German radar jamming. In fact, the escape proved to be a valuable lesson and wake-up call to British countermeasures. Cockburn felt that for RCM, the period from spring 1941 until spring 1942 was largely a period of mental gestation and consolidation. Three important technical conceptions had been established during this gestation period: (1) the use of "noise" as the jamming modulation; (2) the use of simultaneous "barrage" jamming of a large band of channels; and (3) the realization that an aircraft could screen or jam ground radar with only a very small amount of jamming power. Finally, initial qualitative examination had begun on Window (chaff), "certainly the most powerful single countermeasure introduced."[82] That period had been terminated by the *Scharnhorst* and *Gneisenau* episode, which had revealed that the British had 60 percent of their radars on about the same frequency, therefore easy to jam, and that the British operators had been caught off guard, since the Germans had never before jammed so strongly and over such a large area.

Terman also met other TRE staff. Henry Booker was a remarkable mathematical physicist from Cambridge whose PhD dissertation had established solutions for ionospheric radio wave propagation modes. Booker had worked just three years before with Lloyd Berkner and Merle Tuve during a sabbatical year in the United States at the DTM-Carnegie. Booker coached Terman on radar cross-section calculations for aircraft. Martin Ryle, another young student from Oxford who had just decided to do graduate study at Cambridge in ionospheric physics, would cross over to radio astronomy after the war, become Astronomer Royal and subsequently share a Nobel Prize in Physics in 1974. Ryle, only twenty-three at the time of Terman's visit, was Cockburn's group leader in charge of all RCM work. Fred Terman left TRE not only stuffed with the latest British RCM ideas but carrying copies of key TRE reports and background material.

Just after his tour of TRE at Malvern, Terman and his military companions, Detzer and Finch, along with U.S. Naval Captain Solberg met with several British counterparts in the Director of Signals Room, British Air Ministry on May 15, 1942, "to discuss programme of RCM work which it is desired should be undertaken in the United States." The meeting was chaired by Air Commodore O. G. W. G. Lywood, deputy director of Signals for the British Air Ministry. (Lywood was one of the originators of the British encoding machine "typex" but in his encounters concerning radar and intelligence as recorded by R. V. Jones, Lywood appears somewhat misdirected.[83])

During these meetings, the British listed fifteen classes of items they wished to see developed or improved. The Americans ranked as most important the following items on the British list: (1) a jamming device that would allow a receiver to listen through for intelligence-gathering purposes and a device that could allow jamming transmissions to be monitored without stopping the jamming; (2) research and development of airborne barrage jammers, particularly for the 53-centimeter band; (3) development of barrage or selective and tunable jamming transmitters and monitoring receivers for the band 5–50 centimeters, especially 5–15 centimeters; and (4) a device to allow the British to use the same jamming frequencies as the Germans and thus to jam the enemy while not being jammed themselves.

In second order of importance the Americans rated: (5) "Window," extensions of the principle of using artificial reflectors against radar, including the ejection of material from aircraft and ships and the best form of such reflecting material. Also, the possibility of towing reflectors; and (6) improving communications jammers for the medium- and high-frequency radio-operating bands.

The British listed a number of other items—developing improved noise generators, developing automatically tuning jammers, producing large numbers of jammers and receivers, and designing them so that they would fit either U.S. or British ships and planes—and these items, Terman's group agreed, would be considered or were also being planned for U.S. investigation.

The British military suggested that the best and swiftest links between the British RCM board and the U.S. RCM committee would be for all messages to go to and from the United States via Captain Solberg and Lt. Commander Finch.[84] Captain Solberg met with the British RCM board throughout the war.

It was a busy and profitable five weeks for Fred and his two navy colleagues in RCM. Terman wrote to his parents just after his return, "I left England with a feeling that the RAF people, at least in communication, were doing extremely well. . . . I came back with considerable optimism."[85] Among the passengers on his return trip was David Langmuir of the OSRD (son of the noted physicist, Irving Langmuir) with whom Terman enjoyed talking and with whom he would later work. He arrived in the United States after several delays and took the night train from New York to Boston early on the morning of May 28. In his bags was an antique silver tea service for Sibyl. "It is nice to see Fred now and then between trips," she wrote to her mother-in-law. "He brought me a perfectly beautiful silver tea set from England. . . . By Clipper, too. Me and all my girlfriends were bowled over."[86]

Fred's government-allowed per diem was $10 per day in the United States, $7.50 outside the United States, and $5 on the plane. When Fred filled out his official "Office for Emergency Management—OSRD Voucher Travel," he listed his total expenses at $217.06. This ended up being a tale of red tape, and Fred wrote letter after letter to Dr. Caryl P. Haskins, OSRD Liaison Officer, seeking reimbursement. He even visited OSRD's office personally when he was in Washington. He was finally reimbursed nine months later. This was not Terman's last encounter with red tape and RRL business.[87]

Getting Down to Business

On June 11, 1942, soon after Fred returned from his secret visit to England in May, he gave an informal talk to his staff about his trip and followed up with technical talks on July 14 and July 22.[88] He also broadened his weekly staff meetings, variously noted in the minutes as "Senior Staff Meeting" or "Senior Staff Technical Meeting." Fred made his own two-page penciled outlines of the agenda for each meeting, but the actual meeting minutes were taken usually by Don MacQuivey, and the attendees included Terman as chair, Luis Alvarez (during the first two or three months), Howard Chinn, Peter Goldmark, Clark Cahill, John Dyer, Dick Raymond, Don Sinclair, Win Salisbury, Donald Leet, associate directors Robert W. Hickman and John F. Byrne, and business manager N. Preston Breed.[89]

Terman was excited about the additions to his staff who had arrived while he was in England. He had corralled a former MIT electrical engineering grad student and staff member Howard Chinn (who had gone to work for CBS), as well as six or eight men from a CBS television lab in New York City including Peter

Goldmark (the future developer of the LP record), John Dyer (who had been on Byrd's Second Antarctic Expedition), and several other engineers.[90] Goldmark and Dyer were excellent senior engineers and got started right away on modifying a search receiver.

The week of July 14 the RRL officially moved into its new home in the Harvard Biology Building on Divinity Avenue. On that day, Fred gave a staff talk titled "German Radar" to all RRL research associates. He spoke of four types of German land-based radar that had been identified through the end of 1941. (At the time, Terman and the British did not know the radar designations and called them "A," "B," "C," and "D," but the appropriate German names will be used here). According to Terman, the *Freya* radar operated at about 120 MHz and was probably used for long-range aircraft warning. There was a chain of these from Norway to the Bay of Biscay, spaced about fifty miles apart, with a range of fifteen to one hundred miles, depending on the altitude of the target. The *Wurzburg* operated at about 560 MHz and was used for anti-aircraft fire control and probably searchlight control. It was believed that these radars are placed on their target by the *Freya* radars. One of these was captured in the Bruneval raid. Newer models seemed capable of lobe-switching the beam. Cockburn, he reported, knew of four hundred of these along the coast and inland, but suspected there were thousands, and British intelligence reported the Germans to be making them by the thousands. *Wurzburg*, or similar radars, had a range of fifteen to twenty miles and had been found operating in Crete and Sicily. The *Seetakt* radars (primarily ship based, but Terman did not know that) operated on about 375 MHz in the Dover area and were used for gun laying against ships. They had a range of twenty to forty miles. The *Lichtenstein* stations were new, operated on about 450 MHz, and had only been located in the Dover area. Their purpose, however, was unknown. Other radar equipment was suspected, reported both by U.S. and British intelligence. The Germans, Terman suggested, might even have airborne air-to-surface radars (probably *Lichtenstein* or *Hohentwiel* airborne radars).

Terman also reported that extensive search for seaborne radar had not found any naval radars, although photos of the sunken *Graf Spee* indicated it had 50- to 60-centimeter radar antennas, and it was suspected that smaller German warships had 50- to 60-centimeter radar for fire control. There was no evidence that German submarines employed radar or had search receivers that could receive British radar.[91]

It is clear from Terman's talk why Dr. Cockburn concluded that it was of the utmost importance for RRL to concentrate on RCM work in the frequency range of 200–600 MHz. Terman's talk dealt in great detail with the characteristics of the captured *Wurzburg* radar and its weak spots in terms of RCM. While the *Freya* (and its similar models), which operated at about 120 MHz, fell in the range of the earlier U.S. radars, the other radars, both the *Wurzburg* and *Seetakt*, as well as the other still-unknown German radars in 1942 (*Lichtenstein*, *Hohentwiel*, *Kurmark*, *Mannheim*, and related models) operated in the range 350–600 MHz.

That same week, Terman wrote to Bennett Archambault of the OSRD Liaison Office in London, thanking him for seeing to the delivery through diplomatic pouch of the secret notes Terman had taken while visiting the radar centers in England. (Had Terman carried his notes with him and his plane been captured, his notes would have revealed all of Britain's radar secrets.) As for RRL, he confidently explained to Archambault that "we are continuing to grow rapidly and that our program is beginning really to roll ahead." As to RRL products, "the first batch is going to come with a bang in the late summer." He was proud to say that the organization in Cambridge now numbered more than one hundred twenty people, plus twenty more working full time under RRL supervision in CBS laboratories in New York City.[92]

Fred Terman also produced in mid-July 1942 a program of immediate tasks for RRL. He classified the activities under five headings:[93]

I. Development of receivers for intercepting radar signals. These included improvements to the GR P-540 receiver and new receivers for 100–600 MHz, plus 600–10,000 MHz, these receivers to have single dial control, motorized sweep, greater sensitivity, and better image rejection.

II. Development of jamming transmitters. Particular bands included 200, 500, and 3,000 MHz, plus some effort on 100 MHz and 10,000 MHz. All types of modulation would be investigated—am, fm, pulse, spark, barrage transmitters, and IF jammers.

III. Analysis and testing of radar systems from the point of view of RCM, for systems analysis. The eighth-floor roof of the Harvard Biology Building was to be a systems analysis laboratory with complete radar units permanently installed for testing by all kinds of jammers.

IV. Special RCM devices. This included both theoretical and experimental work on "Window" and other devices for producing false echoes. Noise sources for modulating jammers were studied and a new single tube wideband noise generator had already been developed.

V. Special projects and activities, included studies of jamming of navigational systems.

This list of plans and work in progress followed closely the requests given to Terman by the British and his own team's responses regarding priorities, as given during the meeting on May 15. There was no time to waste. Frank D. Lewis, OSRD Liaison, wrote from London that same week, "a first-class RDF jamming campaign has opened up here and the British people are getting anxious for technical assistance from the U.S. Lots of things can happen in a month in this war!"[94]

And lots of things had happened since Fred Terman and Don Tresidder had met at Ahwahnee the preceding December. Terman wrote Tresidder in August 1942:

> When that group in your living room received the news of Pearl Harbor I doubt if any of us appreciated how much our lives would be affected. Certainly I did not imagine that within one month I would have made arrangements to leave my comfortable and very satisfactory place at Stanford for an indefinite time, or that within five I would be in England, and in getting there would have spent two nights north of the Arctic circle, . . . or that by now I would have the responsibility for a research organization which has a budget approximately the same as that of Stanford.

Tresidder replied, "I, too, often think of Sunday morning December 7. I imagine we will always remember that morning on the sixth floor of the Ahwahnee as one of the dramatic episodes of our lives."[95]

Family Life in Belmont

The three Terman children started school soon after arriving, with Bo and Lewis going to the primary school located less than a block from the house and Fred Jr. at the Winn Brook Junior High School just up the road. Fred Jr. wrote to his grandmother Terman that this school was very different from Jordan Junior High back in Palo Alto. Lewis liked his new school better than Peninsula School in Palo Alto, where he had been the youngest and smallest child in the second grade, but Bo liked Peninsula better.[96] Sibyl, however, wished to change both houses and schools.

Soon after she arrived in Belmont, she began visiting nearby private schools and looking for more suitable rental houses. While Fred was in England, she found an "ideal house, old but modernized and beautifully kept up" at 560 Concord Avenue, "right at Belmont Center, very handy to the stores, the bus for Cambridge and the schools, both public and private." The property had almost two acres, with huge trees, which made one feel as if far out in the country. The house had a large living room, front hall, large sun room, dining room, kitchen, pantry, laundry and lavatory downstairs, while upstairs on the second floor there were four bedrooms, two baths, a sun porch, and a maid's room and bath. On a third floor was a big playroom and yet another bedroom. The rent was $150 a month, just what the Termans were getting for the rental of their house on the Stanford campus.[97] And Winifred Elliott, one of Sibyl's best friends, lived just a short walk through the woods. When Fred returned from England it was agreed that the family would move to Concord Avenue on July 1.

Sibyl possibly did not realize it at first, but the new house was adjacent to the estates of William Claflin, the treasurer of Harvard, and Charles Coolidge, of the wealthy and prominent Harvard architectural family. This move would prove to be valuable to Fred. The Claflins and Coolidges began regularly to entertain the

Termans. Fred also would spend many Sundays when he was free talking with Claflin as his neighbor worked outside in his yard and garden. Sibyl was greatly impressed by Bill Claflin. He was "the grandest person you ever met and a great help to Fred. He tells me Fred has done a wonderful job," she wrote proudly. "After all, he is running a show bigger than Stanford."[98]

Claflin (Harvard '15) had been captain of the Harvard varsity hockey team in 1914. Claflin recruited N. Preston Breed (Harvard '29, MBA '32) from his own staff to become RRL's business manager within weeks of Terman's arrival.[99] (Breed also had been on the Harvard hockey team and was at one time a figure-skating champion of New England.) Claflin later assisted Terman by recruiting John Chase to be associate director of ABL-15, the RRL Lab in Britain. Chase, according to Claflin, was the most up-and-coming young businessman in Boston. Chase (also Harvard '29) was from a prominent banking family. He was on fourteen corporate boards, including that of Radcliffe College, and was the treasurer of Wellesley College. Not coincidentally, Chase had been on the Harvard hockey team, as well as captain of the U.S. Olympic hockey team in 1932.[100] In 1944, Claflin and Terman with calls to Vannevar Bush would secure the release of Colonel J. K. Howard from the army to assist Terman in organizing the business side of the ABL-15 lab in Britain. Howard had been a prominent Boston attorney and at the time was supervising Harvard's military-training programs.[101] Claflin proved to be a great help to RRL and to Terman personally. Fred credited Claflin with teaching him how to run a business, how to run a university, and how to handle investments.[102]

In the fall of 1942, Sibyl enrolled Fred Jr. in eighth grade at the private Belmont Hill School, only three-quarters of a mile up the hill from their new home. She wrote to the senior Termans that she had purchased a large quantity of high-quality clothes for the boys, since at Winn Brook and at Belmont Hill, the boys wore collared shirts and ties with coats or suits to school. Academically, the private school was challenging. The school day was long, from 8:35 AM until 5:30 PM, including two hours of sports at the end of the day, and more homework was assigned than Fred Jr. was accustomed to.[103] Bo got out from Winn Brook public school at 1 PM, but he liked to go up to Belmont Hill in the afternoons to play football. Sibyl talked with the Belmont Hill staff and had Bo enrolled in the sixth grade at Belmont Hill by early November. Like his brother, Bo found the new school difficult, but they dug in and saw their work improve. Initially, their grades were poor due to the stricter standards of grading at the private school and to the fact that the boys were behind somewhat in their level of preparation. Sibyl was relieved when the Claflins convinced Fred Sr. that public-school grades given out were much, much higher than at private schools.[104]

Sibyl also looked for housing suitable for her sister Alice Walcutt Somers, and Alice's two daughters, Coralie, a little younger than Lewis, and Myrilla, a little younger than Bo.[105] She located a studio bungalow for Alice just behind the Coolidge estate, very near to the Termans, for only $30 a month.[106]

The Termans had more than one run-in with fire during the year 1942–43. While still living in the house on Richardson Road, the family smelled smoke. Bo went into the basement to play with his blocks and found the ceiling shooting out sparks. The Fire Department was called and discovered an electrical short.[107] After they moved to Concord Avenue, the Termans burned cannel coal as a supplementary source of heating. Young Lewis mistakenly shut the flue damper and the house filled with smoke, but Sibyl managed to put out the coal fire. In November, soon after Aunt Alice moved into the bungalow near the Coolidges, the gas stove supply valve snapped off in the full-on position, and Alice and Sibyl called the Fire Department to put out the stove and stop the gas. Far more potentially serious was the fire back in Palo Alto on November 22, 1942, when Lewis Terman Sr. fell asleep while smoking. The ensuing fire severely damaged the house and nearly killed Professor Terman, who was found on the floor. He suffered severe burns to his back, right leg, and right arm that required skin grafting. Despite several years of recuperation, the injury severely limited movement of his right shoulder and arm.[108]

Illness, too, took its toll. Most of the Terman family in Belmont were sick during the winter of 1942–43. Just before Christmas the temperature fell to -16F. Lewis was hospitalized the week following with a throat and neck infection, and subsequently he missed much of the rest of school during the winter.[109] Fred Sr. was sick for the first time since his trip to England.[110] Many of the family letters show Sibyl intensely concerned with medical remedies and visits to physicians, just as she remained anxious about the boys' schooling. The boys were always pushed by Sibyl to be advanced a grade in school and to excel.

Sibyl realized the intensity and level of study at private schools was considerably above that of the public schools, but Grandfather Lewis argued that private boarding schools seemed to him "just a waste of good money."[111] The boys changed schools more than once. In the fall of 1942, Fred Jr. and Bo were at the private Belmont Hill school, and Lewis at the local public school. In fall 1943, Fred Jr. continued at Belmont Hill, while Bo moved to Cambridge Upper School and Lewis to Cambridge Lower School. By spring 1944, Sibyl had Fred Jr. take entrance exams for Phillips-Andover Academy and he enrolled there as a student in the fall of 1944. Fred and Bo both did well in math and science. The boys' records overall were quite good, while Lewis was an especially good student.[112]

In spring 1944, Sibyl began to teach remedial reading at Cambridge Lower School, and she was teaching there again in 1945. She also encouraged the boys' social development. She and Mrs. Claflin organized a teenagers' square dance group that met sometimes at the Unitarian Church. Although Fred Terman was not formally religious, Sibyl became somewhat involved with Unitarian Church activities while they were in Massachusetts, while Fred Jr. would become an Episcopalian when he was at Andover. Fred Jr.'s. first girlfriends were daughters of his parents' friends: a Claflin daughter and, especially, Elaine Elliott, whose mother was getting a master's degree in reading education at Harvard. Her father, Robert C. Elliott, at Harvard for the year as a Nieman Fellow in journalism, was on the staff of the *San Francisco News*. When the Elliotts' year at Harvard concluded in August 1943, the family decided to return by car to San Francisco and invited Fred Jr. to go with them as company for Elaine. Fred Jr., aged fourteen, sent postcards all along the way, visited his grandparents at Stanford, reported on the state of the Salvatierra Street house, and then returned by himself to Massachusetts on the train.[113] Meanwhile, Bo and Lewis made pals, including the children of Ed Yunker, a colleague at RRL, and several other children who lived nearby.[114]

During their stay in Massachusetts, Fred and Sibyl each wrote to the senior Termans about once a month. The letters were often informative. Sibyl's letters to her father-in-law, like those to her mother-in-law, contained general news of the family, the children's schooling and illnesses, and Fred's work. Particularly with Anna, she discussed details of the houses in Massachusetts, Sibyl's social life, problems of finding maids, gardening, and wartime food and fuel shortages. Fred's correspondence with his father tended to center on news from the Stanford campus, work at RRL, and world affairs, while his letters to his mother were similar but also appealed to her interest in real estate. Anna owned and rented a duplex on Ramona Street in Palo Alto.[115] Anna Terman was especially helpful to them in keeping rented the younger Termans' campus house on 659 Salvatierra Street, reporting on its condition and upkeep.

When Fred wished to invest profits from his textbooks and set up a life trust for Stanford in 1943, it was Anna Terman who scoured the Palo Alto area looking for suitable houses to purchase as investments. In summer 1943, Anna sent Fred three-by-five-inch index cards with her notes on details of houses for sale. In the fall of 1943, she found a small house on Sequoia Avenue in Palo Alto, near the Stanford campus. The family leasing the house knew that it would sell for a bargain, so they would not agree to let prospective buyers inside to examine the premises, always giving excuses. One day Anna met the realtor there and they walked around the premises while the tenants were away, peering in each window. Anna knew a bargain when she saw one and she "signed the contract and paid the deposit" on the spot. She telegrammed Fred and Sibyl, got their approval, and bought the house for them without going inside. She wrote that she had lost her chance on houses in Palo Alto by waiting an extra day or two to close the deal. She also immediately found a tenant for the house, Melita Oden, Professor Lewis Terman's research assistant.[116] (Oden remained Lewis Terman's colleague on the gifted-child research project for thirty years and coauthored and then completed publications on that research.[117])

Part of the increased business and personal correspondence between Anna and her son and daughter-in-law was due to Lewis's inability to write for about a year due to his injuries from the fire. The grandsons, who enjoyed their grandparents' few visits to Massachusetts, wrote each grandparent several times a year, letters impressive for each boy's age. Bo's letters in particular were often reflective and frank. Until his injury, Grandfather Lewis wrote to the boys, frequently including science news or math problems for the boys to study. He took seriously his correspondence with his grandsons, and he engaged them in discussions by letter.

Summer vacations were serious business. Fred Jr. was packed off to summer camp in 1942 and 1943, but the next two summers he worked at Baird Associates, a small Cambridge electro-optical company that manufactured phototube equipment under contract to Harvard for RRL. Fred Jr. had built his own radio soon after he moved to Massachusetts and kept up his interest in electronics. He was quite talented, and the company had him drawing circuit diagrams and wiring assemblies and then building power supplies and amplifiers. He worked forty hours a week, for fifty cents an hour in 1944, moving up to sixty cents an hour in 1945. He saved two hundred dollars the summer of 1944 toward his tuition at Andover.[118]

The real campers were Bo and Lewis. However unhappy they were at the thought of being sent to camp for the two months of July and August, Bo attended summer camp for three years and Lewis for two. Camp William Lawrence was near Mt. Shaw, at Center Tuftenboro, New Hampshire. Like most children, they liked the camp a good deal more once they got there. Bo wrote numerous letters to his mother from camp. Both boys were interested in the various critters (snakes, bugs, and so on) that could be collected by the campers, in the ghost stories told by the camp counselors, and in outings to Lake Winnepesaukee. Lewis was anxious about winning an Indian feather at the camp. Bo was proud of his archery and swimming and played baseball, although he was skittish about being smacked again by the baseball bat. He thought the guys at camp were swell, he told his mother, nicer than the boys at Belmont Hill School.[119]

In 1944, Bo came home a month early from camp and accompanied Sibyl on a visit to friends on Martha's Vineyard. Lewis and Fred Jr. arrived later to visit, and Fred Sr. got away for a weekend. When he came back a week later, he amazed everyone by staying for more than a week. On the island, the three boys did a little sailing in the harbor. The following summer, when the Termans enjoyed a summer at the beach on the Claflin's seventeen-acre estate at East Marion, Massachusetts, the boys sailed a tiny sailboat by themselves.[120]

The big interest in the Concord Avenue neighborhood in 1943 and 1944, however, was Sibyl Terman's vegetable garden. In her first winter in Massachusetts, Sibyl wrote about fears of fuel shortages and said she would keep the house at 55 to 60 degrees. By spring, the food shortages convinced her to plan a big garden.

In March, she wrote to her father-in-law that she was going to have a vegetable garden, chickens, and rabbits "even if Fred does laugh at the idea." To her mother-in-law she complained, "There is little to eat even if you have the [food ration] points, NO chickens to be had."[121] Sibyl was as good as her word. She checked out from the library all the available agricultural pamphlets and consulted all the local truck farmers on crop lore. She persuaded someone with a tractor to plow an area 110' by 120', almost one-third of an acre, on their property near the Claflins and the Coolidges. (Fred suspected her garden was on Coolidge's property.) The boys were supposed to help. Fred Jr. knocked in fifty-eight tomato stakes and planted tomatoes. They put in beets, carrots, potatoes, cauliflower, brussels sprouts, eggplant, celery, and peppers. Sibyl purchased forty hens, roosters, and capons and put them in Fred's tool shed. The biggest hubbard squash weighed thirty-nine pounds, and Sibyl and her sister Alice put up more than five hundred jars of canned vegetables. The beets, carrots, and potatoes were stored.

"Everyone comes around," wrote Fred, obviously proud of Sibyl's garden project. In midsummer, Fred wrote to his father that Sibyl was enjoying several hours a day in the garden and that she had sold dozens of heads of lettuce to the local grocers. Lewis had a pet gray-and-white hen named "Queen Victoria." The family had eaten a dozen of the chickens and had gathered a dozen eggs a day. Sibyl may have enjoyed the garden, but she complained about the load of doing all her own housework, since keeping a maid seemed impossible. Bill Claflin worked in his own garden on Sundays, and it was at these times that he and Fred discussed university management techniques. The next year, 1944, was different for the Terman garden, however. Fred Jr. went off to Baird Associates on his summer job every day, and then in July, Bo and Lewis went to camp; in August, Sibyl and Bo were joined by the boys on Martha's Vineyard. Bo wrote to his grandfather Terman that fall that the weeds in his mother's garden were five and a half feet tall. Without Alice's help, Sibyl noted, little canning was done and the garden got away from them.[122]

The RRL at Harvard

The Radio Research Laboratory's first home was one room at the Radiation Lab in Building 24 at MIT, in February 1942. RRL soon grew to take over one entire floor of the Hood Ice Cream Building at 155 Massachusetts Avenue, leased by the Rad Lab. RRL then moved to the Harvard campus Biology Building at 18 Divinity Avenue, even though some equipment tests were occasionally conducted at the Hood Building.[123] The RRL began moving a few things to Harvard late in the spring of 1942 and completed the move by mid-July.[124] By the time of the move to the Biology Building, the RRL staff had grown to more than one hundred twenty. RRL took over the north wing of the Biology Building, and continued to expand, both vertically and laterally.

The Harvard Biology Building had been built in 1930 in a style called "WPA Modern" or "stripped classic" by the firm Coolidge, Shepley, Bulfinch and Abbott. An eminent campus architect, Charles Allerton Coolidge (Harvard 1881) had had a significant influence not only on the Harvard campus but at Stanford, where he designed the Quadrangle buildings in a distinctive Romanesque style in conjunction with Frederick Law Olmsted's overall campus design.[125] The Biology Building was six floors high, with greenhouses on rear elevations. The top story was windowless. Birds, animals, and fish were incised into the top story's blank walls. The growth of RRL resulted in two wooden stories added above the existing roof, and these plans were already underway by June 1942.[126]

By 1943, with further growth of the lab, a wooden "temporary" utilitarian structure, the Vanserg Laboratory, was constructed just east of the main building, and a test house, the Shannon Building, was later constructed adjacent and to the east of Vanserg.[127] Though the Shannon Building was later removed, the allegedly temporary "ugly wooden" Vanserg Building was still in place a half century later.[128] RRL had hopes for a larger and more elegant structure than the Vanserg and architectural designs were produced for a seven-story Vanserg Building and adjoining garage building, but these were not to come to pass.[129]

The staff was always crowded into the available lab space. On November 22, 1943, E. D. Brooks Jr. wrote to RRL's business manager Preston Breed to ask for more space, noting that an additional floor might be added to RRL. Brooks pointed out that RRL had 80,000 square feet and a daytime staff of 575 on site, a little less than 140 square feet per person.[130] But on December 13, 1943, the RRL Executive Committee decided to defer plans for a new building since the lab apparently reached its peak employment of 813 in August 1943, and by fall 1943 no further growth was expected.[131] After the end of the war, the two upper floors of the north wing of the Biology Building were removed, leaving the eight-story elevator shaft unchanged. In later years Terman was amused to note that the Harvard Biology Building was the only six-story building in the world with an eight-story elevator.[132]

According to RRL staffers in later years, morale was high and Terman was a good boss. The first published laboratory newsletter, which appeared on Christmas Eve 1943, noted that the lab party featured the "Harvard Rhythm Ramblers" dance band, a chorus of RRL carolers, Miss Gladys Johansen in a performance of illuminated baton twirling, and the opening of Christmas presents. Further issues of the newsletter were titled *The R.R.L. Scope* and appeared monthly thereafter. In one illustrated issue, Terman is pictured with the caption "Uncle Freddy." George Hulstede was referred to as "Uncle George." Whatever the humorous references, in later years, several staffers who had been Stanford electrical engineering students recalled Terman being addressed fondly as "Uncle Freddy" when they were not in his presence, just as President Donald Tresidder had been called "Uncle Don."[133] Elizabeth Mudge, Terman's personal secretary, noted that different people in RRL, including the secretaries, expressed how impressed they were with Terman's personal interest in their work and careers.[134] As the lab grew, the machinists and shop people wanted their own Christmas parties. When the question of alcohol at the parties was raised in committee meeting, Terman and business manager "Press" Breed decided that it was better to have alcoholic punch at parties within the lab than to have the machinists have their parties, unofficially, outside the lab.

While the major group of RRL employees were located in Cambridge, there were other physical facilities. At the East Boston Airport, a hangar was leased for airborne test flights. Later, a larger facility was added at the National Guard Airfield at Bedford, Massachusetts, several miles northwest of Cambridge. The Florosa, Florida, RRL field station was seventeen miles from Eglin Air Force Base. The site at Florosa opened in June 1943 and allowed large-scale equipment tests and flights of multiplane formation tests. Florosa began in one Air Force trailer and grew to a normal staff of about nine with additional visiting RRL staffers and others from Bell Labs, General Electric, and Federal Telephone and Telegraph. The local field had a 5,000-foot main runway and two auxiliary runways. In addition to equipment and technique tests, officers were trained in airborne use of radar and RCM equipment for the various war theaters. Single men lodged and ate at the Florosa Inn and married staff lived in civilian housing at Fort Walton, six miles away.[135] The field stations had their additional problems. Terman sent F. Clark Cahill, RRL's associate technical director, to report on things several months after Florosa was opened. Cahill wrote that the Florosa staff felt like orphans. The army air force was very cooperative, he wrote, but RRL needed to send good people down to make sure the equipment got installed correctly in the test planes. And the problem of sufficient spare parts and test equipment needed was a familiar one.[136]

The last, and largest, of the RRL sites outside of Cambridge was the American British Laboratory, of NDRC Division 15, called "ABL-15." This was located on the campus of the Telecommunications Research Establishment (TRE) at Malvern, England, and was established in August 1943.[137]

In addition to permanent field sites, RRL people cooperated with other organizations and made occasional or regular visits to the Naval Research Laboratory near Washington DC, or to Wright Army Air Field in Dayton, Ohio, for field testing of prototypes. In some cases, special visits were made to assist in projects adjacent to RRL specialties. For example, Merle Tuve, of the Carnegie Institution's Department of Terrestrial Magnetism, headed the large and secret U.S. effort in proximity fuzes. Small, rugged transmitters and receivers (tiny radar units) were installed in artillery shells. Special batteries were activated once the shell was fired and a receiver recorded the signal returned to the shell when it got sufficiently near its target. The shell then was made to explode at or very near to the target. This was a tremendous technical advantage to army and navy artillery. But, just as with the fears of the enemy gaining knowledge of "Window" or chaff if it fell over enemy territory, and the fears of the enemy discovering the Allied ownership of 10-centimeter wave radar, there were fears that if a proximity fuzed shell fell as a dud on enemy soil, it could be copied and the enemy would retaliate. This situation occurred frequently during the war. In the case of the proximity fuze, Tuve and staff puzzled about countermeasures to the fuze. They requested RRL assistance on countermeasures, and on September 25 and 26, 1942, Win Salisbury and Dick Raymond visited DTM and observed artillery firings, bringing to RRL fuze designs and firing information.[138] RRL continued some limited assistance to Tuve's group throughout the war, but the proximity fuze project became very large in activities and personnel and developed its prototype jammers, which of course were not needed during the war.[139] RRL personnel also cooperated with a Bureau of Standards proximity fuze project.[140] In addition there was RRL assistance to other NDRC work in a division headed by K. C. Black from Bell Labs having to do with communications jamming.

Window and Chaff

Window (or variations of it called "chaff" or "rope") was the single most important radar countermeasure utilized by the Allies in World War II. It was a metallic reflecting strip, or tape, or rope that was released from airplanes (or exploding shells) and, drifting downward, appeared on enemy radar as a radar-reflecting cloud, masking the aircraft flying within or near it. Window, combined with the jamming transmitter "Carpet" (and its related jammers), was a powerful weapon. German radar experts estimated that 90 percent of their efforts after 1943 went into counteracting Window and jamming and thus they were unable to develop 10-centimeter radar (or 3-centimeter radar). Germany, Japan, Britain, and the United States all developed Window, and each delayed its deployment for a time for fear that it would be copied and used against them by the enemy. Both the Germans and the British had done some work on Window as early as 1940. The Japanese used it beginning in 1943.

The United States probably first learned of it in early 1942 when Commander Malcolm P. Hanson of the navy's Bureau of Aeronautics visited England to learn about countermeasures work there. Hanson was a radio expert, having performed the world's first polar ionospheric sounding experiments on Byrd's First Antarctic Expedition in 1929–30, and, like Lloyd Berkner, was a specialist in navy radio and aircraft.[141] Hanson passed on information about Window to Terman at RRL in February or March 1942. Subsequently, on Terman's visit to England in April and May 1942, he spent several days discussing all aspects of Window and brought back a sample. The original British Window was a paperbacked conducting foil the size of a sheet of writing paper. The British also thought about suspending reflectors from balloons. They dropped some reflecting paper and camouflaged it by printing propaganda material on the tissue-paper side of the foil, but fear of the enemy discovering the secret caused them to stop. They had also considered using wide paper strips with a foil backing.

Terman gave this problem to Win Salisbury at RRL, who worked on it in the spring and summer of 1942. Salisbury thought that since the *Wurzburg* radars operated on rather narrow bands, the best use of the foil would be to cut it into resonant dipole lengths and drop it rolled as cigarette-shaped cylinders. This reasoning came from the fact that fat dipoles have broader resonance curves than thin dipoles. Salisbury had RRL construct a number of these cylinders, cut to different resonant frequencies for the German radars as they were known. Before RRL could test these, whether over land or over Boston harbor, military authorities prevented RRL from testing. The RRL Window program then went dormant, but Terman asked the Rad Lab to lend him Dr. L. J. Chu, the most noted American antenna theorist. Chu made a full theoretical study of the radar cross section of rectangles, ellipsoids, cylinders, and other shapes for varying width-to-length ratios and for varying orientations for all frequencies used by radar. Chu's work took several months and his submitted report was locked in the RRL safe. Several months later, Dr. Fred Whipple, the Harvard astronomer, arrived at RRL. Whipple had been studying meteors, and Terman put him onto again considering Window and Chu's report with an idea to practical applications.

Whipple made an important discovery. Even off-resonance, Whipple found, the narrower the dipole, the greater total radar cross section *per pound of foil*. In the vicinity of resonance, the thin dipole gives a better radar cross section, and the loss at off-resonance is more than offset by the greater total number of dipoles per pound. Thus, this thin Window came to be called "chaff." Whipple was assisted by a noted Dutch astronomer, Dr. Gerard P. Kuiper. The next move was to decide on the optimum frequencies for the dipoles, and in the end bombers usually carried chaff cut to three frequencies used by the *Wurzburgs*. The problem was turned over to the old pro, Harold Elliott. Elliott, who had trouble getting along with colleagues Howard Chinn, Roger Hickman, and others at RRL, was in his element among lathes and milling machines. He had sold more than forty thousand car radios by 1939 using a push-button design he invented. He had greatly simplified the design and operation of Stanford's multifrequency ionospheric sounder in 1941 with his electro-mechanical cam design, and he was involved in the electro-mechanical design of the RRL single-dial tune and motor-driven search receivers. The question to Elliott was: How thin in thickness and how narrow in width can these dipoles be and still withstand being dropped out of planes at high altitude, and how can they be manufactured? Initial attempts used shearing machines (like paper cutters). He began building small prototypes in the RRL shop.

Elliott was given the go-ahead on a crash basis on May 27, 1943. He devised a clever milling machine with alternate teeth being dulled. As the sheets of aluminum foil were inserted into the machine, one sharp tooth cut the foil, the next tooth bent the foil at 90 degrees but did not cut it and then the following tooth cut it. Thus was produced a piece of foil about 10 inches long, bent into a "V," 1/32 inch on a side. Each milling machine with twenty or more teeth (Elliott later called them "chaff cutters") spun at a high rate and produced a lot of foil chaff. The first machine was completed within two weeks and attempts were made to contract the making of more machines. The first twenty machines had to be partially constructed in the RRL shop. Others were ordered from the International Paper Box Company, Nashua, New Hampshire, and the J. C. Rhodes Company in Bedford, Massachusetts. Within three months of starting the project, orders for ninety chaff cutters were placed.

Elliott and the machine shop crew at RRL worked heavy overtime during this period. Loyal to his draftsmen and machinists, Elliott praised them highly. The demand in 1943 for the chaff was so great that RRL sent Elliott and a few machines to England to cut chaff right on the spot. Both Fred Whipple and Elliott spent time in England coordinating the chaff effort, as American chaff materials and American chaff cutters arrived for English use in October 1943. Contracts were let to manufacturers not only to make the machines, but then to others to cut the chaff. Vincent Lane, at Standard Rolling Mills in Brooklyn, recalled being visited by RRL men in 1943 and shown a hand-cranked cutting machine. Later, Lane's company was supplied with many more rugged motorized machines, and they cut the chaff and packed the dipoles into boxes. Standard Rolling Mills operated one hundred machines, each producing six thousand strips a minute. One woman would run about five or six machines, with a mechanic standing by for each ten machines. The machines required constant attendance and honing and sharpening. Everything was secret and, for a while, RRL could not tell the foil companies what length to cut the foil. Shoebox manufacturers were hired to produce cardboard shoe boxes to contain the packets of foil. Standard Rolling Mills and Reynolds Metals each produced about 350 tons of foil per month.[142]

The British began using chaff in July 1943; and the U.S. Eighth Air Force bombers did so in December 1943. Each large bomber carried about 90 lbs. of chaff on every flight. Large B-17 bombing missions carried a total of about 80,000 lbs. of chaff (1,800,000,000 dipoles).[143] Chaff was dropped in many ways, through chutes in the sides of large bombers, and in a variety of ways from smaller planes.[144] Sometimes chaff was glued to paper so that the dipoles "whirled" down. Against the lower-frequency radar encountered with the Japanese, long strings of reflectors, called "rope" were dropped. In the early days of the Mariana Islands-based raids, each B-29 was allowed only fifty bundles of "rope" due to limited supply.[145]

Earlier, however, there was a difficult time of convincing the U.S. Air Corps in Europe that chaff was worthwhile. In daylight bombing in clear conditions, the Air Corps believed that chaff was useless since anti-aircraft fire was directed by visual means. And others claimed that the chaff did not succeed against German fighter aircraft. In fact, much of the bombing over Germany took place above cloud cover, where the chaff was very valuable against radar-directed flak. In addition, as the war progressed, fighter kills against U.S. bombers tended to be against crippled bombers that fell from formation. Chaff drifted down slower than the planes flew and the Germans altered their radar designs to detect the velocity difference or "Doppler shift" between the fast-moving bombers and the slow-drifting chaff. Response to this was twofold. U.S. jamming techniques focused on disrupting the German radars, and lead planes flew higher and above the bombing runs, dropping chaff ahead of the main oncoming flight. Finally, the Allies dropped vast quantities of chaff over miles of flight path. In combination with the eventual use of several Carpet and barrage jammers on each bomber and tons of chaff in the air, the German defense against air attack was stifled.

Carpet

The invention of chaff evolved in the hands of RRL personnel—a radio power amplifier specialist, a mathematician, several astronomers, and an electro-mechanical engineer—into the most valuable radar countermeasure of the war.[146]

Broadloom, Carpet, Cigar, Ground Cigar, Chaff, Dina, Dinamate, Elephant, Elephant Cigar, Jackal, Moonshine, Oboe, Perfectos, Porcupine, Rope, Rug, Tuba, Wind—these were all names for Allied radar or radar countermeasure devices.[147] And each code name also had a military name: AN/APT, ARC-1, APT-2, APR-4, SCR-268, SCR-270, and so forth. But on the RRL honor roll of the 150 or more devices developed by RRL, the *active* electronic countermeasure device "Carpet" shares the place of honor with the *passive* device, chaff or Window.

Carpet was the code name for the APT-2, APT-5, and APQ-9 jammers for the *Wurzberg* 560 MHz band. Carpet was not the most sophisticated equipment to emerge from RRL (certainly not compared to later search receivers) nor was it the biggest and most expensive of units (Tuba, the multikilowatt jammer, filled several trailer trucks). However, Carpet and Window together accounted for more than half the dollar amount of radar countermeasure products produced by manufacturers.[148]

A top priority item for RRL in early 1942, for both Terman and the British, was immediate development of a jammer to counter the German *Wurzburg* antiaircraft radar on a frequency of about 560 MHz (a wavelength of about 53 centimeters). Their jammer for the *Wurzburg* would be nicknamed "Carpet" (it received a military number APT-2, another early jammer named Dina had already received the designation APT-1). Terman's transmitter group was initially headed by Bob Searle, and Searle assigned young William "Bill" Rambo, a recent arrival from Stanford. Rambo had transferred to Stanford from nearby San Jose State College as an undergraduate in 1936 and had finished his BA in 1938 and his EE in 1942. Rambo had taken radio courses from Terman and Karl Spangenberg, who became his thesis advisor. Rambo finished his thesis early in 1942 while working as a broadcast radio engineer at a small station in Oregon. When he wrote the Electrical Engineering Department that he was looking for a job full time elsewhere, the secretary wired him not to do anything until he heard from Terman. Hired for RRL, he arrived straightaway in June 1942.

Rambo's group boss put him to testing vacuum tubes that might generate a little power output at 560 MHz *and* that could be tunable in frequency. (That ruled out the magnetron, which was not tunable.) The jammer unit would have to be small and suitable for installing in an aircraft. Rambo tried tubes by GE, EIMAC, RCA, and IT&T, and finally got a Western Electric "doorknob" tube that put out 1/4 of a watt at 560 MHz. With considerable effort, he raised the power output to 1/2 watt. Through the summer, Searle's group worked on the jammer design and finally worked with two "doorknob" tubes in a so-called push-pull mode, putting out 5 watts of noise power at the *Wurzburg* frequency. A push-pull circuit is one way to get more power by connecting two tubes together. In this case, the grids and the plates of the tubes are connected to opposite ends of a balanced circuit so that at any instant the voltages and currents of one tube are out of phase with those of the other. One feature of this is that the even harmonic frequency modes are canceled out, a feature that slightly increased the desirable power output of the jammer. The main technical reason for using the push-pull circuit was that the voltage to ground in the output circuit is only one-half the value of the voltage in a parallel circuit. This eased the problem of critical economic and supply limits: during World War II, quality high-voltage capacitors were limited in availability. The dielectric material in high-voltage capacitors was subjected to stress, and with the push-pull circuit, capacitors of only half the peak working voltage could be used, compared to those needed for an equivalent parallel circuit. The Carpet was designed to be powered by 400-cycle AC for aircraft use and to fit into a small chassis and case. It could be tuned fairly easily by a technician, and in practice, aircraft radio technicians would tune the Carpet jammers to the latest reported *Wurzburg* operating frequencies.[149]

The Carpet was completed in time for John Dyer to demonstrate it to Robert

Cockburn when he came from England in October 1942 to inspect American countermeasures progress. Cockburn was enthusiastic about the jammer. Major James McRae went out on a limb and bypassed usual channels to order a large quantity of Carpet jammers. A brave thing to do. If Carpet failed, it would have meant serious career trouble for McRae. When Carpet was ready in the early summer of 1943, thirty-five American B-17s were equipped with Carpet to assist by jamming German *Wurzburgs* for the July invasion of Sicily. Unfortunately, when the B-17s arrived in North Africa, maintenance crews there "returned" all but four of the thirty-five planes to their correct specifications as called for by maintenance manuals, thus only those four planes used the Carpet during the invasion. The four B-17s, along with U.S. ships using the "Rug" jammer marked the first use of deliberate radar jamming by U.S. forces in combat. RRL senior staff member Dick Raymond flew in one of the B-17 Ferret aircraft monitoring the effects.

On October 8, 1943, forty-two Carpet-equipped B-17s formed part of the U.S. group bombing Bremen, Germany, where the Carpets were stagger-tuned 1/2 MHz apart so that a "barrage" effect was produced. Overall, during four bombing missions over Germany in October, Carpet-equipped aircraft suffered about one-half the losses of aircraft not so equipped. Although many aircrews still viewed jamming with scepticism, the Eighth Air Force ordered Carpet for all bombers, but it would be some months before a sufficient number arrived. There were only enough Carpets for about one of every ten bombers until U.S. manufacturers were pressed by the military into producing Carpets by the thousands. Rambo's colleagues improved Carpet with newer tubes, and Carpet II became available with a tripling of power output to 15 watts. Another later version of Carpet was more easily tunable, but Carpet I remained the backbone of the *Wurzburg* jammers. In response, the Germans altered *Wurzburg* radars to be more easily tunable and produced different tuning units so that the radars could operate at around 50 MHz away from the original frequency; they even developed a new band, from 440 to 470 MHz. As a result, Carpet had to be manually tunable by the RCM radioman while in the air. ABL-15 in England also modified a receiver so that the radioman could listen for the *Wurzburg*, then tune his Carpet to the correct frequency.

The arrival of Carpet jammers in England was disturbingly slow by May 1944, in spite of the manufacturing surge in the United States. Fred Terman sent his "transition chief" Earl Cullum to spots around the United States to check for bottlenecks, and then he sent Cullum to England. Cullum sent an S.O.S. for Mike Villard to help out. Cullum was an MIT-trained electrical engineer who had worked for American Airlines in the 1930s and then founded his own broadcasting consultancy. He was an effective engineering manager, and Terman promoted him to associate lab director at RRL. Villard acted as an assistant to Cullum as well as Terman. Once in England, Villard was assigned W. H. Hagenbuch, an army air force captain who was invaluable in getting into highly classified installations. Between them, they discovered many crates of jammers whose destination was misunderstood because they were not listed in the standard signal corps catalog. Their coded serial numbers had meant nothing to the warehouse supply officers. In addition to the side-tracked jammers, U.S. aircrews needed to be encouraged and given better instructions on the use of the jammers. Some air officers had been through countermeasures-training courses in the United States, but RRL personnel, notably young John Foster (years later to be U.S. undersecretary of defense), gave presentations to more than twenty thousand airmen over a three-month period.

The Carpet jammer was a great success. As with Window, RRL had shown its talent not only with development of the jammer but by supervising its manufacture, checking on and expediting its deployment into service, and instructing in its correct use.

Overseas Technical Observers

At the laboratory's peak, Fred Terman had eighty-five staff members overseas as technical observers. Although this was a sizable fraction of the total RRL technical-scientific staff, the observers were spread thin. RRL provided the majority of its support to the U.S. Army Air Forces, observers in ones and twos who would accompany air campaigns, landings, invasions, and the occasional special mission. A number of RRL people worked with "Ferrets," the electronic surveillance aircraft, loaded with radios and countermeasures equipment to listen for enemy activity. Don Sinclair went on the first "Ferret" countermeasures B-17 flight to Africa in 1943, and Dick Raymond replaced him three months later. They had narrow escapes, since navigating the Ferrets near the seacoast at low altitude near mountainous terrain was quite dangerous. Other RRL personnel, under the highest priority, flew to the Aleutians to outfit a special Ferret to search for Japanese radar on Kiska. Joe Pettit and others worked in the China-Burma-India theater, installing equipment and preparing Ferrets for mapping Japanese radars over Indochina, China, and Japan. Their work enabled military officers and crews to fly hundreds of navy and air force Ferrets and Porcupine jamming planes on patrol flights and bombing missions. Although there were numerous close calls on flight-testing and Ferret missions, RRL was very lucky in the safety records for its staff.

Wallace Burnside Caufield had been one of Fred Terman's students at Stanford, receiving his AB in electrical engineering in 1941. Wally also was the cousin of Fred's good friend and advisor Melville Eastham of General Radio Corporation. He entered MIT for graduate work in electrical engineering in 1941. Wally was a very likeable guy. After Pearl Harbor, he had tried to enlist in the army air force but was rejected by the military because of his height (six feet six). Wally joined RRL at Terman's request and was put into the receiver group with Bob Soderman under Don Sinclair. Wally met his future wife while she was a secretary at RRL, and they were married in December 1942. Don Sinclair had flown on the first Ferret mission to North Africa; on Don's return, Wally expressed interest in overseas duty. For six months, from October 1943 to April 1944, Wally served as technical observer for the army air forces in the North African and Italian campaigns. Wally later returned to Europe, going to England in May 1944 to assist in preparing for the Normandy landings.

In June 1944, Wally joined ABL-15 and worked with them in England and on the Continent, and in December, he was placed in charge of the ABL Advance Base in Paris. Wally and John P. Chase, associate administrative director of ABL-15, drove in an unmarked military ambulance to the Ardennes region during the Battle of the Bulge in order to investigate radio communication problems that had occurred at various advanced commands. On December 31, 1944, as Chase and Caufield were driving along a road, they passed a group of American trucks. A flight of some five to seven fighter planes marked with U.S. insignia (probably U.S. P-47s) strafed and bombed the convoy of trucks and struck the ambulance with several 50-caliber rounds, severely wounding Caufield. Chase managed to get Caufield to the Thirty-second Evacuation Hospital in Thionville, but Wally died of his wounds the following morning. Chase reported this immediately to military authorities and informed Terman. The *Administrative Report of the American British Laboratory of Division 15 of the NDRC* records that "Caufield was mortally wounded during a bombing and strafing attack," technically true. In spite of Chase's report and other eyewitness accounts of the planes, the American press and official reports later stated that German, not U.S., planes strafed the convoy. It is ironic and tragic that, given that region of Luxembourg during an intense battle and the poor weather conditions, that Caufield was probably killed by friendly forces. He was the only RRL staff member to perish in action during the war.[150]

Secrecy

Secrecy was always an important issue at RRL. In Terman's official letter of appointment of February 16, 1942, Karl T. Compton of NDRC warned him, "I would emphasize the ultra-secret character of this project. The work of the Radiation Laboratory itself is very importantly in the secret category, but the RCM project is of such character that even greater care should be taken, not only to prevent any disclosure of information, but even to prevent every unnecessary intimation that work of this sort is in progress." In a letter to Frank D. Lewis a few days later, with copies sent to Terman, Vannevar Bush, Lee DuBridge, Alfred Loomis, and others, Compton reiterated the ultrasecret nature of Terman's laboratory and the special actions being taken to ensure "extraordinary precautions for secrecy." He acknowledged that the British mission members, Vannevar Bush, and others had emphasized these "warnings" concerning absolute secrecy and that methods recommended by the U.S. Secret Service were being put in place. He specifically stated that RRL members would have access to the Rad Lab but that Rad Lab members not have access to RRL concerning countermeasures. There would be "a one way communication of ideas between the Radar counter measures group and the Radiation Laboratory concerned with Radar developments."[151]

Earl Cullum later recalled that in the first months, staff would take notes during RRL planning sessions and then, at the end of the meeting, guards would gather up and destroy the notes just taken![152] But necessity required some risk-taking. With planning meetings held with military liaisons in Washington, Cullum emphasized to Terman the difficulty faced by RRL staff in getting required plans and documents back and forth, given official document secrecy procedures; Terman replied that RRL simply could not waste the time, they would take them back and forth on the train themselves.

As security efforts relaxed somewhat, the expected things happened. RRL staff sometimes forgot to bring their ID badges to work with them, or they lost their badges outright. This occurred so often that a new set of RRL badges was ordered for all. Two machinists from the Bedford Airport RRL hangar were dismissed for stealing gasoline; a guard at the RRL Cambridge labs was fired for being drunk on duty; Fred himself lost his briefcase in Union Station in Washington DC. On another occasion, Fred and OSRD senior executive Frank Lewis were officially chastised for discussing classified matters in the men's washroom at the Officers' Club at Eglin Air Field. As "penance," NDRC Division 15 Director Guy Suits ordered Fred to discuss security at staff meetings and send security warning letters to all section leaders and research associates. In addition, Suits sent warning notices to all Division 15 contractors about the dangers of lapses in security.[153] In 1943, when writing to Felix Bloch, Terman urged caution and asked Bloch to amend a paragraph in a report to the Stanford trustees referring to "war research on microwaves in Cambridge," worried that "some overzealous individual in the University publishing department will let the stuff out without change to the newspapers and then *all hell will break loose*!" Terman concluded:

> The situation is that the Germans, as far as is known, do not have any microwave radar in use. They may be developing such equipment or they may not be. Our people are very anxious to prevent as far as possible attention being attracted to the fact that we have an extensive program of development with equipment already coming into military use on wavelengths shorter than 40 cm. To date, the

enemy has given no indication that he knows of this activity, although my own personal feeling is that he must know of it but is keeping quiet at present for some reason—perhaps because there is nothing else he can do.[154]

Things had changed since those early days when the OSRD promised that all RRL employees would be cleared by numerous security agencies, including the FBI. By late 1944, it was found that the OSRD had cleared for employment several lower-level employees with jail records. A new process was instituted when the OSRD employed the personnel services of the Retail Credit Company in checking prospective employees.[155] Quite a few military officers and technical representatives from manufacturers were eventually given visitor IDs at RRL for legitimate reasons, which sometimes irritated the staff. In addition, during the last months of the war, selected reporters, including a Nieman Fellow at Harvard, were given some access to the lab. (The Nieman Fellow even helped write some of the RRL press releases after VJ Day.) Stanford University's News Service released an article about Terman and countermeasures work without his knowledge, and this potential security lapse distressed him. Newspaper leaks emerged not from RRL, however, but from a company supplying the aluminum foil "chaff." When Reynolds Metals bragged about their wartime service in a news article and advertisement, "all hell broke loose," as Fred used to say. As a result, RRL canceled their contract with Reynolds and discontinued their business relations.[156]

Taking Care of Business

In the fall of 1942, NDRC decided on a general reorganization, placing RRL into a new countermeasures division of NDRC. Although RRL would remain the major part of countermeasures, the new division would have some other contracts as well. NDRC chose C. Guy Suits, vice president of research for General Electric, to direct the new division. Suits became director of Division F (soon renamed 15) in October 1942. Still commuting to his GE office in Schnectady, he set up division headquarters in New York City's Empire State Building. While Alfred Loomis became director of NDRC's Division 14 (formerly called Division D), superintending Lee DuBridge, director of the Rad Lab, Guy Suits would oversee Fred Terman and the RRL.

Suits had received his bachelor's degree in physics from the University of Wisconsin in 1927, then went to the Swiss Technical Institute in Zurich where he received his PhD in 1929. He had joined the General Electric research labs in 1930, and in 1940 was named assistant to the director of research. (After the war, he would return to GE to become vice president and director of research.) Frequently there on business, Suits was familiar with the Rad Lab and had been highly recommended to Vannevar Bush for the new division post by his boss, Will Coolidge, director of research at GE.

Suits had several years' experience in large-scale technical management. He saw his role as one of facilitating RRL's expansion.[157] In his view, two things in particular loomed on the horizon that fall. First, the previous summer the British had asked for U.S. countermeasures help. Fred had sent two RRL men to England, and things were slowly building toward establishing a permanent RRL presence in Britain, but the work in England was not developing fast enough.[158] Secondly, the NDRC wanted RRL to grow and grow quickly. Having gone from three staff members to some one hundred fifty, RRL had already moved out of its single office at the Rad Lab to an entire floor of a Rad Lab building, and then on to its own facilities at Harvard. Despite RRL's already fast growth, Suits wanted RRL to double in size over the next year.

Obtaining and keeping the technical staff RRL required was a continual problem from the lab's earliest days. Indeed, a major factor in selecting Fred Terman as director of RRL had been his wide range of contacts in radio circles and at engineering schools. Fred was also aware of the value of the relatively young field of television. Television engineers' work was the very closest to the background needed for work in radar and radar countermeasures, he wrote Vannevar Bush during his first weeks at RRL, and such engineers were desperately needed in war work rather than in "such forms of boondoggling as putting on television demonstrations for first aid courses for the benefit of a few thousand television receivers" now required by the Federal Communications Commission.[159]

The search for experienced men grew increasingly difficult by 1943. That spring, Guy Suits, as director of Division 15 of OSRD, asked OSRD on Terman's behalf for funds to pay for sixty scientists (EE graduates, PhD physicists, and physical chemists) with no special training in radio engineering or radar to be enrolled in the three-month courses in radio and radar given at Harvard and MIT, and subsequently to be hired at RRL.[160] Terman was solicitous for the welfare of these new recruits. He sent a memo to all group leaders that most of the large number of new men arriving in June and July "are fresh from college." Terman counseled his senior staff to sensibly utilize these new employees and not just request "top scholarship or Ph.D. men with lots of experience."[161] The men employed at RRL were constantly dogged by draft boards, especially in 1943 and 1944, but RRL actually lost few of its young men to the draft. Fred was proud to note that RRL had the largest percentage of high-priority draft deferments in the Boston area, while in fact at one point, eighty-five of his staff were overseas on special technical assignments.

Like his colleagues in industry, Terman turned to a new source of skilled labor and encouraged women to acquire the skills necessary to become machinists. In September 1942, he proposed to the OSRD that RRL be allowed to hire fifteen "girls" for three months' training, that they be paid fifty cents an hour during training (to cover their room and board), and that following the completion of their course at Worcester, Massachusetts, they be employed at RRL. This request was granted by OSRD and written into the contracts with Harvard.[162]

Expansion of both its physical size and its commitments placed a special burden on RRL's director. Terman already spent much of his time in Washington. Much RRL business and planning, particularly matters concerning the military, took place in monthly "smokers" held in Terman's hotel room in Washington. Here, Terman, military liaison officers such as Commander Finch and Majors McRae and Haller, OSRD men like David Langmuir, and key lab associates talked strategy with Terman. In addition to weekly meetings in Washington and New York for RRL and Division 15 business, Terman was placed on an NDRC Vacuum Tube Development Committee, which met in New York City or sometimes at General Electric headquarters in Schenectady. This committee, which Terman occasionally chaired, usually met monthly to discuss research strategy and procurement decisions on hundreds of millions of dollars worth of tube contracts with RCA, General Electric, Sylvania, Western Electric, and the major tube manufacturers.

During his first year at RRL, Fred spent what little spare time he had left editing the text for his book *Radio Engineer's Handbook*, written with the help of Karl Spangenberg and several other colleagues. He managed to get nearly all the work done by Christmas 1942 (the book appeared in summer 1943). Just as he was hoping for a lighter load, the pressure to enlarge RRL increased. Yet again, more space was needed. Having already added two floors to the top of the Biology Building, RRL constructed the temporary Vanserg Building next door, completed in summer 1943.

At the same time, the RRL field facilities expanded with the addition of hangar space and testing setups at Bedford Airport and the planning of a permanent field station at Florosa, near Eglin Air Field in Florida. Terman learned in August 1943 that Suits had complained to Karl Compton about the operation of the Florosa, Florida, station. Behind-the-back criticism did not suit Terman, who in turn noted that it was Suits who personally had chosen a GE colleague, Dr. Herbert Pollack, for the position as head of the Florosa field station.[163] Three days later Terman distributed Pollack's complaints, comments, and description of Florosa station to all RRL senior staff and group leaders, to make sure all were informed of what was going on.[164]

Terman's many managerial tasks at RRL often involved dealing with large egos and smoothing ruffled feathers. Shortly after the lab was organized, Fred's old Stanford friend Harold Elliott became upset with Howard Chinn because he believed Chinn nosed around too much and tried to organize everything. It was, in fact, Chinn's job. In an early staff meeting, Chinn was designated to coordinate "technical activities and internal organization," and Chinn, along with Elliott and Sinclair, were designated the design committee, charged with checking all items developed from the laboratory as to mechanical and electrical design, ruggedness, and other criteria.[165] Elliott was distressed with more than Chinn and the committee, however. As an engineer with twenty years of experience in electro-mechanics, Elliott wanted a fully equipped shop with top machinists. Soon, he was furious, too, with Associate Director Hickman, whom he believed was not working hard enough to ensure a fully equipped machine shop. Relations worsened with the theft of two machine lathes. In mid-August 1942, two newly arrived machine tool lathes specially ordered by Elliott the previous March and clearly labeled with RRL's name and invoice numbers, along with assorted auxiliary parts, were taken from the loading dock, hustled off, and installed in the Rad Lab shop. The Rad Lab refused to return the lathes. Elliott was furious and felt Hickman did not exert enough muscle to get the lathes returned. Fred Terman stepped in to arrange a compromise wherein two similar lathes ordered by Rad Lab to arrive on September 12 would be delivered to RRL. Elliott's unhappiness with Chinn and Hickman caused him to complain to Terman in writing at least twice, and his irritation increased to the point that he tendered his resignation in the spring of 1943. Terman solved this problem by altering Elliott's position title to "consultant," thereby reporting, more or less, directly to Terman. Harold Elliott's mechanical design innovations and his invention of the chaff-cutting machines were important assets to RRL. The cranky but invaluable Elliott was now out of Hickman's hair, but the loner-inventor could continue to work productively at the lab.

Howard Chinn also proved to be both an asset and personnel problem. Chinn was an electrical engineering graduate of MIT who stayed on there to do radio research work. During his MIT days, Chinn was extremely active as an amateur radio operator. He then moved on to CBS. Chinn was a talented man, but he often complained behind Terman's back about organizational matters. (Terman, for example, initially did not have an organizational chart.) Terman, who viewed this behavior as insubordination, discussed the matter with Guy Suits, Terman's superior when NDRC reorganized in fall 1942. Terman also found out that the undeniably talented Chinn had been released from employment at MIT for similar behavior. With Suits's approval, Terman fired Chinn from RRL in August 1943, although in fact Chinn continued to work full-time on RRL-related problems from the CBS labs in New York City.

A number of Terman's telephone calls were recorded on disc cylinders and transcribed at the time for record keeping. The transcripts make interesting reading as Terman negotiates with manufacturers, military contacts, and NDRC and Division 15 senior administrators. The following gives a sample of a discussion between Terman and R. W. Larson, Guy Suits's chief technical aide at Division 15, just two weeks before D-day regarding Mike Villard's sudden assignment to

Europe to clear up a bottleneck in distribution and installation of radar countermeasures gear:[166]

T: And regarding those men going over there for ABL-15 . . . do you want each one of those cleared individually and reviewed with you people or—

L: Well, here's the way I feel about that. It's your job to man ABL-15 within certain limits—but when we think of manning it—I mean men that are going over for the duration or something like that.

T: Yeah.

L: The thing that ought to be cleared are special expeditions like Salisbury's or this PETTICOAT mission—special trips of that kind.

T: Well now, for instance among the other things yesterday they asked for Villard to come over to do a transition and service liaison job.[167]

L: For the duration or for a short time?

T: No details—not too much details as to how long, I presume for the present emergency which probably during the present planning period means three to six months.

L: Yeah. Well—

T: Probably would go over—probably would be actually attached to ABL as part of their organization.

L: I'd like to discuss that one with you before—or have you discuss it with Suits before—

T: Well, we've got to get it done in the next twenty-four hours.

L: You do!

T: Well, sure, I mean they're getting ready for an invasion—the invasion isn't going to delay at our request. . . .

L: The whole thing is this—I can't tell from this distance—I don't know whether the timing on this thing is such that all this fussing around is going to be any good.

T: Well, I don't know. It seems to me the only thing we can do is to assume that the fellows over there know more about it than we do and not question their decisions on it, . . . with Cullum and Howard and Dyer and Fraenckel over there, it seems to me if we can't have confidence in them we ought to yank the whole thing back and wash out the laboratory.

Terman had sent a number of his men to England (at General D. D. Eisenhower's urgent request) for mission PETTICOAT in early May 1944 to help install radar countermeasures on English naval vessels for the D-Day landings. RRL equipment was installed on 266 naval vessels in preparation for D-Day. Not only was the bureaucracy peeved with Terman, but Larson also disapproved of Terman's plans to send Villard to England before getting appropriate approval from Division 15 headquarters. Terman had mentioned to Larson that William Claflin had already cleared support for all this from NDRC head Conant, but Larson doubted this. When later informed of this, Claflin confirmed that Conant had thoroughly approved of giving every possible aid in sending RRL men to England, and that Claflin was disturbed at Larson's attitude.[168]

Just two weeks later, Terman had another run-in with Division 15 administrators. Director Suits wanted RRL to make, on a crash basis, four countermeasures units of a type that had been developed by the Bureau of Standards under a contract with the navy. These were needed within sixty days, and Suits wanted to do a favor for Captain A. J. Detzer Jr. Terman replied in no uncertain terms that such an effort was not the duty or stated purpose of RRL. The Bureau of Standards could build it themselves in their own shops or in the Research Construction Committee (model shop) (RCC) set up by Division 14 and available to Division 15, Terman insisted, or, if it was so important to the navy, the navy could have NRL build them in the navy's own shop. Suits ultimately had the four built at the RCC shop. Subsequently, Claflin strongly backed Terman in his handling of Suits's request.[169] Earl Cullum, Terman's group leader for transition problems, also had conflicts with Larson and Division 15 headquarters over his reluctance to clear all paperwork through Division 15.[170]

The RCC model shop indeed had been established so that Rad Lab and RRL could build small numbers of units for special purposes. From the beginning, there was the tendency for clients—the military—to ask the Rad Lab and RRL to hand build one, two, five, even fifty or one hundred units of some item for their immediate use. Fortunately, the military services realized that the process, from prototype to production, sometimes took more than a year. For their part, Rad Lab and RRL staff was sympathetic to these requests, and they usually built several of each prototype and took these to the designated manufacturer to assist in production. By 1943, RRL had learned that their own engineers had to accompany their prototypes to the manufacturers and follow the production process in detail. Otherwise, the manufacturer's own production engineers often "cleaned up" the design and, in the process, ruined it. In one case, RRL had used a particular gas thyratron tube as a noise-modulating source in a jammer transmitter. Some of the first sets worked well, but others that followed did not function as designed. A visit to the vacuum tube company chief engineer revealed that the company had proudly redesigned the gas tube so that it was not as noisy, but the change severely weakened the functioning of the RRL jammer. The RRC model shop was established to produce the limited numbers of units needed to serve the prototype needs of manufacturers as well as the "crash" needs of the military. The model shop was located not too far from Rad Lab and RRL.

In interviews late in his life, Suits explained:

> I saw my task as a supportive one, to supply him [Terman] with whatever he needed to expand his laboratory rapidly and make it as effective as possible. He needed the kind of help I could give in dealing with government, seeing to financial matters and generally working with industry. He could have done these

> things, but of course he was very busy with the day-to-day management of the laboratory which included making major technical decisions.[171]

Yet Suits had no love for Bill Claflin, the Harvard treasurer, whom he described as "a very difficult guy to deal with. . . . He was just a dictatorial individual, very strong-minded, very outspoken. . . . Dealing with him like I had to do, was a very tricky thing, and my God, we had a lot of encounters through those years." Although Claflin had spent years as a financial investor, a manager of large sugar plantations, as well as a corporate board member, Suits thought of him as an "academician" who "was always a little bit suspicious of people in industry. . . . The university is all right but you can't trust industry people exactly."

Suits had a better opinion of Terman but was nonetheless condescending. An interviewer later asked Suits what Terman could have brought to technical advisory committee meetings, Suits replied:

> There were always a thousand technical details where Terman could make a contribution. . . . His leadership by virtue of his personality, his acquaintanceship, his knowledge of the trade, was excellent. . . . In the contact I had with him, I found him to be a very reasonable person, very helpful, very cooperative indeed, and I don't have any complaints at all. He was easy to deal with; he didn't have a reputation of being hard to get along with at all; the students, of course, were very fond of him. . . . They held him in the very highest regard.[172]

To another interviewer, however, Suits described Terman as "a student and a teacher," but not innovative as a lab director. According to Suits, "If you're going to have innovative people, you mustn't be stupid about it yourself. I mean, they look to you to have an idea occasionally, and I don't know if Terman ever filed a patent. . . . I would be surprised if he had any patents." This speaks to Terman's modesty. Suits had not bothered to find out much about Terman, who had nearly forty patents by the time he first met Suits in 1941–42, nor was Suits apparently aware of Terman's and Warren D. White's valuable report, "Notes on Power Required for Noise Jamming," distributed May 31, 1943.[173] This report, distributed to both RRL and military personnel, calculated jamming-effective ranges against the small and giant *Wurzburg* radars jammed by Carpet, Carpet Sweeper, and High-Power Carpet jammers as well as by British Rug and Mandrel jammers. The report was produced just as the U.S. Air Corps Eighth Air Force began concentrated raids under attack by *Wurzburgs*.

Radio expert Ralph Bown of Bell Labs, one of the original four of Alfred Loomis's Microwave Committee, had been one of the first to counsel Fred Terman about organization of RRL. In September 1942, Bown was sent by the Joint Communications Board (JCB) of the military and by NDRC to evaluate RRL. This was part of a move by the JCB to urge enlargement of RCM activities and forge closer relations with the military users. Bown reported to Alfred Loomis, with copies to Vannevar Bush, Compton, and Terman that "the Laboratory is now a going concern, tackling the job it has set for itself in an energetic manner . . . and . . . as far as apparatus development is concerned," RRL was progressing satisfactorily. But Bown was concerned that there was no group "for philosophical and analytical study of the subject." Bown thought that such a group was not necessarily appropriate at RRL, but should be established separately. It would require more scientific thought and advice, he wrote, "than is usually available in the regular military organization."[174] It was these concerns that led NDRC later that year to enlarge Terman's RRL from section D-1 in the Rad Lab's Division D to a division on its own. The new Division 15 also would include countermeasures in the radio communications field, a considerable amount already being performed at Bell Labs.

A number of more visible problems—notably Howard Chinn's complaints about Terman's lack of organization and Chinn's subsequent firing, the apparent disarray at the newly forming ABL-15 in England and the inability of the military to get enough RCM gear into the field—generated two important NDRC reviews, the first by John H. Teeter in October 1943, and a second shortly after by John V. L. Hogan.

Visiting RRL on October 26, Teeter spoke individually with Terman, Hickman, Cullum, Byrne, business manager Breed, and several others. At some point, he also spoke with Howard Chinn, who had been dismissed only a few days previously. Teeter viewed Terman's organization as structured vertically, but with too many group leaders reporting directly to him. He noted that Terman recently had reorganized, adding Cullum and Byrne to top posts. He regarded Terman as "acknowledged by all to be a walking encyclopedia of radio knowledge. He has an unusual gift for helping a research associate over some difficult phase of the work." However, Teeter also thought Terman older than he actually was, estimating his age at "about fifty-seven" although Terman was actually forty-three, and "under considerable strain, no doubt from overwork and excessive traveling." He went on to note that "Dr. Hickman was formerly the associate director, but he is not mentally or physically suited for this task and now serves as Director of Information. . . . He is about fifty-seven years old [he was forty-four] and over meticulous about detail." The strain of "his effort . . . appears to have created a nervous disorder." The strain on both Terman and Hickman was showing, revealed in Teeter's misjudgment of their ages. Teeter made similarly frank remarks about others at RRL and went on to confirm the suspicion that ABL-15 was in weak hands with Goldmark and Fraenckel. Teeter was not easy to impress—he also added damaging remarks about the navy and army, noting that he found ample evidence that the competition between the Naval Research Labs (NRL) and the Army Research Labs (ARL) had extended to RRL, whose prototypes were delayed in testing by NRL and ARL staff until their own duplicated efforts could reach a comparative stage. Teeter placed a good deal of blame on the military and expressed the need for an RCM "czar" to govern procurement, planning, and production. He saw a need for more administrative shuffling with a real organization chart approach, and even concurred at one point with the newly installed director Suits that Terman might be replaced as head of RRL and moved to England to run the ABL-15. Even after RCM's establishment, he criticized the military for showing little real interest. "Not until the enemy called the tune did the Services assign General McClelland to RCM activities." Nevertheless, he concluded, "much of the smoke is nothing more than the normal growing pain incident [*sic*] to an organization that went from zero to $21,000,000 and 675 people in eighteen months."[175]

Teeter's memo was the groundwork for John V. L. Hogan's report to Vannevar Bush on November 18, 1943. Hogan's preparation was more thorough, however. He visited RRL twice and talked with all the principals as well as with Division 15 leaders. He read numerous reports, production plans, charts, and letters. Hogan found conflicting opinions, not to mention conflicting impressions of the facts, but in general came away with a more positive impression than Teeter. "The extremely heavy load of administrative duties that Dr. Terman has been handling through this long formative period could probably have been effectively handled by no one else," he wrote. "Dr. Terman is preeminent in this part of the work [scientific aspects of the problems] and could be an even more inspiring leader if he were less harassed by administrative problems." Unlike Teeter, Hogan thought the appointment of Earl Cullum to an administrative post a positive move, and similarly, the recent hiring of D. B. Harris to be a Division 15 Technical Aide for Liaison. He also pointed out that Edward Bowles had since promised to iron out problems by simplifying procurement by army and navy and by loosening tight security restrictions by the military.[176]

Hogan reported further to Bush on January 8, 1944, following conferences with Claflin, Terman, and Suits. He strongly supported RRL's efforts in radar countermeasures (RCM) but now emphasized that the growth in countermeasures (CM) work in radio communications as well as in guided-missile fields required enlarging Division 15 to take control of these additional areas.

> It has been increasingly evident that Harvard, RRL and Dr. Terman personally have all been carrying a tremendous burden. The task of building up so large and successful a countermeasures operation in so short a time, and in the face of the difficulties inherent in the security and procurement procedures first set up by the services, imposed an extremely heavy load of administrative duties on Dr. Terman. I feel that his accomplishments have been far greater than could reasonably have been expected, and I know no one else who could so well have combined administrative and scientific skill in the way that was necessary for the creation of our CM facilities.

Hogan, assured by Terman and Claflin of satisfactory changes at ABL-15 and Florosa field stations, recommended to Bush that there be no change in the contracts.[177]

ABL-15, the American British Laboratory

The pressure to establish a British wing of RRL increased in spring 1943.[178] A scientific mission to England in June 1943 settled the matter. Harvard won the contract when Bill Claflin assured NDRC that Harvard would manage the operation and Fred Terman would oversee it. The first RRL men arrived in England in August 1943. The lab was called the American British Laboratory of Division 15, or "ABL-15." Soon after, the Rad Lab set up its own British wing, called the British Branch of the Radiation Laboratory, or "BBRL." Each of these groups would be positioned on the campus of the school at Malvern, already home to the Telecommunications Research Establishment, or TRE, Britain's foremost radar and countermeasures research center.

By near the end of the war there were seventy people stationed directly at ABL-15. Field observers, who either flew on flights as observers or who worked at advance bases, also thought of ABL-15 as home. As the Allies moved across France in the months following D-Day, RRL was asked to provide support on the Continent, for the army headquarters, for the Ninth Air Force, for the Twelfth Air Force Tactical Air Command, and later for the First Tactical Air Force. By October 1944, ABL-15 also had an advance base in Paris. Assistance centered around various communications problems, mutual Allied radar interference, and assisting the various air commands in problems and methods of dispensing Window or chaff. Weekly or biweekly teletype conferences were set up between RRL and ABL-15 to facilitate discussion of needs and opportunities.

Setting up ABL-15 had not been easy. While the British tried to be helpful, the Americans continued to squawk about housing, gasoline, and food shortages. When the Rad Lab's BBRL branch was set up at TRE, unfavorable comparisons about salary and housing allotments led Terman and his business managers to reach compromise solutions for ABL-15. The biggest problem with ABL-15, however, lay in its on-site leadership. Initially, in August 1943 Peter Goldmark agreed to go to England to act as technical director but he ignored the requirement that he stay in England for a year. Soon after arriving, he announced that he would return to the United States to take care of CBS business at least every three months. When Terman refused to accept this, Goldmark replied that he did not expect travel formalities to apply to him. Terman, however, firmly believed that ABL-15 needed on-site leadership, and Suits strongly backed Terman on this issue. On November 9, Goldmark resigned and returned to New York. Terman now was left with Dr. Victor H. Fraenckel, formerly of General Electric, who served as acting director, but Fraenckel became more and more despondent about ABL-15 progress and also spent a good deal of time away from Malvern. Fred needed a replacement, and at the suggestion of Guy Suits, he hired John Dyer, the talented CBS engineer who already held senior status at RRL. John Dyer went to ABL-15 in January 1944 and officially became director in April. Fraenckel switched positions to become technical liaison for Air Corps General Carl Spaatz.[179]

ABL-15 continued to be a problem. By spring 1944, the Allied air forces were crying for jamming equipment. Located so close to the scenes of battle, its staff was besieged by suggestions and requests. Beginning in spring 1944, Terman wrote a series of tutorial letters to Dyer, counseling him on how to run the operation. Terman worried that Dyer allowed his staff to refine and fine-tune individual projects, to the detriment of outfitting enough aircraft with countermeasures gear. It was the design engineer's classic weakness: continuing to improve a unit instead of seeing that the maximum number of workable units got into the field.

Terman sent additional business management personnel to ABL-15 to help resist outside pressures and to help expedite both the acquisition of parts and product placement in the field. Earl Cullum was sent over to examine the situation, and Claflin assisted Terman in getting Colonel J. K. Howard released from military duty at Harvard to go to ABL-15. The situation improved with the arrival of Clark Cahill as associate technical director of ABL-15 and John P. Chase as associate administrative director to assist Dyer in June 1944.

RRL's Contributions to the Radio War

The Radio Research Laboratory served as the principal U.S. agency concerned with radar countermeasures. Begun in February 1942 with less than a handful of staff, it reached more than two hundred employees by the end of 1942 and grew to approximately eight hundred in 1943, including more than two hundred twenty-five research associates with scientific or engineering training. The RRL produced broadly in four categories of research: jammer transmitters for defeating enemy radar; improved Window and chaff reflectors to produce false reflections in enemy radar; tunable receivers, direction finders, and recorders for searching for enemy radar; and methods of protecting Allied radar against enemy countermeasures. Although RRL started virtually from scratch, by the war's end, the U.S. military had ordered more than $150 million worth of equipment based on RRL design, and had an equal amount under consideration (and canceled at the end of hostilities).

During the last two years of the war particularly, from mid-1943 to mid-1945, RRL-developed units protected strategic bombers against radar controlled anti-aircraft fire, defended the Normandy landings and other invasions, were widely used on shipboard to detect and jam enemy radar, and were used in several theaters of war for reconnaissance of enemy radar from airplanes. Strategic bombers in the European and Mediterranean theaters (Eighth and Fifteenth Air Forces) used combined jamming and Window against ground radar-controlled fire. With the collapse of the German air fighter corps in 1944, anti-aircraft fire remained the only serious Axis weapon against Allied bombing. By late 1944 each heavy bomber carried two jammers and enough chaff to produce false echoes as if from seven hundred to one thousand airplanes. In excess of seven thousand units of the APT-2 Carpet model jammer alone were produced. More than half of Germany's electronic research from late 1943 onward was devoted to saving their radar system from countermeasure efforts. Postwar analysis suggests that RRL efforts may have saved eight hundred Allied bombers and their crews, six hundred in Europe and two hundred in the Pacific. RRL-developed countermeasure support of B-29 bombing in the Pacific theater began quite early in operations against Japan. In addition to jammers and Window on each B-29, "Porcupine" B-29s, each with fifteen jammers, arrived early over the target and circled during the raids, protecting the other planes.

Several hundred ships also were equipped with RRL jamming equipment at the Normandy landings and similar support was used in landings in southern France, Sicily, Salerno, and at Leyte and elsewhere in the Pacific. Radar countermeasures equipment was standard on all navy ships, from submarines and destroyer escorts to all larger vessels, by the end of the war. Each surface vessel carried at least three countermeasure units developed by RRL. The navy had hundreds of PB4Y2 patrol planes, each carrying nine different RRL developments. The army similarly operated many B-17 and B-24 Ferret radar reconnaissance aircraft.

In addition, RRL supported the armed forces in field operations, with seventy staff at the ABL-15 laboratory in England and later in Paris, and with technical observers for the army and army air forces in North Africa and Italy in the Mediterranean Theater, in the China-Burma-India Theater, at Guam, at Okinawa, and with General MacArthur's headquarters in Australia.[180] Terman and RRL received warm congratulatory letters of recognition from Generals Jimmy Doolittle and H. McClelland and from Admiral Furer, as well as from Bush and NDRC leaders. As example, in the fall of 1945 Lloyd Berkner, the navy radio engineer and ionospherist who helped get Terman into the countermeasures job was by now himself a full navy captain in the radio and electrical group of the navy's Bureau of Aeronautics. In a farewell address Berkner said that Terman and his lab had done "a colossal job on aircraft electronic countermeasures," and that he hoped the friendships formed with Terman's staff would be real and lasting.[181]

Meanwhile, on the home front, RRL authors contributed to the technical volume series produced by McGraw-Hill, particularly the two-volume *Very High-*

Frequency Techniques, edited by Herbert J. Reich and Louise S. McDowell and RRL staff, with thirty-five chapters written by John W. Christensen, Seymour Cohn, Matthew T. Lebenbaum, Laurence A. Manning, Jessie Ann Nelson, Robert A. Soderman,T. Gregg Stephenson, William R. Rambo, and numerous additional RRL technical associates.[182] RRL staff made a total of 606 invention disclosures, which were turned over to the U.S. Navy for decision regarding patent application. Forty-six RRL staff submitted invention disclosures. Some RRL staff worked in areas with more potential for patents than others (for example, very-high-frequency and microwave circuits and devices, as compared to those working on Window). Among those with the highest number of disclosures were the Ohio State University antenna expert and engineer John D. Kraus with twenty-one disclosures and nine patent applications, and William R. Rambo, Stanford engineer and electronic specialist with twenty-one disclosures and eight patent applications.[183]

Closing Down

Vannevar Bush felt strongly that OSRD and its subsidiary organizations and divisions should go out of business at the end of World War II. He began preparing for this by early 1944, but while many Americans thought the war would be over by Christmas 1944, events in the Pacific as well as in the forests of the Ardennes intervened. Just as the Germans made a ferocious final stand in Europe, the American military prepared for the invasion of Japan. After two years of relatively few requests from the Pacific Theater and comparative ignorance of Japanese radar capabilities, the U.S. military stepped up surveillance from U.S. submarines. The Japanese, it was soon learned, not only used 200 MHz radar but 10-centimeter radar ("Rope" had been developed mostly to defend against Japanese 100 to 200 MHz radar) and they were using chaff.

RRL's technical observers were being switched from the European Theater to the Pacific and the China-Burma-India Theaters, and plans were underway to augment the Pacific Technical Observers with establishment of a Pacific version of ABL-15, when Vannevar Bush issued demobilization plans in October 1944 for the finishing of projects and phasing out of personnel. By mid-1945, he made it clear that OSRD would shut down at war's end, turning over thousands of tons of equipment to military authorities and, by extension, to a number of American universities.

Worried about the transition of his staff back into the workforce, Terman arranged for job counseling for RRL employees at all levels and invited government and private company recruiters to interview employees at RRL. He kept careful records of all who received job offers. Some 95 percent, he calculated, ultimately received good offers. He also wrote hundreds of letters to companies and to universities recommending his staff for employment positions or, in many cases, for graduate work. One career path led back to academia, but in some cases, careers in government research continued, at least temporarily with research units that continued in altered form. American Airlines, for example, acted as contractor for what became Airborne Instruments Laboratories (AIL) at Mineola, Long Island, New York. John Dyer, Matt Lebenbaum, Bill Rambo, and at least a dozen other RRL staff went to AIL.

As the war ended, Terman hoped to see not only the publication of RRL technical reports, but of popular stories describing countermeasures contributions to the war effort. In late November 1945, Terman called a press conference at RRL for the print and radio press, with staff on hand prepared to demonstrate the lab's workings in a full day of presentations. Mike Villard played a major role in the public presentation of RRL's mission and accomplishments. Villard had been given an array of special assignments at RRL, according to Terman, "because of his effectiveness in dealing with people, his ability to size up and evaluate situations, and his tremendous energy." Among his duties in the liaison division for special assignments, Villard made weekly visits with navy and army offices in Washington. To keep RRL informed, Villard began writing a highly valued "Washington Newsletter" for all RRL group and division leaders. When RRL began to wind down in the summer and fall of 1945, Villard was assigned by Terman to head an editorial group charged with writing the director's final report, the *Administrative History of the Radio Research Laboratory*. Villard wrote much of this report as well as a later publication for the public about countermeasures, "Electronic Warfare," published by the U.S. government. The *Administrative History of the Radio Research Laboratory* was submitted March 21, 1946, for Harvard's Contract OEMsr-411 with NDRC. Although it is a splendid document, it was never published, much to Terman's regret. Harvard University apparently had no interest in publishing either RRL technical reports or a full-length popular account. Villard attempted to interest journals as diverse as the ham radio magazine *QST* and the national magazines, *Time* and *Look*, with little success. In the wake of the bombings at Hiroshima and Nagasaki and the end of the war in Europe, the American public was exhausted with war reporting and the American press wanted articles that looked toward a peaceful future, not a wartime past.

As RRL was closing down, an in-house contest was held for the best stories from the war. Among the many poignant memories of the days of RRL was a short and most precise entry submitted by young Thomas Kuhn, Harvard '43 (who would go on to a distinguished career as a historian and philosopher of science): "The story of Radar Countermeasures," he said simply, "is the story of men who labored, not to build a better mousetrap, but to construct a trap-resistant mouse."[184]

Going Home

In 1944, Samuel Morris had resigned from Stanford to take over management of the Los Angeles Water District. Rumor had it among campus faculty circles, Lewis Terman wrote his son in September, that Don Tresidder wanted Fred to be the university's new dean of engineering.[185] By mid-December, President Tresidder's decision was made official. Fred was appointed dean, while his colleague Hugh Skilling would serve as acting dean until Fred's return to campus from RRL.

Long before Terman's promotion to dean, his family had already begun its own demobilization, preparing as early as mid-1944 for their return to California and Stanford. Much on Sibyl Terman's mind was her boys' education. Andover was selected for Fred Jr., who hoped to eventually enter Stanford. Although at least two years younger than some of his classmates when he entered in the fall of 1944, Fred Jr. quickly adjusted to life there, writing home of how it felt to enter Andover as a college "prep" and of the good-natured rivalries between the other boys and the "preps." Facing a tougher curriculum than he had been used to, Fred Jr. nonetheless did well. Fred Terman approved of his eldest son's ambition to go to Stanford and helped get application materials together. Sibyl, however, was evidently less positive. "I am sorry if you don't entirely approve of it," Fred Jr. wrote his mother, "but it seems best to me."[186] As the family made plans to leave Massachusetts, Terman concluded that entering Fred Jr. at Palo Alto High School in the fall of 1945 would be a waste of time. He must either spend an additional year at Andover or enter Stanford. Fred Jr. opted for Stanford.

Sibyl was tempted to send Bo to Andover as well, skipping him a grade to enter the high school. Andover was a charming, beautiful place, she felt. Bo, however, stayed at Cambridge Upper School, which was more to his liking than Belmont Hill, while Lewis began at Cambridge Lower School. Bo was homesick for California, however. As the date of their return was pushed closer to Christmas 1945, he returned to Palo Alto in the fall of 1945 and enrolled at Menlo School, in neighboring Menlo Park, as a boarder.[187]

A perfect end to their four years in Massachusetts was that summer of 1945 spent at the Claflin's beach property on the coast at East Marion, Massachusetts, "a lovely summer in a beautiful spot," as Sibyl described it. With activities winding down at RRL, Fred was able to spend more time with his family. The estate came complete with guesthouse, servant's cottage, and private beach. Bo and Lewis spent the entire summer at East Marion, while Fred Jr. came down in August after Andover summer school was over. The boys—Fred was now sixteen; Bo turned fourteen and Lewis ten at the end of the summer—were all healthy and busy, and visitors came often. Bo's troublesome hay fever had finally cleared up. Fred Jr. drove his mother to nervous fits, she wrote, practicing driving the family car. The property was located on an enclosed bay, with warm summer water and safe sailing conditions for the little sailboat the boys used. This summer would remain one of the family's happiest memories.[188]

That fall, Fred Jr. and Bo set out on their own for the West Coast on the Canadian Pacific line via Montreal because American train reservations were still difficult to obtain, a trip they both enjoyed.[189] Young Fred's entry into Stanford seemed effortless and his first term went well. Sibyl instead worried about Bo and his adjustment to the food and boarding conditions at Menlo School. Both boys were within five miles of their grandparents, however.

The rental years had not been kind to Terman's house on campus. The large house on Salvatierra Street had been rented to officer's wives and military families, with Stanford students renting the cottage in the back. One officer and family, in particular, seemed to get behind in rental payments, and Anna Terman, managing the property for Fred and Sibyl, finally asked them to leave. Subsequently, the Stanford Mother's Club in 1943 leased the house for a soldier's convalescent home.[190] Thinking of the house's condition, Sibyl wrote, "my heart sinks." Fred concluded that it was time to completely renovate. In 1945, the Mother's Club, which had taken over the lease of the Termans' house in 1943, asked for a five-year lease on the campus home, but Fred refused. The Termans were coming home.[191]

In 1946, the Termans returned to a topsy-turvy campus. Just as Stanford had put behind it the pressures of wartime mobilization and severe housing shortages, it faced new challenges with the boom times of G.I. bill tuitions and yet another dramatic change in student demographics. President Tresidder struggled to take control by drastically reorganizing Stanford's administration and its patched-together, cramped, and often crumbling buildings and classrooms, while he looked out for new sources of financial support and ways to improve undergraduate student life. His actions, however, were not often welcomed by an anxious faculty.

Fred had been back on the Stanford campus for about five months when he corresponded with his old friend, former student, and former RRL staff member Ed Yunker. Yunker, who had returned to the faculty at Oregon State College (now University), shared with Stanford's new dean of engineering data for Terman's comparative salary study of professorial ranks. "The secretarial situation here is not what it was at RRL," Fred added in a penciled note to one typed letter. "Instead of having two secretaries of my own I now have one—shared with 15 other people! It has taken two days to get this letter typed. Guess the war is over."[192]

FIGURE 1. Fred Terman, nearly three years old, in Indiana, March 1903. Courtesy of Coralie Somers and Myrilla Sparhawk.

FIGURE 2. Lewis M. Terman and his family in the garden at their new home in Glendale, Calif., 1908. Left to right: mother Anna; Fred; sister Helen; and father Lewis. Courtesy of Doris Tucker.

FIGURE 3. Ham radio operator Fred Terman, ca. 1917, in his parents' campus home on Dolores Street, Stanford. Courtesy of Stanford News Service and Terman family.

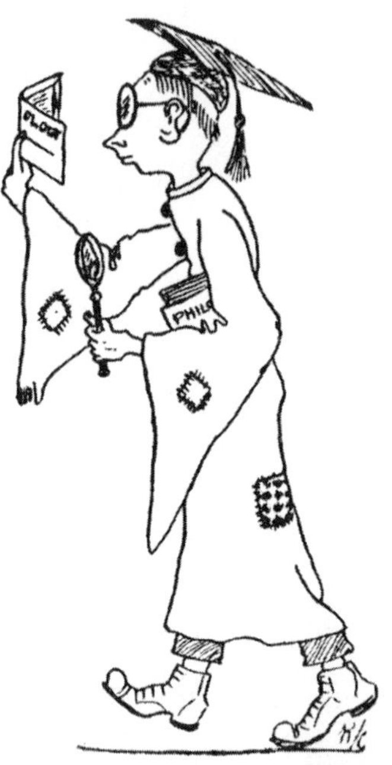

FIGURE 4. A high school caricature of the studious sixteen-year-old Fred Terman, drawn by classmate Kenneth Crowninshield. *Madrono*, Christmas Issue, 1916.

FIGURE 5. In the fall of 1918, many of Stanford's male students posed for their yearbook photographs in their Army Special Training Program uniforms. Here is eighteen-year-old Fred Terman. Courtesy of Coralie Somers and Myrilla Sparhawk.

FIGURE 6. The 1918 track team, with Fred Terman (bottom row, left) and Lloyd Dinkelspiel (second from left). *Stanford Quad*, 1919.

FIGURE 7. Stanford's Theta Xi fraternity house, and especially its many engineers, is caricatured in the yearbook, "Engineers Bunkhouse." *Stanford Quad*, 1920.

FIGURE 8. Fred Terman as a Stanford graduate student, ca. 1922, perhaps taken before leaving California for MIT. Fred began center-parting his hair after graduating with his bachelor's degree in 1920. (After engagement to Sibyl Walcutt in 1927, at her request, Fred gave up the center-part.) Courtesy of Patricia Terman.

FIGURE 9. Wedding-day photograph, March 22, 1928, of Sibyl Walcutt and Fred Terman, taken at Lewis and Anna Terman's house on Dolores Street, Stanford. Courtesy of Terence Terman.

FIGURE 10. Sketch of Fred Terman drawn by Sibyl on their honeymoon, March 1928. Courtesy of Stanford News Service.

FIGURE 11a. The Terman family in their home on Salvatierra Street, Stanford, ca. 1933. Their third son, Lewis, was not yet born. Left to right: Sibyl; Terence; father Fred; and son Fred. Courtesy of Department of Special Collections, Stanford University.

FIGURE 11b. Fred's son Lewis Terman, ca. 1940. Courtesy of Patricia Terman.

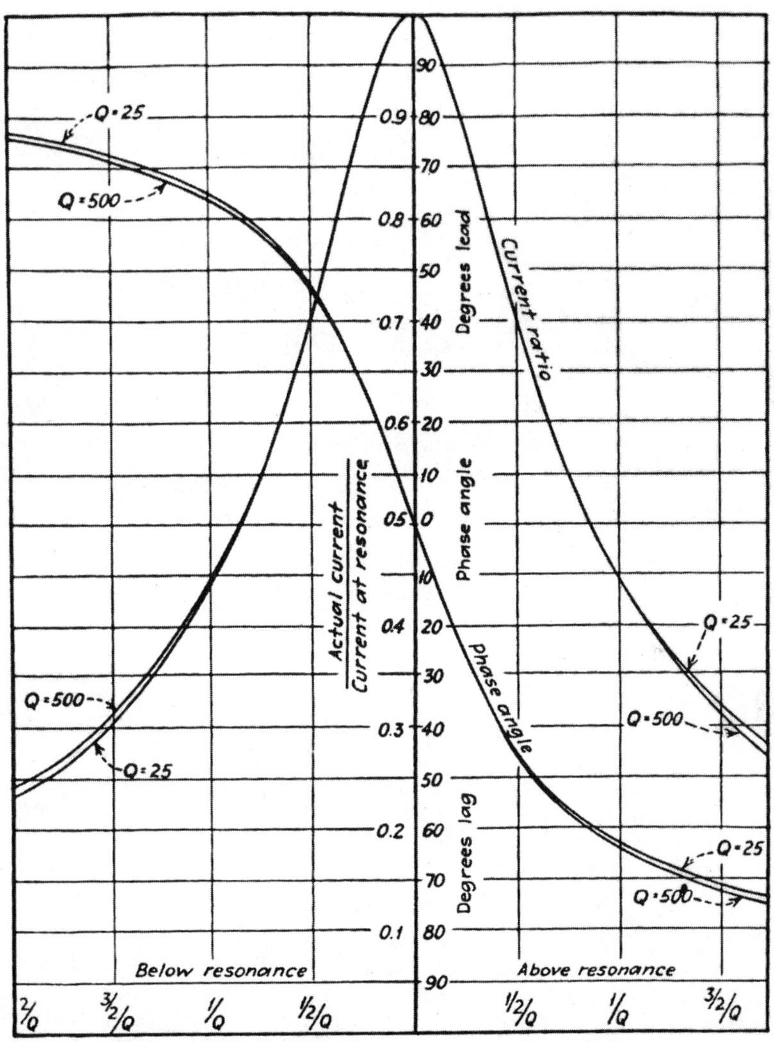

Fig. 29.—Universal resonance curve from which the exact ratio of actual current to current at resonance, as well as exact phase angle, can be determined for any series circuit in terms of the fractional deviation of the actual frequency from resonance. This curve can also be applied to the parallel resonant circuit by considering the vertical scale to represent the ratio of actual parallel impedance to the parallel impedance at resonance. When applied to parallel circuits angles shown in the figure as leading, are lagging, and *vice versa.*

FIGURE 12. "Universal Resonance Curve" as charted in Terman's text *Radio Engineering* (1st ed., 1932).

FIGURE 13. Fred Terman, now chair of the Electrical Engineering Department in his office in the Engineering Building 500, ca. 1938. Courtesy of O. G. Villard, Jr.

FIGURE 14. Bill Hewlett (on left) and Bob Sink playing chess in Terman's attic radio lab in the Engineering Building 500, ca. 1938. Bottles in photo were included as a gag. Segments of the attic were partitioned with wire screening for limiting electrical interference and secured with padlocks. Courtesy of Hewlett Family Archives.

FIGURE 15. Bill Hewlett (on left) and unidentified fellow student (possibly Ed Ginzton), climbing the outer stone walls of the Engineering Building 500, ca. 1938. Hewlett was an avid skier and outdoorsman. Courtesy of Hewlett Family Archives.

FIGURE 16. Dean of Engineering Fred Terman, with Bill Hewlett (center) and Dave Packard, taken during the dedication of the Electronics Research Laboratory's Hewlett-Packard wing, 1952. Courtesy of Stanford News Service.

FIGURE 17. President-Provost's staff meeting, 1961. Left to right: Albert Bowker, Provost Fred Terman, President Wally Sterling, Fred Glover (obscured), and Robert Wert. Terman is obviously making a point, waving his hand, his hair messed up. Wally Sterling is like a bear, smoking, looking at Fred. This is really Fred and Wally in action. Courtesy of Stanford News Service.

FIGURE 18. President Sterling and Provost Terman, in the President's Office, 1965. Courtesy of Stanford News Service.

FIGURE 19. Fred Terman at retirement, 1965. Courtesy of Stanford News Service.

CHAPTER FIVE

Jump-starting Engineering at Stanford

1942–1949

Appointed dean of engineering while still directing the Radio Research Laboratory, Fred Terman's objectives for Stanford's School of Engineering were straightforward. The school, he firmly believed, was at a crossroads. It could settle back and be the fourth- or fifth-best engineering school in California, or it could become "the most attractive and leading School of Engineering west of the Mississippi River, with the possible exception of the California Institute of Technology." Even in this, Stanford could "give the California Institute of Technology real competition by virtue of the fact we are a university, while they are a technical school," Terman wrote President Tresidder just after the war. "It should be a privilege and an honor to be permitted to study engineering at Stanford."[1]

Stanford had been merely a bit player in the war research drama, and Terman was determined to take advantage of federal funding he knew would come available at the end of the war. While significantly strengthening the School of Engineering's three traditional departments of electrical, mechanical, and civil engineering, Terman also initiated new fields (and eventually new departments) of aeronautics, engineering mechanics, and industrial engineering, and encouraged the creation of new programs outside of engineering, such as statistics and, later, computer science. Although postwar federal contracts helped jump-start these engineering programs, Terman in fact was more interested in a broader-based financial improvement of the university as well as the School of Engineering. Even before returning to Stanford, he looked ahead to a twenty-year process of building firm foundations for better faculty salaries, student fellowships and support, and improved teaching and research facilities.

Planning for Twenty Years

During his wartime years at the Radio Research Lab, Fred Terman corresponded with his friend and Stanford fund-raiser Paul Davis about possibilities for establishing a research institute at Stanford. Davis had noticed that Caltech and MIT appeared to have more advantageous organizational structures, he wrote Terman in 1943, and Northwestern had just established a technological institute within their university structure. Electrical, mechanical, and civil engineering at Stanford were organized within the School of Engineering, but the organization of chemistry, physics, mathematics, geology, mining, mining engineering, and aerodynamics at Stanford appeared to be very loosely coordinated. "What about a Stanford technological institute which would include all of these units?" Davis wrote. The end of the war would be the time for Stanford to revise its current school structure, and the plan would be devised then.[2] The system of division of the university's academic departments into schools had been organized by President Wilbur twenty-five years earlier, and there were now at Stanford the Schools of Physical Sciences, Biological Sciences, Engineering, Humanities, and Social Sciences, as well as the Schools of Law, Medicine, and Business.

Fred agreed that reorganization was timely and suggested that Davis and Tresidder visit with his new friend, Harvard Treasurer Howard Claflin.[3] He cautioned against a top-heavy organization, but put off responding more fully for four months. He needed time to organize a careful response, and that summer and fall 1943 was Terman's most stressful time at RRL.[4]

Fred Terman believed that the most important thing for Stanford, for any educational institution, to do at this time was first to develop well-thought-out plans. The immediate postwar years would be critical. Stanford could either create the foundation work to rise toward a position of national prominence, or drop to a level similar to Dartmouth, "a well thought of institution having about 2 percent as much influence on national life as Harvard." Terman would plan a twenty-year program to equal or excel Caltech in the physical sciences and technology (twenty, Terman predicted, because that would probably be the length of Tresidder's administration and because a program such as Terman envisioned could be fully built during that period). "If we achieve anything approaching this, C.I.T. [Caltech] is licked, because after all they are only a specialized school, and Stanford is a complete university."

Pulling the physical sciences and technology together would be a great improvement, but, he warned, any plan must be built "on an irresistible desire to push to the top, combined with an understanding of what it is that being at the top represents. The most important measure of success is in terms of student output, which must be both *large* in number and *outstanding* in quality." Stanford's undergraduate work should be attractive, with high standards, but without "trick curricula or degrees." A strong graduate curriculum would allow Stanford to skim the cream of the undergraduate crop from other universities and keep the best of its own.

"A technical institute," Terman believed, "would provide a splendid opportunity to create a special organization or activity having as its ostensible objective the placing of our students in strategic positions having a future." Such an effort would promote Stanford to employers. Good Stanford people placed in industry as well as in teaching would hire more Stanford people, "and so on ad infinitum." The advantages for fund-raising were also obvious.

Stanford should increasingly concentrate resources on the fields that were of interest to large numbers of students or were particularly important to the western states. For example, the oil industry was important to the western economy, and therefore Stanford should be strong in all things relating to oil, including geology, heat transfer, and chemical engineering. Radio and electronic engineering were rapidly growing fields, as was the field of mechanical structures. Terman began to enunciate his organizational philosophy of "steeples of excellence," which he would lecture about frequently in the 1950s and 1960s, focusing largely on carefully selecting faculty in carefully selected fields. When you formed a track team, he wrote, you did not go after two men who could jump three feet high; you went for one man who could jump six feet. Stephen P. Timoshenko was one of the world's great experts in theoretical and applied mechanics and a marvelous teacher; paid only about twice the salary of an associate professor, he was worth far more.

Economy as well as efficiency came with good planning. Few people in education, Terman wrote to Davis, "really know what counts." Fred looked out at the competition and speculated: How much further ahead would MIT be if it had carefully laid out and well-executed plans in electrical engineering? Caltech, increasingly smug, was revealing cracks in its armor. In these remarks, it is clear that Terman was thinking primarily about the future structure of the engineering and physical sciences at Stanford. Fred wrote to Davis that he had spoken his mind freely and asked Davis to keep his remarks personal and confidential, but Davis was "thrilled" with Terman's letter. Given its attractive display of tremendous opportunities for Stanford, he begged Terman in January 1944 to let him show it to Tresidder and key trustees George Ditz and Paul Edwards, chairs of trustee committees on academic affairs and on planning.[5] Fred responded by telegram that Davis could show the letter using his judgment on "What will be best for Stanford."[6] Davis subsequently asked Terman if he could show the letter to Alvin Eurich, then in line for Stanford's vice presidency.[7] Eurich thought Terman's idea of a technical institute "a grand one" and looked forward to discussing it further.[8]

Tresidder had known of Terman's general views since at least 1942, when as president of Stanford's board of trustees, he learned that Bill Hansen, Fred, and

Felix Bloch were drafting plans for a microwave research lab at Stanford. Terman wanted to bring more science into engineering, and saw physics, mathematics, and engineering working together. Tresidder considered combining the School of Engineering with the School of Physical Sciences in order to create an Institute of Technology, shepherded by a new dean of science and technology at Stanford.[9] Eldridge T. Spencer, Tresidder's newly appointed director of planning, got the impression from a discussion with Eurich in late 1944 that there was "a definite move in the direction of a School of Technology to include Physics, Chemistry, and Engineering," although he saw this as a trend only, without form.[10] Yet where Terman saw a carefully planned technological institute at Stanford as an opportunity to give "the physical sciences group sufficient voice in the affairs of the institution, and some measure of autonomy in solving their educational problems," Eurich wanted to foster an institute focused on serving western industry but virtually autonomous from Stanford's faculty.

To achieve its success in an invigorated Stanford, Terman believed Stanford engineering should develop strength in five basic engineering fields: electronics, engineering mechanics, thermodynamics, fluid mechanics, and structures. Stanford possessed a good name, and particular strength in electronics and engineering mechanics that could serve as a promising foundation. Ten faculty members, Terman wrote, national leaders distributed among these five fields and given appropriate backing and staff would make Stanford one of the greatest engineering schools in the country.

Fred Terman would view his first years as dean of engineering as a chance to jump-start the school, both a necessity and an opportunity. But Terman entered as dean of engineering on the Stanford campus only in January 1946, when his wartime duties were finally finished. He would serve as dean of engineering at Stanford for more than thirteen years and most—in some ways, many—of his wishes for Stanford engineering he would help come true.

Managing Stanford During and Just After World War II

In January 1942, Fred Terman had left Stanford with a new board of trustees head, Donald Tresidder, looking for a new Stanford president. The Electrical Engineering Department was in the good hands of Terman's trusted assistant Hugh Skilling as acting chairman, but there were many challenges still to be met both for Stanford engineering and the university. Stanford was going to lose tuition income from male students sure to go off to war. Some technically trained faculty, especially in the physical sciences and engineering, would serve their country elsewhere than on the campus. If Stanford were successful in obtaining contracts to teach needed skills to military troops, the most appropriate teachers would be those already removed for duty elsewhere. Most of the microwave people had left for Sperry a year earlier, and Terman grabbed both graduate students and recently graduated PhDs in radio and communications—Bob Soderman, Mike Villard, Joe Pettit, and others—for RRL duty. Others had stayed at Stanford to help teach in the Electrical Engineering Department, including "Skip" Athey, Bill Barclay, and young Bob Helliwell. Assistant Professor Karl Spangenberg carried a heavy teaching schedule with courses in electronics and microwaves. Victor Carson was brought back from a year of teaching at the University of Connecticut to help Spangenberg. Athey and Spangenberg would later leave for government service with the military or at RRL. Skilling lined up more electrical engineering faculty to help with the increased teaching. The large number of students coming with the military needed coursework in radio and radar and electronics, and these were not the specialties of the remaining senior faculty. While Spangenberg and the technically advanced younger faculty did the electronics and microwave teaching, Joe Carroll, Ward Kindy, Bill Hoover, and Leland Brown could carry the load teaching electrical motors and machines, also a part of the courses for the military.

Engineering Dean Samuel Morris and Stanford administrators had tried in 1940 and 1941 to get the university involved in national defense research but were not very successful. The big projects went to MIT, Caltech, Berkeley, Harvard, Johns Hopkins, and Chicago. These schools had stronger records in research already underway by the beginning of the war. Caltech would continue work in aeronautics, Johns Hopkins in ordnance (especially the "proximity" radar-controlled bomb and artillery fuze); Berkeley and Chicago in nuclear physics and the atomic bomb; MIT in radar, mine detection, guidance and control mechanisms. Stanford, however, garnered comparatively few military research contracts during the war.

Stanford faculty were in demand—some were in military service, some were in civilian government service away from the United States or at Los Alamos working on the atomic bomb, or working in other government service as was Fred Terman. Stanford's main job during World War II, however, would be to teach several thousand soldiers—enlisted men and young officers. The wartime university ran twelve months of the year, night and day. Soldier-students were housed in dormitories and fraternities.

The Electrical Engineering Department developed courses for the military in two main areas: radio-electronics, and motors and machinery. The department continued some research, mainly taking over the remaining klystron work and some high-frequency radio work sponsored by Sperry and by IT&T.

As the war continued, Wilbur and Tresidder sent Paul Hanna, a prominent professor of education then serving as director of university services, and General Secretary Paul H. Davis to Washington DC to promote Stanford's interests and to generate contracts within the federal government. Hanna opened a Stanford office in Washington. Professor Alvin Eurich, in Washington as a reserve navy officer organizing the nation's V-12 college officers' training courses, also helped with contacts and contracts for Stanford. These men hoped to "Organize Stanford's Resources for Public Service," as a 1942 report posited.[11] Similarly, Fred Terman helped when he could, introducing Stanford people to military planning and procurement officers. Terman and Davis exchanged many letters about university finances, gifts, and bequest possibilities, discussions Paul Hanna later viewed as very influential in Stanford's postwar planning.[12]

President Don Tresidder and his staff worried particularly about radically fluctuating student enrollment. When the United States entered the war, male student enrollment fell significantly. During Tresidder's first quarter as president, in the fall of 1943, civilian student enrollment had dropped to 2,100, two-thirds of them women.[13] Young men in uniform, who were on campus to take special courses that spring, had joined the civilians, however. By fall 1943, the Army Specialized Training Program (ASTP) numbered almost 3,000 enlisted men. To these were added special programs for medical and dental students in a navy V-12 officer candidate program, and a contingent of women WACS in a physical-therapy program.[14] Tresidder was alert to the benefit of financial stipends brought in by this large number of soldier-students, just as President Wilbur had been during World War I, but the sudden influx brought severe pressure on housing and dining facilities as well as staff to teach appropriate old and new courses.

During the early phases of the ASTP at Stanford, visiting military brass were not impressed. The army had expected university presidents to be "cooperative"—to use classrooms at night, increase teaching hours, crowd housing facilities—and expected Stanford to train 3,000 ASTP soldiers. Tresidder felt Stanford was doing its best, but in November 1943, an army report severely criticized the housing and feeding arrangements and reported that Stanford was not equipped to handle more than 2,200 soldiers. The army wanted Stanford to take on more soldiers in engineering, psychology, and in area and language studies, and feared that Stanford's laboratories could not accommodate a sufficient number of engineers.[15]

In order to qualify for an officer's commission, regularly enrolled undergraduate students could accelerate their coursework and graduate in three years. Meanwhile, women not only filled in at key positions in student government and publications but also took war job-related courses. Women took the engineering drafting course beginning in the summer of 1942, and every quarter thereafter women could be found in drafting classes. Forty-five draftswomen in the first group were employed by Consolidated-Vultee Aircraft Corporation. Some women took special courses in chemical analysis and other technical subjects to be equipped for wartime employment.[16]

As at other universities across the country, humanities faculty could be found teaching drafting or introductory mathematics, and professors proficient in foreign languages gave instruction in language and foreign area studies while faculty were added in fields like geography and anthropology. Emeriti faculty came out of retirement—for example, Professor of Machine Design Guido H. Marx, who began his career among the pioneer faculty at Stanford in 1895, returned to help teach, while William Durand, at age eighty-two, returned to the National Advisory Committee on Aeronautics (NACA) committee work to investigate advances in German rocketry.[17]

Stanford's Electrical Engineering Department taught courses late into the evening, including a course for army signal corps officers in ultra-high-frequency radio under the auspices of the government's Engineering Science and Management Defense Training Program (ESMDT).[18] In addition, radio "fundamentals" courses for ESMDT were given at night in San Francisco and hundreds of miles north in Eureka, California.[19]

In June 1942, reported Hugh Skilling, the Army Signal Corps Training Program budget in electrical engineering was about three times the yearly Electrical Engineering Department budget, and he expected the faculty to more than double, to eighteen persons by 1943. Karl Spangenberg, Bill Hoover, and others were carrying a heavy teaching load, and Spangenberg had reported in March 1942 that Bill Barclay, Mike Villard, and Skip Athey "are just putting in super human performances" in teaching and in carrying on the Sperry and other research projects. Villard had finished the 2–5 MHz automatic ionospheric sounder by February 8, 1942, and would have the 5–12 MHz unit finished by the end of spring. Talented undergraduate senior Bob Helliwell would take over when Villard left in late July 1942 to join Terman at RRL in Cambridge.[20]

As the war effort wound down, military need for the special courses subsided, and Stanford worried about lack of tuition revenues brought in by the student-soldiers and empty lecture halls.[21] By VJ-Day in August 1945, Stanford had around 1,500 undergraduates; again nearly two-thirds of the student body were women. The war's end brought new concern—as veterans returned to campus under the GI Bill, beginning as early as mid-1945, the floodgates opened, and again Stanford faced significant housing, classroom, and faculty shortages. Enrollment was 3,726 in autumn quarter 1945 and 4,995 by spring quarter 1946, with three-quarters of them men and more than 2,000 veterans.[22] The GI Bill brought both more mature students and much-needed funding through tuition and living allowances, but the campus needed to provide additional teaching staff, attend to a great deal of deferred maintenance, and undertake new construction.

Fred Terman saw these changes through his rare visits to the Stanford campus and through his regular correspondence with Dean Morris and especially with Hugh Skilling. In Fred's first quarter back on campus, winter 1946, the school estimated that student enrollment in fall 1946 would be 7,000 and there was on-campus dormitory housing only for 4,000. Stanford student enrollment in fall

1947 was a whopping 8,203, including 6,220 men and 1,983 women.[23] Stanford administrators maneuvered successfully to obtain the housing facilities of the former Dibble General Hospital in Menlo Park, built in 1944 to handle navy casualties in the event of a land invasion of Japan. By fall 1945, the new property termed "Stanford Village" housed 1,300 people, mostly single male students, and soon after an additional 300 families with children.[24] A few years later, the new Stanford Research Institute would begin to utilize the Stanford Village grounds and buildings, but Stanford students, married and single, graduate and undergraduate, continued to live in the Village until the 1960s. The Village was literally a lifesaver as student housing for many thousands of Stanford students.

Fred Terman was well aware of such housing problems. Within a few weeks of his return in January 1946, Terman sent President Tresidder a letter outlining Harvard University's efforts to find housing for returning veterans and married students. Terman knew Harvard's plans since he had very recently discussed them with Harvard's administrator in charge of real estate, John Chase, Terman's RRL Business Manager of the ABL-15 branch laboratory in England.[25] Among alumni, David Packard, as chairman of the Veterans' Employment and Service Council, worked to find housing for veterans, especially those married.[26]

Faculty and Student Problems During Tresidder's Administration

Tresidder was an accomplished manager, a talent recognized not only by his father-in-law, David "Pop" Curry, but also by Stanford's trustees and senior administrators. His efforts to reorganize, streamline, and energize the campus were those of a successful businessman, with little patience at times for the internal rhythms of academia.

Tresidder's predecessor, the lanky Ray Lyman Wilbur, had delegated little. Even during his years in Washington DC as Herbert Hoover's secretary of the interior, Wilbur kept a tight rein on Stanford. Robert Swain, as acting president, deferred regularly to Wilbur. Indeed, Wilbur had been criticized for trying to do two jobs at once but when Stanford's board of trustees approached President Hoover, their fellow board member, about a leave of absence from Stanford's presidency, he refused either to let Wilbur return to Stanford, or to let Stanford release Wilbur, however temporarily. Yet, though holding the reins tightly, Wilbur remained remarkably approachable. He kept his busy office open to any faculty who wished to see him.[27]

Less approachable to the faculty (although not to students) than Wilbur, Tresidder also seemed to demand more bureaucratic operations. Lewis Terman wrote to Fred about President Tresidder's ill-advised moves, such as an annoying directive requiring all Stanford faculty to file leave slips or obtain permission to leave the campus, even for a day, during term time. In his choice of helpmates, Tresidder could be precipitous. Early in his presidency, Tresidder selected education professor Alvin Eurich as his new "vice president for academic affairs." Tresidder had been impressed with Eurich when they first met around 1939, and Eurich was anxious to move ahead into a position of administrative importance. In January 1944, in office only four months, Tresidder secured an agreement with the navy to allow Eurich to return to Stanford in the spring of 1944. Eurich's selection proved to be one of the most controversial of Tresidder's administration.[28] Just as Stanford faculty had criticized Tresidder's appointment of Professor of English Clarence Faust as graduate dean because of his alleged lack of scholarly work, the selection of a member of Stanford's School of Education as the university's academic vice president now brought forth a similar insinuation.[29] Tresidder ignored the suspicion that a professor of education could not fully understand the life of scholarship. Having selected a trustworthy executive officer, Tresidder deliberately delegated virtually all faculty affairs issues to Eurich. Two years later, he elevated Eurich to the post of vice president, clearly the president's second in command. Indeed, Eurich's letters were often signed "Acting President."[30]

As he moved forward to reorganize other administrative reporting schemes, Tresidder regularly scheduled meetings with his growing team of administrators as well as with faculty. Faced with the dramatic changes brought by wartime money and government requirements, he moved to modernize Stanford's recordkeeping and budgeting routines. Senator Stanford had placed financial management of the university he founded in the hands of its board of trustees, and they in turn appointed a chief financial officer who reported directly to the board. In 1940, trustee Frank Fish Walker had resigned from the board to become this officer. Early in 1946, Tresidder persuaded the trustees that financial matters, like all other university operations, should report through the presidency. Tresidder instructed Vice President Eurich to inform Walker of the change, and Eurich, in turn, was abrupt in announcing the change to Walker. Walker immediately resigned. Walker's resignation led indirectly to that of General Secretary Paul H. Davis, a close friend of Walker who had not been friendly with Eurich.[31]

Fred Terman found himself in the midst of both minor incidents and major change soon after returning to campus. Newly appointed dean of the School of Engineering, he set about tackling the details. In March 1946, Eurich suggested to Terman that he submit an estimate for certain tasks not budgeted for the current academic year. Terman made the list, but had started already on one task, that of having a part-time secretary acknowledge gifts from the Stanford Appeal. (This secretarial task was the beginning of Terman's three-by-five-inch index card list of Stanford alumni and friends, continuing lists he had kept as an electrical engineering faculty member.) For the secretary's first efforts, Terman had paid her $18.20

out of his pocket. He submitted a receipt, asking Eurich for reimbursement. In Eurich's absence, Tresidder approved the expenditure, but on the vice president's return, Eurich informed Fred that the dean had violated university policy since a petty cash payout of that sort did not properly account for social security and tax withholdings.[32]

It was not just at Stanford that faculty questioned new directions laid out by university administrations. Faculty at both Berkeley and Stanford circulated a document in April 1946 asserting that university administrators were diverting their campuses from their true purpose. A noisy meeting was held at Stanford's faculty clubhouse April 8, 1946, to discuss this document, with the respected professor of mathematics Harold M. Bacon presiding. According to notes of an administration "spy," some sixty faculty members attended; about half were emeriti and about ten were young women. Emeritus Professor Eliot Blackwelder of geology was especially outspoken. Stanford, he argued, was currently "in the hands of the worst gang of administrative blackguards that ever came down the pike." Complaints ranged widely: the Faculty Advisory Board had been bypassed in important matters, including the appointment of Alvin Eurich. Faculty had no individual say in academic matters, and the president and vice president were unreachable. The leave of absence form was an outrage, as was a new biographical questionnaire for faculty. Academic Council meetings should be closed to administrators. The administration's businessmen did not understand scholars and did not support research adequately. Although the criticism was not unanimous—political science professor Edwin A. Cottrell for one firmly defended the administration, although not the appointment of Alvin Eurich—in the end the group endorsed the document on a voice vote.[33] Tresidder received the document but did not respond. On the surface, tempers seemed to cool but not for long.

Soon after, beginning in May 1946, a series of scurrilous postcards circulated widely began an attack on Tresidder. One card stated: "How much longer will we accept the former manager of Camp Curry—Uncle Don—as President? Is not Stanford worthy of a scholar rather than a resort manager as President?" These cards, some mailed anonymously and some signed "Faculty Committee of Five," were sent to individual faculty and to members of the Stanford Associates and the board of trustees for nearly a year. Although at least three specific faculty members were suspected, no authors were ever identified publicly.[34]

Ironically, the campaign revealed significant faculty and trustee support for Tresidder. A formal statement signed by 148 faculty members confirmed that in spite of differences of opinion, the signators believed that Tresidder acted "according to his sincere convictions." As letters subsequently sent to the president revealed, this statement was little more than a general vote of loyalty. While a number of faculty wrote, saying that they had been out of town at the time of the signing, there were others who wanted to argue fine points of logic and still others who stated that, despite their disapproval of the postcard campaign, could not sign the petition of support. Still others said they had not seen the Stanford faculty statement, and until then had stayed out of the fray.[35] Although all of this uproar reflected genuine unhappiness with Tresidder's methods of management on the part of some faculty, Stanford University in the postwar years, with or without Tresidder, required new ways of planning and managing. Tresidder raised faculty hackles in some of his administrative and academic choices, but he drew praise in choosing a new dean of engineering to replace Dean Samuel Morris. He stayed inside the Stanford circle to chose a professor with an outstanding teaching and research record and with more management experience than anyone else in the School of Engineering.

Choosing a Dean of Engineering

In September 1944, Stanford's dean of engineering, Samuel Morris, resigned to accept the position of general manager and chief engineer of the Department of Water and Power of the City of Los Angeles. Morris recommended Fred Terman as his successor and urged Tresidder to appoint Fred as soon as possible, not later than January 1, 1945, since there was need for immediate planning for the postwar period.[36] Meanwhile, Hugh Skilling was appointed acting dean.

Tresidder visited Terman in Cambridge in October 1944 to explore the broad outlines of an appointment. They also discussed the possibility of an institute or "Division of Industrial Cooperation" at Stanford.[37] Terman's appointment, however, was not automatic. Tresidder had narrowed his own list of candidates to two, although officially there was a longer list. One of Tresidder's preferences was from outside Stanford, and the question again arose of whether it was an advantage to select a Stanford man. While in the East, Tresidder discussed Terman's candidacy with Vannevar Bush. On his return to Stanford, the president asked Skilling to preside over a meeting with engineering faculty where Tresidder could present Terman as well as other candidates and ask for faculty comment, verbal or written.[38] Skilling fully supported Terman's appointment, as did most of the faculty, but the nature of the objections—two voted outright against his appointment—is interesting. The Civil Engineering Department's acting head, Leon B. Reynolds, went on record to complain that many of the regular faculty were away on leave for war service (all engineering faculty, instructors, and *temporary* staff apparently had been invited to the meeting); others did not vote, he alleged, because they were young and inexperienced. Summarizing his view of faculty objections to the Terman appointment, Reynolds warned that Terman was experienced in only one field of engineering, his expertise a highly specialized division of that field.

Reynolds also professed to be concerned with Terman's health, wondering if he could stand up to the job. Interestingly, he worried that Terman, who may have become too accustomed to wartime government funding, could not adjust to the traditional frugality of Stanford's budget. And he noted that some worried that Terman might become bored with administration and miss his teaching and research. Some, he finally noted, thought he might be hard to get along with. Contradicting his own arguments, Reynolds also admitted that Terman was relatively young, that his war work must have widened his horizons and, finally, that Terman understood Stanford's tradition of a broad cultural and general engineering training for its undergraduate engineering students. Having come full circle, Reynolds concluded that he could certainly work with Terman.[39]

Tresidder later announced that Terman's overwhelming endorsement by his engineering colleagues had persuaded him to offer Terman the position. The Stanford trustees formally appointed Frederick Terman as dean of engineering just before Christmas 1944, and a publicity announcement was released on Christmas Day. In his statement, President Tresidder said, "Dr. Terman's scholarly contributions in the field of electrical engineering and his administration of one of America's largest war research projects place him among the outstanding engineers in the country. Stanford is very fortunate in securing his services as Engineering dean."[40]

Terman was, in fact, not narrower in training than his engineering colleagues but much *broader* in education: he had completed almost enough credits for a bachelor's degree in mechanical engineering; he completed a bachelor's in chemistry, in the chemical engineering preparatory track; he took twice as many units as needed for his Engineer degree in electrical engineering; he minored in chemistry as a graduate student at MIT. For a man in his forties, Fred's graduate studies in electrical engineering encompassed more physics and mathematics than most of his colleagues of that age had taken. Terman knew a wide range of outside industrial subjects from his years of patent applications, company visits, outside consultancies and his national presidency of the IRE. As for his health, Terman had run in overdrive for four years directing his staff of eight hundred at RRL.

Professor Reynolds's concerns, however, reveal the difficult choices faced by Stanford's new dean of engineering. William Kays, later to succeed Terman as dean, has suggested that there was some reluctance in the Civil Engineering Department to see the deanship go to an electrical engineer. It already was clear that the field of electronics would become an important major, and perhaps the dominant part of the Engineering School.[41] Would the new dean favor electrical engineering over the other departments, and bring change of a new and perhaps threatening sort to the old guard at Stanford?

Jump-starting the School of Engineering

Stanford had hoped to have Terman return early in 1945, but Harvard, technically his employer as head of the RRL, urged a compromise: Fred could take up the Stanford deanship full-time only in summer 1945. Although named dean in December 1944, he continued at the Harvard Radio Research Laboratory through the end of 1945 (with a brief return visit to Cambridge in late January 1946 to wind up odds and ends), while Hugh Skilling continued as acting dean. Fred's achievements were quickly rewarded elsewhere as well. In June 1945 Terman received an honorary doctorate from Harvard University in recognition of his wartime services as director of RRL. On April 24, 1946, Fred was elected to the National Academy of Sciences. Fred and his father then became a rare and almost historically unique father and son pair in the NAS. Later in 1946 Fred was awarded a high honor by the British government for his wartime services, and in 1948 he was awarded the highest award the U.S. government can give to a citizen, the Presidential Medal of Merit.

Nevertheless, as the new dean, Terman immediately sought to educate himself in detail about all the things that had happened at Stanford during his absence, and indeed in the history of the school since its founding. While still in Cambridge, Fred wasted no time asking Skilling to prepare for him copies of budgets of the Engineering School back to its founding in 1925, faculty lists and salaries, president's reports, and copies of the *University Registers* and enrollments for the past few years. He had not formulated plans yet, he wrote Skilling, but wanted to educate himself.[42] Terman's plan for Stanford's engineering and physical sciences had first been outlined in his letter to Paul Davis in late 1943.[43] His "Plan for Twenty Years to Greatness" saw Stanford's engineering and physical sciences departments developing in size and quality of research. He knew that public funds after the war would flow to the modern university for research, especially in fields pursued during the war, and he wanted to build first on the strengths he knew to exist in selected areas of the Stanford School of Engineering. On his return to Stanford he would need to build up his own research and staff in electrical engineering, but he would then focus on the Engineering School's most outstanding areas in mechanics, structures, and thermodynamics. Starting out with a limited budget, he had to find funding and convince top administration to support the school's needs.

During his first month back on campus, January 1946, Terman presented budget proposals for the School of Engineering, including the Military Science Department, to President Tresidder. For the coming academic year 1946–47, Terman estimated a minimum budget of $212,000 to "carry on the program of instruction to which the School of Engineering is committed," based on a predicted increase in overall university enrollment from 4,000 to 7,000, yet the total was less than average annual expenditure during the Depression period of 1932 to 1942. Terman allocated $48,000 to civil engineering, $55,000 to electrical engineering, $75,000 to mechanical engineering, $25,000 to mining engineering, and $8,500 to the dean's office.[44]

Terman asked Tresidder to follow through on promotion commitments already made to A. L. London in mechanical engineering and Karl Spangenberg in electrical engineering, and urged "serious consideration" for promotion of O. C. Shepherd in mining engineering. These promotions were not simply due, but timely—the school was in danger of losing all three men. He was particularly concerned that Hugh Skilling's salary be raised. Skilling had managed the Electrical Engineering Department throughout the war years and had served as acting dean of the Engineering School for fifteen months, yet he still had the lowest salary of any department head in the school.

The budget also included requests for supplemental funds for additional and part-time instructors. Jewels like emeritus professor Stephen P. Timoshenko, who had returned to teach large and popular classes during the war, would not delay their retirement for much longer. Terman and his department heads scrambled to fill teaching slots with experienced graduate students, including Mike Villard, Larry Manning, and Bob Helliwell in electrical engineering. The new dean also asked for funds to hire part-time several experts in the field of aerodynamics from Ames Laboratory at Moffett Field.

Terman also asked for a "floating fund" of $12,000 for discretionary executive funds to increase efficiency "in view of the almost complete inflexibility of the other items in the budget." Such funds had been allocated to the Dean of Engineering in the 1920s but had been squeezed out during the Depression. His "floating fund" request was not granted this time, but Terman persisted.[45]

Given his experience at the Radio Research Lab, Terman immediately took note of the school's space needs. A comparatively large number of graduate students (fifty-five) were doing electronics and more than half of electrical engineering undergraduates were concentrating on electronics courses, yet the electrical engineering facilities were spread across campus, including laboratories in four separate buildings (Room 300 in the Quadrangle, Room 500 in the attic of the electrical engineering quarters, a place called the "Hendy Space" utilized during the war, and in the hills at the Ryan High-Voltage Lab two miles away. In addition, electrical engineering communications work was carried out in two offices in the Education Building, three small field labs scattered around the Stanford foothills, and the Microwave Lab in the Physics Building.[46] Terman wanted to concentrate electronics lab activities in one building. This, he pointed out, would at least free up Room 300—the old engineering drafting room in prewar days in the outer quad—for other valuable university use.[47]

Terman also made initial changes in the degree program. The School of Engineering would now grant bachelor of science (rather than bachelor of arts) and MS degrees, and for the first time in two decades, the bachelor's degree would be designated by department and field of specialty.[48]

Developing Grant Support

Fred Terman kept Tresidder informed of his efforts to generate grant and contract funds for the School of Engineering, as well as for adjacent areas in statistics, mathematics, and physics. In his first six months back on campus, he reported to the president, he had "put in a considerable amount of time on the development of a program of sponsored research projects" and listed projects for which he "acted as the initial man for the University." He had additional projects "under active consideration." He listed projects, as of June 1946, for the Departments of Electrical Engineering, Mechanical Engineering, Physics, and Chemistry totaling about $380,000 per year from the navy's Office of Research and Invention (ORI, later ONR, the Office of Naval Research), the army air force, the signal corps, and the National Bureau of Standards (NBS): $210,000 for electrical engineering, $81,000 for mechanical engineering, $59,000 for physics, and $30,000 for chemistry. The projects, he noted, ranged widely—from Richard Ogg's work in ammonia solutions, Felix Bloch's nuclear induction studies, Bill Hansen's linear accelerator, Alfred S. Niles's aircraft structures, and Lydik Jacobsen's structural dynamics research to Bob Helliwell and Larry Manning's ionosphere studies, and the electronic circuits studies of Mike Villard, Terman, and Karl Spangenberg.[49]

Terman had immediately taken advantage of his wartime contacts, including Captain R. D. Conrad, assistant to Admiral Bowen, the head of the navy ORI, and Commander J. E. Laurance of the San Francisco office of ORI. Terman maintained his close contacts with numerous navy, signal corps, air force, and NBS administrators regarding specific projects but also welcomed more general inquiries and visitors sent to campus by government laboratories. In turn, Terman visited the government laboratories himself or delegated one of his interested professors.[50]

By August 1947, electrical engineering contracts with ONR had reached an annual rate of expenditure of about $130,000, which he felt had improved the quality as well as quantity of Stanford research. He asked ONR's Emanuel R. Piore to consolidate all electronic tasks into a single master task, simplifying operation both for Stanford and for the navy, and the navy agreed.[51] The more focused handling of research tasks for electrical engineering worked so well that other Stanford departments asked to participate in the innovative budgeting and contract administration procedures with ONR.

Stanford's initial postwar success with ONR was due in part to the skill of Leonard F. Fuller. Fuller, Stanford's first engineering PhD recipient, had chaired Berkeley's Electrical Engineering Department during the 1930s and early 1940s, but had moved back across the Bay during the war to work for the Hendy Company near the Stanford campus. After the war, he approached Hugh Skilling about a teaching or research position at the university. Terman and Skilling believed Fuller to be decades behind in technology, and they were unimpressed by both his research and teaching skills, but Fuller's administrative ability was well known. Fuller was hired to coordinate research contracts for electrical engineering. Fuller's success with electrical engineering led other departments to ask him to manage their contracts, and Terman assigned Fuller part of these duties. By May 1947, sponsored research in the School of Engineering had grown to an annual rate of $300,000; by September, that rate would increase to $400,000.

Terman's early grant activity quickly spread out from engineering into related fields. During the war, many of the country's brightest applied mathematicians and economists had worked for the military or the War Production Board in sampling, production management, gunnery and fire control, guided missiles, and operations research, and their work would transform the discipline of economics. As director of research for the Statistical Research Group of the Applied Mathematics Panel of OSRD, Stanford Economics Professor W. Allen Wallis had worked on statistical sampling methods at a government lab at Columbia University during the war. Wallis returned to Stanford with significant navy ORI interest in continuing his research. If Stanford submitted a proposal, ORI suggested to Terman in April 1946, and added the respected mathematician George Pólya as consultant, they were prepared to support Wallis's studies.[52] At this same time, Eugene Grant applied for related work with the army air force at Wright Field, citing Wallis, himself, Pólya, and others as investigators.[53]

Terman tied electrical engineering into the deal. He assumed that the ionosphere contracts in the Electrical Engineering Department could use expert help in statistical data-reduction methods. One intent of Wallis's ORI sampling project was to persuade the esteemed statistician Frederick Mosteller to join the Stanford faculty and run the project with Wallis, while a number of experts from other institutions or labs would be available as consultants. Terman arranged for one-third of Mosteller's time and one-fourth of an assistant professor's time to be charged to the Electrical Engineering Department. But statistics had been taught in the Mathematics Department since the late 1920s and had been of considerable interest to many other departments at Stanford since at least the mid-1930s. An interdepartmental committee of senior faculty—including Quinn McNemar in psychology, Harold Bacon in mathematics, and Eugene Grant in civil engineering—had urged the strengthening of statistics as a discipline at Stanford. Terman also pointed out to the president's office that NACA at Moffett Field and the air corps at Wright Field, Ohio, had expressed interest in statistical research at Stanford, and suggested that Stanford's proposed Research Institute would also need statistical expertise.[54]

Terman cleared all this activity with Tresidder and Eurich, who supported the dean's efforts.[55] Two days later, Terman reported to the president, relevant department heads, and project investigators that he had been informed by Commander Laurance that ORI had mailed out the "master contract with Stanford," which, in its initial form, would include research projects in electronics, nuclear induction, and photosensitive ammonia solutions. "There is no way of getting action," Terman wrote, "like not being content to let nature take its course."[56]

With Tresidder's approval, Terman and Wallis were prepared to move ahead quickly with Mosteller's appointment as professor of statistics. Mosteller's decision to take a position at Princeton did not derail their efforts for long.[57] Instead, in January 1947, Wallis brought a protégé from Columbia, Albert Bowker, who also had been recommended by Mina Rees of ONR. The Department of Statistics was launched in the fall of 1948, with Bowker as its first head. Bowker became one of Terman's most trusted colleagues. Moving into academic administration at Stanford, he went on to senior academic administrative positions in New York and at Berkeley, where he retired as Berkeley's chancellor.

Early in 1948, Terman proudly informed Al Eurich, then acting president (in the wake of Tresidder's death in January 1948), that only three universities had broadly chartered government-sponsored electronics programs—Stanford, MIT, and Harvard. However, he suggested, Stanford should not publicly "brag" about this status.[58] Terman believed that sponsored research in engineering was approaching its maximum capacity, and rather than expand the program haphazardly, he wanted to consolidate the school's operations and develop its position with sponsoring agencies.[59] In this way, Terman argued, engineering replaced and returned to Stanford salary money that the university could use elsewhere.

Planning for Faculty and Students

During his first six months back at Stanford, Terman worked with his new executive committee—Leon Reynolds, Hugh Skilling, Lydik Jacobsen, and Frederick Tickell, the department heads of civil, electrical, mechanical, and mining engineering—to tackle problems brought on by the dramatic increase of enrollment faced by the school.

In June, he presented their report to President Tresidder outlining the school's prospects if undergraduate enrollment was expanded from 50 to 100 percent above its prewar level. Both Terman and Skilling knew that the School of Engineering would be particularly stretched by the influx of veterans returning to school on the GI Bill. With university enrollments skyrocketing, the school felt obliged to train as many students as possible, but this, they felt, threatened to deteriorate the quality of instruction. The School of Engineering budget for 1946–47 was at its lowest peacetime level since 1926. The number of staff was lower than any peacetime year since 1924.[60] A 50 percent student increase could be handled, the committee suggested, if some additional part-time instructors, assistants, and graders were hired. An increase of 100 percent, however, could be handled only at the risk of chaotic conditions in several significant areas. Electrical and mechanical engineering courses already were overloaded at the lower-division undergraduate years and graduate level. The most serious predicted shortage of staff and space, they noted, would not actually come in the School of Engineering but in the Physics Department, where engineering students made up the majority of lab course enrollments. The School of Engineering did not resort to excessively large lecture classes, such as the one to two hundred students frequently found at the University of California, but Stanford's undergraduate engineering classes could not approach Caltech's standard class size of twenty-five.

Enrollments in introductory courses were about forty-five to sixty-five students in mechanical engineering, about forty to seventy-five in electrical engineering and forty to fifty in civil engineering. Some of the midlevel lecture courses were even larger—seventy to eighty—with Eugene Grant's Engineering Economics course reaching one hundred twenty-eight students in the autumn quarter. Nevertheless, increased enrollment during 1946–47 raised the number of senior undergraduate and graduate class sizes of the prewar and war years to more financially efficient and educationally effective sizes.[61] For the senior year and graduate courses, enrollments ranged from a dozen to twenty-five, although Timoshenko's course in mechanical engineering, Grant's in civil engineering, and Lester Field, Karl Spangenberg, and Joe Pettit in electrical engineering had forty or more students per course. Timoshenko alone had more than sixty.

Terman calculated optimum class sizes for varying types of subject material and levels of instruction, with thirty being the desirable size for most lecture classes. (Timoshenko fell outside the rules, it appears—sixty students each learned almost as much from him as if in a class of thirty, wrote Terman.) Given the varying popularity of different majors, the committee estimated minimum desirable numbers of senior students ranged from thirty to forty in mechanical and electrical engineering, and twenty to twenty-five in civil and industrial engineering.

Optimum size was not determined simply by economic factors since incremental costs of any reasonable size increase could be carried by increased tuition income. Rather, in engineering the optimal size for undergraduate courses was determined to be a size that produced a sufficient number of candidates qualified for graduate work, permitting graduate work to be conducted on a "minimum desirable" size basis. For example, in electrical engineering, the maximum number of first-year graduate students should be limited to thirty to forty-five, Terman asserted. Assuming one-third to one-half of these students had done their undergraduate work elsewhere, fifteen to twenty-five Stanford undergraduates might enter as graduate students. If one-third to one-quarter of Stanford graduating electrical engineering seniors wished to continue at Stanford, then roughly sixty students should graduate from Stanford each year. Sixty students in each senior year also would allow the school to offer additional specialized upper-level courses. If undergraduate majors were increased to this number, it would justify the hiring of additional faculty, which could, it was noted, strengthen "some of our weak spots in instruction."

Carrying on the analysis to the graduate level, Terman argued that a total of ninety to one hundred fifty engineering students should enter as fifth-year students, with a total graduate engineering student body of about one hundred fifty to two hundred twenty-five. Prewar graduate registration in engineering had been about seventy-five to one hundred, and these numbers were deemed too small to be efficient. But when enrollments rose to two hundred eighty-five in the winter of 1947, including thirty part-time students at Moffett Field, Terman and his colleagues saw not only the advantages of the newly introduced master's degree but opportunity to raise graduate admission standards.[62] According to these calculations, undergraduate enrollment in engineering had maximized for the 1947 senior class, but the lower-division classes were slightly under-enrolled for an optimum undergraduate engineering division to have one hundred eighty to two hundred seniors. The current graduate enrollment, on the other hand, was too large, two hundred eighty-five rather than an optimal two hundred twenty-five.

Since economic factors did not drive the Terman model, it was all the more important to avoid improvised and continually shifting temporary staffing patterns and to rely instead on instruction by faculty members with continuing appointments and using lecture course sizes of around thirty, based on educational rather than economic determinants regarding optimal classroom teaching and learning conditions.[63]

In future years, Terman's model would yield higher "optimum" numbers of students, but it is interesting to see the relative sophistication of the modeling process in engineering at this time compared to other departments at Stanford, where little planning and analysis was conducted beyond calculating tuition income. Terman's model attempted to find balance between quantity and quality and to add noneconomic factors into the equation.

Grading was another issue that concerned the new dean. Terman cautioned his faculty about grading standards, recommending grading on a curve. For large undergraduate classes he recommended a grade distribution (excluding those who failed) of 15 percent each for A and D grades, and 35 percent each for B and C grades.[64] Tough grading standards in engineering courses were soon recognized across the campus. In the late 1950s, Stanford Business School representatives reassured upper-division engineering students hoping to enroll in the Business School that a B-/C+ average in Stanford's engineering curriculum was good enough.[65]

The new dean firmly believed in staying accessible to students. He regularly held daily office hours for students, the only engineering faculty member to have office hours six days a week.[66] Terman continued to teach his Radio Engineering course through the spring of 1955, when he added the duties of university provost to his administrative responsibilities. For some years, he also ran a one-hour-a-week "topics and literature" course in electrical engineering. Younger colleagues later recalled that he did this to keep current for successive editions of his texts, especially the third and fourth editions of his *Radio Engineering* (1947 and 1955).

The Faculty

At the war's end, all the engineering departments expected a significant increase in students and faced serious staffing problems. New courses had to be added to encompass research innovations introduced during the war. Graduate students would be returning, many from wartime service and with young families; financial support was needed. Terman saw a number of significant differences and opportunities in developing individual departments.

Electrical Engineering: Electrical Engineering clearly had a bright future. As staff decamped from RRL, MIT's Radiation Lab, and other government laboratories in the fall of 1945, many were attracted by Stanford's graduate program in electrical engineering. That year Sylvania, Sperry, and Hewlett-Packard companies offered to fund graduate fellowships. "I would like to see Packard get a very good man for his money on this first organized arrangement with him," Terman wrote Skilling from Cambridge. The HP fellowship went to Jerre D. Noe from RRL, while five of eight graduate assistantships awarded that fall went to RRL (4) or Rad Lab (1) employees. They had fifty others pending, truly a comparative bonanza.[67]

Experienced faculty also returned to Stanford from RRL with Terman, including Karl Spangenberg and Joe Pettit. They were joined by other RRL staff as acting junior faculty, and by others who had remained on campus during the war. The Electrical Engineering Department, more than any other in the university, was deeply involved in contract research, especially projects funded by military agencies and by the NBS. In Terman's opinion, electrical and civil engineering did not need many additional regular faculty appointments for 1946–47 and could get by mostly with junior acting positions.

Civil Engineering: Like most engineering departments, civil engineering had lost faculty to wartime service and retirement. Professor Leon Reynolds served as acting head of the department in 1945. Although Skilling and Terman hoped that Eugene Grant could take over the department, Tresidder kept on Reynolds before he signed the position over to Grant in 1947. The greatest course needs in the immediate postwar years would be in beginning statics and dynamics, surveying, and engineering economics.[68] When Grant took over the Civil Engineering Department, he increased staff and fostered the Program in Industrial Engineering toward becoming a department in its own right.

Mechanical Engineering: Staffing would be a serious problem in mechanical engineering, especially beginning drafting, thermodynamics, and shop courses, which were overloaded. The resignations of Milton L. Weidmann and Arthur Domonoske, and Timoshenko's partial retirement left the department looking for tenure-track appointments in mechanics, thermodynamics, and aircraft structures. Mechanical engineering had a peculiar staffing situation. Since 1920, shop instructors carried the courtesy title of "Teaching Specialist in Mechanical Arts." In prewar days, shop instructors were taken from industrial shops, and manual skill was of paramount importance, but following World War II, shop courses began to emphasize manufacturing strategy, rather than manual skill. No other university in 1946 was using the title of "Teaching Specialist," and the leading universities had awarded academic titles to such persons. Department Chair Lydik Jacobsen pointed out that similar positions in technical high schools and junior colleges paid more than at Stanford, and, strongly backed by Terman, he requested pay raises for the department's three teaching specialists. Six months later he also succeeded in elevating the three positions to the title of assistant professor of mechanical engineering.[69] Within ten years however, such positions would no longer be awarded professorial faculty status.

Mechanical engineering would grow in other ways. During World War II, Dean Samuel Morris and Aerodynamics Professor Elliott Reid had attempted to reinvigorate mechanical engineering's aeronautical activities. Following discussions with President Tresidder, Reid wrote to Lockheed and to Boeing, and Morris to Douglas Aircraft to encourage the aircraft companies to help fund Stanford research and teaching in aerodynamics by giving ten fellowships. The response was not encouraging. The aircraft industry could use aerodynamicists, or men well versed in stress analysis or wind tunnels, but they saw little value in underwriting fellowships in fields that had been overemphasized in most universities. Even with curricular changes at Stanford to train more designers, Douglas Aircraft Vice President A. E. Raymond still had his "doubts as to the willingness of the aircraft companies here to give money."[70]

Reid did not give up. In early 1945, Reid acquainted Tresidder, at Terman's suggestion, with a summary of Stanford's Guggenheim Aeronautic Laboratory research accomplishments since 1940.[71] He succeeded in gaining some research support from General Motors' Allison Engine Division, but in general his efforts were not very successful.[72] Reid was a hard man to get along with, but Terman persisted in supporting him.[73] In 1947, Reid submitted a proposal to the U.S. Air Force for a modest new wind tunnel but, unknown to Terman, his proposal ran afoul of a parallel proposal submitted to the ONR by the newly established Stanford Research Institute. Neither wind tunnel was funded. In mid-1948, Terman was unsuccessful in getting a wind tunnel funded by the NACA. Reid's near retirement and the discouraging response from aircraft companies and funding agencies may have contributed to Terman's decision not to push aerodynamics for further development and outside support at that time.[74] Nevertheless, Lydik Jacobsen and Terman encouraged stronger ties between Stanford and the Ames Laboratory at Moffett Field, and three new faculty members—H. Julian Allen, Max A. Heaslet, and Walter G. Vincenti—were hired as part-time lecturers from Ames to give a course in the aerodynamics of high-speed flight.[75] A few years later, Terman succeeded in establishing a Department of Aeronautics and Astronautics, bringing together Vincenti and Nicholas Hoff to build up aerodynamics and structures as fields of research.

Mining Engineering: Mining engineering was in a somewhat different position from the other engineering departments. Enrollments had fallen off, leaving mining engineering in 1946 far smaller than the other departments. The department's fall quarter 1946 enrollment was 28, as compared to 123 for electrical engineering, 188 for mechanical, and 204 for civil.[76]

Mining had originally been taught as part of the curriculum of the Geology Department. When Theodore Jesse Hoover arrived in 1919, a Department of Mining and Metallurgy was formed, then renamed Mining Engineering in 1925 when the School of Engineering was established. Metal mining declined in interest with the economy, however, while interest in metallurgy and petroleum engineering had grown. Stanford's alumni in the oil and gas industries urged Dean Morris to add instruction in exploratory geophysics to the Stanford curriculum. When he succeeded Morris as dean, Fred Terman saw a solution.

The Geology Department recently welcomed A. Irving Levorsen, appointed professor of petroleum geology in February 1945, to replace the retired Eliot Blackwelder. Levorsen was widely recognized, a member of the National Research Council and a former president of the American Association of Petroleum Geologists. The year after he came to Stanford, he was elected president of the Geological Society of America.[77] Levorsen had the backing of influential alumni in the oil and gas industries and had been persuaded by Herbert Hoover Jr. and others to take the Stanford position. A. C. Waters, a former Stanford geology professor and senior geologist for the U.S. Geological Survey, wrote President Tresidder that many Stanford geology alumni were behind Levorsen. With Levorsen at Stanford, Waters was tempted to return himself; he believed that Levorsen and Tresidder could do much for Stanford geology.[78] Levorsen eagerly began raising funds for new quarters for a future School of Mineral Sciences. They planned to move out of traditional Quad quarters and across the street to a proposed Physical Science Quadrangle. Levorsen recognized that with adequate financial support, mining and petroleum engineering could be added to geology and geophysics in the School of Mineral Sciences.[79]

Like Levorsen, Terman believed metallurgy courses should be a part of mechanical engineering, while mining geology courses ought to be taught in the Geology Department. A first step was made in May 1946 when Frederick G. Tickell, head of mining engineering, presented to President Tresidder a poignant report tracing an industry in decline and other related industries on the rise.[80] "The Mining Department is at present a step-child," Terman acknowledged to Eurich after receiving the report, "with low moral, marking time in all its plans until reorganization occurs." The balance of past areas of expertise with the rise of new specialties posed a serious staffing problem, however. Terman recommended that for the time being, mining not lose its identity entirely until the imminent retirement of Professor Tickell.[81]

In June 1946, Levorsen and Terman discussed a change in status first with Eurich, and then with Tresidder, and suggested a separate School of Mineral Sciences to include both geology and mining. In January 1947, the new school (later the School of Earth Sciences) was formed. Fred Terman had begun as dean with four engineering departments to manage. By 1947, he had only three.[82]

With his first year behind him as dean, Terman summarized the state of the School of Engineering in a report to the president in January 1947. The School had greatly increased its sponsored research over the previous year and had assisted in getting funding for groups in physics, mathematics, statistics, and metallurgy. Several outstanding faculty members had joined or returned to the staff, including John Vennard in fluid mechanics, Lester Field and Joseph Pettit in electrical engineering, and J. N. Goodier, who would ultimately succeed Stephen Timoshenko in theoretical and applied mechanics. The School of Mineral Sciences had been formed, effectively absorbing the Mining Department. Enrollments, however, were nearly three times the prewar average. Part-time graduate students and temporary staff could no longer provide adequate instruction. Laboratory facilities were heading downward to third-rate status, he warned. Stanford's engineering laboratories with the exception of the Ryan High-Voltage Laboratory, were comparatively poorly equipped. Fifteen years of deferred maintenance and nonacquisition of equipment had led to universal obsolescence.

Postwar faculty retirements and resignations gave the school the chance to reorganize some programs and initiate new faculty lines, but Terman wanted to see significant improvement in faculty salaries. Stanford was paying its engineering faculty from 30 to 40 percent less than at Northwestern, UCLA, MIT, and Berkeley, and, in half of the cases, less than nearby San Jose State College. Stanford could securely establish its position in advanced instruction and research in engineering without drawing on normal academic funds. A portion of salary overhead (up to one-half) from government contracts should be directed to a restricted account, he suggested, an account earmarked for long-range development of research and instruction in the School of Engineering.

"Government-sponsored research presents Stanford, and our School of Engineering," Terman wrote to President Tresidder, "with a wonderful opportunity if we are prepared to exploit it."[83] Federally funded support for university research in the immediate postwar years increased the quality as well as quantity of both faculty and students. Whereas capital equipment purchased with government funding reverts to the government at the end of a contract, Terman reminded President Tresidder, foundation and industry grants allowed universities to keep capital equipment purchased for research.

Some faculty members suggested that, compared to the University of California, Stanford offered engineering undergraduates little more "than a rural atmosphere and a bill for tuition." And "when the government stops paying the tuition," Terman warned, referring to GI Bill benefits, "the effect on Stanford will be serious." He concluded, "The decisions not only for now, but for the future, are being made at this time, and this fact cannot be avoided."[84]

An Engineering-Physics Partnership: The Microwave Laboratory

By 1938, Bill Hansen and the Varians' initial work on klystron development grew to involve not only Professor David Webster, head of the Physics Department, but several of Fred Terman's electrical engineering graduate students, including John Woodyard and Ed Ginzton (who pioneered the measuring of klystron characteristics and developed klystron circuits) and David Packard. Bill Hewlett, Joe Pettit, and Otto Smith measured the operating wavelength of the first klystron prototype as an exercise in Terman's electronics lab course.[85] The klystron project had become, Webster worried, an engineering rather than "pure physics" program.[86]

Sperry engineers wanted a larger place in klystron work. The company moved part of their operations to a small plant in San Carlos, north of the Stanford campus. Webster's increasing unhappiness was fed by his paranoia that Hansen, aided by Fred Terman, was trying to take over the Sperry-funded work. Webster resigned from the task, and by Christmas 1939 Hansen was administrator of the Sperry project. Soon after, when Hansen arranged to take a sabbatical year in the East, Sperry announced that most of their klystron work at Stanford after 1940 would be engineering oriented. Meanwhile, in the fall of 1940, Hansen, the Varians, Woodyard, Ginzton, and several others from physics and electrical engineering went to Sperry Gyroscope's new klystron and radar plant on Long Island, New York.[87]

Terman and his electrical engineers were to assume the major role for klystron research at Stanford for the academic year 1941–42, but his appointment to head the Radio Research Laboratory left direction of the klystron work in the hands of Karl Spangenberg. Hansen wanted to build a laboratory to expand the possibilities of the klystron and other devices into the highest frequencies and powers. He knew they would open new doors for physics—pure and applied. Hansen put in heroic hours, splitting his time between two full-time jobs: developing klystrons at Sperry on Long Island and making the trip to Cambridge several times a month to lecture on microwaves at MIT.

At Sperry Gyroscope on Long Island, Sigurd and Russell Varian, Ed Ginzton, and others dreamed of returning to California. In October 1943, they put their heads together and estimated that they could raise $22,000 to form a microwave company after the war. They were the "New Group": Russell and Sigurd Varian, Bill Hansen, Myrl Strearns, Marvin Chodorow, Don Snow, Fred Salisbury, and Ed Ginzton.[88]

Bill Hansen was supportive, but his own wish was to return to Stanford to build a microwave laboratory at the university, expand klystron physics, and use microwaves to accelerate electrons. While at Sperry, Hansen and John Woodyard often speculated on the feasibility of building an electron linear accelerator. Woodyard convinced Hansen that one could use the so-called traveling waves, connecting a bunch of cavities together to make an accelerator.[89]

Hansen, like Terman, hoped to physically tie together the Physics and Electrical Engineering Laboratories in his proposed Microwave Lab. Before leaving Cambridge for California, the newly designated engineering dean and the physics professor worked through a number of possibilities: The Physics Department wanted the space recently relocated by the Psychology Department. Could Terman's Communication Lab and the Microwave Lab move into that space together? Or could the former engineering dean's office, currently being used for another project, be used? There was room for both the Communication and Microwave labs, but that would separate the Microwave Lab from the Physics Department.[90]

Since the first days of his posting to Sperry on Long Island and at MIT, Hansen talked about his microwave lab ideas with Terman and Felix Bloch. An early description of a microwave lab occurs in Bill Hansen's November 6, 1942, letter to Paul Kirkpatrick. Kirkpatrick, acting head of physics, wanted Hansen's suggestions regarding how the Physics Department could better contribute to the war effort. "One sets up, as soon as possible, an organization to be called the

'Stanford Microwave Laboratory' or any other title that may please the maximum number of people," Hansen replied.

> For the moment, Spangenberg would head this as he is the only one at all suitable who is available. Another staff member or two could probably be listed as cooperating in various ways. (Maybe Skilling and perhaps Bloch—to consult on E & M). When peace comes, this lab would have close tie-ups with Physics because I will be in it, and with E. E. because it's a communications field and because Terman is so good at gathering up students.

Hansen goes on to outline the equipment that should be ordered and to describe how to obtain a government contract. "Even if we don't have a dime after the war, good physics can be done if we have a good shop. As another example, Terman's radio lab, which is outstanding, really has very little in it except apparatus for measuring most anything electrical."[91] Hansen suggested Kirkpatrick discuss the matter with Bloch and Terman. By New Year's Eve 1942, Hansen, Bloch, and Terman had developed a proposal—a "Microwave Laboratory at Stanford." Felix Bloch, still at Stanford, presented the plan to Paul Davis, Stanford's general secretary, and to Chancellor Wilbur in January 1943. Wilbur planned to go east soon. Davis recommended that Fred Terman use the opportunity to update Wilbur and provide him with "a copy of Hansen's, Bloch's, and your recommendation."[92]

Hansen worried about David Webster's reaction.[93] "Webster hates Terman," he wrote Bloch.[94] Webster wrote Kirkpatrick about his wish to move Hansen out of physics altogether and to relocate him and his microwave lab in electrical engineering.[95] Terman wrote to Davis to urge some action. "It has been months since I heard anything on the proposed microwave laboratory at Stanford. Is this project still alive or can it be written off as one of the dreams that didn't materialize?"[96] Davis assured him that the idea was very much alive. Hansen was meeting that week with president-designate Tresidder to go over the details. Terman had alerted Davis to the fact that the Polytechnical Institute of Brooklyn had just awarded an honorary doctorate to Russell Varian for his klystron work, adding that, ironically, "our good friend [Webster] of the Physics Department had refused to allow Russ to be a doctoral candidate at Stanford." Davis brought in Journalism Professor Chick Bush, who handled public-relations writing for the university, to get details on the new Varian award to the press and put it into the next issue of *Stanford Alumni Review*.[97]

Hansen's initial meeting with Tresidder went well. In June 1943, Davis asked Hansen, Bloch, and Terman to provide a complete, detailed plan as to how such a lab could be established at Stanford, including its financing, and in a way that would "not cause too much internal opposition." Tresidder wanted to recommend the project to the board of trustees at the earliest opportunity.[98] Two months later,

Davis urged Terman to encourage Hansen to submit the plan soon. None had been received and he wanted it to be the first thing on Tresidder's plate when he took office September 1, 1943.[99]

Hansen, overworked and increasingly ill, finally sent the proposal for a "Proposed Micro-Wave Laboratory at Stanford" to Tresidder on November 17. All major universities, Hansen wrote, would be forced to offer strong instruction in two branches of science—microwave physics and radio engineering. In addition to providing important research in microwaves, a Stanford microwave laboratory would strengthen and reinforce related activities in physics and radio engineering. "It is hard to overemphasize this mutual benefit." Leadership was key, but Hansen was as confidant of the strength in both the Physics and Electrical Engineering departments, as he was proud of the university's past history of microwave research. By planning now, Stanford would take the leading position in microwaves at the war's end.

The plan placed the laboratory within the Physics Department and staffed it with a director, two or three tenured professors, and, at the beginning, two or three nontenured instructors. The faculty also would teach traditional physics courses, microwave courses, and some courses in the Electrical Engineering Department. Good students were a top priority, and Hansen noted Terman's outstanding success in drawing the best students to electrical engineering. One or two machinists, a first-class shop, and a first-class assortment of measurement equipment would be needed. These were key, he wrote, since "these items *are* the laboratory. Given a good shop and good measuring equipment a sound physicist can do wonderful work."[100]

Hansen had acquired definite ideas about industry relations. Terman's and his own experiences had taught them such relations could be touchy. He hoped Stanford would support the microwave lab itself, regardless of outside industrial support, and only accept external contracts on its own grounds. Tresidder, confident that Hansen and Terman had the lab design clearly in mind, replied that Stanford would do "everything within our power to support this proposal."[101]

Little further progress was made, however. Hansen vetted a more detailed proposal with Terman and Bloch, each rewriting a number of sections, and submitted the amended plan to the president in the fall of 1944.[102] Terman followed up with a letter to Tresidder indicating how carefully he and Bloch had reviewed Hansen's proposal. They both felt it would become a "jewel in one's crown," as Harvard treasurer Howard Claflin would say. It was Terman who suggested, however, that "Stanford" be dropped from the laboratory's name, to indicate that the Microwave Lab was unique, a leader, not merely one of several.

Terman urged a speedy decision. The OSRD was taking its first steps toward demobilization. Young scientists at government labs would soon be returning to continue their graduate education; thousands of veterans would return to college to finish their work in electronics. Servicemen and electronics workers, supplied by the military with copies of Terman's books, would be drawn to Stanford.[103]

By December 1944, Terman and Tresidder had worked out the arrangements for Fred to become dean of engineering. Again Terman warned the president that David Webster, tired of working at Aberdeen Proving Grounds, might return to Stanford in a few months. "It is obviously necessary for any plans that you have in connection with physics to be developed rather rapidly."[104]

Webster returned to Stanford for a visit in February 1945.[105] He had several conferences with Tresidder and agreed that after his permanent return to Stanford he would "emphasize research and leave administration alone." His first year back would be a full year with pay to study whatever he wanted. Paul Kirkpatrick wrote Hansen that Webster was "relieved to escape administration of a department which is to be deeply involved in researches which he regards as engineering and which he fears can only have evil influences." Tresidder was solidly behind the department, Kirkpatrick reported, and had asked him to continue as acting department head.[106]

Webster brought with him a proposal for Stanford to undertake a large military research project to develop proximity fuzes, work that had been pursued by the NBS during the war. It was a huge and consuming project, involving both physics and engineering. According to Webster, it would involve two hundred employees and spend five to six million dollars per year. A decision to accept or reject the project was needed in one week, he insisted. It was all a fantasy. Despite his protests against engineering physics in general and microwave research in particular, and his alleged desire to give up administration, Webster was proposing that Stanford run an exceptionally large campus facility dedicated to applied military products in a field with which he was only vaguely familiar.

Kirkpatrick wanted nothing to do with it. Terman and Skilling declined. Terman knew that Merle Tuve and a massive government project managed by Johns Hopkins University had spent the last several years, and several tens of millions of dollars developing highly successful proximity fuzes. Stanford's Electrical Engineering Department had no need to jump into research for which they were poorly prepared.[107] Tresidder placated Webster, side-stepped the proximity fuze project, and continued his support of the Microwave Laboratory.

The Microwave Laboratory was publicly announced in June 1945, with Bill Hansen its first staff member. He was anxious to get going, pressing Eldridge T. Spencer, Tresidder's new director of planning, for a permanent location that reflected a close relationship between physics and electrical engineering.[108] But by the time Hansen had returned to Stanford in 1944, he was extremely ill. He had long been known to take little care of his health, and he had contracted a lung disease later known to be accentuated by beryllium poisoning.[109] Klystron and microwave work had continued at Stanford in the Electrical Engineering Department during the war with Sperry funding of about $20,000 per year, and IT&T's Federal Telephone subsidiary sponsored work at around $10,000 to $15,000 per year.[110] Bill Hansen had been "especially insistent" on keeping electrical engineer Herbert J. "John" Shaw full time on the project during the war, and Hugh Skilling added William J. Barclay and Victor S. Carson to full-time klystron work.[111]

Once the Microwave Lab was founded, Hansen was soon joined by Ed Ginzton, who returned to Stanford early in 1946 as assistant professor of applied physics in the Physics Department. (He later became professor of applied physics and electrical engineering.) Ginzton's first task at the Microwave Lab was to help Hansen convert Room 404 in the Quadrangle's Physics Corner, the site of early klystron development, into the Microwave Laboratory. Marvin Chodorow, a physicist from University of Buffalo who trained under John Slater at MIT, had worked at Sperry Gyroscope. He joined the team at Stanford in the fall of 1946, and the three of them began teaching microwave courses, colisted in physics and in electrical engineering.[112] In 1946, the NDRC-OSRD issued a list of referee experts for various scientific fields. MIT had twenty-eight names on the list. Among other universities included were Harvard with sixteen names, Princeton fourteen, Caltech twelve, Rochester eleven, Yale eight, Berkeley three. Stanford had four names: W. Allen Wallis for econometrics/statistics; Fred Terman for radio; and Bill Hansen and Ed Ginzton for radar.[113]

In 1946 and 1947, Hansen and three graduate students, working with ONR support, demonstrated theoretically and experimentally that an electron accelerator was possible. Their three-feet-long prototype, the Mark I accelerator, was extended to twelve feet. Powered by a magnetron, it generated 7 Mev electrons. Chodorow and Ginzton tried to build a giant klystron to use with future electron accelerators. Chodorow had invented several types of low-power reflex klystrons while at Sperry. These were used in radar receivers, especially valuable in aircraft due to their light weight and in countermeasure radar receivers because, unlike the magnetrons, they were quite tunable in frequency. Now the challenge was to build klystrons capable of delivering millions of watts of power. Planning for a Mark II model was soon underway (it became operational in 1949).

During this same time, 1945–46, Hansen played a joint role in helping Bloch and graduate student Martin Packard design and build the nuclear magnetic resonance experiment for which Bloch, after Hansen's death, was awarded the Nobel Prize in Physics. When the Bloch-Hansen magnetic resonance work was demonstrated at an American Physical Society meeting in New York in April 1946, John Van Vleck (who worked under Terman at RRL and who later also won a Nobel Prize in Physics), described the pair as equal contributors, and told Terman that their work was the hit of the show.[114]

Although now seriously ill, Hansen submitted a proposal to ONR in March 1948 proposing to build a 160-feet-long (Mark III) accelerator, powered by sixteen klystrons, each delivering 30 to 50 megawatts of pulse power, producing billion-volt acceleration of electrons.[115] This accelerator would require klystrons delivering two thousand times more power than those previously built. It also presented challenges in building such a comparatively long accelerator. Hansen's reputation with scientists, and particularly with Dr. Emanuel Piore, head of the ONR office in Washington DC, gained Stanford support for its proposed Mark III linear accelerator.[116]

Bill Hansen's health deteriorated further in 1948. He now walked to class with an oxygen tank. His 250-pound, six-feet-three frame had shrunk to 200 pounds in his earlier lung illnesses, but in the final months he became skeletal.[117] An August 1948 trip to Birmingham, London, and Cambridge, England, for a month to study British work in particle accelerators nearly killed him. Despite their differences and rivalries, Webster and Hansen maintained an unusual friendship. In Hansen's last months, Webster persuaded him to see a doctor.[118] Webster was the executor of Hansen's estate, and Webster, Ginzton, and Terman wrote his faculty memorial resolution.[119]

Hansen passed away on May 23, 1949, at the age of thirty-nine. Only four weeks before, he had been gratified to receive notice of his election to the National Academy of Sciences.[120] Hansen, Terman wrote, was "one of the most fertile and original men I have ever known. . . . He was a rare combination, almost unique, of a theoretical physicist and a thoroughly practical engineer."[121] Close colleague Marvin Chodorow believed Hansen to be a genius, superb at both theory and experiment.[122]

Edward Ginzton assumed directorship of the Stanford Microwave Laboratory after Hansen's death. The Mark III was completed within two and a half years, as promised, and used for research throughout the decade. Robert Hofstadter utilized the Mark III to determine the size and structure of the nucleus, for which he was awarded the Nobel Prize in Physics in 1961.[123]

Terman and the Varian Associates

Russell Varian had returned to California in 1947. The "New Group" assembled into a small company, which they called "Varian Associates." Their first laboratory buildings were located in San Carlos, several miles north of Palo Alto. Varian Associates was incorporated in April 1948, at a meeting in Bill Hansen's home. Russell Varian was frustrated in these early years, as he had been in the 1930s, that he had to spend much of his time researching and writing patents, yet it would be his patent-nose and skill that gave Varian Associates much of its future capital.[124]

Ties between Stanford's Microwave Lab, the Physics and Electrical Engineering Departments, and Varian Associates were close from the beginning. Leonard

Schiff, a theoretical physicist, was among the directors. Schiff, a friend of Ginzton, had been encouraged by Bloch and Hansen to come to Stanford from the University of Pennsylvania in 1947. He became chair of the department in 1948.[125] Professor Marvin Chodorow took on Hansen's role as microwave tube consultant and klystron expert. Chodorow, like Ginzton, continued his duties at Stanford (faculty were limited to the equivalent of one day per week consulting).[126] In addition to faculty interchanges, several Microwave Lab students worked part-time at Varian and others joined soon after graduation.

A few months after incorporation, Fred Terman was added to the Varian board to increase the overall technical capability of the board. Terman was a valued member of the board, for both his technical expertise and familiarity with the nuances of government relations. Interestingly, it was Terman, Schiff, and Ginzton who "took the fall" for other Varian board members when the company (along with Stanford) was investigated during the McCarthy era. Even though Stanford provided expert legal counsel, Ginzton, Terman, and Schiff, among others, lost their high-security clearances for a time. An informal military channel proposed that if Schiff and Terman resigned from the Varian board, face-saving would result, and so they did. The alternative was that Varian would be denied klystron contracts with the military. Terman later returned to the board.[127]

After Hansen's death, Stanford alumnus and Hewlett-Packard executive David Packard was added to the board. Ginzton later noted that Packard was a valuable addition to the Varian board, assisting in discussions of financing, management training, and business orientation.[128] The philosophy of the companies was quite similar. Both the Varian brothers and Bill Hewlett and Dave Packard wanted their companies to be "a good place to work."[129]

Varian's first production contract was to produce a small number of traveling wave tubes; then they gained a contract for making klystrons. Russell Varian later obtained patent rights from Felix Bloch and Bill Hansen to the nuclear magnetic resonance discoveries. Among Varian's early successes were the design and production of the world's first truly high-power klystron in 1951, used in the first commercial UHF television transmitter and in tropospheric scatter communications.[130] In 1952 the first high-resolution Nuclear Magnetic Resonance (NMR) spectrometer system was introduced, opening a new field in chemical analysis and related research.[131]

Varian Associates soon outgrew its modest San Carlos location, and in 1952 the company became the first tenant in the Stanford Industrial Park, the beginning of Silicon Valley.[132] The move was controversial both at Stanford and with the Varian board. Russ Varian and Ed Ginzton, encouraged by Terman, pushed for expansion to the new Stanford location. At Stanford, some administrators expected Stanford Industrial Park land to be given over to seemingly more lucrative leases to commercial property rather than research and development companies.[133]

Fred Terman had a long and involved relationship both with the Microwave Lab and with the beginnings of Varian Associates in his roles as electronics expert, head of the Electrical Engineering Department, and dean of engineering. His ongoing interest in developing a technological institute, however, would be sidetracked by the intentions of other influential Stanford personalities as the university took on establishing a Stanford Research Institute.

Fred Terman and the Stanford Research Institute

In mid-June 1944, President Tresidder and his new academic vice president, Alvin Eurich, had lunch with Hugh Skilling and other Electrical Engineering Department faculty. Fishing for support for the Microwave Laboratory and other ambitious plans, Tresidder posed to them the following question: "What would you do with a gift of $100,000?" Skilling was quick to reply: an ultra-high, microwave frequency lab would be at the top of the list, with support for students and some top-rate visiting professors. Skilling also suggested an idea that he and Terman had discussed—a division of engineering research to embrace the work of all departments. "Dr. Tresidder was very much interested in this idea," Skilling reported to Terman, "which had not occurred to him."[134] A research division would figure in Tresidder's thoughts later in the fall of 1944, both as he considered a successor to Dean Samuel Morris, and as he considered the possibilities of a separate research foundation or school encompassing engineering and physical science research. Terman would figure prominently in both efforts.

Fred Terman's interests in research institutes went back to at least 1927, when he speculated about the prospect of the Federal Telegraph Company setting up a radio research laboratory in their Palo Alto headquarters. Nothing much came of this for Stanford or Terman. Federal was bought out by IT&T, which had its own research facilities in the East, and was moved back east in 1931.

The economic realities of the Depression only temporarily derailed speculation. During those years, Robert Swain and Philip Leighton of the Stanford Chemistry Department talked with President Wilbur and Stanford trustees about the possibility of a Stanford-affiliated research institute, an idea that Swain had first raised more than ten years earlier.[135] They already had at hand the successful establishment of Stanford's Food Research Institute, an interdisciplinary effort initially funded in 1921 by Herbert Hoover but one that had brought in major grants from the Carnegie Corporation and the Rockefeller Foundation in the 1930s to support faculty-initiated and -directed research. By 1945, faculty at Stanford again began to think about a technologically oriented research institute. Donors began to express interest. (One potential donor suggested to President Tresidder in spring 1944 that he *might* be willing to give $100,000 to Stanford for some sort of engineering graduate research institute, although today nothing is known about the donor or the possible gift.[136])

Terman envisioned a Stanford technological research institute centered around faculty and graduate student research interests (similar to the Food Research Institute), not an institute set up to work on behalf of industry. However, this approach was not one shared by influential groups of Stanford business friends, alumni, and trustees who hoped to create a West Coast research institute to benefit western industry, located either in Southern California or near Stanford.

In 1944, incoming Stanford vice president Alvin Eurich may have been excited about Terman's view of research in the physical sciences and engineering, but he soon became more intrigued by the model of the Armour Research Foundation in Chicago. Eurich was concerned with Stanford's postwar relations with industry. "Being a non-technical man he [Eurich] probably doesn't realize that a lot of the so called 'research' at this Institute is routine testing and measurement," a worried Karl Spangenberg wrote Terman.[137] By early 1946, Eurich, Tresidder, and Stanford alumnus and financier Atholl McBean had agreed on an organization and a name: the Stanford Research Institute (SRI). They had at hand the advice of Henry T. Heald, president of Illinois Institute of Technology and the Armour Research Foundation, presented in a report to Atholl McBean in January 1946.[138] Heald proposed a nonprofit research organization to serve western industry, at Stanford and with a large initial gift from the university, with Stanford's president as chairman of the board and with several Stanford trustees as board members. In short, his Armour Research Foundation served as the model for SRI. In the summer of 1946, Tresidder, Eurich, and McBean met with Clyde Williams, director of the Battelle Institute, for counsel on launching the Stanford Research Institute. Tresidder and Eurich also sought the advice of industrial researchers such as Earl Stevenson, a Wesleyan University and MIT graduate and longtime president of the Arthur D. Little Company. Stevenson recommended that the institute should be a profit-making enterprise; Stanford's board of trustees disagreed. SRI ultimately was established as a nonprofit corporation with several Stanford trustees and administrators on its board of directors, and with Stanford's president as the chairman of the board. Both Stanford University and its western business advisors wanted a university tie-in and Stanford's name attached to the institute.[139]

Terman, no doubt, quickly realized that his idea of a graduate research institute in the physical sciences and engineering did not match the plans of Alvin Eurich, Donald Tresidder, and influential trustees. As a result, he had relatively little to do with the actual founding of the Stanford Research Institute (SRI) in late 1946. Indirectly, Terman played a key role in advising Tresidder on actions concerning SRI during its first years and regarding personnel who came to SRI.

Terman's connections were important and stem from his wartime experiences as director of the Radio Research Lab in Cambridge.[140] In 1955 in his position as Stanford provost, Terman became vice chairman of the SRI board.

SRI was incorporated on October 24, 1946. The press announcements read "Research Institute Established On the Campus to Aid Industry."[141] In May 1947, after its first months on the campus, SRI moved its headquarters into buildings in the Stanford Village in Menlo Park and expanded its facilities there steadily in the early 1950s.[142] SRI was among several new western research institutes established in the immediate postwar period. The Mellon (Pittsburgh), Battelle (Columbus, Ohio), and Armour (Chicago) institutes supplied key people to the newer research institutes, but none save SRI were located west of Kansas City and San Antonio. SRI's founders hoped to gather the bulk of western and far west business.

SRI's first director and chief administrator, William Talbot, was previously a chemist with Sun Oil Company. Earl Stevenson, who had worked with him previously, had recommended Talbot but Talbot served only fifteen months. He did not get along with Tresidder and was fired in late 1947, in part because he wanted more freedom to act than Tresidder allowed.[143] Talbot clashed with Tresidder over purchasing authority, and the president became increasingly worried about SRI's cumulative deficit.[144] Talbot had believed that SRI would become a completely separate organization, and as a result, Talbot and others had quite consciously remained aloof from Stanford University and its faculty.[145]

SRI's first years were difficult. Talbot's first quarters in September 1946 were in a small office with no telephone in the Physics Building. Three rooms (399, 399a, and 400) in the Physics Department were rented to SRI for $60 per month.[146] It was clear that both Eurich and Tresidder intended SRI to become, within a very few years, a source of financial support for the university, but the institute was in severe financial trouble and operated in "the red," supported by grants and loans from Stanford and from SRI board members and their companies. By the beginning of August 1948, SRI had contracts of about $60,000 per month in active and $25,000 per month in new work—about 80 percent from commercial and 20 percent from government sources—but this was not enough to offset the red ink.[147]

In one early attempt to find funding, SRI considered operating a government aircraft landing aids testing facility on the northern California coast at Arcata. It seemed to be an ideal source of needed cash for SRI, and the SRI board had apparently approved the Arcata project in September 1947, but it did not materialize.[148] At Tresidder's request, Fred Terman had examined the Arcata situation and advised against the deal. The navy engineer in charge would probably return to Northwestern University and the real operation, Terman suspected, would be out of Stanford's hands; operating such a facility two hundred miles away would bring little benefit to Stanford; and the research work was limited. If such a sweet financial deal was at hand, he suggested, some aircraft company would have taken over operation of the test site. To the contrary, the contract would be for $1.5 million over a five-year period, but Terman learned that it would begin at a monthly rate of only two-thirds of that figure. He estimated that the actual funding to support so many employees would need to be about four times that amount. Terman also found that it was taken for granted that many of the personnel (some one hundred employees) would be accepted by Stanford without question, with a number of them eligible for faculty rank. Yet the university's role was limited: it would run tests, but the navy's Bureau of Aeronautics would retain title to all facilities and the Civil Aeronautics Administration would operate the field. Fred nosed around and learned that Northwestern University had been negotiating on the deal for some time, and that the University of California had also been contacted. Fred suspected that the whole operation might be a postwar activity promoted by its director, the navy engineer, to provide himself with a continuance of his academic career following his upcoming resignation from the navy.

After visiting Arcata, investigating the proposition carefully, and digesting a number of official documents, Terman assembled his response with several accompanying "Exhibit" documents in January 1946. As to Stanford's interest, Terman advised Tresidder, "The activity does not tie in any significant way with an existing program of research now going on at the University. Furthermore, the activity cannot be very effectively integrated with the training of students . . . [and] the University would serve in a capacity which is essentially that of paymaster." He had given no indications of university policy to personnel at the site, he added, and requested that the lieutenant commander in charge speak directly to Tresidder or Eurich.[149]

SRI Director William Talbot acted on several proposals without much consultation with the Stanford University administration. In April 1947, he hired Dr. Maurice A. Garbell as director of aerophysics research. All were enthusiastic about his ideas for projects, Talbot wrote to Garbell, but noted that "no research activities should be undertaken between the Institute and any agency which will conflict with the interests and well being of the various university departments and that every effort will be made to cooperate with these departments."[150] Nevertheless, at the same September 1947 SRI board meeting where Talbot presented the Arcata landing aids project, he presented a proposal that Maurice Garbell had sent to ONR asking for a $4 million supersonic wind tunnel. Again, the SRI board initially approved the idea, but individual directors soon began to express concern.[151] Garbell's proposal, it appears, ignored another proposal in preparation by Stanford's Professor Elliott G. Reid in the aerodynamics section of the Mechanical Engineering Department. Neither proposal was funded.

Stanford trustees were not pleased. Two years earlier, trustee Ira Lillick had sent President Tresidder a letter from F. T. Letchfield, vice president of the Wells

Fargo Bank and an important executive with the Office of Scientific Research and Development during the war, about the importance of aerodynamic research after the war. Letchfield was impressed by the reputation of Professor Elliott Reid at Stanford. Along with Professor William Durand and Dean Frederick Terman, Letchfield wrote, Stanford should be in a good position "when allocations are made to the schools." Reid already had a small government contract and would soon pursue the matter more aggressively, Assistant General Secretary David S. Jacobson assured Lillick. Stanford would surely strengthen its engineering department activities and financial position with the imminent return of Bill Hansen and Fred Terman, he added.[152]

Stanford's Engineering School had been well connected in aeronautics since the arrival of William Durand, the first chairman of NACA. Stanford's aeronautical laboratory was the second oldest in the United States, established in 1916, and its wind tunnel, completed that year, was updated in 1918 and again in 1927. Sixteen Stanford alumni worked at Moffett Field in Sunnyvale on aerodynamics research during the war.[153] As of 1946, Stanford hosted the major American propeller research laboratory. Professor Reid hoped to broaden Stanford's well-known work on propeller design with a new wind tunnel facility and was working with the Army Air Force Aircraft Laboratory at Wright Field, Ohio, to plan the construction of a new, larger tunnel.[154]

Although the two wind tunnel plans differed, it was apparent to the funding agency that the two entities, the Stanford Research Institute and Stanford's Mechanical Engineering Department, had been submitted with little cooperation.[155] As a result, Talbot made no friends with the Stanford Engineering School. In addition, Garbell did not have a significant reputation in aerodynamics and was considered a "lightweight" by experts at NACA's Ames Laboratory.[156] Tresidder fired Garbell in January 1948, upon Talbot's departure.[157] In July, Eurich asked Terman's advice. Garbell had written in early 1948 to suggest that his efforts had not completely removed Stanford's chances for ONR funding for a wind tunnel. Terman went to Hugh L. Dryden, chairman of NACA, requesting that Stanford be considered for a grant for a small, continuous flow, high-speed tunnel (the tunnel originally proposed by Reid). He emphasized Stanford's historical work in aerodynamics, its strengths in related areas of engineering mechanics, thermodynamics, and mathematics, and Stanford's proximity to experts at NACA's Ames Lab at Moffett Field, pointing out the cross-fertilization with Ames staff. (Twenty to thirty Ames staff members were taking courses at Stanford, and Ames experts, including Walter Vincenti, offered courses for Stanford graduate students.) The NACA request was unsuccessful, however. Reid was nearing retirement age, and after the losing battles of the preceding several years Terman himself had doubts about whether aerodynamics should be considered at that time as one of the five highest-priority research areas for the School of Engineering. Some years later, as provost, Terman instituted a separate Department of Aeronautics and Astronautics, drawn from the Mechanical Engineering Department.[158]

Board President Paul C. Edwards, in writing to the newly appointed Stanford University President Wallace Sterling in December 1948 about Stanford's $500,000 loan to SRI, mentioned that "the Industrial Institute problem has been solved for the short range period."[159] By then, Talbot had been succeeded by Jesse Hobson, an electrical engineer with bachelor's and master's degrees in electrical engineering from Purdue and a PhD from Caltech who had served as director of the Armour Research Foundation in Chicago.[160] Hobson had been selected as a nationally outstanding young electrical engineer several years before, and he brought energy and plans to the job when he arrived in the spring of 1948. Fred Terman had taken part in Hobson's selection. He urged Hobson to take the position, telling him that he felt that the Research Institute offered an unusual opportunity to exercise leadership in meeting an important western need, and that "it would be a personal pleasure to have a brother electrical engineer in this position."[161] Thomas C. Poulter, associate director at Armour and a renowned geophysics and explosives expert, followed Hobson to SRI immediately.[162]

Within two months of his arrival, Hobson proposed to Alvin Eurich new and closer relations between SRI and the university, and suggested meeting Terman, as dean of engineering, sciences dean Philip Leighton, mineral sciences dean Irving Levorsen, graduate dean Douglas Whitaker, Business School dean Hugh Jackson, and others to be suggested by the vice president. Hobson invited university faculty to serve as consultants on SRI research.[163] By 1955, SRI had one thousand employees and $10 million per year in contract research. Little known, however, is the further work of Fred Terman in bringing personnel and contracts to SRI.

Fred Terman, SRI, and the ONR "Bird Dogs"

During the war, Navy Admiral Julius Furer, coordinator of research and development for the NDRC, was assisted by several young aides who came to be called the "Bird Dogs." One "Bird Dog," Bruce S. Old, subsequently became vice president of the Arthur D. Little research-consulting firm in Cambridge.[164] Another, Ralph Krause, joined SRI as director of research. Yet another, Tom Morrin, would direct SRI's engineering division.

Furer's wartime Office of the Coordinator of Research and Development maintained close ties to Terman's Radio Research Lab, as well as the MIT Rad Lab and the Underwater Sound Lab at Harvard.[165] Ralph Krause and Bruce Old served as section leaders under Admiral Furer and Captain Robert D. Conrad, with Krause in charge of electronics, and Old in charge of metallurgy and general engineering. Krause worked out of Washington DC and commuted regularly to

Cambridge and Boston. His particular job was to serve as liaison with NDRC Divisions 14 and 15, which included the Rad Lab and Terman's RRL. He soon knew Terman well.

As the war approached its end, Vannevar Bush wanted to dissolve the NDRC superstructure as quickly as possible, but he did not want the United States to lose the experience and trained technical manpower assembled and developed during the war. The Office of Naval Research (ONR) was established to utilize this talent, including helping young engineers and scientists finish their graduate education. The "Bird Dogs" began discussing postwar naval research plans in December 1942 and evolved a design as early as November 1943 for a postwar naval research office (their plan was submitted by Furer to the secretary of the navy late in 1944). Meanwhile, various proposals for a broader national science agency were proposed, studied, and debated.[166]

Furer was well aware that a number of the highest-ranking navy administrators, civilian and military, distrusted scientists. The "Bird Dogs'" proposal for a postwar navy research office was something of an end run around such distrust, and to their amazement, their ideas were strongly championed not only by Furer but by both Captain Conrad and Vice Admiral Harold G. Bowen, who were among those skeptical of scientists. The ONR was established by Bowen, whose relations within the navy, as well as with Bush and the NDRC, were often strained.[167] Initially called the Office of Research and Invention (ORI), the organization was reworked and renamed the Office of Naval Research (ONR) in a bill passed by Congress in August 1946.

In October 1945, Admiral Bowen sent Captain Conrad to visit five select research universities (Harvard, MIT, Caltech, Chicago, and Berkeley) that had enjoyed large wartime contracts and persuade their presidents to accept postwar navy research contracts.[168] Conrad promised that the navy programs would not threaten the integrity of the universities, that only the brightest scientists would be included, and that most projects would be chosen by university scientists. Very little of the work would be classified. He proposed that all fields of science be included and promised continuity of support. All the university presidents agreed to participate. By and large, over the years, ONR kept those promises, to a large number of American universities.[169]

In the years immediately following the war, the ONR became the principal government agency supporting academic science and engineering.[170] As yet, it was the only government funding agency not narrowly defined, and the only major player until the mid-1950s when the National Science Foundation (founded in 1950) began to give really significant amounts of grant funding. ONR senior administrators in its early years would have much influence in their later prominent careers in academia and higher scientific administration.

After their release from the navy, Ralph Krause and Tom Morrin remained in the Boston area. Krause managed more than one job at a time in the immediate postwar years. He helped Harvard phase out its RRL work, and then managed the Engineering Research Laboratory at MIT from 1945 until 1947, while at the same time working at Raytheon Corporation as a vice president. Morrin also went to work for Raytheon Corporation in Massachusetts after the war.

Krause and his wife were from California, however, and wished to return. At an engineering society meeting in New York City in early 1948, he learned from Terman that SRI was looking for new leadership to replace William Talbot. Terman suggested that Krause might want to take a top position at SRI, perhaps as director or as director of research. Krause consulted with Lee DuBridge, the former director of the MIT Radiation Lab and now president of Caltech, about the SRI possibility, but Donald Tresidder moved ahead to offer the top SRI post to Jesse Hobson in late January 1948.[171] Krause joined SRI the following June as director of research. Two months later, fellow "Bird Dog" Tom Morrin joined as director of engineering.[172] Hobson took on the task of building contracts for SRI, while Krause sought to build up the research staff and programs. Krause and Morrin hired at least fifteen persons from RRL for SRI's Engineering Department (about 15 percent of the technical staff in those first two to three years). Krause also frequently offered part-time positions to Stanford graduate students recruited by Terman. Soon after arriving, Hobson wrote Al Eurich at Stanford: "At the suggestion of Dean Terman, and with Krause's enthusiastic endorsement, one of our first steps will be to establish an electronics laboratory and a vacuum tube development laboratory. Both feel there is a large demand for that service, and I'm sure there is. Our work will supplement and complete the excellent research in Electrical Engineering and Physics being done under Terman and others."[173]

The Office of Naval Research, through Krause, Morrin, and Terman, had an important influence in the early development of SRI. ONR funded SRI's first contract in November 1946, a continuation of a study of guayule rubber, a project already underway in Salinas, California, but turned over to SRI.[174] During the war, the guayule project had attempted to find additional sources of natural rubber. Rather than terminate the project at the end of the war, ONR continued the search with a $150,000 grant to SRI.[175]

During SRI's early years, Stanford faculty expected to participate in SRI projects, along the lines of Terman's recommendations and Hobson's overtures to Stanford's administration. Although this generally turned out not to be the case, an important exception involved Terman's field of radio engineering. Among SRI's first big contracts were projects with the navy and the air force to study radar receivers, communications transmitters and receivers, and radio propagation. These projects were similar to early contracts with Stanford's Electrical Engineering Department. In mid-1948, the department's O. G. ("Mike") Villard Jr. worked with the U.S. Army Signal Corps's Camp Coles group to win a single-sideband radio contract for SRI, an endeavor strongly supported by both Fred Terman and Alvin Eurich.[176] This work in radio and communications engineering saw Stanford's Radio Propagation Lab share projects with SRI, a collaboration that has continued for a half-century. Classified radio work was moved off-campus during the campus antiwar demonstrations of the Vietnam War era, but other work still continues, notably studies with "The Dish," the 150-foot radio telescope in the Stanford foothills.

Finding "A Bang-up Good President" for Stanford

In 1943, Fred Terman had imagined that his plan to promote Stanford's rise would take about twenty years, the period of time he assumed Donald Tresidder would occupy the position of president of Stanford. Three years after his appointment as dean, however, an unanticipated event temporarily altered Stanford's course.

Despite the turbulence of Tresidder's presidency to date, the year 1947 had been a good one, Tresidder felt, and Stanford was clearly on the rise. There was talk that Tresidder might become a candidate in the upcoming California gubernatorial race if Governor Earl Warren were to run for the U.S. presidency. Or perhaps Stanford's president might seek a senate seat in 1950.

At the beginning of the year, President Tresidder headed east on Stanford business, visiting Harvard first, then on to Washington DC, and finally to New York for the Association of American Universities meetings. Late on the evening of January 28, 1948, President Tresidder died in bed in his room at the St. Regis Hotel in New York City. He was only fifty-three years old. Mary Tresidder, on a skiing trip in Utah at the time, returned in shock to the Stanford campus and found the students and staff in a similar state.[177]

William Parmer Fuller Jr., president of the board of trustees, appointed Vice President Alvin C. Eurich to the post of acting president. Fuller told him, "You're running this place," Eurich later recalled. "Don't forget you're not only acting, you're running." Eurich added, "Don and I had our plans for the university, so I went right ahead with them."[178] Fuller resigned from the board presidency in May 1948 due to ill health and was succeeded by Paul C. Edwards. (Edwards also had known Tresidder well and was a distant relation.) Fuller, who had been extremely close to Tresidder, in fact suffered a nervous breakdown and was obliged to withdraw entirely from Stanford affairs for some time.[179]

It was the purview of the board of trustees to appoint Stanford's president. Their search would take nearly a year, and Fred Terman soon became centrally involved.

The board's presidential search committee included Herbert Hoover, who took an active role despite his advanced age and governmental responsibilities. Other trustees on the search committee were Chairman Ira Lillick, Lloyd W. Dinkelspiel, George A. Ditz, Paul C. Edwards, Seeley G. Mudd, and Herman Phleger.[180] All resided in California, save Hoover who spent most of the year in New York City. Hoover was sagacious and earnest in his task on the trustee committee. His influence on the board, in his fourth consecutive presidential search, was as powerful as ever.

The board committee received names submitted by trustees, and by search advisory committees of the Stanford faculty and the alumni. In February 1948, Parmer Fuller had asked Eurich to appoint a faculty committee to advise the trustees.[181] Eurich conducted an election for a seven-person committee along traditional divisional lines with a member plus two alternates for each place (in the same fashion as members of the Academic Council's Faculty Advisory Board were elected).[182] This committee, formed in April, consisted of Loren R. Chandler, dean of the Medical School; R. F. Jones, head of the English Department; Marion R. Kirkwood, former dean of the Law School; George S. Parks of chemistry; Edgar E. Robinson, head of history; Fred Terman, dean of engineering; and Victor C. Twitty, head of biology.[183] Alternates included other respected senior faculty members Charles H. Danforth, John W. Dodds, Eugene Grant, Philip A. Leighton, Ralph Lutz, George E. Osborne, Hugh Skilling, and Douglas M. Whitaker.[184]

After Marion Kirkwood declined to serve as chair, a second ballot elected Fred Terman by a large majority. The faculty committee met more than a dozen times between April and September and began recruiting immediately. They invited Stanford colleagues to suggest candidates and to inquire of their close colleagues at other institutions for suitable names. They sent out letters to more than sixty-five universities and colleges. Members wrote personally to colleagues. Terman worked out an arrangement with Ira Lillick that all names being considered with any seriousness by the trustees would be passed on to the faculty committee for evaluation from the faculty viewpoint.[185]

The faculty committee worked with a statement listing the qualities they perceived to be important for Stanford's next president. They felt strongly that the position required an academic man, a university man with teaching and administrative experience and the long view of the profession of education, and a recognized scholar among scholars. He must be a capable executive who could work with collective wisdom and successfully delegate; a man possessing the various necessary personal qualities. Most important of all, the president must be a man who would have the full respect and confidence of the Stanford faculty.[186] Their initial wording of age requirements (between forty and fifty-five years of age) was amended to the more felicitous phrase: someone who could expect to serve at least ten years, but not more than twenty.

A parallel alumni committee appointed by the trustees, and chaired by former treasurer Frank Walker, met several times in the early summer of 1948 to vet lists of candidates from the trustees and faculty committees. The alumni group wanted a Stanford man for the presidency, but approved a number of names including Lawrence Kimpton (their top choice by a narrow margin), followed closely by Fred Terman and four other names, and, in twelfth place, J. E. Wallace Sterling.[187]

The faculty committee presented to trustees a list of candidates, as first and second choices. Terman felt his committee had to give the trustees a slate of at least five or six names to reduce the possibility of an embarrassing deadlock. Their "first" of six names contained no one from Stanford's faculty.[188] Then the committee had voted six to one to place Fred Terman's name on the list. He objected—he did not want the position, he told them—but he was overruled. His name was added to the first list, and he soon resigned from the committee. As chair, he was replaced by Edgar Eugene Robinson, and his place on the committee was taken by alternate Hugh Skilling. (Once again, as in 1941, Fred Terman was the Stanford faculty committee choice for president, among candidates from the faculty.)

The trustees were anxious to move ahead. No one name, as yet, appeared as a frontrunner on the combined lists of the trustees, the faculty and the alumni committees. In mid-July, Ira Lillick asked the faculty committee to submit to the trustees their "screened down" list of most desirable candidates no later than August 1.[189] Terman summarized his thoughts for incoming chair Robinson and commented on the top names (absent his own). In order to maximize the committee's influence, he suggested that no single faculty committee member's vote should veto a name; the committee should indicate to the trustees their full willingness to reconsider names submitted to them by the trustees' committee, and be willing to consider new names. He also urged the committee to stand firm on the need, "at this rather critical time," for faculty support of any nominee. He indicated to Robinson that Frank Walker had the alumni committee quite united and could help the faculty and alumni committees maintain a solid front on policy matters. Finally, Terman advised, "if the question of Tresidder's regime comes up with the Trustees Committee, facts should be stated impartially and frankly in such a way that makes it clear that Stanford simply cannot stand another period of stress." The committee should not "beat around the bush with respect to Eurich."[190]

A penciled list in Fred's hand made in 1948 suggests that he summed up the pros and cons, as was his custom, as he thought about his own nomination.[191] He was complimented that George Szego, mathematics professor, had nominated him. He was not looking for the position, however, nor had he been cultivating key trustees Lillick and Edwards. Nevertheless, he would not be afraid of the task—he had run the Radio Research Lab (RRL) during the war, a "big show" with more than eight hundred employees and a larger budget than that of

Stanford University—but he was not "itching" to move into big administration. He had already shown he could do the job when he put new life into the IRE as its president and ran the RRL. He also recognized that there were some things he could do well and with enjoyment, things he could do "o.k." but considered a chore, and other things he would have to delegate or struggle with. If he were appointed to the presidency, he would work with the knowledge that there is no monopoly of brains in the president's office, indeed, that there were many bright people in the university smarter than him.

He was not motivated much by the personal spotlight, he admitted. As director of RRL he was rewarded by seeing his organization "tick." He was not impressed by "mixing with the Great"—he had seen enough of Conant, Bush, Compton, Ray Lyman Wilbur, and the military brass to satisfy his ego. He would have a longer, perhaps happier life, he speculated, certainly a life with fewer crises without taking on Stanford's presidency. His personal ambitions were satisfied by remaining with engineering and related work. He wanted to associate with Stanford all his life. He preferred the "working level" in an organization and looked forward to working under a "bang up good President that one respected and liked and would serve as a real help instead of an impediment and millstone."[192]

Fred could have insisted that his name be dropped from the list after it was sent to the trustees. Perhaps he admitted his reluctance to Herbert Hoover when he visited him in New York.

New committee chair Edgar Robinson stressed to Ira Lillick, by phone and in writing, that the faculty committee believed that a large proportion, possibly a majority, of the faculty would not support Eurich's selection, and the committee urged his name be dropped.[193] The faculty was apparently not as united as Robinson suggested. In late July, medical dean Loren Chandler and five other deans (or soon-to-be deans) wrote directly to the board of trustees to extol the strengths of Eurich, while admitting that most of them had been appointed to their deanships by Tresidder or Eurich.[194] It was Chandler who had originally nominated Eurich, and the dean subsequently resigned from the faculty committee.[195] In response, Robinson reported to the trustee committee that the faculty committee had been contacted by numerous faculty members who complained about Eurich as a candidate. The trustees received a number of similar critical letters, along with letters lauding Eurich. One letter claimed that Tresidder had taken the blame for poor innovations at Stanford that were, in fact, Eurich's doings; another claimed the opposite, that good innovations at Stanford attributed to Tresidder were due to Eurich's efforts. Eurich was an honest guy, Robinson told Lillick, but he could not inspire faculty confidence. Professors of more traditional fields could not hold in high esteem a professor of education.[196] Considered an administrator rather than a scholar, Eurich also was seen by some faculty as a meddler and a hatchet man of Tresidder.

Robinson was himself a thorny character. He was an outspoken department head, and as years went by he not only fell out with Tresidder and Eurich, but also had reservations about future president Wallace Sterling. Robinson and Board Chairman Edwards were close friends, however. (They later coedited the autobiography of Ray Lyman Wilbur.) Robinson could express his concerns freely with Edwards and Lillick, including the faculty committee's frustration in feeling their recommendations were not seriously considered by the trustee search committee.[197] But as Edwards wrote to Paul Davis, Ray Wilbur had expressed to Edwards his feelings that it was a mistake to have either a faculty or an alumni committee, that "it's a Trustee's job."[198]

As of late summer 1948, two names, Fred Terman and Philip C. Jessup, law professor at Columbia University, were on the "first" list of both the faculty and the alumni advisory committees. Five names, including J. E. Wallace Sterling, were on the "second" lists of both faculty and alumni.

By the end of the process, Hoover had personally removed approximately sixty names from further consideration. His reasons included inexperience, personal character flaws (alcoholism, marital problems, or erratic behavior), and political beliefs (including any leaning toward "Rooseveltism"). Hoover also vetoed the names of current Stanford faculty members, just as he had done in the search for Ray Lyman Wilbur's successor.[199] Other trustee committee members also had the right to veto candidates.[200] Paul Edwards noted in his Presidential Search Notebook: "List of names remaining after eliminating from our list those as to whom Mr. Hoover has objections, coupled with those as to whom other members of the committee have expressed objections." These remaining names, as of September 22, 1948, were: J. E. Wallace Sterling; Deane W. Malott, chancellor of the University of Kansas; F. L. Hovde, president of Purdue University; General John J. McCloy (nominated solely by Vannevar Bush); Dean G. Harrison of MIT; and Swarthmore President John W. Nason.[201]

Hoover and other trustees were well aware of personal differences between Stanford faculty and a number of Tresidder's administrators. As in any close community, personal and working networks were intertwined and multidimensional. People took sides. When Tresidder's reorganization of Stanford's financial management necessitated the demotion of Frank Fish Walker, Walker's friend Paul Davis took his side. Davis, who had been at Stanford for much of Ray Lyman Wilbur's later presidency, had very close relationships with other Wilbur appointees, including business manager Almon Roth and registrar J. Pearce Mitchell; he also worked closely with trustees George Morell and Louis Roseberry on Stanford fund-raising.[202] Faculty who had risen to prominence during Wilbur's era—such as Edgar Robinson—tended toward this camp. Tresidder appointees tended to support the charismatic president's vision for Stanford's future and his proactive attempts to grapple with change. Tresidder and Eurich were supported by David S. Jacobson, who had little personal liking for his boss, Paul Davis, and who would take over much of Davis's work after Sterling's arrival.[203] Some managed to take a middle line. Professor John Dodds was a close friend of Walker, but understood Tresidder's organizational motives in altering Walker's position. Dodds, like many on the faculty, personally liked Tresidder, but did not support Al Eurich.[204] Fred Terman similarly took a discretionary tack. Terman had an influential place among the more senior faculty, both in terms of his own and his father's long commitment to Stanford. He was respected and admired by Ray Lyman Wilbur and Don Tresidder alike, and remained a personal friend of both Tresidder and Paul Davis.

Although some suggested that Eurich's academic background as a member of the education faculty was not up to snuff, Eurich's managerial style alienated many. Influential Professor of Education Paul R. Hanna, a friend of Fred Terman's, also felt Tresidder's appointment of Eurich was a mistake, and like Terman, Hanna remained close friends with Paul Davis.[205] Eurich left Stanford embittered, later recording that he could not get along with Paul Davis and thought Edgar E. Robinson, as chair of the faculty presidential search committee, "stabbed me in the back."[206] Eurich probably learned of Fred Terman's lack of support of him as well when Fred was chair of the committee, but Eurich and Terman remained on friendly terms, and Terman later performed a number of educational consulting tasks at Eurich's request.

By October, J. E. Wallace "Wally" Sterling, the director of the Huntington Library, emerged as the front-runner and a favorite of Herbert Hoover.[207] The Canadian-born Sterling came to Stanford as a graduate student in 1932 and received a PhD in history in 1937. Sterling joined the faculty at Caltech in 1937 where he quickly rose to prominence. He became a full professor within five years and was elected chairman of the faculty. During World War II, Sterling became a popular network radio news analyst and broadcast his comments over a weekly fifteen-minute program on CBS radio. Early in 1948, he was named director of the Huntington Library and Art Gallery in Pasadena. The Huntington board was chaired by Robert Millikan, and included Stanford alumni Herbert Hoover and Seeley G. Mudd.[208] Hoover wrote to Mudd in May 1948 that Sterling "might be looked into" for the Stanford presidency. Both Hoover and Mudd threw their support behind Sterling as did Ray Lyman Wilbur. By August, Sterling had become their lead candidate.[209]

The faculty committee thought Sterling had high ethical standards, good common sense, and a fine personality. He was an excellent public speaker. However, he had little large-scale administrative experience, they felt, and his published scholarly output was negligible—three manuscripts remained unpublished, although he hoped to finish some of them at Stanford.[210] (Sterling's work in progress included a treatise on British foreign policy since 1783, a volume on Canada and the United States, and a book on Canada and the refugee problem.[211])

Sterling mentioned this work during his final interviews. (He made at least one visit to Stanford, in October, to meet the trustees, visit the Hoover Library, and attend a football game.) Seeley Mudd warned board president Paul Edwards in September 1948 that Sterling's ideas about doing further research, writing, and teaching while at Stanford were a mistake. The job of Stanford president was a full-time task. Stanford's president must be fully and completely in the public eye and, he added, "participate intimately and fully in the lives of faculty, students and all those who live on our Western shores."[212] Writing on the eve of Sterling's acceptance of the position, Mudd again wrote Edwards that the president's job was essentially "one of academic *administration*." During Robert Millikan's presidency, he noted, his name "was synonymous with Caltech and Caltech was synonymous with Millikan. The twenty-four hours available to a President belongs to the University and to its over-all educational program."[213]

Whatever Seeley Mudd's feelings about Sterling's scholarly hopes or the faculty's concern about his previous experience and scholarship, the trustees' search committee moved ahead to appoint J. E. Wallace Sterling Stanford's fifth president in mid-November 1948. Nearly a year later, Paul Edwards outlined the process for an alumnus. More than a hundred names were considered by three committees, representing trustees, faculty, and alumni; perhaps six names appeared on the lists compiled individually by the three committees. Dr. Sterling's name was one of those on all three lists. Edwards went on to write that the faculty committee had emphasized scholarly accomplishment; the alumni committee stressed administrative experience and hoped for a Stanford alumnus; and the trustees hoped for a "happy combination of the three," plus enough youth to serve at least ten years before the retirement age of sixty-five. Two board members previously knew Sterling and others came to know him. "It was evident to all that he possessed the additional and important qualities of warm personality, quick friendship, serious intent with regard to advancement of education in America and a genuine and wholesome family background," wrote Edwards. "The appointment was received with universal approval from all segments of the Stanford community—faculty, alumni, students and interested friends."[214] Sterling's appointment was also approved by academics outside the Stanford circle. Lee DuBridge wrote Paul Edwards just after the appointment, "many of us thought Wallace Sterling a *logical* choice for President of Stanford University."[215]

Anne Marie Shaver Sterling had also impressed the trustees. Anne and Wallace Sterling had met as students at the University of Toronto. Anne had worked at Stanford as assistant director of the Roble dining hall during Wally's graduate years, and she, too, would soon become a notable presence on campus.[216]

The announcement of Sterling's election by the trustees was received well on campus. Published statements of welcome and support appeared from Chancellor Ray Lyman Wilbur, from the presidents of the Stanford Alumni Association and board of trustees, and from the chairman of the faculty and the alumni presidential search committees.[217] December's *Stanford Alumni Review* reported that the president-elect intended to continue his writing. Sterling felt the president should share in the intellectual leadership of the university. The three volumes in progress, however, were never finished.[218]

Wally Sterling would not arrive on campus to take up his duties as president until late March 1949.[219] Alvin Eurich had decided to move on and was due to take up his new position managing New York State's program of university reorganization on January 1, 1949. Who would serve as acting president in the interim? The trustees asked Clarence Faust to take the post, even though Faust had not been warmly welcomed by the English Department when he arrived from the University of Chicago to serve as director of the university library (with an appointment as professor of English).

Board of Trustees President Paul Edwards advised the Faculty Advisory Board, "as a courtesy," of the board's plan to appoint Faust as acting president. The Faculty Advisory Board, in turn, notified Edwards that they could not approve the move. Alvin Eurich "went to the bat magnificently," Edwards reported to Sterling, and "talked with all the deans." Two hours before the trustees' meeting to approve Faust's appointment, Eurich got enthusiastic endorsement of all the deans, with the notable exception of Fred Terman (who was also a member of the Faculty Advisory Board).[220] As a result, Fred Terman's first entry into President Sterling's business correspondence logged him in as a defender of the English Department faculty in opposition to the board of trustees and a Tresidder-Eurich era administrator.

Nevertheless, a new era had opened for Stanford. Fred Terman would get his wish: Wally Sterling turned out to be "a bang-up good President," one whom Terman both liked and respected.[221] And as Terman's own career now progressed from dean to provost, he and Sterling would develop a legendary partnership and friendship.

CHAPTER SIX

From Building a Discipline to Building a University

1949–1959

When Engineering Dean Fred Terman welcomed a new university president into office in 1949, he could look back on three roller-coaster years for Stanford. The sudden drop in student enrollments at the end of the war had been just as rapidly replaced by a wave of new and returning students, many of them supported by the new GI Bill. Just as Stanford began to deal with related issues of student housing and curriculum changes, graduate student admissions fell and GI Bill tuition assistance faded. Yet, as other departments struggled with fragile budgets, floundering faculty morale, and student admissions questions, the School of Engineering faced the sweet dilemma of how to outfit new research projects, teach unprecedented numbers of undergraduates and graduate students, and attract and retain top-flight professors.

As department head and dean, Fred Terman had been astute in seeing the possibilities of cutting-edge fields in engineering and related disciplines, and he continued to look for means to facilitate their establishment and growth at Stanford. Utilizing his ever-growing circle of former students, faculty, and industry colleagues, he attracted support to the engineering departments under his care. Regardless of the source of that funding, be it from government sources like ONR, companies like Lockheed, or successful alumni like Bill Hewlett and David Packard, he insisted that those funds be directed to research projects that would advance the knowledge, experience, and careers of Stanford's students and faculty.

Dean Terman shared with President Wallace Sterling a deep love for Stanford and an ambition for its future. If Terman began his deanship with Stanford's traditional vision of "Service to the West," he had quickly broadened his view to national, and even international, horizons.[1] The San Francisco Peninsula would grow mightily in the years following World War II, and Terman and Sterling felt certain that Stanford University should not simply grow with the area, but be an engine of growth.

Sterling readily understood that what Terman had done with the School of Engineering suggested one means to accomplish greater things for the university. Like Terman, Sterling believed strongly that a top-ranking university required an exceptional faculty and student body. To get this, Stanford had to find new sources of funding and to improve dramatically its endowment. Early in 1953, Sterling expressed his "appreciation and deep gratitude" to Terman, who had continued to build at Stanford "an engineering school that is already great."[2] Two years later, the president would appoint Terman as his second in command, provost of the university (which Terman would overlap with his responsibilities as dean until 1959). The duties and authority of the provost were still nebulous in 1955, but the provost's office would hereafter bear the imprint of Fred Terman's goals and expectations.

Engineering in a New Era

In the mid-1940s, Terman had concluded that Stanford's School of Engineering demonstrated significant strength in the fields of communications, electronics, thermodynamics, and mechanical structures. He saw potential in the field of engineering economics, or industrial engineering, in the Civil Engineering Department, and possibilities for the development of engineering mechanics and aeronautics within the Mechanical Engineering Department. In his first years back on campus as dean, these were the areas he focused on developing first.

During this period, Fred was also anxious to move the Engineering School toward what would later be called solid-state and materials sciences. And while he would continue to support microwave research at the renamed Hansen Labs, he would see new research efforts get underway at the Electronics Research Laboratory and the Applied Electronics Laboratory as the 1950s began. He would also be able to turn to the development of new academic programs in statistics, computer science, and applied mathematics.[3]

Faculty and student needs were a top priority. Terman held steadfast to the Wilbur tradition of a broad common program for undergraduate students in engineering. Compared to typical engineering curricula at other universities, there was relatively little departmental specialization until the senior, or fourth undergraduate year, and a student's coursework typically included a relatively large number of social sciences and humanities courses. The School of Engineering faculty had already put up a fight over this issue in an accreditation battle in the early 1940s and continued to back this philosophy of engineering education. In one of his early annual reports to President Sterling, Dean Terman emphasized that his faculty wished to maintain this broad plan.[4] Meanwhile, Terman also considered the development of an undergraduate and graduate major in engineering science (with additional emphasis on statistics, mathematics, and physics) for promising students likely to go on to graduate school. In 1949, Fred's eldest son, Frederick W. Terman, was among those to get a bachelor of science degree in engineering science at Stanford.[5]

The population of the West Coast was growing rapidly, and the West's postwar economy booming. Terman intended to make sure that Stanford's faculty participated in that regional development. He knew that Vannevar Bush, wartime chairman of OSRD, was planning to transfer formerly war-related federal research funds to American universities now that the war was over, and he was certain that the several armed forces research divisions planned to support research, especially in electronics, engineering mechanics, applied physics, and aeronautics. To begin planning for such actions, Terman chartered an Electronics Research Laboratory (ERL) committee in April 1947 to coordinate electronic research operations in the Department of Electrical Engineering. Terman served as chair, with Karl Spangenberg as vice chair, and Lester Field, Joseph Pettit, Leonard Fuller, and department head Hugh Skilling as members.[6]

Terman kept up his contacts with electronics companies as well, just as he had done throughout the 1930s. He sought to encourage their employment of Stanford students and his professional colleagues, but fellowships also remained a top concern now that the war had ended. The fellowships were a part of the ongoing linked process of research, training, and employment. When asking General Electric executives to support fellowship awards in 1949, for example, Terman described the work of Charles B. Crumly, whom he regarded as the most outstanding graduate applicant. Crumly, he noted, was working with the "terrific" network theory expert David F. Tuttle. He similarly described graduate student Dean A. Watkins's traveling wave tube work with Lester Field in the last six months as "sensational."[7] In detailed and frank letters, Terman always seemed to make a strong and positive connection between Stanford and the company. Soon, a number of those electronic firms would establish branch laboratories within ten miles of Terman's Electrical Engineering Department.

Also as Terman expected, as Stanford's Electrical Engineering Department became better known, offers to hire away Stanford's faculty became more frequent. In late 1950, General Electric offered to double Professor Karl Spangenberg's $7,500 salary if he would head General Electric's vacuum tube laboratory. Lester Field was offered similar deals with several companies that same year.[8] Fortunately for Stanford, both Spangenberg and Field stayed for a few more years. As the electronics industry developed in the surrounding area, Stanford had similar problems keeping highly skilled electronic and electron tube technicians on campus. Like faculty, they were being lured away by much higher salaries at Varian,

Sylvania, and General Electric.[9] Salaries, Terman knew, had to be better balanced and competitive with industry as well as with other universities.

Industry salaries had been double, even triple, those of academia since the days of Harris J. Ryan and Leonard Fuller in World War I. To make matters more difficult, however, salaries for full professors in engineering were still below the mean for salaries for full professors at Stanford University ($7,572) in 1951. The top salary in the School of Engineering ($8,750) was well below the maximum salary set for full professors at Stanford ($12,500). Engineering exceeded only the humanities in this. Among assistant and associate professors, by contrast, engineering salaries were above the means for Stanford salaries (at $4,382 and $5,497, respectively) although higher salaries could be found in the Schools of Business and Medicine.[10] But Terman's faculty, he was obliged to point out to President Sterling in 1950, included a number of long-serving young teachers, Mike Villard and Bob Helliwell among others, who had served too long as "acting instructors" carrying heavy teaching loads at low salaries. They deserved promotions, as did associate and assistant professors like Lester Field, David Tuttle, and Ed Ginzton.[11]

Despite the potential pilfering of faculty, the association between Stanford and neighboring firms was viewed as healthy and positive, and Terman continued to encourage development of local industry relations. "I am quite interested in your letter," he wrote to a magnetic amplifier developer from Pennsylvania who was thinking of moving to Palo Alto to be near Stanford's Electrical Engineering Department, "because I have always had a soft spot in my heart for small personal businesses. The Hewlett-Packard Company, for example, really started in the radio laboratory at Stanford."[12]

Dean Terman's efforts at promotion could, of course, run afoul of campus bookkeepers. Stanford's assistant controller complained in 1948 that Fred had two unauthorized bills at the Stanford Union amounting to $4.97 and $7.79 for "entertainment." In response, Hugh Skilling wrote directly to Acting President Eurich to point out that the Electrical Engineering Department usually spent about $75 per year on luncheon seminars featuring nonuniversity speakers. After one such seminar, General Electric executives had presented Dean Terman with a check for $6,000 over the lunch Fred hosted at the Stanford Union. To avoid skirmishes, Terman arranged a year later with newly arrived President Sterling that $600 per year be set aside by the Engineering School for travel and development purposes by engineering faculty.[13]

Early in 1949, Terman pointed out to Sterling's new administration what he viewed as a significant budget imbalance. Tuition fees received from students enrolling in engineering courses were now considerably more than the school's actual instructional budget allocation (whereas before the war, the reverse was the case). He attributed this situation to careful balancing of class sizes and course offerings, and by carefully integrating into the department's government-sponsored research contracts. He also noted that due to tuition-fee increases at Stanford in 1948–49, an additional $59,000 had been raised from engineering students' credit units that year, but only $20,000 of this (or one-third) had been returned to the School of Engineering for salary increases. The short-fall between apparent income and costs was particularly annoying since during Fred's second year as dean (1947–48) alone, the School of Engineering had received six research contracts in the Departments of Mechanical and Civil Engineering ($112,000) and eight in Electrical Engineering ($321,000) totaling $433,000 per year, including $94,000 in overhead to the university.[14]

In 1952, Terman reorganized the dean's office to promote, intensify, and better systematize fund-raising and development for the school. He appointed Hugh Skilling as associate dean of engineering and obtained the part-time services of Farrell McGhie of the general secretary's office as assistant to the dean. McGhie also helped supervise electronics engineering research contracts.[15] McGhie's efforts began to "pay dividends" immediately with increased support from industry for engineering scholarships, fellowships, research funding, and, in some cases, general university expenses. As part of the reorganization, supervision of engineering alumni volunteers in Stanford's annual giving program was transferred to the "Stanford Engineering Fund." An engineering alumni committee, chaired by Fred's old colleague Harold F. Elliott ('16), set to work to increase contributions from alumni.[16]

Although the university budget was no longer operating at a deficit, the university's finances had yet to improve sufficiently as the 1950s began. In preparing his Engineering School budget for 1951–52, Terman wrote to President Sterling that he accepted the hard times with its predicted decrease in overall student numbers. As a result, he outlined potential cuts in staff and programs to the extent of $22,000. But, he reminded Sterling, the Engineering School in 1951 was educating four times as many students as it had in 1928 for the same budget (in constant dollars). "We have thus not built up fat during the post-war period that can now be worked off."[17]

By the time he prepared his budget requests for 1954–55, however, Terman could point out that the continuing enrollment increases, particularly in electrical engineering, now required him to ask for a 19 percent increase in budget (15 percent for faculty additions). Despite earlier pessimistic predictions, the number of men entering college in the United States between 1950 and 1953 who intended to major in engineering had risen by 59 percent, and at Stanford, this number had risen by 106 percent. In 1953 alone, graduate enrollment in electrical engineering had risen 50 percent. The department's 187 graduate students made the department nearly as large in number as the combined number of graduate students (195) in all of Stanford's physical science departments (chemistry, physics, mathematics, statistics, and mineral sciences, including geology). By the end of 1954, undergraduate enrollment in engineering courses had risen 33.5 percent in the previous year, while graduate enrollment was up nearly 15 percent, most of this driven by student interest in electrical engineering.[18] (Overall university undergraduate enrollment was up only 1 percent and graduate enrollment down by 3 percent.) With no corresponding increase in budgets or staff, the expenditure per full-time student had fallen sharply. Among the top ten engineering schools (rating relative expenditure per student at Stanford as 1.0), Terman estimated Stanford's major competition as: MIT 1.6; Cornell at 2.2; Berkeley 2.4; Caltech 2.6; and Columbia 2.7. Only Illinois was close to Stanford, but still slightly higher at 1.2 in expenditure per student. Stanford was falling behind Berkeley in class size, and the quality of instruction would deteriorate unless he could increase the staff.[19]

Honors Co-operative Program in Engineering

The initiation of the Honors Co-operative Program with its industrial financial support—companies paid double tuition to enable top technical employees to study for graduate degrees—was one solution Terman found to finance additional staff without placing further demands on university general funds. Since normal tuition did not pay the entire cost of a graduate education, Terman persuaded companies to pay the student/employee's tuition plus an equal sum to the university. In 1953 he argued that this allowed the university to hire additional faculty, train more good students, and strengthen local industry "in a most effective manner."[20]

Employees accepted to the program registered for courses on a fee-per-unit basis. Their registration provided a new source of income to the university, and the connection with participating companies provided mutual advantages to the university, its graduate students, and local employers. Even before the program was formalized in 1954, in its first informal years it served as a model for other departments. Albert Bowker, head of the new Department of Statistics, requested of the graduate dean Ernest Hilgard, that a similar program be allowed for his department. Writing Sterling, Hilgard suggested that the Engineering School plan might "serve as our policy."[21] The Honors Co-operative Program had its beginnings as early as 1945 when Terman suggested to Hugh Skilling that Radio Research Lab employees coming to the Stanford area (for example, as employees of Hewlett-Packard) might be given a research assistantship at Stanford if paid for by their company. "At least I am going to attempt this," wrote Terman.[22] Government employees from Ames Aeronautics Laboratory at Moffett Field had begun attending classes in the 1940s, with aerodynamics courses taught at Stanford by Ames staff. By 1952, some technical employees of Stanford, of the Stanford Research Institute, and of several nearby engineering firms were allowed to register for part-time graduate work in engineering. Hewlett-Packard and Westinghouse, both of whom husbanded "good relations" with Stanford (including the donation of fellowships), were brought on board the honors program. Several other companies requested similar arrangements. As tenants took up facilities in the Industrial Park taking shape on campus borders, Terman expected tenant companies also to request participation in the Honors Co-Op for their employees. Looking up the corporate ladders, Terman commented, "we might reasonably look for some additional financial support from the sponsoring company organizations."[23] Other companies participated, including new members General Electric, Dalmo-Victor, Ampex, and Varian, to a total of thirteen companies by 1956.[24]

The first sixteen regularly registered Co-Op students who entered for the 1954–55 academic year came from Sylvania, Hewlett-Packard, and the Stanford Research Institute. Since they were still working at least part-time, they normally took two-fifths of a regular course load and received a master's degree in eight quarters. Most Co-Op course enrollment was in electrical engineering, followed by courses in mathematics and physics, but a number also enrolled in courses in mechanical engineering, engineering mechanics, and the other engineering disciplines as well as in statistics and chemistry.[25]

By 1957, 243 part-time graduate students were enrolled in the program.[26] As the program grew, enrollments steadily increased in the new Division of Aeronautical Engineering, in the Departments of Mechanical and Industrial Engineering, and in the Departments of Mathematics and Physics. Terman eventually rewarded those departments that built up the program by returning matching tuition directly to them.[27]

Electrical Engineering and Electronics Research Laboratories

At the end of the war, Fred Terman and his colleagues in electrical engineering began securing a number of major research contracts from the federal government, primarily from the ONR and from the U.S. Air Force and Army Signal Corps.[28] Terman had begun experimenting with a new way of managing government contracts as early as 1946 with the celebrated "Tri-Services Contract" (all army, air force, and navy electronics work was managed under a single contract by the school's coordinator of research contracts, Leonard Fuller).

The work was predominantly in the Electrical Engineering Department's radio propagation section, investigating natural phenomena (meteor scatter, wave propagation phenomena from very low to very high frequencies), and research that would lead to practical breakthroughs in radar (backscatter and long-distance over-the-horizon radar), and in electron tubes. Research by Lester Field and Karl Spangenberg on electron tubes was among the most outstanding of its kind in the nation. Spangenberg was Terman's first hire as Electrical Engineering Department head in 1937, and Spangenberg carried the brunt of the electronics and klystron teaching and research on the Stanford campus during the war until 1943. At that time he left to perform government service as an electronics consultant to the army air force and then joined Terman's Radio Research Lab at Harvard before returning to Stanford following the war. As a graduate student, Lester Field had worked during the pioneer days of the klystron before World War II. After receiving his PhD at Stanford in 1943, he went to work at Bell Labs (his work led in the invention of the traveling wave tube, which had significant advantages over the klystron) and then returned to Stanford in the fall of 1946.

The outbreak of hostilities in Korea in 1950 significantly increased both the pace and the amount of government-sponsored radio and electronics research at Stanford.[29] In July 1950, Terman received a telephone call from ONR headquarters in Washington, DC. Fred was told that, informally, ONR looked to Stanford as a center for tube research and radar countermeasures. This was certainly a logical assumption considering Terman's leadership of the Radio Research Laboratory during WWII, the numerous former RRL and MIT Radiation Laboratory engineers working at Stanford, and the quality of Stanford's postwar radio research. Stanford, Terman was told, ranked "about first in usefulness" to the navy in defense electronics. Most importantly, the ONR was planning to spend a million dollars for fast-paced electronics research activity at Stanford, and this support would continue regardless of the outcome of the Korean conflict.[30]

Terman, believing this to be an excellent field for university research, made preliminary plans for facilities that would also provide a nucleus for expansion should a general war develop in Korea. President Sterling was enthusiastic. In a meeting with Sterling, Karl Spangenberg, and campus planner Ted Spencer, Terman called for preliminary designs of a laboratory of some ten to twelve thousand square feet, to be located near the new Microwave Laboratory. Things moved quickly from there. President Sterling took Terman's proposal for a new electron tube center to the trustees on July 20, 1950, and they quickly approved it. Two months later the trustees approved the expenditure of $160,000 for the new Electronics Research Lab building. They also committed Stanford to undertake research in applied electronics under the direction of Dean Frederick Terman at an annual rate of between $300,000 and $450,000.

By mid-November, the navy indicated it would enter into a contract by December 1, whereby the trustees authorized completion of working drawings by the architectural firm of Spencer and Ambrose for the Electronics Research Laboratory (ERL). By December, the board had authorized an additional wing to the proposed building, to be funded largely by the pledge of a gift from the Hewlett-Packard Company. This wing, the first large construction gift to Stanford by William Hewlett and David Packard, was designed to provide space for classrooms, teaching labs, and offices, rather than research. (Six months later, the trustees accepted Sterling's recommendation to name the building wing after Hewlett-Packard.) The firm of Wagner and Martinez was hired in February to build the new ERL building and teaching wing. Estimated that it would cost $252,625, the 21,000-square-foot building was actually completed by August under budget ($224,000—at a remarkable cost of only $10.67 per square foot). On September 20, 1951, the Electronics Research Laboratory building was occupied.

Within two months of the building's completion, the annual funding for the research program in electronics was estimated at $700,000 per year, and the air force asked for further expansion. That month, November 1951, the board of trustees authorized a 10,000-square-foot expansion to the middle wing of ERL. In 1955, the first part of a third wing was constructed with a $50,000 gift from Terman's long-time friend Sennett W. Gilfillan ('12), and that same year Hewlett and Packard gave additional funds to further expand their wing, ERL's first, by adding an additional 7,500 square feet. Sennett Gilfillan doubled his gift to complete the Gilfillan wing of the ERL in 1956, adding some 9,000 square feet to the lab. By fall 1957, with the final part of the Gilfillan wing extended, the entire ERL building had cost a total of $529,000, of which $230,000 was paid for by alumni gifts (principally Hewlett, Packard, and Gilfillan) and $295,000 from university general funds (amortized over five years and paid for from overhead on research contracts).[31]

By 1955, electrical engineering had edged out mechanical engineering as the largest undergraduate engineering student major; it had been larger at the graduate level since the late 1930s. The department had grown so rapidly that the ERL, home to many undergraduate and graduate classes, along with research and teaching labs, faculty offices, and after January 1956 the university's IBM 650 computer, was jam-packed. Fred Terman now needed an additional building to house the growing applied electronics research program, including its classified research. Completed in 1958, this new facility was the 12,000-square-foot Applied Electronics Laboratory (AEL). Its cost, $238,000, like that of ERL, was amortized over seven years using overhead from research contracts.[32] By 1958, the year before Terman resigned as dean of engineering, there were some eighty-five undergraduate seniors majoring in electrical engineering, three hundred fifty master's degree candidates, and well over one hundred PhD candidates, all studying and doing research in the ERL and AEL buildings.

The ERL and AEL buildings, which Terman later combined administratively to be known as the Stanford Electronics Laboratories (SEL), were typical of buildings constructed at Stanford during the 1940s and 1950s. Utilitarian and far from elegant, they were of concrete or concrete-block and wood construction, with simple wooden office doors and trim, wood-backed theater seats for the larger classrooms and chairs for the smaller classrooms, lab benches and stools in the numerous teaching labs, and standard wood office desks. The buildings served Stanford well, providing space for thousands of electrical engineering students for forty years until they were razed in the late 1990s and replaced by buildings in the new Stanford Science and Engineering Quad.

The original purpose of the Hewlett-Packard wing of the ERL was for student classrooms, offices, and teaching laboratories. Rapidly growing electronics research needs put great pressure on the available space in ERL. The newer AEL building was designed primarily for faculty and graduate student research, including classified research, particularly in microwave electronics.

In 1951, Terman hired William Rambo, one of his Stanford-RRL protégés, for the Electrical Engineering Department. Rambo soon after took over as head of the Applied Electronics Laboratory, and in 1958 took over the combined Stanford Electronics Lab. "Fred Terman ran the labs, even from a remote distance," said Rambo. Terman was an administrator, he noted, who would never overorganize or "clutter up" a lab with unnecessary organizational structure. Terman was a "GREAT monitor," both as a teacher and as an administrator. (Terman sometimes began his class with a fifteen-minute quiz, Rambo recounted. It was possible to do well on the quiz if you had read the text, or you could figure it out by yourself if you were enormously smart. "I used to hate it," Rambo recalled, "but it made me read the book." Rambo continued the practice in his own teaching.)[33]

Terman's concept, said Rambo, was that Stanford people could help the U.S. government, and in turn, Stanford faculty and students would benefit from the experience. The student component was very important to Terman. According to Rambo, "Terman was very rigid about that. He was out counting noses to be sure there was a full complement of graduate students involved and that they were doing useful things, not Mickey Mouse things."[34]

The now-combined SEL offered an annual four-day campus conference for military service contractors, members of other service laboratories, and industry people. Three to four hundred visitors would listen to presentations by Stanford faculty principal investigators on the fifteen to twenty projects going on at SEL. The projects had been designed by individual faculty, although Terman and after 1958, Dean Joseph Pettit, oversaw proposal budgets and made sure that the faculty members did not promise something Stanford could not deliver. This faculty-contractor interchange was extremely important. The navy, air force, and army signal corps had first-rate senior research directors, men with PhDs in their appropriate fields, and advisory committees composed of recognized experts, of the likes of respected astronomer Fred Whipple from Harvard.

In 1956, with the ERL building full and busy, Terman prepared a report on space needs for the School of Engineering for the next five years. The need was still acute in electrical engineering where research contracts now brought in some

$2 million per year, and the number of electrical engineering graduate students alone was expected to rise from two hundred to some three to four hundred within five years. Space, however, was at a premium throughout the School of Engineering. Mechanical engineering and its developing aeronautical section, along with civil and industrial engineering, had filled the reclaimed "attic, basement, and under-the-eaves space" in the Quadrangle.[35] By 1958, Stanford's electronics research within the Electrical Engineering Department had hit more than $3 million annually and was still growing. Research in space science and electronics, both civilian and military, had raised the level of research in radio wave propagation, and the ERL and AEL buildings again needed expansion.

Transistors

Terman's interest in the future of the transistor can be found in his notes as early as 1948. By the early 1950s, Terman began planning for development of the study of solid-state (transistor) electronics at Stanford. Terman discussed the need for funds to start a program in transistors with Sennett W. Gilfillan in 1952.[36] Gilfillan had placed few bounds on the $50,000 gift he gave to Stanford that year. In thanking his friend heartily for the gift as a "welcome Christmas present," Terman recommended that $15,000 could go to undergraduate (freshman) scholarships for those intending to major in electronics, while $35,000 should go to develop a "program of instruction and student research in *applications of the transistor*." He added, "The transistor is a great new force that will revolutionize many aspects of electronics in the next five to ten years." Terman had long wanted to get into this area more heavily, but "the problem, however, has been how to do so on a fixed budget that does not permit expansion into new fields of activity."[37] The Gilfillan gift allowed Terman to search for a gifted transistor expert to underpin the new field at Stanford.

Terman carefully searched for an outstanding teacher at the associate professor level. He looked especially for two things: a proven and popular teacher, and an outstanding scholar in transistor research. He found both in John G. Linvill, who had been an assistant professor at MIT. Linvill had recently left MIT for industrial research at Bell Laboratories, but he missed working with students. Lured by Terman to Stanford, Linvill arrived at the beginning of spring quarter 1955.[38] A very popular teacher at Stanford and a strong booster of the new Honors Co-Op Program, Linvill initiated Stanford's full-scale research into transistors and subsequently became executive head of the Electrical Engineering Department.

Instruction in this field actually had begun in the Electrical Engineering Department in 1953, when Karl Spangenberg began teaching transistor electronics in his graduate electrical engineering course, Electron Devices, and Joseph Pettit in his course, Advanced Electronic Circuits, in 1954. With Linvill's arrival, transistor electronics could be studied in undergraduate electrical engineering courses as well.

Terman had also discussed his plans for the field of transistors with William Shockley as early as 1954.[39] Fred Terman had known Shockley, who had also grown up in Palo Alto, for years. Terman played a pivotal role in advising Shockley to come back to the Bay Area from Bell Labs to found his own transistor company.[40] Backed by funding from Beckman Instruments, Shockley formed Shockley Semiconductor Laboratories in Palo Alto in 1956. Arnold Beckman had wanted Shockley to operate out of Southern California, but Shockley wanted to set up shop near Stanford, moving eventually into the Industrial Park. Shockley and his Bell Labs colleagues John Bardeen and Walter Brattain would share the Nobel Prize in Physics later that year for inventing the transistor. (Shockley's prize was for the junction transistor, an improvement over the point-contact transistor developed by Bardeen and Brattain.)

Like Terman, Shockley knew talent and recruited a team of remarkable engineers and scientists, among them Robert Noyce and Gordon Moore. But unlike Terman, he had little experience in, or patience with, managing a complex operation. In a now-famous split in September 1957, eight of Shockley's key employees, the "traitorous eight," resigned in protest of his heavy-handed management. Staying together, they subsequently formed their own company with backing from Fairchild Camera and Instrument. The new outfit, called Fairchild Semiconductor, had just been established in a modest Palo Alto building when in 1959 Noyce led the group in the invention of the first commercially practicable integrated circuit.[41]

Shockley found refuge at Stanford. Terman had appointed him a lecturer in electrical engineering at Stanford in 1955, and Shockley was named the Alexander M. Poniatoff Professor of Engineering Science in 1963. Shockley's tenure at Stanford was not simply a celebrity promotion. He lectured at electrical engineering colloquia and assisted John Linvill and young Jim Gibbons in installing a Solid-State Electronics Lab at Stanford.[42] A team was in the making. Terman brought Gibbons (MS '54, PhD '56, Stanford), on a Fulbright Fellowship in England, back to Stanford in 1957. Terman and Linvill then lured John Moll from Bell Labs in 1958, and Gerald L. Pearson from Bell on a "sabbatical" leave (he was persuaded to stay in 1960). Moll was an inventor of the MOS transistor and Pearson a senior coworker with Bardeen, Brattain, and Shockley at Bell.[43]

Mechanical and Aeronautical Engineering

Mechanical engineering had always been a strong department at Stanford, and it was the school's largest until surpassed by electrical engineering in the mid-1950s. In 1949, the Mechnical Engineering Department had thirteen tenured professors and associate professors and ten junior faculty members. Lydik S. Jacobsen, a leader in applied mechanics, had been executive head for several years.

During Terman's years as dean, he nurtured three traditional strengths in mechanical engineering: engineering mechanics, thermodynamics, and aeronautics. Years later, when Terman was asked if he had to do particular balancing among faculty in the various engineering departments, he replied, "The balance was pretty much controlled by the numbers of people who wanted to study in these fields. It turned out to be a reasonable balance."[44]

In 1955, the Mechanical Engineering Department developed a program in nuclear engineering under Professor George Leppert and took over portions of the little-used Ryan High-Voltage Laboratory for nuclear work. By 1957, Stanford was awarded an Atomic Energy Commission grant to purchase a full-scale nuclear reactor for teaching purposes. This award was supplemented by private gifts. Stanford soon rose to fourth in the number of AEC Fellowships awarded to students. In 1956, John Arnold from MIT was appointed to head a new program in engineering design, a field little known previously at Stanford.[45]

With an eye to those who would retire in the 1950s, Terman and Jacobsen looked ahead to build up faculty particularly in the fields of engineering mechanics and aerodynamics. James N. Goodier succeeded renowned engineering mechanics expert Stephan P. Timoshenko, who had taught well into his seventies.[46] Two other notable figures in structures and dynamics were Professors Wilhelm Flügge and Irmgard Flügge-Lotz. Alexander L. London was the key figure in thermodynamics in the department, and that field was enlarged with the addition of William Kays in heat transfer studies. Kays went on to become dean of engineering at Stanford in 1972, succeeding Joseph Pettit, and in turn was succeeded by Jim Gibbons in 1984.

The Division of Engineering Mechanics was established in the Department of Mechanical Engineering in 1948. Planning also to revitalize the aeronautical program, Terman determined to strengthen the faculty in the field of fluid mechanics. Engineering mechanics had developed first as a graduate-level program and was especially strong in theoretical fluid dynamics, including aerodynamics and nonlinear mechanics, with the intent of revitalizing the aeronautical program.[47]

Aeronautical engineering was established in 1951 as a graduate program within mechanical engineering but the program had almost collapsed by 1954.[48] There were few students and almost no research was being performed (Professor Reid's efforts to enlist the help of the aircraft industry had failed in the years just after World War II).

With Reid's retirement in 1954, the situation had to change one way or the other. Terman and his staff, backed by Stanford alumni in the industry, devoted three years of intensive work to win financial support of six companies who subscribed a total of $130,000 over the next five years. Dean Terman's participation was crucial. "Terman's being there made all the difference," Stanford's man in Southern California wrote to Sterling's assistant, Frederic Glover, after Terman met with Los Angeles aircraft engineers in February 1955. "Top engineers from the six local aircraft companies were there. . . . These guys mean to get the whole pot for him. Remarkable man."[49]

As a department report noted, several events occurred in 1957 to firmly reestablish aeronautics at Stanford: Lockheed decided to establish its Missile System Division near Stanford; the Soviets launched Sputnik I on October 4th; and Nicholas Hoff and Walter Vincenti joined the Stanford faculty.[50] "I'm gratified at the progress Fred Terman has made in trying to revivify the [aeronautical] department here," President Sterling reported to Caltech scientist Ernest E. Sechler.[51] Aeronautics was reestablished as a division in 1957.

With funds donated by Southern California aircraft manufacturers and from Lockheed, Stanford brought Walter Vincenti, Nicholas Hoff, and Daniel Bershader to quickly build the Division of Aeronautical Engineering into a department. Terman made good progress working with a committee of four engineering faculty in mechanical and aeronautical engineering, along with Hugh Skilling and Phillip Coleman of Lockheed, an outside expert.[52] By 1958, the aeronautics faculty consisted of newcomers Hoff, Vincenti, and Bershader, who joined old-timers Alfred Niles and Elliott Reid, Irmgard Flügge-Lotz (professor of both aeronautical engineering and engineering mechanics), and three young assistant professors, Max Anliker, Chi-Chang Chao, and Krishnamurty Karamcheti. Professors Robert H. Cannon Jr., Wilfrid H. Horton, Howard S. Seifert, and Milton Van Dyke were added at more senior rank in the next year or two. The Lockheed and United Technologies Corporations paid portions of the salaries of Hoff, Bershader, and later Siefert.[53] The division became a graduate department in 1959, costing the university $30,000 in general funds, but it would be supported by annual gifts of about $50,000 and contract overhead of $60,000.[54] When the Electrical Engineering Department moved out of Building 530 altogether (construction of the Applied Electronics Laboratory building had allowed this), the new aeronautics engineering program filled it in. Aeronautics research subsequently grew from $4,500 in 1956–57, to more than $300,000 in 1958–59, while the number of graduate students grew from eleven to forty-five in that two-year period, and to one hundred ten by 1960–61.[55] In 1959, the division was made a department.

Aeronautics became the Department of Aeronautical and Astronautical Engineering in 1963. By that time, the number of graduate students enrolled and degrees awarded annually since 1956–57 had grown by a factor of twenty, research support by a factor of nearly two hundred, and the equivalent full-time faculty from 2 to 15.8. With two hundred graduate students, the department had a greater number of majors than any department in the university except for electrical engineering.[56]

Civil and Industrial Engineering

The Civil Engineering Department continued strong throughout the 1950s in structures (a field close to engineering mechanics), hydraulics and fluid mechanics, and civil engineering administration. Like mechanical engineering, the Department of Civil Engineering was transformed with the evolution of new programs and the breakout of new departments.

As elsewhere in engineering, faculty retirements offered the chance to look at new opportunities. Leon B. Reynolds in hydraulics and James B. Wells in structures retired in 1950 and 1954, respectively. Each was a popular teacher, but neither man had done much research nor was he a leader in newer developments. Two men, John K. Vennard and Jack R. Benjamin, had recently been added to the civil engineering faculty, but Terman hoped to add two more young professors of promise, particularly in hydraulics and in structures.[57] Donovan H. Young, who complemented Stephen Timoshenko's work in mechanical dynamics, had been at Stanford since 1937 in engineering mechanics, closely related to civil engineering. Young would strongly support Benjamin. In the end, Stanford graduate instructor Joseph B. Franzini, BS and MS from Caltech, was promoted to assistant professor in hydraulics when he finished his Stanford PhD in 1950. And, Terman found a second, but senior hydraulics expert, Ray K. Linsley, also in 1950. Linsley, brought a strong record of national prizes. With extensive previous government experience in the Weather Bureau, he became executive head of the department within a few years. Finally, James M. Gere, a National Science Foundation Fellow during his graduate work at Stanford and a specialist in structures, replaced Wells in 1954 when Gere finished his PhD.[58]

Stanford had awarded a bachelor's degree in industrial engineering since 1945, even though it was neither a department nor a division. Faculty within the Civil and Mechanical Engineering departments handled coursework in industrial engineering for a decade, led by Civil Engineering Executive Head Eugene Grant (whose text in the field was a national best-seller in use at many universities). In 1951, W. Grant Ireson joined the civil engineering faculty and added to Grant's strength in engineering economics. Suspecting this area would grow, in 1954 Terman provided a separate budget mechanism for industrial engineering (although secretarial services were provided by civil engineering).[59] This move made it easier to see how the industrial engineering program operated and facilitated its evolution into departmental status.

Early in 1955, Terman wrote Sterling that industrial engineering needed more staff to assist in teaching its rapidly growing undergraduate clientele. At Terman's suggestion, Eugene Grant wrote to President Sterling that spring. Industrial Engineering had granted about one-sixth of the Engineering School bachelor's degrees for the past ten years, he reported, adding that his own two texts in engineering economics and statistical quality control each had 60 percent of the national sales market in the field, while Grant Ireson's textbook on factory planning was one of two leading texts in the field. Ireson had received two invitations in the past six months to become a candidate for position of Dean of Engineering at other institutions, and Gerald Lieberman had large research contracts and was much in demand. Grant proposed that industrial engineering be made a department. On Sterling's and Terman's recommendation the board of trustees voted in June 1955 to make it a separate department within the School of Engineering, combining the Mechnical Engineering Department's faculty interest in production and management with the Civil Engineering Department's interest in project administration. In preparation for the change, the industrial engineering faculty of three (Grant, Ireson, and Lieberman) was increased to 4.5 FTE, with the addition of temporary appointments.[60] Significantly, Robert V. Oakford, a specialist in the new field of electronic data processing, joined as a part-time lecturer in the spring of 1955 and later was appointed full-time after industrial engineering became a department. Lieberman, a Stanford product, was promoted to associate professor of industrial engineering and of statistics in 1957. The new department was especially careful to watch the caliber of entering students as there had been, wrote the department's head, "a tendency in other universities for poorer students in other engineering curricula to transfer to industrial engineering."[61]

The work in data processing offered by Lieberman and Oakford contributed materially to the development of the industrial engineering graduate program. In 1955, industrial engineering joined the Departments of Electrical Engineering, Statistics, and Mathematics to promote a graduate program in data processing and scientific computations, including operations research.[62]

Statistics and Computer Science

As dean of engineering, Terman remained particularly concerned with encouraging areas outside the school that were close to the interests of engineering faculty and students.[63] He astutely used government-contract funds and industry gifts and contracts to allow expansion of faculty and facilities for statistics and computer science.

Fred Terman, writes one historian, formed the Statistics Department to exploit military money available just after World War II.[64] Although true in part, this emphasis misses both the extended history and the extent of statistical activity at Stanford. Few universities had statistics departments in 1945. Statistics and computer science were, in fact, the only new disciplines added to most major universities in the fifteen years following World War II. Nonetheless, Terman and economist Allen Wallis recognized that Stanford already had a community of interest that could support statisticians. They were aware that faculty at Stanford were ready to put to use available project funds to build a viable and coherent academic program.

Stanford's mathematics faculty had long included a number of statisticians, including famed statistician Harold Hotelling in the late twenties; James V. Uspensky, who taught probability at Stanford from 1929 until his death in 1946; and George Pólya, who joined the faculty in 1942.[65] In addition, faculty interested in applied use of statistics in the Departments of Biology, Psychology, and Civil Engineering, and at the Food Research Institute (FRI) and the Graduate School of Business, had shared similar interests with faculty in the Mathematics Department as early as 1934. That year, Stanford President Wilbur appointed three men to the newly formed Committee on Instruction in Statistics. This committee would draw its members over the years from departments or schools concerned with both the teaching and use of statistics. Subsequently, a minor in statistics was approved for PhD candidates working in any field.[66]

The statistics committee remained active throughout the 1930s and early 1940s (in 1946, the name was changed simply to Committee on Statistics). Stalwarts in the early days of the committee included John B. Canning of economics, Holbrook Working of the Food Research Institute, Harold Bacon of mathematics, and Eugene Grant of civil engineering. In 1944, thirteen men representing ten departments (anatomy, biology, physiology, zoology, economics, mathematics, psychology, the Business School, civil engineering, and the Food Research Institute) participated in statistics discussions.[67] Also during the war, campus military training courses featured Eugene Grant's short course on statistics.

Trends in American business and industry as well as military research indicated more need for applied statistics training after the war. Influential foundations, such as the Rockefeller Foundation and the Ford Foundation, stressed the importance of developing the science and applications of statistics in higher education. Government-funding agencies would eventually back them. For nearly five years, congressional debate had stalled over funding of a National Science Foundation.[68] Into the breech stepped the navy's Office of Research and Invention (ORI) (which became the Office of Naval Research, or ONR in 1946). The ONR played a critical role in supporting broad-based university research in science and engineering, and for some twenty years, it would fund basic research in academia—often with little obvious connection to specific navy military needs or devices.

When the ONR assisted Stanford in its development of statistics, computer science, and mathematics at Stanford, Fred Terman was, as usual, centrally involved. "Fred Terman had the view that the intelligent use of government money in those days . . . could be used to support faculty and could be used to support a department," Albert Bowker recalled.

> The real question was whether Stanford would try to go first rate or whether it would continue as a kind of respected regional university. . . . Stanford when I went there was first rate in physics; it was first rate in psychology; it was strong in engineering; it had some strength in English and History. . . . [President Sterling] had a long talk with me about. "Do you think we can really go first rate?" [I said] "Sure, why not?" but I didn't know what I was talking about.[69]

In 1945, Allen Wallis returned to Stanford's Economics Department after spending the war years as scientific director at Columbia's Statistical Research Group (SRG).[70] He and Terman learned from Mina Rees, then in charge of the navy's mathematical research funds at ONR, that the navy was interested in funding further work in statistical sampling—which happened to be a field of special interest of Wallis and Eugene Grant, as well as to faculty in the Graduate School of Business.[71]

In late 1945, Holbrook Working of FRI proposed to Vice President Alvin Eurich that a master's degree program in engineering statistics be developed for the 1946–47 academic year. For budgetary reasons, Eurich counseled waiting. Nonetheless, a group of faculty came together as a committee to plan a Centralized Statistical Laboratory to benefit academic departments, the university library, administrative offices, and facilities offices.[72] Working found his talks with the ONR in spring 1946 encouraging, those with the Rockefeller Foundation less so, he reported to President Tresidder.[73]

New faculty hires were much on their minds. Perhaps they could lure applied mathematician John H. Curtiss to Stanford's Business or Engineering Schools when he returned to Cornell from the navy.[74] Or perhaps Frederick Mosteller would come to Stanford. As it turned out, Curtiss went back to Cornell, and Mosteller chose Princeton. Then, in the midst of this initial planning, Wallis left Stanford for the Economics Department of the University of Chicago (where he later created a Department of Statistics) but he continued to advise Terman and the statistics group.[75]

Changing course, Terman, encouraged by Allen Wallis and George Szego, head of the Mathematics Department, offered Albert Bowker a position in the department. Bowker had followed his advisor Jack Wolfowitz from Columbia to the University of North Carolina in the fall of 1946. Even though Bowker had not quite finished his PhD dissertation, Terman, assisted by Wallis and by Szego, asked him to come to Stanford to build up a program in statistics.

It was a rewarding solution. In 1948, soon after he arrived at Stanford, Bowker brought Abraham Girschick to Stanford from the RAND Corporation as professor of statistics, and then persuaded the Economics Department to appoint

Kenneth Arrow to a joint position in economics and statistics. Bowker continued to creatively use joint appointments, eventually bringing aboard statistics other faculty already at Stanford, including psychologist Quinn McNemar and philosopher-logician Patrick Suppes.[76] At one time, nine out of sixteen statistics faculty had joint appointments with other departments in humanities and sciences, the Medical School, the Engineering School, the School of Education, and the Stanford Linear Accelerator Center (SLAC).

In 1950, Bowker became the first director of Stanford's Applied Mathematics and Statistics Laboratory. As mathematician and former dean of humanities and sciences Halsey Royden expressed it, "Not only did mathematics and statistics prosper through involvement with the [Applied Mathematics and Statistics] laboratory, but also computer science and operations research grew out of activities of the laboratory." According to Mina Rees of ONR, Royden wrote, the ONR's major support of mathematics in the late 1940s was concentrated in five centers: "NYU, MIT, Stanford and Berkeley in classical analysis, and Tulane in modern analysis and topology."[77] Support from government contracts, especially from ONR, allowed Stanford also to expand its Mathematics Department and conduct research in game theory, mathematical economics, logic, complex analysis, partial differential equations, functional analysis, measure and ergotic theory, and harmonic analysis and to move into other major areas of mathematics, such as topology.

The Applied Mathematics and Statistics Lab was more than a sort of holding company for government contracts; it was also a center for increasing campuswide academic and administrative use of electronic computational equipment. In the summer of 1952, Terman got together with Al Bowker, mathematician John Herriot, and electrical engineer Allen Peterson to formally plan the Computation Center.[78] The center began operation in March 1953 as a joint activity of the Electronics Research Laboratory and the Applied Mathematics and Statistics Laboratory.[79] In fall 1953 Herriot began teaching computer mathematics (numerical analysis) while Peterson taught computer electronics (analog and digital electrical circuits), and soon after the Departments of Industrial Engineering, Electrical Engineering, Statistics, and Mathematics jointly developed a graduate program in data processing and scientific computations.[80]

In 1955, Terman took on additional duties as provost, and he and Bowker continued to work to develop computer science at Stanford. A major catch for Stanford was George Forsythe, to fill a position in the Mathematics Department designed specifically for computer science. Forsythe had been working at the Institute for Numerical Analysis (INA) at UCLA on a National Bureau of Standards (NBS) and military contract. (The NBS work by then had been led by John Curtiss, whom Stanford had tried to get from Cornell in 1946.) Political changes at the national level made the work environment difficult for the National Bureau of Standards, however, and by the mid-1950s, a number of good people left the INA. Terman and Bowker persuaded Forsythe to come to Stanford in 1957 to build up an academic computer science program.

Forsythe became professor of computer science and chairman of the Division of Computer Science (a division within the Mathematics Department) in 1961. (He was later named director of Stanford's new Computation Center.) Forsythe was a visionary and an extremely hard worker. He quickly added John McCarthy, Gene Golub, and Niklaus Wirth to the faculty, and in 1965, the division was established as a full department. Under his leadership, Stanford's Department of Computer Science became the most influential such department in the country, attracting almost as many National Science Foundation graduate fellows as all other computer science departments combined.

After his appointment as provost, Fred Terman's interest in computer science and statistics remained strong. Terman figured centrally in proposals and correspondence seeking funding and faculty, or planning curricula. Whether assisting Allen Wallis in obtaining ONR funds or searching for new faculty, assisting the Math Department in meeting huge student demand for instruction or starting computation instruction in math and electrical engineering, Terman's interest was ongoing.

In 1964, with Forsythe overseeing a committee to find a computing leader for the Stanford Linear Accelerator Center, Terman chose physicist William F. Miller. Miller had done an excellent job directing the high-energy physics computations at Argonne National Laboratory. Miller was made jointly professor in SLAC and professor of computer science.[81] In 1971 Miller became provost of Stanford.

Terman's line of vision was wide, taking into account not only personnel needs and operating funds, but also the growing need for large computing equipment. He astutely used government contract funds and industry gifts and contacts to allow expansion facilities for statistics and computer science. As provost, he came up with a number of innovative ways to recoup costs. By 1956, the Hewlett-Packard wing of the Electronics Research Laboratory housed Stanford's new IBM 650 computer and peripheral devices. With industrial engineer Gerald Lieberman, Terman arranged to sublease the IBM 650 part-time to recoup the machine's purchase cost. Several years later, when Stanford purchased a large IBM 360–67 time-sharing computer, George Forsythe reportedly said, "If we can't afford a large computer at Stanford, we might as well buy an even bigger one we can't afford."[82] But in fact, the IBM 360–67 ultimately cost the university nothing—IBM gave it to Stanford for one-third retail cost, then leased computer time back from Stanford from midnight to 8 AM each day for a price that just happened to equal Stanford's purchasing costs. As a result, Stanford got its computer, at least for sixteen hours per day, at no cost.

Bowker's relationship with Terman also remained an important and ongoing partnership. Holding down a joint appointment as dean of engineering and university provost between 1955 and 1959, Terman relied heavily on Bowker's talents as an astute administrator and facilitator in the provost's work as well as in development of statistics and computer science.

From ERL to "CroMem"

Fred took a very personal interest in the Stanford campus, including the way it looked. (Al Bowker remembers Fred recommending to Business Manager Alf Brandin what kind of lawn clippers to use at Stanford.) Fred always considered site planning, tree and shrub locations, and other details as well as a building's space allocations and financing. Fred's first major chance as dean to rework the physical space of engineering had been the building of the Electronics Research Labs and then the Applied Research lab buildings.[83] Crothers Memorial Hall—CroMem—would be his last.[84]

Terman found campus planner Ted Spencer easy to work with. Spencer's work did not suit everyone, but his utilitarian approach was perfect for the kinds of buildings Terman wanted for engineering research. Tresidder had appointed Eldridge "Ted" Spencer, a prominent San Francisco architect who had worked for the Yosemite and Curry Company, as Stanford's director of planning in 1945.[85] Spencer was immediately hit with accommodating waves of military and then postwar student needs.

Still waiting for an overall campus plan, Tresidder turned to architectural critic, social philosopher, and planning advocate Lewis Mumford for his views about Stanford's future campus growth.[86] Mumford may have admired the original campus design of Frederick L. Olmsted, but was little impressed with what had happened in the interim since the turn of the century. Stanford's heavy masonry construction, he believed, was too expensive and limited in its adaptability, and he called for a fresh effort at unity in future campus building design.[87] Tresidder and Spencer agreed, and so began a brief architectural period one trustee disparagingly called "Early Marinship Architecture" (after the wartime Kaiser ship-building factory to the north in Marin County). In 1949, Spencer's first effort at student housing earned a public outcry for his design and construction of Stern Hall. Built of the light and inexpensive building materials recommended by Mumford, Stern appeared to Stanford alumni and other critics as merely squat, flat faced, flat roofed, and gray. The board responded with a ruling that "any future building should, so far as possible, blend and harmonize to form a pleasing whole," that is, maintain Stanford's historic sandstone and tile ambiance.[88] Despite the controversy, Spencer continued as director of planning until his retirement. He worked very effectively with Fred Terman in expediting design and construction of research buildings like the Electronics Research Lab, just the sort of buildings that required a utilitarian approach.

Crothers Memorial Hall was the last major contribution in a long life of service to Stanford by Judge George E. Crothers ('95). Crothers, a member of the Pioneer Class, had been an influential trustee (1901–11), a confidant of Jane Lathrop Stanford, and important advisor of five presidents. Crothers Hall, a dorm designed by Spencer and Ambrose for Stanford law students, had been constructed in 1949. Crothers, like his classmate Herbert Hoover, was a product of Leland Stanford's philosophy of "direct usefulness" and was especially interested in helping students who planned to go into the professions. He would raise additional funds for a second dormitory, he proposed, this one for engineering students. Crothers and Terman exchanged letters for years about this plan. When outside prospects fell through, Crothers decided to fund the project himself.[89] In November 1955, Crothers Memorial Hall, a facility for 213 graduate engineering students, was dedicated. The dorm was actually named for Crothers's mother, Mary Jane Crothers.[90]

The projected cost had been $724,000 (Crothers donated $352,000 toward the project) but the construction firm unexpectedly brought the project in at $44,000 under cost. University officials assumed they could use the unexpended funds for general purposes, but Judge Crothers had long been involved in the mysteries of university finances, and insisted that this windfall was in fact a portion of his original donation. The $44,000, he insisted, would be split into two funds, one for the libraries and the other for the furnishings of the two Crothers halls. Law Dean Carl Spaeth and Engineering Dean Fred Terman would administer the funds. Crothers, a prickly if wise man, loved Stanford deeply—the university promptly agreed and honored him at a dinner at the Bohemian Club and again on campus at the dedication.[91] At a luncheon for fifty persons, with Fred Terman the speaker, the guests included President Sterling and President of the Board of Trustees Lloyd Dinkelspiel, Fred's old buddy from the 1918 track team. Fred then accompanied Judge Crothers to the football game.

One might assume that this was the customary routine with a major donor, but it meant much more to Terman. Before the construction of Crothers Memorial, Terman had wandered over to Crothers Hall, the law student dormitory, on numerous occasions to closely examine the outcome of bedroom design, bathroom design, hallways, and other details, to ensure that the new engineering students' project would benefit from lessons learned in earlier construction.[92] He enlisted his sister, Helen Terman Mosher, who worked in Stanford's student services, in studying the layout and the use of Crothers Hall. He consulted questionnaires, compiled by the resident advisors in the law dorm, about student likes and dislikes. He discussed with Judge Crothers the wisdom of prepouring foundations for a possible extension wing to Crothers Memorial. He discussed the subsurface problems in soil around that part of the campus.[93] After talking with law students, he called for a lawn and playing fields to be built for the mutual benefit of residents of the two buildings (together they would form the Crothers Quadrangle). Fred also wanted a room in the basement of Crothers Memorial to serve as an office for the student chapters of the engineering societies, a room for the amateur radio club, and a room with simple shop tools where engineering students could construct devices.[94] Assistant Engineering Dean Farrell McGhie worked with Fred on all these details.

Terman was delighted to report to Judge Crothers that only a month after the students moved into the dormitory, he found a party underway in the building. On a Wednesday night, Fred had left his office about 9:30 and had gone over by Crothers Memorial Hall "as I do several times each week just to see what is going on." He was thrilled to discover about sixty couples at a party, some dancing to a phonograph, others talking in the lounge or outside the building. The engineering graduate students had arranged a mixer with some women's living groups. "I was particularly pleased," Terman wrote, "because before the time of Crothers Memorial Hall, the graduate engineers at Stanford have never had an opportunity to develop wholesome informal social activity of this type, which can contribute so much to young people."[95]

Land-Use Planning and Development

As Stanford moved out of the Depression and war years to blossom in the 1950s, it desperately needed money, and Leland Stanford had pointed the way. He purposefully endowed the university in 1885 with more than 8,000 acres of valuable peninsula land, along with more than 100,000 elsewhere in California. Jane Stanford had been the first to rethink how that land was used. She modified the founding grant to authorize land sales (with the exception of the Palo Alto farm) and suggested various changes in use of her ranch lands and other properties. Since her death in 1905, Stanford family wheat ranches and vineyards elsewhere in the state had been gradually sold off, but the Palo Alto Farm remained, by legacy legal and traditional, inviolate.

The question remained, however: Could land beyond the central campus—the Quadrangle and the few buildings surrounding it—be developed for income purposes? President Tresidder, faced with dramatic waves of new students (from a wartime low of 1,500, the student body jumped to around 5,000 in 1946) and new pressures on teaching and research facilities, took up where Mrs. Stanford left off. In hiring Alf Brandin in 1946 as his new business manager, Tresidder expanded the position's duties to include responsibility for housing and feeding the horde of incoming students and returning servicemen; construction, operation, and maintenance of buildings and grounds; police and fire; managing the faculty residential area; working with architects, landscapers, and building contractors; labor negotiations; and operation of the farmlands. Most challenging of all, however, was to find the money to pay for everything, at a university that had run a deficit budget annually between 1942 and 1945.[96]

Brandin decided to "talk about the land" with three influential trustees, who in turn brought in Colbert Coldwell, founding partner of the real estate firm Coldwell-Banker (and an ardent University of California alumnus) as an unpaid advisor. Brandin had several ideas in mind, including a shopping center and a site for light industry. Coldwell agreed to support Brandin in his quest for trustee approval. Brandin presented his ideas to the board in the spring of 1950: to develop Lot 41 near Page Mill Road for "light industrial use," and Lot 76, along El Camino Highway for commercial use.[97] Brandin argued that the peninsula's great postwar population increase pointed to a potentially large market for goods and services.

The trustees agreed, setting aside 50 acres for the shopping center and 80 acres for the Industrial Park. They then commissioned Elmore Hutchison, of Peres, Punett and Hutchison, to prepare an overall commercial-use study. Shortly after this meeting, Brandin's first proposed tenant for the shopping center—The Emporium, then San Francisco's largest department store—expressed definite interest. By March 1951, the board had also approved a ninety-nine–year lease for Varian Associates, the first tenant of the proposed new Industrial Park.[98]

Due to the complexity of the issues now being raised, in 1952 the board created the Committee on Land Development, of which Board President Paul C. Edwards took personal charge, while Alf Brandin combined executive officer of land development with his duties as business manager. Leasing was an especially important issue. University land could not be sold, but the board could lease land for up to ninety-nine years (except for agricultural leases, which were limited by state law to fifteen years) if such a lease was judged to be in the best interest of the university.[99] Such arrangements were already in use—faculty who were given permission to build houses on campus land did not, in fact, own the land itself but leased it for the duration of their habitation. For many years, shorter term agricultural leases had been granted for Stanford land in the hills for use by dairy and feed cattle operations, hay production, and flower and vegetable gardening. By 1952, many companies and institutions were expressing interest in moving onto Stanford land. Paul Masson Wineries, the U.S. Geological Survey, and several housing contractors quickly made proposals.[100] One Redwood City firm wanted to build single family houses with fifty-year leases, and proudly proposed that Stanford would receive as income the grand sum of $25,732 per acre (disbursed over twenty-five years).[101]

The Hutchison plan essentially supported the two developments but had also recommended additional residential developments in the foothills.[102] The plan may have been accepted "in principle" by the trustees, but President Sterling still had serious doubts. Brandin's office subsequently hired Skidmore, Owings, and Merrill (SOM), a well-known San Francisco architectural firm, to prepare a detailed master plan for the university. A preliminary report of August 1953 agreed with the sites already set aside for the shopping center and the Industrial Park, a good thing since the shopping center had already been announced to the press more than a year earlier.[103] Stanford's administration had been quite concerned about the reactions of city and county officials and local chambers of commerce (Palo Alto merchants were especially nervous about competition just across El Camino).[104] Construction moved forward at both locations while SOM conducted its full study. By 1953, the Stanford Shopping Center had been designed to cover sixty acres with a wide variety of stores and parking for five to six thousand cars. (Coldwell-Banker Company would develop the site.) Three major San Francisco department stores—the Emporium, Joseph Magnin, and Roos Brothers—served as anchor stores, along with three banks and a grocery store, all signing leases early in 1954. (Leases for some thirty stores were signed during fiscal year 1954–55.[105])

Varian Associates signed the Industrial Park's first lease in October 1951 (Varian's first lease would be for 9.546 acres for ninety-nine years at $4,295.70 per acre). Varian was followed in November 1952 by Eastman Kodak (for a Kodachrome processing plant on a ten-acre site at $12,000 per acre).[106] Within another four years, they were joined by Hewlett-Packard, Preformed Line Products, Scott Foresman, and Beckman Instruments.

For Stanford as a whole, however, more controversial issues during the first years of intensive land development would arise regarding residential housing developments. In his 1947 recommendations to President Tresidder, Lewis Mumford had urged the establishment and maintenance of a greenbelt around the perimeter of the campus to preserve academic isolation and prevent nonuniversity incursions. (He had also recognized that residential construction on campus was inevitable and suggested that the overall density be no more than fifteen houses per acre.) "The land Stanford does not develop for its own purposes," he warned, "should not be developed at all."[107] This overall concept was, if not ignored outright, off the table for discussion. (Hutchison's design had called for a town of around 44,000 people to be built on 5,600 acres in the Stanford hills, while throughout their studies, SOM promoted intensive development of several self-contained nonuniversity residential communities on 2,933 acres in the nearby Stanford foothills to house an estimated forty thousand people. In general agreement with the SOM plan, the trustees approved several smaller nonuniversity housing developments, but they began to waver when strong objections were voiced by a new faculty committee on buildings and land.[108]

The Committee on Land and Building Development, chaired by art professor Ray Faulkner, had been established by President Sterling in 1951. It included administrators and faculty members from engineering, arts, humanities, and sciences.[109] Fred Terman was among its original members, and chaired the Subcommittee on Campus Size and Boundaries (his fellow members were presidential assistant Robert Wert and campus planner Ted Spencer). Terman had been involved peripherally in land-development issues up to this time. A member of the Varian Associates board, he had encouraged Russell Varian's quest for land near the campus and had urged other companies to consider similar moves, but he would now play a decisive role as a member of Sterling's new faculty advisory committee. Terman's subcommittee report would have a long-lasting influence on the amount of land set aside for residential use.[110]

The Skidmore, Owings, and Merrill master plan was studied carefully by the faculty committee. The committee's lengthy and very critical report on the plan was submitted to the trustees in June 1954. While they praised the university's efforts to plan for growth, they took issue on a number of the plan's recommendations. The committee particularly objected to the SOM recommendation for extensive residential development. Skidmore, Owings, and Merrill, they charged, viewed Stanford as a vast potential subdivision, which, only incidentally, had a university occupying a portion of the area. The consultants had repeatedly minimized faculty suggestions to extend the area reserved for academic use. Even if the bulk of Stanford's six thousand available acres became a reflection of Palo Alto housing developments, with comparatively high-cost houses on ample lots, the university had no guarantee of maximum financial return, yet it would have lost land that might be needed for future academic growth. The faculty committee foresaw that as Stanford became increasingly important as a research center and focus of related governmental and professional activities, a more lucrative and manageable use of land could be exploited.

Terman's subcommittee report in particular pointed out the need to increase, not decrease, land reserved for academic use. He noted that in 1934, the trustees had defined the "legal" campus (academic reserve) as 1,022 acres, which excluded not only the golf course but the Ryan High-Voltage Laboratory and the Carnegie Institution's Laboratory of Experimental Taxonomy and Genetics. Not only was space needed for faculty research facilities but for student and faculty residences. Terman argued that over the next twenty-five years, student enrollment at Stanford was predicted to increase 50 to 100 percent with the greatest increase being in graduate students and in undergraduate women, both of whom needed new housing facilities. Faculty housing on campus was in short supply, as was additional housing for married students. Terman also raised the question of water supply for the campus. Searsville Lake was not protected by the SOM plan, and they had also neglected provision for a second reservoir below Searsville that would be needed in the near future. Terman recommended "that a minimum of 3,700 acres be set aside for campus purposes . . . [and] that this entire acreage be withdrawn from the development program at this time, since once land is dedicated to commercial use it is for all practical purposes forever after lost to campus applications."

Although Fred Terman had loved to hike, hunt, and fish in the hills and lakes above the campus when he was growing up, the value of that hilly land was its potential for the future of Stanford University. Terman was not fighting to preserve green hills per se, but rather to reserve land for future uses central to the university's teaching and research functions, for example, for biological and ecological studies; for space for radio physics, radio astronomy research, and aero-thermodynamics research; and for the possible site of a "multibillion volt linear accelerator" project percolating in the minds of Stanford's physicists. Terman's own Engineering School was already using the hills for radio propagation field research, and for the past two years, Biology Department faculty had lobbied for a biological preserve. In June 1954, in the same week as the faculty land committee completed their report, Victor Twitty, executive head of biology, submitted a lengthy memo by biologist Donald Wohlschlag on the present and future utilization of Stanford's lands as a biological resource.[111] Again, in 1956, just as Terman was preparing his report for the trustees, the curator of the Dudley Herbarium, Richard Holm, who was also a professor of biology, wrote to Terman about his need for a nearby reserve for his teaching and plant collecting, suggesting "the Jasper Ridge area, extending down to and including Searsville Lake."[112] It is clear that Terman's subcommittee was rounding up the biology troops for support, since Terman had alerted them. Terman's view was persuasive. While SOM preferred 2,500 acres and the faculty committee in 1954 had recommended 3,218 acres be set aside, the trustees went along with Terman's new proposal to reserve more than 4,000 acres of land for university research purposes.[113] By 1960, 4,800 acres was set aside.[114]

Throughout the 1950s and 1960s, Stanford's trustees, administration, and faculty each argued that their view of land-use planning was best for the university's welfare. Over time, the means grew closer as they took the long view of the university's future needs, and as the trustees worked more closely with Sterling's administration. This growing understanding was due in part to the influence of Lloyd Dinkelspiel, a board member from 1947 to 1959, and its dynamic president during the 1950s. But it was also due to the background of a new generation of trustees, especially David Packard, who served for many years as a trustee and as president of the board between 1958 and 1960.

As his own responsibilities expanded from dean to provost in 1955, Terman continued to argue for the use of Stanford land for important research projects. He continued to use university land as a magnet for faculty, not only for research but also for suitable faculty housing. It was Terman who engineered an innovative approach to campus with 4 percent thirty–year mortgages for the Pine Hill faculty housing area.[115] He remained an active member of the committee until 1959, when his responsibilities expanded yet again.

Terman, Stanford, and Silicon Valley

Stanford's Industrial Park by the mid-1950s was already a center point between the campus to the immediate north and the burgeoning electronics and avionics centers growing in Mountain View to the south. Engineering and science students remember friends working at Ampex in San Carlos, at the Stanford Research Institute in Menlo Park, at Lockheed and Philco-Ford in Mountain View and Sunnyvale, and at the ever-developing laboratories of Hewlett-Packard, Varian, General Electric, and Lockheed Research in the Industrial Park itself. College Terrace, the modest neighborhood adjacent to the southeastern edge of the Stanford campus on Stanford Avenue, in turn, extended all along the northwestern edge of the Industrial Park on California Avenue. College Terrace had been home to many young faculty couples in the 1920s and 1930s. By the 1950s it was increasingly popular as home to numerous graduate students who could ride their bicycles both to class and to their part-time jobs in the Stanford Industrial Park. Housing complexes from Redwood City south to Mountain View were springing up to accommodate workers and students alike.

Over the years, Alf Brandin later recalled, he rejected far more applications than he accepted for inclusion in the Industrial Park.[116] Even so, he was not about to wait for offers to come in and missed few opportunities to seek out good clients. Fred Terman, in touch with electronic executives around the country, happily gave him tips. Following up on one such tip, Brandin wrote to David Sarnoff of RCA that he had heard rumors that RCA was thinking of opening a research laboratory on the West Coast. He extolled the value of the Stanford Industrial Park, its closeness to the Microwave Laboratory at Stanford, the Honors Co-Op Program, and Stanford's great graduate students in electrical engineering.[117] Not all worked out as the Stanford team expected; in this case Brandin's efforts did not succeed.

The *Industrial & Housing Review*, a peninsula-area realtors' magazine sponsored by nearly thirty real estate firms and housing developers from San Bruno south to Santa Clara, considered the Stanford Industrial Park great news.[118] By 1956, the Stanford Industrial Park had a dozen research and manufacturing companies (several East Coast-based companies were in the process of signing leases). A special issue of the magazine in September 1956 featured the park, prominently displaying photographs of three individuals: university founder Leland Stanford and the university's Fred Terman and Alf Brandin. The magazine credited Terman with attracting key electronics and research firms with his School of Engineering. Mutual interests between the firms and the university were emphasized—faculty advised the companies in research, and top scientists at the companies acted as consultants at Stanford. Due largely to this working arrangement, the magazine said, the midpeninsula area had grown to become a "Mecca for electronics industries." The magazine assured its readers that the Stanford Industrial Park had "very sharp teeth" to protect the surrounding residential areas; construction did not mar ridgelines, excessive noise and obnoxious odors were strictly banned, and the park resembled a "blue-chip" professional center more than a thriving industrial area. (Maintaining absolute architectural control, Brandin required facilities to be designed with deep landscaped setbacks, parking screened from view by trees and shrubs, no heating or smoke stacks, and especially lawns that flowed from property to property with no fences, "one long sweep of lawn," as one of Brandin's staff later described it. "This came to be known as the "Brandin Theory on Lawns."[119])

In addition to technology firms, the park's tenants included prominent publishing houses like Houghton Mifflin, which boasted that it was the publisher of some of Stanford's most illustrious authors, including Lewis Terman, Maude Merrill, Paul Hanna, J. B. Sears, and Wallace Stegner.

By spring 1958, the Palo Alto Chamber of Commerce counted 123 electronics and electronics-based firms on the Peninsula: 56 firms and laboratories in Palo Alto and at Stanford, and 67 others from San Bruno in the north, down to San Jose. Over the years this development tended to move outward. A number of the earliest firms, founded in the 1930s and in the immediate post–World War II years—Eitel-McCullough, Litton Industries, and Ampex—kept growing in San Bruno, San Carlos, and Redwood City to the north of Stanford. Dominating the area to the south of Stanford, in Mountain View, Sunnyvale, and San Jose, were the giants Lockheed, Sylvania, General Electric, and IBM.

At the center of this growth was the Stanford Industrial Park, still separated from the main Stanford campus by several blocks of the residential College Terrace neighborhood. By the time the Stanford Shopping Center and the Stanford Industrial Park were both filmed for display in the U.S. Pavilion at the 1958 World's Fair in Brussels, Belgium, Stanford Industrial Park included Hewlett-Packard, Varian Associates, Lockheed Research Laboratories, General Electric Microwaves, and the Shockley Semiconductor Laboratories of Beckman Instruments Company, among others.[120] In the words of one author at the time, the "creative center of this great scientific activity is Stanford University. . . . The name of Dr. Frederick E. Terman . . . is the magnet that continues drawing renowned scientists to the faculty and nationally known electronics research firms to the Palo Alto area."[121]

The success of the Stanford Industrial Park and electronics-based industry in the surrounding area challenged Stanford's salary scales both for faculty and for highly qualified technicians. Just as in the 1990s, when computer science faculty succumbed to high-salaried industrial offers, a number of engineering faculty left Stanford in the local boom of the 1950s, some to join the electron tube divisions of corporate giants like General Electric's Microwave Division, some to form their own companies. Stanford, in turn, found new recruits. Terman's traveling-wave-tube whiz Lester Field, for example, was replaced with graduate student Dean Watkins when Field left for Los Angeles. Several years later, Watkins left to cofound the Watkins-Johnson electronics company in the Stanford Industrial Park, and Watkins was replaced by Anthony E. Siegman (PhD in electrical engineering, Stanford '57). As Terman predicted, the potential for poaching from Stanford was repaid in industry support, but by 1960 the question had become: Was it enough? Almost a decade after the first lease was offered for the Stanford Industrial Park, Ken Cuthbertson's new Office of Development reviewed the support the university was receiving from the corporations listed as park tenants as of fall 1960. Seventeen of the twenty-eight corporate tenants actively supported Stanford, they noted, with General Electric, Standard Oil of California, Hewlett-Packard, Varian Associates, and Lockheed logged in as the major donors. Fifteen companies, including the several book publishers, however, had given nothing or, at most, several hundred dollars. In a confidential memo, the Office of Development suggested that special attention should be paid to those not currently supporting Stanford, especially the book companies, to increase their support of the university. Terman, now full-time university provost, thought the suggestion interesting, but not very meaningful. The fact that Standard Oil had a gasoline station in the park, he responded, bore little relationship to the company's $284,000 gifts to Stanford, while the $150,000 per year of extra tuition paid to the Honors Co-Op Program came in large part from tenants in the park.[122]

Terman nonetheless believed firmly that while the income received from leases in the Stanford Industrial Park was useful, it was not the driving reason for the existence of the park. Rather, such arrangements must benefit Stanford University's educational programs and intellectual contributions. Building a strong research base near the campus provided an important interchange between faculty, students, and neighboring scientists and engineers.[123] Much more than most academic scientists and engineers of his era, Terman valued these cross-benefits and fostered the knowledge exchange between academia and industry.

Since the 1970s, Terman's name has taken on a legendary quality in the area, even as the core technologies of what has come to be called "Silicon Valley" have varied over the decades. Terman's striking influence on Stanford's development, and Stanford's subsequent relationship to the evolution of the phenomena surrounding it has prompted much speculation about whether he deserves to be called "the father of Silicon Valley."[124]

Neither Fred Terman nor Stanford can be credited with discovering silicon transistors, nor with centering their development in the San Francisco Peninsula. The term "Silicon Valley" was not, in fact, coined until 1971—six years after Terman's retirement from Stanford.[125] Nor, indeed, is silicon the key component in the area's extraordinary role in American technology. The boom in radio experimentation and radio-manufacturing activity on the peninsula before and after World War I blossomed into electron tube and electronic instrument manufactures, avionics, and radar countermeasures. From there it moved through transistors, to personal computers, and, more recently, into logic design, software and internetworking, and biotechnology. Today, the valley could just as logically be called "Ferrite Valley" for the extremely large-scale design and manufacture of ferrite materials such as magnetic memory storage devices, hard-drives, and memory "sticks."[126]

The geographic location ascribed to Silicon Valley is also contested. Some of the area's earliest hi-tech firms—Litton, Eitel-McCullough, Varian Associates, Ampex—were first located north of Stanford University in San Carlos and Redwood City. As the Stanford Industrial Park took shape and became the Stanford Research Park, Palo Alto and Stanford appeared to be the center of Silicon Valley. Today, the city of San Jose, as civic and governmental center of the region, claims the overall title of capital of Silicon Valley, while technology-oriented venture capital, research, and production alike are spread from San Mateo in the north along a nearly sixty-mile corridor to Gilroy in the south.

If, however, one is looking for the mind, or perhaps the heart, and the institution that fostered the phenomenon known today as Silicon Valley, then the answer is surely to be found in Fred Terman and Stanford University. In 1991, electronics pioneer William Hewlett wrote, "The presence of Stanford University was a key factor in the development of the technology enterprise now known as Silicon Valley. More than anything, it was Terman, his students, and the encouragements and opportunities that he gave them that enabled this great enterprise to flourish. The Annex (Building 500, Terman's original lab in the 1930s and 1940s) was an important part in this process."[127]

Former Stanford dean of engineering James F. Gibbons reminds us that Silicon Valley (which is really the Santa Clara Valley) was formerly nicknamed the "Valley of the Heart's Delight," an exceptionally fertile land known for its orchards and gardens that welcomed small farmers and big producers alike. Stanford, too, has been a fertile soil for hi-tech startup companies, while replenishing existing companies with an intellectual pool with outstanding graduates. The development of the Stanford Industrial Park enabled many firms to locate in the area and to develop innovative products. In some cases—Hewlett-Packard, Varian, Cisco Systems, Sun Microsystems, and Silicon Graphics—the prototype for the first product was developed on the Stanford campus.

Like Hewlett, Gibbons credits Terman with an instrumental role in the formation and long-term development of the region. "It was [Terman's] frustration with the lack of jobs for graduates of the Stanford electrical engineering department that led him, beginning in 1936, to energetically encourage several of his former pupils to start their own businesses," Gibbons writes, "thus initiating Stanford-related high-tech entrepreneurship in the region. He saw that the growth of these companies could provide agreeable employment for new graduates and consulting opportunities for faculty."[128]

The Dean Becomes Provost

When Frederick E. Terman became provost of Stanford University on September 1, 1955, he began helping Wally Sterling vigorously rebuild the university's faculty, increase its endowment, and seek further outside funding. Sterling had been drawn to Terman's philosophy and ambition for Stanford, so similar to his own, but he was also drawn to proven results displayed in Terman's School of Engineering. The transition would not be an easy one. Resentments flared up initially, provostial assistant E. Howard Brooks later recalled, when other deans found themselves reporting to Dean Terman, and to a "mere engineer, a mere engineer! It took awhile," Brooks added, "but Fred took over." Remembered one of those deans, Ernie Arbuckle of the Graduate School of Business, "Fred was a challenge. He challenged me to exert my very best efforts. He really built the Provost's Office."[129]

Soon after President Wallace Sterling took office in April 1949, he had asked all departments to prepare summaries of their present status and future prospects. The resulting picture did not look good. The problems represented by the Chemistry Department were not unusual. Chemistry appeared to be floundering over faculty appointments. Chemistry Professor Frederick Koenig sent in his resignation in August 1951 (after inheriting nearly a million dollars), and the department promoted acting assistant professor Eric Hutchinson to fill Koenig's place. Koenig's letter of resignation, however, was not acted on by the department (no one among Sterling's staff was quite sure why), and Koenig was reappointed (he would remain at Stanford until his retirement in 1968) even though Dean Douglas Whitaker thought Koenig had become "more of a luxury item."[130] When Philip Leighton (a member of the faculty since 1928, and executive head since 1940) resigned as department head in August 1951 to return to teaching, Sterling's search for an "outstanding young chemist to head the department" quickly became complicated by competition between the biochemists and the chemical engineers (both groups complaining that they were treated as poor stepchildren within the department).[131] So George Parks, at Stanford since 1925, then served as head of chemistry from 1951 to 1960.

In 1952, Sterling decided that he needed a high-ranking academic post to assist him in rebuilding Stanford. He could look back at Stanford's tradition of using vice presidents to take the lead on academic affairs rather than simply serve a place-keeping administrative role. As vice president for David Starr Jordan, Professor John Casper Branner had helped his friend Jordan, notoriously bad at dealing with faculty conflict, deal decisively with more than one serious faculty controversy. Professor Robert Swain was less acting president than busy academic vice president during the years that Ray Lyman Wilbur served double-duty as Hoover's secretary of the interior and absentee president of the university. Don Tresidder had relied heavily on his vice president, Al Eurich, to handle faculty affairs. Often, this delegation of duty had been unpopular among Stanford's faculty, and emotions still ran high about Al Eurich's particular way of dealing with faculty issues. Perhaps, as Stanford legend has it, that is why Sterling decided on the new designation of "provost."[132]

In 1952, Sterling named Douglas Whitaker (Stanford AB '26, PhD '28) to the position of Stanford's first provost.[133] Whitaker, who had been on the Stanford faculty since 1931, had served as executive head of the Biology Department and dean of the School of Biological Sciences (from 1945 until the school was absorbed into the new School of Humanities and Sciences in 1948). He then served as dean of graduate studies until 1951 when he was promoted to dean of humanities and sciences. Whitaker was also a respected scientist. He was among the leading biologists on the army-navy expedition to Bikini to inspect the effects of atomic radiation on marine and animal life at Operation Crossroads and had taken a sabbatical leave in 1950–51 as chairman of the National Research Council.[134]

Sterling announced Whitaker's appointment to this newly created post to a special meeting of the Academic Council with little fanfare or elaboration. The provost, he explained, would act as the second-ranking administrative officer of the university and would assist the president in the direction of academic affairs and serve as acting president in Sterling's absence from campus. Not one for elaborate job descriptions or organizational charts, Sterling left it up to Whitaker to charge ahead.[135]

In 1953, Whitaker oversaw a "self-study" of the behavioral sciences at Stanford. In the end, the committee surveyed many of the departments in the School of Humanities and Sciences and some of the graduate schools.[136] The effort revealed that little improvement had been made since Sterling's 1949 survey. Departments complained about lack of space, low salaries, staff shortages, declining enrollments. A year earlier, history executive head Thomas A. Bailey had already complained to Whitaker that the history faculty found it difficult to attract good people to teach required Western civilization courses. "Eastern PhDs, whom we could use with profit, are increasingly reluctant to come West, and we are inclined to get only the culls among those who are prepared to move this distance."[137] By the 1953 study, the History Department had experienced a significant increase in undergraduate majors and found that they tended to be better students than their graduate students. Yet when they raised their admissions standards for their graduate program, the size of their graduate population clearly fell off.[138]

The report from Ernest Hilgard, Whitaker's successor as graduate dean, reflected this same trend: graduate enrollments were down for nearly all departments. Art, history, and political science were down by 40 to 50 percent in the past two years, while biology, chemistry, English, geology, speech and drama, and law were down 15 to 30 percent over the same period. The only upward trends were in mathematics, up 15 percent, and electrical engineering, up an impressive 50 percent.[139] Part of the cause lay in the fact that GI Bill subsidies for graduate students had declined, while faculty efforts to improve graduate standards further thinned out the ranks of incoming graduate students. Collapsing graduate enrollments meant both decreasing tuition income and problems for some departments that relied on using graduate students as teaching assistants.

In 1953, however, Wally Sterling had his hands full already with his plans to relocate the Stanford Medical School and hospital from San Francisco to the campus. After several years of faculty debate on the move, Sterling's proposal for new, greatly improved facilities was approved by the board of trustees in November 1953, and he was anxious to move on with his new twenty-man committee to work out issues relating to faculty moves from San Francisco to Palo Alto, space planning and design, outside funding sources, and hospital negotiations. The president could see significant programs elsewhere on campus. The Engineering School was going extremely well, in terms of both graduate students and faculty and incoming research grants. The board was busy rethinking Stanford's master plan, while the shopping center and the Stanford Industrial Park were now underway. He remained confident that Provost Whitaker could move ahead on needed general academic improvements, particularly to improve the quality of faculty and the student body, and explore solutions to funding and space problems.[140]

Faculty issues, especially in the humanities and sciences, remained troublesome. In 1954, Ray Faulkner, then acting dean of humanities and sciences, brought to Sterling's attention the fact that Princeton and Yale had each significantly raised their faculty salaries across-the-board. In the humanities and sciences, 75 percent of Stanford's full professors and 86 percent of its associate professors were now paid below the minimum salaries at Princeton.[141] The Biology Department's problems were emblematic. The department had received a $250,000 matching grant from the Rockefeller Foundation, but by 1953 they were afraid they were going to lose their star, microbiologist Ed Tatum, to more lucrative offers from East Coast schools. The department's faculty was relatively strong in fields of systematic biology and botany, but with the exception of several recently hired young faculty, department head Victor Twitty worried about the quality of the work of other of the ecologists and systematists.[142]

Political science represented another ongoing dilemma: warring faculty. Divided between behavioral scientists and those with more traditional approaches, the department was having difficulty recruiting for senior vacancies. One outside examiner pointed a finger at the department's executive head James T. Watkins IV, who tended to isolate the Political Science Department from potentially fruitful interactions with faculty in the Departments of Economics, Sociology, and Philosophy. As late as 1956, Watkins would complain about the problem of hiring a "few outstanding men," adding, however, that he would be content to hire faculty even "if not so good."[143]

The prospect of a budget freeze early in 1955 badly affected faculty morale, even in strong departments like history. As Tom Bailey wrote to Provost Whitaker, "An extremely serious morale problem has developed within our Department as a result of the so-called budget 'Freeze,' and so much animus is being directed at the Administration, whether rightly or not, as to threaten real harm to the University as a whole."[144]

Sterling had taken time over his first years in office to reorganize his presidential staff into a strong team. Wally and Alf Brandin hit it off immediately. Brandin, '36 and a member of Stanford's Vow Boys football team, had known Sterling as a student in the 1930s. Hired by Tresidder in 1946, Sterling had entrusted him with Stanford's land-development program by 1950. Fred Glover, '33, had also known Sterling as a student. An experienced newspaper editor and navy intelligence officer, Glover had come back to campus in 1946 as Stanford's first director of information (the first regular employee of the university, rather than the Stanford Associates, devoted to getting out the news). Sterling tapped Glover to be his assistant in 1952. Robert Wert, '43 (MBA '50, PhD in education '52) worked as presidential assistant while completing his graduate studies. "The distribution of staff work in the president's office was very simple," Glover later remembered of those days. "If it was academic, it went to the provost; if it had dollar problems, it went to Bob Wert, and anything that didn't have any dollar signs came to me."[145] More to the point, Sterling was building a team that felt as intensely about Stanford and about working well together as he did, a team that would include Fred Terman instead of Douglas Whitaker.

When Wert left for the Carnegie Corporation in New York in 1954, Sterling hired Ken Cuthbertson ('40, MBA '47) as budget control officer. Although Glover and Sterling joked about the president's initial reluctance to hire yet another one of Glover's fraternity brothers, Sterling had in fact known of Cuthbertson's leadership in that year's Alumni Conference and his ongoing interest in Stanford fund-raising since serving as a student volunteer for Dave Jacobson. Wally's assistants, Glover, Wert, and Cuthbertson, along with business manager Alf Brandin, "made up a hard-working, effective, fun-loving team," Sterling later recalled.[146] Teamwork, and the trust and dependability it implied, was important to Sterling. So was decisiveness and getting results. A significant change was made to the Sterling team in 1955. When Provost Doug Whitaker resigned to become vice president of administration of the Rockefeller Institute for Medical Research in New York City, Sterling took pains not to appear relieved. Whitaker's leaving was a blow, Sterling politely wrote to Rockefeller Institute President Detlev W. Bronk, but added that Whitaker should leave as soon as possible, for the best for the Rockefeller Institute.[147] Sterling already had a replacement in mind. Fred Terman would be provost, Sterling happily wrote a former colleague at Caltech, but would continue "for the time being" as dean of engineering. The "time being" turned out to be four years.[148]

Years later Sterling reminisced:

> My first appointee [as provost] was quite popular with the faculty, but, unfortunately, he was unable to take responsibility and make decisions. . . . He was delightful company,—but he was not doing what I expected and needed him to do. . . . Then I struck it rich. In 1955, Fred Terman became Provost. Never have I worked more harmoniously with an extremely able colleague. He *did* take responsibility. He had an extra sense for spotting younger men of real ability. Work was his hobby, and it was after his appointment as Provost that Stanford really began to make headway.[149]

There are several versions of just how Wallace Sterling offered Fred the job of provost. Sterling's own version was offered in late 1978 when Fred was awarded Stanford's highly prestigious honor, the Uncommon Man Award (the closest honor Stanford has to an honorary academic degree, which it does not grant).[150] "I went to Terman's office to ask him to be provost," Sterling recalled.

> He looked at his watch and his desk calendar and asked what I'd be doing at 2:15 PM two days later. Fred came to my office two days later at 2:15 PM with a stack of 3" by 5" cards wrapped in an elastic band. On each card was a question. Fred then put the cards back in a bundle and said, "Well, that's that." I replied, "What's that? You haven't said yes or no!" Fred said, "Oh, I'm sorry, it's yes."

When Sterling asked Fred why he agreed to become provost, Sterling added, "He said he'd enjoyed helping build a stronger School of Engineering, and he thought it'd be fun to help build a stronger University." To help with all the doings in the School of Engineering, for the time being, Fred immediately recommended two men be appointed his associate deans, civil engineer Ray K. Linsley and electrical engineer Joseph M. Pettit. Each would spend two days a week in the dean's office doing the school's day-to-day business. They took office the same day in 1955 that Fred became provost.[151]

As Terman told a Stanford chapter meeting of the American Association of University Professors in 1957, he had learned much about individual departments, each with its own personality and its own problems. But, he concluded, there were few if any problems at Stanford that the generous application of funds wouldn't solve, and few problems that could not be solved over time.[152] There were problems, however, that he was too discreet to mention, problems involved in the ongoing renegotiation of power between the faculty and the administration.

Making Headway for a Stronger University

As Fred took up the duties of provost, Stanford was in the midst of a two-year study of the undergraduate curriculum, sponsored by the Ford Foundation. President Sterling hoped to raise the level of intellectual engagement of Stanford undergraduates generally. Although obvious strides had been made to improve Stanford's rankings in terms of graduate students and faculty, the university still fought against its lingering country club image for undergraduate life. For most students, little had changed since Ray Lyman Wilbur raged against the "sideshows" of student life. The 1950s brought a new sort of college prank to the public eye—a machine gun was fired from one of the Zeta Psi fraternity house windows. Students later stole a fire truck from the campus fire department. The head football cheerleader appeared at games wearing a toilet seat as a collar.[153] Student radio station KZSU disrupted the annual Spring Sing concert, broadcast shows of questionable taste (including the Stanford "Sadie Show," with its risqué topics and the seductive voice of a mystery Stanford coed), and operated at illegal power levels, thus interfering with other local stations. In 1958, it was banned from the airwaves for two years. The student humor magazine *Chaparral* produced a "Layboy" issue in 1961, complete with a burlesque of the Virgin Birth. The editor, Bradley Efron, was suspended. (Years later, Efron became professor of statistics and chair of the Stanford Faculty Senate.[154])

The *Stanford Study of Undergraduate Education* (1954–56), sponsored by the Academic Council and led by Stanford psychologist Donald W. Taylor, was one attempt to revitalize the undergraduate curriculum. This series of investigations and surveys was the most thorough such effort at Stanford in thirty-five years. In 1956, the study recommended replacing the lower and upper divisions with an integrated four-year curriculum. This led to adoption of the General Studies Program, allowing more freedom to select courses for the bachelor's degree but increasing the range of general education courses required. The study also recommended the senior colloquia. These studies were carefully laid out and discussed at length by Academic Council's Executive and Advisory committees, meetings chaired by either Terman or Sterling.[155] Although Terman had been a member of numerous faculty committees since the 1930s, this was his first experience in a leadership role working closely with humanities faculty.

Terman encouraged Admissions Director Rixford Snyder to increase efforts to upgrade the undergraduate standards.[156] Stanford began a more vigorous effort to draw high-quality students from beyond the borders of California and to recruit more minority students (even fewer minorities were among the student body in the 1950s than had been decades before). The combined median SAT scores for the entering freshman class of fall 1956, Snyder reported, were 1,186 for men and 1,128 for women, an increase of 9 percent over the class that entered two years before. One half of the class entering in the fall of 1951 would not have been admitted for the autumn of 1956.[157]

The *Study of Undergraduate Education* also underscored the need to fill the position of dean of the School of Humanities and Sciences as soon as possible. The School of Humanities and Sciences, Stanford's largest, had been assembled in April 1948 by acting president Alvin C. Eurich from the twenty departments that formerly made up the Schools of Biological Sciences, Humanities, Physical Sciences, and Social Sciences.[158] Eurich appointed Clarence M. Faust, formerly dean of graduate studies, as its first dean. Faust had had administrative experience at the University of Chicago before coming to Stanford at the behest of Don Tresidder to head the library. He had not been a popular faculty appointment, however, since his tenured faculty position was apparently forced on the English Department by the administration. Fred Terman had been among those who disapproved of Eurich's recommendation that Faust be appointed acting president between Eurich's departure and the arrival of Wally Sterling.[159] When Faust left Stanford in 1951, he was replaced as dean briefly by Douglas Whitaker, and then in 1952, Professor of Art Ray Faulkner became acting dean, a position Faulkner would fill for four years.

In searching for a new dean, Sterling was drawn to candidates from Ivy League schools. His favorite was Whitney "Mike" Oates, a classicist visiting for a year at Stanford. Oates had originated the national Woodrow Wilson Fellowship Program, aimed at students intending to enter the field of teaching (particularly in the humanities) and had provided valuable insights during the *Study of Undergraduate Education*. But Oates was not interested in leaving Princeton.[160]

Bob Wert then suggested Phillip Rhinelander (Harvard AB '29, and LLB '32). Rhinelander had practiced law for several years, served in World War II, and returned to Harvard to complete his PhD in philosophy in 1949. He was on the staff at Harvard as an undergraduate tutor at Eliot House, then director of the General Education Program, and held a nontenured position as lecturer in philosophy. He was apparently unhappy with the Philosophy Department at the moment since it was likely he would not get a tenured position.[161] Although Rhinelander had, in fact, a rather modest academic reputation, McGeorge Bundy had nominated him for the presidency of several colleges, Wert noted.[162] Fred Terman was not involved in this process.

Phil Rhinelander knew from the outset that he would report to Fred Terman as provost, and they saw eye-to-eye on many, if not all, things. Rhinelander, for example, agreed with Terman that departmental faculties needed to be seriously strengthened, and commented that it was necessary to "tighten up" the screening procedures, especially for senior appointments.[163] Terman cautioned Rhinelander, however, that when seeking to fill any faculty vacancies, it was best if the Provost's Office had the opportunity to review the dockets of the short list (the top two to four names) of department candidates before a final selection was made and sent to the provost for his approval.[164] However kindly it was phrased, this was a clear warning. Nevertheless, when Terman suggested some sort of award to honor good teaching (outstanding faculty, he thought, could be designated "master teachers"), both Rhinelander and his associate dean, Ray Faulkner, discouraged the idea due to possible discord it might cause among the faculty. Terman dropped the idea.[165]

In late 1957, Rhinelander asked his assistant, William M. McCord, a Stanford sociologist, to confidentially assess all of the school's departments. McCord interviewed each of the department heads and some eighty additional faculty members and wrote particularly frank reports in confidence to Rhinelander in a final revised version of April 1, 1959.[166] He reported faculty complaints of heavy teaching loads, faculty disunity, poor library resources, insufficient research funds, and lack of clarity in tenure standards. Faculty members resented the power of the administration, even though, as McCord noted, "the relation between Stanford's faculty and its administration is probably happier now than at any time in the University's history." And they complained about the students' lack of seriousness: according to a rather amorphous definition and little evidence, they noted that at Harvard, 25 percent, and at Swarthmore, 60 percent of the students became "intellectuals," whereas at Stanford only 4 percent became "intellectuals" while some 70 percent went into "technical trades" (that is, the professions of law, business, engineering, and medicine). By 1959, feelings were, at best, strained between the dean and Sterling's administration as Rhinelander fought with Terman, Cuthbertson, and Wert over budget matters and resorted to stormy sessions in Wally Sterling's office.

Ironically, it had been Terman and Cuthbertson's strategy to move budgeting out of the President's Office and back into the hands of the deans. Wally would "go over individual salaries when I first came here," Cuthbertson remembered.

> Everybody would submit their budgets, and the controller's staff would add them up and say it's a half million dollars over, or two million dollars over. And then old Wally would go to work to see how you might get a couple of million out of it. He would know individual faculty salaries and he'd say, "gee, I think that's a little high" or "that's a little low" or maybe, "we can't do that much this year." It was ridiculous. It was one of the first things I had to go to work on. We went through that procedure of my helping him increasingly, and trying to anticipate what his judgments would be and make it a bit easier. But it was still an awful way

> to do it. It wasn't until Fred Terman began to get hold of the budget, around 1956, that Wally was relieved of that way of working. Fred certainly agreed it was ridiculous.[167]

Terman and Cuthbertson agreed that the administration should make it clear ahead of time what the ground rules would be and determine the size of the budget, "and not let people come in thinking they can shoot for the sky, and [then] force them to make the tough decisions." Cutherbertson believed that Fred's "beautiful idea" of leaving budget savings in the hands of the budgeting unit "is what really got the entrepreneurship of Stanford going. We moved the responsibility for the budget to the academic side and off of Wally's desk."[168] This worked best, however, when the deans did not see budgeting as a battle, or when key budget staff felt that a dean either misunderstood, or ignored, certain financial figures.

Sterling took faculty morale very seriously and maintained an open-door policy, thus Rhinelander's resort to a private conference with the president surprised no one in the President's or Provost's Office. A more serious confrontation between Rhinelander and Terman was two years down the line. The dean, however, was rapidly losing Sterling's confidence, while the president kept faith with his administrative team. "One of the strengths of Wally's presidency was the strength of the team," Howie Brooks recalled. When he picked people like Fred Terman or Ken Cuthbertson for key positions, he backed them up. "Wally surrounded himself with strong people. He didn't want weak people, he wanted the strongest people he could have," Dean Ernie Arbuckle commented. "And he recognized in Fred Terman a person who could get the job done that needed to be done while Wally was attending to things that he did best."[169]

Upgrading Stanford's Administration: The Corson Report

As Sterling approached his tenth year in office, Stanford underwent a major, if delicate, realignment of its administration and faculty committee structure to enable the president to devote more time for external affairs while making faculty input into planning and policy making more effective.

As the university grew in size, and fund-raising and contracts grew more complex, Sterling continued to oversee everything with a close hand. "Wally had everyone in the university reporting directly to him for a long time," Ken Cuthbertson commented about those years. "Wally had to have it that way until he got a handle on what was going on."[170] Relenting to his staff's pressure, advice from friends among the trustees, and his own common sense, he called on John J. Corson, executive vice chairman of the well-known management consulting firm McKinsey and Company, to review Stanford's administrative organization.[171]

John Corson was already somewhat familiar with Stanford. He had served on the Ford Foundation College Grants Advisory Committee in 1955 (as a result of that committee's work, Ford gave a half billion dollars to 630 institutions in American private higher education, including about $3.4 million to Stanford).[172]

Corson was asked to concentrate on two problems: How can the burdens now devolving on the President be reduced? And how should the top executive staff be developed to relieve the President of tasks that can be as well or better handled by others? Between October 1957 and May 1958, Corson studied numerous Stanford procedures, by-laws, and manuals, interviewed at least fifty faculty members and a number of trustees, talked with Alumni Association officers and alumni fund-raising volunteers. Corson's first draft was then studied by some twenty Stanford staff, and their comments and criticism led him to prepare first a second, then a third draft.[173] During the spring and summer of 1958, the third and final draft was discussed widely by Stanford's administrators and by members of the Academic Council's Advisory Board and Executive Committee, while Sterling and his staff worked with Corson to prepare a report for the board of trustees.[174]

Sterling presented the report formally to both the Academic Council and the trustees, but the choices to be made and the speed of implementation remained in Sterling's hands. Few disagreed with the problems and deficiencies outlined by the Corson Report: as Stanford had grown, in faculty and students, teaching and research programs, the ensuing demands on its aging physical plant called for new approaches to land use and development, fund-raising, and management. The existing university administration was overloaded.

The university's business affairs functioned relatively well, the report noted, although differently from other universities in part due to its particular land-development opportunities and problems. Stanford's financial organization needed more unification and strengthening; the university did not have sufficient or correct data with which to work, nor did it use objective data-gathering techniques to maximize performance in several areas. Fund-raising goals were confused and responsibilities were too diffused, requiring much of the president's time. Student affairs needed more attention and greater centralization.

Although originally intended as a review only of Stanford's administration, Corson's study grew to survey how the university's academic program was managed. Existing faculty committees were not working toward clear academic goals, nor were responsibilities among department heads, deans, and other officers clearly defined. Weak departments appeared to perpetuate weakness by recommending mediocre candidates, and Sterling's administration had not yet learned to overcome this tendency. Some department heads and faculty bypassed their deans and the provost to go directly to the president. The twenty-three departments of the School of Humanities and Sciences, in particular, were not working together productively. Communication between faculty and senior administration, including budgetary officers, was often inadequate and ineffective.[175]

Corson made it clear that the president needed substantive administrative help. The report proposed redistributing the major responsibilities for administration among the president and five principal officers—by beefing up the provost's role, raising his business and financial managers to top posts, and adding positions responsible for students and for development—and engaging larger faculty participation in policy consideration and formulation. Corson had put it simply to Sterling, as Ken Cuthbertson later remembered it: "Look, Wally, you've got to come to grips with delegating some of this responsibility and grouping some functions together."[176]

Over the next year, 1958–59, Sterling set about reorganizing and enlarging his team to best advantage, putting into motion a balancing act between easing faculty anxiety and Corson's advice to move as rapidly as possible on reorganizing planning and development functions (Stanford was in the midst of a Long-Range Planning Study by the Kersting and Brown Company).[177] His three trusted senior staff became his three "vice presidents": Fred Terman, as provost and vice president of academic affairs; Alf Brandin as vice president of business affairs; and Kenneth Cuthbertson as vice president of finance. (The recommended post of development officer would soon after be added to Cuthbertson's duties.) By 1958, Fred Terman, as provost, was fully acknowledged to be the prime academic officer of the university, with responsibility for the affairs of each of the university's schools, libraries, and eventually all institutes.[178] With the role and responsibilities of the provost considerably broadened, Terman gave up the position of dean of engineering on September 1, 1959, passing on that post to his protégé, associate engineering dean Joseph Pettit.[179]

A key point in broadening the provost's position was the creation of a new position of vice provost while strengthening that of dean of graduate studies. Bob Wert was enticed back from the Carnegie in the summer of 1959 to serve as Terman's vice provost. Wert was seen by administration insiders like Al Bowker as Wally's special link to the provostial staff.

Some faculty had favored discontinuing the post of graduate dean altogether, turning the position into a kind of vice provost, but Sterling argued against this. Others saw the position as an important channel between faculty and the president, whereas the provost was the voice of the president down to the faculty. Terman, among others, wanted the graduate dean to work more closely with the provost and his staff, and this was to happen with the appointment of Albert H. Bowker.

Al Bowker, Terman's assistant since 1957, succeeded William Steere as graduate dean.[180] Terman and Bowker became an especially effective duo, working closely together until 1963 when Bowker resigned to accept the chancellorship of CUNY. (He later returned to California as chancellor of UC Berkeley.) Fred also brought in E. Howard Brooks in 1957 as assistant to the provost and director of the Summer Session. Brooks (AB '42, AM history '47, PhD history, '50) was an acting instructor in history in 1949 when he first met Wally Sterling and had become assistant director of admissions. Brooks was Terman's man for detailed jobs, data gathering, and, at times, sensitive tasks. (Brooks served as vice provost at Stanford from 1965 to 1971.)

Terman was determined to better utilize the position of graduate dean. The position had been held by at least three people (Faust, Whitaker, and Hilgard) between 1949 and 1955, Sterling later recalled, which suggested a "lack of continuity which, in turn bespeaks at least some degree of weakness." Al Bowker's appointment in 1955, Sterling believed, was a significant improvement. Terman brought the graduate dean into the center of academic policy and budget-making decisions. Like Terman, Bowker was a fair but tough negotiator and indefatigable in his work, Sterling observed, and deserved a share of the credit for Stanford's advance in comparative rankings of American universities. In 1963, Bowker was followed by Virgil Whitaker. Ironically, Whitaker (while head of the English Department) had been among those who had tried to sidestep Terman by going directly to Sterling. However, once Wally "carefully edged Virgil over to Fred," Howie Brooks recalled, "Fred and Virgil became strong collaborators." (Virgil Whitaker served as associate provost and dean of the Graduate Division, 1963–69.[181])

Since his arrival, Sterling had made notable efforts to seek input from faculty and had been praised for his relationship with the Academic Council's Advisory Committee. When the Corson Report encouraged such efforts at involving faculty in policy decisions regarding broad university issues, Sterling experimented with a new Committee on University Policy (COUP), made up of each of the deans, with Sterling as chair and Terman as vice chair. Although the COUP lasted less than five years, it served as an important means of easing the deans into a working relationship with each other, much less key administrators. The deans, Cuthbertson later recalled, had not been exposed to universitywide problems, or problem solving. By the time he came to them for serious work on Stanford's development planning, these important senior faculty members were used to working together.[182] Its purpose proved to be largely informational, and the COUP was discontinued in favor of a more pragmatic deans' council.

The Corson Report did not fulfill everyone's intentions. Sterling was, inevitably, bitterly criticized by some of the faculty members for adding more staff layers between himself and the faculty.[183] The president appeared by some to be taken further from academic matters, while the roles and relationships between the dean of humanities and sciences and the dean of students were left unclear. Of the principal officers now reporting to Sterling, only one, wrote one faculty member, was "an academic man," while the "Dean of Students Office, and its associated faculty bureaucracy . . . constitutes one of the major foci of anti-intellectualism at Stanford."[184] (Faculty politics was clearly at work; the post of dean of students was held from 1950 to 1967 by H. Donald Winbigler, a professor of speech and drama, who helped establish the Faculty Senate in 1967 and subsequently served as academic secretary until 1974.[185]) These complaints from several humanities and sciences faculty reported by Associate Dean Halsey Royden to Dean Rhinelander reflect fears of some faculty that the new administration plan would go further from faculty concerns and toward bureaucracy. When economics head Lorie Tarshis urged that final decisions regarding hiring, promoting, firing, and budgeting should be made at the lowest possible level (in the hands of department heads) with little interference from deans or provosts, Terman noted in pencil in the margin to Sterling that matters were hardly so simple anymore.[186]

Terman had already taken up this issue in a long, detailed comment to one of Corson's drafts written in March 1958.[187] Drawing on his own experience, he commented that the job of provost was "primarily but by no means exclusively an inside job" that dealt with all phases of education at Stanford (though only secondarily with the Medical School, the Hoover Institution, and the Law School). The provost, he observed, should ensure that departments and schools were treated equitably and that the overall educational operation was coherent, working toward long-term objectives rather than operating on a year-to-year basis. The provost should continually evaluate the quality and character of the academic operation, including budgeting, and he recommended his own study, "School of Engineering Needs for 1958–59" as an example to show what could be done to extract the most from each educational dollar.[188]

The provost's most important function, however, was the selection of new and promotion of existing faculty, he stated. To its disadvantage sometimes, Stanford had tended to favor the man on the spot over outside candidates in tenure positions. Terman believed that faculty review had been much more thorough at the provostial level during his recent years in that office than ever before. Yet despite the review of candidates done by Terman and his assistant, there was still a tendency for department heads and deans to try to handle an appointment with "getting it by the Provost." Terman hoped to establish an arrangement within the School of Humanities and Sciences whereby the provost became involved in a faculty search only when the list of candidates had been narrowed to two to four names, thus entering the picture without arousing resentment from a dean or department head already committed to a particular position. By way of confirming a more positive role for the provost, Terman also outlined efforts underway by his office and by the Graduate Studies Office to obtain financial support for research programs that built individual faculty reputations while giving prestige to the university.

Terman may have been reluctant to give up the dean's office, but he now intended to significantly improve conditions in Stanford's largest school, humanities and sciences. Terman kept prime responsibility for the natural sciences and mathematics and assigned to Bob Wert responsibility for the humanities, social sciences, fine arts, and undergraduate general studies.[189]

Terman believed that he *had* been encouraging each dean and each department head to work as autonomously as possible. The problem, he believed, was that although humanities and sciences (like the School of Engineering) appeared to have workable department structures, it had had strong central leadership for less than two years while engineering had had strong central leadership from a dean for more than thirty years. Terman thought it best that the dean, rather than the provost, work directly with department heads, thus strengthening the dean's position, and this had been his practice over the past year and a half working with Dean Phil Rhinelander.

The expansion of the provost's responsibilities, however, would lead some department faculty in the School of Humanities and Sciences to complain about Terman's actions in the years ahead. Often enough the issue was style rather than substance. "Even though you know more about the budget," Glover remembers Wally cautioning Fred, "and know more about the department than the head of the department, let them tell you their story before you jump in first." Fred would jump in early on, nonetheless.[190]

Taking Stock: The School of Engineering in 1958

In 1958, before stepping down after thirteen years as dean of engineering, Fred Terman submitted an extensive report to the president on the status of engineering at Stanford, and what he viewed as the school's current needs.[191] The year before, the *Chicago Tribune* had published a series of articles ranking the academic programs of various national universities.[192] However flimsy the newspaper's survey methodology may have been, Terman realized that the report was influential. Stanford had been rated as tenth overall, and its engineering school rated fifth. Terman disagreed, ranking Stanford second behind only MIT in graduate work in engineering, but he reckoned that at least fifteen other schools had comparable undergraduate programs.

In its building phases, Terman had been proud of Stanford as a lean operation and undergraduate morale remained high. One-third of freshmen male students at Stanford stated that they planned engineering as a major. Results of the 1955 universitywide *Study of Undergraduate Education at Stanford* showed that engineering students were consistently better satisfied with their Stanford experience than the average undergraduate. Faculty morale was good, too. Lester Field had, so far, been the only engineering faculty loss (among those "we wished to keep") in the last eleven years.

In his 1958 report, Terman therefore took aim at two things. First, faculty salaries were improving but were not yet adequate, and additions to the faculty were needed. Large classes, overloaded advisors, lack of student seminars, and insufficient laboratory work were now significant weaknesses. With additional faculty hires, class sizes could be brought down, and faculty would have more time for advisees, including, he suggested, lunching once each quarter with each individual student advisee.

Secondly, Terman was concerned about the excessive commitment of faculty time to research in electrical engineering. He noted that a number of electrical engineering faculty devoted as much as three-quarters of their budgeted time to contract research. Although initially this had been an important strategy to improve the engineering school without drawing further on university general funds, Terman now felt that individual faculty who taught only one three-unit course a quarter due to heavy research loads benefited only their graduate research students and had little, if any, time for wider departmental service. Beginning in 1958–59, Terman proposed that no engineering department would allocate more than one-half of an individual faculty member's time to a research project during the school year.

Stanford's Engineering School now ranked among the top graduate schools in the country, and Terman thought it was time to improve the undergraduate engineering experience as well. The extensive *Study of Undergraduate Education* and subsequent establishment of a universitywide General Studies Program in 1956 had turned attention to undergraduate education. Terman had encouraged better integration of the General Studies curriculum into the engineering program. A joint committee representing engineering, physics, and mathematics had worked out changes in course sequences beginning in 1957.[193] (Engineering undergraduates were required to take one year of history of Western civilization, a year of English literature and composition, a course in public speaking, a selection of courses in the humanities and social sciences, plus general courses in physics, mathematics, chemistry, and introductory courses in all the engineering departments.) In some "options," students could substitute additional physics and mathematics courses for some of the general engineering courses. Mathematics was now utilized in the engineering curriculum more effectively, he felt. With the exception of chemical engineering majors (still administered by the Chemistry Department), which nationwide required an extra eighteen or so quarter units of credit for the BS degree, no undergraduate course at Stanford required such extended and rigorous preparation for all its majors as did the School of Engineering.

Over the course of his deanship, Stanford's engineering curriculum and research agenda had changed markedly. Engineering mechanics had been established in 1948, then enlarged and strengthened, and industrial engineering had grown from a part of civil engineering in 1945 into a strong program by 1954 and then department in 1955. Engineering science had been established as a degree program. Aeronautics was brought from an aging program into vitality and on the brink of becoming a department (in one of Terman's last acts as dean, it became so in 1959). Metallurgy had left the School of Engineering for the School of Mineral Sciences in 1947 and would return to engineering as the Department of Materials Science in 1960.

Development of further research in microwaves and the electronics of transistors continued to be on Terman's mind. When key Physics Department faculty showed little interest in the further development of Stanford's high-energy physics research facilities, or in further pursuing semiconductor and solid-state physics, he helped these important areas of pure and applied physics evolve into new and separate enterprises and departments elsewhere on campus: the Stanford Linear Accelerator Center (SLAC), evolving out of the microwave and accelerator work at the Hansen Labs, the new departments of Applied Physics and Materials Science, and in new programs in the Departments of Electrical Engineering and Computer Science.

With Al Bowker's help and the help of others, Statistics and Computer Science Departments had been established at Stanford, with strong links to engineering. The Microwave Laboratory had grown beyond expectations, splitting into the two laboratories, one of High-Energy Physics, the other Microwaves, which were now grouped together as the W. W. Hansen Laboratories. Terman's own discipline of electrical engineering had become a colossus, contesting MIT for the best program in the country, providing stellar research in electron tubes, radio wave propagation, microwaves, and geo-space research, and entering strongly into the new fields of "transistors" (solid-state physics), masers, network theory, and computer design.

In the academic fiscal year ending August 31, 1955, the School of Engineering brought in a total of $465,000 of earned overhead from research contracts, including $86,000 in nondefense contracts in the Microwave Laboratory. A total of $314,000 in overhead came from Electrical Engineering Department and Microwave Lab defense projects, while $104,000 came from basic research in electrical engineering (mostly radio wave propagation); another $32,000 from mechanical engineering, aeronautical engineering, and engineering mechanics; $12,000 from civil engineering; and $2,000 from industrial engineering. The bulk of this support came from contracts with the navy and air force, but other contracts were funded by the National Science Foundation, the National Bureau of Standards, the U.S. Public Health Service, the American Cancer Society, General Electric, and Hewlett-Packard.[194]

The bar chart illustrates Engineering School research contracts from 1949 until 1959, the year Fred Terman resigned as dean of engineering to become vice president as well as provost. The chart shows the high growth rate and very high absolute level of research contracts in electronics in the Electrical Engineering Department and, beginning in 1957–58 (the year of arrival of Nicholas Hoff and Walter Vincenti), the high take-off growth in aeronautics research contracts. It also helps illustrate how Dean Terman funded the additional electronics buildings and considerable improvements in faculty salaries through overhead on the research contracts.

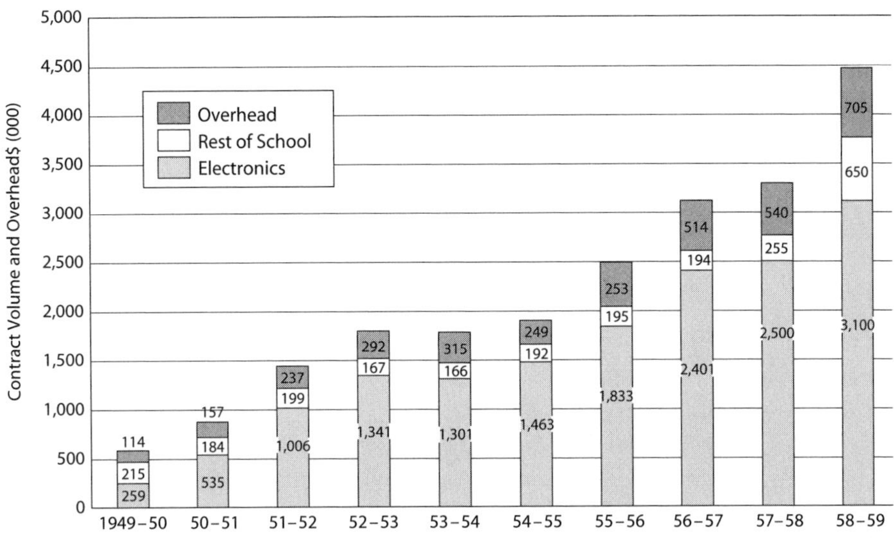

By 1959, the Sterling-Terman team was in full stride. If at times overly impressed by the Ivy League, they nevertheless aimed high. "With the exception of Harvard, we are catching up fast with California, Princeton and others," Sterling had commented in 1957. "Our problem is to stay caught up."[195]

The expansion of the provost's responsibilities, and particularly Terman's single-minded insistence on raising faculty hiring and promotion standards, would lead some department faculty to complain about Terman's actions in the years ahead. Some faculty feared Fred Terman, a few disliked him outright, but as psychologist Ernest Hilgard said "although some joked that Stanford was becoming Terman Tech, he was concerned with all aspects of the University."[196]

Recalling their efforts at comparing Harvard's endowment and spending per student to Stanford's in 1957, Bob Moulton later quipped, "And we wanted to compete at their level? Our hurdle was clear. It was a marvelous atmosphere at Stanford, with optimism, risk-taking, and momentum in all directions—including the possibly world leadership in high-energy physics. Why not?"[197] Indeed, on the horizon was the opening of Stanford's new campus Medical Center, the creation of the Stanford Linear Accelerator Center, and a trend-setting fund-raising campaign, along with significant strides in the quality of Stanford's humanities and sciences departments.

CHAPTER SEVEN

Raising Steeples at Stanford

1958–1965

In February 1961, *Newsweek* magazine featured a photo of thirteen new Stanford professors, all brought from prominent eastern schools like Harvard, MIT, Yale, and Columbia. Five more, it said, were scheduled to arrive that fall. "We want Stanford to be the Harvard of the West," President Wally Sterling was quoted as saying.[1]

President Sterling and Provost Fred Terman knew, however, that in 1961 Stanford was trying to do a great deal with much less—less endowment money and lower spending per student—than leading rivals. But their ambitions for Stanford had already caught fire on campus. "Every department which I have contacted wishes to expand," reported Assistant Dean of Humanities and Sciences William McCord.[2]

By the end of the 1950s, Stanford had fully entered the era of "Big Science." The reevaluation and relocation of Stanford's Medical School between 1954 and 1959 provided a fast learning curve for Sterling's administration, as did initial negotiations and planning for the Stanford Linear Accelerator Center. As the 1960s opened, Stanford embarked on an in-depth analysis of the university's academic and financial problems, possibilities, and ambitions. This, in turn, placed the university in a position to conduct a trend-setting national fund-raising campaign. Throughout these busy times, Terman kept trustees, administrators, and faculty focused on the central goal of the Sterling administration: the improvement of Stanford's academic program through the attraction and retention of top faculty and students. According to some on campus, the provost's assessments were cold and calculating, while to others, Terman's approach was welcomed as astute, wonderfully flexible, and exhilarating. In either case, Stanford was a far different place in 1965 than it had been in 1955.

With his responsibilities broadened in 1958 and his staff beefed up, Fred Terman turned his attention to the condition of the humanities and sciences at Stanford. Terman was especially interested in the Departments of Biology, Chemistry (and Chemical Engineering), Mathematics, Physics, Psychology, and Statistics and their overlapping interests in the School of Medicine. Yet while he assigned his vice provost, Robert Wert, primary responsibility for the remaining seventeen humanities and sciences departments, Terman nevertheless became closely involved in the development of a number of humanities and social science departments as well.[3] The Departments of Physics, Biology, Chemistry, Political Science, English, and History will illustrate here the variety of problems and opportunities Terman, his staff, and his faculty worked with. Between 1955 and 1965, each of these departments received different kinds of attention, and different levels of assistance, but each was a substantially different place by Terman's retirement in 1965.

The Lessons of Relocating Stanford's Medical School

On September 18, 1959, after more than six years of planning, the new Stanford Medical Center on campus was dedicated. Moving and rebuilding the Stanford Medical School proved to be an especially valuable experience for Sterling and his staff. It required careful planning, extensive public and internal negotiations, close work with the trustees, attentive facilities and site design, and management of a complex construction site. It also required raising more than $21 million.

The move of the Medical School also was a pivotal step for Stanford in that in coming years the National Institutes of Health (NIH), not the Department of Defense (DOD), would be the prime federal lever for Stanford. Those who argue that military radar and aeronautical contracts primarily determined the path of Stanford during the cold war ignore the rise of academic medicine. In 1946 the Hill-Burton Hospital Survey and Construction Act began a massive federal program of hospital and medical school subsidies. Funding continued with the growth of the NIH budget and then Medicare and Medicaid. The NIH has long been the largest sponsor of academic research in American universities.[4] It is true that at one time in the early 1950s, during the Korean War, more than 90 percent of government-sponsored research at Stanford was funded by the Department of Defense. By 1963, this figure was reduced to 40 percent, and the largest single commitment of government funds at Stanford was to the Medical School for clinical sciences and radiotherapy.[5]

By 1959, the university had honed its fund-raising and public-relations skills, but the process had also revealed management inadequacies. The enormity of the task was one of the major reasons Sterling was finally persuaded to seek the advice of management consultant John Corson of McKinsey and Company and to put in motion Stanford's administrative reorganization of 1958–59. Similarly, the complexities of the Medical School fund-raising campaign and resulting public-relations issues led to valuable consultations with Kersting, Brown, and Company and gave Stanford the confidence to embark on a new, even bigger university-wide fund-raising campaign.

The moving process began in 1953 when President Sterling persuaded the board of trustees of the necessity of moving Stanford's Medical School from crowded, outdated quarters in San Francisco some forty miles southward to the Stanford campus.[6] This decision was not an easy one—faculty physicians with good practices and personal ties to San Francisco resented having to move, while some campus faculty were equally resentful that what they saw as a cash sinkhole was to be moved closer rather than eliminated. Nonetheless, Sterling envisioned this as an important opportunity to build both the medical sciences and basic sciences on campus.

Terman, first as engineering dean and later as provost, saw important opportunities in the move for chemistry, biochemistry, and genetics as well as for physics and electrical engineering. A much-discussed example of Terman's encouragement of interdepartmental interests (and ultimately, commercial value) was the teaming of accelerator engineer Ed Ginzton and radiologist Henry S. Kaplan. In 1952, Ginzton, director of the Microwave Laboratory, and Kaplan, chair of the Radiology Department, began work on a new tool for cancer treatment—a compact 6,000,000-volt linear electron accelerator to be used to shoot X-rays at deep-seated cancerous tissue. By January 1954, the Medical School began an ambitious program on cancer research with twenty-eight projects funded by five agencies and eighteen principal investigators. Kaplan and Ginzton's machine, built and installed by 1956, made national headlines January 1957 when it was used to treat a two-year-old patient. (The "Clinac" was later developed for commercial use by Varian Associates.[7])

Given the enormity of the fund-raising required to relocate the school, the trustees and Stanford's development staff reconsidered the best way to gather and present the relevant information and explored new possibilities for private and foundation funding.[8] In a three-year period from 1956 to 1959 about $14 million was raised in gifts, grants, and pledges toward Stanford's $17 million share of the cost (largely from the Commonwealth Fund, Ford Foundation, Rockefeller Foundation, several federal funds, and individual major gifts to the Stanford Medical Center Fund), and $4 million raised through a Palo Alto city bond issue. The Medical School endowment itself was increased from $2.5 to $12 million.[9]

Stanford's School of Medicine traced its origins to the first medical school on the Pacific Coast, founded in 1858 by Dr. Elias Samuel Cooper. Renamed the Cooper Medical College, the college added various classrooms, a library, a hospital building, and a nurses' school by 1895. Financial woes drove it into the arms of Stanford University in 1908, a move promoted by trustee Herbert Hoover. As Stanford's School of Medicine, the school graduated its first class in 1913, with Ray Lyman Wilbur (AB '96, Cooper MD '99) named as its first dean.[10]

Sterling's 1953 proposal was not the first time Stanford reviewed the question of the medical school's location and the value of associating medical education with the university. In 1910, Abraham Flexner's influential report, *Medical Education in the United States and Canada*, had called for medical schools to be organic parts of and geographically close to their parent universities, but at Stanford debate ensued over whether Stanford should reject altogether its recent acquisition of the Cooper Medical College.[11] When President John Casper Branner protested vigorously against retaining the medical school in 1913, he was outflanked by trustee Hoover and medical dean Ray Lyman Wilbur. During his own term as president, Wilbur considered moving the school to the Stanford campus, as did President Donald Tresidder (Stanford MD '27) during the Second World War.[12] In 1944, Tresidder sought the advice of Alan Gregg of the Rockefeller Foundation, who urged Tresidder to involve the Medical School in the latest scientific research and to consolidate the school on the campus rather than isolate it from the "undisputed and essential contacts" in biology, chemistry, and physics.[13] Gregg also noted increasing use of mathematics, sociology, anthropology, and psychology, and predicted future use of techniques of pedagogy and education in public health information. Proximity to campus faculties would facilitate this, but he also recognized that only major population centers could provide sufficient clinical patients for medical teaching and research. Despite the mobility brought by automobiles (and despite the Peninsula's fast-growing population), Gregg understood that specialists in medicine, surgery, obstetrics, and pediatrics would protest leaving lucrative practices in the city. "If you doubt their ability to exert pressure," he warned, "you haven't long to wait for proof, for they need the school more than the school needs them." Nevertheless, Gregg wrote, in the future "the medical school may need the skill and loyalty of the University administration more than it will need anything other cities will provide." He advised Tresidder that "any other place than the University campus is the wrong, the cheap, and the troublesome place to put the medical school of the University."[14] The trustees, struggling with wartime budget deficits and military needs, decided to leave the medical school in San Francisco. Tresidder concurred, largely because he was afraid the population of the surrounding area was not sufficient to support a clinic and hospital. Many of Gregg's recommendations, predictions, and warnings would reappear in discussions on the topic throughout the 1950s.

In 1951, President Sterling, under heavy pressure from Dean Loren Roscoe "Yank" Chandler and medical faculty, initially endorsed the board's 1944 decision to continue the Medical School in San Francisco. Within months, Sterling regretted the decision. The medical school grabbed his attention, and he would not let go for another ten years. Sterling closely studied documentation regarding earlier decisions and various alternatives, then broached the subject again with Dean Chandler. The president raised many of the issues that had come up in the past (the vital role of scientific research in medical education and the potential presented by the Peninsula's fast-growing population and changing demographic profile) while adding a new enticement: the growth in medical benefits provided by medical care plans (with eighty million subscribers nationwide by 1953) reduced the number and proportion of indigent patients in medical school clinics.[15]

Chandler was willing to cooperate with Sterling, but added the understated comment that the president viewed these issues "from a perspective which we may not fully appreciate."[16] The dean nonetheless had given the president an opening. Sterling appointed a Committee on Future Plans of the Medical School and launched himself into compiling data and advice for a proposal to the board of trustees. A letter to each of some four hundred members of the medical faculty resulted in only thirty responses and mixed results, but Sterling's subsequent visits with twenty leaders in medical education outside Stanford pointed strongly to the benefits of relocation.

By 1953, Sterling saw no value in discontinuing the school (as some on campus still hoped). It was ranked among the top ten of seventy-nine accredited medical schools in the country, and it had its own endowment of $4.4 million and future bequests of $9.6 million. But he also concluded that the circumstances that had earlier discouraged the move were no longer significant. He recognized that some physicians on the school's faculty might not choose to move, but took note that 20 percent of the current clinical faculty already lived on the Peninsula, and another 213 physicians had practices within a twenty-minute drive of the campus.

Early in 1953, Sterling proposed to the board of trustees dramatic renovation of the Medical School program through relocation and rebuilding faculty, facilities, and endowment. He acknowledged significant problems needed to be overcome, in San Francisco, on campus, and in the local medical community. Stanford would require a great deal of new funding to build a new teaching hospital and medical school, with its associated library, classrooms, laboratories, nurses' and medical students' dormitories, and to build up an adequate endowment for operations and faculty salaries. Sterling therefore recommended a $15 million campaign over three to five years (approximately $2 million more, he estimated, than the cost of rebuilding facilities in San Francisco). He pointed to shared academic interests of physicists, chemists, and statisticians in new departments like radiology, pharmacology, and bacteriology, of the importance of changes occurring on the Peninsula, of national changes underway in medical care and education. These were the opportunities, he concluded, "to be plucked by courage and vision from these changing circumstances."[17]

Having convinced the trustees to approve the relocation in July 1953, Sterling now had to put the plan into motion. Doubts were quickly voiced among his supporters as well as among the medical community. The prospect of having to raise many millions for this single effort was daunting. Some worried that because many of the individuals capable of helping to fund the move lived in San Francisco, they might be resentful of losing the school to Palo Alto. Others feared that raising funds for a new medical facility would cut heavily into funds that would otherwise be directed at other university needs. Still others were anxious about the reaction of medical staff in San Francisco, physicians on the Peninsula, and physicians among the alumni.[18]

Sterling wasted no time in getting started, however. He had laid the groundwork in his notes for "Medical School Plans," roughed out only three weeks after the trustees' decision.[19] Among twenty topics on his list were financing considerations; "heavy money"; a Curriculum Study Committee; a Clinical Material Committee; and a Site and Construction Committee. He wanted a "strong" committee of trustees, administrators, and faculty behind him. He wanted Dr. Russel Lee, an internist, a founder and the executive director of the sixty-five–member Palo Alto Clinic, and president of the Stanford Alumni Association as a key advisor.[20] He would enlist faculty with ties to outside funding organizations (such as biochemists Ed Tatum and Murray Luck, radiologist Henry Kaplan, psychologist Ernest Hilgard, medical statistician Lincoln Moses, and anthropologist Bernard Siegel). He wanted influential medical faculty members on board, such as surgeon Frank Gerbode and immunologist Sidney Raffel, and expected further discussions with regional medical planners regarding patients for the campus hospital. Finally, Sterling noted the aid of an unofficial and exclusive group called the "Clay Street Marching and Chowder Society"—Medical School friends (among them, Alvin J. Cox Jr., Windsor C. Cutting, Henry Kaplan, and Sidney Raffel) who wanted to make the new school one that would "open eyes."

Four months after the trustees' decision to move the school, an extensive advisory network had been organized. Board president Lloyd Dinkelspiel, a prominent San Francisco businessman and influential philanthropist, appointed a new Committee on the Medical School, naming as its chair George A. Ditz, the board's vice president, who like Dinkelspiel was devoted to Stanford and to relocating the Medical School to the campus. The committee's membership was carefully picked: Ditz and Dinkelspiel were joined by veteran Medical School committee trustees W. Parmer Fuller and George Morell, and by Herbert Hoover and Seeley G. Mudd MD (strong Sterling advocates on the board since 1948). Among the six medical faculty committee members were acting dean Windsor Cutting, Russel Lee, and W. L. Rogers, chairman of the Stanford Medical Alumni Fund. Other appointments to the committee included former Stanford administrators Frank F. Walker (now president of the Stanford Associates) and Louis B.

Lundborg, Dave F. Dozier, president of the Stanford Medical Alumni Association, and several prominent judges and businessmen from northern California, including Walter A. Haas and Paul C. Wilbur.

A committee of twenty-two faculty was charged with evaluating Stanford's long-term objectives for medical teaching, while an additional group of faculty studied ways to attract sufficient numbers of clinical patients. Yet another faculty group considered the construction of the new plant on campus and the disposition and future use of the old Medical School buildings.[21]

Throughout his study of the status of medical education, Sterling was particularly struck by the argument that medical education was more and more dependent on close interaction with research in the basic sciences, and "even more so on the social sciences." Windsor Cutting (who would take over as dean in 1953) agreed that the Stanford Medical School should be a "highly academic one . . . not a trade school turning out largely practitioners of medicine, but a University school whose product includes new knowledge as well as trained practitioners."[22]

The Provost's Office had been little involved in planning for the new medical school as yet. Provost Douglas Whitaker simply confirmed in a letter to the Medical School faculty that the board had voted unanimously to relocate the school, that President Sterling had consulted with medical authorities across the country, and that the administration was genuinely concerned for the welfare of the medical faculty.[23] Terman, entering the scene as provost in 1955, took a different approach and insisted on appointments of the highest quality to both the clinical and basic medical sciences faculty.

Senior leadership at the school underwent several changes during the process. Yank Chandler, dean since 1933 and "a good soldier," retired in 1953 to make way for the change.[24] Dean Cutting, a gentle, friendly man who worked effectively with the administration, stepped down in 1957. Pediatrician Robert H. Alway, briefly acting dean, became dean of the Stanford Medical School in 1958.

Under Provost Terman and Dean Alway, the medical faculty doubled in size and research funds tripled during 1957–1964. To counteract the criticism that the university had encouraged too much scholastic "inbreeding," they brought in new department chairs from elsewhere: pediatrician Norman Kretchmer from Cornell; biochemist Arthur Kornberg from Washington University, St. Louis; geneticist Joshua Lederberg from Wisconsin; immunologist Halsted Holman from the Rockefeller Institute in New York; hand surgeon Robert Chase from Yale; psychiatrist David Hamburg from the National Institutes of Health. Remaining in their departmental positions were pharmacologist Avrum Goldstein and radiologist Henry Kaplan, who had come to Stanford from Harvard and from the National Institutes of Health.[25] Dean Alway also created new Departments of Anesthesiology and Dermatology.

Alway and Terman worked hard to bring the best people. While seeking to attract the interest of Arthur Kornberg, for example, they started with numerous letters and phone calls. After Stanford selected Kornberg as their first choice, he was invited for a four-day visit in June 1957 that began with a conference with the provost, then talks with the Basic Science and Clinical Medical department heads, each of the university's deans, then visits to the Chemistry Department, the Biology Department, the Carnegie Plant Biology facilities, the Hopkins Marine Station in Pacific Grove, and back to President Sterling's office, interspersed with several dinners and cocktail parties and a trip to UC Berkeley. Terman, Goldstein, Kaplan, and Alway did the heavy lifting during Kornberg's visit.[26] Relocating the school required more than in-house rearrangements. Negotiations had to be carried out with local and county governments, local physicians, and hospital staff. More than routine contract negotiations, the issues raised were very "human problems," remembered Fred Glover, secretary of Sterling's Medical School committee. Wally, who was under medical care for diverticulitis problems, would "get two minutes of medicine and an hour of medical politics," Glover recounted. "I was having a routine physical . . . and the nurse started to heckle me about the move of the medical school, and my rate picked up so much they had to do the cardiogram over."[27] By 1956, Glover, financial officer Ken Cuthbertson, and public affairs administrator Lyle Cook were trying to see how "some order can be brought out of our current chaotic medical communications problem." Glover prepared for Sterling a list of thirty-four items of "Misunderstanding and Disagreement Relating to the Medical School Move."[28] Press conferences featured Sterling and Dean Alway; articles appeared in *Newsweek*, *Look*, *Reader's Digest*, *Good Housekeeping*, and *Cosmopolitan*. Edward R. Murrow interviewed Sterling.[29]

After three years of fund-raising, the new Stanford Medical Center and Hospital broke ground on campus in June 1957. It began operation in the summer 1959. Designed by Edward Durell Stone, its original three hospital (with 440 beds) and four medical school buildings cost $21.5 million. The opening of the new Stanford Medical School did not end the school's funding problems, however. "The hospital continues to be in grief," presidential assistant Fred Glover wrote to trustee Paul Edwards a year later, "as a matter of fact there is a heavy debt, although we think we see daylight ahead."[30]

In the center's 1959 dedication booklet, President Wallace Sterling repeated what he had been saying for years: "Central to this new Stanford program is the concept that the future progress of the medical sciences is inextricably linked with progress in the basic physical and biological sciences and increasingly with progress in the social sciences."[31] Once the Medical School was settled in, however, several trustees, notably Thomas Pike and Herman Phleger, questioned whether the Medical School faculty—and the Stanford faculty in general—was doing too much research as opposed to teaching more medical students. The trustee's discussion of this issue was amplified a few months later by a *Wall Street*

Journal assertion that too much federal money was being spent on medical research and medical researchers rather than on the training of physicians or on undergraduate education.[32] Fred Terman attempted to deflect this criticism by pointing out that research was often linked to the teaching of graduate students.[33] By 1964, Stanford medical students rated number one nationally in each of the six preclinical sciences tested by the National Board of Medical Examiners.

Forecasting Stanford's Minimum Financial Needs: "The Red Book"

Between 1953 and 1959, President Sterling and his staff learned a great deal about Stanford's strengths and weaknesses while dealing with the relocation of Stanford's Medical School and the rebuilding of its research and teaching programs. By the end of this period, Stanford's trustees, administrators, and much of the faculty had digested the extensive comments and recommendations of two influential management consultants. As a result, starting in 1958, Stanford reconfigured its senior administration and readjusted the administration's means of working with both trustees and faculty. In October 1959, a new long-range planning effort was initiated to rethink the university's academic goals and objectives and to evaluate their cost. "Stanford's Minimum Needs in the Years Ahead," dubbed "The Red Book," would help propel Stanford into a new era.

Forecasting was not new to Wallace Sterling. Shortly after his arrival in 1949, he had asked each of Stanford's schools and departments to prepare five- and ten-year forecasts. In 1959, in preparation for his tenth year of service as president, Sterling had again asked for forecasts. Part of this effort went into his unpublished ten-year report, "Mark X," and part was melded into a report for the board of trustees.[34]

Although the Corson Report had originally recommended two separate officers for finance (budget planning and management) and development (fund-raising), Sterling was reluctant to add more positions and was determined not to have a vice president of development. He well understood, however, that development functions needed better planning and staffing, and he concluded that Cuthbertson should manage both duties. (Sterling, in fact, had also wanted to lump in university relations, but Cuthbertson agreed to take on that responsibility only until they could get a good person to report directly to the president. Lyle Nelson's arrival in 1961 as director of university relations solved that problem.[35])

Years before settling in as vice president in charge of fund-raising and development, budgeting and financial planning, Ken Cuthbertson had started a process of financial forecasting.[36] His top man was his Stanford classmate Robert Moulton. Moulton and Cuthbertson both graduated in the class of 1940 as economics majors. Cuthbertson had been student body president, Moulton chairman of the student council, and both had worked as student fund-raising volunteers for Dave Jacobson and the Stanford Annual Fund.[37] After working briefly for the CIA, Moulton had joined the Ford Foundation as assistant to Rowan Gaither from 1953 through September 1957, when he was chosen by Sterling as presidential assistant for long-range planning at Stanford.

Early in the forecasting process, Moulton and Cuthbertson calculated that Harvard University had an endowment large enough to enable it to go tuition-free and yet still spend more per student than Stanford could. Moulton's ensuing ten-year forecasts for Stanford were the germ of the "Red Book."

In the spring of 1959, Moulton began preparing tables of financial needs, illustrating the gap between existing funds and projected needs. Moulton enthusiastically accepted Sterling's proposal that there should be a full-scale presentation to the trustees and suggested that each dean and key administrators give presentations. Reflecting Sterling's tradition of providing the trustees with adequate background well before asking them for a decision, Moulton recommended that these presentations should be prepared ahead of time and presented in a notebook for each trustee.[38]

The financial forecasting itself was done by Stanford's three men most familiar with the university's financial problems and practices: Bob Moulton, Ken Cuthbertson, and controller Ken Creighton.[39] They produced conservative figures, since they hoped to convince the trustees that ongoing growth of expenditure should be expected. As Fred Terman explained in the opening pages of their final report, Stanford needed to provide for the long-term future a strong salary structure, a healthy rate of growth, and adequate physical facilities. Cuthbertson, Moulton, and several colleagues joined Provost Terman and Stanford's deans in a day-long session with the trustees in October 1959.

Terman began the morning's discussions and was followed by deans and financial officers who discussed specific university programs. The provost, however, set the pace and the theme: Terman asserted at the outset that if Stanford kept its sights high, its very successful past would be nothing compared to its future. He noted the great gains in rankings made by Stanford in the previous decade (Stanford was fourth nationally among schools chosen by winners of the most recent National Merit Scholarships, and it was second after Harvard in the General Motors National Scholarship competition). He also pointed out that the ratio of applicants to positions in the freshman class was higher at Stanford than at Harvard (4.2 versus 3.3), while the proportion of Stanford's freshmen from the East and Midwest during the past five years had risen from one-eighth to more than one-fifth of the incoming class. Stanford's graduate student body was larger, more national in character, and better qualified.

Terman went on to praise particularly Stanford's Departments of English, Physics, Psychology, and Electrical Engineering, and its Schools of Business, Law, and Education for competing well nationally with the best institutions in their fields. The new Medical School was attracting national attention for its educational program, its facilities, and its faculty. The rising prestige of Stanford among students, Terman said, was in substantial measure a result of the growing stature of the Stanford faculty and of individual departments and schools.

Terman's remarks were exhilarating, but the provost then went on to remind the trustees that Stanford had achieved these gains with a minimum of financial resources. Stanford's endowment income per student was lower than any Ivy League school (except perhaps Cornell) and was only one-fourth the size of the endowments of Harvard, Yale, and Princeton. All three of those institutions charged higher tuition than Stanford. As a result, Harvard, Yale, and Princeton were able to spend twice as much per student as Stanford. Stretching resources was one thing, he commented, but any significant further progress required a substantial increase in Stanford's resources. Stanford's goal, he recommended, should be to raise itself to be on a par with the best eastern private universities and to be the most prestigious university in the West.

Stanford could not, and need not, compete at every point, he added, nor at every level. However, in those fields where Stanford chose to make a serious effort to be good, it must strive to be the best. To do so meant that Stanford had to have a progressive strengthening of its faculty salary structure, a healthy and steady growth of the faculty, substantial plant additions and rehabilitations, and improved housing for undergraduates, graduate students, and junior faculty.[40]

Terman's stirring speech powerfully affected the trustees. Although still inclined to conservative steps, they concluded that being satisfied in reaching minimum needs was no longer adequate.[41] Stanford needed a clear strategy for academic development and physical plant and financial improvement.

The various discussions that took place among Stanford's trustees, administrators, and faculty members were summarized six months later by Vice Provost Robert Wert.[42] Stanford's *minimum* financial needs—as presented to the trustees by Cuthbertson, Terman, and other university officers—totaled a whopping $150 million in addition to expected tuition income and gifts already pledged. This was a great deal of money. The trustees asked for recommendations as to how to meet this great need. "By sheer coincidence," according to Sterling, shortly after the trustees' meeting, Ford Foundation Program Officer James Armsey and Secretary Joseph McDonald met with Sterling and several university officers on campus.[43] The Ford executives mentioned that they had not found universities to be thinking much about long-term financial planning. "They asked what are you going to do ten years from now," Fred Glover recounted, "and Wally said, 'Ken, get the *Red Book*.'" A delighted Wallace Sterling thereupon presented to his astonished guests a copy of Stanford's self-assessment and ten-year forecasts.[44] The Ford officials were so impressed, the story goes, that they proceeded to award Stanford a $25 million matching grant.

Wally Sterling loved a good story, and the tale of his revealing the "Red Book" like a magician to astound the Ford Foundation was one of his (and his staff's) favorites.[45] But Sterling's disarmingly simple tale clouds his astute leadership and Stanford's determination. Although by late fall 1959 Sterling and his staff were aware of Ford's interest in making large seed grants to a selection of universities, Stanford's self-assessment and forecasting were already well underway when Ford's men decided to make the visit in the spring of 1960. Nor were Armsey and McDonald specific about their reasons for visiting. Trying to finish up their forecasts before the Ford visit, Sterling's staff had to scramble when the visit was suddenly rescheduled for three weeks earlier than originally planned.[46]

A "Plan of Action for a Challenging Era": The PACE Campaign

In April 1961, President Sterling publicly announced Stanford's initiation of a three-year, $100 million fund-raising campaign with the impressive name of "A Plan of Action for a Challenging Era." The PACE campaign, Sterling pronounced, is "our boldest venture since the University was founded." A campaign brochure, prepared by communications professor Wilbur Schramm, highlighted one of author (and Stanford English professor) Wallace Stegner's many memorable phrases: "Stanford is a university trembling on the edge of greatness."[47]

The campaign was firmly grounded in a $25 million, three-for-one matching grant from the Ford Foundation. The Ford gift, awarded to Stanford in September 1960, was the largest single grant yet given to a private university. Four other universities received Ford grants at that time, ranging from $4 to $6 million. Stanford's faculty and staff received the good news in a letter from Wallace Sterling, enclosed in their pay envelopes.[48]

Despite the pathbreaking work encompassed in the "Red Book," Ford officials had counseled Stanford not to jump too quickly into announcing plans to seek the necessary $75 million matching funds, but to take time to think further about Stanford's needs. That summer, Ken Cuthbertson had taken a working vacation, driving across country with his wife and kids to visit nineteen other private colleges and universities to survey financial planning in higher education.[49] Over the fall and winter of 1960–61, Bob Wert and Dean of Humanities and Sciences Phil Rhinelander pulled in forecasts from each of the schools and departments to make more fully the "Case for Stanford." Stanford's full needs for the next decade, they concluded, actually amounted to $346 million, including $91 million for improved faculty salaries and faculty additions; $42 million for scholarships; $23 million for libraries; and $115 million for facilities. Approximately $100 million, they estimated, would come from expected sources, but $246 million would have to come from additional gift support.[50]

The PACE campaign effort was, in essence, a kick-off to these much larger fund-raising goals, with $71.5 million of the initial $100 million goal destined for capital objectives. Stanford's "plan for action" called for an across-the-board strengthening of virtually every major university activity, from the improvement of undergraduate education with increased honors courses, tutorials, and more small classes, to continued emphasis on the university's graduate programs and professional schools through improvement of faculty and facilities.

As Ken Cuthbertson later said, the PACE campaign "was clearly a watershed in Stanford's fund-raising history and put the university into high gear on the fund-raising front."[51] The campaign benefited significantly from the experiences of General Secretary David Jacobson and his fund-raising staff in generating funds for the Medical School. (In fact, the books were not quite closed on the $22.5 million Medical Campaign.)

Cuthbertson, backed by the advice of Kersting, Brown, and Company, organized a large campaign staff under his direction, with some regular staff taking on additional tasks, some new staff added, and a large and well-organized body of faculty and alumni volunteers.[52] The Ford grant was, in itself, an extremely important point in attracting donors, Cuthbertson recalled. Stanford's development staff and volunteers were "unused to asking for big gifts; it gave them confidence and opened doors." Cuthbertson also noted the value of careful planning. Stanford's focused development staff now "pushed" the volunteers rather than relying on a volunteer-driven program that "pulled" the staff. With more than five thousand volunteers plus an expanded and increasingly experienced development staff, in 1964 the PACE campaign topped out in less than the planned three years at $114 million.[53] One-third of the $100 million had been raised within the first nine months.[54]

Fred Terman had set as his primary task for 1959 and 1960 the establishment of Stanford's financial needs for faculty salaries, student scholarships, and improvements in the university's physical plant for research, teaching, and housing, not only in the sciences and engineering but in the humanities and social sciences. During PACE, he articulated these broader needs frequently to key PACE committees and in speeches to alumni and industry groups across the country. Funds brought in by the PACE campaign also were quickly put to work. By October 1962, Terman could approve funds for renovation of all classrooms in the Quadrangle's History Corner (used by the Departments of Economics, Sociology, and Political Science as well as the History Department). Student aid was increased that same year. Nearly 38 percent of Stanford freshmen were now on financial aid using university funds (compared to 31 percent at Harvard and 36 percent at Princeton).[55] In an interim report of January 1964 to the Ford Foundation, Sterling showed that Stanford's plans had called for an addition of 125 faculty members, and within two and a half years, the university had added 170. Faculty salary increases, originally planned for a cumulative 35 percent over five years and 75 percent after ten years, had already reached 27 percent after three years. Stanford faculty salaries now ranked just below the top five in the country. Fifteen new endowed chairs were sought; ten of these chairs had been filled.[56]

The PACE campaign was taxing for many.[57] President Sterling, much in demand by alumni, carried the heaviest load, while Terman was often dispatched for special meetings with potential corporate donors and wealthy individuals. On a December 1962 trip to New York City, Fred's task was to meet with International Nickel, Texaco, and National Lead Corporations and with wealthy investment banker Charles Allen Jr. On another New York trip four months later, Fred was scheduled to meet with executives at General Dynamics, Fairchild Camera, Reynolds Metals, and General Electric.[58] Terman made eighteen trips outside the Bay Area during the 1961–62 academic year and was gone from campus eighty-two days. On one ten-day trip, Fred worked for PACE in Wichita, Kansas City, St. Louis, Cincinnati, Chicago, and Pittsburgh, in addition to visiting Washington DC and Chicago on national science committee business for NASA and for President John F. Kennedy.[59]

Wallace Sterling's health soon showed the strain of his busy schedule. Ill with diverticulitis, he was hospitalized several times during the campaign years. In late summer 1962, Dr. Russel Lee "gated and grounded" him in hopes of helping him keep well.[60] Early in 1964, when Sterling became seriously ill with acute peritonitis, Terman served as acting president from February to September while Sterling recuperated.[61]

The PACE campaign's very success raised criticism among some alumni of the directions that Stanford seemed to be taking. Was it building the sciences at the expense of the humanities, facilities and faculty at the expense of undergraduate education? Mixed into this argument was current popular discussion of the effect of the infusion of federal money, both civilian and military, on the balance of university interests—whether, as University of California President Clark Kerr put it, "A university's control over its own destiny has been substantially reduced." The growth of the "Super University" (exemplified by Kerr's fast-growing University of California system of campuses) and a new emphasis on graduate education and research was seen by some as creating a new tension "between humanists and scientists," and coming at the expense of undergraduate education.[62] These same issues produced great unease among a number of prominent Stanford faculty who anxiously watched the progress of Stanford's two-mile-long linear accelerator project, "The Monster."[63]

The Purity and the Politics of Physics: SLAC and the Physics Department

Nestled into the Stanford foothills about a mile and a half southwest of the Quadrangle, the Stanford Linear Accelerator Center (SLAC) was opened in 1966 after nearly twelve years of planning and building.[64] SLAC was both the most expensive nondefense federal research project of its time (at $114 million for construction, with an additional $18 million in preconstruction research and development) and the most spectacular single project (a five-year construction project across some five hundred acres and employing several thousand people) at Stanford during the Sterling-Terman years.[65]

As a "national facility operated by Stanford University on behalf of the U.S. Department of Energy," SLAC was also perhaps the era's most controversial undertaking. Even more than the Medical School's relocation, the creation of SLAC raised important questions regarding the balance of federal funding and university research agendas and commitments. It also evoked delicate—and at times unsuccessful—negotiations among faculty members regarding access to research facilities, as well as to students about affiliation and status. SLAC exemplified growing concerns not only about the balance of the humanities and the sciences but also about the future of Big Science on college campuses.

What would eventually become SLAC grew out of the dreams of Stanford physicist William Hansen and his work on Stanford's first linear accelerators in the early years of the Microwave Laboratory. In March 1948, Hansen submitted a proposal to the Office of Naval Research for the development of a billion volt (BeV) linear electron accelerator with a length of 160 feet. Hansen's 12-foot-long Mark I accelerator had already produced a six MeV electron beam. Although Hansen died in the spring of 1949, his accelerator work was continued by klystron expert Edward Ginzton, professor of applied physics and electrical engineering and now director of the Microwave Lab, and Marvin Chodorow, a Sperry colleague who joined the Stanford faculty.

Stanford's Mark III accelerator, first operated in 1950, grew as funds were juggled between research and construction costs. By 1957, it had gone well beyond its originally planned 160 feet to 300 feet, hitting the laboratory wall. Physics professor Robert Hofstadter used the Mark III for his study of the structure of atomic nuclei, work that earned him the Nobel Prize for Physics in 1961, but as soon as the Mark III began to show its usefulness in his electron scattering studies, Hofstadter stimulated interest at Stanford in building an even longer electron accelerator. Ginzton wanted to push the technology further as well. In April 1953, he suggested development of a "*much* larger accelerator."[66] With the Mark III devoted to research, he successfully won AEC funding for a smaller Mark IV that would be used both as the test components for the next generation of electron linear accelerator, and used for initial studies of electron cancer therapy under Henry Kaplan.[67]

In October 1954, Ginzton, Hofstadter, and two other physics faculty members, high-energy physicist W. K. H. "Pief" Panofsky (director of Stanford's new High Energy Physics Laboratory) and department chair Leonard Schiff, made a formal proposal to President Sterling and the trustees: in order for Stanford to keep abreast of the latest progress in high-energy physics, they argued, it was necessary to construct a new large electron accelerator within the next five years. A preliminary study by Robert Hofstadter had recommended a 25 to 50 BeV machine, but the group now proposed a two-mile-long machine (guessing that that was the longest that could be accommodated by Stanford's terrain) adding that the AEC already had expressed interest in the construction of a very large linear accelerator. Stanford's track record in constructing and operating such machines was excellent. Equally appealing, they thought, was the availability of land on the Stanford campus.

The Stanford group worked through nonbinding discussions with the AEC in Washington DC in mid-October 1954, followed by further discussions at Stanford with Sterling and Terman in November.[68] Sterling's notes indicate that at this point the administration expected the project to take five to seven years to complete, with $25 million for design and construction and with an annual operating budget of $2 to $2.5 million. Since Stanford was expected to pay a portion of the cost, this was no inconsiderable undertaking at this point in Sterling's presidency.[69]

"With a bee in our bonnet and Mark IV under construction," Ginzton later remembered, "ideas for a much larger machine began to take more concrete form." The serious work began with a small project group from the Physics Department and the Hansen Laboratories, including Ginzton, Panofsky, Schiff, and Hofstadter. The project was named "Project M" for "Monster"—both a comment on its size and on its somewhat ungainly and unpredictable quality—at a meeting at Panofsky's house in April 1956 (although some people who were at that meeting still maintain that the "M" originally stood for "Multi-BeV" and that Monster was a later, cuter nickname).

Having determined that such a project was feasible, scientifically justified, and economically practical, the group determined its academic and administrative parameters. Its object was basic physics research, and would *not* be used for classified or military research. It would be administered separately from both the Physics Department and the Hansen Laboratories. Ginzton agreed to serve as the project's director, Panofsky as its assistant director, and Schiff and Hofstadter agreed to serve as consultants.[70] Meanwhile, Stanford civil engineers and geologists, along with consultants from Varian Associates, Bechtel, and Utah Construction, assisted with project and site studies, confirming that a two-mile machine would be the longest that could be accommodated on Stanford land. Its initial site, suggested by Ed Ginzton, ran roughly parallel to Foothill Road (present-day Junipero Serra Boulevard), beginning near the golf course, with the beam switch yard, the end stations, and beam dump near Page Mill Road. (The site was later moved back into the foothills along Sand Hill Road due to geological considerations.)

Many of the meetings of the group and their various consultants took place at Rossotti's beer parlor on Alpine Road. "There was a sense of excitement, of promise, and of personal pride in participating in a project of great importance," Ginzton wrote. "Good beer didn't hurt any."[71] At a dinner given years later by Lloyd Dinkelspiel for the president's staff, Fred Terman spoofed the Rossotti's connection by producing, much to everyone's surprise and delight, a large architectural drawing showing SLAC as an elaborate plan to bring beer down to the campus, with klystrons pumping beer along the way. Sterling enjoyed it so much, Fred Glover later recalled, that he asked Terman to bring it to the next board of trustees meeting.[72]

In April 1957, Stanford submitted a formal proposal to the U.S. Atomic Energy Commission, the National Science Foundation, and the Department of Defense. (By 1959, the AEC became the "cognizant" or sponsoring agency.[73]) Although no one knew for certain that the two-mile-long machine would work, scientific advisory panels acknowledged its scientific merit and desirability and supported the design and proposed location. Confidence in Project M was high. The major problem to be surmounted was its huge cost—each year getting closer to $100 million—but funding for science and engineering during the late 1950s and early 1960s seemed plentiful, and the project appeared to have American scientists on its side.

A few months after the proposal was sent off to Washington, Fred Terman dropped in to see newly arrived Bob Moulton, then hard at work on university financial forecasting. "Bob," Terman said, "because your schedule has more flexibility than most, I'd like you also to track the status of a proposal that Stanford has before the federal government to build and operate a two-mile-long linear electron accelerator on our campus." Moulton later recalled, "I had no idea what a linear electron accelerator was, but I didn't ask the provost that question. I am sure it was just as well."[74] "Tracking the status" of the project turned out to be an understatement. Moulton soon found himself Terman's man at the center of the storm.

Stanford's proposal first had to run the gauntlet of Washington politics. Although Terman was well known in federal science circles and Sterling known in similar academic foundation settings, Stanford was neither well connected within Washington DC political networks, nor experienced in belt-way politics. Moulton's several years at the Ford Foundation and a brief stint staffing a presidential bomb-shelter committee made him a comparative Washington insider. As Moulton found, Stanford's few contacts were Republicans (trustees President Tom Pike was an original backer of Richard Nixon) and the largely Democratic Congress viewed Stanford as a "Republican Country Club." President Eisenhower's endorsement of the Stanford project before a meeting of the American Association for the Advancement of Science in May 1957 appeared to confirm the project's

Republican credentials. Members of the Congressional Joint Committee on Atomic Energy, annoyed that they had not been informed of the public statement earlier, held the Stanford proposal political hostage.

Stanford's team in Washington (Ginzton, Panofsky, Moulton, Richard B. Neal, SLAC's technical director, and Frederick Pindar, its administrative director) was grilled by committee chair Senator Clinton P. Anderson of New Mexico. Anderson prodded for cracks in the Stanford dike: Why build tunnels in California instead of using already-existing railroad tunnels or mine shafts in other states? How could Ginzton serve as project director while also serving on the board of the company (Varian Associates) that might be the major supplier of klystrons to the project? What were the terms of lease or sale of Stanford land proposed for the project?

Soon after the hearings got started, Edward Ginzton made a painful decision. At the death of Russell Varian, he resigned as project director to become chairman and CEO of Varian Associates. President Sterling was dismayed and initially accused Ginzton of disloyalty, but Ginzton assured Sterling that he would be nearby in case of need (Ginzton remained on the faculty until 1968) and expressed his firm faith in Panofsky's management skills.[75] As Ginzton predicted, Panofsky not only was an accomplished scientist but also proved to be an inspiring leader. He became an influential member of the international high-energy physics community, a much-sought-after government advisor on questions of national science policy and arms control, and a highly respected participant in Stanford university affairs. Terman was especially proud of Panofsky's accomplishments and gave him, as he had given to Ed Ginzton, free rein over the mushrooming project.

The congressional committee was satisfied for the time being with Stanford's answers and authorized an initial $3 million architectural and engineering study. However, the question of Stanford land use and leasing policy arose again. Moulton, on the spot in front of the Joint Committee, had explained that while Stanford could not legally sell its land, it would merely lease the necessary acreage for $1 a year. However, Stanford's trustees, who were happy with progress on the shopping center, the Industrial Park, and other leasing ventures, expected income from government use of nearly five hundred acres of Stanford land. (The new accelerator site had, in fact, put an end to a residential development venture in that area.) The board balked at Moulton's $1 a year recommendation and insisted on a 5 percent annual return of the land's market value. Moulton was in a fix—he had assured the Joint Committee that no such reimbursement would be expected. "A number of trustees still had the impression," he later wrote, "that the government was imposing the accelerator on Stanford and that, therefore, the trustees could expect the university to be properly reimbursed for accommodating the government." Fred Terman stepped in. At a dramatic trustees' meeting, the provost stated bluntly "that it was time to decide whether Stanford was a research institution or a real estate operation." Terman saved his neck, and the project's future, Moulton remembers, for "everyone involved trusted Terman's assessment of SLAC's importance to Stanford."[76]

David Packard also stepped in when negotiation with the AEC bogged down over construction contracts. AEC head John McCone, a Southern California businessman little impressed by basic research, wanted the center built entirely by private companies rather than, as Ginzton and Panofsky insisted, by Stanford's already experienced accelerator crew.[77] The Stanford group compromised: private contractors could contract for the nonscientific elements (buildings, roads) but not for the accelerator itself. McCone, however, pushed hard. Would Stanford refuse to continue if the AEC insisted on private contracts for the whole venture? Calling his bluff, Packard (now president of the board of trustees) said, "Yes," standing by the Stanford compromise. McCone gave in.[78] Moulton and his colleagues quickly learned to work the human side of beltway politics. Hearing that a visiting Joint Committee staff member desperately wanted to meet Fred Terman, "author of the definitive text for radio engineers," Moulton recounts, Terman gladly obliged. (Moulton also arranged for one of the visiting wives to meet child star Shirley Temple Black, a resident of nearby Woodside.[79])

Brushfires and Sniping: Taking the SLAC out of Physics

In June 1963, Wallace Sterling could report to the trustees that SLAC was moving along well.[80] With a staff of more than six hundred, on schedule and within budget, SLAC was set for completion in 1966.[81] Stanford's expertise in governmental relations—local and federal—as in public relations and development, had grown rapidly during the early 1960s, but the problems that arose now with the emergence of SLAC highlighted questions raised during the PACE campaign. What would be the relationship between Stanford and the federal government regarding research agendas? And equally important, what was the relationship to be among Stanford's physicists—on campus, and at the emerging "National Facility" regarding faculty status and tenure, teaching roles, not to mention research arrangements? Just what did it mean to be a national facility operated by Stanford University?

Faculty involved in the original SLAC proposals had assumed that its leading scientists would direct physics PhD students. In 1960, while still director of the SLAC project, Ed Ginzton had agreed with a suggestion of Graduate Dean Al Bowker that "having an Institute of High-Energy Physics as a degree-granting agency of the University seems a good one."[82] But Ginzton also assumed that the Physics Department would be agreeable to joint appointments with SLAC, allowing faculty to share teaching and advising. Serious disagreements soon developed, however, between the Stanford physicists involved in the SLAC project (both original participants like Panofsky and new appointments, like theorist Sidney Drell, who looked forward to working on the project), and Physics Department individualists (Bloch and Walter Meyerhof, later Hofstadter, and eventually Schiff), who feared that the potentially large budget and personnel roster would distort the university's teaching and research commitment and, equally important, non-SLAC faculty influence in the department.[83]

Felix Bloch had been opposed to the giant accelerator project from its first discussion in the Physics Department in the summer of 1954.[84] Schiff wrote to Bloch several times in the fall of 1954 about Terman and Sterling's support for the project and of the favorable response of AEC, but Bloch was not impressed. He responded to both Schiff and Hofstadter that he was "strongly opposed to the idea of undertaking the project at Stanford." "To do physics on a large scale and yet in 'University Style' was impossible."[85] It was not that he did not appreciate the interactions offered by such lab work. Bloch had worked with Fred Terman at the Radio Research Lab, where he had learned radio techniques, receivers, antennas, and noise. Such war work, he said in a later interview, exposed physicists to other parts of science; part of the "sudden quick development of physics after the war was due to this phenomenon."[86] Bloch also had signed on with Ginzton, Hofstadter, Panofsky, and Schiff in the department's first formal step to initiate SLAC within the university in 1956, but soon after removed himself from any association with the project. Robert Hofstadter had been very active in the first planning stages of a very large accelerator, but his concerns grew when he realized that he would not be able to claim a major portion of beam time on the Project "M" machine as he had with the Mark III accelerator at the Microwave Lab. Hofstadter and Bloch took the lead in fighting off SLAC's influence on the department, although they were hardly alone in their distrust. As a result, the Physics Department, which had strongly supported the initial SLAC proposal, now not only refused to give faculty appointments to Stanford physicists resident at SLAC, but also lobbied to keep them from using Stanford's existing accelerator at the Hansen Labs.

In the summer of 1961, the Academic Council's Advisory Board adopted policies and procedures for appointment of key people in all of the university's research laboratories and institutes, including SLAC.[87] This was meant to clarify and yet impose more overall faculty control over research appointments that involved faculty status. In May 1962, however, the Physics Department adopted its own policy: there would be no joint appointments between SLAC and physics faculty, and no joint PhD degrees were to be granted. Whatever other departments in other parts of the university might do, physics made an ultimatum. Ignoring their own precedent of sixteen PhDs awarded to nondepartment members out of the department's one hundred one PhDs between 1955 and 1962, several influential physics faculty members effectively built the wall between the department and SLAC ever higher.

Graduate Dean Bowker thought their behavior outrageous, selfish, and foolish. Bloch and Hofstadter, he later remembered, "came in and argued that it was immoral and irrational and so forth to let them [SLAC] use the existing accelerator; that it was against values and principle. . . . There was a terrible fight, and they threatened to resign if we forced the issue. Fred (Terman) and I wanted to call their bluff; but Wally overruled us, maybe correctly."[88] But the bitter dispute soon took its own course. The year before, Panofsky had worried that Sid Drell would leave Stanford if Hofstadter's antagonism to the project did not change.[89] Instead, Panofsky and Drell tendered their own resignations from the Physics Department in May 1962, to become professors at SLAC.[90] That same month, the Physics Department had passed a resolution that "there should be no joint appointments between SLAC and the Physics Department," and also that "the staffing of SLAC should not involve the Physics Department either in whole or by powers delegated to a committee." Graduate Dean Albert Bowker wrote at the time that "No problem at Stanford has been as difficult for me and other University authorities as taking on the linear accelerator project. I have had many sleepless nights on this matter."[91] The following December, the physics faculty (in a close vote of seven in favor, four against, and four absent or abstaining) established an even more restrictive policy. The four absent or abstaining votes were faculty in applied physics sympathetic to SLAC but who had tried to avoid taking sides. Even so, the department was now badly split.[92]

Despite attempts by the president to heal the breach, relations between SLAC and the Physics Department remained sour. Proudly independent, SLAC was no longer simply an extended interest of Stanford's Physics Department, but an organization of some five hundred physicists, engineers, and technicians with a national outlook. (As Panofsky was reported to put it, referring to Bloch, experimental physics was no longer merely the setting up of a few magnets in the basement of the Physics Building.[93]) SLAC's physicists also had the confidence of the university's administration. By 1963, nearly all of the university's administrators who worked with SLAC (from Terman and graduate deans Bowker and Whitaker, to the associate provost for research Hubert Heffner (and son of speech and drama professor Hubert C. Heffner) and Robert Moulton, who had been reassigned as SLAC's associate director of administrative services) aligned themselves with Panofsky and his associate director Sid Drell.

Physics Department partisans, by contrast, drew support from among campus faculty who feared that the prerogatives of academic departments were threatened and who argued for limiting the scope of extradepartmental, government-sponsored research institutes like SLAC.[94] With their eyes on Stanford's engineering departments and laboratories, some blamed Fred Terman. Even though Panofsky made himself unpopular in some government circles as he firmly refused to allow classified research at SLAC, other faculty continued to express their concern that the government would unduly affect academic research agendas.

Most of Stanford's departments, in fact, looked forward to growing and improving with the help of outside funding, but control remained a primary point of honor. Felix Bloch, for example, had refused on principal to "salary split," even though salary splitting could be used to support a significant part of a faculty member's salary with outside research accounts and reallocate general funds elsewhere in the department or university. Interestingly, Bloch was among those who, for several years, billed the air force or navy for one-third of their annual salaries. When his actual research time rose well above one-third, however, he refused to raise the rate of reimbursement. It was unethical, he said, to build salary schedules on "soft" money. Not all saw it that way, particularly in the business office. Stanford was inequitably supporting faculty research programs in Physics, believed Business Manager Alf Brandin, while other departments tried to pay their way. From Brandin's viewpoint, the reliance of physics faculty on general funds deprived those other departments that, unlike physics, had little chance of obtaining large amounts of research support. (Brandin calculated that one of Bloch's ONR contract renewals had, in fact, cost Stanford $24,990 per year.) Also, in effect Bloch carried a lighter teaching load than, for example, professors in the language departments, Brandin concluded, yet Stanford was not reimbursed for its generous research time allowances to physics. Nevertheless, the frustrated Brandin was forced to admit, Stanford continued to make an exception for years for physics "in deference to certain personalities and threats of resignation from that department."[95]

The department had not bowed out of high-energy physics altogether—work continued on at Hansen Labs—but physics faculty watched anxiously as their field changed dramatically in a number of directions and not simply because of the "monster" in the foothills. The fields of solid-state and plasma physics, as well as materials sciences and electronics, were opening up rapidly and suggested various courses for joint work. Very good people were engaged in these fields elsewhere on campus, but Stanford's Physics Department was leery of engaging further in any of these areas.[96]

Ever the conciliator, Sterling had decided to treat the Physics-SLAC breach as a series of brushfires. As a result, bad relations between the department and SLAC smoldered throughout Terman's last five years as provost (though nearly flaming up in 1961, 1963, and 1965). Influential Physics Department faculty continued to express their concern that a huge laboratory might overwhelm a university department. Even before SLAC was dedicated, they limited the number of graduate students who would be allowed to do PhD dissertations in physics using SLAC's faculty and facilities. Meanwhile, just as SLAC's directors hoped to attract top talent to the facility, it became increasingly clear that few of SLAC's physicists, regardless of the value of their academic experience or quality of their research, could expect to become tenured or adjunct members of the Physics Department.

Faculty recruiting was the substance of yet another serious skirmish, this time on unexpected ground. In January 1964, George Forsythe, head of the Computer Science Division, asked Terman to establish a search committee for a joint SLAC/Computer Science position. SLAC would soon be the heaviest user of university computer time for complex data analysis and required excellent computer staff and facilities for data gathering, data storage and retrieval, and pattern recognition.[97] The search committee's choice was physicist William F. Miller, who had previously managed Argonne National Laboratory's high-energy physics computation center. One advisor described Miller as "a terrific administrator who really understands scientific computing problems. Has built Argonne's applied mathematics and computing from chaos to prominence in a few years." Forsythe argued that SLAC would eventually have greater computing needs than even they could imagine and thought Miller was the best choice for Stanford. As part of the deal to bring Miller to Stanford, Terman arranged to appoint Miller to the faculty of the Computer Science Division of the Mathematics Department.[98] Forsythe (in the process of negotiating the division into departmental status) and his CS colleagues welcomed the idea.[99] Miller would be one of four tenured professors in the department-to-be (the others were Forsythe, John G. Herriot, and John McCarthy) along with junior faculty that included Edward A. Feigenbaum, Gene H. Golub, and Niklaus E. Wirth. His teaching could cover large-scale data processing and pattern recognition. Joint appointments in computer sciences were the norm in major universities, Forsythe argued, and all save Miller would split their time between Computer Science and the Computation Center; Miller, of course, would split his with SLAC.[100]

Miller's appointment was approved by the dean's office and sent on to Terman.[101] Unpredictably, it got caught up in the Physics Department's arguments about joint appointments with SLAC, even though it did not involve a Physics Department appointment. Although Miller had been judged not only as the best candidate for SLAC's proposed computing facilities, but also by his peers as the most desirable candidate to serve as a tenured professor in computer science, several faculty—not in the computer science program or field—complained to the president about the offer of a tenured position. Miller's PhD was not in computer science, but in nuclear physics (as Forsythe had already pointed out, virtually no one had a PhD in computer science but came to the field from mathematics, physics, or engineering), and critics saw it as the crack in the dam. SLAC had been granted a certain limited number of joint positions, Leonard Schiff complained, *regardless* of departmental affiliation; by hiring Miller, SLAC was expanding unfairly.[102] Terman approved the appointment, but it was one of the few battles the

Physics Department lost, and it would not be soon forgotten.[103] Physics put the lid down on SLAC tightly—severely limiting their teaching of physics courses and advising of graduate students.[104]

When the "tension" between SLAC and the Physics Department was described in a 1964 article in *Science* magazine, however, Sterling finally became peeved.[105] He had learned elsewhere that physics faculty had been extensively lobbying with faculty outside the department, he wrote Terman in the spring of 1964, and he was angry at the overt bias shown by physicist Walter Meyerhof against some pro-SLAC graduate students. The inequity and lobbying, he warned Schiff, must stop.[106]

Leonard Schiff tried to keep some balance within the department, for personal as well as professional reasons. (Schiff's wife, Frances, was the cousin of Ginzton's wife, Artemas; it had been Ginzton who had persuaded Schiff to leave Pennsylvania for Stanford.) Letters of complaint, however, continued to fly across Terman's desk, some aimed higher at Stanford's ever-approachable president. In 1965, Terman's last year as provost, the conflict flared up again. SLAC was now clearly at a disadvantage in its attempts to hire staff because rival high-energy physics institutions could tell highly desirable candidates (as then graduate dean Al Bowker had been told by SLAC senior personnel), competitor academic institutions were recruiting against SLAC by telling candidates "don't become a second class citizen at SLAC."[107] Associate Provost Hubert Heffner wrote to Sterling about his concern that even though Matthew Sands, SLAC's deputy director, was a coauthor of the most exciting and most widely employed new text for undergraduate physics, the Physics Department would not allow him to teach.[108] Sands had rejected an offer to be head of physics at the University of Minnesota, Heffner said, because Sterling had promised him the SLAC-Physics controversy would be over by Christmas 1964. If Sands left, SLAC's remaining faculty might resign in a group, thus placing the future of the SLAC program in danger.[109]

Sterling asked the new graduate dean Virgil Whitaker that summer to ride herd on the Physics-SLAC situation.[110] Panofsky, Whitaker reported back, was working under enormous tension getting SLAC up and running, but the Physics Department showed no glimmer of understanding, much less sympathy, for the tough spot in which they put him.[111] The controversy was eventually resolved, but bitter traces remained for years.

In the fall of 1966, a year after Terman's retirement, the SLAC-Physics fire seemed to have gone down for good. Sterling gathered together the many documents, protests, resignations, threats, lobbying letters, and proclamations, and gave them to his secretary, Jessie Applegarth, with a note: "9/66. Jessie—I guess this can go to files now. May it R.I.P.—WS." Applegarth, too wise to the history of the entire affair, passed the bundle to an assistant secretary with her own note: "Jane—Watch this carefully—It may not R.I.P.—Jessie."[112]

Building Biology and Chemistry

Stepping from engineering in 1955 to provostial responsibilities across the university's academic program, Terman viewed the School of Humanities and Sciences as an amorphous operation, lacking coherence, discipline, and guidance. Lest he be accused of taking an engineer's yardstick to another school, Terman knew, as a longtime member of the Stanford faculty with personal as well as professional ties to a number of other nonengineering departments, that the school had emerged from decades of vague relationships and periodic regroupings. Since Stanford's founding, the twenty-three departments now included in the school had a strong history of autonomy and marginal cooperation, rather than any singularly strong and centralized tradition typical of Stanford's "professional" schools—education, law, engineering, and medicine. Autonomy continued apace as "school" boundaries shifted at least three times between the 1920s and the late 1940s.

A number of schools had been created by President Wilbur in the 1920s—biological sciences (1922), social sciences (1924), physical sciences (1925), and letters (1926)—but with the possible exception of the biological sciences, they never seemed to fulfill the promise of more efficient planning and operation, or simplified curriculum and degree-granting arrangements. As Sterling had hoped, Terman felt that he should mold the ill-defined position of provost to better fit the university's overall needs. Terman therefore attended to the School of Humanities and Sciences with the same energy and ambition as he had as dean of engineering. His crucial task, he felt, was, first, to pick and to promote the very best faculty, and secondly, to improve departmental teaching and research facilities. He had already set new patterns for fields closely related to engineering, in statistics and mathematics, computer science and physics. Given his own expertise and interests, Terman retained direct responsibility for the natural sciences and mathematics while his associate provost, Bob Wert, oversaw the humanities, social sciences, fine arts, and undergraduate general studies.[113]

Terman believed that as provost he must dispassionately assess the university's various strengths and weaknesses. This was precisely what President Sterling expected. Wally not only admired "Fred's great capacity for getting work done," remembered presidential assistant Fred Glover, but also he counted on the fact that "Fred didn't give a damn what people thought about him or whether he stepped on toes. Wally was perfectly willing to accept that in Fred, because Wally could come in afterwards and clean up the messes with his wonderful personality."[114]

Terman understood that not all Stanford faculty wished to see their departments cold-heartedly assessed or "improved," particularly by those outside their field. Others, he felt, had become accustomed by slim budgets and other obstacles to setting their sights too low, both in terms of faculty choice and student recruitment. Thus, among his first actions, he sought to access faculty quality and to institute independent, thorough reviews of all faculty applicants and promotions. (Initially, he did this himself for all departments, until he developed a provostial staff entrusted with such assessments.)

Within the School of Humanities and Sciences, Terman purposefully sought to make a disproportionate number of appointments of eminent people at high rank. These were not to be persons taking "early retirement" elsewhere to live out their sunset years at Stanford, but rather vigorous individuals with the promise of making significant contributions to their fields and of bringing major changes to their departments.[115] Two science departments—biology and chemistry—were quickly targeted for such redevelopment.

The changes brought about in biology and chemistry in the late 1950s and early 1960s are stories complicated by the departments' long traditions at Stanford, by their ongoing ties with colleagues in the sciences, engineering, and the Medical School, and, in the case of biology, by historic affiliations with natural history museum collections and a marine station. Both were long-established departments at Stanford in the mid-1950s, but their fields were rapidly diversifying in the postwar years.

The Transformation of Biology at Stanford

Stanford's pioneer years included a strong faculty in the biological sciences, starting at the top with university president, David Starr Jordan, a respected naturalist and ichthyologist, to faculty colleagues in zoology, botany, and physiology. In 1892, less than a year after the university's opening, Jordan commissioned two young faculty members in the new biology department to establish a marine laboratory on the Pacific Coast (later renamed the Hopkins Marine Station). Five years later, Stanford's first PhD was completed, based on biological research at Jasper Ridge in the Stanford foothills. Over the next five decades, Stanford would remain focused largely on systematic biology and physiology, while faculty research tended toward pragmatic contributions to important Western industries: the fisheries, the forests, and the fields (especially canning and fruit growing).

The arrangement of "biological sciences" at Stanford remained fluid. The School of Biology had been organized from some seven departments in 1922–23 (and renamed the School of Biological Sciences in 1929). Over the next twenty years, the school was variously composed of Applied Botany, Entomology, Botany, Zoology, Physiology, Bacteriology, Anatomy, Experimental Pathology, Biochemistry, Paleontology, Experimental Psychology, the Natural History Museum, the Hopkins Marine Station, and the Food Research Institute. The school blossomed under Dean Charles V. Taylor. The annual number of graduate students increased from eighty-five to two hundred fifty between 1920 and 1928. With the help of a

Rockefeller Foundation grant, a major addition was made to the facilities at Hopkins Marine Station. In 1929, the Carnegie Institution of Washington completed its Experimental Taxonomy and Genetics Lab on campus.

As elsewhere on campus, the Depression put academic plans on hold. In the 1930s, the Departments of Botany and Zoology discontinued, and the Departments of Anatomy, Bacteriology, and Physiology were moved up to San Francisco to the Stanford Medical School. An important link was made with the medical school at this time, however, with cooperation in undergraduate teaching and faculty research. Finally, in 1948, the School of Biological Sciences was demoted to the status of a single department and fused together with faculty of the humanities, social sciences, and physical sciences into the university's largest school, Humanities and Sciences.[116] The Biology Department was portioned into three sections for instructional purposes: General, Botany, and Zoology, although some faculty taught in more than one section. Modern genetics, cell biology, and biochemistry were listed under "General" biology.[117] For administrative purposes, the department was divided into three divisions: the "General" Biology Division, housed in Jordan Hall in the outer quadrangle; the Natural History Museum, housed a short walk from the Quad in the old museum building; and the Hopkins Marine Station, located on Monterey Bay, some ninety miles southwest of campus.

Over the next decade, biology as a field would begin to change markedly. "The biologist of today might even go unrecognized by his colleagues of fifty years ago," department head Clifford Grobstein commented to the board of trustees in 1963. Grobstein reported, "There is a 'ferment' in biology which has changed the subject rapidly and radically. . . . The glamour of physiology has passed to biochemistry, genetics and bioengineering. . . . Some biologists at work in their laboratories nowadays are hard to distinguish from mathematicians or physicists, others from chemists or psychologists." By 1963, the department (with advice from a national Commission for Undergraduate Education in the Biological Sciences) had restructured its undergraduate teaching in line with modern approaches focused on the biology of the cell.[118]

By the time Terman took over as provost, the Biology Department could point to a distinguished past, while it remained one of Stanford's strongest departments in the School of Humanities and Sciences. Work by George Beadle, at Stanford from 1937 to 1947, and Ed Tatum, on the faculty 1937–45 and 1948–57, in the basement of Jordan Hall would earn them the Nobel Prize in 1958, but Beadle had left for Caltech (later he became president of the University of Chicago). It was Tatum's departure for the Rockefeller Institute in 1956 that set in motion Provost Terman's process of evaluation and faculty recruiting. Between 1956 and 1965, Terman made the best of several opportunities to build the biological sciences at Stanford, both in the School of Humanities and Sciences and in the Medical School, particularly in cell and developmental biology, genetics, biochemistry, and ecology. Terman's preference for new fields of research (particularly those that brought substantial federal grant money) over older, more traditional areas was not always roundly applauded, but the provost was determined to raise the department from one of the top twenty to one of the very best.

When he became provost in the fall of 1955, Terman set out to learn about the various departments outside the Engineering School. In early December, he visited the Biology Department in Jordan Hall. He was given a tour around the labs, met with the faculty, and discussed with both students and faculty the department's three divisions. His questions were careful and respectful, geneticist David Perkins later observed. That night, Terman compiled his notes into seven pages of well-written prose, documenting his thoughts on the students and faculty, their problems and needs, their research grants, faculty visitors, their specimen collections and facilities. He concluded that the Biology Department seemed to be getting on pretty well. Morale seemed good. He agreed that the department needed more space for labs, offices, and classrooms. The department, however, needed to build the number of more promising graduate students, but Terman felt that this problem could be solved partly by finding more money for graduate student assistantships.[119] A 1958 assessment by the Dean's Office concurred, pointing out that graduate student enrollments had dropped by two-thirds since 1950.[120]

Stanford had been afraid of losing biologist Edward Tatum for several years. Tatum and Beadle were known to be leading candidates for a Nobel Prize. Victor Twitty, head of the Biology Department, informed President Sterling in January 1956 that Tatum had been offered the directorship of the Microbiological Institute at Rutgers University. In an attempt to keep Tatum at Stanford, Sterling (with Terman's cooperation) proposed the creation of a new Department of Biochemistry with Tatum as its executive head.[121] Reorganization of teaching and research into a separate Department of Biochemistry would, of course, ruffle some feathers on campus, but the idea was received warmly by J. Murray Luck, biochemist in the Department of Chemistry. Tatum was delighted with Sterling's offer, but wanted the new department located in the Medical School, a suggestion enthusiastically endorsed by Medical Dean Windsor Cutting as well as Sterling, Twitty, and Graduate Dean and plant biologist William Steere. Tatum nonetheless left Stanford a year later for the Rockefeller Institute.[122]

Over the course of two years, Terman confidentially discussed the talents and characteristics of each biology faculty member with Steere, with biologist and former Stanford provost Douglas Whitaker, and with Ed Tatum, the department's lost star.[123] Meanwhile, Twitty provided Terman with the Biology Department's wish list to replace Tatum.[124] Their short list included Clifford Grobstein of the National Institutes of Health, Clement L. Markert of Michigan, and Joshua Lederberg of Wisconsin. The search committee invited both Grobstein and Lederberg to visit. Twitty reported to Dean Rhinelander that it appeared that both Grobstein and Lederberg might accept a position. (Steere, however, warned Twitty not to act on his own without clearing invitations or offers with the administration. Stanford was moving toward a more formal search technique, using ad hoc committees to assist in choosing top senior candidates.[125]) The search was further complicated by Stanford's intent to create a new Biochemistry Department, on hold with Tatum's departure. As it turned out, possibilities opened up first in biochemistry and genetics, which would in turn bring new faces to biology.

Terman wanted Arthur Kornberg, eminent biochemist at Washington University Medical School in St. Louis, for what he assumed would be Stanford's new Medical School Biochemistry Department, and he set off to get him. Terman, Goldstein, and Kaplan played major roles in persuading Kornberg to consider Stanford. They offered him biochemistry (instead of microbiology, as he had been directing in St. Louis) and the chance to help select a new head of Stanford's Chemistry Department. They held out the possibility of adding a "first-class" biophysicist and a new joint appointment in biology/biochemistry. They pointed out that coming to Stanford would get him away from St. Louis weather and that he would not be saddled with those already teaching biochemistry at Stanford. Dean Alway tendered Stanford's official invitation to Kornberg in June 1957, and three weeks later Kornberg sent his acceptance to Terman and Alway.[126]

In late summer 1957, San Francisco newspapers announced that Arthur Kornberg had decided to come to Stanford University, a major coup for Stanford's new Medical Center, then under construction on campus.[127] Kornberg was internationally known, and his laboratory was doing very exciting work. Soon after his decision, a colleague wrote to Kornberg to say, "The professional facilities and surroundings which are being developed there completes what seems to be a practically ideal picture."[128]

Kornberg quickly got into the swing of things. In fall 1958, months before arriving on campus, he wrote to Barry Wood Jr. at Johns Hopkins that Stanford's Medical School was looking for department heads for medicine, pediatrics, surgery, and psychiatry, and he noted curricular changes to integrate university and medical school training. There was momentum at Stanford, he commented, to create a fine medical school.[129] That same year, Kornberg requested $148,000 from NSF to equip his microbiology unit, which he proposed to move on July 1, 1959, from Washington University to a new building under construction at Stanford. (He would arrive at Stanford himself in June.) In building the new department, Kornberg brought with him Melvin Cohn and Paul Berg (who would win the 1980 Nobel Prize for Chemistry), along with three assistant professors (two more biochemists to be appointed later).[130] Stanford University would contribute about $200,000 toward laboratory equipment, but Kornberg brought in additional funds: $139,000 from NIH, $85,000 from NSF, and $60,000 from the Public Health Service for equipment.[131] Terman also found housing for Kornberg's new assistant professors. Terman, Alway advised Kornberg, was "a very useful man."[132]

Kornberg was delighted with his reception at Stanford and especially excited about prospects for research. As he wrote to Henry Kaplan a few months before he took up residence at Stanford, "We have had an avalanche of excellent applications for graduate and post-doctoral work."[133]

Kornberg's arrival overwhelmed the small and long-suffering campus biochemistry faculty, made up of Hubert Scott Loring (who worked on chemistry and metabolism of nucleic acids), J. Murray Luck (protein chemistry), Laurence O. Pilgeram, and Emeritus Professor Robert E. Swain.[134] Loring had been at Stanford since 1939, Luck since 1926, young Pilgeram had just arrived in 1955. Their future was in something of a muddle, caught between the Chemistry Department and the Medical School. Key Medical School faculty (Henry Kaplan, Avram Goldstein, and incoming Dean Robert Alway) had already assured Terman that Luck, Loring, and Pilgeram would not be included in the new Med School Biochemistry Department unless Kornberg asked for them. As it turned out, he did not want them, nor did chemistry chair Eric Hutchinson.[135] When Dean Alway asked who was going to teach biochemistry to the undergraduates and non-medical school graduate students, Kornberg answered simply, "We will."[136] Pilgerim left in 1957, and Loring and Luck fully joined the Chemistry Department (Loring became emeritus in 1974, Luck in 1965).

Fred Terman and Dean Alway brought Kornberg on board to assist in strengthening various science departments, particularly chemistry.[137] Kornberg wrote letters, served on committees, gave speeches, and worked scientific meeting hallways to build Stanford. He was discouraged to find that graduate students had not much knowledge of Stanford, he wrote after a visit to Harvard. "We need to immediately start a program to correct this."[138] Seeking to boost minority enrollments, Admissions Dean Rixford Snyder asked Kornberg to find faculty volunteers to write to prospective black students. (Since Terman took over as provost, Snyder explained, the Admissions Office had been trying to increase the number of black students applying to and enrolling at Stanford.) Kornberg reported that all seven of his biochemistry faculty members were *eager* to help with student recruitment.[139]

Once Joshua Lederberg learned that Kornberg was going to Stanford, he rethought his position. (He had initially resisted the Biology Department's efforts to bring him to Stanford.[140]) Lederberg knew Stanford well, and his wife, Esther Lederberg, had received her MS in biology at Stanford. Henry Kaplan and Kornberg joined in recruiting him, and in July 1958, Alway proposed that Lederberg take the position of professor and executive head of the Medical School's new Department of Genetics.[141] An "emergency" committee of the trustees, polled by

Sterling, approved Lederberg's joint appointment as professor of biology in the School of Humanities and Sciences, and head of the Department of Genetics, to take effect January 1, 1959.[142] Esther Lederberg also accepted a research appointment in genetics. Three months after deciding on Stanford, Lederberg learned that he was to share the 1958 Nobel Prize in Physiology/Medicine with George Beadle and Ed Tatum. (Three months after his arrival in 1959, Kornberg similarly learned he was to share the Nobel Prize in Physiology/Medicine for his work in synthesizing DNA.[143])

Terman had been a strong supporter of inviting Clifford Grobstein to fill the vacancy left in biology by Ed Tatum in 1956.[144] When Joshua and Esther Lederberg originally had decided to stay at Wisconsin, and Grobstein seemed unavailable, Twitty approached Charles Yanofsky, a Yale PhD in molecular biology then teaching bacterial genetics at the Western Reserve Medical School, to be a candidate for an assistant professorship in microbiology.[145] Yanofsky later recalled that he was not very impressed with Stanford's facilities, but found the grand promises made by Sterling, Terman, and Dean Rhinelander to be sincere. Terman approved increasing the salary offer to Yanofsky to persuade him to accept, and the department's most noted bacteriologist, Cornelis van Niel, became the department's "point man" to woo him. Returning to Cleveland from his California visit in the midst of a horrible winter, Yanofsky learned that Arthur Kornberg and his entire staff, including Paul Berg, were moving to Stanford's new Medical School Department on the campus. Yanofsky was convinced and accepted the position in June 1957. (He and his family arrived in fall 1958.[146])

Only a day before Yanofsky accepted, Stanford learned that developmental biologist Clifford Grobstein would also entertain an offer from the Biology Department. Grobstein was a potential successor to Twitty as department head, but he was being offered jobs elsewhere, including Berkeley. Nevertheless, he agreed to come out for a visit early in 1957.[147] By this time, Lederberg and Grobstein both knew that their friend and colleague Arthur Kornberg was seriously considering a move to Stanford. Terman, Twitty, Rhinelander, and Sterling set about to persuade Grobstein to join the Stanford faculty, and by June, Grobstein too had accepted Stanford's offer.[148]

Twitty thought of Clifford Grobstein (who became Twitty's associate executive head of the department) as his logical successor. When the time came, the department's faculty committee agreed. But when Twitty reported to the dean's office that the department's faculty unanimously recommended Grobstein for the position, Terman agreed but felt compelled to remind Twitty as an aside that at Stanford, department heads were chosen by the President's Office, not by the faculty.[149]

Twitty would have other disagreements with the administration about department affairs. In 1961, he complained about salary imbalances within the Biology Department, whereby a second-year assistant professor was given a salary higher than that of several others senior to him in rank and years of service.[150] That assistant professor, neurophysiologist Donald Kennedy, a promising researcher who had performed exceptionally well as a teacher in the General Studies Program, was also in considerable demand. Kennedy was promoted to associate professor, although without a large salary increase. A year later, Caltech hinted to President Sterling that they were going to try to steal Kennedy. Terman felt that Kennedy was too valuable to lose and asked Dean Robert Sears to act "promptly and generously."[151] (Kennedy later became provost and then Stanford's eighth president.)

Natural History and Systematics

Biology at Stanford had long been identified with taxonomy and related descriptive disciplines.[152] Terman would later be criticized in some biology circles for his "heartless" treatment of systematic biologists and his neglect of the Natural History Museum. It is true that he took a dim view of the potential research value of some of the older faculty who followed in the steps of Stanford's noted naturalists David Starr Jordan, William Dudley, and Leroy Abrams. Responding to a complaint of one such faculty member, the temperamental George Myers, Terman wrote Fred Glover in the President's Office: "Myers is a hard-working but not particularly bright biologist in the Jordan tradition who specializes in fish. . . . Systematics is the present-day version of the old naturalist type of biology of Jordan, Campbell, Peirce, etc., and I know that the people in this field at Stanford (and also elsewhere) are on the defensive and feel underprivileged and underrecognized."[153] Terman had little patience with whining, but he also recognized that faculty changes in systematics and at the Natural History Museum offered opportunities for the department to excel in new fields of growing interest: ecology, ethnobotany, and population studies.

Faculty changes in the mid-1950s offered several opportunities to plan for the development of general biology and systematics. Along with Tatum's leaving, entomologist Gordon R. Ferris, at Stanford since 1916, was set to retire in 1956 (his wife, botanist Roxanna Ferris, considered a "mainstay" of the herbarium collections, would retire in 1963). The department's short list of candidates consisted of Charles D. Michener of Kansas and Charles L. Remington of Yale at a more senior rank, and E. O. Wilson of Harvard and Paul R. Ehrlich of Kansas (he had recently completed a postdoc at Chicago) at the junior level.[154] The department leaned toward Wilson, who appeared to have great teaching and research promise.[155] With the full support of Terman, Rhinelander, and Sterling, Twitty invited Wilson to Stanford in early March 1958. Wilson, an untenured assistant professor in the second year of a five-year contract at Harvard, was very impressed when Provost Fred Terman of Stanford brought President Wallace Sterling into his office at the Harvard Museum to convince him to accept Stanford's offer of promotion, assistance in buying a house, and tenure.[156] Harvard responded, however, with the unthinkable for Harvard; within the amazingly short period of a few weeks, Wilson was boosted in rank and salary to keep him in Cambridge.[157]

The Stanford team quickly moved on to recruit Charles Michener. Michener preferred to stay at Kansas, but highly recommended his colleague, entomologist and population biologist Paul Ehrlich.[158] Ehrlich visited in January 1959, was hooked, and soon after began his long and illustrious career at Stanford.[159] Ehrlich and others, including Peter H. Raven, were to build Stanford's Ecology and Population Biology Division up to top rank nationally among graduate programs. To date Ehrlich has published more than a dozen books on ecology, population, resources, and the environment, including the worldwide best-seller *The Population Bomb* (1968).[160]

In 1959, Ira Wiggins, a highly respected expert on Pacific Slope botany, was made scientific director of the Belvedere Scientific Fund, essentially allowing him to serve as a specially funded full-time research professor at Stanford, freeing up university funds for the department to create a new faculty position. Stanford hired the outstanding young botanist Peter Raven.[161] Shortly after coming to Stanford in 1962, Raven conducted innovative ethnobotanical research in Chiapas, Mexico, and later became an internationally known leader in the conservation movement to protect the tropics. Also added in those years was the promising young plant physiologist, Winslow B. Briggs, who while a member of the Biology Department went on to become director of the Carnegie Institution of Washington's Department of Plant Biology, located on the Stanford campus.

Ehrlich and Raven may have quipped that they told Terman that they were coming to Stanford to do *modern* systematics and ecology, as one of their students remembers, but they worked well with colleague Richard Holm, curator of the Dudley Herbarium collections and, following Wiggins, director of the Natural History Museum from 1961 to 1971.[162] Holm coauthored with Ehrlich a book and numerous articles on population biology. Ehrlich, Raven, and Holm inspired students and the public alike with new conceptions of ecology and conservation biology. Although Raven left Stanford in 1971, Stanford's Division of Systematic and Ecological Biology under Ehrlich's leadership was judged to be the outstanding graduate program in its field in the country by the 1990s.[163]

As early as 1960, Victor Twitty had considered some sort of outside review committees to evaluate the Natural History Museum and the Hopkins Marine Station program. Terman gladly offered to pay more than half of the costs from the president's discretionary fund and wrote personally to the individuals on Twitty's list of well-known biologists to ask them to perform the evaluation.[164] A primary reason for the outside visit was that the museum's director, Ira Wiggins, was resigning from administration and teaching as of fall 1961, to devote himself to full-time research with outside funds. Similarly, senior faculty at the Hopkins Marine Station would be retiring as would department head Twitty, and the long-range direction of the Biology Department in general needed to be discussed.

Nothing came of the effort, however, before Twitty stepped down as department head. In late 1962, Terman, Humanities and Sciences Associate Dean Halsey Royden, Graduate Dean Al Bowker, and Twitty again discussed the needs and opportunities of the Biology Department, with special concern for the Natural History Museum, the Hopkins Marine Station, and the Division of Systematics, as well as connections with molecular biology in the Medical School and the Physics Department.

Museum Director Ira Wiggins got along well with Fred Terman. Wiggins had a distinguished record of research. Backed by a wide array of private and public funding, he had conducted field research from South America to Alaska (where he had served as scientific director of the Navy's Arctic Research Laboratory at Point Barrow). His arrangement with the Belvedere Scientific Fund (supported by Bechtel family money) was precisely the sort of entrepreneurial approach Terman appreciated. Richard Holm, Wiggin's successor in 1961 as director of the museum, was similarly respected. Terman took seriously Holm's 1956 suggestion about extending the Jasper Ridge area.[165] (Ehrlich would put Jasper Ridge to especially good use in his population studies.)

Despite this, Terman gave the Natural History Museum little support and viewed it as something of an albatross to a modern biology department that he envisioned. The Natural History Museum, containing more than 650,000 specimens in 1965, had grown from the large personal collections of plants, fish, and insects brought back from hundreds of field trips by faculty members over more than sixty years. Botanist William Russell Dudley, one of the more esteemed members of Stanford's pioneer faculty, gave his large collection of botanical books and specimens to the university in 1911. The "Dudley Herbarium," added to President David Starr Jordan's extensive collection of fish specimens, was the backbone of the Natural History Museum. Having long since outgrown rooms in Jordan Hall, the museum was housed in a rickety part of the Stanford Museum (what one administration insider, Registrar J. Pearce Mitchell, dubbed an inadequate but safe arrangement in 1941). For years, a number of faculty hoped to see the museum housed in a new building planned for Biology, since efforts at raising funds for separate facilities failed, but competition for space and resources, among other internal faculty differences of opinion and personality, placed the museum at a disadvantage.

Aside from Terman's view, faculty within the Biology Department, especially among the younger faculty and those working in molecular biology and biochemistry, gave the Natural History Museum only lukewarm support. Lawrence Blinks and Rolf Bolin of Hopkins Marine Station, in responses to President Sterling's office, noted confidentially that a case could be made for centralizing the museum collections of both Stanford and Berkeley with those of the California Academy of Science in San Francisco. While the botanical and fish collections were extraordinary, collections in areas closer to their own fields such as herpetology, microentomology, and invertebrata were, in their view, "unimportant."[166]

In 1976, the Herbarium and Jordan collections were moved to a new, state-of-the-art facility on long-term loan at the California Academy of Sciences in San Francisco.[167] Although the move took place eleven years after Terman retired as provost, a few systematic biologists still blame him for giving away, as a sort of parting shot at the naturalists, a Stanford treasure and important research resource and threatening the very future of systematics at Stanford.[168] What is more significant, however, is that the bitter feelings that arose over the Natural History Museum had their roots in fundamental changes underway in the sciences. In biology, as in physics, faculty whose work took them into "big science," with its big money, big laboratories, and big awards, both openly and quietly confronted faculty whose culture of teaching and research were based in long-standing traditions of the individual in the field. However, Donald Kennedy, Paul Ehrlich, and Peter Raven are examples of field biologists who agree that the move of the museum collections was the correct thing to do. Both entomologist Ehrlich and botanist Raven, working in the 1960s in new techniques and approaches of systematics, population studies, and ecology, always supported the idea of moving the museum collections away from the campus.[169]

This clash of cultures within science was exemplified in biology by the reaction of George Myers. Myers, who joined the Stanford faculty in 1926, was a respected ichthyologist with a Stanford PhD who had raised grant money, advised many PhD students, and published in his field. He was also short-tempered and prone to letter-writing campaigns (his letters of protest to the administration go back decades before Terman became provost). He was generally unhappy about the worldwide turn of biology toward cell biology, molecular biology, and biochemistry, which he viewed as coming at the expense of Stanford's traditional strength in natural history. In one scathing 1960 letter, Myers protested Terman's lack of support for the Natural History Museum. The reaction within the department to this letter is more telling than that of the provost. "I have just received a copy of George Myers' letter concerning his plight, partly imagined and partly real, at the Museum," Twitty wrote Terman. "George is a great letter writer, and fulminations of this sort are not new to us. In fact, his moods and his tantrums have long been a problem at the Museum, . . . unfortunately he dissipates his energies and talents, and for several years I believe that his published contributions, though numerous, have been less major in scope than they used to be." Twitty went on to write that he and Dudley curator Holm agreed that the department needed to "contain" Myers for the "benefit of the rest of us." Their strategy was to ask the provost to give Myers a full-time secretary (instead of half-time) to protect the other museum staff "from irritation and conflict." Terman drafted a written response to Myers but decided in the end to have a pleasant chat with him, which he did two weeks later.[170]

As the years progressed, the rise of Stanford's biochemists and the influence of new definitions was unmistakable. In 1962, Richard Holm even nudged the Biology Division of the museum into a new form as the Division of Systematic Biology (due to what he saw as the misleading and archaic connotations of "Natural History" and "Museum") but by the mid-1960s the future of systematics as well as of the museum looked cloudy.[171]

Biology by the Sea

The future of Hopkins Marine Station was also somewhat misty. Founded in 1892, the Hopkins Seaside Laboratory (renamed Hopkins Marine Station in 1917) in Pacific Grove focused on summer teaching but was available year round to researchers from Stanford and elsewhere. Research was not centered on marine biology, but rather on the use of Monterey Bay's rich biological diversity for studies ranging from parthogenesis, embryology, and electrobiology, to invertebrate zoology, oceanography, and pesticide pollution.

Expansion of the lab's facilities in the late 1920s with help from the Rockefeller Foundation attracted prominent biologists as summer visiting professors. Cornelis van Niel, an internationally noted microbiologist, began as a summer visitor, but stayed on as one of Hopkins's most notable faculty. An exceptional teacher, his course inspired such students as Arthur Kornberg and Paul Berg. When Terman became provost, van Niel was still the station's most prestigious faculty member. Hopkins's director was Lawrence Blinks, a creative researcher in electrobiology and photosynthesis, and like van Niel and biology head Victor Twitty, a member of the National Academy of Sciences. Blinks was assisted by Rolf Bolin, a noted ichthyologist and fabled teacher of comparative anatomy. The faculty was rounded out with phycologist Donald Abbott (and until 1971, unofficially by his wife, Dr. Isabella Abbott).

Terman was well aware that the budgets of the National Science Foundation and National Institutes of Health, as well as private philanthropies such as the Ford Foundation, in the 1950s and 1960s were aimed at the hot spots of biological research: the intersection of biology, chemistry, and physics, and the emerging fields of molecular biology, biochemistry, and now marine biology and oceanography.[172] In 1958, the National Science Foundation expressed interest in sponsoring a center on the West Coast similar to Woods Hole, Massachusetts, focusing on marine biology and oceanography. Biologists at Berkeley wrote to Blinks to suggest that Stanford and Berkeley cooperate in operating such a marine station. Blinks was leery of the suggestion, fearing that Berkeley would take over the Hopkins Marine Station. He asked Terman for advice, who in turn asked Sterling's advice. Sterling counseled a careful and noncommittal approach, and Terman provided Blinks with a draft response.[173] (Ironically, years later Blinks wrote that he found the prospect of cooperating with Berkeley interesting, but that it was Fred Terman who spoiled the deal.[174])

But the issue was not dead. Soon after this exchange, Terman sent Al Bowker out to visit the Hopkins Station. Cornelis van Niel told Bowker that if Berkeley's faculty came to Monterey Bay, they would indeed soon dominate. However, van Niel also felt that Stanford should be actively involved if any major expansion of marine biology and oceanography occurred in the area. Blinks, by contrast, continued to oppose a Stanford-Berkeley coalition, complaining to Terman that Berkeley was no good at cooperation. (They had been very bad partners, he commented, during a summer of joint work at Hopkins Station.)

Blinks and Terman discussed the NSF's plans for a $650 million program for oceanography, proposed for 1960–70. Blinks still was interested in getting some of that money for marine biology at Hopkins, but he was not interested in developing oceanography.[175] Terman, who as chair of the NSF Committee for Mathematical, Physical, and Engineering Sciences, already knew of the NSF proposal and did his best to help Blinks obtain some $225,000 in NSF funding for the Hopkins Station facilities.[176]

Marine exploration was attracting increasing interest in the early 1960s. If Blinks was not keen on deep-ocean work, Assistant Director Rolf Bolin jumped at the chance for further support. Bolin proposed to obtain a small ship and, with NSF funding, participate in the International Indian Ocean Expedition. Bolin was eager, Blinks told Terman, and had deep-ocean experience. Twitty wrote to Dean Rhinelander to assure him that both the NSF and Bolin were ready to cooperate, although Rhinelander and Terman both felt that more planning was needed. Terman agreed, nonetheless, to endorse the proposal so long as it did not cost the university money and so long as the funding was guaranteed for the long term.[177]

Bolin submitted a proposal for $462,000, which NSF granted in full in April 1961. Although NSF oceanographic biology administrator (and Stanford alumna) Dixie Lee Ray supported the project, Blinks was losing confidence in the project. The plan relied on using philanthropist George Vanderbilt's 327-ton yacht *Pioneer*, but the Vanderbilt executors were balking on the deal on the grounds that the *Pioneer* was old and out of condition. Oregon timber executive Harold A. Miller, who had attended Stanford in the 1920s and had maintained a special interest in Hopkins, came to the rescue. On the spur of the moment, Blinks later wrote, he asked Miller for a ship. Miller offered his 135-foot, 242-ton yacht, the *Te Vega*. Bolin and Dixie Lee Ray visited the *Te Vega* in New York harbor. It was beautiful, in top shape, and ready for use by May 1962.[178]

The *Te Vega* set out on its first cruise in June 1963 and participated in Pacific Ocean cruises for several years before retiring, "ancient in years and expensive in habits," as Blinks remembered.[179] The ship was a mixed blessing from the outset. However beautifully outfitted as a yacht, it had to be refitted into a research vessel. Its first voyage caused some anxiety in the President's Office when it was discovered that both men and women students were on the cruise without a "chaperone." ("Well, Fred," Sterling told Fred Glover, "don't worry about it, it's the ship's 'maiden' voyage.") One cruise was troubled by an inebriated cook, another by a drunken captain. One time, the ship vanished for five days, making no radio contact. From the administration's perspective, "it was an ill-fated venture," Fred Glover later reminisced. "We just weren't equipped to operate a ship like that."[180] The *Te Vega* was sold. She was briefly succeeded by a "very ugly but much more efficient tuna clipper" renamed *Proteus*, but this, too, was a discouraging experiment. After Bolin's retirement and hard financial times for the Marine Station, Stanford was out of the oceanography business.[181]

Van Niel retired in 1963, Blinks in 1965, and Bolin in 1966. Al Bowker urged some long-range planning for the Marine Station. Indeed, some campus faculty (notably Kornberg and Lederberg) argued that since van Niel's work and interests were technically "unrelated to marine biology," they should be allowed to replace the distinguished microbiologist with a new appointment for the main campus.[182] The Hopkins Marine Station "fell on hard times in the early 1970s," wrote biologist David Epel, associate director of the station, in the station's centennial year. "Environmental work, although important, did not garner the level of federal support for research that everyone expected would come. Activity at the station reached its nadir." A blue-ribbon committee, chaired by W. D. McElroy, chancellor of UC San Diego and a Stanford alumnus, urged Stanford not to let go of an "important treasure." The Harold Miller family continued to make major contributions, including an endowed chair, while Packard family funds provided much needed renovation of the facilities. In 1976, Colin Pittendrigh, a well-respected campus biologist, was appointed director. By the 1980s, Hopkins enjoyed a renaissance, supporting faculty research in cell biology, ecological sciences, neurobiology, and, by the 1990s, in biomechanics, molecular biology, and biotechnology.[183]

Biophysics

In spite of the incredible fund-raising efforts of the 1960s, not all blossoming scientific crossover fields were destined to become full-blown departments. Despite the support of a number of influential professors and the kind eye of the provost, Stanford did not develop a Department of Biophysics, but instead created a highly regarded graduate program.

In 1955, the Microwave Lab initiated a program within the Department of Biology, overseen by Ed Tatum of biology, Henry Kaplan of radiology, and Ed Ginzton of the Microwave Lab, to use microwave phenomena to study biological systems.[184] Kaplan and Ginzton had developed an extremely close personal as well as professional relationship during their highly gratifying joint work on the medical linear accelerator for cancer therapy.[185] Their 6 MEV linear accelerator, which began functioning at Stanford Hospital in January 1956, operated nearly full time each day, treating patients with the greatest chance of permanent cure—carcinoma of the cervix, bladder, and prostate, retinoblastoma, nasopharynx tumors and pituitary adenomas, and brain tumors. Seventy-five patients were treated in its first year (each treatment lasting from five to eight weeks) and these initial experiences had been extended by adapting beta-rays from the Mark IV accelerator, then in development at Stanford.[186]

In 1957, at Ginzton's suggestion, Kaplan was appointed director of the Biophysics Laboratory, housed within the Hansen Laboratories (which was now made up of three constituent laboratories: High-Energy, Microwave, and Biophysics).[187] There were good prospects that a biophysics program at Stanford could quickly grow, perhaps becoming a department. Initially, Stanford tried to get Robert Sinsheimer from Caltech to head a new department or division in the Biology Department, but Sinsheimer also was being recruited by Berkeley.

In 1964, however, Terman decided that Stanford should not attempt large-scale growth in the field of biophysics in the near future. Although he would have loved to see that field grow at Stanford, particularly with its ties to Kaplan and Ginzton, Terman concluded that it was simply too expensive.[188] By Terman's retirement, the Biophysics Program had instead a highly regarded graduate program with an outstanding faculty of joint appointments, chaired by medical radiologist Mitchel Weissbluth and that included Associate Provost for Research Hubert Heffner, biologists Donald Kennedy, Joshua Lederberg, and Philip C. Hanawalt, chemist Harden McConnell, physicist Leonard Schiff, and Engineering Dean Joseph Pettit.

Biology in 1965

Stanford's Biology Department, expanding its faculty, its research agenda, and its facilities (a large new building, long in planning, would open in 1966), experienced another readjustment just before Fred Terman's retirement. Clifford Grobstein, who some credit with getting the department moving again, left Stanford in 1964 (largely due to personal, not professional reasons) to head the Biology Department at the new University of California in San Diego.[189]

With Donald Kennedy as acting chair, the department searched for a successor. Without adequately checking with either the dean or the provost, the committee announced their selection to the preferred candidate, and everything came to a halt. The Sterling administration, angered that the department had bypassed their assessment, stopped the process. Lederberg, Kornberg, and biology colleagues in the Medical School were angry, complaining that the proposed candidate was not, in their view, the optimum one. The Biology Department faculty, both angry and embarrassed, could make no appointment.

That June, President Sterling created a "Committee on Long Range Plans for Biology" to review Stanford's program in the biological sciences, as well as the program's connections to the Medical School and to the Chemistry Department. The committee was the idea of Fred Terman and Humanities and Sciences Dean Robert Sears. Sears served as chair, with members Donald Kennedy (as acting head); Richard W. Holm, representing the Systematics Division; Charles Yanofsky, representing general biology; John H. Phillips, representing the Hopkins Marine Station; Joshua Lederberg, for both biology and genetics; Carl Djerassi for chemistry; and Robert Glaser, the new Medical School dean. Associate Provost for Research Hubert Heffner and Arthur Kornberg were named "consultants."[190]

George Myers, for one, immediately criticized the committee membership as imbalanced, but Sterling launched the committee because he felt that biology, biochemistry, and biomedicine were on a threshold that required reevaluation of Stanford's directions.[191] Another, if unstated reason, was the need to take back control of the faculty appointment process. The week before he retired, Terman sent committee chair Sears a letter of advice. He included a number of documents concerning the structuring of the search committee that he had used during the rebuilding of the Chemistry Department several years earlier.[192] Sterling's committee studied the situation for some months, and suggested biochemist Paul Berg be made department head. Berg countered by requesting nine new faculty appointments and construction of a major laboratory facility, but then withdrew his candidacy. Donald Kennedy, who had wide support within the Biology Department and considerable diplomatic skills, was appointed department head in 1966.[193]

It appeared that biology had fulfilled its promise. Stanford's new formulation of "biological sciences"—biology, biochemistry, biomedicine, and biophysics—had made giant strides during the Sterling-Terman decade of 1955–65. In 1965, Stanford received typewritten excerpts from Allan M. Cartter's new study, *An Assessment of Quality in Graduate Education*, made for the American Council on Education.[194] In it, faculty were rated in each of five general divisions: humanities, social sciences, biological sciences, physical sciences, and engineering. Cartter's report concluded, "In the biological sciences Stanford has taken a giant stride from thirteenth in 1957 . . . to fifth position."

Years later, Terman told Joshua Lederberg that he had always respected both the Biology Department and the role that Charles V. Taylor had played in the 1920s and 1930s in building up a very strong department. Terman felt that his own role as provost was to turn around Stanford's inferiority complex—by the time he retired, the Biology Department could recruit the best rather than accept those who were available.[195] Fred Terman also supported within biology not only those who wanted to strengthen the "modern" biological areas but also those in the systematics area, as it was reorganized by Ehrlich and Raven.

Rebuilding Chemistry

Fred Terman's proudest achievement as an administrator was the rebuilding of the Chemistry Department. Terman, of course, had a special interest in the department. He had received his BA at Stanford in chemistry and had minored in chemistry for his ScD at MIT.

Stanford's Chemistry Department approached the 1950s with an aging, overcrowded building, a modest "frill-free" laboratory and a good executive head, Philip Leighton. Photochemist Leighton was an excellent experimentalist with prolific publications and had worked to establish the Stanford Research Institute, whose early contracts were for chemical research.[196] As the decade opened, chemistry, like many of Stanford's science and engineering departments, had already embarked on research programs backed by outside funding. Stanford had forty research contracts with government agencies in 1950 (twenty-three of which were with the Office of Naval Research alone). Eleven contracts—and two-thirds of Stanford's total research dollars—went to the Departments of Electrical Engineering and Physics, and to the Microwave Lab. By comparison, chemistry had two research contracts, its research funds making up about 6.5 percent of Stanford's total federal research support (approximately the same as the Departments of Mechanical Engineering and Statistics, while the Department of Medicine had about 2 percent of the total, and anatomy, biology, and physiology each had less than 1 percent of the university's federal income, which was the bulk of outside financial support).[197] Leighton's research projects accounted for much of the department's outside funding. Although the Chemistry Department's research contracts and contract funds more than doubled over the next year, they remained relatively small compared to those awarded to engineering departments, physics and the Hansen Labs, the Electronics Research Lab, and the Mathematics and Statistics Lab.[198]

The Chemistry Department held together three functions often assigned to three separate departments in many other universities: chemistry, biochemistry, and chemical engineering. The basic or preclinical chemistry courses were taught on the campus for premeds, and medical students moved to San Francisco for further training. Over the decades, there had been talk of moving the biochemistry teaching to San Francisco (just as some portions of biology had been moved to the Medical School) and some talk of moving chemical engineering over to the Engineering School. By 1949, however, the Chemistry Department faculty was "unanimously" against moving either biochemistry or chemical engineering out of the department. Indeed, one-half of Stanford's undergraduate chemistry students majored in chemical engineering, and the chemistry faculty had no intention of giving up these enrollments to the engineers.

Responding in the spring of 1949 to the new university president's call for department scenarios of current status and future (ten-year) ambitions, the Chemistry Department called attention to an American Chemical Society report. Stanford's Chemistry Department was ranked among the top 30 percent of American university chemistry programs, but had not made it into the top 10 percent. The solution, as Executive Head Philip Leighton saw it, was not in faculty changes, but in facility improvement. He would not trade his faculty for any other in the country, he wrote, even though he had no Nobel winners, "no Paulings, no Woodwards, or Pitzers." He had seven tenured professors, eight assistant professors, and one instructor, and his plan was to build with the personnel he had. His sixteen faculty members best represented the areas of physical, inorganic, and organic chemistry, and he therefore hoped to see some growth in biochemistry (an additional faculty position) and in chemical engineering (two positions). The department's greatest needs, however, were for additional space, improved facilities, research funds, and the means to attract high-quality graduate students.

As yet, the department still relied on the old chemistry building—first occupied in 1903, severely damaged in the 1906 earthquake, repaired and modified several times thereafter—for classroom, laboratory, and library space.[199] The building was extremely crowded and, given the needs of maintaining chemicals and laboratory equipment for students and faculty alike, not very safe. Leighton hoped for at least four new buildings that would occupy about 100,000 square feet (which he estimated would cost a little over $2 million dollars). The department could then remodel (or replace) the old chemistry building with modern lecture rooms, undergraduate laboratories, a library, and a shop.

When he wrote his report to Sterling, Leighton mentioned the small, single-story organic research laboratory, slated for completion by the end of 1949 (it was actually occupied in January 1950). Even so, wondered Leighton, how could Stanford compete with Caltech or UCLA, then each spending $5 million for new chemistry buildings, when it took fifteen years to raise the $225,000 Stanford needed for the modest little lab building? To move Stanford up to the top 10 percent among national chemistry departments, Leighton called for a $2 million initial outlay and an annual addition of $100,000 to the budget.[200]

In August 1951, Leighton resigned as executive head to devote more time to his research and teaching. "I suspect that Phil, if asked for advice, would push some of the younger men now in the Department," President Sterling wrote to American Cyanamid Company chemist and executive Robert C. Swain. But Sterling was hoping to attract someone from outside campus circles. Leighton's resignation "seems to me to be a possible opportunity which, if capitalized, could achieve some re-vitalization of the Department. I write now to ask you if you have any names of up-and-coming, competent, imaginative young chemists whom I should consider for the Executive Headship of the Department."[201]

Stanford's attraction at the time was seriously limited, as Leighton had pointed out, by its limited facilities. In the end, Leighton's colleague George Parks, who had served as acting graduate dean in 1950–51, moved back to take over chemistry. The Berkeley-trained Parks, whose interest lay in thermodynamics (particularly calorimetry), had first joined Stanford's faculty in 1920 and had devoted his entire career, save one year at Caltech, to Stanford.[202] Parks inherited from Leighton the department's awkward position on the brink of changes in science and in academic funding, as well as internal problems swirling around the department's weakest fields, biochemistry and chemical engineering.

The biochemistry faculty was in limbo as plans were made around them in the Biology Department and the Medical School. The needs of biochemistry were "far more pressing" than those of any other parts of chemistry, biochemist J. Murray Luck complained to Medical School Dean Windsor Cutting, and the biochemists continued to complain to Parks that they were overworked, underpaid, and generally unappreciated. Associate professors were badly underpaid, Luck asserted to Dean Cutting (although George Parks disagreed).[203] Given potential changes in the department, including Parks's inclination to help out the chemical engineers, Luck, for one, worried that biochemistry was in "grave danger" of being subordinated to chemical engineering.[204] Chemical engineering was in a real bind. Its serious shortcomings led, in 1953, to its loss of accreditation. When J. S. Walton assessed the chemical engineering program for an accreditation board in late 1952, he pointed out that Stanford, like other private universities, drastically needed more funds for chemistry in general. He noted Dean of Engineering Fred Terman's interest in building up chemical engineering, but for the present, Stanford's chemistry building and its chemical engineering equipment and staff were minimal. Stanford was turned down for accreditation in chemical engineering.[205]

Chemical engineer R. R. Paxton subsequently wrote Provost Douglas Whitaker that as of fall 1954, there were more undergraduate majors in chemical engineering than in chemistry, yet the department devoted less than the *minimum* in staff to the program to be accredited by the Engineer's Council for Professional Development. Paxton proposed a plan for the immediate development of chemical engineering, but his ambitions fell by the wayside when his appointment was terminated in 1955.[206]

Whitaker was hardly pleased to learn that Paxton and a former Stanford chemical engineer had been ridiculing the department to Standard Oil, a potential major donor. Standard Oil's Stanford contacts, however, apparently not only agreed that chemical engineering needed much improvement at Stanford, but preferred to see it moved out of the Chemistry Department and into the School of Engineering. With the right moves, Stanford might expect at least ten chemical and oil firms to give as much as $5,000 each over five years toward chemical engineering, Whitaker reported to Sterling. Whitaker was delighted with the appointment of David Mason, coming to Stanford in the fall from Caltech and the Jet Propulsion Lab. Mason, he told Sterling, was expected to rejuvenate the chemical engineering program.[207]

By 1955, with a few exceptions, changes had been few and modest. In his assessment for President Sterling, Parks reported that the chemistry faculty still numbered sixteen, as it had in 1949–50, but there were now thirteen tenured professors and associate professors, rather than seven. Parks believed that at least three of the four junior faculty replacements had led to significant improvement. The need for facilities continued to rank high, while the department's wish list of new facilities was largely unfulfilled. Incoming research grants continued to bring in around $125,000 per year, but the department graduated only about twenty-five bachelor's degrees annually, in chemistry and chemical engineering combined. Indeed, at the undergraduate level, Parks commented, the department appeared to be largely a service department for engineers, premeds, and biology students. The graduate student population, too, had remained about the same, and graduate fellowships were sadly lacking.[208] The quiet, cautious Parks would later be credited with effective building of chemical engineering. "It was on Parks's initiative—which was persistent rather than forceful—that chemical engineering at Stanford took on its present form," wrote fellow chemist Eric Hutchinson.[209]

By 1954, General Secretary David Jacobson had concluded that the Chemistry Department's overall expansion plans were hastily drawn, and neither very imaginative nor well developed.[210] Provost Douglas Whitaker continued to search, though not very actively, for an up-and-coming chemist to head the department. When it appeared that Arthur Cope, the top candidate on the list, was unlikely to leave MIT (he was department head there), Robert Swain had recommended several other chemists for what he considered to be the difficult but important job of rebuilding the Chemistry Department.[211] Six names, led by Cope, made up Whitaker's shortlist, with an additional list of sixteen more possibilities (including Melvin Calvin of Berkeley, Paul Doty of Harvard, and William Doering of Yale).

Whitaker passed on the lists to his successor as provost, Fred Terman, in the fall of 1955.[212] Terman found that Cope had already told Whitaker that he was not interested in leaving MIT. In fact, Whitaker had communicated with only two of the candidates, and little additional information had been gathered on most of the people on the list. Terman decided to start over. Rather than revisit the department's past failures to attract interest, he passed the word around that Stanford was "starting a search" toward the appointment of a new chemistry head.

In the spring of 1956, Terman appointed a nine-man ad hoc committee to assist him in searching for a new head of the Chemistry Department. He named to this committee Graduate Dean William Steere as chairman, three Stanford chemists (Department Head George Parks, Eric Hutchinson, and Carl Noller), physicist George Pake, biochemist Edward Tatum, trustee Monroe Spaght (vice president of Shell Oil), Robert C. Swain (director of research at American Cyanamid), and Douglas Whitaker, vice president of the Rockefeller Institute. Physics Nobelist Felix Bloch would substitute for George Pake until Pake arrived on campus in late summer (in fact, Bloch stayed on the committee as well).[213]

Terman explained the search:

> Our problem here is to build the Chemistry Department up to the point where its scientific stature compares with that of our Physics, Mathematics, Statistics, Biology, and Biochemistry Departments. We look upon this as a long range job, but feel that a real transformation can be accomplished in a period such as 10 years, as judged by our Physics Department, which in a decade has risen from obscurity until its staff, though small, has an average quality that is one of the best in the country. We could do likewise in chemistry if we have the kind of leadership that builds soundly and skillfully.[214]

In order to provide the flexibility in appointment that would be needed to attract truly top-notch outside candidates, Terman blocked a number of tenure billets coming open in the department and filled the positions with temporary appointments. Terman was determined to bring to Stanford scholars with strong, established reputations, just as the department had recently recruited David M. Mason and Cornelius J. Pings into the chemical engineering program.[215]

Sterling was pleased with Terman's approach. Writing to Eric Hutchinson, away in Britain on sabbatical, Sterling reported that real progress was being made with the review of Stanford's undergraduate program, although little could be done until Stanford significantly improved faculty salaries and library and laboratory facilities. Fred Terman, he added, "is fitting very well into the Provost's job. . . . We have much to be thankful for."[216]

Terman, Sterling, and the search committee worked very hard to attract a major leader in chemistry. Stanford's new short list was: Bryce Crawford (a Stanford alumnus and head of chemistry at the University of Minnesota), William S. Johnson (an organic chemist at Wisconsin), and E. Bright Wilson (a molecular spectroscopist at Harvard).[217] Nuclear chemist Willard F. Libby, a member of the Atomic Energy Commission, soon moved to the top of the list.

Terman conducted extremely thorough background checks and examined all possible problems in attracting each of the desired candidates. A good example of the committee's methods is their effort to recruit nuclear chemist Willard F. Libby in 1957–58 (Bryce Crawford had turned down Stanford in March 1957).[218] Libby very nearly came to Stanford. In the summer of 1957, Terman had worked out the best offer he could provide: a salary of $15,000 for nine months (soon "sweetened" to $17,500, since Chicago was going to offer Libby $20,000 to return there) and enough funds to let Libby hire *four* other faculty, distributed through the ranks. Terman advised Sterling to point out to Libby that he could earn another $5,000 with summer grants and could obtain a consulting retainer at Stanford Research Institute or elsewhere for about $4,000 per year. Monroe Spaght and Robert Swain promised to raise $35,000 to $70,000 per year for five years from industry, while Ken Cuthbertson assured Terman that at least $150,000 would be used to upgrade the old chemistry building. Libby could even take two years to arrive on campus—three, Terman privately told Sterling, if necessary.

The Libbys, Terman found in his preliminary discussions, were very favorably impressed with Stanford's benefits—medical, housing, tuition remission, and admission preference for faculty children. Libby had gone to the AEC in Washington DC from the University of Chicago, but Libby's wife, Leonor, wanted to return to California, her home state, and Terman worked that angle. (Chemist Kenneth Pitzer at Berkeley cued Terman to this fact.) Terman thus advised dinner for four and encouraged Anne Sterling to sell Leonor Libby on Stanford and California as strongly as Sterling sold Stanford to her husband. Terman stressed to Sterling Libby's national importance as a chemist; he was also a good possibility for a Nobel Prize.[219] "If we plan [*sic*] our cards properly I feel we will probably be successful."[220] Terman discussed Libby's ideas for Stanford with Sterling, and the president liked their boldness. Felix Bloch also was a keen supporter of Libby. Wally and Anne Sterling subsequently visited the Libbys in Washington in late October.[221]

Despite Stanford's institutional and personalized enthusiasm, Libby reluctantly declined Stanford's offer two months later and chose UCLA. Libby expressed his full understanding for Stanford's limited resources, but as he told Terman, he believed that the financial support for physical chemistry at Stanford was "inadequate for the rate of development to which I want to devote myself, to achieve world recognition [within five years]."[222]

There were not enough funds to do everything, but Terman's willingness to use what was available for his faculty steeple-building plan was a significant factor in the development of departments like chemistry. Stanford had recently received an unrestricted gift of $25,000 from Proctor and Gamble, with the expectation that a similar gift would follow for each of the next five years. Sterling and Terman decided to use these funds as seed money to rebuild faculty in chemistry, but as his next set of searches would reveal, far more would be needed if Stanford were to obtain the new facilities and equipment needed to attract the kind of people for whom Terman aimed.[223]

As Libby's final decision underscored, conditions in the department had not improved much by 1958. In a confidential report to Humanities and Sciences Dean Philip Rhinelander, Assistant Dean William McCord reported, "During the last years the Chemistry Department has fallen on evil days. Staff problems plague the department. The faculty has deteriorated and few high-caliber graduate students are entering the department." Several senior faculty members, he reported, had stopped working actively in chemical research, while others refused to accept their proper teaching burden. As a result, Associate Professor Eric Hutchinson was teaching four times the load of some others, an imbalance acceded to by Department Head Parks. Faculty disarray and poor facilities did not help the student situation, McCord added. Although undergraduate enrollment had grown in the past two years (with three-fifths of the majors in chemical engineering), the quality of graduate student work was not good. In the preceding year, not one chemistry student won an NSF graduate fellowship, compared to twenty-two NSF fellowship winners in the Physics Department.[224]

Johnson and Djerassi

Terman reactivated his search committee on March 3, 1958, substituting Pief Panofsky of physics and Arthur Kornberg of biochemistry for Pake and Tatum (who had left Stanford).[225] Stanford had searched for a top physical chemist to fill the position for several years, but was clearly hampered by the seriously inadequate facilities for physical chemistry research. Returning to his committee, Terman asked them instead to recruit an organic chemist.

William S. Johnson had been on the short list compiled two years before by Whitaker. Through the winter of 1958 and early spring of 1959, Terman and his committee worked on attracting the forty-six-year-old organic chemist from the University of Wisconsin. Johnson was celebrated for his work in steroid synthesis. Fred Terman made the first contact when he telephoned Johnson in late 1958 to ask him to accept the position of head of chemistry and to lead Stanford's plans to upgrade the department. Johnson was not interested in administration, he responded, and had just built a new house in Madison. Terman then asked Johnson and his wife to at least come visit Stanford and give him some advice. The gamble paid off. Johnson later recalled that he was immensely impressed by both Sterling and Terman, who "ran the university in a benevolently despotic manner." Johnson believed that "Stanford's early 1960s administration was ideal for effecting rapid, dramatic changes; indeed, several departments such as Biochemistry, Mathematics, and Physics had already become great under this regime. Sterling and Terman assured me that it was now chemistry's turn. I also found that the department, already consisting of a number of talented scholars, was highly supportive of the new plan."[226]

In a major-league deal, Terman offered the position of executive head of chemistry to Johnson and invited Johnson's former student, thirty-five-year-old Carl Djerassi of Wayne State University. Djerassi, too, was persuaded in a "lengthy conversation with the legendary Stanford provost F. E. Terman," as he put it, "who promised the construction of a new laboratory building for the two of us." (Joshua Lederberg, Arthur Kornberg, and Henry Kaplan also spent a good deal of time in the courting of Johnson and Djerassi.[227]) As Terman noted to President Sterling, Djerassi had 246 publications on the subjects of steroids, antibiotics, and antihistamines and had most recently won two of the major prizes given in chemistry. The combination of Johnson and Djerassi, he wrote, would cause Stanford to be recognized immediately as one of the leading academic centers in the country in the chemistry of natural organic compounds. "It would give us national distinction overnight."

Djerassi felt that Terman welcomed his ties with biomedical and biochemical research companies. At the time, Djerassi was research vice president of Syntex Pharmaceuticals. He later brought the research headquarters of Syntex to the Stanford Industrial Park and initiated other research there as well, particularly Synvar. Synvar (later "Syva"), a collaboration of Syntex and Varian Associates, included as consultants Edward Ginzton, Harden McConnell, and Avram Goldstein, thus joining together the consulting talents of applied physics, chemistry, and pharmacology.[228]

Johnson and Djerassi brought some forty graduate students and postdocs with them, and the immediate need for 10,000 additional square feet of space (at an estimated building cost of about $350,000). Djerassi's team alone consisted of seventeen graduate students and postdoctoral fellows brought from Wayne State. How to justify the costs of a new building? Terman provided Sterling with a list of seven reasons to bring before the board of trustees that included the great strengthening of the Chemistry Department overall, the doubling of its graduate student population, the probable tripling of research support within two years, and the likelihood of industrial and major donor support. Terman's conclusion: "If constructing the [new] building will bring Johnson and Djerassi to Stanford and thereby give us a national position such as we so desperately need, *how can we afford not to do it*?"[229] The board of trustees agreed, and Johnson and Djerassi were offered positions immediately. Shortly after the offer, Sterling wrote to Johnson saying:

> Thanks to Fred Terman, I have kept in close touch with the Chemistry situation. . . . I hardly need to repeat what I said to you when you were here: that we need leadership in Chemistry, and that we mean to have it, not only because Chemistry is a fundamental science with a great tradition, but also because it is so

> intimately related to such fields as Biology, Biochemistry, Physics, Biophysics and the Medical Sciences in general, in all of which Stanford has a strong position and a fundamental stake. . . . Fred Terman and I have done all that can reasonably be done to secure a proud place for Chemistry at Stanford until we get you on the job.

Sterling assured Johnson that he and Terman carried high hopes for helping Johnson "rebuild Chemistry at Stanford to its rightful and central place of distinction among its sister sciences." A week later Sterling received Johnson's letter of acceptance with "great rejoicing."[230] At almost the same time, Sterling announced John Stauffer's agreement to fund the (first) Stauffer building.[231]

Building Further

As soon as he became head of the department, William Johnson took up the search for a physical chemist. Outside reviewers Herbert Gutowsky and Bryce Crawford (who had themselves at one time been on Stanford's wish list) along with Carl Djerassi recommended Samuel Weissman of Washington University in St. Louis. However, as Eric Hutchinson warned Johnson, Stanford's chemists were not keen on Weissman—they preferred Bruno H. Zimm, who had been at General Electric's research labs in Schenectady, New York. Terman advised Johnson not to worry about Hutchinson's warning but rather to ask the country's most outstanding physical chemists to compare Weissman to the best in the field. Johnson judiciously replied to Hutchinson to ask him for supporting facts and reasonable alternates.[232]

Weissman came to Stanford in August 1959 for a visit and was subsequently offered the Stanford position. George Pake (former Stanford faculty physicist having returned to Weissman's institution) reported to Terman that Weissman had some hesitation about leaving St. Louis. Perhaps Weissman had learned of the less than enthusiastic support of some of the Stanford department members. Nevertheless, in an effort both to attract Weissman and to assuage the department's faculty, Terman agreed to offer both Weissman and Bruno Zimm full professorships, with the added attraction of offering a position to yet another outstanding physical chemist, "such as Harden McConnell" in two years. Ironically, Stanford ended up with neither Weissman nor Zimm. Weissman rejected the offer.[233] That fall of 1959, Bruno Zimm visited a number of California institutions and had informal discussions with Berkeley, UCLA, Stanford, and UC San Diego; he accepted UCSD's offer in the spring of 1960.[234]

Eric Hutchinson wrote to Sterling that with Johnson and Djerassi, and two new junior physical chemists soon to arrive at Stanford, "It is going to be exciting, and I must confess that Stanford has taken the wind out of the sails of those of us who have complained for some years that chemistry has been a step-child. . . . No one can deny that in the last year we have been given a good chance to get firmly re-established."[235]

Later in 1960, Terman's "fighting fund" of discretionary money was used to capture the celebrated polymer chemist Paul Flory. Newly recruited Chemistry Head William Johnson was attending an NSF committee meeting in December 1960 in Washington DC when he heard from Al Blomquist, chairman of Cornell's Chemistry Department, that Flory, director of the Mellon Institute in Pittsburgh, was resigning to accept an academic position, most probably at Cornell. As soon as he returned to Stanford, Johnson collared Terman who, within fifteen minutes, gave him the authority to offer Flory a position. Johnson telephoned Flory, who indicated it was awfully late to change his mind. Johnson remembered Terman's strategy in his own case when at Wisconsin, and he asked Flory at least to come out to Stanford and give him some advice. Two visits to Stanford convinced Flory to change his plans. (Flory would receive the Nobel Prize in Chemistry in 1974 for research on the chemistry and physics of giant molecules, or polymers.)

The personal approach also influenced Henry Taube, who had been vacillating over whether to leave the University of Chicago for Stanford.[236] Taube came to Stanford in 1962, and again John Stauffer expressed his willingness to help Stanford build a new building suitable to both Flory and Taube's research needs. Taube received the Nobel Prize in 1983 for discovering basic mechanisms in chemical reactions, ranging from how enzymes and batteries work to the critical energy processes that maintain life.[237]

Bill Johnson continued to work hard to attract top faculty. Physical chemist Harden McConnell wrote from Caltech in 1962 to say that he'd decided to stay in Pasadena, even though he suspected that over the long haul Stanford would be better for him. Echoing Terman's approach, he added some advice: to improve physical chemistry at Stanford, do not make any "mistakes" in hiring. Stanford was reaching the position to demand the very best. "If you can't get the very best today, don't get anybody," McConnell wrote Johnson. In the meantime, he suggested, hire two top theoretical chemical physicists. Get "thinkers," not "calculators," that is, get theorists first since outstanding experimental chemical physicists require sophisticated equipment that Stanford, as yet, did not have.[238]

Johnson succeeded in building Stanford's chemistry faculty much more often than he failed. Early in 1962, Fred Terman wrote proudly to donor John Stauffer, "Professor Johnson has done it again. He has persuaded Dr. Eugene van Tamelen to join the Stanford faculty." Stauffer and his niece Mrs. Mitzi Briggs had provided funding for construction of the John Stauffer (General) Chemistry Building in 1961. When Paul Flory and Henry Taube moved from that first Stauffer building into the new Stauffer Physical Chemistry Building, van Tamelen would take their old space. Terman assured Stauffer that Stanford "continues to be the most talked about chemistry department in the nation." He specifically noted to Stauffer that the acceptance of van Tamelen, a brilliant young organic chemist, came about largely because of the physical facilities available with the upcoming completion of the John Stauffer Laboratory for Physical Chemistry.[239] Even Harden McConnell, who had remained interested in Stanford's progress, reconsidered Stanford and accepted an offer to come in 1964.[240]

With a growing stable of eminent chemists, egos sometimes clashed and opportunities elsewhere frequently arose. In seeking to keep Paul Flory from going to Cornell, Johnson referred to Fred Terman's further plans for building chemistry. "From my previous experiences with Fred, I have a strong feeling that he now really means business. When he does mean business, he seldom fails to get action."[241]

Once William Johnson had brought the Chemistry Department around, he turned attention to undergraduate (general) chemistry facilities and curriculum. As a department alumnus himself, Fred Terman was also worried about the state of chemistry undergraduate teaching. By 1964, when the Stauffers and other donors had guaranteed funding for chemistry's three new buildings, Richard Eastman (director of the General Chemistry Program), Eric Hutchinson, and others turned their attention to improve undergraduate education in chemistry.[242] Writing Johnson about Eastman's proposal for general chemistry, Arthur Kornberg agreed that undergraduate facilities were in need of much improvement. General chemistry facilities were "scandalous," he wrote, but he also criticized the content and format of the introductory year.[243] By the mid-1960s and after, undergraduate teaching in chemistry at Stanford had improved visibly, Henry Taube later concluded.[244] The coursework was improved, and undergraduates as well as graduate students benefited from the new facilities and faculty. In spite of setbacks, Stanford's Chemistry Department had made obvious strides.

During the Sterling-Terman decade of 1955–65, chemistry, like biology, had made important improvements in the breadth and depth of the department's faculty, research and teaching. In 1957, national surveys had ranked the Chemistry Department fifteenth. By 1964, it was ranked fifth, and by 1969, it was tied for third. Chemical engineering was ranked in a tie for ninth in 1964, and it tied for fourth in 1969.[245] "California and Stanford have done remarkable things," University of Wisconsin President (and biochemist) Fred Harvey Harrington wrote to a colleague in spring 1964. "They have gone forward so far, in fact, that many people in the Middle West feel that we cannot compete."[246]

By the time Terman retired in 1965, Stanford's Chemistry Department had attracted seven regular faculty members (plus an eighth with a courtesy appointment) who were or would soon become members of the National Academy of Sciences: William S. Johnson (arriving in 1960), Carl Djerassi (1959), Paul Flory (1962), Henry Taube (1962), Eugene van Tamelen (1962), John Brauman (1963),

Harden McConnell (1964), and Karl A. Folkers (1964, courtesy). Of those who arrived between 1959 and 1964, Flory and Taube won the Nobel Prize, while Flory, Djerassi, Taube, Johnson, and McConnell would receive the National Medal of Science.[247] From the appointment of Stanford's first chemist in 1891 until 1959, there had been only one member of the Chemistry Department elected to the National Academy of Sciences. That was Edward C. Franklin, who arrived in 1903, Terman's teacher and the father of Terman's boyhood friend, Jack Franklin.

Chemical engineering had also undergone significant changes. Under the leadership of David Mason, the program evolved into department material. In September 1960, the board of trustees heeded the advice of outside reviewers and moved the program out of chemistry into the School of Engineering. The following spring, the new Chemical Engineering Department, now numbering four full-time faculty members, gave diplomas to students with some twenty BS degrees and a half-dozen MS degrees, and had begun work with PhD candidates.[248]

Although criticism surfaced as early as the PACE campaign that chemistry's rapid growth in the early 1960s must have been at the expense of other departments, particularly those in the humanities, the evolution of chemistry came at a time of general growth throughout the university. As Eric Hutchinson points out in his history of the Chemistry Department, improvements were made with growing external research funds, through the judicious use of the Proctor and Gamble gift funds, and the creation of endowed chairs. Increased annual giving propelled by the PACE campaign and significant gifts of major donors like the Stauffers were not peculiar to chemistry. By way of comparison, the Chemistry Department's budget in 1954–55 was $189,000, or 9.1 percent of the total humanities and sciences budget. By the 1969–70 academic year, chemistry's budget had risen to $698,000, yet it had fallen to 6.9 percent of the total School of Humanities and Science budget.[249]

When Fred Terman spoke in 1963 on the touchy subject of higher education and the federal government, he acknowledged that Stanford had used government programs, that is used government funding available to other institutions on the same basis as it was to Stanford, to turn itself into one of the top institutions in the country. The difference was, he argued, that from the beginning Stanford had a clear concept of the type of government programs that could best contribute to its educational objectives. The key, he believed, was faculty quality, a point most other schools were slow to realize. "Our success in physics, math-stat, electronics, and more recently in the Medical School and in chemistry illustrate the value of emphasis on faculty quality."[250]

There would always be those who chafed at Terman and Sterling's "benevolent despotism," as William Johnson called it. Some newer faculty joined the old guard in wishing for more faculty autonomy in departmental decision making. Physicist

George Pake wanted the faculty to have more say in the running of things, and he and Johnson argued over Stanford's advantages and disadvantages. Yet, after Pake returned to Washington University in St. Louis and became its provost, Johnson later recalled, "George told me he had come around to my view."[251]

Johnson himself was a treasure. Years later, emeritus chemistry professor Harry S. Mosher recalled that Johnson ran the department beautifully and that all faculty liked him.[252] Several years into Terman's retirement, Terman and Johnson exchanged correspondence about what a pleasure it had been to work together to build up chemistry at Stanford. "The transformation that you have achieved in Chemistry at Stanford is probably without parallel in the history of education in Chemistry," Terman wrote Johnson, "since it was done with only a modest injection of new funds, and without producing a swollen oversized Chemistry Department. You certainly exploited the basic principle understood by so few that the quality of an educational program depends much more on the person on whom one spends his money, than on how much money is spent, or the gross number of new appointments made!" Johnson responded, "You give me entirely too much credit for the success in building up the department. . . . Whenever I receive praise in this connection, I never fail to point out that you were the *sine qua non*."[253]

The Provost and the Social Sciences and Humanities at Stanford

Terman looked at the School of Humanities and Sciences in 1955 as an amorphous operation, lacking coherence, discipline, and guidance. He knew that over the years the school had gone through periodic regroupings, and the twenty-three departments now included in the school had a strong history of autonomy and marginal cooperation.[254] Terman suspected that many of Stanford's academic departments did not always wish to be "improved" too much, particularly by those outside their field. Many at Stanford, used to slim budgets and other obstacles, still set their sights too low, both in terms of faculty choice and student recruitment. Thus, among his first actions, he sought to assess faculty quality and to institute independent, thorough reviews of faculty applicants and promotions that included the advice of those expert in the field under consideration. Secondly, he developed a provostial staff that he could trust with assessments, particularly Bob Wert, Al Bowker, and Virgil Whitaker. Given his own expertise and interests, Terman largely retained direct oversight of the natural sciences and mathematics, and in 1959 turned over to Associate Provost Bob Wert responsibility for the humanities, social sciences, fine arts, and undergraduate general studies.[255]

Appointing and promoting faculty was hardly a straightforward process, and the new layers of decision making inevitably irritated faculty accustomed to more autonomous roles. Stanford's broad ambitions to improve the quality of the social sciences and humanities as well as the sciences and engineering, however, compelled a broader appraisal of the availability of current and potential funds, balance within and among departments, balance across competing subfield specialties, and proper apportionment among senior and junior faculty throughout the school.

Within the School of Humanities and Sciences, Terman purposefully sought to make a disproportionate number of appointments of eminent people at high rank. As mentioned above, these were not to be persons taking "early retirement" elsewhere, but rather vigorous individuals with the promise of making significant contributions to their fields and of bringing major changes to their departments.[256] Within his first years as provost, however, Terman would find that perceptions of "improvement," "promise," and "quality" varied across campus. Differing perspectives on the relative balance of research and teaching, for one, entered into the equation of "quality." According to the *Stanford Study of Undergraduate Education* (1956), faculty in all of the university's schools *except* the School of Humanities and Sciences felt that their departmental policies on the balance between teaching and research fell somewhere between the two extremes, but most of them personally favored research. Although there was a good deal of variance by department, the humanities and sciences faculty by contrast felt that departmental policies too heavily favored research over teaching and overall wished for more emphasis on teaching.[257]

Part of the problem lay in salary disparity. While Douglas Whitaker was provost, the university salary scales revealed the Departments of Physics, Statistics, Psychology, Special Humanities Programs, Economics, Mathematics, Biology, and History to have the highest mean salaries at the full professor rank, while near the bottom, in descending order, were the Departments of Art, Sociology and Anthropology, Speech and Drama, European Languages, Philosophy, and Asian Languages with the lowest.[258] Thus, with the exception of the History Department and the Special Humanities Programs, the humanities fared less well than the biological and physical sciences within the School of Humanities and Sciences. The social sciences were somewhat mixed: Psychology and Economics were near the top, Sociology and Anthropology near the bottom. Recognizing this situation, in his last year as provost Whitaker assigned the biggest *percentage* salary raises to the European and Slavic languages, geography, art, speech and drama, sociology and anthropology, and the Natural History Museum (averaging 8.2 to 13 percent), whereas the physical sciences and math departments received the smallest raises (averaging from -0.5 to +2.7 percent).[259]

Disparity was, at least in part, the result of the continuing great autonomy among the school's many departments. As one undergraduate education subcommittee on teaching and research policy concluded, *less* departmental autonomy and stronger administration participation in staffing decisions could solve serious imbalances.[260]

Six years later, the need to raise the quality of the faculty and faculty salaries remained key issues, but the question also remained about how that would be done. In surveying their needs for the upcoming PACE campaign in 1961, department heads from the school's physical sciences asked for endowed chairs for existing faculty; those from the humanities called for endowed chairs for new faculty. As usual, the social sciences were a mix, requesting endowed chairs for both new and existing faculty.[261]

Two departments—one in the social sciences, one in the humanities—provide important studies of how Terman worked with nonscience/engineering faculty to carry out the Sterling administration's goals for raising the school's overall quality through new faculty appointments. In the rebuilding of the Political Science Department, Terman dealt with a particularly contentious appointment case that aggravated bitter feelings between older department faculty and the administration. The History Department, at the time the largest undergraduate major in humanities and sciences, also underwent significant faculty changes, but these were driven from within by the established faculty in a cooperative effort with the administration.

Stanford's Political Science Department

Political scientist Robert Rosenzweig argues that, as in other academic fields at Stanford, significant changes in the field of political science, and not the personal agendas of either Terman or Sterling, drove the rebuilding of Stanford's Political Science Department.[262] Behavioralist methodologies were the major developing trend in the social sciences in the immediate postwar decades. Stanford's attempts to build on its strengths in several areas among social science departments were particularly successful, resulting not only in stronger departments but also in productive interdepartmental programs and the creation of Stanford's Center for Advanced Study in the Behavioral Sciences. Stanford's Political Science Department in particular underwent a renaissance in the 1960s.

As he passed the provostial baton to Terman, Douglas Whitaker left his successor with comments about several "hot hot spots" in the school—among them, the Political Science Department. At least one faculty member in the department recommended abolishing the department altogether (after he retired, of course).[263] The department's quandary went beyond prickly faculty tempers, however. Terman was ultimately faced with deciding whether to push the department into new territory and higher ambitions, or accept it as a productive but not particularly well-respected undergraduate program—a valley among the schools' steeples. Throughout the 1950s, the Political Science Department had attracted little outside faculty research funding and granted comparatively few PhDs (one-quarter to one-third as many as either the English or History departments).[264]

The study of politics was, of course, firmly grounded in the Enlightenment gentleman's classical education, but its growth as an academic field began in the late nineteenth century in the study of history, constitutional law, political economy, and philosophy. (The American Political Science Association was founded in 1903.) Many history departments—including Stanford's—focused on the evolution of political institutions and the influence of political men. The study of American political science in particular was dominated by legal, philosophical, and historical methodology. Although the Department of Political Science was not formally established at Stanford until 1918, courses in the emerging field were something of a forte of the History and Sociology departments, particularly during the Progressive era, under men like George Howard and Edward Ross, among others. The Political Science Department thus inherited a strong tradition in historical studies, international relations, and political theory.

The field was significantly influenced by faculty at the University of Chicago's School of Political Science, who emphasized concrete empirical studies, interdisciplinary research strategies, quantitative methodologies, and the benefits of organized research support. The Chicago School also brought attention to the study of political law, political parties, elections and public opinion, interest groups, international relations, and comparative politics.[265]

As in other fields, war-related research during the Second World War introduced political scientists to the "behavioral sciences" and brought about increased use of deductive and mathematical methods and economic models during the 1950s and 1960s. University political science curricula expanded rapidly as the cold war fed the demand.

Social science institutes at the universities of Michigan, Columbia, and Chicago recruited and trained new "behavioral" sociologists, economists, and political scientists. Most influential was the University of Michigan's Institute of Social Research, which began its summer training institute as early as 1947. Equally important was the influence of talented émigré scholars who arrived from Europe in the years surrounding the war and into the cold-war era. It was in this context that Stanford sought to build up its Political Science Department.

Connections with the Ford Foundation during the 1950s strongly encouraged greater cultivation of the behavioral sciences at Stanford generally. Ford Foundation officers and consultants such as Rowan Gaither and W. Allen Wallis assisted Stanford in self-studies in the behavioral sciences and in establishing the Center for Advanced Studies in the Behavioral Sciences in 1954. This center brought to the campus scholars in history, political science, sociology, and other related fields who shared an interest in the behavioral sciences with Stanford faculty like Kenneth Arrow in economics, Patrick Suppes in philosophy, and Wilbur Schramm in communications. As it turned out, the center also served as a means to attract prominent or promising faculty who might be considered for positions on the Stanford faculty.

Throughout the early 1950s, various studies and assessments of teaching and research, particularly relating to new interest in the behavioral sciences, focused attention on the comparative inadequacies of the Political Science Department. In 1951, Stanford accepted a Ford Foundation grant of $100,000 to develop resources for research in individual behavior and human relations. In examining the "core" areas of Stanford's social sciences—namely, psychology, anthropology, sociology, economics, and political science—a committee appointed by Provost Whitaker and Graduate Dean Ernest Hilgard estimated that only the Psychology Department was in a relatively good position to support such research.[266]

Across the School of Humanities and Sciences, liberal promotions had been offered to make up for poor salary increases, leading to a disproportionately high proportion of full and associate professors who devoted much of their time to undergraduate teaching. This was clearly the case in political science. In December 1953, Acting Dean of Humanities and Sciences William McCord reported to Provost Whitaker that while the political science faculty taught a comparatively large number of undergraduates, they showed little evidence of leadership in their field and enjoyed little genuine cooperation with other related programs (a view shared subsequently by an external reviewer), including the Hoover Institution.[267] McCord's views were echoed in a 1954 Ford Foundation assessment of graduate study, whose political science consultant criticized the department for maintaining close ties only with the History Department but virtually no association with economics, sociology, anthropology, and other social sciences.[268]

Searching for Leaders

In November 1956, Provost Terman appointed a five-man committee to conduct searches for present and prospective vacant positions in the Political Science Department. (Alfred de Grazia, a political behavioralist and Chicago PhD who had spent several years at Stanford, was leaving.) Terman appointed Dean Phil Rhinelander as chair and the department's executive head, James T. Watkins IV, as vice chair. (Its three other members were Albert Bowker of statistics, who was also Terman's assistant in the Provost's Office, C. E. Rothwell of the Hoover Institution, and Robert A. Walker of the Political Science Department.[269])

Several excellent political science prospects had been at Stanford's Center for Advanced Studies, among them Robert Dahl in 1955–56 and Gabriel Almond in 1956–57. Dean Rhinelander approached such distinguished visitors and discussed Stanford and possible positions in the department. Heinz Eulau, on leave from

Antioch College and at the Center in 1957–58, was among those who gave Rhinelander a positive response. Eulau, a 1941 Berkeley PhD, had worked for the federal government during the war and then went into teaching. Eulau was one of those political scientists who had "retooled" his skills and approaches at Michigan during the early 1950s. Rhinelander proposed Eulau to James Watkins and Robert Walker at a dinner in the fall of 1957. Prompted by Terman and Rhinelander, the Political Science Department went along with the proposal. Eulau took up his appointment as professor in the fall of 1958.

At about the same time in 1957, a productive scholar and good teacher, Arnaud Leavelle, died unexpectedly, opening up a slot in "political theory." The Department of Philosophy also eyed this political theory slot with the reasonable argument that the study of political philosophy and theory had long been a legitimate subfield in classical philosophy. Terman and Rhinelander now determined to attract a major figure in this field, in addition to Eulau, such as the young and promising political theorist David Easton from Chicago (then visiting at the Stanford Center for Advanced Studies) or the well-established Louis Hartz of Harvard to replace Leavelle. Terman also supported the candidacy of behavioralist David Truman from Columbia.

The department rejected outright the candidacy of David Easton for the Leavelle position.[270] Having given way on the Eulau appointment, the political science faculty wanted to fill this slot on their own and sought the go-ahead to invite Mulford Quickert Sibley, a political theorist from Minnesota then visiting the department for the year. Sibley had become especially popular with undergraduates that year. Several years before, he had coauthored a prize-winning book on conscientious objectors during World War II. Reactions outside Stanford's department about his record at Minnesota, however, were mixed.[271] Sibley, a likeable person, a Quaker, and a vociferous pacifist, was considered by some at Minnesota as a public relations problem.[272] By spring 1958, the "Sibley Case" soon after became a cause celebre at Stanford.

On February 25, 1958, Watkins reported to Rhinelander that the department faculty had unanimously voted to recommend Sibley for the political theory post along with Heinz Eulau for the political behavior post. Rhinelander subsequently sought opinions outside the department: social psychologist Leon Festinger, formerly at Minnesota, did not support Sibley's appointment and suggested names at Minnesota for a better assessment of Sibley's record. Ithiel de Sola Pool (formerly at the Hoover Institution) liked Sibley personally, but felt that he would not advance the department's quality, would not make significant scholarly contributions, and was likely to confuse his role as a citizen with his role as a scholar.[273] Louis Hartz at Harvard (who Rhinelander considered an excellent candidate for a professorship at Stanford and head of the department) also reported that he had reservations about Sibley as a scholar.[274]

Rhinelander suspected, rightly as it turned out, that Hartz would not accept an offer from Stanford. "I am not happy about the Sibley recommendation," he wrote Bowker, "but I have signed it on a tentative basis because if our pitch to Louis Hartz should come to nothing it may be that Sibley is the best candidate we can get at the moment. . . . If there is any substantial hope of getting [Hartz] then I should certainly exclude Sibley."[275]

A week later, however, Rhinelander informed Watkins that while he had forwarded Eulau's recommendation to the President's Office, he had not endorsed that of Sibley. The dean went on to note that at the time of their recommendation of Sibley, none of the senior members of the department had read Sibley's chief work, nor had the department's recommendation contained any systematic statement of the specific grounds on which Sibley had been judged superior to the other candidates being considered. Both Hartz and Sibley might be lost to the department, he told Watkins, but "I think this is a risk which for the long-term good of the Department and the University we must be prepared to take."[276] Watkins did not accept Rhinelander's reasoning and was willing, as he had told Rhinelander the year before, to hire candidates even "if not so good."[277]

This was not the first time Watkins and Rhinelander had clashed, and the dean now recommended his replacement as executive head. Terman recommended Robert Walker, and Rhinelander agreed. Predictably, President Sterling's letter to Watkins discussing the removal was generous; Watkins, gentlemanly by nature, replied that he was pleased that his dismissal was for entirely personal reasons (as explained to him, "personal incompatibility" with Dean Rhinelander).[278]

The search committee met again. Having learned that Hartz, who was to leave Harvard, expected a salary offer far above what Stanford could afford, they again discussed Sibley. Rothwell, Walker, and Watkins strongly advocated Sibley as the best candidate "available," while Bowker abstained. Rhinelander went along "without a firm conviction" and reluctantly forwarded Sibley's recommendation to Terman.[279]

Al Bowker felt compelled to explain his abstention in a two-page report to Terman and Sterling the day after the committee meeting. He explained that he was present at only one meeting when Sibley had been discussed and commented that Sibley's name had not been on their list the year before. (Like Rhinelander, he thought Sibley's record had been incompletely compiled for the committee's consideration.) Bowker felt that there were better people in other, competing fields of interest—public administration, political behavior, public law—and even questioned the definition of political theory as used by Watkins and his colleagues (he felt they really meant philosophy). Although Sibley's scholarly work was good by the standards of Stanford's political science, he added, it appeared mediocre by the standards of philosophy or social sciences. Sibley might be considered an undergraduate teacher, he conjectured, but if so, the department would have to decide among Kurt Steiner and John Bunzel (junior faculty already in the department) and Sibley for a tenured appointment. "One possibility," wrote Bowker, "is to abandon the Political Science Department to mediocrity at the graduate level but insist that it be a good undergraduate department."[280]

Bowker also sent to the files a memo on an April discussion with Wallace Sterling, in which the president stated that if the administration went ahead with Sibley's appointment on grounds of expediency it would be one of a "chain of such events." Sterling was irritated that the committee was seeking to undercut his authority as president.[281]

Stanford's Department of Philosophy had been discussing the appointment of a political theorist for the last three years (in either philosophy or political science) and the possibility of a joint appointment. John Goheen and the Philosophy Department already had canvassed the field. Rhinelander, himself a philosophy professor, and Bowker approved of this strategy and further explored the possibilities of a position in political philosophy.[282] Rhinelander was disturbed, he told Terman, at the way Robert Walker brushed off John Goheen's proposal of a joint political philosophy appointment between political science and the Philosophy Department. Rhinelander doubted that political theory was as central to the Political Science Department as some contended, but Walker told him that "some members" of the department would resign if Sibley were not appointed (although he did not specify who these faculty were). If they were the "right ones," the dean quipped to Terman, it could improve the department. In his note on the conversation, Terman concluded that Rhinelander supported the Sibley appointment only on the grounds of expediency.[283]

Terman also had at hand the decidedly luke-warm comments of scholars like Ithiel Pool, Louis Hartz, Heinz Eulau, Leon Festinger, and John Goheen. Historian Tom Bailey, a noted scholar of political parties and elections, threw in his two cents as well in a letter to Rhinelander, advising against Sibley.[284] Finally, Sterling asked Terman personally to visit the University of Minnesota to inquire about Sibley's standing. Terman discussed Sibley's record with a half dozen senior scholars and administrators at Minnesota, including the associate dean of the Graduate School, the assistant dean of Humanities and Sciences, the head of the Political Science Department, and several senior faculty in the social sciences. All agreed that Sibley was intellectually sharp and a popular teacher, but that he had contributed little to the field of political theory. (Sibley taught mostly in general studies and in American studies and about one-third in political science.) Political scientists at Minnesota characterized Sibley's professionally significant publications as meager for a full professor—one book, three articles, and possibly a book chapter. Terman went on to discuss with them some twenty-eight items on Sibley's bibliography, but his advisors listed two-thirds of these as insignificant or unrefereed newspaper-type publications. Most of his writings were for a lay public rather than scholarly publication. Sibley was fair to students, reported several, and did not insist on agreement with his own socialist, pacifist views. Another commented that the majority of the Minnesota faculty regarded Sibley as a "slight screwball." He was biased against empirical studies, but interested in mental telepathy and psychical research, according to the associate graduate dean at Minnesota (a psychologist). Sibley ranged widely in his courses and got out of his areas of competence in lectures in American studies. If the department needed undergraduate interdisciplinary teaching from a humanist standpoint, he suggested to Terman, or if a department was "stuffy and needs a gadfly," then Sibley would be good.[285]

Stanford economist Kenneth Arrow had also been asked earlier in the search to inquire among colleagues at Minnesota. Dean Rhinelander noted that Arrow reported to him that an eminent economist at Minnesota thought Sibley was not regarded as a strong faculty member and was surprised that Stanford was considering him.[286] Sterling, too, personally inquired about Sibley. On Sterling's behalf, President Grayson Kirk of Columbia (a political scientist) made enquiries of his Political Science Department and reported to Sterling that Sibley was considered a good teacher but that his writing did not indicate distinguished scholarship.[287]

By early May, Rhinelander pressed Sterling for a decision, one way or the other, on Sibley.[288] According to Al Bowker, Heinz Eulau, and others, the question now was whether Stanford would build up the comparative strength of the Political Science Department, or leave it largely a teaching department. The latter state of affairs was no longer acceptable to Rhinelander, Terman, *or* Sterling.

The Sterling administration refused to offer Sibley a permanent position and soon took public as well as campus heat for the decision. The *Stanford Daily* student paper severely criticized Sterling and Terman, and the case was taken up by the local press. A number of political science faculty, especially some younger members, smarted under the administration's decision on Sibley.[289] Campus feelings cooled down, but the Political Science Department was left bruised. Interestingly, the department next swung to a candidate politically opposite of Sibley and invited Wilmoore Kendall of Yale, a conservative, to Stanford for the 1958–59 year. Kendall, too, had strong student support, although his teaching and personal habits while at Stanford got mixed reviews. As President Sterling put it in a letter, "He panicked at large classes and drank. He improved, but we're not keeping him."[290] If, as one scholar has suggested, Sibley was declined primarily because of his leftist political views, Kendall, distinctly conservative, was hardly considered an attractive alternative by that same administration.[291]

Were the administration's actions concerning the Political Science Department faculty taken primarily due either to political discrimination or a preference for behaviorial sciences? Assistant professor John Bunzel, it is also alleged, was denied tenure in 1963 because of undue influence exerted by conservative trustees

David Packard and Thomas Pike.[292] It should be noted, however, that the School of Humanities and Sciences tenure review committee, including senior members from economics, history, psychology, and sociology, had already voted against Bunzel's promotion to tenure on grounds of scholarship before receiving or knowing of any statements from Terman or Sterling.[293]

As elsewhere at Stanford, changes in approach and methodology in the field of political science, rather than personal political agendas of either Terman or Sterling, brought about reassessment of the effectiveness of the department's teaching and place nationally in the field. The first key move to revitalizing political science at Stanford, argues Robert Rosenzweig, was the hiring of Heinz Eulau; the next move was not to seek out another behaviorist, but to find a *leader*.[294]

Shortly after Robert Sears succeeded Rhinelander as dean of humanities and sciences in September 1961, he too concluded that vacancies in political science created an unusual opportunity to strengthen that department, both from the standpoint of national visibility and its vitality at the graduate level. The most recent four additions to the faculty (Robert C. North, Heinz Eulau, Arnold A. Rogow, and Jan F. Triska) had worked well with this strategy. Stanford should seek to attract a star appointment, Sears hoped, as had been so brilliantly done in history, English, psychology, and chemistry. Or it could continue to build from the bottom up with younger people, but in doing so must select such persons on the sole criterion of research and scholarly promise, as well as vigor of intellect. Sears suspected, however, that some of the older department members would assert that coverage of particular subfields should predominate over brilliance and promise.[295]

Among his first steps, Sears asked Robert Walker to step down from the chairmanship of the department. In 1956, Walker had chaired the Committee on General Studies and devoted much of his time subsequently to organize support for and firmly establish Stanford's overseas studies program. (The first campus was opened in Germany in 1958, with additional sites established in France, Italy, Austria, and England by 1966.[296]) Walker turned his full attention to the program, serving as its director until 1972.

Sears could now vigorously recruit Gabriel Almond of Yale, but while Almond lingered over the decision to accept, Sears speculated about appointing Heinz Eulau as interim executive head of political science. Eulau got along splendidly with Sears, but Walker, Watkins, Steiner, and Hubert Marshall were against the appointment. Eulau would be a disaster as head, Robert Horn wrote in an impassioned letter to Sears.[297] Instead, the dean installed Nobutaka Ike for a year.[298] Almond accepted the position of professor and department head later in 1963.[299]

Sears nonetheless continued to seek Eulau's advice. Asked by Sears in 1962, "What does Political Science want?" Eulau asked for four junior positions, regardless of field, and the best young scholars one could get. Sears agreed, and the department chose Richard A. Brody, Richard R. Fagen, Martin Shapiro, and

Raymond E. Wolfinger.[300] (Brody and Fagen enjoyed long and excellent careers at Stanford; Shapiro and Wolfinger each left after several years to make bright careers at Harvard and Berkeley, respectively.)

By 1963, Sears wrote Associate Provost Bob Wert that he was elated over the improvement of the Political Science Department. Sears felt that Almond's appointment had paid off "beyond my wildest expectations or hopes," and he described the department's hiring of junior faculty Brody, Fagen, Shapiro, and Wolfinger as acquiring "four crackerjacks all at once."[301]

With Gabriel Almond's arrival in 1963, the department also broadened, moving toward international relations rather than strictly quantitative studies as some have believed.[302] In 1964, celebrated specialist in comparative politics Sidney Verba came to Stanford from Princeton. He had just published, with Almond, a well-received book on civic culture in five different nations that became a classic in twentieth-century political science.[303] In addition to Verba, Almond succeeded in bringing Alexander L. George and John W. Lewis. Shortly after his arrival, Almond used a $50,000 grant from the Ford Foundation's International Program to form an Institute of Political Studies. The institute was a coalition of four faculty interests—Heinz Eulau (American), Almond (comparative), Robert North (international), and Jan Triska (Soviet and Eastern Europe)—and was a major support for the department.[304]

The Department of Political Science was well on its way. It became more balanced in area studies and comparative politics, and quantitative approaches were strengthened without dominating. With the support of the dean and provost, Eulau helped bring in promising younger scholars, while Almond brought in well-established figures. Almond worked well with Sears and felt that Terman always supported candidates of very high quality, without regard to subfield or personal political persuasion. (When Bowker proudly brought Almond to the Provost's Office to show him off to Terman, Almond discovered that Fred really did still wear high-button shoes.[305])

As the dean gained confidence in the high quality of his choices, Almond recalled, departmental budgeting and position allocation also became much easier. For example, in 1964, Almond asked if Stanford could hire C. U. Pritchett of the University of Chicago for the winter quarter 1965–66 as lecturer in American democracy. Terman funded the visit out of the Provost's Reserve Fund. (Terman also used his reserve fund of $130,000 that year to give expeditious support to earth sciences, international studies, undergraduate general studies, overseas programs, salary increases, an appointment in chemistry, and women's physical education.[306])

In 1964, Stanford's Political Science Department was ranked ninth in the nation in the quality of its faculty and sixth in effectiveness in the graduate program. This survey had included a much larger number of universities than the previous (1957) study that had placed Stanford thirteenth out of only twenty-five. Similar survey data taken again in 1969 increased Stanford's ranking to a tie for sixth in terms of faculty and a tie for third in effectiveness of graduate program.[307] This was a striking validation of the improvement of the Stanford Department of Political Science during the Sterling-Terman years.

It is interesting to note that of the five political science candidates favored by Deans Rhinelander and Sears and Provost Terman (Gabriel Almond, Robert Dahl, David Easton, Heinz Eulau, and David Truman), all five served as president of the American Political Science Association. Stanford succeeded in getting Almond and Eulau, and nearly succeeded in getting Truman to succeed Fred Terman as provost.

The Humanities at Stanford

Although respectable, the humanities at Stanford by the late 1950s were not highly regarded nationally. Fred Terman knew this and was glad to promote their improvement. Much of the credit for improvement of the humanities, however, lay in the ambition of the faculty itself.[308]

Just how Stanford defined the "humanities" had changed quite a bit over time, but the grouping consisted roughly of history, religion, philosophy, and the languages and literature departments as one part, and the fine arts of art, music, and drama as another. A new School of Humanities had been formed in 1941, absorbing "letters" (Classics, English, and the Germanic, Romantic, and Slavic languages departments), along with history, philosophy, and religion, and the departments of a languishing and only half-recognized School of Fine Arts created five years before (art, music, and drama). Just to make matters more confusing, several departments were overseen by more than one school. History and philosophy were members of both humanities and social sciences; speech and drama had floated between English and the Fine Arts School; graphic art found a home in the School of Education.[309]

In response to a 1955 American Council of Learned Societies (ACLS) study, Ray Faulkner, then acting head of humanities and sciences, surveyed the most pressing needs of the humanities at Stanford. Faulkner summarized for ACLS data regarding the Classics, English, History, and Philosophy departments (since other departments apparently did not take his request for information seriously). Faulkner concluded that the major humanities needs at Stanford appeared to be for more graduate fellowships and travel funds; brighter and better-trained faculty; a better library; and funds for translation of language materials.[310] These would largely be Stanford's ongoing targets for improvement over the next decade.

The English Department was among those that soon prospered. Its faculty doubled during the Terman years.[311] In 1957, Virgil Whitaker, then head of the department, reported to his faculty that while administrative reports, surveys, and red tape seemed to be on the rise, "a number of things are getting done that should have been done before." Acting instructors in English had been given lightened teaching loads, for example, and were henceforth automatically given a half-tuition scholarship. A few months later, Whitaker saw good progress toward gaining ten fellowships for four years of graduate study in English.[312] Bliss Carnochan, who joined the English Department in 1960 and later served as department head, looks back at the Sterling-Terman years as good for the English Department and for the humanities in general.[313]

As Whitaker pointed out, however, decision making had indeed become more complex. Unlike engineering and the sciences, where changes were often top down affairs, the humanities, like the social sciences, exchanged the neglect that often accompanied autonomy for layers of attention and scrutiny. Stanford-trained humanists were well represented among the administration—Rixford Snyder, dean of admissions, came from the history faculty, and Ray Faulkner (art), acting dean of humanities and sciences through the mid-1950s, and his successor as dean of humanities and sciences, 1956–61, Phil Rhinelander (philosophy) were from the humanities. Assistant Provost and later Vice Provost Howard Brooks (history) and Graduate Dean Virgil Whitaker (English) were both Stanford PhDs, as was Wallace Sterling, who retained an emotional tie to the History Department and continued to meet frequently with humanities department heads.[314] (As for the social sciences, Bob Wert, who had both an MBA and Stanford PhD in education, was interested in political theory, while Bob Rosenzweig was a political scientist.)

As soon as the PACE campaign got underway in the fall of 1961, questions were immediately raised about Stanford's commitment to the humanities. A public panel discussion on "The Sciences and the Humanities," moderated by law professor Herbert Packer (and featuring representatives from biochemistry, philosophy, physics, electrical engineering, and the administration) fielded questions about support for the humanities.[315] During the campaign itself, Terman took pains to point out the need to support the humanities and argued that the popular idea that large government programs in science and engineering at the university took resources from the humanities and social sciences was a myth. Without government funds, there would be "irresistible" pressure to take support for science and engineering out of university general funds, resulting in a smaller proportion for the humanities and social sciences, he said.[316] Stanford's plan was to build the humanities in tandem with the sciences, social sciences, and engineering.

Interestingly, on that Stanford Today panel, the humanities were represented by the recently resigned dean of humanities and sciences, philosophy professor Phil Rhinelander, whose strong opinions on the topic and clashes with the provost were campus news itself. Rhinelander had worked strenuously to increase the prestige and the resources of the humanities. A 1961 study from the Stanford Humanities Council, appointed by Dean Rhinelander to investigate the humanistic disciplines at Stanford and chaired by John D. Goheen of philosophy, reported that "There has been a significant—in some ways dramatic—change in the status (relative and absolute) of the Humanities during the last five years. . . . We have indeed reached a point where we can truthfully say that the Humanities have finally turned a difficult corner."[317] In percentage terms, the humanities at Stanford received 41 percent of the humanities and sciences budget, compared to 34 percent at Harvard, 35 percent at Swarthmore, and 39 percent at Columbia.[318] Nevertheless, while recognizing the significant—"in some ways a dramatic"—improvement in the humanities since Terman's joining the Sterling administration, the report asked for further assistance in obtaining better faculty, a renovated and expanded library, and graduate fellowships.[319] Less than a year later, the council and new dean of humanities and sciences, backed by ten pages of statistics provided by Terman's office, asked the administration more forthrightly for assistance.[320]

Salaries and research funds, especially in physics, mathematics, and economics, were substantially higher than in humanities, but the humanities faculty realized that possibilities for outside support were much fewer than for similar support for the sciences and social sciences.[321] Although in 1962 the highest maximum and highest median salaries for full professors at Stanford were paid to faculty in the School of Humanities and Sciences (followed by those in Law and Business), these statistics were skewed by the high salaries paid to newer natural science and economics faculty.[322] Over the next two years, the Provost's Office, along with the deans of the Department of Humanities and Sciences and of the Medical School, worked persistently to establish tenure guidelines and promotion policies aimed at giving fair evaluation and balanced remuneration to faculty and to effect major improvements in the humanities.[323]

Terman put his Graduate Dean Albert Bowker onto another way to approach the problem of parity.[324] Bowker interviewed a number of younger faculty members and found that among the twenty-five to thirty research-oriented assistant and associate professors in the humanities, the greatest perceived need was for paid time off for research. Bowker proposed to the Humanities Council and the president that the university increase paid faculty fellowships and provide better office space, common rooms, and study rooms for advanced graduate students.

Letting History Take Off

One of the largest (in both student enrollments and faculty size), oldest, and most esteemed departments in the humanities at Stanford was the Department of History. Although the department largely stuck to traditional studies—ancient, medieval, and renaissance history, English, American, and modern European history—it entered fairly early into some less-charted quarters such as the history of the Pacific Slope and Asian and Pan-Pacific studies. It also took an active part in building the collections of the Hoover War Library. Its Problems in Citizenship course, which evolved into a year-long History of Western Civilization course required of all undergraduates, became one of the school's most popular, if more complicated, teaching programs.[325]

The History Department faculty had been quite comfortable in the School of Social Sciences and was so reluctant to be drawn into the new School of Humanities in 1941 that they suggested the creation of their own School of History. As a concession, this haughty department was allowed to straddle both schools, while its long-time executive head, Edgar Eugene Robinson, carefully guarded his department's territory.

Contrary to the situation in the Political Science Department in the late 1950s, the History Department appeared to be in rather good shape. Graduate work in history flourished during the GI Bill years. By 1955, the History Department was the largest producer of bachelor's degrees within the university, and among the largest producers of PhDs (although with rising qualifications, graduate enrollments were falling).[326] Nearly half of the Humanities Honors Program enrollments were students in history.[327]

By all evidence, history was still a scrappy department. Department Head Thomas A. Bailey reacted quickly, and predictably tartly, to comments of the university's 1953 self-study committee by suggesting that its authors knew little about history or about the department.[328] His faculty bristled at the suggestion, he said, that their teaching was outdated, overly concerned with "places and periods," and not adequately involved with interdisciplinary courses. Nevertheless, a year later, a Ford Foundation visitor reported that the History Department had not taken advantage of opportunities to appoint the strongest possible candidates and needed to focus its teaching efforts, utilize more fully the resources of the Hoover Institution Library, and increase the number of courses on other cultures more "remote in time and space."[329]

History had fared well in an extensive 1955 survey of undergraduate student teaching satisfaction. Graduating members of Stanford's class of 1955 were given an eight-page questionnaire on teaching evaluation and more than 60 percent of the 865 seniors responded.[330] The results were calculated separately for women and men. Women rated psychology highest, and men chose physics, chemistry, and chemical engineering above the rest, but for *both* men and women, the Departments of History, Humanities Special Programs, Biology, and the Engineering School in general were highly rated. The History Department's year-long, required History of Western Civilization course was judged by the seniors as far and away the most valuable course taken during their undergraduate years.[331] (In contrast, among the most unsatisfactory teaching experiences at Stanford for women were journalism and the Romance languages, and for men the Reserve Officer Training Corps instruction; for *both* men and women, the Departments of Sociology, Anthropology, and English rated most unsatisfactory.)

The 1955 survey, however, illuminated ongoing problems at the graduate student level. Housing, fellowship and scholarship aid, and teaching loads continued to be significant problems for graduate students in general. But while science and engineering graduate students had a better chance of working on research projects and gaining work-study assistance, humanities graduate students were more or less limited to instructing in freshman English or Western Civilization courses and grading papers. Undergraduates were also affected by this trend: the large (often more than one hundred students) first-year Physics 50 classes were taught by senior faculty, and graduate students were limited to running labs and grading homework; English and history students enjoyed smaller sections to accompany lecture classes, but these were often taught by relatively inexperienced graduate student instructors.

The administration was well aware of the need for increasing graduate fellowships. In 1958, Al Bowker had advised Terman that history was a prime candidate to apply for three to five of the new National Defense Education Act (NDEA) fellowships.[332] The following year, Terman congratulated Bailey on the progress of the History Department in attracting an increasing number of good undergraduate majors and suggested that the heavy advising load of the department and the increase in student course enrollment earned the department "some special consideration" for faculty slots and other assistance.[333] By 1959–60, Stanford had eighteen humanities graduate students with NDEA fellowships, and with the addition of social sciences, Stanford had twenty-six NDEA fellows in 1960–61.[334]

Clearly, by 1960 the self-confident history faculty considered itself a prime candidate for additional faculty. Gordon Wright of the University of Oregon had been among several senior people who had turned down the Europeanist position eventually offered to H. Stuart Hughes (grandson of the former U.S. chief justice) of Harvard in 1952. Hughes was a productive young scholar and a good administrator (he had excelled in administration with the State Department during World War II), and thus was a real catch, Sterling believed, for a middle-level position.[335] Hughes served as head of the department and worked out so well that the president considered offering him a deanship or associate deanship in 1955, but this brought forth the charge of "robbery." (The department had already lost British historian Rixford K. Snyder, who became dean of admissions and took with him young Howard Brooks.[336]) When Hughes returned to Harvard in 1957, Bailey reluctantly took over as head until a successor could be found. Stanford again turned to Gordon Wright, who had earned his PhD at Stanford in 1939 and had a distinguished reputation as a scholar of French history. Wright replaced Hughes and eventually succeeded Tom Bailey as head of the department.[337]

Few other changes, however, had occurred in the department during the later 1950s. Arthur Wright, with his wife, Hoover Institution scholar Mary Wright, formed a valuable duo in Chinese history, but Stanford was slow to promote Arthur Wright. As events played out, the couple left Stanford for Yale where they were promised an unbeatable offer of salary, rank, and a research program backed by a splendid document collection.[338] A more fruitful route to improvement now appeared to be use of funds from a major donor. In the early 1950s, Tom Bailey had cultivated William R. Coe, a wealthy and conservative philanthropist interested in American studies. Some years before, Coe had supported American studies at Yale, and he was impressed with Stanford's American history summer program in secondary-school teacher education. In his will, Coe left Stanford funds for American studies, which could be applied to American political, social, or economic history, or American literature. But President Sterling had decided to use the Coe funds to buttress weaker social science departments—prominent political scientists Clinton L. Rossiter, Robert A. Dahl, and Louis Hartz were among those who turned down offers that would have used Stanford's Coe funds. History, not being one of the weaker departments, was instead offered the chance to name Otis Pease (already on board) as "Coe Associate Professor." Some portion of his salary was, in fact, paid with Coe funds, which took some pressure off Sterling—the Coe Foundation was edgy that Stanford had not yet succeeded in attracting an outstanding scholar as Coe Professor.

At this point, the administration actively sought an economic historian who would be acceptable to the faculty of both the Economics and History departments, a highly unlikely feat. When an associate professorship in economic history was offered to Sigmund Diamond of Columbia in the early spring of 1960, History Department Head Gordon Wright and former head Tom Bailey simultaneously cried out in anger. Each assumed that this would cost the department a full-time slot (Diamond would not *permanently* be offered Coe funds, which the administration preferred to use on a flexible yearly basis). Even though history (actually, Tom Bailey) had done the work to secure the Coe funds, they asserted, the department was forced to stand aside while Coe Professorships were being offered to other departments. Otis Pease, they believed, had been given a name only with Coe money, at no manpower or permanent salary gain to the History Department. Why were the Political Science and Sociology departments getting appointments, they asked, but not a stronger department like History?[339] Although this might appear overly excited, the history faculty had good reason to feel that their department had been the victim of a fast shuffle, and that somehow they were losing out—either funds or a tenured slot—on the deal.

In a brief handwritten memo stapled to this correspondence, Terman wrote to

Sterling, "This annoys me in light of [the] Tom Bailey letter and [the] fact that in 1958–59 Phil Rhinelander had set up History budget with Coe [funds] paying Pease salary and paid most or all in 1959–60 from Coe."[340] And so Terman responded to Wright and Bailey, explaining the administration's actions but asking them to come to his office to discuss their complaints further.[341] He reminded them of the Coe funding two years before but more importantly, he discussed Stanford's efforts to attract truly first-rate scholars and said in effect, "when have you brought me a proposal to invite a top senior scholar and had me turn you down?" As Bailey later recalled, the two of them left Terman's office and immediately discussed the situation with their colleagues.[342]

When, in the early weeks of April 1960 Sig Diamond turned down Stanford's offer, the History Department had a quick response. Braced with Terman's remarks of a few weeks earlier, it had not taken them long to settle on forty-nine-year-old David Potter, Coe Professor and head of the American Studies Program at Yale as their candidate. Potter had published six well-received books and had an international reputation for his pathbreaking 1954 book *People of Plenty*. He was an outstanding lecturer and conversant in southern history, constitutional history, historiography, and American economic history, as well as American studies. He was a perfect fit for a Coe Professorship. Fortunately, his family had loved Stanford during a previous year spent in Palo Alto (he had taught for two summers at Stanford in the Coe summer program), and Potter welcomed the offer.[343]

By April 27, Dean Rhinelander wrote to Bob Wert (who was Potter's friend) that after unsuccessful searches for an Americanist in political science and in economics, Stanford ought to get the best Americanist possible; if Potter were available, he should be offered a Coe Professorship.[344] The following day, Tom Bailey pressed both Terman and Sterling to make the appointment.[345] "The speed with which things have been happening around here this week," Wright wrote Potter, "proves, I think, that there's life in Stanford yet." The department was being authorized to bring a formal offer, he added, and the administration was very enthusiastic.[346] They were so enthusiastic, it turns out, that Terman and Sterling agreed on a salary for Potter some 15 percent higher than what Bailey and Wright had originally proposed. Terman made the final arrangements with Potter in early August 1960, and Potter arrived at Stanford for the fall semester of 1961. Potter followed Wright as department head and took a leading role in reassessing and improving the graduate program in American history and a strong hand in further faculty improvements.[347] Fred Terman's "go-ahead" signal for top quality led the History Department to another important appointment less than three months later. At a history convention in Seattle in September 1960, Tom Bailey learned that German historian Gordon Craig of Princeton would be interested in moving West. Wright immediately approached Craig, who replied that he was very impressed with the History Department's present high standing and bright future prospects. Craig was offered a professorship in late October, and he accepted the offer within two days (he arrived on campus early in the summer of 1961). This was a coup of the first magnitude, Bailey wrote Terman, and on behalf of the whole History Department, he complimented Terman and "the entire front office" for their magnificent cooperation in making possible the Potter and Craig appointments. Bailey was convinced that Craig's interest in the Stanford offer was closely connected to Potter's acceptance.[348] It was certainly reminiscent of the lustrous tandem arrival of Arthur Kornberg and Joshua Lederberg in the biological sciences a year earlier. Gordon Craig believes that the provost and deans during the 1960s and 1970s had the better vision and creativeness, and that the History Department and the School of Humanities and Sciences were certainly amazed when Sterling and Terman raided the East for faculty in the early 1960s. But Craig gives top marks to David Potter, who was excellent with personnel, for building the History Department. He credits Potter with making the History Department "really good" in a second phase, bringing along the younger people who came in the later 1960s.[349]

In the spring of 1961, Terman followed up with Wright on an experiment to see how teaching could be improved in the larger classes.[350] His remarks to Wright at a recent cocktail party, he quipped, were not the result of "a couple of gin and tonics," but founded on a more solid basis. Terman suggested additional funding for such things as preparation of graphic or written material for handouts; summer pay for a faculty member to rework and improve the course material; paying graduate student readers for short essays on reading assignments; and additional weekly conferences between teaching assistants and undergraduate class members. Terman stressed that the details would be up to the department. He was looking for imaginative proposals that might well differ from one faculty member to another. Since history had so many excellent teachers, Terman thought it would be a good place to begin the experiment. Three history professors took up the invitation; two tried the experiment in 1962 and reported considerable success in their efforts.[351] In 1961, at the request of Dean Rhinelander, Gordon Wright reported on the state of his department. Wright was proud to mention that Stanford stood approximately tenth in the nation in the number of history doctoral candidates and that it continued to be the largest undergraduate major department in the university. Equally important, the quality of the history undergraduate majors had improved: Stanford's current two Rhodes Scholars were both history majors; Stanford's two finalists in the Marshall Scholarship competition were both history majors; and Stanford's nominees for Woodrow Wilson fellowships included a large plurality of history majors. Stanford was attracting more graduate fellowship winners from other universities and the nine Woodrow Wilson fellows in history exceeded that of any other department at Stanford.[352]

Fred Terman, too, was proud of the department's recent achievements and appointments, from the young and promising Richard Lyman to the better-established Potter and Craig.[353] He pointed out such triumphs in speeches he gave to alumni during the PACE campaign. Although Terman considered himself no expert in the humanities, he remained interested in history throughout his life. His avocation during his latter years as an administrator was reading Roman and medieval history (administrator E. Howard Brooks recalled that Terman had read Gordon Craig's work on German history *before* Craig had been invited to Stanford).[354]

The Provost and the Dean

Planning and decision making for the School of Humanities and Sciences at Stanford depended on a smooth working relationship between provost and dean. This was an especially important relationship as the 1960s opened up, as the provost and his staff took an increasing load off the President's Office and now attended to planning, development, implementation, and policy regarding faculty, students, and facilities in the Schools of Medicine, Law, Business, Education, Mineral Sciences, and Engineering, as well as Humanities and Sciences. The dean, in turn, was faced with administering the largest, most diverse, and historically least manageable of Stanford's academic programs at a time of great change and opportunity.

Terman's proclivities, as an engineer, a highly successful dean of engineering, and the son of Lewis Terman, were to quantify means of assessment and seek clearly definable goalposts. A favorite faculty anecdote pictures Terman sitting quietly each year on stage at graduation ceremonies, mechanical pencil poised, carefully using his program to calculate and compare doctoral production statistics. Fred preserved these annotated graduation programs for nearly all years 1951 through his retirement in 1965 in his files.[355] Fred nearly always put these data jottings to use in some way. He noted in a report, for example, the early productivity of economist Kenneth Arrow, who in his first years at Stanford produced about twenty times as many PhDs as a particular and mediocre senior member of the department.

Faculty in the humanities did not always appreciate Terman's penchant for measurable results, and some thought he lacked empathy with their own goals and methods. However, while Terman may not have understood the humanists, Robert Sears later recalled, he considered Stanford's humanities departments to be an important part of the university and firmly believed that they should be encouraged to be as strong as other campus departments. Fortunately, Terman was good at taking advice about things he did not understand, another colleague, Bob

Rosenzweig, commented. Stanford, as a great university, had to be broad in its greatness.[356] "I wasn't sure he could do the job," said Lillian Owen, Wallace Sterling's executive secretary and Fred's 1920 Stanford classmate. "After all, he had only been involved with the engineering side of the university. But he studied, he studied . . . he always had the humanities people come and talk to him so he could know as much as possible about what they were doing. He was a fine administrator."[357]

Terman's alleged difficulties with the humanities is more a final legacy of his working relations with Dean Phil Rhinelander than his success or failure in supporting humanities programs or goals. Indeed, Terman and Sterling had worked well with Rhinelander for several years, jointly working on such goals as improving faculty salaries and making major new appointments, developing the Project "M" accelerator project, and attracting better-qualified entering freshman and graduate students.

Rhinelander, however, personally felt that Stanford's administration worked harder for the sciences and engineering than for the humanities, for graduate students and faculty research more than for undergraduate needs. His own inclination was to protect the school. Humanities and sciences taught two-thirds of Stanford's undergraduates, he complained to Sterling after a year in office, yet the school received only two-thirds of this tuition income back for humanities and sciences uses.[358] Sterling subsequently raised the school's budget by $340,000, with half of that amount set aside for new faculty slots or for promotion raises.[359] Rhinelander's strategy is reminiscent of that of Dean Fred Terman, who had similarly written President Sterling two years before to point out that while overall university student growth was static, engineering graduate, and especially undergraduate, enrollments had risen significantly. One-third of the lower-division undergraduate men were enrolling in engineering. Of the additional $150,000 in tuition this had brought to Stanford, $90,000 (60 percent) went into general university funds, and only 40 percent into the engineering school.[360]

Rhinelander annually pressed Sterling for additional funds for his school and reminded the administration that the monetary allowance per each humanities and sciences student was far lower than that for any of the other schools in the university.[361] By December 1959, Rhinelander was so frustrated over budget affairs that he came to Sterling's office more than once "really in a tizzy," remembers Sterling's assistant Fred Glover. Later that month, he engaged in a bitter debate with Vice President for Finance Kenneth Cuthbertson.[362]

Rhinelander's working relationship with the Provost's and President's offices began to deteriorate seriously with the pressure of assessment and planning efforts of 1959 and 1960 that evolved into the Red Book and the PACE campaign. In January 1960, each of Stanford's deans and department heads was asked to help with the planning document, "Stanford's Needs and Opportunities, 1960–70" (the funding proposal planned for the Ford Foundation visit in April 1960).[363] Philip Rhinelander was furious with an early draft of this report and composed a sarcastic response to Fred Terman, including the comment that higher administrators would again learn only from their mistakes. He bitterly complained that while the report was full of building plans and salary needs, his ideas regarding improvement of undergraduate programs had received very little note. Rhinelander sent a draft of this letter to Ray Faulkner, associate dean of humanities and sciences, with the note: "Maybe I shouldn't send this?" Faulkner replied, "You're right." The letter was filed away rather than sent, evidence of the depth of his suspicions.[364]

Instead, in March 1960 Rhinelander submitted to Sterling a seven-page proposal for strengthening the undergraduate curriculum, with undergraduate majors to be decided by groups of topics, rather than courses, and with a general examination at the end of the senior year. He proposed greatly enlarging the number of honors programs, and undergraduates doing senior honors theses, and suggested replacing graduate teaching assistants with postdoctoral faculty. He imagined a better undergraduate library, faculty resident members in coeducational student residences, and special residential honors colleges.[365] Many of his ideas would be explored and implemented over the next two decades, but his document had little place in the effort underway to prepare for the Ford Foundation visit now only a few weeks away. Humanities and sciences department heads were instead rallied at the last minute by Associate Dean Sandy Dornbusch to submit lists of urgent requirements and ten-year forecasts.[366]

That summer, with the Ford Foundation's support almost assured, Robert Wert had two long discussions with Rhinelander about the humanities in general and more specifically about undergraduate education. Planning for undergraduate education at Stanford left much to be desired, and Wert encouraged Rhinelander to add an associate dean ("as near equivalent to Pat Suppes as possible"), but Rhinelander disliked the idea of establishing a position responsible for undergraduate studies. They also discussed some of the departmental wish lists. Both agreed, for example, that plans for the Theater Arts Center and for the Fine Arts Building had been based on no clear planning or interaction by the departments concerned and that much work needed to be done.[367] In the months following, Stanford's administration continued to push for a dean of undergraduate education, and Rhinelander continued to resist.[368]

As planning for the PACE campaign took shape, Rhinelander formed his own Development Committee of the School of Humanities and Sciences. Ken Cuthbertson wrote Rhinelander of the potential helpfulness of such a committee to the larger campaign effort, but cautioned the dean against going out on his own with "position papers" without going through channels.[369] Clashes over departmental autonomy brought forth criticism within the school itself. When he spoke to the heads of the three fine arts departments, Dornbusch reported to Rhinelander, they all "expressed disbelief" at the notion that they should be expected to cooperate in an integrated plan for a new fine arts building.[370] Humanities Professor John W. Dodds, in turn, complained to Rhinelander about Dornbusch and "ad hoc . . . Super Policy-making" committees of a few people trying to tell individual departments what to do.[371]

Budget battles erupted again in the summer of 1961, when Rhinelander charged that Stanford's administration only talked about undergraduate education and the liberal arts but would not put any money toward them.[372] Rhinelander then sent Terman a letter charging the Provost's Office with five serious faults, complaining especially about the provost's staff changing budget figures without departmental consultation and giving the dean insufficient consideration. Further Rhinelander insisted that he and Terman negotiate the matter.[373] According to Rhinelander, Terman agreed to lunch to discuss the letter. In Rhinelander's mind, the lunch was pleasant, but Terman did not budge on "negotiating."[374]

On July 10, Fred Terman replied that over the past two weeks his office had received six memoranda from Rhinelander requesting various revisions of the humanities and sciences budget, but with both Wert and President Sterling away, further staff work would be required before any more changes or decisions could be made. (Rhinelander's proposed salary changes for fifteen individuals and two departments were in areas that fell under Wert's responsibility.) Although polite, the text of Terman's letter clearly reveals his frustration.[375] That same day, Rhinelander wrote Sterling to say that relations had gotten so bad between himself and Terman's office that he was resigning as soon as possible.[376] Sterling was surprised at the turn of events and continued to exchange letters and phone calls with Rhinelander when the dean left for his summer home in Maine. Rhinelander had told Sterling that the less said the better, and that if a reason for his resignation were needed, to say "differences of policy." Meanwhile, however, someone leaked the news of the tendered resignation to the local press by early August.[377]

Faculty began to complain about Rhinelander's resignation, even though Sterling had not yet accepted the resignation nor had word about the resignation left his own office. The popular version of the story was that behind it all was the fact that Fred Terman's office could not get along with Rhinelander. Sidney Drell of physics, Wilfred Stone of English, and several other faculty wrote Sterling in support of Rhinelander, who stood, they believed, for core values of a traditional university. Physicist Walter Meyerhof, still bitter about SLAC, complained about an unnamed high administrator who wanted to put on a research "show" and about the large number of administrators and development office people who had little understanding of a true university.[378] Not all were supportive of Rhinelander, however, and were worried more about his replacement. The new dean of humanities and sciences, warned Lorie Tarshis of economics, must have a "clear understanding" of budget matters or things would go badly for humanities and sciences.[379]

Terman said little about the matter while Sterling met in early August with "not fewer than seventeen of our colleagues," including ten executive heads of humanities and sciences departments and four colleagues outside the school. After this discussion, Sterling wrote Rhinelander, "I accept your resignation as of today" (August 8, 1961).[380] In responding to Sidney Drell, Sterling commented, "The situation was not as simple as you may have concluded."[381]

Philip Rhinelander continued to teach in the Philosophy Department for some years and continued to support strengthening of the humanities and undergraduate education. Sterling immediately appointed a committee to recommend a new dean of humanities and sciences, and when urged to ask Stanford psychologist Robert R. "Bob" Sears, Sterling quickly did so. Sears accepted the office on August 18.[382] Sears's father had been a colleague of Lewis Terman in psychology, and the Sears and Terman families had become close decades before. Young Sears was among the "gifted children" studied by the senior Terman, who encouraged his career in psychology. After receiving his PhD at Yale in 1932, Sears had risen in the Social Relations Department at Harvard. He had returned to Stanford in 1953 to become executive head of psychology. His wife, Pauline Sears, was also on the faculty.

Terman trusted Sears's judgment and appreciated his high academic standards, and Sears worked easily with both Sterling and Terman.[383] Sears also had the support of Stanford's deans. Albert Bowker, graduate dean in 1961, thought Robert Sears better prepared than Rhinelander, both in terms of experience and academic reputation to be dean of humanities and sciences.[384]

Like Terman, Sears divided supervisory duties according to personal expertise. He took charge of some of the social sciences, English, and the mathematical sciences, while Associate Deans Halsey Royden (of mathematics) handled the physical and natural sciences, psychology, and philosophy; and Virgil Whitaker (formerly head of the English Department, with a special interest in drama) managed the arts and humanities.[385]

In looking back a quarter century later at the summer's events, Fred Glover said simply that Terman and Rhinelander just had different approaches. Wally Sterling was doing more than backing Fred Terman when he accepted Rhinelander's resignation. Just as he had done in 1955 with the provost's position, he sought a successor as dean who would be both a team player and an effective administrative leader, as well as a dean who could look beyond his own turf to consider the broader needs of the university as a whole. Although he had supported Rhinelander's 1957 request for a larger share of the budget, Sterling also insisted it was not possible financially for Stanford to have the "every-tub-on-its-own-bottom" policy in every school (as Rhinelander had seen at Harvard). Sterling went further: "Nor am I sure that faculty morale is as bad as you suggest. Perhaps I labor under the disadvantage in this particular of a tired, rather than a fresh, look, and on some awareness of morale nine years ago. And with the exception of Harvard, we are catching up fast with California, Princeton and others. Our problem is to stay caught up."[386]

The Provost at Work

As provost, Terman continued an almost ruthless working schedule. Staff and faculty alike tell stories of his working late into the night, then telephoning them at midnight to discuss financial figures. One night Terman telephoned Engineering Dean Joseph Pettit who was hosting a late evening dinner party. As Sanford Dornbusch, who was at the party, recalls, Fred asked Pettit for a few minutes time to discuss budgets. It was inconvenient, Pettit responded, he was having a dinner party. Fred persisted. It was very late, near 11:30 PM, Pettit responded. Fred still insisted. Pettit finally answered: "Dammit Fred, it's New Year's Eve!"[387]

"I got a telephone call from Fred Terman at 11 o'clock one New Year's Eve," remembered Fred Glover. "He wasn't aware it was New Year's Eve." On another occasion, Glover found Terman coming down to the office the day after Christmas with a caddie full of dictating roles. "He'd worked all week. He just worked constantly."[388]

Terman's quiet and serious demeanor was interpreted many different ways. Fred Glover described Terman as "difficult" and impatient with Wally's health problems, but then quickly added, "I was always astounded that he and I were such good friends, and how much he came to me for help on some of these things. . . . Fred had the knack of knowing what you were going to say before you said it."[389] Bob Rosenzweig recalled his boss as intimidating and formidable, yet shy and very likeable.[390] To Esther M. Lederberg, a professor of medical microbiology, he was a "kind and humble man," while Albert Hastorf (head of psychology and later dean of humanities and sciences) never knew Terman to be mean or vindictive, or to lose his temper.[391]

Staff members also recount that Fred was always willing to help, was very courteous and considerate with his own staff, and gave staff members a free hand to complete tasks without micromanaging.[392] He sought to learn something not work related about every new staff member—hobby, favorite sport—so that he could cultivate a more personal relationship. Burnice Bourquin, his secretary as head of the Electrical Engineering Department, recalled "a very fine spirit in the Department," while Elizabeth Patton, his secretary during the vice presidential years (1959–65), recalls Terman's office as "a busy happy place."[393]

Terman was not above jumping into things physically as well as intellectually. Laurence Manning recalls coming upon a fire at a fraternity house on Lasuen Street in the late 1940s and finding Dean Terman on top of the Stanford student fire truck operating the water cannon himself.[394]

Terman, like Sterling, never seemed threatened once he had placed a strong person into an important job, or by others in influential positions at the university.[395] Rather than collide, Terman and Alf Brandin, who had quite different views about managing land resources, proved to be a "powerful combination" in land-development matters as one former staff member calls them.[396] Asked in a later interview if he thought Terman was "a genius," Brandin answered: "There's no question about it. He was a dynamic and energetic person—a great asset to the university. He not only got the policy set and things organized, but then he followed through to be sure things were carried out as he intended. That's the trick. That's a great combination."[397]

Neither Terman nor Sterling was uniformly praised on campus. Some faculty vocally disagreed at times with the provost's *methods*, and in other instances with his *goals*. Charles Park, head of geology, would return to departmental meetings fuming about his encounters with Fred Terman.[398] Some disliked the university's new methods of fund-raising and budget analysis (yet did not hesitate to ask for more funds for their own individual departments); others were dismayed by the pressure and intervention of the Provost's Office. Latin American specialist Ronald Hilton does not think of Terman with either fondness or respect.[399] Even so, the equally prickly chair of history, Tom Bailey, could conclude, "I give Fred Terman credit for straightening us out."[400]

Some of Stanford's faculty frankly harkened to an earlier age of university tradition and an ambiance they associated with faculty prestige: small seminars; collegial comradery; abundant faculty travel allowances and sabbaticals; clubby offices with walnut paneling, casement windows, and fireplaces; bench-lined walks under maple trees; the residential colleges with suites and serving staff. During his sabbatical at his alma mater Cambridge University in 1955–56, chemist Eric Hutchinson, a Scot, wrote wistfully to President Sterling (whose British sympathies were notoriously strong). British pageantry was splendid, and he suggested that Sterling should have a more "handsome gown" as university president. But, Hutchinson complained, how things had changed from his prewar days at Cambridge when the faculty were unmarried and lived with the students in college, and college life was more gentlemanly. Now, even at Cambridge, it was "no longer enough to be a good college man! One now has to put out research to get on in the university. . . . Research and the education of the young now conflict as much here as anywhere else, and the undergraduate is the loser."[401]

Ironically, Stanford had never had many of these luxuries of an earlier age and could acquire them now only through assiduous development and aggressive self-promotion. Wally Sterling and Fred Terman simply could not provide the comforts of Harvard, Yale, or Princeton, something that incoming stars from the Ivy Leagues quickly noticed.

Nor was faculty discontent directed solely at the administration. The newcomers themselves, brought by Terman, could also be the targets. Historian Gordon Craig, who came from Princeton in 1961, found some Stanford faculty openly resentful both of new ways and new arrivals such as himself, including David Potter from Yale, Albert Guérard from Harvard, and Al Hastorf from Dartmouth. As Craig later wrote:

> A long period of lean years had accustomed the Stanford faculty to live like troglodytes. When a large piece of meat was thrown between them they darted out in order to seize as big a portion as possible and then scuttled back into their departmental caves. . . . Stanford occasionally reacted as the Boers in the Transvaal had reacted to the Uitlanders in the 1890s, with suspicion and with a jealous resentment of any implied criticism or any questioning of accepted tradition or methods.[402]

Some faculty felt Terman relied too much on narrowly defined quantitative evidence in faculty selection.[403] In several cases, Terman questioned the suitability of faculty candidates in psychology and in biology because they had received mediocre grades in undergraduate calculus classes. At least in the case of the biology candidate, as biologist (and later university provost and president) Donald Kennedy suggests, Terman turned out to be right in the long run.[404] Some did not expect him to be better prepared than they were when discussing a proposed faculty candidate, and they jumped to their own conclusions. The political science faculty thought their candidate "was being turned down because he was a conscientious objector. The truth," Fred Glover remembered of the Sibley case, "was that Terman knew more about the man than the department did." The provost had not only called for advice from former colleagues and leaders in the field in this case but had read everything the candidate had written.[405]

Although some faculty at times thought him heartless in his decision making, he did not make negative decisions without feeling. Although he fully supported the decision of Dean Rhinelander and Associate Provost Robert Wert to discontinue the Geography Department, for example, he worried about its impact on department faculty careers and feelings.[406] (Two faculty members close to retirement were allowed to continue, while two younger men were transferred to other departments close to their fields of expertise.)

Others criticized Terman for taking an engineer's dim view of the liberal arts.[407] As associate dean and later graduate dean, English professor Virgil K. Whitaker faced "glaring deficiencies" in the humanities. "Terman backed me to the hilt. . . . One of the things I learned from my experience in the Summer Festival [Stanford Shakespeare Festival] is that I got far better support from the sciences that I did from the humanities at Stanford. This was a disillusioning experience for a humanities professor, but it's nonetheless true."[408] Terman continued to respect a certain breadth of general knowledge from engineers and scientists as well. When he recruited physicist William Spicer from RCA Labs in 1962 for solid-state work in electrical and applied physics, Terman knew that Spicer had a bachelor's degree in liberal arts from William and Mary College. During their hour-long job interview, they discussed mostly the liberal arts, Spicer remembers, which Terman clearly hoped to build up at Stanford.[409]

While attending administration staff meetings for a number of years, Virgil Whitaker came to admire President Sterling's ability and thought Sterling extremely able in dealings with both the faculty and the public. However, Whitaker stated, "I must say my personal favorite among the administrators that I worked with was Fred Terman, who I thought was a superb administrator and who had a vision of the University with which I thoroughly agreed, and which he carried out." Whitaker was particularly concerned about the Stanford Library—its collections were poor, its book-ordering system in chaos. He had "long and fairly rigorous" discussions with Terman about the library, but "I learned one of Terman's characteristics that I was subsequently to value. If you had evidence on your side, you could convert him. I did. The changes were made in the library and the library has been growing ever since."[410]

Fred and Wally: The Way They Were

There are many staff anecdotes about the way Sterling and Terman worked together, often reflecting Wally's charm and Terman's single-mindedness.[411] A central story is "The Staff Meeting." Sterling ran a sprightly ship at Monday morning staff meetings, although it sometimes took a while to get things going. "Wally would start out usually telling a joke," Fred Glover remembered, or sometimes a rambling story, and then ask if others had stories or comments. "And there would be Fred Terman, sitting there with his papers and just anxious to get going."[412] Terman was often quiet during Wally's long stories and the banter of the staff, with a countenance that could be easily interpreted as "we're wasting time" as he took his mechanical pencil and stirred the coffee in his plastic cup. Yet Terman openly admired Sterling. "Wally could do things I could never do," he admitted. Terman cautioned younger senior staff, however, "never to leave Wally alone with a Dean." Wally might too easily end up giving in to a request.[413]

Stanford faculty and alumni have remarked that Wally and Fred acted rather like "Mister Outside" and "Mister Inside," the two Heisman trophy winners in 1945 and 1946 on Army's nationally ranked West Point football team just after World War II. (Army halfback Glenn Davis ran outside and caught the passes downfield for touchdowns. Fullback Felix "Doc" Blanchard bloodied himself plunging inside the line for the necessary first downs.) A more recent comparison is the "Good Cop-Bad Cop" duo. Certainly, Sterling purposefully chose Terman as his partner for his counterbalancing strengths. "He recognized in Fred Terman," said Ernest Arbuckle, "a person who could get the job done that needed to be done while Wally was attending to things that he did best. And he used Fred so astutely, . . . Wally could come in afterwards and clean up the messes with his wonderful personality and sense of fairness."[414] Just as certainly, he recognized that Fred Terman shared his basic philosophy: "Just try to get the best possible faculty and the best possible students together. . . . You get the right people interested in learning together, and you've got what it really takes to make a university."[415] Paul Hanna, influential professor of education and fund-raiser, put it this way: "I think the concept of Stanford's growth and move to eminence is the result of Wally Sterling and Fred Terman, not of Tresidder's concept of the university. Together, Sterling and Terman built this university from a regional institution into a national and worldwide institution. . . . Sterling and Terman together . . . they captured the enthusiasm and energy of the faculty."[416]

Their partnership was, they knew, special as well as productive. "Ours was truly a team operation—and a happy one, too!" Sterling wrote shortly after Terman's death. "There were long hours of hard work but there was also time and occasion for healthy laughter."[417] Although "Fred was not given to much small talk," Sterling remembered, "he could laugh at a good story." The rare occasions when he purposefully evoked laughter from others were a special delight to the staff—Fred's beer-pumping linear accelerator design presentation ended up making the rounds of the trustees after it had been shared with a small group of staff. Similarly, when he took Sterling's place as commencement speaker in 1965, Terman gave an amusing speech written for him by presidential assistant Don Carlson (known for his witty writing). Nobody expected Terman to go through with it, Glover recalls. "It was just wonderful, he had everybody laughing. The faculty couldn't believe it."[418]

The Bohemian Grove brought out these complementary sides in Stanford's president and provost.[419] Even off duty at Bohemian Grove encampments, Wally was often in the limelight, entertaining and charming. He was a marvelous entertainer, a popular piano player and singer with a wide repertoire of songs ranging from popular to Gilbert and Sullivan. Fred cherished the opportunity to relax a bit and to enjoy the comradeship of good friends among academics and businessmen. Even so, between the two of them, Stanford progressed bit by bit at the Grove even though the club forbids the conduct of business.

Fred had joined the Bohemian Club early in 1946, soon after returning to Stanford from wartime duties as director at the Harvard Radio Research Lab. The Bohemian Club, as originally founded in 1872 by San Francisco journalists, was a meeting place for writers and artists. In time, the City's wealthy were allowed in to help with finances, but the male-only club continued to focus on fun, fellowship, and "high jinks." Members were expected to take part in rhetorical and musical activities, and over the years the club organized a chorus, an orchestra, and several groups for dramatics and musical entertainment. By the early twentieth century, however, the club included among its members California's most powerful businessmen, with membership gradually but carefully spreading up and down the Pacific Coast. A few from the East Coast were allowed to join, particularly as Herbert Hoover's contacts spread to national and international proportions.

By the time Terman joined the Bohemian Club, there were about 1,900 members, an initiation fee of $900 and a very long waiting list of applicants. A number of luminaries had been elected as "Honorary" members—for example Herbert Hoover, California Governor (and later U.S. Chief Justice) Earl Warren, Chancellor (then President) Clark Kerr of Berkeley, General Dwight Eisenhower, and, in 1950, Stanford President J. E. Wallace Sterling. There was a class for "professional" artists and entertainers, for example Bing Crosby, Morton Downey, and Lawrence Tibbett. There was a "regular" list (prominent examples are Kenneth Bechtel, William W. Crocker, and Dean Witter), and a "nonresident" category (including James F. Burns Jr., Norman Chandler, and Leonard K. Firestone). There were honorary associates and associate members, who paid lesser dues but who contributed primarily as the artists, musicians, and theatrical producers. And there were a number of senior retired military officers and consul generals of foreign states. Other prominent figures were invited as summer guests. In 1939, shortly after Vannevar Bush became president of the Carnegie Institution of Washington (and thus in charge also of the Carnegie Division for Plant Biology, located on the Stanford campus), Stanford President Ray Lyman Wilbur, a member, invited Bush to the Grove Summer Encampment.[420]

And there was Fred Terman's category, the "faculty," considered an intellectual stimulant to the club. In 1960, there were sixty-one members in this category: thirty-nine from Berkeley, fifteen from Stanford, and the seven remaining from Caltech, UC Davis, UCLA, Mills College, Menlo College, Cornell University, and San Francisco State University. A number of academics, such as Ernest O. Lawrence, Robert G. Sproul, and Stanford presidents Ray Lyman Wilbur, Donald B. Tresidder, and J. E. W. Sterling had been elected as honorary members. Many of these other academics were, in fact, also university administrators. Stanford alumnus Lynn T. White Jr., in 1960 the only member from UCLA, had been elected in 1946 when he was president of Mills College. Lee A. DuBridge was president of Caltech. Among Stanford's other members, Robert E. Swain (1931) was elected when he was acting president of Stanford; Carl B. Spaeth had been graduate dean at Stanford, and Ernest C. Arbuckle, the dean of the Stanford Business School as well as a prominent San Francisco businessman. Fred Terman was the newly appointed dean of Stanford's Engineering School when he was elected in 1946. Professor of speech and drama Norman Philbrick was an important contributor to club theatricals. (Due to the club's stubborn hold on all-male membership, Stanford president Richard Lyman, along with other college and university presidents, gave up his membership during the 1970s, but Stanford men still aspire to membership and attend Grove Summer Encampments.)

Frank Fish Walker, Stanford's financial vice president in 1946, was a member; so was Stanford vice president Alvin C. Eurich and a number of Stanford trustees. Walker, who had recently sponsored Eurich's application, offered in the summer of 1945 to help Terman get past the four-year wait.[421] Interestingly Terman, whose application was sponsored by Ray Lyman Wilbur and others, did not mention either President Donald Tresidder or Walker among those Bohemian Club members that he knew, although he wrote Walker, "I appreciate very deeply your interest in this matter. . . . The association of the Bohemian Club is something that can mean a great deal."[422]

The Bohemian Club itself kept year-round quarters (restaurant, clubrooms, library, entertainment rooms) on the side of Nob Hill, not far from San Francisco's financial district. Terman met at least several times a year at the Bohemian Club for business meetings and occasional social evenings, but his most valued activity was at the annual two-week summer encampments at the Bohemian Grove.[423] In 1898, the club established the "Bohemian Grove" on 160 acres of California Redwood forest in Sonoma County some sixty-five miles north of San Francisco, increasing the acreage to some 2,700 by 1945. The Grove grew to include a store, a bar, a telephone and message center, a small healthcare center, jitney busses for travel around the Grove, and large central dining and kitchen areas with living quarters for the several hundred summer employees.

At each encampment, daily noontime "Lakeside Talks" by guests or members, begun in 1932, dealt with science, literature, or world affairs. President Herbert Hoover, a member since 1913, for many years gave the final Lakeside Talk at each Grove encampment. Among others who gave Lakeside Talks were Lee DuBridge, E. O. Lawrence, and Fred Terman.

The entertainment varied, from "high jinks" (the serious plays) to "low jinks" (slapstick and musical reviews). The main entertainment, the Grove Play, had originated in 1902. Some spectacles could involve a cast, crew, and orchestra of several hundred members. A pipe organ was installed near the stage. A chorus was formed in 1905, an orchestra in 1922, and later a band. A good number of club members gained their membership through their literary, musical, or dramatic ability and their willingness to undertake responsibility for the drama, music, artwork, production, and writing tasks. As the years went on, a larger number of entertainers were professionals who performed at variety nights for the entire club, or at smaller functions at one of the 120 or so "camps" or living areas within the Grove.

Even though "high jinks" and "low jinks" might seem out of character, Fred

Terman enjoyed the encampments, and he carefully marked them into his appointment calendars. In the early years, a few Bohemians spent the entire summer at the Grove, but Fred Terman was typical of postwar members who could, at best, spend the full two weeks at the encampment or perhaps just make it to the encampment's three weekends. Terman attended every summer encampment at the Grove from 1951 through 1976, although he often could not stay the full two weeks while he was Stanford provost. Several times during the 1950s and 1960s, Fred planned on a two-week vacation at the Grove only to have to cut it back due to university or national committee duties. (He reluctantly resigned in 1977 due to poor health.)

The Grove is divided into some 120 living areas or "camps," each camp ranging from a few to more than a hundred members. (Camp election often followed after several years of membership.) By Fred's time, the cots and simple tents or log cabins of the early days were gone. Some of the camps had grown rather luxurious—country lodges with indoor plumbing with hot and cold water, finished and heated rooms, and piano lounges. Camps varied not only in size and appointments but also in membership. The "Lost Angels" and Santa Barbara camps reflected the geographical base of their members; Mandalay camp and Caveman camp included many corporate and political figures (including Herbert Hoover, Ray Lyman Wilbur, and Wally Sterling). There were the Silverado Squatters, the Rattlers, the Cliff Dwellers, and the Stowaways. Faculty members and scientists gravitated to the Sons of Toil, Swagatom, and Wayside Lodge.

Fred Terman's camp, the Sons of Toil, was a small and unpretentious camp formed in 1905 by engineering faculty members of the University of California. For some two decades, the camp had consisted simply of two canvas tents with cots and chairs, later replaced by four small rustic wooden cabins. A larger central lounge was built in the mid-1950s, along with improved sanitary and electrical facilities. Membership in 1951, when Fred joined, was sixteen, and it grew little over the next years. Many of its members were noted scientists: the brothers Ernest and John Lawrence, chemists Edwin McMillan, Gilbert N. Lewis, and Melvin Calvin, and physicists Lee DuBridge and Charles Townes. Most of its other members, at least until the late 1960s, were engineers or medical school professors. Fred Terman was usually the only member there from Stanford.

Campers at the Grove, of course, were never restricted from making friends or seeing old friends at the other camps, and indeed, with the daily band and orchestra concerts, the lectures, and the busy preparations for the Grove play and other musical events at individual camps, it was a wonderful release for Terman. While he is well remembered for spectacular presentations to trustees and business leaders about Stanford's potential and for his speeches to national engineering groups about the challenges facing modern engineering, Terman did not feel comfortable with the banter of cocktail parties or hosting social gatherings. A shy, often quiet man, he was at his best among small groups of students or in conversation with his peers—be they academics or businessmen. The Grove, however, was a place where he could enjoy and be himself.[424]

The conducting of business is forbidden within the confines of the Grove. Indeed, the Grove's logo bears the phrase from Shakespeare's *A Midsummer Night's Dream*: "Weaving Spiders, come not here." Yet business connections are undoubtedly made and strengthened at the Grove, and university affairs certainly promoted. In 1936, UC President Robert Gordon Sproul did not hesitate to introduce Ernest O. Lawrence to University of California regents, William H. Crocker and John Francis Neylan, who subsequently secured large financial backing for construction of Lawrence's 60-inch cyclotron.[425] In a secret meeting in the Grove clubhouse in mid-September 1942, James Bryant Conant, Division Chief of the National Defense Research Committee, met with Lawrence, Arthur H. Compton, Harold Urey, J. Robert Oppenheimer, Lyman Briggs, and several other scientific luminaries, to decide on the future of the American nuclear-fission program for the atom bomb.[426]

In the 1950s, a Bohemian Grove event occurred of less national importance, but that provided significant aid to Stanford University. John Stauffer and the Stauffer family had long been benefactors to Stanford but Terman and Sterling now hoped to obtain a large gift from the Stauffers to support Terman's efforts to strengthen chemistry faculty and research. Stauffer was to be at the Grove encampment, and Wally Sterling intended to work his celebrated persuasive magic on Mr. Stauffer. Wally was "dynamite" at persuading visitors of the potential of Stanford, especially under such disarming conditions. Sterling planned a visit with Stauffer at Stauffer's camp to finally persuade him of the wisdom of donating a building to Stanford. But when Wally Sterling went up the wooden stairs to meet Stauffer on the porch, he found Fred Terman and Stauffer on their hands and knees reviewing architectural drawings of the proposed chemistry building. Terman had already sold Stauffer on the deal. Stauffer is reported to have said, "Wally, look at the great chemistry building Fred has laid out, it's perfect!"[427]

Terman's Retirement: Wherefore the Provost's Office?

Fred Terman retired as provost on August 31, 1965, at the end of the fiscal year, when he had reached the age of sixty-five (mandatory retirement age at Stanford at the time). At a university convocation in his honor the previous May, Terman commented:

> With my affection for Stanford, I have obtained great satisfaction from the emergence of Stanford during the last 15 years as one of the really great universities in

> this country. . . . With my 40 years of perspective I can appreciate more than most of you the extent to which Stanford's star has been rising during Dr. Sterling's administration and the continued progress that can be expected in the years ahead as a result of the forward momentum that is now present.[428]

"His 10 years as Provost have been a decade of markedly increased growth and stature for Stanford," Sterling commented about Terman that summer. "He has stimulated much of this increase and monitored much more of it."[429] (Stanford's operating budget had reached nearly $36 million in 1965–66, nearly four times its budget a decade earlier.) Peter Allen, university editor and former director of Stanford's News and Publications Service, remarked, "Fred, although everyone is not aware of this, is one of the country's master planners of the modern university which has evolved since World War II."[430]

Under Terman's leadership, the Provost's Office had evolved as dramatically as the university. The office had taken on a wide role in planning, developing, and implementing academic programs, but Stanford now faced a time of a less dynamic era of moderate, rather than spectacular growth, and the need to smooth rough edges and the anxieties produced by rapid change.

In remarks to the Faculty Advisory Board, Sterling praised Terman's organization of a superb staff that was capable of budgeting, review of research, management of space, and oversight of graduate and undergraduate affairs, while allowing the provost to carry out a number of assessments and studies of great significance to the university. Terman's staff was readily available to the president and worked well with his own staff. The existence of such a well-developed staff, commented Sterling, suggested that the next provost might have a different role.[431] What that new role might be was as yet unclear. The president offered several suggestions of ways the provost could be of direct assistance to himself: to assist more directly in fund-raising and working with volunteers; to assist in preventing "de-personalization" of relations between administration and faculty; and to take part in an ongoing review of academic policy. In sum, Sterling said, he was searching for a person who, in an anticipated period of moderate growth for Stanford, would share with the president and the faculty in a broad range of academic leadership, including cultivation of financial resources and social activities, inside and outside the university. As usual, Sterling wanted to search for the right man without being pinned down to a job description.

It took nearly a year and a half to find a successor to Fred Terman, in part because of the flexibility the president sought in making an appointment, and in part due to the severe toll recent operations had taken on his health.[432] Wallace Sterling discussed the succession to the provostship with the Faculty Advisory Board just before Christmas 1965. Many names had been proposed of candidates, both inside and outside the university, but not until spring 1966 was a short list prepared. One important question remained throughout the search: Should the new provost be an inside or outside candidate?[433]

Fred Terman had offered his own counsel to Sterling about a successor, leaning toward an insider. After an early August 1965 visit with philosopher Pat Suppes, Terman wrote, "My feeling is that Pat is superb Provost material, and probably has the makings of a first class president."[434] But Sterling was edging toward an outside candidate; his top choices were Princeton economist William Bowen, former Princeton chemist Donald Hornig, as of 1964 President Lyndon Johnson's special assistant for science and technology, and political scientist David Truman, dean of the college at Columbia. Princeton made Bowen their own provost while he was being considered by Stanford. Hornig was not interested in Stanford without guarantees that he would remain provost after Sterling's retirement, something Sterling could not promise.[435]

Sterling's discussions with Truman are especially illuminating. Truman and his wife Ellie visited Stanford, and were much taken with the opportunity. After discussing the Stanford offer with Columbia University President Grayson Kirk, Truman inquired further about the relationship between president and provost at Stanford, and the provost's role in external relations, particularly with alumni.[436] Sterling had worked so closely and so well with Terman as provost that (as was his fashion) he expected to work out with the new provost a mutual understanding as to how they would share the work, but Sterling also felt that each should be able to pinch-hit for the other as need arises, he told Truman. Sterling also wanted to continue the provost's central role in budgeting, where the president's role was essentially limited to early planning stages. The provost was the key player, the president believed, in evaluating "priority academic needs and, if necessary, in defending these as Deans of Schools and non-academic officers may argue for a larger piece of the budget pie." Sterling had no fixed ideas about the provost's role in external relations, particularly with alumni, but he would encourage the provost, he said, to participate "to some degree" in external relations. Sterling saw Stanford's future financial problems to lie in maintaining a large budget base while making costly improvements to buildings and facilities. Finally, Sterling proposed that Truman be appointed professor of political science as well as provost.[437]

After Truman declined the offer, Sterling and his search committee turned to Stanford insiders. The leading candidates were historian and associate dean Richard W. Lyman and law professor Herbert Packer, who had played an impressive role in the "Study of Education at Stanford" but whose recent book on the Alger Hiss case made him a controversial choice. Lyman had not been particularly interested in administration when he first joined the Stanford faculty, but he soon changed his mind.[438] He was a talented administrator as well as a keen intellect and productive scholar. Wally was impressed with how Lyman had performed as associate dean of humanities and sciences, Fred Glover later recalled, and thought him bright, able, energetic, and straight shooting.[439] (Lyman had successfully handled some tough personnel tasks.) Lyman had had two offers to leave Stanford that year, as Sterling knew, including the offer of the presidency of Haverford College.[440] In November 1966, Lyman accepted the position as vice president and provost of Stanford, and Packer was named vice provost.

When Dick Lyman became Stanford's third provost in 1967, he inherited a well-established office with substantial authority. Busy with an array of consulting tasks, Terman made a point of standing back from Stanford's administrative affairs. Yet the campus, however much it had grown physically, financially, and in the esteem of its peers, was also a troubled campus. Like Berkeley and its other rivals, it was now in the midst of student unrest, national discord, and financial downturn. Terman's ongoing contributions to higher education, not only at home but now on an international scale, would not always be appreciated in the climate of discord, but his pace was unrelenting.

CHAPTER EIGHT

"If I Had My Life to Live Over Again, I Would Play the Same Record"

1965–1982

Terman maintained a ferocious pace from 1926 until his retirement in 1965. He went right into retirement at the same pace, noting in 1966 that "the trouble with retirement is that you become so busy with committees, and with part-time jobs and projects that your disposable time disappears."[1] His youthful hobbies of ham radio, card playing, fishing, hunting, and running had long since been given up due to illnesses of his youth and later his rigorous work schedule. His consulting work for educational institutions, governments, and private firms continued and, in some ways, increased after retirement.

For more than a decade after his retirement, Fred was extremely active intellectually and on the road a great deal. By the mid-1970s, however, his race through life began to slow down markedly. In 1975, Fred lost his wife Sibyl, whose health began seriously to decline in 1970. Although he continued to receive many awards and commendations, Stanford moved on without him. Nevertheless, looking back over his busy life, the seventy-seven-year-old Terman wrote his friend Cecil Green, "Stanford has been good to me. . . . If I had my life to live over again, I would play the same record."[2]

Philosophy of Education and Life

During his first four years in retirement, he continued to speak publicly and privately about university planning and building and the importance of faculty and student quality, technical innovation and university-industry cooperation, and the goals and efficient management of engineering education.

Famous professors and text writers presumably dash off a quick speech to a few students, but Fred Terman prepared as careful an outline for his remarks to a 1967 seminar course of Professor Hugh Skilling as he would a plan of action for university trustees. And he critiqued his own presentation just as ruthlessly. "I failed to review notes adequately," he recorded, "and as a result was too wordy and took too much time. Next time—Review, Rehearse, Rewrite, and make it a tight talk." When Fred spoke again to Skilling's seminar two years later, the talk was similar in topic but, in his view, more tightly organized.[3]

Terman's remarks, delivered to Hugh Skilling's teaching seminar of about a dozen graduate students, provide one of the best expositions of Terman's philosophy of education just as they provide insight into his personality and character.[4] His advice to prospective teachers was highly pragmatic, confirming his firm belief in industry, perseverance, and the trickle-up affect of ambition. The teacher, he said, must develop genuine competence in something important, beginning narrowly, perhaps out of one's own PhD work. Terman firmly believed that teaching and research were complementary, not competitive. Teaching was a process, not an exhibition of how much you know, and the teacher must tune in on a student's wavelength and use feedback. He advised: do something individual in research, or develop a distinctive course, or write a book. There simply was no substitute for getting on with the job, for being productive, whether in teaching, advising, or research. Finish your research and write it up. Direct PhD students and get them out into the world. One's time, he warned, is precious so it should be used well—do not waste it on trivial activities or on too few students.

Secondly, learn what others are doing in the field by getting yourself into circulation. Get acquainted with people at meetings or in their laboratories. It is easy, he said, to get people to talk about what they are doing, and professional meetings are an especially good place for doing this.

Above and beyond publishing books, receiving awards, and moving up in his career, Terman felt his biggest personal rewards had come from the opportunity granted to him to build things—the Electrical Engineering Department, the School of Engineering at Stanford, the Harvard Radio Research Lab during the war, and, finally, Stanford University itself. Terman also appreciated the opportunity to help others build their careers and the institutions with which they became involved. Terman listed a number of former students and younger colleagues whom he was especially proud of assisting, people who later became university teachers and researchers, manufacturers, businessmen, or administrators.

Although there were always disappointments in teaching, its rewards, he said, also came from the freedom to allocate your efforts toward something you really like and the opportunity to make something out of it. University work was demanding, but it had been for him, so fun and so varied, he told them, that he believed one "can keep at it terribly intently without getting worn out."

Many of these same ideas can be found back in his comments in the 1930s and 1940s, but Fred would reiterate them consistently in speeches, letters to students, and consulting reports carried out later in life: develop personal and institutional excellence by targeting areas of potential strength; do not accept mediocrity and generality; help your students succeed after graduation as well as before; strive to make a significant contribution by being personally productive, efficient, and well informed; make and keep up with contacts beyond the confines of classroom and laboratory.

Terman's concept of developing a successful career closely resembled his strategy for a successful university. Two of Terman's oft-noted phrases in his talks and articles were his idea of "Steeples of Excellence" or "Steeples of Talent," and his idea of a "Community of Technical Scholars."[5] Although his own career had been built around these ideas, they emerged particularly in his speeches given during his time as provost when his attention turned from engineering to university strengths in the sciences, social sciences, and humanities. Personal values of systematic hard work and ambitious, but quantifiable goals, easily transform into institutional ones.

Just a week before he retired, Fred gave a talk he entitled "Governing the University: The Administrator's Role in Building a Strong University" to a Society for Religion in Higher Education group on the Stanford campus.[6] Fred began by pointing out that any idiot could compile a list of goals—the real problem was implementation. He described Stanford University before 1950 as a respected regional university suffering from financial pressures. Fifteen years later, the university could attract undergraduates from a much wider geographical spread. Both the undergraduate and graduate student body were much better qualified than in the past, as national ranking indices showed. But, Terman stressed, the key element making up a fine university is the quality of its faculty.

The most expensive faculty member, he warned, is the one who is merely adequate. The university may save a little on his salary, but it loses in every other way—the quality of education provided and of graduate students attracted, in the stature of his department, in the amount of support attracted through grants, contracts, and gifts, and in the ability to attract other excellent faculty. Terman mentioned Senator Ernest "Fritz" Holling's recent statement to the same effect, that his state of South Carolina needed to build around a few outstanding college professors, as its "one shot left in its effort to gain status among the states."[7] The steps in faculty recruiting, Fred said, are simple: conduct an arduous search for potential talent, backed by the fullest information; do not set artificial restrictions on the position; do not be satisfied with the merely good, but keep standards extremely high. Being "tough" later on tenure is no substitute for the most exacting search procedures.

Fred went on to explain his theories of "Steeples of Excellence and the Mainstream." One sought to build peaks or steeples, but one must build them in the mainstream, not in an eddy. He recited "Terman's Law"—that is, "the quality of an educational program and its educational productivity are only incidentally related to the money being lavished upon it"—and he gave several examples of university spending on other campuses that had led to nothing. He warned his audience of factors that could influence costs—the organization of curriculum, proliferation of offerings, fragmentation of the core offerings, and exotic specialties of little importance and no student interest.

At a Stanford Alumni Conference in 1968, Fred Terman gave away what he jokingly called "my secret" to developing Stanford engineering.[8] Although he was simply playing on the same themes he had expressed before, his comments became better known in the world of engineering education when they were published simultaneously in the *Journal of Engineering Education*.[9] According to Terman, three important events influenced pre–World War II engineering education at Stanford: the first was the establishment of Stanford's general education requirements in 1920, which exposed the Stanford engineering student to wider cultural values and skills; the second was the organization of the School of Engineering in 1925, which decreased the rugged independence and rigidity of the individual departments; and the third was the decision that a four-year program was not sufficient to produce a professional engineer. A six-year program was instituted so that the bachelor's degree was followed by a two-year graduate degree of Engineer.

After 1928, Terman pointed out, at least one-third of the engineering faculty's effort was devoted to the graduate program, yet there was no systematic effort to recruit students. By World War II, Stanford's School of Engineering was "good" but not one of the outstanding engineering schools in the country. When he returned to Stanford as dean of engineering, Terman knew that graduate study in engineering, particularly at the PhD level, would assume new importance, and that, for the first time, there would be "real money" available to support engineering research and graduate students. Fred took advantage of what he had learned at MIT and at Harvard; beginning in 1946 he developed a plan that would stay much the same over the years.

Terman described the plan's seven major points:

1. Sponsored research would be a part of the educational operation; it would be performed by students and faculty with a minimum of full-time professional staff, and only projects having substantial academic value would be undertaken.
2. Sponsored research would be built around the competence and interests of the individual faculty members.
3. Under no circumstances would administrators obtain a project, and then *assign* faculty members to work on it.

4. The faculty member would make his principal contribution to the project as a researcher, not as a manager of others; in particular, no faculty member would serve only as an assistant to another faculty manager.
5. Sponsored research was of central importance to the university; accordingly, a faculty member involved in a research project would be given a reduced teaching load, and would be eligible for a summer salary adequate to serve as an inducement to stay on the campus during the summer.
6. In the interest of academic integrity, no *extra* salary would be paid to faculty members for service on research projects during the academic year.
7. Graduate students would be recruited to work part-time on research projects, would be paid for this service from research funds, and could use research results for dissertations as appropriate.

Fred went on to describe his "Steeples of Excellence" policy, a strategy he enunciated many times over the years: build up great faculty strength in a few important but very narrow areas at the expense of broad but modestly productive coverage. Since the faculty is central to this process, he reiterated, Stanford did not use gift income to invest heavily for equipment. Instead, it invested in faculty themselves. Terman also discussed the measurement of academic productivity (the ratio of output to input costs). It is not individual faculty productivity, he noted, that is measured, but the total cost or "teaching load." Using such measures, he argued, can result in outstanding school or department quality and productivity, with graduate class sizes as large as those of undergraduate courses and yet with relatively light faculty teaching loads. In 1966–67, Fred noted, the Engineering School faculty of 133 had produced 3.7 MS and 1.1 PhD degrees per faculty member, something of a record.

Fred traced the history of Stanford's growing relations with industry and the coupling of academic engineering with the "real world." Immediately after World War II, Fred had encouraged companies to become better acquainted with the School of Engineering, just as he encouraged faculty to get to know their opposite numbers in industry. The Honors Co-Operative Program, created in 1953, was devised along just these lines. Employers could use Stanford to upgrade the skills of promising employees and the Stanford connection to recruit top new employees. In return, Stanford made important contacts and received double tuition revenues with the scheme. Similarly, the Affiliates Programs, begun first in aeronautics, directed financial contributions from a selection of companies to the training of graduate students. Like the Honors Co-Op Program, it benefited both Stanford and industry. (By 1968, solid-state electronics and construction engineering Affiliate Programs had been added.)

From his earliest days as a professor, Terman had argued for more science and mathematics courses in the engineering curriculum. His *Science* magazine article of 1927 advocating such a policy had scandalized some of his elders, but now, he admitted, engineering had finally overshot the mark. He called attention to Engineering Dean Joseph Pettit's efforts to bring back the "real world of engineering" by introducing philosophy of design and systems engineering to the school. Among his other trade "secrets," Terman insisted on the importance of the social sciences and humanities to undergraduate engineers.

Terman was proud to note the rise of Stanford engineering nationally as reflected in various national ranking surveys. He refuted the claim that government research funds perpetuated a separation between "have" and "have-not" institutions. It had been a few able faculty members in the "have-not" Stanford of 1946, he said, who took advantage of postwar opportunities for upward mobility. A corps of highly qualified faculty with sound plans and willingness for hard, systematic work can help any institution move upward.

When he received the Stanford Alumni Association's Herbert Hoover Medal in 1970, Fred defended academic research in general, which he felt was too frequently castigated as the "bad boy of academia." He summarized the charges: faculty research leads to poor teaching and a transfer of faculty loyalty from the university to the granting agency, which in turn leads to campus unrest. These, Fred responded, were half-truths and myths. While some researchers are indeed poor teachers, there are also poor teachers to be found among those who did no research. The best teaching, he asserted, is done by the scholar or researcher who enjoys teaching but who also has something authoritative and fresh to say. Every faculty member in Stanford's Engineering School taught classes and worked closely with a group of students. As to the charge that the research professor's loyalty had been lured away from the university, thus leading to the neglect and frustration of students, Fred observed wryly that the current campus unrest seemed to come mainly from students *and* faculty in humanities and social sciences, areas where research funds were scarce or nonexistent. In the natural sciences and engineering, where research funds had been available for years, one found, he said, a greater loyalty to Stanford among both faculty and students.[10]

By the early 1960s, Provost Fred Terman was being acclaimed in the media for his efforts to build both Stanford's faculty and high-technology industry in the Bay Area. Even the *Reader's Digest* was interested, publishing an article on Terman, "He Searches for 'Steeples of Talent'" in 1962.[11] Regional newspapers and magazines continued to write about Fred after his retirement. Terman "is generally recognized as the man responsible for making the San Francisco Bay Area a leading international center of electronics research and industry," commented the Bay Area IEEE magazine *Grid* in 1966, "largely through his leadership in engineering education."[12] Perhaps his favorite article, however, appeared in a national magazine before the rush of books about Silicon Valley (a term coined in 1971). Although he said that the portions about him were exaggerated, Fred often recommended the 1974 *Fortune* magazine article "California's Great Breeding Ground for Industry."[13]

Fred took the same pride in his role in the transformation of the Santa Clara Valley's farmland to a suburban, technology-based economy, as he did in the transformation of Stanford University. Shortly after his retirement, Fred was awarded Palo Alto's Distinguished Citizen Award. In his acceptance speech that November evening of 1965, Fred stated that Palo Alto had been lucky as communities go and should better appreciate its association with Stanford University.[14] In the old days, he reflected, you had to commute to San Francisco to earn a decent living unless you worked for Stanford University or were a local merchant "taking in your neighbor's wash." Most likely, your children would have to move away from Palo Alto when they sought to make a living. He was acutely aware of this problem, he said, because until after World War II, he had to send his most promising students "into exile in the East." Fred admitted the bustle and traffic of the present-day Palo Alto could be annoying, but accountants, secretaries, marketing people, machinists, and other skilled workers, engineers and scientists could now find interesting and well-paying work in surrounding industries, and these now provided business for local merchants and bankers, clients for lawyers, and patients for doctors and dentists.

The developments that had taken place around Palo Alto since World War II were inextricably bound up with the transformation of Stanford from an essentially regional institution to one of the greatest universities of the country. Stanford, after MIT, was the largest producer of advanced engineering degrees in the country, he pointed out, and Stanford served as a beacon to attract the brightest graduates from elsewhere. Terman then spoke of the "community of technical scholars," of high-technology industries working together with a strong university that was sensitive to the creative activities of local companies. Fred chided Palo Altans for their community indifference toward the Stanford Linear Accelerator Center, then nearing completion and an integral part of this interrelated technology community. Out of the dreams of two Stanford professors, this huge project had come to town without the community putting up a dime or doing any political lobbying. Terman contrasted this situation to that represented by two British cabinet officers, who had recently visited Stanford to see how England could duplicate what was happening around Stanford and Palo Alto. He also mentioned the efforts of companies and legislators from Dallas and from New Jersey who were putting together large sums of money to attempt to replicate what Stanford was already doing for the Santa Clara Valley. Some 126 applications from forty-six different states had been submitted to the U.S. government, he told them, just to win the *next* proposed national accelerator center. "All I can say is that you should count your blessings, and should take great pride in what has been created here as a result of the combined efforts of local leaders and a cooperative university."

It was vintage Terman, straight from the hip and would be soon challenged from a variety of directions. Some would target Stanford's place in the military-industrial complex; others would question whether the urban sprawl brought to Santa Clara Valley represented a better way of life. Still, for many, the valley continued to be a dream spot for working and living.

Consulting for Stanford

Fred Terman continued to consult for Stanford, working both for President Wallace Sterling on several projects between 1966 and 1968, and for President Kenneth Pitzer on a financial planning study in 1969–70. His two most important studies concerned Stanford faculty: an analysis of faculty size and retention, and a review of faculty pensions and retirement pay. Terman was disappointed that his study on faculty retention in the 1970s seemed to have little influence, partly due to the distractions of campus disruptions during the last few years of Sterling's administration and over the next several years. His evaluation of the sorry state of Stanford pensions, however, resulted in an important upgrading of emeriti pensions as well as a change in Stanford's TIAA-CREF policies.

In December 1966, Wally Sterling asked Terman's advice on two matters: the control of faculty billets, and the Faculty-Staff Benefits Program. With resources becoming "a bit" scarcer, the university's need to carefully allocate and control faculty billets was perhaps obvious, but how could Stanford go about correcting for these needs, he was asked. Given possible changes in Stanford's retirement program, should Stanford take over the medical and hospital insurance program, or change the tuition-waiver program for faculty and staff children?

Terman studied the faculty-planning problem through the spring and summer of 1967, editing a September draft report into his document, "A Program for Faculty Planning."[15] Fred first pointed out that during the decade 1956 to 1966, the Academic Council had grown dramatically from 460 to 883 persons, but this sort of growth was not expected for the coming decade. How, then, could Stanford's faculty continue to grow in quality and reputation overall, continue to adapt to changing trends, and not lose that important component of vitality and youthful enthusiasm? Reflecting his own past strategies, Terman recommended that each dean have a plan and a competitive priority list, but these plans should be approved by the President's Office. The deans should expect a search for a truly outstanding senior faculty appointment to take at least three years, he reminded them. As much as Fred and his staff had improved the faculty search process during the late 1950s, he thought even better procedures should be established. Stanford could learn from Harvard, where both the president and the dean of arts and sciences were personally involved in each tenure vacancy.

This was familiar ground, but Terman went on to recommend that Stanford's administration rigorously control senior faculty positions (billets) and closely monitor junior and part-time positions (assistant and adjunct professors, lecturers, instructors, and teaching assistants). Openings at the senior level could no longer be guaranteed to stay in the same department, he believed, and any expansion of the senior faculty should be based on *new* funding. (Fred offered up an old Cambridge saying: "Harvard did not become great by reusing old money.") Nor should senior positions use short-term or soft funds.

Senior appointments must reflect clear opportunities in academic fields, but they should reflect the future, not the past. Stanford's increased reputation during Terman's years as provost had resulted from the appointment of prominent, older senior faculty. Now, he suggested, Stanford should lean toward senior appointments of very promising younger faculty, under the age of forty. In the humanities, arts, and sciences, Stanford's ratio of junior to senior faculty was too low: 0.28 at Stanford, as compared to 0.38 at Yale, 0.40 at Harvard, 0.50 at Princeton, and 0.55 at MIT.

While faculty growth had slowed considerably, Terman found a sharp rise in nonfaculty staff growth over the years 1963–66. The Academic Council grew by 12.5 percent and the student body by 9 percent during this period, while the non-Academic Council staff had risen 33 percent. In 1965 alone, some 534 additional staff had been added. The point Terman was making was that Stanford was entering a new era. The years were over of "ramping up" sharply in quality of faculty and size of affiliated programs (Medical School and SLAC, for example). Stanford was a much bigger operation in 1967 than in 1950. Staying at the top of academic excellence was going to be a difficult job.

Throughout his report, he used comparisons of salary data by rank and by department and total actual and proposed departmental budget figures at Stanford from the years 1955 through 1969.[16] In compiling his reports Fred collected data not only from Stanford but from colleagues at Harvard, MIT, Berkeley, Yale, and Princeton. Fred was annoyed that since his retirement, no one at Stanford had continued to collect academic statistics and argued that the collection and comparative use of statistics ought to be continued.

Fred concluded that the 1966 Cartter Report had made Stanford too cocky when it showed Stanford had made more progress than any other American academic institution. Stanford had much to do, he warned, before it would be where it would like to be.[17]

Provost Richard Lyman found the report of enormous interest and usefulness, he told Terman, but due to campus disruptions through 1968 further discussion was set aside until 1969. In fact, nobody seemed to like the Terman report. Vice Provost Howard Brooks tipped off the various deans in April 1969 when he hinted that perhaps Terman's plan was too harsh for Stanford. The deans discussed the report among themselves, and then with department chairs. Reactions across campus were predictable. Economics Chair Lorie Tarshis thought Terman's reliance on central planning "pathologic." Terman's analysis was correct, he added, but his solution was wrong; department chairs should have the primary say on spending of monies. The deans, Brooks reported to newly appointed President Kenneth Pitzer, did not want the provost to centrally control faculty billets or spending, but expected to exercise such control within their own schools. Running a university faculty is somewhat like trying to herd cats, so it is not surprising that at each level, there was reluctance to share power over billets and budgets.

In autumn 1969, the *Stanford Daily* mentioned that the recommended changes in university tenure policy in the "Terman Report" had been discussed in faculty councils. Their assumption was simply that faculty levels at Stanford would be held constant in coming years, but Fred believed his effort had little influence on university policy or procedure.[18] Terman talked with the deans himself, and, Lyman later told him, the deans had appreciated his straight talk as coming from the man who "more than any other single person, built the Stanford faculty of today and is responsible for the great improvement in quality that it represents."[19] But as had always been the case at Stanford, department heads and deans were reluctant to share power over appointments and budgets, even for what Terman viewed as the overall good of the university.[20]

In the fall of 1966, Fred began a second study for President Sterling, which resulted in his October report, "A Study of Faculty Retirement at Stanford." An edited and expanded version of the report was presented to the trustees in the spring of 1967.[21]

Terman's study made an important contribution to the financial security of Stanford's retired faculty, as well as those in service and those to come. His report had two aspects: a concern for the genuine need of those already retired, and future retirement plans at Stanford. Stanford had participated in the Teachers Insurance and Annuity Association (TIAA) retirement plan for many years. TIAA had been established about 1920 for employees of academic and nonprofit organizations and was a trusted, conservative investment fund giving a safe but modest dividend. Before 1948, TIAA received 10 percent of a faculty member's salary until retirement (with 5 percent contributed by Stanford and 5 percent by the employee). After 1948, the total portion allocated was increased to 15 percent (with Stanford contributing 10 percent). As an avid student of the stock market, Fred knew that TIAA had formed a more aggressive wing, the College Retirement Equities Fund (CREF), in 1952 to allow more choice in stock market investment. That same year, Social Security was applied to university employees. Fred knew that some of the more elderly retired faculty members were having severe financial difficulties (some were no longer able to afford coming to the Faculty Club). In 1966, he began to correspond with TIAA-CREF officials and to research alternative and more fruitful methods of investing for faculty pensions.[22]

Professor Virgil A. Anderson, president of the emeriti faculty, conducted a survey of annual income in the spring of 1967. Of about one hundred replies, 20 percent reported total annual incomes *under* $4,000, and were "doing badly."[23] Anderson sent the anonymous survey forms to Terman who found that some reported annual incomes in the range of $5,000 to $9,000, with several reporting incomes more than $20,000. Fred easily figured out the identities of most of those polled; the questionnaire asked for total years of service to Stanford and their year of retirement. Thus, he could see that senior science and engineering faculty like Paul Kirkpatrick and David Webster in physics, Gabor Szego and George Pólya in mathematics, Philip Leighton in chemistry, Loren Chandler in medicine, Lydik Jacobsen in engineering were doing very well, and these provided a basis for further study. In David Webster's case, social security provided a yearly income of $1,464 and his Stanford pension $2,335, but these were augmented significantly by other income of some $24,000. Thus it was painfully clear that some of the oldest faculty, who had no income other than social security and their Stanford pension, would have a tough time making ends meet.

Fred's proposal worked toward two ends: in 1959, the board of trustees had authorized supplemental pensions for emeriti to put a "floor" under total retirement income; they raised the floor again in 1961. Fred recommended another raise to fill the gap (but only for those emeriti whose total income fell below the new "floor"), arguing that his plan would cost the university only about $40,000 per year in 1967 and would lessen each year after. Similar, though lesser amounts were set as the "floor" for retired associate and assistant professors. While professors with additional income made through patents, textbook sales, and other investments—like Fred Terman as well as David Webster—received nothing from this amendment, it nearly doubled the retirement income of some of the oldest emeriti.

A second part of Fred's proposal intrigued officers at TIAA-CREF. With assistance from TIAA-CREF, Fred used Stanford's 7090 computer to study *all* faculty who had retired since 1950, and made a case-by-case study of the 125 living emeriti. Fred determined that the 15 percent paid toward TIAA retirement was insufficient, since it provided only 30–40 percent of an individual's equivalent salary during retirement. Each dollar invested in TIAA in 1952, he revealed, was worth only $1.48 in 1966 whereas a 1952 dollar invested in CREF was now worth $4.00. Terman believed that the academic community should be grateful to William Greenough and his associates for establishing CREF and should take better advantage of it. Fred proposed that in the future Stanford should put one-half of its 10 percent contribution into CREF, and that the individual faculty member should be counseled that he or she could put some portion of one's 5 percent contribution into CREF. Fred also recommended that the TIAA-CREF plan should be mandatory for tenured faculty over the age of forty. TIAA-CREF Vice President George K. Harrison agreed and wrote Fred that a few universities already were investing some of their retirement contributions in CREF.

Fred was pleased, he told Harrison, that the Stanford administration had received his proposal so warmly. Both he and President Sterling had been surprised at how Stanford's pension, only minimally adequate at retirement, could become so very inadequate over time. Fred personally presented his proposal to the trustees, who approved it. The new plan became effective in August 1967.[24]

A year later, Fred wrote to Provost Richard Lyman suggesting implementation of a health or medical care program for active faculty members—possibly the entire university staff. He regretted not having done this during his own years as provost. By shaving faculty salary increases for two or three years, he felt he could have financed a medical plan that would have pleased everyone.[25] (Stanford implemented a faculty-staff health plan by the 1970s.) Stanford began to tighten its belt again toward the end of Wallace Sterling's presidency and into the term of Kenneth Pitzer (1968–70). In the fall of 1969, the administration announced the need to cut back $2.5 million over four years from its $52 million operating budget, due largely to the decline in federally sponsored research. Within a year, the cut was increased to $6 million as Stanford faced funding new undergraduate programs but a new federal cut in graduate fellowships. Stanford was far from alone among universities that faced budget problems and these only grew worse as the country experienced double-digit inflation, a worldwide oil shortage, and a declining stock market by 1974.[26]

In November 1969, Stanford President Pitzer asked Terman to help the university determine whether certain schools (medicine, business, law, and engineering) should operate under a General Fund Ceiling (GFC) program. The GFC allocates university general funds to a budget unit according to a formula that is not negotiated annually. A school would operate under the allocation, supplementing this with its own endowment, gifts, grants, and sponsored research income. The Stanford Medical School already operated with a GFC, although the administration was not sure the formula was optimal. To succeed with a GFC, an individual school needed fund-raising ability and enough income (from tuition, fees, gifts, and research support) to virtually go it alone. Stanford's administration was not sure that either the Law School or the Business School were in a position to do so. On President Pitzer's behalf, Howard Brooks asked Fred to consider whether the Business School, the primary concern, and secondarily, the Law School, should adopt a GFC program.[27] (The Engineering School was certainly strong enough to do so, but it was not of major concern to the administration.)

Within four months, Fred compiled two thick notebooks of figures and estimates. His fifty-four-page "Study of General Fund Ceiling as Applied to the Graduate School of Business" was submitted in February 1970.[28] Once again, Fred used Harvard as a model.[29] Fred supported the idea of the Business School operating on a GFC model, and Dean Arjay Miller concurred with most of Fred's points.

Terman met with Provost Lyman and other staff, including Howard Brooks, Richard Lyman, Kenneth Cuthbertson, and Raymond F. Bacchetti in March 1970 to consider the proposed model. Brooks and Bacchetti worked further on the model, and Cuthbertson modified some of the weighting of Terman's factors.[30] According to the GFC formula, the Ceiling is equal to (A) income "earned" from tuition, fees, conference profits, and so forth, plus (B) income from some number "Z" of shares of the overall university unrestricted endowment. The factor "Z" once decided on would remain constant for some years. The factors (A) plus (B) plus those gifts, grants, and program endowments unique to each school would equal the total funds available to a school. The plan was intended to allow a school to operate under the GFC while giving it more flexibility within a long-range plan that need not be renegotiated with each annual budget. In addition, by knowing the allocation, the university could better plan for itself.

Fred extended his study to Stanford's Law School after he visited the Harvard comptroller and officials in the Harvard Schools of Law and Business in May 1970.[31] Terman had reminded Stanford officials that Harvard's financial philosophy was "every tub on its' own bottom," but in his discussions at Harvard, Terman pursued both the positive and negative aspects of this every-school-for-itself philosophy.[32] Carl Janke, Harvard's comptroller, stated that he had yet to hear a valid objection to the approach. Perhaps it encouraged the university's schools to pull apart from each other, but it insulated against mediocrity, he argued, and increased the total funds received by the university. Terman's Harvard contacts felt that the independence of the various schools was best for Harvard. Their policy involved minimum central coordination, they told him, and eliminated from the top administration the internal politics and headaches caused by attempting to be King Solomon. And, they said, it stimulated fund-raising tremendously. Besides, if a given school had trouble with its General Fund Ceiling operation, the university could "loan" reserves (as Harvard was then doing to its School of Education—at about 6 percent interest).[33]

Fred submitted a similar, but shorter report concerning the GFC idea and specifically about the Stanford Law School early in July 1970.[34] Harvard's Law School operated with much larger general class sizes than Stanford's Law School, he noted, and offered very few specialized classes having small enrollments. As a result, Harvard Law was very successful in "standing on its own bottom." Its budget "surpluses" were, in fact, being used to enlarge Law School buildings. In contrast, Stanford Law was spending considerably more money per student.[35] Fred concluded that at Stanford's Law School, fund-raising abilities and "earned" income from tuition, fees, and other sources were not yet sufficient, nor would they be in any foreseeable future. It was prudent to defer the GFC for the Law School until the administration could see how the GFC was working for the Business School.

Several years later, one of Fred's last consulting services for Stanford senior administration again related to the GFC. In 1975, he was asked by a committee chaired by Daniel Bershader to share his experiences in producing the GFC reports on the Business and Law schools. The Bershader Committee was considering similar financial plans for the humanities and sciences. "Nothing came of this" at the time, Fred noted for the files in 1977.[36]

Fred continued to give his candid opinions about Stanford past, present, and future privately. When alumnus and presidential cabinet member John W. Gardner was invited to become a Stanford trustee in 1969, he wrote Fred, asking for information about the board. The board, Fred told him frankly, continued to lack adequate knowledge of the activities, plans, and dreams of the operating academic segments of the university. As an illustration, Fred asserted that in all the years during which he was a department head and then dean of engineering (1937–59), there was never a single trustee who was really well informed about the academic activities for which he had been responsible. Fred suggested that the board divide itself into small teams that could become adequately familiar with different portions of the university's activities (the social sciences, or engineering, for example) so that at least two of each of the twenty-three trustees would be familiar with any given activity. He also told Gardner in confidence that he believed there was a growing sense of factionalism within the faculty. Faculty spent a disturbing portion of their time on committee work that was too often aimed at other faculty groups. Meanwhile, the central administration had relaxed its vigil over the quality of faculty appointments. In retirement, he said, he tried to stay out of things on campus, but he honored Gardner's specific request for information and expected his response to be treated as strictly personal and confidential.[37]

In September 1970, Richard Lyman succeeded Kenneth Pitzer as university president. In congratulating him, Terman advised Lyman that tough times of tight budget problems and campus unrest were no reason to "mark time." Stanford should not lose its forward momentum and settle back to becoming just another "good" institution.[38]

Lyman subsequently appointed computer science professor William F. Miller as provost. Miller recalls, when he had come to SLAC years earlier, Terman's confidence in him and in George Forsythe and creation of the Computer Science Department.[39] Terman wrote to the new provost in 1971 that Stanford must never forget that faculty quality is the sine qua non for a great university. "Hard times" are just the time when a great university can move ahead, he added. (James B. Conant brought Harvard to the top between 1933 and 1943, during the depths of the Great Depression, Terman could not help pointing out.) Terman raised for Miller specific points from his 1967 report on faculty hiring and tenure policies: improved procedures were necessary for the selection of tenured *and* nontenured faculty alike; department offerings needed to be simplified, with

Stanford offering fewer but higher-quality courses; and overhead activities needed to be thoroughly scrutinized. During hard times, the first thing a company does is to cut back on overhead services; why can't a university do the same, suggested Terman.[40]

During Lyman's presidency, Stanford counterbalanced its financial woes with the "Campaign for Stanford." Launched in 1972, this five-year fund-raising drive sought to raise $300 million, the largest goal yet again for any university. (The campaign topped out by $4 million and made major contributions to buildings, endowed chairs, student loans and scholarships, and a $132 million boost to the university endowment.[41])

Studies in American Engineering Education

Fred was fiercely proud of Stanford's School of Engineering. As he wrote to Paul Davis a month after he retired, Stanford ran the best low-cost engineering education operation in the country. The teaching loads were very light for the faculty (with only three lectures a week for most) and the salaries were as good as at MIT and Harvard. Stanford was among the leaders both in prestige and in producing PhD and MS degrees, while Stanford's costs per student credit hour were low compared to the competition. "Terman's Law" still seemed to fit the data.[42]

It is hardly surprising that others turned to Fred Terman to review engineering education. In the late 1960s and early 1970s, many American universities were experiencing budget cuts. Major cutbacks occurred in science and engineering program development, such as those at Brown University. It is only natural to find that Fred Terman, who had built Stanford's Engineering School to such heights, would be asked to bring his measuring tools to other campuses. After retiring from Stanford, Terman was commissioned by state regents and state education councils, by individual universities, by several university-industry groups, and by Alvin Eurich's consulting company, the Academy for Educational Development. His task might be a two- or three-day visit to the campus, a two- to three-thousand-word report, and a discussion with the campus president or provost or dean of engineering, but Terman also conducted several much larger studies. Some of these studies made front-page news in the capitals of California, Florida, New Jersey, and New York. Some of the most significant of these studies include:[43]

"Excellence in Science and Engineering in Colorado Universities," January 1967, assisted by Robert Hind and George Masek.

"A Study of Engineering Education in California," March 1968, assisted by Robert Hind and L. F. McGhie.

"Engineering Education in New York," March 1969, assisted by Glenn E. Reeling.

"The Polytechnic Institute of Brooklyn," March 1969.
"Education in Engineering and Engineering Technology in Colorado," August 1970, by Archie Higdon, M. R. Lohmann, F. E. Terman.
"A Study of Engineering and Engineering Technology Education in Florida," August 1971, by F. E. Terman and Archie Higdon.

For most of these tasks, Terman received a modest consulting fee, typically, travel expenses and two or three days' consulting fees at $150 to $200 per day. In his longest and most complicated effort, a study for the State of California, Terman worked for several months on the project, and his fee of $11,000 included the costs of publishing three hundred copies of the report, secretarial work, travel, and per diem consulting fees. (He actually billed the state for only one-half of the number of days he spent on the project.)

Terman was a member on a President's Science Advisory Committee manpower studies commission in the early 1960s and again in 1970.[44] During the years 1967–70, Terman gathered operating costs, student course load, faculty load, departmental activities, and other data for more than seventy U.S. engineering schools, including nine of the top ten engineering schools as ranked in the 1969 Roose-Andersen report.[45] Nearly all schools cooperated with Terman when he sought additional data. One uncooperative administrator at Purdue, however, wrote Terman that his study was useless to Purdue and that Purdue collected no such statistics as direct instruction costs per student credit hour because "such data are misleading and dangerous."[46] Terman was quite surprised that such a huge, publicly funded engineering school saw no need for such a study. If no such data had ever been collected at Purdue, he responded, how could they know that the results would be misleading and dangerous? Some months later, a different high-ranking Purdue official asked Stanford's Engineering Dean Joseph Pettit for copies of Fred Terman's reports, stating that Purdue had learned that these were very valuable. Pettit alerted Terman, and Fred responded with glee.[47]

Southern Methodist University

Shortly before his official August 31, 1965, retirement from Stanford, Fred Terman was approached by a group from Dallas, Texas. They offered him the presidency of the Southern Methodist University Foundation for Science and Engineering, recently established to improve the academic engineering program at Southern Methodist University (SMU) and to benefit the greater Dallas area, the state of Texas, and the Southwest in general. Leading engineers, industrialists, and bankers from the Dallas-Fort Worth area wanted to boost the academic backup for the large and growing number of high-technology firms in the area, including Texas Instruments, Ling-Temco-Vought, Collins Radio, and General Dynamics.

The existing engineering program at SMU had never awarded a PhD. Only a trivial amount of sponsored research was conducted there, and there was no apparent leadership coming out of the engineering school. Nevertheless, SMU was chosen, as Fred recalled, because it had other, excellent programs in the university, and it welcomed development of a new, vigorous engineering program with strong emphasis on graduate work at the PhD level.[48]

Fred Terman was an obvious choice. He was nationally known among engineers and university administrators; indeed he was at the top of his form. He also was well known among the engineering-business innovators of Dallas, men like the heads of Texas Instruments, Cecil Green (Stanford's great benefactor) and Erik Jonsson (later mayor of Dallas), and William P. Clements Jr., president of Southeastern Drilling (and later governor of Texas). His old and very good friends, A. Earl Cullum Jr., and Eugene Fubini were in the group—Cullum had been Fred's right-hand man at the RRL during the war, and Fubini (former assistant secretary of defense and by then a vice president of IBM) also had served under Fred at the lab. Also on the board was Jesse Hobson, former director of the Stanford Research Institute, now SMU's vice president for Coordinated Planning.[49] When the group came to Fred, they were already convinced that he was the one for the job. The board offered Fred an annual salary of $30,000, along with a commodious Dallas apartment and travel expenses for what was expected to be a half-time job.

Fred accepted this intriguing position, convinced that the high-level industries in Dallas, particularly Texas Instruments, were prepared to actively support the SMU Foundation with substantial annual gifts as well as moral support. He insisted, however, on returning to SMU at least $12,000 per year as a financial gift to the program. (Seven years later, when his duties lessened, he returned one-half of his then $12,000 salary each year.[50])

For the first four years, Fred visited Dallas twelve times per year for the monthly Executive Committee meetings and the quarterly full board meetings. His first job, however, was to take over as ghost dean of the School of Engineering and to find a strong dean to lead SMU to the high level expected. In this task, Fred traveled a good deal to speak with many individuals at major schools, including Georgia Tech, Harvard, MIT, Florida, Brooklyn Polytechnic, and Case, and he talked with others at Bell Labs and the National Bureau of Standards.[51] One of his own consultants was Thomas L. Martin Jr., a Stanford PhD in electrical engineering, who had been dean of engineering at the University of Arizona for five years where he substantially revamped their operations. At age forty-two, Martin became dean of engineering at the University of Florida, a large school and, along with Georgia Tech and Texas, one of the three best engineering schools in the South. Although Fred had been talking with Martin only as a consultant, he found out from other sources that Martin might be leaving Florida to become president of a small engineering school in the Northeast. Fred pounced. He invited Martin to visit Dallas and arranged a luncheon with the top men from Texas Instruments and other large electronics companies and with other influential members of the SMU Foundation Board. Martin was convinced and arrived to take the helm at the School of Engineering in the fall of 1966.

One of Martin's biggest achievements at Florida had been to construct an educational television system, "GENESYS." This system was used throughout the Florida university system (Cape Kennedy, West Palm Beach, and Orlando, as well as Gainesville). Martin had been instructed by the University of Florida administration to provide graduate degree engineering programs at each of those locations, but had not been told how to implement the program. He had decided to use television. Within two years of coming to SMU, Martin installed a similar system called "TAGER"-TV and was offering more than forty television courses, thirty-nine of them in graduate engineering topics with nearly nine hundred course enrollments per term.[52] (SMU's instructional TV system was financed by Cecil Green.)

Fred was intrigued and thought the system could be implemented at Stanford and on the Peninsula. He asked Stanford's Engineering Dean Joe Pettit to stop off in Dallas and examine TAGER. Pettit liked it, especially when equipped with auxiliary talkback. Back at Stanford, Pettit found Peninsula companies to be very interested, and he raised $1 million in industry gifts to set up the Stanford system. Stanford installed a TV system with four campus classrooms. The signals were beamed to Black Mountain and then sent out in a fan beam across Santa Clara Valley to south of San Jose, and also into Berkeley and parts of San Francisco. It was so successful that Peninsula companies asked for video tape recordings of the classes to use for their employees at locations remote from the Peninsula. One young Stanford electrical engineering professor, James Gibbons (later to become dean of engineering at Stanford), improved the usefulness of the course tapes by having a group of remote users meet together with a "tutor" for instant feedback and support.[53]

Back at SMU, the foundation's board members, through their companies, were now contributing about $600,000 per year to its engineering program. In his first year as president of the foundation, Fred energized a program of undergraduate recruitment. The freshmen engineering class at SMU increased by 33 percent in one year. He also sought to increase the number of full-time day students in the master's degree program. In a "booster" talk to an industry-faculty group to introduce Dean Martin to the area, Terman indicated that the best-known examples of the effect a strong university can have on the economic growth of a region were the Boston area and MIT, and the San Francisco Peninsula and Stanford. But, Fred added, many other regions were seeking to do likewise—Portland, Oregon, had just announced the formation of a Graduate Center; Colorado was looking to do so; Bell Labs, Standard Oil, Union Carbide, and others were planning a graduate Institute for Science and Technology in northern New Jersey. (He did not mention it, but Fred was an executive committee member of the New Jersey planning group as well from 1966 to 1969.[54]) A good university *can* make many contributions to a region, he told the Dallas group, but it does not come automatically. (There were other good universities that had little direct impact on the world of industry, he pointed out, such as Princeton University and several excellent schools in the Midwest.) A good engineering school needs leadership but also partnership with the industrial community. The formation of the Graduate Research Center of the Southwest in Dallas was a significant first step. The recent establishment of the SMU Foundation was an important next step. He now heralded the arrival of Dean Thomas Martin and concluded that what they wished to do for Dallas and Texas was "no idle dream. The opportunity is here for the taking, the time and location are right, and the requisite industrial base already exists, and the necessary leadership is on the scene." All that remained to be off and running, Terman emphasized, was the tangible support of the community and the SMU Foundation.[55]

Martin soon got SMU off and running. With Fred's assistance, he quickly attracted to SMU experienced faculty with good research records. He taught several younger faculty the ways to develop graduate research programs and increased the number of graduate students. Within two years, 998 graduate students were enrolled in engineering, one of the largest enrollments in the country. PhD candidates increased by a factor of five, and by 1970–71, SMU expected to award about thirty PhDs per year in engineering. The number of undergraduate engineering majors more than doubled, and joint programs were established in biomedical engineering and computers in health care systems. The TAGER-TV system had grown to include lower-division engineering courses offered to a half-dozen Texas schools, allowing their students to take a preengineering program. Active research grants to SMU had grown from $30,000 in 1965 to more than $1 million. In a 1968 letter to Texas Instruments' Chairman Erik Jonsson, Terman wrote that "The SMU Institute of Technology is today's 'hottest' engineering stock in the country's educational market."[56]

Naturally Fred had his run-ins with the SMU administration. As president of the SMU Foundation, Fred was unhappy to find that some foundation funds were used to plug-up leaks in the university's general operation and supplement salaries of some of the more unproductive faculty.[57] Overall, however, he worked well with SMU officials, and the engineering program progressed well.

Terman continued to advise Dean Thomas Martin. Martin was not as fond as Terman of the "each tub on its own bottom" philosophy of Harvard, but Fred argued that the alternative "King's Decree" system, as he called it, ignored a faculty's distrust of arbitrary authority from above. The "King's Decree" approach generated intense internal competitive entrepreneurship with the king at the center of pressure, Terman maintained. He warned Martin that administrators of an educational institution do not have full freedom to choose and control the direction of an institution, but are under the influence of private donors, foundations, government agencies, public moods, and educational fads.[58]

Martin was very grateful to Terman for his years of effort. In 1973, he wrote to Fred that by that summer, SMU had produced 131 PhDs and 1,307 MS degrees in engineering since 1967, and "this was possible largely through the support, both financial and moral, that you have given us."[59] Fred felt that his task at SMU was now largely accomplished and asked to resign as president of the foundation. He suggested that Martin himself, as chief operating officer, should take on the post of president of the foundation, but Martin demurred and suggested the president should be a member of the Dallas community, not one of the SMU faculty. Fred resigned as president but stayed on as a member of the board.[60]

Within a year after Terman stepped down, Martin crossed swords with a new SMU provost and felt that the Engineering School had been denied some support promised to it. Martin resigned from SMU to accept presidency of the Illinois Institute of Technology, and Fred was once again asked to find a dean. Fred wrote to SMU Chancellor Willis Tate that he was worried that SMU, after having built itself up so much in nine years, was now losing momentum and was about to lose some key faculty.[61] Nevertheless, Fred worked with the new SMU provost and its new president, James H. Zumberge, a noted geologist, to attract F. Karl Willenbrock, whom Fred had known for some years, as the next dean of the SMU School of Engineering. Willenbrock was former director of the Engineering and Applied Physics Labs at Harvard, then provost at SUNY-Buffalo, and then on the senior staff of the National Bureau of Standards. After Willenbrock settled in at SMU in 1976, Fred "dropped out" of the picture due to increasing health problems. In 1977, SMU awarded Fred Terman an honorary degree of Doctor of Science.[62]

Straightening the Course in California and All Points East

Among Fred's earliest educational consulting jobs had been his work in 1952 for the State of California. Asked to study engineering education programs in California's state college system, Fred had visited a number of schools over a five-month period.[63] A new task for the State of California unfolded in 1967–68 while Terman was studying engineering school design and efficiency and national manpower needs in engineering. Fred's State of California report attracted nationwide attention.[64]

In 1959, the California State Legislature had created a ten-year "Master Plan" for the development of public and private institutions of higher learning in the state. By the 1960s, the University of California, at the top of the state's educational system, and California's State Colleges had long since outgrown the limited role originally foreseen for them. The state's "junior colleges" had also grown rapidly since the 1920s.[65]

In April 1967, the Coordinating Council for Higher Education (CCHE), contracted with Fred Terman to undertake a "Study of Engineering Manpower and Higher Education in California." The Terman project could count on the advice of a distinguished group of California educators (including seven deans of engineering from public and private colleges and universities), and six representatives from state agencies and from industry, including the vice presidents of Litton Industries, Lockheed Aircraft, and Pacific Lighting Corporation.[66] Fred gathered two Stanford administrators, Robert Hind and Farrell McGhie, as his assistants and visited the eleven campuses that, collectively, accounted for 70 percent of the BS degrees in engineering awarded annually in California. They sought advice from another fifteen deans and educational consultants.[67]

Thirty-five public and private California institutions offered the BS degree in engineering. New York State was next with twenty-two and Pennsylvania with fifteen. Limiting the count to public schools, California led with twenty-two, with Texas next at nine and Ohio with six. Between 1958 and 1968, California *quadrupled* the number of campuses in the mushrooming University of California system authorized to offer a BS in engineering. Four campuses (Riverside, Irvine, San Diego, and Santa Cruz) were so new that they had yet to award a single BS degree. Of the thirteen existing state colleges with BS engineering programs, only five, Terman would calculate, had an output that approached the minimum economic size.

Fred's study concluded that after a decade of extensive campus building throughout California, the facilities and programs for engineering at the University of California campuses and the California State Colleges were excessive. The total number of bachelor's degrees in engineering, as a percentage of all bachelor's of science degrees awarded in the United States had been slowly diminishing since 1959 (from 17 to 13 percent). Advanced degrees, both the MS and PhD, however, had been growing rapidly in proportion to the BS degrees. BS degrees, he also noted, were awarded more or less constantly by geographical region, whereas graduate engineering degrees were concentrated within a few regions and at fewer schools. Fred argued that this reflected changes in the engineering profession since World War II and the resulting increase in the sort of advanced knowledge required of engineers. (The President's Science Advisory Committee already had concluded in 1962 that the major need of the country was for more graduate engineers with MS and PhD degrees, rather than for more at the BS level.)

Three of the top five engineering schools in the country were in California (Berkeley, Stanford, and Caltech), and two other California schools (UCLA and USC) had some national visibility. The state college campuses provided a sound undergraduate education, Fred added, but they lacked any national distinction. He found that interest in engineering varied greatly among California campuses. It was high at Berkeley, UCLA, and Davis, and at Cal Poly-San Luis Obispo and San Jose State among state institutions, and, in the private sector, at Stanford, Caltech, USC, and Santa Clara. Elsewhere in the state, interest in engineering was either low or practically nonexistent. Among engineering specialties, chemical engineering, nuclear engineering, petroleum engineering, and naval architecture drew few students.

Fred used his famous "instruction cost index" in his study. This is defined as the total teaching payroll of the educational unit involved, divided by the total units of credit that students receive. It was not a perfect index, Fred admitted, but was very useful in educational manpower and planning studies. His model was based on the assumption that unless each engineering field at a school (civil, electrical, and so on) produced at least forty to fifty BS degrees annually, and, for graduate programs, thirty to forty MS degrees each year, the operation is not very cost-efficient, and the instruction cost index rises considerably.

Fred's lengthy report discussed many factors in cost effectiveness: the location of industrial employers, the needs of part-time students, the differences between engineering and engineering technology curricula, facilities, and the likely population/economic growth of various regions in the coming decade.

Terman advised the discontinuation of several California engineering programs, or close monitoring on an annual basis. Similarly, he proposed that marginal specialties be closed out, such as the naval architecture programs, and some mineral technology programs at Berkeley. (Privately, Fred indicated that MIT's Naval Architecture Program was ten times larger than the one at Berkeley, which graduated only five students per year. Since some of those five graduates surely were foreign students, Fred thought the Berkeley program had negligible effect on U.S. shipbuilding.[68])

A more innovative recommendation was his proposal to increase interdisciplinary degrees and interuniversity degree granting at the PhD level. He proposed strengthening graduate programs of the several state colleges most active in graduate work (that were also located in or near large population areas). And he urged the CCHE to develop a consistent program for collecting and studying statistical data concerning California engineering programs.

Fred's report was sent to hundreds of faculty and administrators. (He paid to have three hundred copies printed when the CCHE asked for more copies, although technically his contract called only for one copy to be prepared.) Thus, many people were familiar with his findings when the report was discussed in May

1968 by the CCHE Committee on Educational Programs. One of Fred's advisory board members was on the CCHE committee, so the committee itself was also well aware of Fred's findings two months before its hearings. The CCHE committee discussed the findings, voted to accept Fred's study in principle, and asked for comment from all interested observers before the overall CCHE would hear recommendations in October.

Understandably, there was already some concern on the part of California university and state college administrators. Fred thought the CCHE administrative staff prepared a rather too lengthy (eleven pages) and rudely instructive memo on the upcoming hearings, and that this memo would needlessly irritate the educators.[69] Fortunately, a new CCHE staff director was appointed in late summer, and Fred was pleased that suggestions he presented in September for a more flexible and polite summary memo were adopted.

Fred was rather pleased with responses from the state college system, but he thought University of California President Charles Hitch to be obtuse and evasive in his response.[70] Hitch ignored a number of Fred's recommendations and misstated several others, Fred wrote. He believed that President Hitch had been badly served by his own staff, who had inadequately researched the issues and had produced a poorly written response.[71] Nevertheless, Hitch had acted quickly to defer plans for programs at Riverside and Santa Cruz.

A two-page document was submitted by the CCHE staff, which adopted most of Fred's plan.[72] The CCHE committee resolutions concerning Fred's report were then unanimously approved by the full council. No more engineering programs were to be approved until nearly all current programs were filled to the minimum desirable level. Minimum desirable level guidelines, as suggested in the study, were to be adopted. The state colleges and the University of California should be encouraged to discontinue those engineering specialties that were marginal as to size and need. More specifically, the council ruled that remotely located Humboldt State College should phase out its engineering program as quickly as possible, while engineering programs at Chico State and San Francisco State were to be monitored annually and phased out three years hence if there was insufficient growth. The CCHE accepted the University of California decision to defer the engineering programs at the university campuses at Riverside and Santa Cruz; the engineering programs at Davis, Irvine, San Diego, and Santa Barbara should be designed to work toward size goals. Finally, the CCHE requested its staff to compile annually statistical data to permit it to develop a clearer picture of California public higher education in engineering.[73] The press reported it all, although not always accurately, and Fred's report became widely read around the nation.[74] Fred sent more than one hundred copies to various universities across the country.

The California study was an especially timely one. In 1969, the University of California alone forecast a total enrollment for the academic year of 1978–79 of

150,000 students. By 1973, the total enrollment had reached 119,000, but enrollments would plateau by 1982. In the field of engineering, the "super campuses" of the University of California would continue to be Berkeley and UCLA.[75] Fred Terman's report was an early signal that the great campus building of the 1950s and 1960s had its limits.

The situation in New York State was somewhat different than in California. Unlike California, most of the engineering schools in New York were private institutions that were often insufficiently funded and needed special attention. Fred visited a number of New York schools in 1968 for the Regents of the New York State System and personally delivered his report to the regents that December.[76] New York needed no more engineering schools, he told them, and would not for another decade. As he found elsewhere, a few schools produced most of the degrees while many others were too small to be viable. At best, Fred felt that eleven of twenty-one BS programs and five of eighteen MS programs were large enough to be cost efficient. Part-time education at the MS level was good, he found, but full-time program enrollments were weak. Enrollment figures for PhDs were also surprisingly weak for a state as industrialized as New York. The New York schools in general, he added, were nearly all completely lacking in top leadership. Fred recommended that faculty, not buildings or improved equipment, should be the state's highest priority, along with increased funding for graduate fellowships. He also recommended that public and private graduate programs be treated alike in the allocation of state funding.

The Polytechnic Institute of Brooklyn (PIB) was a special case, an excellent school but now nearly bankrupt. Fred wrote a separate study of PIB and recommended, as one solution, that it merge its engineering offerings with New York University. In 1974, incoming PIB President George Bugliarello commended Fred on his "magnificently perceptive" 1969 report on PIB. The previous year, the NYU School of Engineering merged with PIB, and Bugliarello reported that things had "turned around."[77]

Each state Fred visited seemed to have special needs and particular strengths or weaknesses. Nevertheless, certain themes prevailed in Fred's engineering education studies. He favored quality over quantity. He supported people (faculty and students) ahead of buildings. And his recommendations, comparisons, and criticisms did not make everyone happy.

In 1970, Fred was asked to examine the engineering schools in Florida. His subsequent report outraged several Florida regents and perhaps smacked of Yankee interference. Fred's report stated that the University of Florida (UF) engineering school needed ten years of single-minded persistence to improve. His criticisms were succinct: UF spent too much money per student for too few students and too few classes. There were too many peripheral courses, not enough core courses, and a thicket of devious strategies and red tape. The faculty should be improved. The GENESYS TV system, installed in 1964, was very good but should be improved and expanded. UF made it into the top thirty-five engineering schools in the country, but not into the top twenty-five. Even the University of South Florida, the report stated, was doing better with its engineering program.

Fred stepped on a hornet's nest. The *St. Petersburg Times* headline read "Report Criticizes UF College of Engineering." The university's president and vice president went on record stating that they were tired of the criticism of UF in the press, and the vice president further argued that UF was better than Georgia Tech, Syracuse, and Colorado.[78]

Fred fully understood what was happening. Before he sent his report to the state authorities, he sent a copy to each of Florida's several deans of engineering and to all of the academics who would be participating in a subsequent meeting to discuss the report so that they could feel prepared. In a long letter to his colleague Robert Uhrig, dean of the University of Florida College of Engineering, he admitted that he did not think it likely that he would make many friends at the university, nor become the most popular man in Florida education.[79]

Fred went on to explain his view to Uhrig. The University of Florida had too many courses, curricula, and departments of engineering. (UF offered more areas of engineering than MIT, with fewer students and resources and considerably less prestige.) UF was overextended in proportion to its resources, size of the student population, and state needs, and someone other than local engineering faculty needed to pare courses down to the essentials. (Bill Everitt, Fred's University of Illinois friend for more than thirty years, had prepared a report for Florida back in 1965 which leveled essentially the same criticisms.) Fred refused to accept the argument that some of today's "tiny rivulets" might well become tomorrow's "raging mainstreams" of engineering and that the mainstream would become the rivulet. Of the six major areas of engineering, only aerospace had joined in the past fifty years and it was still the smallest of the six areas. Nuclear engineering was not growing very quickly, while environmental engineering would probably modify civil engineering departments the way electronics modified electrical departments. Computer science *would* become a major field, he thought, but would probably be classified apart from engineering. In his letter to Uhrig, Fred also stuck to his well-known analyses that showed that forty to fifty BS degrees per year per field, with about the same number of MS degrees, were normally needed to deploy teaching resources most efficiently, and he criticized the lack of progress with the GENESYS TV network.

Fred was interested in Florida's engineering future, he assured Uhrig, not in its past. The University of Florida's long-range goal in engineering should be to become the outstanding engineering school in the South and to be numbered among the top fifteen engineering schools in the country. This could be done with well-planned efforts persisted in over a span of years.[80]

In July 1971, Fred spent several weekends at the Bohemian Grove where he had long discussions with Michael O'Brien, who had been dean of engineering at Berkeley (1943–59) at roughly the same time Terman had been dean at Stanford. In an eleven-page, typed memo to Uhrig, with a copy to Fred, O'Brien had criticized Fred's analysis of the Florida situation, saying that Fred had not investigated the *kinds* of engineers needed in Florida and that Fred was overdoing it to bring cost factors and productivity considerations into the picture. Fred responded with a quote from Marshall Robinson of the Ford Foundation: "The modern American university is the most inefficient instrument man has ever devised, including the Federal Government." O'Brien had written that Fred was "naïve in the extreme" and "overwhelmingly biased toward Electrical Engineering" and not knowledgeable about other fields of engineering. Fred defended himself against these charges by detailing how he had, for example, built Stanford's aeronautical engineering from two men to a department that out-produced MIT and Caltech in production of PhDs. As provost, he pointed out, he had had responsibility for the entire spectrum of Stanford's curricula, and Stanford had made more progress than any other institution in the country. Fred commented wryly to Uhrig that O'Brien did not seem to notice that by the late 1950s, Stanford had been awarding more graduate degrees than Berkeley in civil and mechanical engineering, and that Berkeley's engineering production improved after O'Brien retired.[81]

Advisor to the U.S. Government

Fred Terman served as an advisor to the U.S. government for almost forty years, beginning in the late 1930s with his help on textbooks for the military academies. During World War II, he had served the war effort as director of the Radio Research Laboratory, and as member of a joint military-industrial committee on vacuum tubes. He also served on naval research and army signal corps advisory committees during his time as dean of engineering and as provost.

During these same years, Fred served on National Academy of Sciences and National Science Foundation boards for mathematical, physical, and engineering sciences. Twice, from 1959–63 and from 1970–73, he was a consultant to the President's Science Advisory Committee. While provost, he was also a member of the U.S. State Department Board of Foreign Scholarships. In retirement, Fred was a member of a visiting committee to evaluate the National Bureau of Standards. As one would expect, in most of these positions Fred's expertise was valued in education, electronics, and communications.

One of Fred's most extensive consultancies both before and after his retirement was his work with the Institute for Defense Analyses (IDA) from 1955 to 1973.

This nonprofit think tank was established with Ford Foundation support at the request of the Department of Defense (DOD). During Fred's seventeen-year service, IDA provided advice to the DOD and to numerous nonmilitary agencies of the government. IDA and its associated group "Jason" became controversial during the Vietnam War era, however, and Fred's IDA trusteeship would become tangentially involved with antiwar disruptions on the Stanford campus.

In 1949 Secretary of Defense James Forrestal had established a civilian operations research group in the Pentagon called the Weapons Systems Evaluation Group (WSEG). This group reported to a military commander and served the Joint Chiefs of Staff (JCS) by performing operations research on choices of weapons systems, tactics, and so forth. As time passed, it became more difficult to recruit talented staff for WSEG due to limitations of civil service salary scales, and questions were raised regarding the quality of the WSEG staff and their long delays in getting timely advice back to the DOD.[82]

In 1955, the DOD asked for assistance from MIT's president, James R. Killian Jr., to manage the WSEG as a contract operation. MIT staff proposed that, rather than take on the responsibility itself, it should organize a consortium of universities to sponsor a new nonprofit organization. It was decided to choose private rather than state universities in the initial group. Admiral E. L. Cochrane (retired), MIT's vice president for government and industrial relations, convened the group, by inviting Caltech, Tulane, Case Institute, and Stanford to join in the effort. In July 1955, Sterling agreed and asked his newly appointed provost, Fred Terman, to represent Stanford.[83] Fred knew Admiral Cochrane well. He accepted and served as trustee of the Institute for Defense Analyses (IDA) until 1973.

IDA had its first full meeting at the Pentagon in April 1956.[84] Each university had two trustees on the IDA board, an academic officer (usually the university president) and a business officer. (For several years, Thomas Ford represented Stanford as business officer.) A scientist was named operating head of IDA with the title of director of research, and a retired admiral or general usually served as the president. The initial director of research was the MIT physicist Albert G. Hill. (Terman was offered the post in later years but declined.)

At the first meeting, Albert Hill outlined the main areas of military interest: continental defense, nonmilitary effects on an enemy, and peripheral warfare. Topics needing attention, he told them, included electronic countermeasures, ballistic missiles, technical surveillance of atomic and other tests, anti-countermeasures, relations with allies, and effects of other types of attack (chemical, biological, radiological).[85]

Within a few years, Killian, who was IDA board chairman and MIT president, suggested that some nontechnical men be added to the IDA board as "public" trustees. Among the first appointed was William A. B. Burden, investment manager for the Vanderbilt fortune and influential advisor to the U.S. government.

(Fred Terman and Burden became friends, and as a result Terman acted as technical advisor on the electronics industry to Burden's investment firm.) Other noted public trustees included Laurance Rockefeller, C. Douglas Dillon (former secretary of the treasury), and James Perkins (later president of Cornell). Fred and the IDA academic trustees got along especially well with Laurance Rockefeller, and in his later years Fred loved to tell a story of being flown in Rockefeller's private plane.[86]

By 1962, six other universities had joined as sponsors and with Berkeley's addition in 1967, the total membership reached twelve. (Additions were Illinois, Columbia, Michigan, Princeton, Penn State, Chicago, and Berkeley.) Chief executives of these universities attended regularly, including Presidents Robert Goheen of Princeton, Grayson Kirk of Columbia, and Eric Walker of Penn State.

IDA performed military work only for the Joint Chiefs of Staff of DOD and did not consider contracts from individual military services or branches and so avoided getting caught in interservice rivalries or competitions. It did a number of studies for nonmilitary agencies, however, including the Departments of Agriculture and Justice, the Post Office, the Federal Communications Commission, the Urban Mass Transportation Agency, the Corps of Engineers, the State Department, the National Science Foundation, the Federal Aviation Administration, and the Atomic Energy Commission.

In its early years, the IDA board often discussed the fact that it seemed that former wartime colleagues from the MIT Radiation Lab, Fred's Radio Research Laboratory, Los Alamos, and the other major federal World War II projects, made up the majority of those drawn on for advice. In 1959, Charles Townes (who succeeded Hill as director of research) proposed forming a group of younger academic scientists and engineers. This group was called the Jasons. Eminent Princeton physicists John A. Wheeler and Eugene Wigner and mathematician Oskar Morgenstern had also recommended that IDA increase opportunities for the scientific community to serve its country.[87] The Jasons were a highly select group who met for one month each summer, where they were briefed on IDA problems. They were generously paid and were brought in on many important situations. Allen Peterson of the Electrical Engineering Department, and Sidney Drell and Wolfgang Panofsky of physics were Stanford members of Jason.

By 1960, the Jason group was up to twenty-four persons and numbered nearly forty by 1967. They were an extremely talented group, most of them physicists, but they were not all so young; the Jasons included not only Freeman Dyson, Val Fitch, Marvin L. Goldberger, Murray Gell-Mann, Subrahmanyan Chandrasekhar, Steven Weinberg, Fredrik Zachariasen, and Edward Salpeter, but also Wheeler and Wigner, Hans Bethe, and Edward Teller.

Fred's service to IDA included studying the possibilities of IDA fellowships, research leaves for faculty, and postdoctoral internships. He was skeptical of the value of sending established faculty on paid leave to IDA, except for operations research people, where perhaps young faculty could benefit from a postdoctoral year. Short-term institutes and special meetings, he thought, would be more useful to acquaint faculty with IDA problems. He also felt that certain regular IDA employees might themselves benefit from educational leave to universities for further training. Fred's proposals were adopted by the IDA board in September 1959.[88]

In the mid-1960s, the Students for a Democratic Society (SDS) began to pressure the administration at the University of Chicago and at Princeton University to resign as university members of IDA. The IDA building at Princeton was besieged on several occasions, and ultimately the faculties at Princeton and Chicago voted to ask IDA to be removed. Some members resigned individually due to personal harassment. At least one Jason summer study group location was changed to the Naval Postgraduate School at Monterey, California, in order to circumvent possible demonstrations or harassment.

Opposition to the war in Vietnam had first arisen at Stanford in 1965, but things heated up early in 1967 with protests against the draft. At Stanford, antiwar activists in 1967 printed broadsides and news sheets criticizing connections between Stanford's faculty and trustees and the "war contractors" in Stanford Industrial Park. The broadsheet *Resistance* attacked Stanford's ties with military contractors. Although IDA was not mentioned, names among the indicted included electrical engineering faculty members then conducting classified research (including O. G. Villard Jr., William R. Rambo, Dean Watkins, and Allen Peterson), various administrators of Stanford and SRI, and trustees William Hewlett and David Packard. Central to the article's complaints, however, was the name of former provost Fred Terman.[89] A mass rally near the center of campus in White Plaza on April 13 was followed by a march to Stanford Research Institute (SRI) to protest weapons and chemical warfare research.[90]

In spring 1967, Terman wrote to a retired friend that the Vietnam situation was miserable, with no easy or attractive solution in sight.[91] In early November the SDS sponsored another protest, its hint of violence sparking an all-night peace vigil of some two thousand at Memorial Church, the largest demonstration yet at Stanford. Terman was interviewed by a student reporter about IDA activities shortly after for an article in the *Stanford Daily* (and Fred thought the reporter did a pretty fair job of writing up the interview).[92]

By the following spring, events turned distinctly worse. In March, the *Stanford Daily* returned to interview Terman on the IDA, focusing on recent actions at Princeton and Chicago (in February, the Chicago and Princeton faculty had urged disassociation with IDA).[93] By midsummer 1968, the campus experienced several large demonstrations, arson (fire destroyed President Sterling's office), and disruptions at the Old Union. Nevertheless, in record-breaking turnout during student spring elections, 70 percent voted that forceful occupation of university buildings was "unacceptable behavior."

The *Los Angeles Times* ran a feature on SDS activity against the IDA on several campuses, and even *Science* magazine looked into the issue, publishing an article contributed by Daniel Greenberg.[94] The IDA board was greatly concerned about finding some solution. Board members did not want Chicago, Princeton, or any others to resign yet many of the academics faced serious pressure back on campus. In June 1968, one sort of solution was found when IDA became independent of university sponsorship. In nearly all cases, the IDA trustees simply changed hats and became private trustees. Fred Terman continued on as trustee, legally becoming a Trustee at Large, a position he held until he retired from the board.[95]

Fred Terman considered his service on IDA to be beneficial to Stanford, even though the university had a minimal institutional role in IDA activities. He and business manager Thomas Ford, for example, learned a great deal about how top-ranking officials at other institutions were handling government research programs. In his opinion, his seventeen years as consultant and trustee to IDA, "although not central to the functioning of the University, nevertheless was an activity of substantial public importance and one to which Stanford can look back upon with satisfaction as having made a worthwhile contribution to the national welfare."[96]

Across the country, more violent campus protests against American involvement in Southeast Asia were just beginning. On April 3, 1969, a mass meeting at Stanford demanded an end to classified research and war-related research on campus, and the end of chemical and biological warfare and counterinsurgency studies at SRI. Several days later, several hundred "April 3rd Movement" protesters occupied the Applied Electronics Lab, disrupting its operation for nine days (and they, in turn, had been surrounded by another hundred or so students counter-demonstrating against "mob rule"). A convocation of more than eight thousand at Frost Amphitheater subsequently attempted a peaceful discussion of classified and war-related research at the university and SRI, but on April 30, the university's main administration building, Encina Hall, was occupied overnight and administration offices ransacked. That May, Stanford's board of trustees severed the university's ties with SRI—contrary to the demands of protesters who had wanted SRI brought under closer scrutiny and control—but several small classified research projects continued on campus in microwave electronics and communications. (The over-the-horizon long-distance radar study moved to SRI.[97]) In 1973, Jason activity at Stanford was moved to the Stanford Research Institute for administrative purposes.

As Terman saw it, the connections between Stanford and SRI were, in any case, nominal. During his last year as provost, he had served on a joint SRI-Stanford committee to consider their institutional relationship. All of the Stanford members concluded that the two should split since SRI's activities were basically unrelated to Stanford's goals. Aside from current events, SRI's association with Stanford seemed to be confused in the public mind, which more than once had hurt Stanford's fund-raising activities. The SRI people on the committee, however, liked the prestige of having a connection with Stanford University, Terman wrote. Equally significant, Stanford's trustees felt SRI and Stanford should remain together. The board's final decision to separate was, therefore, a difficult one.[98]

Fred Terman was not out of the sight-lines of the antiwar movement yet, however. In the spring of 1970, as the United States moved into Cambodia, campus violence escalated. A sit-in at Old Union erupted into rock-throwing, arson, and a barrage of tear-gas when several hundred students faced off against some 250 police. Protesters confronted each other when some 300 nonviolent demonstrators tried to block protesters in front of Encina. Rocks flew over their heads into office windows and the protest moved on across campus to White Plaza and other campus sites. Yet another group of more than fifty "Free Campus Movement" students, including many engineering and science students, surrounded the Durand Engineering and the Earth Sciences buildings to protect them from damage.[99] Nonetheless, over two days at least fifteen other major campus buildings, including Encina Hall, the Bookstore, and Tresidder Union, and the homes of President Ken Pitzer, Provost Dick Lyman, and Provost-Emeritus Fred Terman were damaged with rocks and red paint. The damage, outside and inside, to Terman's home amounted to more than two thousand dollars.[100]

Protests in various forms would continue at Stanford through 1972. Peaceful convocations, teach-ins, petition signings, and the periodic boycotting of classes jockeyed around protesters blocking everyday activity at Encina, the ROTC office in the athletics building, the Hoover Institution, the ERL and other engineering labs, and in 1971, the Computation Center, the Hansen Labs, the Old Union. Ironically, Stanford would not only go to, but win the 1971 and 1972 Rose Bowls during these difficult years.

In 1973, *Science* magazine reporter John Walsh wrote that the campus demonstrations of the past years had had a particularly dispiriting effect at Stanford "because no American university, public or private, had made a more intense effort at organized self-examination and reform."

> Stanford has made big advances since World War II, and they can be attributed to the dynamism of Sterling and Terman. . . . Ironically, the means the university has used to gain its prominence—its relations with government and industry, its land development practices, its quest for academic excellence—have been primary targets for militant critics. . . . There are, in fact, few signs that more than a small minority of students and faculty approve of violence or fully accept the radical analysis, which, in effect, claims that success has spoiled Stanford.

Terman, as Stanford's academic vice president, "presided over the effort to make Stanford an institution in which excellence in the sciences and engineering was matched in the humanities and arts," Walsh continued. "There is little question that just as Sterling was the architect of a super Stanford, Terman was, in the same figurative sense, its engineer."[101]

Fred had retired at just the right time, he remarked, "just before the storm hit."[102] Wally Sterling's last two years in office had been extremely difficult, capped as they were with the destruction of his books and personal possessions, collected over some four decades, in the July 1968 President's Office fire. Provost Richard Lyman had his hands full on the front lines in more ways than one. In June 1970, Kenneth Pitzer resigned as president, frustrated at the disruption of the educational process, and Lyman took over as Stanford's seventh president. He was widely backed by faculty, alumni, and student leaders and was intent on putting Stanford's house in order.

Fred tried not to give backseat advice to those now running the university. In 1972, Fred Terman was quoted in the press as saying that though he was the oldest continuous inhabitant of Stanford University (resident since 1912), "it's unwise for a retired person to throw his weight around," and that he tried not to involve himself in university activities anymore.[103] Yet while he turned his attention to help other American and foreign universities and to serve as senior statesman in professional society affairs, he never considered moving away from the Stanford campus.

Consulting Abroad

Fred Terman's interest in engineering education took on an international perspective after his retirement. Although an initial look at Soviet higher education was more in terms of checking up on the competition, his interest in engineering training in Asia grew into an especially significant contribution to the educational system and economy of the Republic of Korea.

Only three months after Fred Terman retired as vice president and provost of Stanford, he accompanied a small U.S. Office of Education mission to observe engineering and technology education in the Soviet Union. During the month of December 1965, he visited Moscow, Leningrad, and Kiev to study both higher education in science and engineering and training for elementary and secondary-school teachers in these subjects. The team visited many universities and technical-training schools but, as Fred noted, they were taken only to the very best. (Their request to see newer or more parochial institutions was turned down.)

Fred prepared a lengthy report for the Department of Education shortly after his return.[104] Soviet students were prepared in calculus, physics, and chemistry at a somewhat earlier age than in the United States, and motivating students seemed to be no problem, he reported. Although there were only some fifteen to twenty subspecialties in physics in university training, he found, there were more than two hundred in engineering, a fact he attributed to the very narrow technical categories in which Soviet technology operated. Even allowing that he saw only the best, Terman was generally impressed by the general level of Soviet education, but concluded that this should not be seen as a challenge to the United States. The rigid educational boxes in which young people were trained was a factor of the planned Soviet society, not a result of optimum engineering education. The Soviet educational system, he believed, could stifle creativity in a society like that of the United States.

Terman delivered at least thirteen talks regarding his Soviet experience in the two years following his trip, giving them titles such as "Engineering Education in Russia," or "Some Observations on Soviet Education," or "Education in a Planned Society."[105] His themes remained largely those he had presented in his trip report; in short, his belief that Soviet educational gains seemed impressive but fit their particular (and rigid) system. Problems in American education, he stressed, could not be solved by imitating Soviet education.

Fred began a period of consulting in Asia in 1968 that continued through 1975, just about to the end of his physical ability to travel overnight. In June and July 1968, he journeyed to Taiwan to deliver the keynote speech, "The Expanding Partnership Between Industry and Engineering Education in the USA," in a university- and government-sponsored seminar on modern engineering and technology. He gave two other lengthy talks during this trip to the same audience.[106] Terman was with a high-level visiting group of twenty-six Chinese engineers from the United States and elsewhere, who met for an eighteen-day seminar with engineers and scientists from Taiwan. (President and Madam Chiang Kai-Shek entertained the group.[107])

Part of Fred's keynote remarks would develop themes he would touch on again and again: first, that modern engineering needs required serious study of mathematics, physics, and chemistry; and second, that it was more important to train for the highest quality than for quantity. But some points were aimed especially at a developing Asian economy. It was critical to stress creativity, he advised, and not emphasize mere memorization. Leave the ivory tower of academe to acquaint the student with actual industry situations. Go beyond imitation of foreign ideas and products; new, self-initiated ideas and techniques must be valued. One should strive to be a leader, not a follower in technology. Fred returned to Taiwan four years later in 1972 to deliver a similar keynote address.[108] He emphasized particularly the necessity of preparing engineering MS and PhD candidates for nonacademic careers. From his extensive manpower studies performed for various government and educational panels, Terman had become convinced that a teacher could no longer offer a very narrow research track as the model for his graduate student. The new PhD, perhaps a doctorate in engineering, needed greater breadth and less specialization, but no less intellectual rigor, than in the former days. Real-world skills must be in the tool bag of newly finished engineering PhDs. The better engineering school of the 1970s, he reiterated, was not "in a little world of its own" but aware of the outside.

As he had been telling audiences back home, industry-funded research and development would grow during the 1970s at twice the overall national research and development rate, but that would not fill the gap from the declining support from governmental defense and space programs better funded during the 1960s.[109] Just as the U.S. educational system needed to find new places and new opportunities for its graduates, a similar need would arise in Asia, with the additional angle that Asian countries needed engineers and applied scientists who could design competitive original products, would know materials and manufacturing processes, quality control, factory design, and cost effective operations, and as a result, who could become successful business leaders. While a sophisticated American high-technology industry could teach its young engineers some aspects of industrial management and production techniques on the job, this was less likely in a developing country. Technological education in Asia thus must acquaint students with the current problems of industry and teach them to become supervisors and managers of plants.

Fred would impart much of this wisdom to South Korea from 1970 to 1975, in his most extensive consulting effort in Asia. In 1965, the United States had assisted the Republic of Korea in establishing the Korea Institute of Science and Technology (KIST).[110] In early 1970, Korean President Park Chung Hee authorized a study with respect to the establishment of a new graduate school of applied science and technology. Working with a design plan for such an institute prepared by Professor Kun Mo Chung of the Polytechnic Institute of Brooklyn, the Korean cabinet passed a special law to establish the Korea Advanced Institute of Science (KAIS) and requested the support of the U.S. Agency for International Development (AID). The U.S. government decided to send a U.S. team to evaluate the Korean plan. Hubert Heffner, former Stanford electrical engineering professor and associate provost for research, had gone to Washington, DC, in 1969 to serve as deputy science advisor to President Nixon. Heffner recommended that Fred Terman head the evaluation team, along with Thomas Martin Jr., dean of engineering at SMU; Franklin Long, chemist from Cornell; Kun Mo Chung of PIB; and an AID representative, Donald Benedict. Chung and Benedict went to Korea in early summer 1970 to prepare the way, and the others arrived in August for a three-week visit. It would be the first of Terman's five trips to Korea over the next five years, and this in turn would lead to a Stanford advising office and cross-faculty visits between Stanford University and KAIS.

South Korea was Asia's second-fastest growing nation after Japan. Since 1962, Korean exports had increased an average of 40 percent per year, mostly in textiles, but there continued to be a severe shortage of technical, scientific, and managerial manpower. Fred's team was specifically asked to investigate a proposal for the establishment of a new institution that would take engineering and science graduates of Korean universities and put them through a two-year graduate-level MS program to provide the type of experience needed to make those individuals directly useful to Korean industry. In addition, the proposed KAIS would emphasize problem solving, and courses would include lecturers from industry, visits to industrial plants, and extensive laboratory activities. Korean industry was highly in favor of this concept, and the Korean government was prepared to proceed with the plan, with or without U.S. assistance.

Korea's need for such an institute was the result of several distinct weaknesses in higher education in science and technology. Academic advancement in Korea was heavily tied to seniority; faculty taught from a perspective far removed from the actual world of twentieth-century engineering and technology; and university teaching was still heavily oriented to rote memorization. Universities in Korea that covered science and engineering had spread themselves very thin. In 1969, the country awarded nearly five thousand BS degrees in science and engineering, but the nation's total of only six hundred MS graduate students in science and engineering was spread over 152 departments in twenty-two different colleges and universities. Universities were "hamstrung" by traditional rigidity and government bureaucracy. Only 5 percent of the research money in Korea went to Korean universities and very few advanced (PhD) degrees were given. Most Korean students who went abroad for graduate training did not return. As a result, Korea's graduate schools in science and technology seemed to have little impact on the Korean economy.

Fred's team made good progress during their initial visit, but Fred was delayed in submitting the report when one member, Franklin Long, was in a serious auto accident and another member became seriously ill.[111] Fred therefore wrote most of the report himself, with the assistance of Donald Benedict. The report focused on several main points: Korea had made remarkable economic progress since 1962, through careful planning and execution and extensive use of imported technology. In the future, however, Korea must learn to use imported technology with increasing effectiveness. The decade of the 1970s would be critical. In addition, the report recommended strongly that KAIS be free from the Ministry of Education.

Fred's final team report was submitted to AID and the Korean government on January 5, 1971.[112] Fred's team had been received warmly, and their report was implemented quickly and with enthusiasm by the Korean government. KAIS was formally founded on February 16, 1971, with ground breaking less than two months later at a site in the Seoul, Korea, Research and Development Complex on April 14, 1971. A U.S. AID loan of some $5 million assisted the Korean government. Much of this money went to the Battelle Memorial Institute for technical assistance, but Fred established a contract for Stanford to provide educational guidance concerning policy, curricula, and faculty recruitment and to coordinate U.S. activities. For a five-year period, Fred spent some two days a month on the project, plus an annual visit of a week or so to Korea. Industrial Engineering Professor W. Grant Ireson handled the bulk of the Stanford work, but Electrical Engineering Professor William Rambo and other Stanford faculty or alumni on occasion visited KAIS to report to Fred on planning.

KAIS proposed in its first formal publication to open the campus and its buildings in September 1972.[113] Its first president was physicist Dr. Sang Soo Lee, who had been director-general of the Korean Office of Atomic Energy. He began to work on KAIS in the fall of 1971. Terman was made one of the trustees when Lee was formally installed as institute president by Korean President Park Chung Hee in Park's office in February 1972.[114] In his early correspondence with Dr. Lee the previous fall, Terman had worried about the timing of the opening. Fall 1972 did not seem to leave nearly enough time for proper planning. The buildings would not be ready, faculty recruitment surely would not be finished, and plans seemed to have been changed to allow too many different programs. Perhaps he was unduly nervous, he wrote, and suggested KAIS consider the advice in his team's survey report for a phased start-up. (He was also concerned about the lack of entrepreneurship taught in Korean institutes.[115]) Six months later, in January 1972, Terman was pleased to report that Professor Bill Rambo had visited KAIS and given a positive update on progress. Stanford had signed the contract with KAIS and AID, and Hubert Heffner, Franklin Long, and the highly regarded oceanographer Roger Revelle (formerly dean of science and engineering at UC San Diego) were soon to arrive in Korea under the auspices of the U.S. National Academy of Sciences for an evaluation of Korea's new five-year plan for science and technology. Fred was quite pleased to learn that KAIS had delayed its opening another year and now planned it for September 1973.[116]

But all was not going as easy as it appeared. Grant Ireson had begun to spend one-third to half of his time with the KAIS project, and then he spent much of 1973 in Korea. Chung and Ireson reported to Fred that KAIS lacked good planning. Many faculty seemed not to have understood the concept of KAIS, and initial expenditures were extravagant and not well conceived. In Fred's view, KAIS was attempting to do too much with limited funds, once again making the same mistake as other Korean universities by spreading few students across far too many programs.[117] Ireson and Terman now concluded that KAIS should offer a larger industrial engineering curriculum than had originally been planned—perhaps adding more courses in quality control, quality assurance, inventory control, plant layout, and the rudiments of accounting and time and motion study. If they were correct in this, Fred wrote, KAIS could very quickly make a contribution to the country that would be highly visible in Korean industry and government.[118]

In September 1972, Fred gave a pep talk, titled "Role of Advanced Graduate Training in Industrial Development," to an important audience of government, business, and industry executives in Seoul.[119] He stressed the need for coupling technical education to real-life industry, and the importance of moving Korea's "ivory tower" faculty toward some knowledge of Korean industry. Korean technical education, should produce "doers" rather than philosophers or meditators, and that was the purpose of KAIS.

Bureaucratic problems continued, however. Stanford had trouble getting reimbursements for its faculty for travel expenses; some Korean visitors to the United States were left without funds; required forms proliferated.[120] Faculty politics bubbled up within KAIS as professors fought over turf.[121] President Lee fell from favor with the minister of science and technology and resigned to return to teaching physics. Within a year, rumors circulated that the minister was unhappy with Lee's successor, Dr. Joseph D. Park, a Korean-American chemist.[122]

All these problems eventually worked themselves out. In 1974, Terman gave a sort of valedictory talk to KAIS faculty then training the first class of MS students. He emphasized yet again the need to keep clear in their minds the purpose of KAIS, its strategy for achieving that purpose, and the jobs for which KAIS students were being prepared. He stressed the need for more core courses, more interdepartmental courses, and fewer peripheral courses. Faculty must recognize, he said, that *they* as well as the students needed to work with the outside world, and that faculty had a *responsibility* to help their students get jobs and to follow-up with their students' careers. Faculty reputations would be determined by what their students did in the outside world, not by how many square feet of lab space they controlled at KAIS, nor by how many titles they held, nor how much apparatus they had in their labs. A title is not a substitute for lack of achievement, he told them bluntly, and KAIS would ultimately be known by what its students contributed to Korea.

Fred thought of KAIS as a pioneering institute not just in Korea but also in the world. His 1971 report and the KAIS brochure published later that year both expressed the ambition that by the year 2000 KAIS would be intimately identified with the industrial and technological development of Korea, and that KAIS alumni would be in positions of leadership throughout Korean industry and government. Over the next decades, he noted, there must be continuing interplay among KAIS, government, industry, and educational institutions as Korea itself became a prosperous, modern nation and an inspiration and model for developing nations. In his

1974 speech, Fred added that if by the year 2000 the KAIS faculty had helped make the dream come true, they would have contributed more than their share to the welfare of Korea and of mankind.[123]

KAIS indeed prospered. By 1975, KAIS graduated its first class of some ninety-two MS students and planned to develop Engineer and, later, PhD students, according to the minister of science and technology, Hyung-Sup Choi.[124] The minister expected KAIS to involve itself with industry and to allow other Korean science and technology professors to share in research projects. KAIS was *not* to be a stepping-stone for students to study abroad, and KAIS graduates were required to serve some time at home in education, industry, or domestic government service. In 1979, Franklin Long reported back to Fred that though there were still problems at KAIS, there were 360 students in the MS program, and industry was snapping up all KAIS graduates, whereas Seoul National University continued on a slow course to improve its engineering programs.[125]

In 1981, KAIS merged with the Korea Institute of Science and Technology (KIST) to become Korea Advanced Institute of Science and Technology (KAIST), and this duo was further merged with the Korea Institute of Technology (KIT) in 1989. (KIT had been an undergraduate college established in 1985 for scientifically gifted students.) The new KAIST campus was built in the Taedok Science Town about one hundred miles from Seoul, at the center of Korea's most advanced scientific activities.

Today, KAIST is an institution with about 2,500 undergraduates and more than 4,000 graduate students. Its graduates have founded more than seventy modern high-technology enterprises. In 1992, KAIST was evaluated by the Accreditation Board for Engineering and Technology, an American organization that assesses science and engineering programs in the United States and elsewhere through on-site and written reviews. According to the evaluation, KAIST ranked as a top-quality educational institution. Its graduate school was considered comparable to that of the top 10 percent, and for its undergraduates, in the top 30 percent of U.S. universities.[126]

Fred's role as chief advisor is well remembered in Korea a quarter century later. Professor Sang Soo Lee remembers Terman warmly. Despite his earlier run-in with the ministry, Lee was appointed president of KAIST in 1989 and served until mandatory retirement. It is his opinion that KAIST developed over the last thirty years with the spirit of Terman's report, and that this "should be appreciated continuously by all future KAIST Presidents and Ministers of Science and Technology in Korea."[127] President Park Chung Hee awarded the Korean Order of Civil Merit, the Dongbarg Medal, to Fred Terman for "his valuable dedication and service to the Korean people." This high honor is rarely awarded to foreigners and was personally presented to Terman by Prime Minister Kim Jong-Pil in Seoul on December 10, 1975.[128]

Corporate Boards and Consulting

Fred's board memberships tended to be with electronic firms with which Fred had had firsthand experience, and with whom he had personal ties. Varian Associates, Watkins-Johnson, Granger Associates, and Hewlett-Packard were not only important neighbors in Stanford's Industrial Park, but also companies led by his boys. Of the four presidents of the IRE or IEEE living west of the Mississippi, he pointed out to John Granger in 1969, three had been his students or protégés Bill Hewlett and Barney Oliver (of Hewlett-Packard) and John Granger. (The fourth, of course, was Terman himself.[129])

Fred Terman's first significant corporate board membership was with Varian Associates, which he had joined shortly after Varian was incorporated in 1948. Fred had directed his graduate students (Ginzton, Packard, Stearns) to assist Hansen and the Varian brothers back in 1938 in the first klystron developments. He had played a major role in establishing the Microwave Lab at the end of World War II and had encouraged Russ Varian's desire to move the company nearer to Stanford, to the fledgling Stanford Industrial Park. And because of his technical expertise, Fred was added to the Varian Associates board in its first year. He was among those who resigned from the Varian board in 1953, as a scapegoat in a military security clearance episode during the McCarthy era.

Fred joined the board of Ampex Corporation, a maker of magnetic tape recorders and electronic devices in Redwood City, California, in 1953. Fred had known and respected the company's founder, Alexander M. Poniatoff, for some years. Fred resigned from the Ampex board in 1964 only because Hewlett-Packard began making magnetic tape-recording products, and Fred (by then on the HP board) felt there could be a conflict of interest for him.

Dr. John V. N. Granger had served with Fred at RRL during the war and then later at SRI. He founded Granger Associates to design and manufacture communications and radar antennas and transmission equipment. Fred joined the Granger board in 1963 and remained on it for most of the remainder of his active life. The case was similar with the Watkins-Johnson Company, whose board Fred joined in 1957. Dean A. Watkins was an energetic and brilliant electrical engineer at Stanford who developed the traveling-wave tube, a high-frequency device of much use in microwave frequency radar and transmission sets. When Watkins's interests consumed an increasing amount of his time as a Stanford professor, the one-day-per-week consulting rule was applied. Watkins became an adjunct professor and left the university to start his company with H. Richard Johnson. Fred joined the young Watkins-Johnson board immediately, became a large stockholder, and remained on the board for most of his active life.

In a somewhat tangential business move, Fred Terman was one of several professors from Stanford University who helped organize a local bank, the Stanford

Bank. Fred served on its board from 1964 to 1971, helped the bank stave off an unfriendly takeover, and then aided the bank when it merged with the larger Unionamerica Bank (Union Bank of Los Angeles).[130] For a time after the merger, Fred served on the Union Bank's regional board of directors.[131]

Fred's greatest off-campus love, however, was Hewlett-Packard. HP went public in 1957, and Fred was one of the first three outside directors added to the board, where he served until age limits required his resignation in 1973. In very unusual cases, HP has created the title of director emeritus, with the privilege of attending HP board meetings with voice but without vote. Fred relished the title of emeritus director, and he attended HP meetings until at least 1979.[132]

In planning his other duties during retirement, Fred listed his corporate board meetings in order of increasing priority: the Stanford Bank Trust Committee met monthly, but was of moderate importance; the Stanford Bank board met monthly, and it was desirable for him to attend, but not a must; the Granger Associates board meetings were important for him to attend, but not a must; and the Watkins-Johnson Company board also met monthly, and while it was more important than the bank meetings, it was *not quite* a must. Finally, he always listed the bimonthly meetings of the HP board as "A *must* for me."[133]

In those last years, Fred's attendance was more often tolerated, as he sometimes dozed in meetings, but the other directors understood his stature in the company.[134] Perhaps more important, company founders Bill Hewlett and David Packard felt closely connected to Terman as friend and teacher, and as a pillar of Stanford and its environs. David Packard stated publicly on more than one occasion his belief that "Fred Terman, more than any other single individual," was responsible for the growth of the San Francisco Bay Area electronics industry from less than $1 million in 1934 to $700 million in 1965. "It was his vision that the academic community of a university and the business community of the adjacent area could and should work together for the benefit of both." Terman was a great teacher, Packard felt, who had the unique ability to make a very complex problem seem the "essence of simplicity."[135]

Just as he had done in earlier decades, Fred consulted for a number of companies after his retirement from Stanford. He was a member of the Encyclopedia Britannica Science Yearbook advisory group with a panel of distinguished figures including the astronomer Jesse Greenstein, biologists Bentley Glass and George Beadle, physicist Robert Glaser, and geophysicist Frank Press. (Fred was on the initial panel and served for six years before suggesting that new blood would be welcome.) This work was similar to Fred's consulting on journal and review boards, since he developed ideas for the yearbook and vetted authors' proposals and articles submitted. Some of his reports are incisive and amusing. Regarding Buckminster Fuller and his fans, Fred wrote that he felt they were mostly full of hot air but a proposed manuscript on Fullerisms was harmless and might as well be published.[136]

Much of Fred's consulting grew out of friendships he had with industry and organization leaders. For example, Eugene Fubini, George Haller, Paul Klopsteg, Bennett Archambault, and others Fred worked with during WWII subsequently attained high positions in government or industry. When Haller became manager of General Electric's Laboratories Department, he asked Fred to consult for GE. Similarly, Alvin Eurich founded the Academy for Educational Development in New York to provide consulting services to educational and research enterprises. Eurich asked Fred on several occasions to help with educational studies for the Academy in Ohio, Louisiana, Colorado, and Massachusetts.

Fred was particularly valuable in pointing companies toward talented engineers or engineer-executives. He had stayed in touch with many working engineers as dean and provost and remained alert to senior executive talent. By the early 1970s Fred tended to decline from advising industry in technical matters, although he continued to recommend persons as candidates for deanships or university presidencies and to nominate persons for national science and engineering awards. He would write to the effect, "My last technical engineering research was in 1955, when I became Provost, and thus I have not had recent experience in the technical area but . . . "

One of his most interesting, and perhaps longest, consultancies, was his work for the Television Shares Management Company (TSMC), an early technology investment fund group.[137] From 1948 through 1978 Fred contributed quarterly and then monthly reports to the Television Shares Management Company (it used several names over the years). Fred's hundreds of pages of letters and detailed notes to TSMC, carefully preserved in his files, form a valuable but as yet neglected history of postwar electronics and the so-called Silicon Valley.[138] Televisions Associates, Incorporated was founded in Chicago in 1946 by Captain W. C. Eddy, and it acted as technical consultant to the Television Fund, Incorporated, an investment trust. Eddy was an Annapolis graduate who had worked with Philo Farnsworth in early television, then in radar during WWII, and then in television management. The Television Fund was put together by nine prominent Chicago bankers and industrialists with funds from sixteen Chicago-area "subscribers" from a number of wealthy Chicago families.

TSMC established a technical advisory board of three: Fred Terman (on the West Coast); his friend and influential electrical engineering professor W. L. "Bill" Everitt (in Illinois); and former Federal Communications Commission Chief Engineer George P. Adair (in Washington). Terman and Everitt carefully "checked-out" the TSMC before joining (Everitt through Chicago banking friends, and Fred through Frank Fish Walker and associates at Dean Witter and Company and others).

Terman lent his wide experience by giving advice in the Fund's early years on TV tubes, microwave relay systems, the potential growth of UHF TV and color

TV and on the emerging transistor electronics. His textbooks had been published before the explosion of solid-state electronics, but he was well aware in the 1940s of numerous specific technical challenges and possibilities, for example, with respect to UHF TV (the design of new antenna types and new tuning strips for TV sets, and the market development of UHF tubes capable of operation at 900 MHz). He was knowledgeable of the limitations then experienced with the transistor: its high noise level, its limited upper-frequency limits, and its power-handling capacity. Because of his contacts, he could bring to the fund the latest information from electronic research and development circles. "I visited RCA Labs at Princeton last week and talked with [Vladimir] Zworykin," he wrote, or "I heard General [David] Sarnoff say last week."[139]

Fred counseled in early 1952 that while transistor technology would experience huge growth, its real markets would come in new areas and new products, such as in telephone company central switching offices. He forecast that television sets would primarily still rely on vacuum tubes until the mid- and later 1950s.[140] Far more companies would put in money toward transistor marketing than will ever survive, Fred believed. In 1953, he wrote that magnetic tape would come to be central in television use but would not replace film in movie houses for many years.[141] Fred was quite prescient in these and other predictions.

Fred suggested that someone from the Boston area be added to the advisory board. On his list of several appropriate candidates was Jerome B. Weisner, electrical engineer at MIT (later an MIT executive and U.S. presidential advisor). Weisner was added to the board.

The Television Fund's high take-off rate continued. After eighteen months, the fund assets grew from the initial $151,000 in September 1948 to more than $4.5 million by February 1950; from 28 stockholders and 12 dealers in 11 states, to 3,600 stockholders with 504 dealers in 37 states; while the fund shares price rose from $9.93 to $12.31.[142] It became obvious to TSMC that television as such would be only a small portion of the electronics industries, and in 1952 the fund changed its name to the Television-Electronics Fund, Inc. as it saw its total value grow to $20 million by August 1952 and $100 million by June 1955.[143] By 1952, the fund owned shares in about 70 hi-tech companies, including IBM, NCR, GE, Philco, CBS, Raytheon, Sperry, RCA, Walt Disney, Sylvania, and Westinghouse. When asked about investing in electronics, Fred commented that it was a highly speculative field and that if one did not have enormous amounts of time to invest in study, that the Television-Electronics Fund was about the best and perhaps the only way to go.[144]

In the first years with the fund, Fred received $500 per year for four quarterly reports and responses to specific questions from TSMC officers. By 1952, his compensation was up to $1,000 per year. Between 1955 and 1978, when Fred increased his reports to monthly, his compensation rose from $2,500 until it hit

$5,000 per year by the 1970s. Interestingly, sometime in the mid-1950s, Fred also managed to have TSMC award an annual electronics fellowship worth $2,000 to Stanford. The grant was specifically for a PhD graduate student who had already taught for several years at the MS level and for whom further training would assist his or her own teaching career and benefit his or her home university.[145]

In 1962, Kansas City Southern Industries bought 40 percent of TSMC, and shortly after that TSMC became Supervised Investors Services. The Television-Electronics Fund, Inc. changed its name to Technology Fund, Inc. in 1968 to reflect its true status as an investment fund for high technology and industry in general. At that time, twenty years into the fund's history, holdings were in about 130 stocks in numerous sectors, including aerospace, airlines, autos, broadcasting and entertainment, construction, consumer goods, insurance, metals, and chemicals, with about 30 percent of the total stock holdings in electronics and computers. A sum of $10,000 invested in the fund in 1948 would have increased to $169,000 before taxes in 1968, with dividends and distributions reinvested, a compounded return of 15.2 percent interest for the two decades.[146] In the mid-1970s, it became Kemper Financial Services.

Fred Terman earned for TSMC many times over the consulting fees he received over three decades. In September 1978 he resigned from the advisory board due to the decline in his state of health, and his resignation was received "with regret and great gratitude for [his] services."[147]

That same year, David Noble, chairman of the Science Advisory Board for Motorola Corporation wrote to Fred that his contributions had been so varied and so significant "that I consider you one of the great 'Generalists' of our time." Noble specified Fred's systems thinking, his effective leadership, his students, his writing, his anticipation of trends, and finally that "all who know you consider you one 'helluva nice guy.'"[148]

Professional Associations

From the first decades of his career, Fred Terman's primary interest in professional organizations rested with the American Institute of Electrical Engineers (AIEE) and the Institute of Radio Engineers (IRE), which combined in 1963 as the Institute of Electrical and Electronics Engineers (IEEE) to become the largest professional technical organization in the world. As his career broadened, so too did his interest in other professional associations.

Fred joined the American Society for Engineering Education (ASEE) during the 1930s, but he increased his activities after his retirement from Stanford and published some of the results of his manpower studies and his studies of engineering education in ASEE journals. Elected to the National Academy of Sciences in 1946 (Engineering Section), Fred chaired the Engineering Section for several years. Fred was Founding Member of the National Academy of Engineering when the organization was founded in 1965.

Among his earliest professional association memberships, however, was with Sigma Xi. Fred was elected to the scientific research honor society, Sigma Xi, on receiving his Engineer degree from Stanford in 1922. He served as president of the Stanford chapter during his first year as dean of engineering. In retirement, he became active in the society's national organization and served as national president in 1975.[149]

Although it has never gained the national prestige of Phi Beta Kappa, Sigma Xi is a venerated society with more than one hundred thousand members, mostly in North America. Sigma Xi emphasizes promise and performance in research in a scientific or technical field. It was founded at Cornell in 1886, and its several hundred chapters and clubs today are strongest in smaller institutions. A portion of the organization is also active in industrial research laboratories. Although Fred served a term on the Sigma Xi national executive board in the mid-1950s, he began his principal association when he was reelected to the national board in 1968. In 1973 he was chosen as president-elect for 1974 and served as president for 1975. (He was well aware that William F. Durand had been national president of Sigma Xi in 1936–37.)

Just as he had campaigned for more West Coast participation on the boards of AIEE and IRE, Fred canvassed for representation outside the northeastern states in Sigma Xi. He argued for wider geographic representation in his first term on the Sigma Xi board, and a system of regional directors was in place by the time of his presidency. By 1975, one of his principal goals was to strengthen the role of these regional directors. He presided at chapter installation ceremonies at several colleges and universities in the Midwest and West, both during his presidency and after. Fred encouraged the return to active status of many inactive members and was successful in promoting the authorization of an International Chapter of Sigma Xi, created near the end of his term in November 1975.

Sibyl's illness and death in mid-1975 curtailed some of Fred's activities as president, however. Nevertheless, he was quite pleased when Dixie Lee Ray (a Stanford PhD in biology), chairman of the Atomic Energy Commission, later assistant secretary of state and governor of Washington, was awarded the society's highest prize, the Proctor Award.[150]

Although he had joined the American Society for Engineering Education (ASEE) in the 1930s, Fred became more active in the organization during his years as dean of engineering.[151] During the Korean War, the Association of American Universities had endorsed the military draft. Terman, then a vice president of ASEE, along with most of the committee members of the Engineering College Administrative Council in the ASEE opposed drafting technical and science students, echoing Stanford President Ray Lyman Wilbur's World War I philosophy that modern wars would be won by brains and technical know-how, but these brains should not be sent to the trenches when they could be better used elsewhere.[152]

Nearly all of Terman's post–1965 research was on the subject of excellence in engineering education and in manpower studies in engineering. Thus, his research and consulting interests fit neatly within the boundaries of ASEE, which had long been concerned with manpower, faculty teaching loads, and facilities needs.

In retirement, Fred was a member of the ASEE Committee on Institutional Development, which was particularly concerned with assisting historically black colleges and other "developing institutions of engineering" in the United States to become accredited by the Engineers Council on Professional Development, the national accrediting agency. Committee members, working without honoraria, visited colleges and advised on possible improvements. The committee proposed institutional faculty exchanges with Tuskegee University (Alabama), Southern University (Louisiana), and four other black colleges and universities. In the committee's discussions with the schools, however, most asked to be helped solely on the basis of being developing institutions, not as what was then termed "Negro" schools. The ASEE also assisted them with by providing visiting advisors, assistance from nearby accredited institutions, and invitations to faculty from the developing institutions to become visiting teachers at accredited institutions. It raised $125,000 from Western Electric and other corporations to fund some of the program ideas.[153]

In his work on the ASEE Engineering Manpower Statistics Committee, Fred tracked for a number of years the national degree and enrollment data for engineering and engineering technology students, including women and black students.[154]

In 1964, Fred was awarded the ASEE Lamme Medal for "excellence in teaching and for contributions to the art of teaching," and in 1968 he was elected to the ASEE "Hall of Fame." (These were not Fred's only national teaching awards. In 1956 he had been the first winner of the Education Medal awarded by IRE.) The year 1969, however, saw the creation of the Frederick Emmons Terman Award in ASEE, sponsored by the Hewlett-Packard Company, which is presented annually to an outstanding young electrical engineering educator. In his remarks on HP's donation of the award in 1969, Fred addressed particularly the younger teachers, that as he looked back over forty-eight years, he realized that teaching was the high point of his many experiences. The rewards to him as a teacher came not just from successes like Bill Hewlett and Dave Packard, he said, but with the boys for whom he found jobs in the Depression and others whom he helped get into administration. Helping students is something like placing a deposit in a savings bank, he said, the Savings Bank of Life. It is amazing how those helping deeds to students built up considerable compound interest over the years.[155]

Fred derived a great deal of pleasure from attending the ASEE awards banquet each year and presenting the Terman Award to the young teacher selected. He attended nine of the first ten presentations and was especially sorry that his health did not permit him to attend after 1978, since the 1979 recipient, Martha Evans Sloan of Michigan Tech, had received her BS and MS degrees in electrical engineering from Stanford while he had been provost.[156] Martha subsequently went on to become the first woman president of the IEEE. She was not the first Stanford figure to win the ASEE award, as a young associate professor of electrical engineering at Stanford, Joseph W. Goodman, had been the third winner, in 1971.[157] Goodman later became chair of electrical engineering at Stanford, and associate dean of engineering.

Fred's primary activities in the National Academy of Engineering during the first years after its founding in 1965 were to build up the initial twenty-five members into a body of about one hundred. He corresponded widely and frequently to discuss possible nominees.[158] One of Fred's aims was to have the academy reflect the relative importance of the various engineering fields in the present and the near future, rather than the past. In the same way, he cautioned against overloading the academy with elder statesmen and urged the selection of a good number of candidates in their middle years, those who had recently done outstanding work. He sought to avoid the situation of the Académie des Sciences in France, where in the 1960s the average age at election was the late sixties and the mean age of the academicians was considerably higher than that.

Fred Terman achieved great distinction in his home society, the Institute of Electrical and Electronics Engineers.[159] President of IRE in 1941, he won the society's highest award in 1950, the Medal of Honor, "for clearly exceptional contribution to the science and technology of concern to the Institute." He then won its education medal in 1956 and was given the IEEE Founders Award in 1963 for his "leadership, planning and administration" in serving both AIEE and IRE as they merged.

Fred served on the editorial board of the IEEE general magazine *Spectrum* and advised on various submitted manuscripts. His written reviews are particularly perceptive and complete. By 1969, however, he became more interested in the history of engineering. He had kept a file for many years on the history of radio and electronics, and in retirement he was increasingly asked to speak on these topics at electronics conventions, or manufacturers' associations or at "old-timers'" ham radio gatherings. He wrote IEEE executive Donald Fink to ask whether the IEEE was developing an historical archive, but went right on to tell them how IEEE should do so. The IEEE already had a history committee and its chair was Fred's old good friend, Haradon Pratt, who had assisted Fred in his election as president of the IRE in 1941. Pratt subsequently contacted Fred and asked him to join the IEEE History Committee as chair (Pratt was terminally ill). Fred agreed to join the committee, but begged off as chair.[160]

In thinking more about the history of electronics, Fred cast around for a location to build a history of electronics and engineering archive in California. At Stanford, he found little or no interest in his ideas. Things at Stanford in the spring of 1970 were so upset, he wrote, that no one had time to pay attention. "I am moreover, rather dubious about Stanford's interest because we do nothing in the history of science or the history of technology, and thus such a collection would not serve any faculty interest at our institution."[161] The situation remained the same at Stanford for much of the early 1970s, evidenced by Fred's correspondence with Professor Charles C. Gillispie, noted historian of science at Princeton. Given the financial squeeze at Stanford, he wrote Gillispie in 1973, there was no interest in the history department and no possibility in the engineering school for a regular faculty position in history of technology.[162]

Fred knew of history of science and technology activities at UCLA and talked with a colleague there, but the situation was more promising at Stanford's archrival, UC Berkeley. A former Stanford electrical engineer, Charles Süsskind, was teaching engineering and engineering history at Berkeley and had a professional interest in electrical history. Fred received a warm response from Berkeley's Bancroft Library Director, James D. Hart, and Hart and Süsskind offered Bancroft as a center for the history of electrical and electronics engineering.

Fred was pleased to learn from W. Reed Crone at IEEE that Süsskind was to be the next chair of the IEEE History Committee. Recently named the chairman of IEEE's Life Members Fund Committee himself, as well as a member of the History Committee, Terman intended to see that the IEEE further support institutional history.[163] The Life Members Committee offered several thousand dollars to help get IEEE history started by supporting oral history interviews, compilation of a list of active historians of electricity and electronics, and the location of repositories around the country interested in preserving papers and artifacts. An effective force on the History Committee was historian of technology and electrical engineer James Brittain of Georgia Tech. Brittain supported the idea of establishing a national center for history of electrical engineering, similar to the Center for the History of Physics at the American Institute of Physics. The IEEE History Committee also discussed publishing a biographical dictionary of several hundred historically prominent electrical engineers. Fred was acutely aware of the weakness of amateurish articles written by elderly engineers and constantly argued that any published products sponsored by the History Committee should be of high quality and done by professional historians. The Smithsonian's electrical curator Bernard S. Finn and Brittain agreed with Terman, but Fred saw no likelihood of such a product appearing in the near future.

Fred also tried to get historical sessions placed on the national IEEE convention program, but the IEEE Technical Program Committee showed little interest. He then tried to get the IEEE to form a regular divisional group on history, but did not succeed. Fred remained on the History Committee, although his efforts lessened after 1974 because of his activities as president and past president of Sigma Xi. He finally resigned from the IEEE History Committee in 1977 because of health reasons, but Fred's efforts to help preserve engineering history did not end there.[164]

During the 1970s, Fred supported the efforts of the Bancroft Library's Office of the History of Science and Technology, beginning with his own oral history interview. In 1975, three Berkeley historians conducted an extensive interview of Fred regarding his engineering career and the electronics industry in California. The resulting 175-page document was later completed and made available to scholars in a joint effort between the Bancroft and the Stanford University Archives.[165] Terman and former colleague Albert Bowker (chancellor of the University of California at Berkeley) assisted the Bancroft in acquiring the papers of a number of people and corporations significant in the history of electronics.[166] Fred also assisted the Bancroft in obtaining financial assistance through a matching grant from Bill Hewlett and David Packard, raising $300,000 for a five-year study at the Bancroft to collect materials and study the history of electronics in the Bay Area.[167]

Nor did Fred give up entirely on Stanford. By the mid-1970s, Stanford's University Archives was better prepared to handle his voluminous records, and in 1977 he began working with archives staff to arrange and describe the collection. By this time Fred had begun to realize that his own papers were not only an important resource regarding electrical engineering, but engineering education, university affairs, and the evolution of Stanford University over the course of some six decades. Much of the lengthy and informative descriptions included in the guide to the Frederick E. Terman Papers was written by Fred himself. He also set aside $15,000 in his will for the archives to help complete the project. Although Terman gave up on developing a history of science and technology faculty at Stanford, the university itself soon after began to slowly build such a program, using Terman's own strategy of joint appointments between history and physics, American studies and engineering, and history and philosophy.[168]

"I Would Play the Same Record"

When he retired as provost in September 1965, Fred moved into a modest office, room 174, on the ground floor of the Jack A. McCullough Building near the old ERL building.[169] He worked there most mornings for nearly fifteen years. Using fully the services of a part-time secretary, Fred kept up a serious pace well into his late seventies, sending out some thirty-five letters per month.[170] He was still meticulous with his records and made out checks to the university financial offices for any long-distance personal telephone calls or for those dealing with his consultancies. But by the mid-1970s, the pace was beginning to take its toll.

The year following his retirement, Fred dealt with his first major health problem since his youthful bouts with tuberculosis. Around Christmas 1966, Fred learned that he needed cataract operations on both eyes. The first was scheduled for January 1967 and was reasonably successful, though Fred was preoccupied with his recovery in letters he wrote to friends.[171] He noted in several letters that his father had undergone cataract surgery at almost exactly the same age. The convalescence slowed him down somewhat, and he tended to stay away from crowds and read less than usual.[172] His second cataract operation, late in June 1968, was a success. By early August, he felt that for the first time in six months he enjoyed having two working eyes.[173] Fred was back in full swing.

The Termans had donated their Salvatierra house to the university in 1966 to benefit the Terman Engineering Fund, and the house became the home of the university's chaplain. Fred and Sibyl had purchased the former home of Business School Dean Hugh Jackson at 445 Escarpado Street, just off Gerona Road and directly behind the campus and Lagunita. It was a large house, and Sibyl set about modernizing it.[174] It was decorated with practicality but understated elegance, showing Sibyl's touch.[175] Fred assembled for his study a collection of photos of people who had been "uniquely important" to his life and career, among them H. J. Ryan, Wallace Sterling, William Claflin, and Vannevar Bush.[176]

In the garage were the Terman's distinctly practical cars. Fred never drove a flashy car. During his years as provost, he drove an old Dodge, while Sibyl had her Ford Fairlane. When his sister Helen decided in 1968 that she did not like her 1966 Chevrolet two-door, Fred bought it from her.[177] He gave the Chevy and the Ford to his son Terence in 1972, and replaced them with a new Chevy Nova. (He kept the old Dodge.) In his last years, the garage housed one large, boat-like 1964 Pontiac Bonneville sedan, which had been appraised at Sibyl's death as being worth $100.[178]

Fred was loyal in retirement to his Stanford alumni class. In 1965, he served on the class forty-fifth reunion committee that arranged dinner and festivities on Big Game weekend at the Mark Hopkins Hotel with entertainment by the Stanford Band, the cheerleading Dollies and the Yell Leaders, and remarks by President Wallace Sterling. For his fiftieth reunion class activities, in May 1970, Fred was again on the reunion committee and attended all of the functions except the campus tour (a round of cocktails at Rickey's Hyatt House, lunch at an alumni home, morning coffee at President Kenneth Pitzer's office, a campus conference on "The University and Society: Education for What?" and dinner at the Faculty Club).[179]

Sibyl was able to attend only the morning coffee that reunion weekend. She missed such socializing far more than her husband, although she was never known as an easy-going personality. The topic of children's reading was evidently a lively one at faculty dinner parties in those days. Sibyl did not hesitate to take on other parents over the subject, and a noisy and unpleasant argument just might ensue. Fred, who disliked arguments, would sit at the table and say not a word.[180]

Sibyl had taught part-time at San Jose State and had continued her interest in child development. Especially concerned about the teaching of reading, she advocated the use of phonics and disagreed with contemporary alternative methods. During the 1950s, she had decided to write a monograph on the errors in reading instruction. She asked her younger brother, Charles Child Walcutt, a professor of American and British literature who had published a number of monographs and articles, to assist her in writing the book. Their book, *Reading: Chaos and Cure* (1958), was published by Fred's publisher, McGraw-Hill.[181] In her book, unnamed university centers—but clearly including Stanford's School of Education—were chided for their misleading and harmful methods. Sibyl did not hesitate to defend her point of view.

Early into Fred's retirement, she began having serious medical problems.[182] Although she had kept her slim figure, she smoked heavily and drank more than Fred approved.[183] By the late 1960s, Sibyl began experiencing dizziness and difficulties with her balance when walking, and she had regular long bouts with bronchitis.[184]

Nevertheless, Sibyl accompanied Fred to Europe in the summer of 1969, where they visited Hewlett-Packard company plant sites in Switzerland, Germany, Scotland, and England with other board members, and then went on their own to the Mediterranean for two weeks in Greece, Turkey, and Italy. Sibyl remained in Italy for two more weeks with her sister.[185] Fred was very happy that Sibyl could join him on this trip since she was able to do less and less. Beginning in 1965, Fred had retained a large apartment in Dallas near his consulting work at Southern Methodist University, but by 1969, Sibyl rarely visited Texas with him. They gave up the apartment, and Fred stayed in a hotel thereafter during his visits.[186]

Sibyl, too, underwent cataract operations, both in 1970, but they did not work out nearly as well as Fred's surgery. She required an additional operation for a detached retina after the first operation; the second cataract operation proceed a little better but required a convalescence that kept her away from social functions at Christmastime.[187]

Terman's extensive traveling took a toll on him in his later life. Fred had traveled eighty thousand miles a year during his first years of retirement, and during the early 1970s he was still traveling annually some forty thousand miles.[188] He began to fly first class when he went cross-country. He would pay the difference himself, he explained to staff at the President's Science Advisory Committee offices in Washington, using the $75 per day consulting fee they paid him to make up the difference between economy and first-class rates.[189]

During his first five or six years in retirement Fred kept up a whirlwind of activity, but after 1972 things began to slow down considerably. Fred missed the action and turned his attention to professional societies and the history of engineering. It is difficult to believe that he really wanted to take on, again and again, more assessments of engineering education in the various states and more work for his professional organizations, but he was driven to stay in the game. He was miffed when *Electronics* magazine listed his 1971 subscription as from one "other than those engaged in electronics technology." He responded that he had been a charter subscriber to the magazine in the early 1930s, that he was still on the HP, Watkins-Johnson, and Granger Associates corporate boards, and that his McGraw-Hill author's and editor's royalties topped $15,000 per year! In another exchange with a military official, he noted that after many years, his top-secret government clearance (which he had held through Stanford University) had been downgraded to secret. Should he get it raised again, he wondered?[190]

Fred's activities were so much off campus after his first couple of years of retirement that he missed eating with his friends at the Faculty Club. He noticed, however, that faculty now seemed to arrive in groups, and there was no social table for "singletons" (a phrase taken from his passion for bridge card playing), no clearly identified community table where an individual arriving alone could sit with others and have a sociable lunch. Fred wrote to the Faculty Club's treasurer to propose that Stanford have such a community table or two as was done in the Faculty Club at Harvard where, he recalled, he came in one day and sat next to McGeorge Bundy, who had arrived alone.[191] (Such a community table was later instituted.)

Fred's books had been translated into Spanish, Italian, Hungarian, Polish, Korean, Chinese, Finnish, and in pirated Russian editions not even bearing his name, and by 1965 he had sold more than six hundred thousand legal copies.[192] During the early 1970s, McGraw-Hill began to drop Terman's texts one by one from their book list. Fred had been a magnificent producer for McGraw-Hill for more than four decades but annual sales of his *Radio Engineer's Handbook*, first published in 1943, had fallen in recent years from one thousand to four hundred copies per year. In 1971 McGraw decided to pass it on to the Michigan Microfilm Corporation (wherein a customer can purchase a photocopy of an out-of-print book).[193] The next year, Fred learned that McGraw-Hill was dropping his *Electronic and Radio Engineering*. This was a harder blow, since it was his favorite book. He explained to McGraw-Hill that he had hoped to update his fourth edition (1955) a decade later, and in 1961 he had tried to get three different Stanford faculty to assist him in putting out a fifth edition but each was unavailable. Once he became provost in 1955, his time for editing books was gone. He went on to admit that a one-volume comprehensive work intended for a year-long senior undergraduate course would now be impossible, since the transistor and the integrated circuit had changed electronics so much. Nevertheless, Fred hoped that McGraw-Hill would keep the volume in print for at least a few more years and let it die a "gradual but graceful death."[194] A year later, in 1973, McGraw-Hill announced that *Electronic Measurements* by Terman and Pettit (1952) was to be dropped. The international student edition was still selling, they said, but not the U.S. edition, and the book was now twenty-one years old.[195]

Sibyl's health continued to decline.[196] By 1973, she was using a wheelchair, and a stair-assist elevator was added to the Escarpado home. Fred took her to the St. Helena Hospital and Health Care Center in Deer Park, California, for a month's rest and physical therapy, but she did not like it and returned home within the week. Fred then arranged for home care and physical therapy, suggested by his old friend Dr. Russel Lee.[197]

In the fall of 1973 Sibyl had hoped to accompany Fred to Tokyo, Kyoto, and Hakone, Japan, for HP board meetings, but it was not to be. The next spring, Fred reported to his Bohemian Grove friends that Sibyl's health prevented him from driving her up to the Grove for the Spring Picnic and Show.[198] When Fred went east for four days to SMU board meetings and to the Sigma Xi national board meeting (as president-elect) that summer, he left a typed schedule for Sibyl's care, involving Carol Marr morning and night and during the day: "Anna" on Sunday, the housekeeper Myrtle Pound on Monday and Tuesday, and "Mary Beth" on Wednesday. Carol Marr, a young student in inhalation therapy, began living at the Terman's in June 1972 and continued until after Sibyl's death. She coordinated several workers who came to the house for five or six hours per day. Sibyl and Fred were very fond of Carol.[199]

Always sharp-tongued, Sibyl became increasingly critical of others as her illness progressed, but she missed Fred's sister Helen, who died in November 1973 of a stroke at the age of seventy in her home near campus. Sibyl and Helen had enjoyed talking together, usually over the telephone.[200]

Sibyl lost her voice and was in the hospital twice in the fall of 1974. Her general physical weakness and unsteadiness continued unabated, and physicians found her throat problems were due to a malignant tumor on the vocal chords. She began six weeks of radiation therapy December 13 at the "Clinac" Linear Accelerator at Stanford Medical School.[201]

Fearing for them both, Fred added the Terman names to a reservation list for the new Pearce Mitchell Houses condominium project, aimed at retired faculty, on campus. He felt that this would be a step toward easier home care for both of them. But the radiation treatment seemed to work extremely well and the tumor shrank away, "encouraging and something of a miracle." So much so that Fred removed their name from the Pearce Mitchell list. Sibyl was well enough to go to Carmel to see granddaughter Kathy in a school play in April, but then things reversed rapidly.[202] The tumor location remained sore and antibiotics could not control a resulting lung infection. Sibyl's last month, Fred wrote, was rather miserable. Her last happy evenings were spent in Carmel. She saw Kathy deliver the Carmel High School valedictory speech and knew that Kathy was going to the University of Chicago as a National Merit Scholar. They had then attended a dinner party at Ernest Arbuckle's house for HP board members and spouses who had visited Japan the year before.[203]

Sibyl entered Stanford Hospital in June. Fred hoped that he could go up for at least a weekend of the summer's Bohemian Grove encampment, but he reported to "Sons of Toil" camp that Sibyl's health might not permit it. He had wanted the opportunity to talk about Sigma Xi affairs with engineering educator Athelstan Spilhaus, who would be at the Grove, and Fred planned to come up for one weekend. He motored up on Thursday night July 17, but received a call from the hospital that Sibyl had taken a turn for the worse and he returned the next morning.[204] Sibyl Walcutt Terman died on July 23 at the age of seventy-three. They had been married forty-seven years.

Fred Terman kept appointment calendars on his desk while he was provost and then in retirement. These annual calendars report in pencil and in ink, his appointments, board meetings, and duties. Among the many calendars preserved in his papers, only one pair of sheets is mottled and smeared, as if water had been overturned onto the pages. The date is July 23, 1975.

Fred returned to the office on Friday, two days after Sibyl's death, to dictate letters about her legal and financial affairs to her lawyers and to his bankers in Boston.[205] At her memorial service in the Stanford Memorial Church, the eulogy was read by the Reverend B. Davie Napier, former Stanford chaplain and then-president of the Pacific School of Religion. The Napiers had been the first tenants of the donated Terman house on Salvatierra and they had come to know Sibyl very well. Fred was extremely appreciative of Napier's remarks and subsequently made a donation to the Pacific School of Religion of HP stock worth more than $1,000.[206]

When the Termans had moved from Salvatierra Street, their donation of the house was worth approximately $50,000, intended for the Terman Engineering Fund. Two years after Sibyl's death, however, Fred started a Sibyl Walcutt Terman Memorial Fund in the School of Education for the purpose of supporting teaching and research in methods of reading. This had been Sibyl's lifelong interest, and the subject of *Reading: Chaos or Cure*, the book she coauthored with her brother Charles. Contributions to Sibyl's memory began arriving, and Fred was especially pleased with two large donations, from Professor and Mrs. O. G. Villard Jr. and from Fred's son Lewis Terman and his wife Bobbi. It was Villard and his wife who urged the formation of a fund for the School of Education. Fred now arranged to donate the Terman house on Escarpado to Sibyl's Memorial Fund with life tenancy for himself. The house was appraised at $200,000, and Terman received an estimate that after his death and with depreciation, the amount would be $150,000 to Stanford.[207] By fall 1977 Sibyl's Memorial Fund was thus worth about $180,000. The following fall of 1978 the Education School held a well-received Sibyl Walcutt Terman Memorial Conference and invited her brother Charles "Bill" Walcutt to give one of the welcoming addresses.[208]

Fred missed Sibyl and perhaps tried to cover the loss with keeping busy with letters and yet more business matters despite his own declining health. In his last years, receiving and answering his mail became increasingly important to him. To care for Sibyl, the Termans had arranged for one or two young women to live in the house, in addition to the two part-time housekeepers. This was not unusual, since the Termans, like many faculty homeowners, had almost continuously had two students or a married student couple living in their cottage behind the house on Salvatierra. A few months after Sibyl's death, young Carol Marr left for a period of Mormon missionary work; Jill Baxter, a former Stanford student, left not long after. Carol and Jill were replaced by a recent Stanford graduate Marci Lee Smith and graduate student Susie Rathman. There was a nice apartment on the ground floor, plus a small bedroom on the main floor of the house next to the kitchen and garage. Their basic job was to prepare dinner for Fred and keep him some company over dinner. Initially, Fred was not picky at dinner, but loved to tell old stories, they later recalled, some they heard on several occasions. His stories concerned his pride in his former students, of his insights gained during World War II about the possibilities of university-industry cooperation, of his educational consulting, and of his provost years. And he talked often and fondly of Sibyl.[209]

By the later 1970s, few came to the house to visit. Dave Packard, Bill Hewlett, and Dr. Russel Lee were among his more frequent visitors. Arthur Fong, longtime Hewlett-Packard engineer, would drive Fred to IEEE section meetings in San Francisco and chat with him and listen to his stories.[210] Old campus friends and acquaintances were passing away. Fred's longtime friend Paul Davis lost his wife Helen just three weeks after Sibyl died, and Davis himself began to go downhill soon after. Davis had provided much guidance to Fred over the decades, helping him understand the fund-raising process at Stanford and giving Fred the key, as he told Davis, to understanding Ray Lyman Wilbur in the late 1930s and early 1940s. Fred recalled the many discussions the two had had regarding Donald Tresidder, which helped Fred gain "the understanding required to get through a very troubled period successfully."[211]

Now in his mid-seventies, Fred's own health began to fail. He had overextended himself in some of those trips to Korea and Texas, and to Sigma Xi and IEEE meetings on the East Coast. Soon after Sibyl's death, Fred began to experience nearly continuous digestive problems until the end of his life and became obsessed with his diet. (Each morning for breakfast he now ate canned peaches covered with Metamucil; every day for lunch it was a hamburger patty, a serving of cottage cheese, and a tomato.) At one point around 1978, when Fred was in the Palo Alto Medical Clinic, a physician telephoned to ask Marci and Susie to clean out all of Fred's medicine cabinets since he suspected that Fred might be self-diagnosing and overtaking Metamucil and Milk of Magnesia. Fred had apparently been experiencing periods of confusion, perhaps from taking a sleeping pill and then, as often happens with the elderly, forgetting and taking a second. Marci and Susie then strictly laid out daily doses of his medicine and he seemed to improve. He very likely suffered some small ischemic strokes, for sometimes his speech was slurred and his balance was bad.[212] By 1979, Fred was taking Ritalin for his problems with confusion, Benadryl for sleeping, Dalmane and Cephulac for his stomach problems, plus Vitamin B-12, and Tinactin and a cortisone cream for a skin itch. He also took drops for his eyes, prescribed by his ophthalmologist, O. R. Tanner.[213]

Fred was quite fond of all of those who stayed with him, and he wrote letters to them after they went on in their careers elsewhere. Fred wrote a special letter in 1974 to Foothill College requesting that Carol Marr be allowed to receive her inhalation therapy diploma in September, since she had completed her work, rather than wait until the following June graduation. This would permit Carol to take the National Registry Examination in Inhalation Therapy immediately, rather than to wait a full year.[214] When Sibyl had learned of Carol Marr's engagement of marriage, she suggested that Carol have the wedding reception and party at the Terman house and gardens. After Sibyl's death, Fred remembered the promise and reminded Carol of the offer. In September 1977, Carol Marr had her wedding party at the Terman home.[215] Carol's mother recalled Fred as extremely kind, and after Marci and Susie's departure for a business career and graduate school in late 1978, Carol Marr Gange and her new husband returned to live with Fred Terman while they renovated a house.[216]

In his last years, Fred's correspondence was more and more limited to his answering of Christmas cards, writing about medical bill payments, discussions of genealogy with distant cousins, the occasional professional letter, and his preoccupation with helping Stanford prepare his papers for the archives. He wrote to the National Academy of Sciences, asking that O. G. Villard Jr. write his NAS biographical essay. (Villard did so and it was published in 1998.[217]) Evidently by early 1979, Fred suspected that he might become incapacitated at any time, for he wrote a note stating that if someone (such as his attorney Nathan Finch) had to prepare his 1978 tax report, that he had expenses of $630 for prescriptions, $950 for dental bills, and $3,750 for the one month in 1978 when he required nurses around the clock.[218] He suffered further mild strokes: one in February 1980 left him in Stanford Hospital for two days and precluded him from driving his automobile.[219] He was forced to use a wheelchair when he went out, such as when he met his good friends Cecil and Ida Green at the dedication of the reconstructed Green Library on campus in April 1980.[220]

In 1979, a team from Hewlett-Packard set out to make a film of Fred's career. He corresponded about this with his Radio Research Lab secretary and extremely valuable assistant, Elizabeth Mudge.[221] Fred's take on the HP movie crew was that some "young people" at HP thought up the idea and went ahead without his permission. They filmed him talking, but when they appeared in Cambridge to film Bill Claflin and Charles Coolidge, their wives refused to allow it.[222]

Fred had won many other awards in retirement, including a regional Boy Scout award and a regional Brotherhood Award from the National Conference of Christians and Jews (1979).[223] On campus, his name had become a cliché view of engineers. He especially enjoyed a spoof in the winter issue of the 1975 humor magazine *Chaparral*.[224] Titled "The Virtuous Engineer," it features three photo panels. In panel one, a young man is seated at a table with his slide rule, Hewlett-Packard calculator, and textbooks, working on a problem set. A young woman is saying to him, "Come on, it's Friday night," and "You never take me anywhere." The young engineering student thinks, "If she doesn't leave me alone, I'll never finish this problem set." By panel three, she has physically picked him up and hauls him off over her shoulder. With his calculator, pencil, and paper still in his hands, he thinks, "I wonder if Frederick Emmons Terman ever had this problem?"

Yet more honors were coming his way, among them several he valued most highly. In October 1976, President Gerald Ford personally presented him with the National Medal of Science for 1975. The citation on the National Medal of Science read, "For his principal role in creating modern electronics and his ability to document his knowledge so that it could be effectively communicated to his many students who now populate the worlds of industry, academics, and public service."[225] His closest faculty and administrative colleagues gave him an honorary dinner at the Bohemian Club on May 6, 1977, and in October of that year, he attended the dedication of the $9.2 million Frederick Emmons Terman Engineering Center, built through the generosity of his students William Hewlett and David Packard and their spouses. "Many years ago we were walking out of the old Engineering Building, and Terman said he was looking forward to the day when I gave my first million dollars to this laboratory," William Hewlett said at the dedication. "I remember this, because at the time I thought it was so incredible."[226]

Marci Smith recalled that in her four years at the Terman home, however, she had never seen Fred as excited and happy as when he told her the news that he had been chosen for Stanford's Uncommon Man Award. He asked Marci and Susie to get all dressed up, and he reserved a table for them at the dinner. It was at this dinner, December 7, 1978, surrounded by many of his friends from Stanford and from around the country that Fred delivered a splendid speech on Stanford's history and planning during his lifetime. It was that same evening, while introducing Fred, that Wallace Sterling's voice broke on two occasions when he spoke of what Fred Terman had meant to Stanford and to him personally.

On that evening, Fred Terman gave the last substantive speech of his life. Fred titled his talk, "Stanford's Growth to Greatness" and termed Stanford an "Uncommon University."[227] Fred's description of Stanford's growth to greatness underscored just how he himself wanted to remember Stanford.

As a child at Stanford in 1912, he came to know many of Stanford's faculty and to learn early on of its ways and history. The university had begun under very favorable circumstances, backed by Leland Stanford's fortune and the wisdom and talent of its first president David Starr Jordan. From the beginning, Stanford was respected and had a fiercely loyal alumni body. It could have continued as "the nicest, smallish college in the country offering a program of liberal arts ornamented with trimmings of science and technology," but this was not to be. Ray Lyman Wilbur reoriented Stanford with an emphasis on faculty scholarship, research, and the training of graduate students, while retaining as much as possible the student camaraderie and the Stanford spirit. Under Wilbur, he went on, the medical school in San Francisco was firmly attached to the university, and the Graduate School of Business, the Hoover Institution, and the Food Research Institute were founded, as were the Schools of Engineering and Education. A strong Psychology Department was developed, he recalled, remembering his father. Undergraduate enrollment increased and graduate enrollment tripled. The physical plant was eventually expanded with student housing, additional laboratories, a new library, and the Frost Amphitheater and Stanford stadium were constructed. The Stanford Associates began its fund-raising work in the mid-1930s. Even during the Depression, Terman asserted, Stanford kept its head above water.

Terman saw that firm foundation built at Stanford greatly strengthened during the third quarter of the century under the of leadership of Wallace Sterling and Richard Lyman. Significantly, Terman thought the most important single change was the movement of the Stanford Medical School from the City to the Stanford campus, a tremendous undertaking in physical and in personal terms. Next in its impact was the federal government's policy, established after World War II, of supporting basic research at universities, first in the sciences and engineering and later in the social sciences and humanities.

It was at this point that Terman became more personal in his remarks. Stanford skillfully utilized government support, he said, and accepted only research projects of academic value. Most research work was carried on directly by faculty and graduate students; "job shops" and research not oriented toward the training of graduate students was rejected or discontinued during his years as dean and provost. Stanford greatly increased the vigor of its searches for new faculty members, particularly after 1955 when he became provost. Before 1955, he reminded them, there was not a single faculty member who had come to Stanford already a member of the National Academy of Sciences, but this would dramatically change. The Center for Advanced Study in the Behavioral Sciences and the National Bureau for Economic Research, established on campus during that era, also assisted in attracting better faculty.

As Stanford grew in quality there was a corresponding increase in the quality of its undergraduate students and the widening of their geographic spread. Some 93 percent of male undergraduate applicants to Stanford in 1951 were admitted, but after Stanford recruited harder, only 22 percent of male applicants were admitted by 1978. This was a clear indication of Stanford's high visibility among the most superior high school graduates, he said. Concurrently, Stanford began a systematic and aggressive pattern of recruiting the best graduate students as teaching and research assistants. Academic ratings in the late 1970s reflected these changes, placing Stanford at or near the top in the nation in the fields of business, engineering, education, the sciences, history, English, economics, and journalism.

The public's regard for Stanford and the intense loyalty of its alumni was indicated, Terman said, by the successful completion of the recent $300 million Campaign for Stanford, the largest capital campaign ever undertaken by a university, and during the previous five years Stanford's endowment fund growth outperformed that of all major universities, including Harvard.

In effect, Terman's "Uncommon Man" acceptance speech was a toast to Stanford, illustrating his deep love for Stanford and his obvious pride in its success.

The Very Last Years

Fred Terman was, no doubt, a lonely man at the end. He loved going to HP board meetings, but his presence there became awkward. He was not always easy to get along with, and at times treated his young house helpers with insensitivity. Yet while he could be quirky, Marci Smith later recalled that he far more often acted very kindly toward them. Now approaching his eightieth birthday, he was no less frustratingly single-minded at times and took a while to warm up to people, yet he loved the people living in his home and remembered some in his will.

Sandra Torval Dyer was his secretary for the first seven years of retirement; she was succeeded by Donna Soderberg, and in the last year and a half (when Fred mostly was housebound), by Elsie Leach. Fred was particularly devoted to Donna Soderberg, and she to him. She wrote strong letters to the university administration concerning his needs. She made one or two trips a day between his home and the office in McCullough and also drove him several times a week to the post office, bank, and Palo Alto Medical Clinic.[228]

Susie Rathman recalled that the Terman annual Christmas card had always been an elaborate Sibyl production. With Sibyl gone, Fred asked his young helpers to give him advice on how to produce the Christmas card, but he seemed unhappy if they gave him suggestions differing from his own. The Christmas card seemed to be a way, Susie remembered, for him to tell his friends what he had accomplished during the year, but when he accomplished less, the card seemed more difficult to produce. After receiving the Uncommon Man Award, Fred told Susie that there would only be one more Christmas card to produce, since he would not be getting any more awards.

Some people took advantage of the elderly, ill man. The son of one of his housekeepers would come over to the Terman house during the day and pilfer objects—a stolen check later forged, the young women's jewelry, three television sets, and, incredibly, thirteen spare tires from Fred's Pontiac. For almost a year, Fred would simply reorder the missing object and say nothing. Finally, he discharged the housekeeper, but wrote her a reference in support of her next job application.[229]

Marci Smith tells two touching stories of Fred Terman in his very last years, one involving his love of Hewlett-Packard and one reflecting his concern for young people and his faith in his old friends. Terman was no longer allowed to drive when, late one night, Marci Smith and Susie Rathman heard a noise from the garage. Fearing a prowler, they went to investigate and found Fred returning the large Pontiac but having knocked over some things in the garage. They asked why he had been out driving in the night, and Fred responded that he was going to an HP board meeting. He had gone over to the HP offices on nearby Page Mill Road, but when the security guard told him that the board meeting was the next day, Fred replied that he was just there to make sure about the arrangements.

One time, Marci came down with the flu. Fred heard her moaning and coughing in the middle of the day and came downstairs to find her still in her nightgown and looking quite ill. Marci thought Fred was concerned about her health, but also about who would be cooking his dinner that evening. He told her that he would call a friend to examine her and not to be worried about answering her door at a knock. Sometime later, Marci indeed answered the door to a very elderly gentleman who asked whether she was "Marvin." No, she said, she was Marci. Without concern, he asked to enter but neglected to identify himself. He asked her to sit down on a couch and lower her nightgown so that he could examine her chest. She was ill and quite likely could get pneumonia, he told her as he wrote out a prescription. The medicine would pretty much knock her out for two days, he added, but she would get much better and feel fit as a fiddle.

At that point, Fred Terman entered, and it was obvious the two were old friends. When Marci went to the Palo Alto Clinic pharmacy and gave the pharmacist the prescription, a long wait ensued. The pharmacist returned to ask her if the prescription was on the up-and-up and then retreated to make a telephone call. The delay had been caused, he later told her, because the physician ordering the prescription had not practiced medicine in more than ten years! The suspicious pharmacist had then telephoned the physician's son (who was also a physician) to verify that the prescription was correct for her symptoms. He finally explained to Marci that her visitor had been Dr. Russel Lee.[230]

Lengthy memos dictated for the Stanford Archives as late as 1980 reveal that his mind could still be quite sharp, very accurate as to detail, and written in well-structured prose. But in May 1981, Fred fell unconscious at home and was taken by ambulance to the hospital where he remained for three days. He was too ill to attend the "SEMICON/West '81" electronics conference that spring, where David Packard presented an award to Terman, and Electrical Engineering Professor John Linvill accepted it on Fred's behalf. He fell ill again in late July and was taken by ambulance to the hospital. (His last two letters date from September 1981 and concern his ambulance bill and his prescription drug list.[231])

Fred Terman died of a heart attack in his sleep on the morning of November 19, 1982, at his home on campus. His memorial service was held January 4, 1983, in Stanford's Memorial Church with eulogies by Stanford President Donald Kennedy, David Packard, and Engineering Dean William Kays.

The *San Francisco Chronicle* headline read "Stanford's Terman Dies—He Launched Silicon Valley." The *Peninsula Times Tribune* called Terman "the architect of Silicon Valley." In his eulogy, Donald Kennedy commented that Terman's "capacity to think about the future was the most remarkable thing about him." While mentioning Terman as the "father of the modern School of Engineering" at Stanford and the "academic architect of the high-technology industrial area of Silicon Valley," the *Stanford Daily* editorialized that the most helpful lesson that "college administrators can learn from Terman is the importance he placed on taking actions in the present that would strengthen the depth and quality of education in the future."[232] His family asked that memorial contributions be made to the Terman Deanship Fund at the Stanford School of Engineering.

Interested observers have asked just how much Fred Terman was worth when he died. They wonder how much money he left to relatives and how much he gave to Stanford. Fred Terman's main rewards in life were not financial. Rather, Fred was largely rewarded by seeing Stanford University and his students succeed. In later life, he enjoyed talking about his role in these successes, but what might seem like bragging is far outweighed by the many hundreds of letters he wrote in praising Stanford's rise and many more he wrote to support and praise his former students. Nevertheless, Fred Terman died a fairly wealthy man, at least in 1982 financial terms. He left each of his three sons about $750,000 after taxes.[233]

Throughout the 1960s and the first years of retirement, Fred's earned income (based on federal tax returns) was about $70,000 to $90,000 per year. About $30,000 came from royalties, another $30,000 to $40,000 from his salary (at

Stanford, then at SMU and his part-time duties at Stanford), and the rest from his income from consulting, membership on various boards, and investments. Fred's estate was self-earned. Lewis Terman's estate had gone largely to Fred's sister Helen, with some to Stanford.

Terman's income from his publishing royalties and consulting far exceeded his university salary for several decades, and he had made a number of wise investments. While he was at the Radio Research Lab, William Claflin of Harvard had persuaded Fred to form a stock portfolio and to contribute regularly and steadily to that fund. Fred took that advice and studied investment as thoroughly as he studied any engineering problem. The thirty years during which Fred wrote monthly reports to the Television Shares Management Company investment group were thirty years of appraising potential markets for technology stocks in general. In 1965, Fred's portfolio consisted of twenty-three stocks, with holdings in electronics, chemicals, utilities, oil and gas, pharmaceuticals, timber and paper products, insurance, autos, and steel. In that year his dividends reported were $12,082, with HP being his largest single dividend producer.[234] By 1969, Fred had 15,000 shares of Hewlett-Packard stock, then worth about $85 per share, and during the 1960s he also had about 5,000 shares of Watkins-Johnson and 1,900 shares of Granger Associates stock.[235]

For many years Fred and Sibyl had given gifts to Stanford (and, for some years, to Southern Methodist University) in the form of stock. To the extent possible with the existing gift tax laws, Fred and Sibyl also gave stock to their children and grandchildren. Fred hoped, he wrote, to give each of his five grandchildren enough to pay their college tuition through graduate school and to have enough extra for a nest egg.

Fred's annual salary as dean of engineering during his first year was $8,500; just before he became provost in 1955 it was $14,000; and his final salary in 1965 as vice president and provost of the university was $37,500. (The sum of all the salary paid to Fred at Stanford from 1925 to 1965 is about $450,000, plus perhaps a half-salary for another three years when he counseled for Sterling.) Over his long career, Fred gave back to Stanford considerably more than he received in salary. He began giving small gifts during the early 1930s when he, like his father before him, funded a tuition scholarship for a graduate student. During World War II, he gave Stanford the future ownership of his *Radio Engineer's Handbook* (after a period of years of royalties to him and his family), which sold more than three hundred thousand copies in the 1940s.

At times during the later 1940s, Fred gave Stanford in annual gifts more than the amount of his salary as dean. He provided steady gifts of stock to the Terman Engineering Fund, hoping to build the fund to an amount equal to the level for endowing a professorship ($500,000). In 1960, he endowed ten annual Engineering Scholastic Awards of $50 each to leading undergraduate seniors, not large amounts but enough to provide publicity and encouragement to top students who were entertained at a luncheon, each with his or her favorite high school teacher as a guest in attendance.[236] He provided $131,000 to pay for the refurbishment of the old engineering labs in Building 500, his laboratory and office home for twenty years.[237] When it was modernized in 1965 for Mechanical Engineering, it was named (not by his request) the Terman Engineering Laboratories.

When he and Sibyl gave their Salvatierra house to the university in 1966, the gift was estimated to be worth $50,000. They established the Terman Scholarship Fund in 1943 and the Frederick Emmons Terman Engineering Fund in 1959, and had then amended these in 1966 with the hope that Fred's estate gifts would be enough, combined with the earlier gifts, so that they could be combined to endow a professorship in the School of Engineering.[238] After Sibyl's death, he gave the Escarpado house as well to the university for the Sibyl Walcutt Terman Memorial Fund in the School of Education. With life tenancy, this gift was estimated in 1977 as worth $150,000.

It is difficult to say exactly how much Fred and Sibyl gave to Stanford—perhaps some three-quarters to a million dollars by 1982. As he and Sibyl had requested, some of their donations were aggregated and reaggregated by the university over the years. In the end, about half went to endow the Terman Engineering Professorship, and the other half to Sibyl's memorial fund in the School of Education. The Escarpado house, reappraised at $200,000, was actually sold by the university for a half million dollars. Thus, Fred and Sibyl's donations to Stanford rise to a million dollars.[239]

Following a university tradition, Fred gave most of his library to Stanford, sending some of his duplicate volumes to Korea. More importantly, he gave his voluminous personal and professional records to the Stanford University Archives and provided months of his personal time to their arrangement and description.[240] The papers, totaling well over one hundred linear feet, are a truly valuable gift to Stanford. They document more than sixty years of the university in many of its facets. These, too, are an investment, for over the years, the F. E. Terman papers continue to increase in scholarly value.

EPILOGUE

Building, Momentum, Waves, and Networks

In 1985, shortly after Wally Sterling's death, nine former Sterling and Terman staff members met to record their memories.[1] As they concluded their many stories and accounts of the 1950s and 1960s at Stanford, Howard Brooks commented, "I run into so many people who have had jobs sort of like I've had down through the years, who have never had the exhilaration of Stanford in that building period. That's an incredible thing."

"It's something that the people nowadays really can't have here," answered Don Carlson, "because they're building on something that's already established."

"But," added Ken Cuthbertson, "the momentum's still there. That's what makes it so great."

Concepts like building and momentum would have appealed to Fred Terman had he been able to attend that luncheon. Between his arrival at Stanford in 1910 as a faculty child until his death seventy-two years later as Stanford's provost emeritus, Fred Terman proved himself a master builder of a career, a profession, a university, and a regional economy. He would also look back proudly on his years as a member of that remarkable team, at their hard work, their intensity, their ambition for Stanford.

He had returned to Stanford with his MIT doctorate driven not only personally to succeed in the new field of radio engineering but also to forge a place for Stanford's electrical engineering program among the best in the country. A popular teacher and accomplished text writer, he championed and built three important research areas in electronic circuits, radio wave propagation, and electron tube design. Waves and networks were prophetic as well as technical terms, for Fred not only saw the potential in such fields in electronics and radio engineering but applied the concepts to the relationships he built among teachers, students, alumni, employers, and the university. Despite the Depression's grueling impact on Stanford's budgets, Fred pulled together the Electrical Engineering Department by staying alert to the newest fields, by integrating teaching and research, by securing jobs for students, and by seeking out funding for student support, faculty salaries, and facilities.

Accused later in his career of being "merely an engineer," Terman in fact fully endorsed Stanford University's philosophy of providing a broad undergraduate engineering education that must include not only a number of approaches to engineering but also some background in the sciences, social sciences, and humanities. He was determined that his students would be able to communicate and took a special interest in how engineers should be taught to write. Indeed, more than once he fought on behalf of his university to defend its broader approach when national accreditation boards urged its engineering departments to specialize more narrowly. Accomplished in chemistry, mathematics, and mechanical engineering as well as electrical engineering, Terman remained especially interested in the multifaceted interdepartmental approaches to academic planning and research. His abilities to look outward and to build up his own familiarity with new fields served him well in later years when he was university provost.

Fred broke into the electrical engineering text market with textbooks in new and upcoming areas. His books were well written and concise, introducing students to the latest in research and teaching by way of relevant and current case study problems. Able to write for alumni magazines and popular magazines such as *Radio* as well as for highly specialized technical journals, Terman produced classic texts in radio engineering in a variety of formats. Thus, "Terman" had already become the byword, for specialists and laymen alike, for the authoritative works on radio engineering and electronics by the time the United States entered World War II.

Early in 1942, the forty-one-year-old Terman took on the directorship of the Radio Research Lab for radar countermeasures at Harvard University. Fred's RRL was a great success, saving thousands of army air force fliers with numerous radar devices and procedures. His wartime experiences working with a large staff, managing a budget larger than most universities, and producing under tremendous pressure created by the war effort greatly broadened his managerial skills and his personal contacts. He brought back to Stanford many talented engineers and scientists, along with the advice of Harvard and MIT neighbors and friends who encouraged his inclination to aim high. Certain that Stanford University could take advantage of federal support that he knew would become available for postwar university research, he already had plans in mind for electrical engineering, for the School of Engineering, indeed, for Stanford itself, when he returned home in 1946.

As Stanford's engineering dean, Fred built up its engineering departments, including newer areas of industrial engineering, aeronautics, and materials science, and worked closely and supportively with allied sciences, especially physics and chemistry. New programs in statistics and computer science would begin to take shape under his coaching.

Stepping from leadership of his department to that of his engineering school, Terman had taken good advantage of his broad concept of the interaction of engineering and science at the university. A far greater leap, perhaps, was his promotion to university provost in 1955, certainly a leap in the eyes of many humanists and social scientists at Stanford. Yet again Terman's willingness to broaden his own horizons and his intense loyalty to Stanford and its self-conception as a university, and not as a technical school or institute, made him a valued and highly effective player on President Wally Sterling's team. Terman and Sterling worked well together, balancing each others' strengths and weaknesses and moving toward a seemingly very straightforward goal: to put Stanford in the very highest ranks of a handful of the best universities in the United States by judiciously building its faculty and recruiting the best among graduate and undergraduate students alike.

As these chapters have shown, Terman's philosophy of targeting academic strengths, promoting the talents of faculty and students, providing the best research and teaching facilities, and actively involving alumni and other benefactors in the university's welfare, paid off for Stanford's humanities, social sciences, and sciences as well as its various professional schools and its engineering program.

Retiring from Stanford in 1965, Fred Terman had earned a place among the senior statesmen of higher education. He remained especially interested in engineering education, however, and in the relationship between academia and industry. During the next fifteen years, he counseled many private and state universities and academic-industry groups on strategies for the development of engineering and technology centers. His evaluations were not always popular with local politicians, but they often resulted in significant improvements in both undergraduate and graduate teaching across the country. His work with the SMU Foundation for Science and Engineering in Dallas, Texas, and the Korea Advanced Institute of Science (and Technology) was especially rewarding for Fred.

Terman was also asked his advice on how to replicate the academic-industrial phenomenon dubbed in 1971 "Silicon Valley," and he often obliged. Terman's "model" has been described by Stuart Leslie and Robert Kargon as "a strong research university with close links to industry, entrepreneurial corporate and academic cultures, aggressive venture capital markets, supportive government institutions, a pleasant climate, a technology park."[2]

Many ambitious technology parks and university-associated technical centers, however, did not rise to the same level of national or international prominence as Stanford and the Silicon Valley. As a result, some scholars have questioned the wider applicability of Terman's "model" for university-industry cooperation. They argue, for example, that generally universities have not been prominent sources of technological spin-offs, but provide, rather, a necessary pool of technical personnel and well-educated potential entrepreneurs. Venture capital, they assert, plays a more important role in today's market in some (but certainly not all) geographic or economic regions.[3]

Leslie and Kargon assert that Stanford's and Silicon Valley's growth depended much more than Terman himself realized on the special circumstances of the early cold war years. In their view, Terman simply assumed that what was good for Stanford and Silicon Valley was good for everyone else, and indeed what was good for Silicon Valley frequently was good for Stanford.[4] However, they argue, success clearly required both geography and history: high-tech industry and high-tech academic research institutions had to grow and evolve together, just as they did around Stanford and the Santa Clara Valley. As this biography has shown, Fred Terman had no intention of being a business modeler, nor did he believe that what was good for the goose was good for the gander. Terman worked to maximize Stanford, not the Stanford Industrial Park, or Silicon Valley. His methods, if applied consistently and fully, certainly do not speak against the success of a given high-tech academic-industry center but should be viewed as a strategy for academic planning, not corporate profit.

Terman's alleged subservience to military money in the development of a somewhat skewed academic program at Stanford has also been a theme raised repeatedly by several scholars.[5] It is certainly true that Fred Terman and his colleagues at Stanford were exceptionally successful in attracting key government grants to university research projects. And it is certainly true that Terman and others worked hard to get government and corporate support for research on electron tubes and radar electronics, aeronautics, solid-state physics, high-energy physics, bio-medicine, computer science hardware and software, and more recently, bio-engineering, all of which have served as driving engines. But by 1964, government support for clinical bio-medical sciences and radiotherapy research at Stanford easily surpassed military support for engineering.

Terman's essential strategy was hardly so narrow, his concept of Stanford hardly so self-centered. He did not have to fawn on military and corporate contractors, but rather sought to attract support from an array of sources and to apply such funds creatively to build on university strengths. He did not force contracts on faculty, but expedited faculty research and student teaching by helping to find them the funding they needed. Nor was he at work alone, somehow single-mindedly driving Stanford toward government dependence, but was part of a hard-working team whose aim was to dramatically improve Stanford's financial base. As a result, between 1946 and 1965, Stanford not only substantially increased its project-related funding but also attracted funding for new facilities and buildings, faculty salaries, and student fellowships, and dramatically increased the financial base of its endowment. Such funds came less from military and civilian government contracts, than from large, and in some cases landmark, grants from private and corporate granting agencies, and from major gifts of alumni and other benefactors.

Some historians also have suggested that as provost, Fred Terman unfairly emphasized engineering and a selection of the science departments, to the detriment of humanities and social sciences, in fostering Stanford's now legendary growth spurt of the 1950s and 1960s.[6] Fred Terman can be charged with not sympathizing with those who wished Stanford to stay the comfortable, self-satisfied, and slower-paced campus of earlier days. He can also be charged with cold-heartedly pointing out strengths and weaknesses in a department—any department—and for valuing the cruel evidence of quantifiable data regarding a department's curriculum success, or its production of bachelors and graduate students, or of a faculty member's research and teaching accomplishments and potential. He had little patience with anecdotal evidence and personal biases, and little taste for the intrigues and inter- (and intra-) departmental battles that had captivated his father, Professor Lewis Terman.

These chapters suggest, rather, that a department or an individual faculty member's promotion at Stanford during this era had less to do with the academic field of choice, and much more to do with what Fred Terman saw as fields on the cutting edge of higher education, relevant and effective as instruments for both top-notch teaching and productive research. Be it in high-energy physics, European history, biochemistry, or political theory, Terman was willing to be persuaded to back a department fully, if he was given adequate evidence from which to work. There are numerous examples of academic departments across the university that rose significantly in national rankings between the mid-1950s and the 1969 studies that ranged across the breadth of the university's degree-granting programs.[7]

As an undergraduate student at Stanford from the fall quarter of 1956 to the fall of 1960, I believe my years were both socially and academically rewarding. As an undergraduate, I was given the experience of doing research with four different professors. Genuine interest in me shown by faculty and research staff helped me to undertake my own research project lasting a year and a half. Similarly, a fellow student (for many years now, my wife) wandered over to Joshua and Esther Lederberg's new lab, and although an undergraduate, she was welcomed to help with research in genetics.

Efforts to reorganize and invigorate undergraduate education at Stanford had just begun when I arrived—and yet more changes would occur as a result of the campus unrest of the next generation of students. That the process took more than a decade is hardly surprising, for change within a university can be glacial.

My classmates and I could see the results of some of these changes in our own classrooms. Better graduate student teaching assistants invariably led to more interesting interchanges between graduate and undergraduate students in my classes. Within a year or two of my graduation, significant increase in faculty size, a benefit of quickly putting to work funds earned from the PACE campaign, also led to more small undergraduate seminars and better facilities.

By the time I left in 1960, Stanford was no longer just a popular undergraduate school of some reputation with regionally respectable professional schools. Nevertheless, Stanford by 1965, the year Fred Terman retired, was not the mega-university that the University of California had become, with its crown jewel still sitting across the bay in the city of Berkeley. Yet, Stanford in 1965 could give Berkeley a good run for its money, and today it jockeys with Berkeley, Harvard, MIT, and Caltech, as its peers.

Sterling and Terman and their talented colleagues, from Al Bowker and Ken Cuthbertson on the administration, to leaders among the faculty like Henry Kaplan, Arthur Kornberg, David Potter, and Walter Vincenti, knew that Stanford was attempting to compete with older universities with much larger endowments and greater national prestige, and with the top few well-established but narrowly focused technical institutions. Sterling and Terman's vision for Stanford, however, included broadening as well as strengthening the university: to a remarkable degree, Stanford has achieved that vision.

REFERENCE MATTER

APPENDIX A

Fred Terman's Salary, 1925–1965

As Professor at Stanford 1925–41

1925–26	$1,250	Instructor, half-time
1926–27	$1,800	Instructor, "less than full-time"
1927–28	$2,500	Assistant Professor
1928–29	$2,750	Assistant Professor
1929–30	$3,000	Assistant Professor
1930–31	$3,250	Associate Professor
1931–33	$3,350	Associate Professor
1933–35	$3,015	Associate Professor
1935–37	$3,350	Associate Professor
1937–39	$4,275	Professor and Head of Electrical Engineering Department
1939–41	$5,000	Professor and Head of Electrical Engineering Department

As Director at Radio Research Lab During World War II

1942–45 "Base Salary" $6,000; apparently $8,000 on a twelve-month basis

As Administrator at Stanford, 1946–65

1945–46	$8,500	Dean of Engineering
1946–48	$9,000	Dean of Engineering
1948–52	$12,000	Dean of Engineering
1952–55	$14,000	Dean of Engineering
1955–57	$21,500	Provost and Dean of Engineering
1957–59	$24,540	Provost and Dean of Engineering
1959–60	$26,000	Provost and Vice President
1960–63	$30,000	Provost and Vice President
1963–64	$35,000	Provost and Vice President
1964–65	$37,500	Provost and Vice President
September 1, 1965		Provost Emeritus

APPENDIX B

U.S. Patents of Fred Terman, 1930–1947

The following list and brief description of thirty-six U.S. patents held by Frederick E. Terman was compiled with the assistance of O. G. Villard Jr.

Patent No.	Patent Description	Date
1,782,588	Galvanometer needle deflection increases as the square root of current.	Nov. 25, 1930
1,784,119	Use of a vacuum tube to drive the above galvanometer.	Dec. 9, 1930
1,812,066	Vacuum tube frequency changer.	June 30, 1931
1,816,448	Coil with spacing between turns least at the outside ends.	July 28, 1931
1,825,105	Inductance coil for radio frequencies.	Sept. 29, 1931
1,846,043	Amplifier with input connected to grid and output to plate.	Feb. 23, 1932
1,858,349	Generates two rotating fields, one inside the other. The second has a different number of poles and generates a different frequency	May 17, 1932
1,915,558	Derive ratio between crest voltage and mean voltage=degree of modulation.	June 27, 1933
1,933,773	3-element tube—rectification at input and output circuits.	Nov. 7, 1933
1,950,759	Reactance tube (triode) controlled by screen grid tube.	Mar. 13, 1934
1,976,904	Loss metering circuit.	Oct. 16, 1934
1,978,918	Thermionic tube, concentric cathodes with grids in between.	Oct. 30, 1934

2,000,304	Thermionic tube, use of secondary emission to reduce current draw with positively biased grid.	May 7, 1935
2,000,362	Frequency multiplier—nonlinear action in triode at input.	May 7, 1935
2,000,673	Electron tube—voltage-reducing vacuum tube, with outside anode shield.	May 7, 1935
2,037,202	Variable resistance—a method of operating a tetrode.	Apr. 14, 1936
2,055,736	Basically a single-sideband-generating modulator.	Sept. 29, 1936
2,079,134	Oscillating radio receiver; push-pull oscillators with adjustable variable feedback.	May 4, 1937
2,152,753	Absorber modulator. Choke in d-c.	Apr. 4, 1939
2,167,162	Means for avoiding non-linearity in standard metering circuit.	July 25, 1939
2,215,672	Linear amplifier with means for varying potentials.	Sept. 24, 1940
2,218,487	Directional radiating system, with W. W. Hansen	Oct. 15, 1940
2,238,236	Modulation system using impedance-inverting lines. Carrier tube to peak tube.	Apr. 15, 1941
2,252,049	Linear amplifying system. Envelope is rectified and re-supplied.	Aug. 12, 1941
2,270,394	Modulation system. A means for supplying grid power during modulation peaks.	Jan. 20, 1942
2,276,119	Loop antenna plus dipole to cancel dipole pickup. (Must be at right height above ground.) With Joseph Pettit.	Mar. 10, 1942
2,287,280	Detection arrangement and negative impedance. Negative admittance for use across diode.	June 23, 1942
2,293,180	Detection system for klystrons (special collector electrode).	Aug. 18, 1942
2,293,181	Sound-absorbing device; exponential horn.	Aug. 18, 1942
2,305,911	High-efficiency loss modulator.	Dec. 22, 1942
2,318,268	Diversity receiving system, FM and AM simultaneous detection.	May 4, 1943
2,372,231	Frequency modulation system. Two plates put out an oscillating circuit. A variable signal current is superimposed on d-c voltage between plates.	Mar. 27, 1945
2,429,652	Coupling system for power amplifiers. Audio frequencies are a means for building out the response of a transformer.	Oct. 28, 1947

APPENDIX C

Amateur ("Ham") Radio Operators at the Radio Research Laboratory

Out of approximately 225 technical staff at RRL at its full size in 1943–44, at least 102 were known to be current or former "hams" (amateur radio operators), including, of course, Terman himself.[1] From the earliest days of U.S. government-issued ham radio calls, about the time of World War I, until the 1970s, calls were issued by geographical area. The numbering order was not strictly east to west: New England region was "1"; New York and New Jersey "2"; the Mid-Atlantic, South, and Southeast "3" and "4"; the Southwest "5"; California "6"; and the Northwest, Midwest, and Rocky Mountain areas "7," "8," "9," and "0." In the earliest years, the operator simply used his or her initials, then the government-issued calls beginning with a region number plus two letters, for example, "6XE." Subsequently, the "W" was used as a prefix, followed by the number, then two or three letters. By the 1950s, the "W" prefix was exhausted in some regions and the prefix "K" was used. In recent years many prefixes have been used, for example, "WA," "WB," "A," "N" and the numbering system no longer has a geographical meaning. In the following table, "Ex," in common ham usage, means the holder of a call now relinquished. When hams moved from state to state, or gave up a call for a time, their permanent call could be changed; thus, John Dyer by 1945 had held three different calls in the New England region.

Hams were extremely valuable to Fred Terman at RRL, since many of them had extensive experience in radio transmitter, receiver, and antenna design, at a time when such knowledge was uncommon in many university circles. For example, J. D. Kraus, W8JK, for many years was an antenna expert at Ohio State University and developed the university's radio astronomy program after the war.

Adams, M. B.	W4EGL
Albrecht, H. W.	Ex-W9CRZ
Anderson, R. E.	W9VZT
Anger, H. O.	W6OZP
Artman, R. G.	W9KYY
Ayer, H. C.	W1IIP
Baldwin, C. P.	W1EPF
Barnard, R. C.	W7EWO
Barnes, F. R.	Ex-W8KXH, W9YGO
Barnes, R. B.	Ex-W5BTX, W6EFX, W6DRI, W6DQ
Barrett, E.	W8PHF
Beraducci, S.	W2IWB
Bisby, J. F.	Ex-W6NCO
Boynton, W. H.	W1AYI
Bridgeford, G. R.	W7GRV
Brooks, E. D., Jr.	W1TL
Campbell, J. P.	W7DYQ
Carles, R. C.	W1NR
Christensen, J. W.	W6EZD
Clark, J. L.	W2HTV
Clark, L. G.	W9LAG
Cohn, S. B.	W1JPV
Collins, R.	W5TA
Cooke, L. S.	W1NLU, Ex-8BQN, Ex-9BQN
Crispell, H. L.	W6TZV
Cullum, A. E.	W5CS
Davis, K.	W8WAC
Dowell, M. R.	W9LGN
Duffy, D. P.	W9VKU
Dyer, J. N.	Ex-W1BJD, W1GD, W1CCZ
Eames, A. L.	W1KFE
Early, H. C.	W8ING

Eggers, C.	W1MMY
Eldredge, J. H.	W9WVG
Ellis, A. R.	W7FCA
Erickson, R. J.	W1FPR
Evans, G. E.	W1JJB
Gibson, P. M.	W1HRF
Grant, L. E.	W1AQD, AHC, EUT
Hagen, G. D.	Ex-W7EFX
Harring, D.	Ex-W9FMM
Harris, D. B.	W9BTJ
Haskell, M. W.	W1VV
Hok, G.	SM3ZQ
Hunt, J. M.	W1CCL
Jacobs, G. B.	W8REM
Johnson, R. A.	W8NUX
Kaisel, S.	W9QBE
Kamphoefner, F. J.	W6OOC
Kell, R.	Ex-W9UXR
King, R. C.	W2KJX
Kinsman, R. C.	W1JPL
Kraus, J. D.	W8JK
Lawlor, W. J.	W1ITP
Lee, C. F.	W1UX
Loebel, L.	W9UMP
MacKechnie, H. K.	W1ADP
MacQuivey, D. R.	W7BAL
McCouch, G. P.	W3GGS
McGuigan, W. D.	W9ZOP
McSheehy, W. H.	W1KPZ
Monroe, R. B.	W2UN
Moran, J. M.	W2IVI
Morehouse, G.	W9JRV
Moyer, R. C.	W1ANY
Newcomb, L. A.	W3GMD
Norton, R. S.	W1AZZ
O'Brien, R. S.	W6OEU
Oliphant, C. W.	W1MSC
Pearson, P. A.	W7DOX
Pendergrast, C. F.	Ex-W1AFF

Pettit, J. M.	W6HDB
Phillips, A. B.	W1IQG
Plotts, E. L.	W1NVV
Powers, E.	W1BFG
Preston, G. D.	W1UL
Raburn, L. E.	W9KWE
Rakestraw, D. L.	W3FOR
Reynolds, D. K.	W6MRL
Rhiger, R. R.	W7CNV
Riemitis, C. F.	No Call (Operator's License)
Robbiano, P. P.	W6PKM
Ross, C. C.	W5RK
Schuech, D. R.	W6LIC
Silliman, R. M.	W9VO
Smith, E. C.	Ex-W8AFC
Stephenson, J. G.	W1DGC
Sturges, D.	W1GP
Sullivan, J. C.	W1EXU
Sutherlen, G. R.	W2IAA, W6DUF, W6NIT, HZ1AA
Terman, F. E.	Ex-W6FT, W6AE, W6XH
Towle, M. L.	W1DEG
Turner, A. T.	W1AHB
Vermillion, R. K.	W4JM
Villard, O. G., Jr.	W1DMV
Ward, D.	No Call (Operator's License)
Webster, R. R.	W6VCY
Whitby, O.	VE2PH
Wilhoit, D. J.	W7APL
Wilson, V. P.	W1JWG
Yunker, E. A.	W7EZL
Zeidler, H. M.	W1NVC

APPENDIX D

Stanford in the Rankings

During Fred Terman's decade as provost (1955–65), Stanford rose from its usual position of around fifteenth among American universities to rank with the top three or four most distinguished universities in the United States. No other university, it can fairly be said, made so great a rise over such a brief period.

In 1957, Hayward Keniston surveyed the top twenty or so graduate departments in twenty-four disciplines in the United States. In the Keniston survey, Stanford University ranked generally about thirteenth to fifteenth, an unsurprising result for the time. (In earlier surveys in 1925, Stanford had ranked fourteenth nationally in a study of graduate schools, but had dropped somewhat by a 1935 survey, the victim, it was said, of its "country club" image.[1]) In a somewhat slapdash Chicago *Tribune* survey poll of selected academics in that same year, 1957, Stanford had ranked as the tenth overall best university, combining undergraduate and graduate ratings.[2] But by including medical, law, business, and agriculture schools, the *Tribune* survey had placed a few major universities such as Princeton (with none of these professional schools) at a disadvantage in the survey rankings.[3] Although not a very thorough survey, nor an all-inclusive one, the Keniston study has been used instead as an important signpost of the development of graduate education.[4]

In 1964, Allan M. Cartter of the American Council on Education conducted a much more extensive survey based on responses of four thousand faculty members in thirty disciplines.[5] The results, published in 1966, rated both the quality of graduate faculty and the effectiveness of the doctoral programs in each discipline. Five years later, Kenneth D. Roose and Charles J. Andersen, also of the American Council on Education, repeated and extended the Cartter survey using data collected in 1969, with responses from more than six thousand faculty members in thirty-six disciplines.[6]

Keniston (1957 data), Cartter (1964 data), and Roose-Andersen (1969 data) rankings of individual graduate programs at Stanford are shown in the table below. In the table, the "1957" column represents the rank granted Stanford in Keniston's 1957 study of the top fifteen graduate departments in each field. (The Keniston study omitted specialized or technical institutions, and excluded engineering fields.) NR means the department rated lower than the top fifteen in the Keniston study, or was not ranked in later studies, while an asterisk (*) means the department was not included in the particular study. A "T" equals a tie in rank between Stanford and another institution; a dash (—) indicates that Stanford had no doctoral program in that discipline. A range (for example, "17–26" for Spanish) indicates a large group all given the same approximate ranking. The columns "1964F" and "1964P" and "1969F" and "1969P" indicate, respectively, the Cartter and Roose-Andersen study rankings for leading graduate departments, by rated effectiveness of, respectively, Graduate *F*aculty, and effectiveness of Doctoral *P*rogram.

Rankings of Graduate Programs at Stanford, 1957–1969

	1957	1964 F	1964 P	1969 F	1969 P
Humanities					
Art History	NR	—	—	11T	9T
Classics	15	NR	NR	4	5T
English	15	7	5	6T	4T
French	NR	12	10	8	4T
German	NR	15	13	5T	3T
Linguistics	15	—	19	19	24
Music	NR	—	—	10T	8T
Philosophy	NR	10	10	11T	10
Spanish	NR	17–26	14	17T	14T
Social Sciences					
Anthropology	14	10	10	9T	7T
Economics	5T	6	4	7T	6T
Geography	NR	—	—	—	—
History	15	7T	6	5T	4
Political Science	13	9	6	6T	3T
Psychology	5	2	1	1	1
Sociology	NR	12	12	15T	13T
Biological Sciences					
Bacter/Microbiology	*	7	7	8T	7T
Biochemistry	*	3	3	2T	1T
Botany	14	10	7T	11	9T
Pharmacology	*	13	9	1T	4
Physiology	*	24	21T	30–54	55–79

Population Biology	*	*	*	9T	7T
Zoology	14	4	3	3T	2
Sciences					
Chemistry	15	5	5	3T	3T
Geology	6	7	4	4T	3
Mathematics	9	6	4	6	5T
Physics	6	5	3	5T	2
Engineering					
Chem. Engineering.	*	10T	9	4T	5T
Civil Engineering	*	5	3	4T	3T
Elect. Engineering	*	2	1	2	1T
Mech. Engineering	*	3	3	2	1T

If "overall" rankings are summed for the leading universities by general area of study, in the 1964 survey, measured by quality of faculty, Stanford ranked in the top ten in humanities, ninth in social sciences, sixth in physical sciences, fifth in biological sciences, and third in engineering. University rankings place Harvard in first, Berkeley in second, Stanford in third, with Yale and Princeton more or less tied for fourth and followed by a cluster of Illinois, Michigan, and Columbia. Looking at it another way, Berkeley appeared in the top rankings in all five General Areas of Study, Harvard and Stanford in four of the five. Cartter thus noted that among the country's most distinguished universities, Berkeley could claim to be the best-balanced university in the country.[7] Along these same lines, Stanford could claim that the 1964 data revealed it to be one of the top three universities in the country. Roose and Andersen attempted to remove the notoriety of "pecking order" ranking in their 1969 survey. (Even so, with the exception of increasing the total number of academic fields measured to thirty-six, their study was based directly on the approach of the earlier study of Cartter.) As the 1969 rankings in the table illustrate, Stanford continued its overall rise in strength throughout its graduate programs, including the humanities and social sciences as well as the sciences and engineering. No department that survived the decade showed any considerable decline. (The program of linguistics was reorganized in the 1960s; the Department of Geography closed its doors in the early 1960s, and Stanford had no departments of astronomy, entomology, or Russian. Physiology, no longer a strong part of biology at Stanford, was taught largely at the Medical School.) The Roose-Andersen survey subdivided biology into a number of subfields, yet did not subdivide other fields more relevant to Stanford's program to a similar extent (for example, Physics was not subdivided into theoretical physics, high-energy physics, plasma physics, or solid-state and condensed-matter physics). A number of Stanford departments had made significant improvements in the ratings, among them classics, French, German, political science, pharmacology, geology, and chemical engineering. Strongholds, such as psychology, electrical and mechanical engineering, and physics, remained at or near the very top.

Such surveys carry both a "halo effect" and a lag time. The "halo effect" accounts for the appearance of a mediocre (or even no longer existing) department at an excellent university to be ranked higher in surveys than it deserved. The 1957, 1964, and 1969 data gathered for these studies might indicate more closely the program's standing in the several years before—1954, 1961, and 1966—for example. Nevertheless, the surveys were published and made more generally known to the public in the several years after—1970–71, for the 1969 Rosse-Andersen study, for example, and have a resulting after-affect on fund-raising and student recruiting.

Student ratings of desirability offer another comparative index that Fred Terman found especially useful. Again, Stanford had moved up dramatically between 1956 and 1969. In one year alone, between 1956 and 1957, Stanford rose from ninth to fifth among choices of undergraduate National Merit Scholars and from third to second among undergraduate General Motors Scholars. During those years, Stanford rated highly in graduate NSF fellowships and in Public Health Service fellowships. Yet, as Graduate Dean William C. Steere pointed out early in 1958 to Dean of Humanities and Sciences Phil Rhinelander, Stanford had fallen back "a bit" in these ratings among students choosing the social sciences and humanities. Steere revealed unpublished data that ranked Stanford as ninth in the country among four thousand students applying for Woodrow Wilson National fellowships but only thirteenth at the university of choice among those actually elected fellows for 1957.[8] By 1965, Terman could proudly report that Stanford had risen in the number of Woodrow Wilson fellowships awarded (primarily to those in the humanities) from around tenth place in 1955–57 to fourth by 1964–65 (behind only Harvard, Yale, and Columbia). As for NSF fellowships, Stanford had worked itself up from tenth in 1955, to third or fourth by 1963, remaining at or near the top through the rest of the decade.[9] Between 1959–60 and 1963–64, Stanford had also dramatically increased the number of NSF fellows and Woodrow Wilson fellows awarded to its graduate students.[10] Yet Terman also cautioned students to consider department strengths wisely. "The organizational form, degree structure, etc. . . . are much less important than the people in the faculty. . . . If one has strong people who have outstanding qualifications, the program will be good even if archaic in its form." Terman used the MIT undergraduate program of his day (the mid-1920s) as an illustration. It was a reactionary curriculum, he noted, with a minimum of flexibility and minimum of humanities taught, yet it was staffed with an excellent faculty. As a result, it turned out great students on the strength of its faculty.[11]

Putting good students together with good faculty was, after all, what a good university was all about. In summing up President Wallace Sterling's "simple" philosophy, vice president for finance and development Ken Cuthbertson spoke for the entire administrative team: "Try to get the best possible faculty and the best possible students together. . . . You get the right people interested in learning, together, and you've got what it really takes to make a great university."[12]

Notes

All archival materials are located in the Department of Special Collections and University Archives, Stanford University Libraries, unless otherwise noted.

INTRODUCTION

1. Recently, and most notably, Roger L. Geiger, *Research and Relevant Knowledge: American Research Universities Since World War II* (New York: Oxford University Press, 1993). See also Hugh Davis Graham and Nancy Diamond, *The Rise of American Research Universities: Elites and Challengers in the Postwar Era* (Baltimore, MD: Johns Hopkins University Press, 1997).

2. For example, Henry Kissinger, *Nuclear Weapons and Foreign Policy* (New York: Harper, 1957); Robert Gilpin, *American Scientists and Nuclear Weapons Policy* (Princeton, NJ: Princeton University Press, 1962); Daniel S. Greenberg, *The Politics of Pure Science* (New York: New American Library, 1967).

3. For the United States, see Peter Galison and Bruce Hevly, eds., *Big Science: The Growth of Large-Scale Research* (Stanford, CA: Stanford University Press, 1992); Jessica Wang, *American Science in an Age of Anxiety: Scientists, Anticommunism and the Cold War* (Chapel Hill: University of North Carolina Press, 1999). For the international context, see for example, Michelangelo de Maria, Mario Grilli, and Fabio Sebastiani, eds., *The Restructuring of Physical Sciences in Europe and the United States, 1945–1960* (Singapore: World Scientific, 1989). See also C. S. Gillmor, "Federal Funding and Knowledge Growth in Ionospheric Physics," *Social Studies of Science* 16 (1986): 105–33; Paul Forman, "Behind Quantum Electronics: National Security as Basis for Physical Research in the United States, 1940–1960," *Historical Studies in the Physical and Biological Sciences* 18 (1987): 149–229.

4. Rebecca S. Lowen, *Creating the Cold War University: The Transformation of Stanford* (Berkeley: University of California Press, 1997), 9.

5. See especially Stuart W. Leslie, *The Cold War and American Science: The Military-Industrial-Academic Complex at MIT and Stanford* (New York: Columbia University Press, 1993); Lowen, *Creating the Cold War University*.

6. Leslie, *The Cold War and American Science*, 5; Lowen, *Creating the Cold War University*, 41–42.

7. SC160/XIV/5/4, FET to C. H. Green, November 7, 1977.

CHAPTER ONE. CALIFORNIA BOY

1. May V. Seagoe, *Terman and the Gifted* (Los Altos, CA: William Kaufman, 1975), 13. Lewis Madison Terman is the subject of two good biographies by fellow psychologists: Seagoe's *Terman and the Gifted*, and Henry Minton, *Lewis M. Terman, Pioneer in Psychological Testing* (New York: New York University Press, 1988). Seagoe was Terman's graduate student.

2. Seagoe, *Terman and the Gifted*, 1–2. SC160/XII/1. James and Martha Terman were married in 1854. The Termans were of Scots-Irish, Welsh, French, and German ancestry. Most had become farmers after arriving in the American colonies. The name Terman itself is probably Scots in origin but various ancestors and relatives spelled it Tarman, Terman, Turman, Tearman, among other variants.

3. SC38/8, Folder "Invitations, 1925–1935," Lewis M. Terman (LMT) to W. Wood, February 28, 1933.

4. SC160/XII/1/2.

5. Reuben and Sarah had married in 1873. SC160/XII/1, Frederick E. Terman (FET) to F. N. Duncan, November 16, 1949; FET to P. C. Emmons, September 1, 1959.

6. SC160/XII/1; Lewis Terman discusses his ongoing battle with tuberculosis in his manuscript, "I was lucky," 1953, in SC38, LMT Papers, Box 8, Folder 18 (reprinted in Seagoe, *Terman and the Gifted*, 239–44).

7. Seagoe, *Terman and the Gifted*, 18.

8. Ibid., 19.

9. Ibid., 21–23.

10. Ibid., 133; Minton, *Lewis M. Terman*, 23–24.

11. Seagoe, *Terman and the Gifted*, 26–27; L. M. Terman, "Genius and Stupidity: A Study of Some of the Intellectual Processes of Seven 'Bright' and Seven 'Stupid' Boys," *Pedagogical Seminary* 13 (1906): 303–73.

12. Minton, *Lewis M. Terman*, 28. See also Lewis M. Terman, "Trails to Psychology," in *A History of Psychology in Autobiography*, vol. 2 (Worcester, MA: Clark University Press, 1932), 297–331.

13. L. M. Terman, "I was lucky."

14. Founded in 1891 on the present site of the Los Angeles Public Library, the campus was taken over by the Regents of the University of California in 1919, who turned it first into the University of California's Southern Branch. It was renamed UCLA in 1927. The campus was moved out of the city of Los Angeles to a beautiful, more rural site in Westwood in 1929.

15. SC160/XII/1.

16. Seagoe, *Terman and the Gifted*, 33.

17. SC160/XII/3, A. L. Gesell to FET, October 5, 1942. Arnold Gesell recalled in later years retrieving a scrap of brown paper dated June 5, 1908, from inside the bungalow walls on which Fred had written the name "Turman." Seagoe, *Terman and the Gifted*, 37.

18. Minton, *Lewis M. Terman*, 36. The job was first offered to Terman's friend E. B. Huey, but Huey declined and suggested Lewis Terman. G. Stanley Hall sent Stanford a splendid letter of recommendation regarding Terman.

19. Terman, "Trails to Psychology," 323.

20. On Stanford's early history, see Orrin Leslie Elliott, *Stanford University: The First Twenty-Five Years* (Stanford, CA: Stanford University Press, 1937); Margo Davis and Roxanne Nilan, *The Stanford Album* (Stanford, CA: Stanford University Press, 1989); Karen Bartholomew, Claude Brinegar, and Roxanne Nilan, *A Chronology of Stanford University and its Founders, 1824–2000* (Stanford, CA: Stanford Historical Society, 2001); Karen Bartholomew and Roxanne Nilan, "*Stanford Observed [Centennial Supplement to the Stanford Observer]*," Stanford University News Service (June 1991).

21. The University of California, across the bay at Berkeley, had 520 students in the fall of 1891. "Cal" had experimented with the "specials" category but kept it for mature students (twenty-one or older). "Specials" were expected to qualify and move on to a degree-granting program. The faculty, who admitted and mentored these students, were generally in favor of the policy. Elliott, *Stanford University*, 94–97.

22. "Specials" were expected to make up their academic deficiencies promptly, thereby changing to regular status. A student's expenses were estimated at two hundred dollars a year in the 1890s. Student wages averaged fifteen to eighteen cents an hour and many found jobs on campus and in neighboring towns. Bartholomew, Brinegar, and Nilan, *Chronology*, 17.

23. Davis and Nilan, *Stanford Album*, 41.

24. Elliott, *Stanford University*, 326–78.

25. Cubberley carefully invested his own savings from earnings from writing and editing to amass more than $350,000. At his retirement in 1933, Cubberley gave this money to Stanford for the construction of the new education building. Bartholomew, Brinegar, and Nilan, *Chronology*, 66.

26. Sears and Terman became good friends as well as professional colleagues, and Lewis served as a mentor to Sears's son, Robert, who subsequently joined Stanford's Psychology Department. Robert R. Sears served as dean of humanities and sciences under Provost Fred Terman.

27. Bruce Bliven, "The Innocent Decade," in *Stanford Mosaic: Reminiscences of the First Seventy-Five Years at Stanford University*, ed. Edith R. Mirrielees, 58 (Stanford, CA: Stanford University Press, 1962); also quoted in Davis and Nilan, *Stanford Album*, 107.

28. As late as 1906 there were only six registered campus automobiles. (In 1900, there were only eight hundred cars registered in the state of California.)

29. Ward Winslow, *Palo Alto: A Centennial History* (Palo Alto, CA: The Association, 1993), 64–65.

30. Elliott, *Stanford University*, 113.

31. *Frederick Emmons Terman, Interviews by Arthur L. Norberg, Charles Süsskind, and Roger Hahn, 1975*. Transcript, a joint project of Bancroft Oral History Project on the History of Science and Technology and [the] Stanford Oral History Project, 1984 (hereafter, *Terman Interview*), 174.

32. Ward Winslow, "Tall Trees: The Palo Alto Stanford Connection," *Sandstone & Tile* 18, no. 2 (spring 1994): 11–12.

33. Winslow, *Palo Alto*, 202; C. F. Elwell, *Der Poulsen-Lichtbogengenerator*, trans. A. Semm and F. Gerth (Berlin: Springer, 1926).

34. Lee de Forest, "Recent Developments in the Work of the Federal Telegraph Company," *Proceedings, Institute of Radio Engineers* 1 (1913): 37–51; L. F. Fuller, "Continuous Waves in Long-distance Radio-telegraphy," *Transactions, American Institute of Electrical Engineers* 34 (1915): 809–27.

35. Alfred P. Morgan, *Wireless Telegraph Construction for Amateurs* (New York: D. Van Nostrand Co., 1910). This book, with Terman's sign-out signature, is in the private collection of Ludwell Sibley.

36. Winslow, *Palo Alto*, 202.

37. *Terman Interview*, 174.

38. Lists of the young Stanford engineers at Federal during its first decade are given in *Daily Palo Alto Times*, January 29, April 28, June 9, 1916; April 30, 1919; and May 25, 1922.

39. An informative history of the region's early electronics industry is Jane Morgan, *Electronics in the West: The First 50 Years* (Palo Alto, CA: National Press Books, 1967). See also Ward Winslow, ed., *The Making of Silicon Valley: A One-Hundred Year Renaissance* (Santa Clara, CA: Santa Clara Valley Historical Association, 1995).

40. *Palo Alto Times*, January 29, April 28, and June 9, 1916.

41. *Madrono* (December 1, 1915): 71.

42. *Madrono* (October 15, 1916): 33.

43. *Palo Alto Times*, October 4, 1915.

44. Rugby had replaced American-rules football at Stanford in 1905, and Palo Alto followed soon after. Rugby, it was argued, stressed individual skill rather than coaching strategy, and American-rules football smacked of a professionalism not true to the spirit of college athletics. "Ric" Templeton was among Stanford star athletes who toured the Pacific Coast lecturing on the merits of rugby football. Bartholomew, Brinegar, and Nilan, *Chronology*, 41.

45. Sources include *Madrono*, 1916 issues, and *Palo Alto Times*, April 20 and 24, May 5 and 7, September 15 and 18, November 17, and December 16, 1916.

46. Frederick E. Terman, Palo Alto High School transcript, December 15, 1916; Frederick E. Terman, Stanford University transcript; access to both courtesy of Patricia Terman.

47. Winslow, *Palo Alto*, 123–29; Birge Clark, "An Architect Grows up in Palo Alto," Palo Alto Historical Association files, Palo Alto City Library, 1982.

48. Author interview with Robert A. Helliwell, 1998. Helliwell's wife's uncles, the Perham brothers—well-known figures around Palo Alto and Stanford in those days, called Fred "Boots" Terman. They knew Fred as both a high school and a college student.

49. *Terman Interview*, 174.

50. Birge Clark, "An Architect"; Winslow, *Palo Alto*, 128.

51. Davis and Nilan, *Stanford Album*, 159–66; Ray Lyman Wilbur, *The Memoirs of Ray Lyman Wilbur, 1875–1949*, ed. Edgar Eugene Robinson and Paul Carroll Edwards, 224–25 (Stanford, CA: Stanford University Press, 1960).

52. SC160/VIII/3/6, FET to Stanford Phi Beta Kappa Chapter, April 9, 1964.

53. F. E. Terman, "William Frederick Durand," *Biographical Memoirs, National Academy of Sciences*, 48 (1976): 153–93. Durand replaced another Cornell engineer, Albert W. Smith, who served on Stanford's faculty from 1891 until 1902. Even after his retirement in 1924, Durand continued to serve on government committees. In 1941, at the age of eighty-two, he headed a project to develop jet propulsion. Durand was one of three Stanford engineering faculty members to be elected to the National Academy of Sciences before World War II.

54. The history of the difference between the degree of "Engineer" and that of the bachelor of arts in engineering is somewhat confusing. For several decades after the turn of the century, engineers normally worked toward the degree of "Engineer." In most cases, this was considered a more advanced degree than the bachelor of arts degree. In the early years of the century, the bachelor of science degree in some fields was also considered a

higher degree than the BA. Indeed, in some engineering fields, one could not earn a bachelor's degree. At Stanford, in order for a student to work for the degree of Engineer in electrical engineering or in chemical engineering, one first earned respectively, a bachelor's degree in mechanical engineering or in chemistry. (The master's degree was usually not available for engineers.) Thus, in the early days, "C.E.," "E.E.," "M.E.," "Min.E.," and "Chem. E." meant the degree of civil engineer, and so forth. During Fred Terman's years as a student, the degree of Engineer at Stanford required about one year of study beyond the bachelor's degree. By 1926, it required two year's work beyond the bachelor's. Following World War II, the degree of Engineer lost favor at most universities. The master's degree became the normal graduate professional degree for most engineers, and by the 1950s, the master's required one year of work past the bachelor's. The degree of Engineer represented an amount of study and research somewhere between the degrees of master's and the doctorate. Most engineering school faculty in the United States educated before 1925 did not have nor were expected to have earned a doctorate degree.

55. SC129. Guido H. Marx Papers, Stanford University Archives, Biographical Information.

56. In addition to Charles D. Marx (who had followed his Cornell studies with graduate study at the Karlsruhe Polytechnicum), the Civil Engineering Department at the time included Professors Charles B. Wing and John Charles Lounsbury Fish, both with Engineer degrees from Cornell, along with Assistant Professors John Harrison Foss and Charles Moser, both with bachelor's degrees from Stanford. In electrical engineering, Professor Harris J. Ryan (ME, Cornell) was supported by Assistant Professor James C. Clark (who had a master's degree in electrical engineering from Harvard) and instructor Fred S. Muluck (AB, Stanford).

57. Hoover won commendation by Scotland Yard for his efficiency and management skill. Wilbur, *Memoirs*, 227–28; Jordan, *Stanford Alumnus*, October 1914.

58. Mark Sullivan, *Our Times: The United States, 1900–1925* (New York: Charles Scribner's Sons, 1926–35), 5: 417–18.

59. *Stanford Illustrated Review*, February 20, 1917; Wilbur, *Memoirs*, 236.

60. Sullivan, *Our Times*, 5:392.

61. *Madrono* (December 1, 1916): 47. Another short story in the issue, "With the American Legion" by Ronald Heath, featured an American pilot who saves a French town by ramming his little biplane into a German bomber.

62. Sullivan, *Our Times*, 5: 392–403.

63. Wilbur, *Memoirs*, 238–39.

64. *Stanford 1920 Quad* [yearbook], vol. 26 (1919); *Palo Alto Times*, January 14, 1919.

65. Ray Lyman Wilbur reported that 3,393 Stanford men and women (students, alumni, faculty, and staff) served during the war in American and foreign service or war-related civilian posts, and that 77 were killed. Stanford University, *President's Report* (August 1921): 7.

66. Camp Fremont covered 7,203 acres, including what is now SLAC and stretching as far as Foothill Park. The main part of Camp Fremont, some 1,300 acres, was bounded by El Camino Real, Alameda de las Pulgas, Valparaiso Avenue, and San Francisquito Creek.

67. F. E. Terman, Stanford University transcript.

68. Sources used include Kenneth W. Crouch, '20, "Students' Army Training Corps," *Stanford 1920 Quad*, vol. 26 (1919): 84–89. Crouch was one of Fred Terman's Theta Xi classmates.

69. *Daily Palo Alto*, October 4 and 7, 1918; *Stanford 1920 Quad*, vol. 26 (1919).

70. Bartholomew, Brinegar, and Nilan, *Chronology*, 51.

71. Sullivan, *Our Times*, 5:652; *Daily Palo Alto*, October 21 and 28, 1918. *Stanford 1919 Quad*, vol. 25 (1918), issues of *Daily Palo Alto* (Stanford) and *Palo Alto Times*.

72. Wilbur, *Memoirs*, 251.

73. *Daily Palo Alto*, October 3 and 7, 1919.

74. *H. J. Ryan, Edison Medallist, 1925* (New York: AIEE, 1925), 14 (copy in SC165/I/2/27). Ryan was elected to the National Academy of Sciences in 1920, but there is no written biographical memoir in their published series. There is an entry in the IEEE online archives at www.ieee.org/organizations/history-center/legacies/ryan.html.

75. (Stanford University) *Annual Report of the President*, July 31, 1917; *Annual Report*, August 31, 1918.

76. Davis and Nilan, *Stanford Album*, 164; Bartholomew, Brinegar, and Nilan, *Chronology*, 49.

77. Sources used include: *Daily Palo Alto*, 1917–20; Archives of the Stanford University Athletic Department (courtesy of Lloyd McGovern); *Stanford Quad* yearbooks, 1918–20; Don E. Liebendorfer, *The Color of Life Is Red: A History of Stanford Athletics, 1892–1972* (Stanford, CA: Stanford University, Dept. of Athletics, 1972); and SC160/XIII/1/23, FET to H. Hoover Jr., April 22, 1927.

78. *Daily Palo Alto*, February 15, 1918, and April 7, 1919.

79. Author interviews with Payton Jordan, 1999, and with Robert Helliwell, 1998. William A. Wambsganss (1894–1985) was an infielder in the major leagues from 1914–26, mostly for the Cleveland Indians. He finished out his career with the Boston Red Sox and Philadelphia Athletics. Source: Baseball-Reference.com.

80. *Terman Interview*, 6–7.

81. Davis and Nilan, *Stanford Album*, 162.

82. Incidental fees had been raised earlier to $15 per quarter, and tuition imposed on graduate study (*Daily Palo Alto*, October 14 and 16, 1919). When caustic editorials appeared in the *Daily*, Hoover responded that tuition was absolutely necessary to maintain the university and raise faculty salaries to match those at other universities. Hoover calculated that the cost to educate a Stanford student was about $525 per year, yet while other prominent schools asked $150 or more yearly tuition, Stanford was asking only $120. Bartholomew, Brinegar, and Nilan, *Chronology*, 43, 53; Davis and Nilan, *Stanford Album*, 166.

83. *Daily Palo Alto*, May 12, 1920; *Stanford 1923 Quad*, vol. 29 (1922): 12.

84. Swain received his BA in 1899 from Stanford, his PhD in 1902 from Yale. From 1928 to 1932, Robert Eckles Swain would serve as the tight-fisted acting president of Stanford during President Ray Lyman Wilbur's service in Washington as Herbert Hoover's secretary of the interior.

85. Eric Hutchinson, *The Department of Chemistry, Stanford University, 1891–1976: A Brief Account of the First Eighty-Five Years* (Palo Alto, CA: Stanford University, Chemistry Department, 1977), 10.

86. Ibid., 6.

87. FET Stanford University transcript file; access courtesy of Patricia Terman.

88. Terman's official transcript notes his completion of 181 quarter units of academic credit, just 1 unit over the 180 necessary for graduation (although his units in fact add to 183 and one-third hours). Edith R. Mirrielees, *Fifty Years of Phi Beta Kappa at Stanford, 1891–1941* (Stanford, CA: Stanford University Press, ca. 1941), 110.

89. *Daily Palo Alto*, May 27 and 28, and June 1–3, 1920; *Stanford Quad*, various years.

90. SC160/VIII/3/6, FET to Stanford Phi Beta Kappa Chapter, April 9, 1964.

91. Course and degree work and student lists are available in Stanford University *Registers* (course catalog).

92. Paper #2 in the series Leland Stanford Junior University Publications.

93. Carmen received his AB '83, AM '86, and DSc. '85 from the College of New Jersey (later called Princeton University).

94. Following British tradition, Princeton at this time awarded the master's degree three years following the receipt of a bachelor's degree, provided a small amount of paperwork was completed. The doctorate of science, however, required two years of coursework following the bachelor's, a set of *rigorous* exams, and acceptance of a research thesis presenting results of original work. (Information on DSc requirements and awarding of degrees for Carmen and Perrine from Princeton University Board of Trustee minutes, Princeton University Archives.)

95. Like Carmen, Perrine received his AB '83, AM '86, and DSc '85 from the College of New Jersey. F. Perrine, *Municipal Monopolies* (New York: T. Y. Crowell and Co., 1899); F. Perrine, *Power Plants of the Pacific Coast* (New York: New York Electrical Society, 1902); and F. Perrine, *Conductors for Electrical Distribution* (New York: Van Nostrand, 1903).

96. In 1926, Mabel Macferran (BS '25, MIT) was the first woman at Stanford to receive the degree of Engineer in electrical engineering. After World War II, Fred Terman hired her in the Electrical Engineering Department at Stanford.

97. Leonard Franklin Fuller (ME '12, Cornell) was also the first Stanford PhD to work with radio research as well as the first PhD awarded for cooperative work with an industrial company and under a classified U.S. Navy contract. A major figure at nearby Federal Telegraph Company, Fuller later chaired the Electrical Engineering Department at the University of California, Berkeley.

98. Information from Stanford University *Registers*, various years.

99. Harris J. Ryan, "The Conductivity of the Atmosphere at High Voltages," *Transactions, American Institute of Electrical Engineers* 23 (1904): 101–34, and Discussion, 135–45, 168–70.

100. Shannon Moffat, "Stanford's Power Line Research Pioneers," *Sandstone & Tile* 12, no. 1 (fall 1987): 3–7.

101. By 1922, significant roles in Federal's work had been performed by Stanford graduates, including Leonard F. Fuller, chief engineer, PhD, EE, Stanford '19; Ralph R. Beal, AB, EE '12; Roland G. Marx, AB, CE '11 (son of engineering professor Charles D. Marx); Harry J. Rathbun, AB, ME '16, EE '20 (and later JD '29 and Stanford professor of law); Adrien L. Anderson, AB, ME '17; Harold F. Elliott, AB, ME '16, EE '25; Milton P. Baker, AB, ME '16; William L. Parker (B.Engr. '12, New Zealand), Stanford graduate student '17; William A. Hillebrand, graduate student in electrical engineering 1905–6 and assistant professor of electrical engineering 1907–11; Herman P. Miller Jr., AB, ME '17; James A. Miller, AB, EE '13; and Carl E. Scholz, AB, ME '17. In addition, Sumner P. Wing, AB, CE '14 (son of engineering professor Charles B. Wing) worked with Elwell and followed him to England when Elwell left Federal to establish an international consulting practice in London.

102. J. Cameron Clark and Harris J. Ryan, "Spark Gap Discharge Voltages at High Frequencies," *Transactions, American Institute of Electrical Engineers* 33 (1914): 973–87.

103. At the time, the Elwell scholarship was one of only six graduate scholarships in the university—two general, two in medicine, one in law, and one in electrical engineering. A year later, the two "general" graduate scholarships were enlarged to thirty.

104. They measured differential frequency propagation effects between San Francisco and Honolulu to support the idea of a Kennelly-Heaviside Layer, or upper reflecting layer (or ionosphere, as it would later be named). These interpretations were published ten years before the similar work of Edward Appleton, who won the Nobel Prize in 1947 for his contributions to ionospheric physics. De Forest, "Recent Developments"; Fuller, "Continuous Waves."

105. Sources include Terman's Stanford University transcript.

106. Additional advanced coursework included: Electrical Engineering Technology, Advanced Electrotechnics (given with the assistance of the Physics Department and the Applied Mathematics Department), a weekly graduate literature seminar, an additional physics course and one in applied mathematics, three to five elective courses, and completion of a thesis.

107. Seagoe, *Terman and the Gifted*, 126; information regarding Winifred Johnston from the Johnston family; author interviews with Donald J. Carpenter, 1998, 1999.

108. F. E. Terman, *Characteristics and Stability of Transmission Systems* (unpublished DSc dissertation, MIT, 1924), 290–91.

109. Stanford University, *Report of the President* (1921–22), 144–45.

110. F. E. Terman, "The Measurement of Transients," *Transactions, American Institute of Electrical Engineers* 42 (February 1923): 389–93, and Discussion, 393–94.

111. See C. H. Sharp and E. D. Doyle, "Crest Voltmeters," *Transactions, American Institute of Electrical Engineers* 35 (1916): 99–107; and other references in the same volume (particularly Chubb; Work; Whitehead and Pullen).

112. Philip C. Clark and Charles E. Miller, "The High-Voltage Wattmeter," *Transactions, American Institute of Electrical Engineers* 43 (1924): 1124–29.

113. Terman, "Measurement of Transients," 393–94.

114. *Terman Interview*, 5, 27.

115. This section relies on the excellent volume by Karl L. Wildes and Nilo A. Lindgren, *A Century of Electrical Engineering and Computer Science at MIT, 1882–1982* (Cambridge, MA: MIT Press, 1985).

116. SC38/14/28, LMT to T. L. Kelley, September 18, 1922.

117. *Atlas of the City of Boston*, 1928.

118. SC38/14/28, LMT to T. L. Kelley, November 6, 1922.

119. MIT *Catalog*, 1922–23, MIT Archives.

120. *Terman Interview*, 22.

121. The committee also included Frank B. Jewett, the chief engineer of AT&T. MIT Archives, MC5, Dugald C. Jackson Papers, Box 3, MIT Archives.

122. Dugald C. Jackson Papers, MIT Archives, MC5, Box 4, Folder 271, MIT Archives.

123. Vannevar is pronounced "Vuh-neever," rhyming with "Beaver."

124. Materials for this section utilize Terman's academic transcript from MIT, obtained from the MIT Registrar, the MIT *Directory*, and MIT *Courses of Study* materials, located in the MIT Archives.

125. Fred Terman commented on this in a letter to Stanford Engineering Dean Theodore Jesse Hoover in 1926.

126. Tenney L. Davis and H. M. Goodwin, *A History of the Departments of Chemistry and Physics at the M. I. T., 1865–1933* (Cambridge, MA: MIT Press, 1933).

127. SC160/V/11/1, FET report, prepared September 1923 for Western Electric, "Given to M. J. Kelly."

128. SC38/13/18, E. G. Boring to LMT, January 31, 1924.

129. SC160/XII/1, FET to E. Morris, December 30, 1977.

130. Materials in this section drawn from the Arthur Edwin Kennelly Papers, HUG 1479.70 to 1479.80, Harvard University Archives; Vannevar Bush, "Arthur E. Kennelly," *Biographical Memoirs, National Academy of Sciences* 22 (1941): 83–119; C. S. Gillmor, "Wilhelm Altar, Edward Appleton, and the Magneto-Ionic Theory," *Proceedings, American Philosophical Society* 126, no. 5 (1982): 395–440.

131. By the time he retired from Harvard in 1930, his texts included *The Application of Hyperbolic Functions to Electrical Engineering Problems* (London: London University Press, 1912), and *Artificial Electric Lines* (New York: McGraw-Hill, 1917); plus Kennelly's published tables *Tables of Complex Hyperbolic and Circular Functions* (Cambridge, MA: Harvard University Press, 1913), and *Chart Atlas of Complex Hyperbolic and Circular Function* (Cambridge, MA: Harvard University Press, 1913).

132. Dugald C. Jackson interview, January 22, 1941, in Arthur Edwin Kennelly Papers, HUG 1479.80, Harvard University Archives.

133. *Terman Interview*, 19.

134. Norbert Wiener, *Cybernetics, or Control and Communications in the Animal and the Machine* (Cambridge, MA: MIT Press, 1961).

135. SC160/V/11/1. Terman's homework for Wiener, submitted on February 8, 1924, explores a special problem on the J. Fischer-Hinnen method of harmonic analysis.

136. This section benefits from G. Pascal Zachary, *Endless Frontier: Vannevar Bush, Engineer of the American Century* (New York: Free Press, 1997); Karl L. Wildes and Nilo A. Lindgren, *A Century of Electrical Engineering and Computer Science at MIT, 1882–1982* (Cambridge, MA: MIT Press, 1985); and from the Frederick E. Terman Papers, SC160, Stanford University Libraries.

137. MIT Archives, MIT Graduation Exercises, June 14, 1916. Vannevar Bush, "Oscillating Currents, With Applications to the Coupled Circuit and the Artificial Transmission Line," D.Eng. dissertation, MIT, 1916. Zachary, *Endless Frontier*, 31–32.

138. Zachary, *Endless Frontier*, 311.

139. See Bush's portrait by the noted photographer Yousuf Karsh, reproduced on the book jacket of Zachary, *Endless Frontier*.

140. Vannevar Bush, *Pieces of the Action* (New York: William Morrow, 1970).

141. Vannevar Bush files, MC78, bibliography, MIT Archives. For example, see, *Trans. AIEE* 42 (June 1923): 878–93; *Jour. AIEE* 42, Pt. II (November 1923): 1155–58; *Trans. AIEE* 44 (February 1925): 80–103; and *Jour. AIEE* 44, Pt. I (March 1925): 229–40.

142. *Terman Interview*, 165.

143. Terman, ScD dissertation, 1–2.

144. F. E. Terman, "The Circle Diagram of a Transmission Network," *Transactions, American Institute of Electrical Engineers* 45 (1926): 1081–92; William Suddards Franklin and Frederick Emmons Terman, *Transmission Line Theory and Some Related Topics* (Lancaster, PA: Franklin and Charles, 1926).

145. The "Superpower Transmission" papers were published in *Transactions, American Institute of Electrical Engineers* 43 (1924): 1–103.

146. V. Bush and R. D. Booth, "Power System Transients," *Transactions, American Institute of Electrical Engineers* 44 (1925): 80–97, and Discussion, 97–103.

147. F. E. Terman, Commentary on "Superpower Transmission" systems papers, *Transactions, American Institute of Electrical Engineers* 43 (1924): 84–85.

148. *Terman Interview*, 166.

149. Among those graduating with their doctor of science degrees with Fred was Manuel Sandoval Vallarta of Mexico City in physics. Vallarta had earned a bachelor's degree from MIT in electrochemical engineering and moved on to graduate work in math, physics, and electrical engineering, and a dissertation on Bohr's Atomic Model. Vallarta became a renowned theoretical physicist.

150. SC160/XIII/1/32, H. J. Ryan to R. L. Wilbur, August 2 and 6, 1924. Ryan had set up the appointment for Fred Terman before Fred's bout with tuberculosis: SC38/14/11, LMT to A. L. Gesell, February 27, 1925.

151. Seagoe, *Terman and the Gifted*, 126–27.

152. *Terman Interview*, 160.

153. SC38/14/11, LMT to A. L. Gesell, February 27, 1925; SC38/13/18, E. G. Boring to LMT, October 7, 1924; SC38/17/2, R. M. Yerkes to LMT, December 24, 1924.

154. SC38/17/2, LMT to R. M. Yerkes, June 13, 1925; author interview with Terence Terman, 1999.

155. *Terman Interview*, 159.

156. Ibid., 161.

157. SC160/XIII/1/23, FET notes on H. Hoover Jr., March 3, 1980.

158. SC160//XIII/1/23, H. Hoover Jr. to FET, September 14, 1929.

159. SC160/XIII/1/23.

160. Sullivan, *Our Times*, 5:383.

161. Tom Kneitel, *Radio Station Treasury, 1900–1946* (Commack, NY: CRB Research, 1986). Aside from which U.S. city provided the first radio broadcasts, the first stations granted U.S. government licenses were September 15, 1921, WBZ, Westinghouse, Boston; September 19, WDY, RCA, Roselle Park, New Jersey; September 29, WCJ, A. C. Gilbert Company, New Haven, Connecticut; September 30, WJZ, Westinghouse, Newark, New Jersey. KDKA, Westinghouse, obtained its license in Pittsburgh in November. In December 1921 alone, the following California stations were licensed: in Hollywood, KGC; in Los Angeles, Leo J. Meyberg's KYJ, and KOG; in Oakland, KZM and KZY; in Sacramento, KVQ; in San Jose, Charles D. Herrold's KQW; in San Francisco, Leo J. Meyberg's KDN at the Fairmont Hotel, KGB, and KYY; in Stockton, KWG and KJQ; and in Sunnyvale, KJJ. Most had previously operated as experimental stations with calls such as 6XE or 6XG, indicating they were located on the West Coast, geographical area "6."

162. *Palo Alto Times*, January 29, April 28, and June 9, 1916; April 30, 1919; May 25, 1922. Winslow, *Making of Silicon Valley*, 8.

163. Kolster, formerly at the U.S. Bureau of Standards, had developed a radio direction-finder in 1913 and worked on a radio compass, radio receivers, and big parabolic antennas.

164. *Palo Alto Times*, March 24, April 12 and 13, August 11 and 26, and October 25, 1921, and May 1, 1922.

165. Ibid., May 5, 1922.

166. Ibid., various issues, 1920–24; and Kneitel, *Radio Station Treasury*. In 1923, there were two hundred radio stations in the United States, the only country in the world where regular radio broadcasting occurred. Local newspapers owned major stations in Los Angeles, Seattle, and Portland. Washington State College in Pullman and the Oregon Agricultural College in Corvallis operated stations.

167. *Terman Interview*, 161.

CHAPTER TWO. THE STANFORD PROFESSOR

1. Published by McGraw-Hill in New York and London in 1920.

2. William Franklin was also the uncle of Jack Franklin (BA, EE '26, Stanford), who was one of Fred's ham radio buddies.

3. SC160/X/5/7, W. S. Franklin to FET, January 19, 1924.

4. SC160/5/1, FET to H. E. Carson, April 18, 1929.

5. Franklin wrote that two thousand copies of the book could be printed in London for $1,709 as opposed to $3,031 in Lancaster, Pennsylvania. Including taxes, shipping, and so forth, the production price per book would be $1.20 from England versus $1.51 from the United States and would sell for $3 a copy. Of course, distribution and discount costs of about 30 percent would also apply. Fred agreed to the English printer, with the book to be distributed by Franklin and Charles publishers in Lancaster, and their agents Constable and Company in England. SC160/XII/3, FET to Sibyl Walcutt Terman (SWT), September 21, 1927.

6. SC160/X/5/7, W. S. Franklin to FET, December 6, 1925, and February 12 and November 2, 1926.

7. SC160/X/5/7, FET to W. S. Franklin, May 14, 1926.

8. SC160/X/5/7, FET to W. S. Franklin, May 27, 1926, and March 21, 1927. It is difficult to know exactly the income produced since Franklin seems to have gotten increasingly forgetful with age and neglected to keep correct records of his own payments to the publisher (or lack thereof).

9. Wilbur, *Memoirs*, 215.

10. Ibid., 580.

11. According to *A Study of the Graduate Schools of America*, cited in Bartholomew, Brinegar, and Nilan, *Chronology*, 56.

12. SC64A/75/7, R. L. Wilbur to H. J. Ryan, May 16 and June 24, 1925.

13. SC165/I/6/21, T. J. Hoover to R. L. Wilbur, April 17, 1925.

14. SC165/I/10/7, minutes of School of Engineering Executive Committee, n.d. but ca. late 1925.

15. Wilbur, *Memoirs*, 281–91. Social sciences and humanities departments were more difficult to organize, and several school configurations were tried before the final merging of the Schools of Biological Sciences, Humanities, Physical Sciences, and Social Sciences in 1948. Bartholomew, Brinegar, and Nilan, *Chronology*, 73. On organization of Stanford's various schools, see also J. Pearce Mitchell, *Stanford University, 1916–1941* (Stanford, CA: Stanford University Press, 1958), 77–94.

16. SC165/I/6/21, T. J. Hoover to R. L. Wilbur, April 17, 1925.

17. Davis and Nilan, *Stanford Album*, 221.

18. SC165, T. J. Hoover notes for a talk on April 16, 1925; T. J. Hoover to R. L. Wilbur, April 17, 1925; and T. J. Hoover to R. L. Wilbur, October 15, 1925.

19. SC165/I/6/50, memo notes by T. J. Hoover, n.d., but ca. December 1925.

20. SC165/I/4/40, T. J. Hoover to R. S. Lewis, February 11, 1936.

21. Theodore J. Hoover, "Training the Engineers of Tomorrow," *Stanford Illustrated Review* (May 1926).

22. SC160/V/11, for example, see T. J. Hoover to FET, April 22, 1926.

23. SC165/I/7/28, T. H. Morgan to T. J. Hoover, April 28, 1926; W. B. Kindy to T. J. Hoover, May 8, 1926; H. H. Henline to T. J. Hoover, April 30, 1926.

24. SC160/V/11, FET to T. J. Hoover, April 26, 1926.

25. SC64A/89/17.

26. SC160/XIII/1/30, H. J. Ryan to R. L. Wilbur, August 2, 1924.

27. SC160/XIII/1/31, excerpts from H. J. Ryan's 1926–27 report to R. L. Wilbur. Ryan noted to Wilbur that since he had arrived at Stanford in 1905, three electrical engineering faculty had died prematurely, two of tuberculosis and one of pneumonia.

28. SC160/XIII/1/30, excerpts from H. J. Ryan's 1925–26 report to R. L. Wilbur.

29. SC160/XII/I/1, D. C. Jackson to FET, March 16, 1925; and V. Bush to FET, August 5, 1926.

30. SC64A/123/1, T. H. Morgan to R. E. Swain, June 22, 1931; and R. E. Swain to H. H. Skilling, August 14, 1931; SC64A/13/1/2, R. E. Swain to H. H. Skilling, September 11, 1931.

31. *Terman Interview*, 161–63.

32. SC64A/159/5, H. C. Moreno to T. J. Hoover, May 10, 1935.

33. Data in table from Stanford University *Registers*, and from SC165/I/3/3.

34. SC160/II/6/7, FET to H. J. Ryan, August 16, 1929.

35. SC64B/74, "Stanford Faculty Salaries."

36. SC64A/117/7, R. E. Swain to R. B. House, March 5, 1930.

37. SC160/XIII/1/30, excerpts from H. J. Ryan's 1928–29 report to the president, prepared during the 1927–28 academic year.

38. SC160/XIII/I/31, "E.E. Budget Documents."

39. SC160/XIII/I/30, H. J. Ryan to R. L. Wilbur, December 27, 1927; and T. J. Hoover to R. L. Wilbur, December 8, 1933.

40. SC160/XIII/1/30, T. J. Hoover to R. L. Wilbur, January 11, 1935.

41. SC64A/75/7; SC64A/106/15; SC64A/114/13; SC64A/149/4.

42. F. E. Terman, "The Electrical Engineering Research Situation in the American Universities," *Science* 65 (April 22, 1927): 385–88.

43. *New York Times*, June 5, 1927.

44. SC160/II/6/3, R. E. Swain to FET, May 2, 1927.

45. SC160/II/6/3, D. C. Jackson to FET, June 8, 1927.

46. SC160/II/6/3, H. J. Ryan to C. E. Magnusson, August 30, 1927.

47. SC160/II/6/3, FET to C. E. Magnusson, September 4, 1927.

48. SC160/XII/3/3, FET to SWT, September 3, 1927.

49. SC160/II/6/3, FET to C. E. Magnusson, October 10, 1927.

50. *The Thermionic Vacuum Tube and Its Applications* (New York and London: McGraw-Hill, 1920).

51. *Terman Interview*, 159–60.

52. SC165/I/6/39, T. J. Hoover to R. L. Wilbur, March 22, 1922; SC64A/53/1, H. J. Ryan to R. L. Wilbur, April 1, 1922.

53. SC64A/53/1, R. L. Wilbur to H. J. Ryan, March 27, 1922; SC64A/56/8, H. J. Ryan to R. L. Wilbur, January 8, 1924.

54. SC160/II/4/17, FET to R. L. Wilbur, October 29, 1936.

55. SC165/I/6/39, T. J. Hoover to R. L. Wilbur, July 2, 1924.

56. SC165/I/6/39, E. E. Robinson to R. L. Wilbur, July 18, 1924.

57. SC64A/69/4, H. J. Ryan to A. E. Roth, June 10, 1924.

58. SC165/I/6/39, H. H. Henline to P. C. Chambliss, October 9, 1924.

59. SC165/I/6/39, T. J. Hoover to R. L. Wilbur, March 23, 1922; *Science and Invention* (June 1924): 181, listing of Stanford radio station KFGH; correspondence between U.S.

Bureau of Standards and Henry Henline, summer and fall of 1924; H. H. Henline to C. F. Elwell, Ltd., October 8, 1924; H. H. Henline to G. K. Burgess, October 9, 1924.

60. SC165/I/4/9, T. J. Hoover to R. L. Wilbur, February 14, 1934.

61. SC160/XIII/1/30, FET report, "Recommendations for the Development of the Communication Laboratory at Stanford," dated "approx. Sept. 1927"; also SC160/II/6/7.

62. Sibyl Terman interview in *Link* (Stanford ERL Bulletin), December 1955, copy in SC160/IX/1/1.

63. SC160/XII, Box 2.

64. Measuring in at 5'3" and 115 lbs., Sibyl kept her slim figure for nearly her entire adult life. This entire Walcutt section utilizes SC160/XII/2, and SC160/XII/5, various folders.

65. SC160/XII/5.

66. SC160/XII/5, H. L. Walcutt to SWT, September 17, 1921.

67. SC160/XII/5, H. L. Walcutt to SWT, February 4, 1921.

68. SC160/XII/5, "Winkie" to SWT, February 4, 1921.

69. SC160/XII/5, "Winkie" to SWT, June 2, 1921.

70. SC160/XII/5, "Winkie" to SWT, August 21, 1921.

71. SC160/XII/5, "Winkie" to SWT, June 5, 1922.

72. SC160/XII/5, "SWT—School Papers."

73. SC160/XII/5, "Winkie" to SWT, October 18 and 21 and November 27, 1926.

74. Lewis Terman's annual income in 1926 was an impressive $18,000, including his $3,500 Stanford faculty salary, with the remaining income from book and test royalties and lecture fees. SC38/19, "Invitations, 1920–25."

75. Sibyl Walcutt, "An Attempt to Provide a Basis for Grading and Classifying Red-Green Color Blindness," unpublished master's thesis, Stanford University, 1928.

76. SC160/XII/5, J. A. Weir to SWT, April 22, 1925.

77. SC160/XII/5, "Correspondence from Friends and Relatives"; and "Harry" to SWT, October 4, 1926.

78. SC160/XII/5, "Connie" to SWT, November 22, 1926; see also "Winkie" to SWT, November 27, 1926.

79. SC160/XII/5, "Connie" to SWT, January 20 and March 30, 1927.

80. SC160/XII/5, "Correspondence from Friends to SWT"; and "Louise" to SWT, July 25, 1927.

81. SC160/XII/3/3, SWT to FET, August 22, 1927.

82. SC160/XII/3/3, FET to SWT, ca. September 4, 1927.

83. SC160/XII/3/1, FET to SWT, August 19, 1927.

84. SC160/XII/3/3, FET to SWT, September 3, 1927.

85. SC160/XII/3/6, SWT to FET, September 18, 1927.

86. SC160/XII/3/6, SWT to FET, August 28, 1927.

87. SC160/XII/3/6, SWT to FET, August 31, 1927.

88. Ibid.

89. SC160/XII/3/3, FET to SWT, September 6, 1927.

90. SC160/XII/3/6, SWT to FET, September 17, 1927.

91. SC160/XII/3/6, FET to SWT, September 17, 1927.

92. SC160/XII/3/6, C. C. Walcutt to FET, December 3, 1927.

93. SC160/XII/3/6, SWT to FET, September 18, 1927.

94. SC160/XII/3/7, "SWT Formal Invitations."

95. SC160/XII/5, "Connie" to SWT, March 19, 1928; and "Winnie" to SWT, February 29, 1928.

96. SC160/XII/5, "Formal Correspondence to SWT"; and C. K. Sumner to SWT, May 7, 1928; and John Breuner Company to SWT, May 17, 1928.

97. Author interviews with Byron and Nelle Phillips, 1998, and with Walter Vincenti, 1999.

98. SC160/XII/5, various folders.

99. See Chapter 8, below.

100. C. S. Gillmor, "The History of the Term 'Ionosphere,'" *Nature* 262 (1976): 347–48; C. S. Gillmor, "Threshold to Space: Early Studies of the Ionosphere," in *Space Science Comes of Age*, ed. Paul A. Hanle and Von Del Chamberlain, 101–14 (Washington DC: Smithsonian Institution Press, 1981); C. S. Gillmor, "Wilhelm Altar, Edward Appleton, and the Magneto-Ionic Theory," *Proceedings, American Philosophical Society* 126, no. 5 (1982): 395–440.

101. SC160/XIII/1/23, FET to H. Hoover Jr., May 6, 1929. Herbert Hoover Jr. and Jack Franklin were then executive engineers at Western Air Express in Los Angeles and both were teaching part-time at Caltech. Hoover soon resigned from the aircraft radio design business and went into the geophysical instrument business. He did this so that there might be no conflict of interest in that his father, Herbert Hoover Sr., as secretary of commerce and then as president, was technically in charge of the Federal Radio Commission. (The romance of radio and aircraft is suggested by the 1920s popular song, "Big Boy Jess, of the Western Air Express" [Brewster-Raph, composers, 1929].)

102. SC160/II/6/7, FET to H. J. Ryan, August 16, 1929.

103. SC64A/114/13, Plan, including sketch of proposed radio site, 1929.

104. SC160/II/4/4, FET to A. E. Roth, August 5, 1929; and FET to H. J. Ryan, August 5, 1929.

105. SC160/II/4/4, FET to R. E. Swain, August 14, 1929.

106. SC160/XIII/1/23, FET to H. Hoover Jr., September 20, 1929.

107. SC160/II/4/4, FET to H. J. Ryan, T. J. Hoover, and R. E. Swain, November 26, 1929.

108. SC160/XIII/1/30, H. J. Ryan to T. J. Hoover, December 31, 1929.

109. SC160/II/4/4, R. E. Swain to A. E. Roth, January 23, 1930; SC64A/114/13, R. E. Swain to A. E. Roth, with R. L. Wilbur's note, January 10, 1930.

110. SC160/II/4/4, FET to H. J. Ryan, May 4, 1930.

111. On the impact of the Depression on the Stanford community, see Davis and Nilan, *Stanford Album*, 217–26.

112. SC64A/139/4, H. J. Ryan to W. B. Kindy, March 25, 1933.

113. SC160/II/4/4, T. J. Hoover to R. E. Swain, March 24, 1930; SC64A/123/2, T. J. Hoover to R. E. Swain, November 5, 1930.

114. SC165/I/15/17, various correspondence between T. J. Hoover and film studio executives, 1929–30. San Francisco *Call*, May 9, 1929, "Stanford Offered Aid for Courses in Movies."

115. SC160/II/3/1, J. N. A. Hawkins to FET, December 22, 1938, and November 21, 1939.

116. SC160/II/4/4, FET to T. J. Hoover, March 11, 1930.

117. SC160/XIII/1/30, W. B. Kindy to T. J. Hoover, December 18, 1931; FET to W. B. Kindy, December 21, 1931.

118. SC160/II/1/2, FET to W. B. Kindy, September 16 and November 20, 1932; SC160/XIII/1/30, FET to W. B. Kindy, December 8, 1932, with Swain's note thereupon.

119. SC160/XIII/1/30, W. B. Kindy to R. L. Wilbur, January 10 and 11, 1934; SC160/II/1/7, R. L. Wilbur to FET, January 6, 1934.

120. SC160/XIII/1/30, T. J. Hoover to R. L. Wilbur, January 11, 1935.

121. SC165/I/6/20, FET to T. J. Hoover, June 2, 1931.

122. SC165/I/6/20, memo from Electrical Engineering Department to Physics Department, "December 1931."

123. SC165/I/6/20, T. J. Hoover to R. E. Swain, June 1, 1931.

124. SC165/I/6/20, P. Kirkpatrick to S. B. Morris, February 23, 1937.

125. *Terman Interview*, 18–20.

126. SC160/II/1/6, FET to City of Los Angeles, Water and Power Department, October 8, 1934. Terman gave the transmission lines course for a number of years and built up a complete written syllabus that he intended to turn into a textbook by the late 1930s, but events involving the Institute of Radio Engineers and subsequently World War II terminated the project. His colleague Hugh Skilling subsequently took over the course and published texts on electrical transients and transmission lines. *Terman Interview*, 17. Hugh Hildreth Skilling, *Transient Electric Currents* (New York and London: McGraw-Hill, 1937); and Hugh Hildreth Skilling, *Electric Transmission Lines* (New York: McGraw-Hill, 1951).

127. SC160/II/2/4, "Report of Special Committee on English for Engineers," October 9, 1931. (Given its style, the report was probably written by Terman.)

128. SC160/II/2/4, S. S. Seward Jr., "English for Engineers," n.d., but written in the 1931–32 academic year.

129. SC160/II/2/4, FET to T. J. Hoover, June 17, 1932.

130. SC160/II/2/4, "Report of Committee on English" (Terman, L. B. Reynolds, and E. P. Lesley), n.d., but 1932–33 academic year.

131. SC160/II/2/4, G. Hinkle to FET, June 7, 1933; and FET to T. J. Hoover, n.d., but 1933–34 academic year; SC64A/149/2, minutes of Engineering School Faculty, January 15, 1934.

132. SC160/V/4/8, FET to L. S. Lyon, April 21, 1926; SC160/V/3/5, FET to L. S. Lyon, May 13, 1926; and FET to R. F. Lyon, June 23, 1926.

133. SC160/V/3/2; SC160/V/3/4.

134. SC160/V/3/3, FET to R. F. Lyon, June 23, 1926.

135. SC160/V/3/3, FET to R. F. Lyon, April 22, 1927.

136. SC160/V/1/2. U.S. patent no. 1,782,588 was filed for on February 13, 1928. After being amended several times, Fred was allowed five claims, and the patent was issued on November 25, 1930.

137. SC160/V/4/6; SC160/V/4/3 and 4; numerous letters between FET and Wired Radio, 1928–29.

138. SC160/V/5/8.

139. SC160/V/9, FET and Frank Reiber, Inc., 1929.

140. SC160/V/5/1, FET and Alco Products of San Francisco, 1932.

141. SC160/V/5/13.

142. Ibid.

143. SC160/V/3, Folders 6 and 12, FET to R. V. A. Lee, 1930–39. Contract of September 12, 1930.

144. SC160/V/3/12, FET to R. V. A. Lee, February 10, 1932.

145. M0049, Cyril Frank Elwell Papers. Containers 1–4. Container 1 includes two ver-

sions of Elwell's unpublished autobiography. Photos of Elwell and several of his radio stations and antennas from 1910–36 are included in BP, Box 9, Folders 7–8.

146. SC160/V/1/3; SC160/V/1/6.

147. SC160/V/3/6, C. F. Elwell to FET, July 29, 1936.

148. SC160/V/3/6, C. F. Elwell to FET, April 19, 1936; SC160/II/1/9, C. F. Elwell to FET, January 4, 1936, and April 9, 1938; and FET to C. F. Elwell, September 28, 1937.

149. SC165/I/2/24, Clipping from *Palo Alto Times*, June 18, 1941.

150. Letters in author's collection: R. Hanbury-Brown to R. N. Bracewell, July 22, 1999, and L. Brown to C. S. Gillmor, July 19, 1999.

151. Curtis G. Benjamin to William Kaufmann, April 26, 1982, copy in author's collection (copy courtesy of William Kaufmann); SC160/VIII/3/6, FET remarks on receiving Theta Sigma Phi (Journalism Honorary Society) Matrix Award for Public Service, May 18, 1965.

152. *Terman Interview*, 161.

153. John Harold Morecroft, *Principles of Radio Communication* (New York: Wiley and Sons, 1921); J. H. Morecroft, *Experimental Radio Engineering* (New York: Wiley and Sons, 1931); J. H. Morecroft, *Electron Tubes and Their Application* (New York: J. Wiley and Sons, 1933).

154. William Kaufmann, letter to the author, August 2001.

155. SC160/X/5/1, FET to H. E. Carson, April 18, 1929.

156. SC160/X/5/1, H. E. Carson to FET, March 29, 1929.

157. SC160/X/5/1, FET to H. E. Carson, April 18, 1929.

158. SC160/X/5/1, J. S. Thompson to FET, April 27, 1929.

159. SC160/X/5/1, FET to J. S. Thompson, February 16, 1930.

160. SC160/X/5/1, R. M. Triest to FET, June 3, 1930; and FET to R. M. Triest, June 14, 1930.

161. SC160/X/5/1, J. S. Thompson to FET, April 24, 1931.

162. SC160/X/5/1, FET to J. S. Thompson, March 20, 1931.

163. F. E. Terman, *Radio Engineering* (New York: McGraw-Hill, 1932; 2nd ed. 1937; 3rd ed. 1947), ch. 3.

164. SC160/X/5/1, FET to J. S. Thompson, October 20, 1931; and J. S. Thompson to FET, July 26, 1932.

165. SC160/X/4/10, FET to C. G. Benjamin, October 27, 1932; C. G. Benjamin to FET, November 3 and 14, 1932; H. J. Kelly to FET, November 19, 1932; J. S. Thompson to FET, January 6, 1933; and C. G. Benjamin to FET, February 25, 1933.

166. SC160/X/4/10, Wiley advertising sheet, n.d. but 1933 or 1934.

167. SC160/X/4/10, J. S. Thompson to FET, May 22, 1934.

168. Terman saw his competition as R. R. Ramsey's *Experimental Radio*, Morecroft's *Experimental Radio Engineering*, H. A. Brown's *Radio Frequency Electrical Measurements*, E. B. Moullin's *The Theory and Practice of Radio Frequency Measurements*, and A. Hund's *High-Frequency Measurements*.

169. SC160/X/4/10, FET to C. G. Benjamin, April 5, 1935.

170. SC165/I/2/24, Stanford University, "Stanford on the Job in Electrical Engineering," February 1941, pamphlet, 12.

171. In the first edition of *Radio Engineering* (1932), former students Philip G. Caldwell, Nathaniel R. Morgan, Horace E. Overacker, William R. Triplett, Harry Engwicht, and D. A. Murray were acknowledged for drawing figures and checking manuscripts and proof. A. L. Cook, I. E. Wood, D. H. Ring, D. E. Chambers, E. H. Fisher, N. R. Morgan,

T. M. Googin, P. G. Caldwell, J. S. Low, and C. R. Skinner were cited for research on triode amplifiers, vacuum tube detectors, transformer characteristics, and audio frequency devices. Eight of these former students had already published articles on their own or with Terman in the *Proceedings* of the IRE or the *Transactions* of the AIEE, within a four-year period. Two of Terman's favorite students, Nathaniel Richard Morgan and John Stewart Low (both earned a BA in 1928) died within three weeks of each other in 1931. Low's parents established an electrical engineering scholarship at Stanford. Many more of Terman's graduate students published articles after 1932, which were noted in succeeding editions of his texts.

172. William W. Hansen and J. G. Beckerley, "Concerning New Methods of Calculating Radiation Resistance With or Without Ground," *Proceedings, IRE* 24 (December 1936): 1594.

173. SC4/8/101, manuscript dated March 25, 1937; also SC126/1, Folders 1–3; SC160/VIII/3/2, FET remarks to Palo Alto Rotary Club, May 27, 1963. Hansen always had several irons in the fire, so to speak. His further research and his deep friendship with Terman will be examined in succeeding chapters.

174. Norris E. Bradbury received his PhD in physics from Berkeley in 1932 and then did postdoctoral work at MIT for two years. He came to Stanford in 1935 and left for navy service from 1941–45, including serving at Los Alamos on the Manhattan Project beginning in 1944. Bradbury succeeded J. R. Oppenheimer as director of Los Alamos National Laboratory from 1945 until his retirement in 1970. Harold M. Agnew and Raemer E. Schreiber, "Norris E. Bradbury," *Bibliographical Memoirs, National Academy of Sciences* 75 (1998): 58–69.

175. Norris E. Bradbury, "Electron Attachment and Negative Ion Formation in Oxygen and Oxygen Mixtures," *Physical Review* 44 (December 1933): 883; Norris E. Bradbury, "Fundamental Mechanisms in the Ionosphere," *Journal of Applied Physics* 8, no. 11 (November 1937): 709–17; Norris E. Bradbury, "Ionization, Negative-Ion Formation, and Recombination in the Ionosphere," *Journal of Geophysical Research* 43 (March 1938): 55–66; Norris E. Bradbury and W. T. Sumerlin, "Night-Sky Light and Nocturnal E-layer Ionization," *Journal of Geophysical Research* 45, no. 1 (March 1940): 19–24.

176. It was common for Terman's students to minor in physics. John R. Woodyard and Robert R. Buss, among others, did so.

177. SC160/II/1/6, FET to C.-H. Chang, May 11, 1937.

178. F. E. Terman, "Resonant Lines in Radio Circuits," *Electrical Engineering* 53 (1934): 1046–53.

179. SC160/II/3/1, FET to N. Hall, December 28, 1937.

180. SC160/II/3/7, FET to J. K. Lewis, May 11, 1936.

181. SC160/II/3/13.

182. SC160/II/3/1, March 23, 1936.

183. SC160/II/3/2, letters between Hamilton M. Jeffers of Lick Observatory, and FET, 1935–39.

184. SC160/V/1/2, FET to R. D. Hickok, June 19, 1933.

185. For a brief biography of Bill Hewlett and Dave Packard, see David Packard, *The HP Way: How Bill Hewlett and I Built Our Company* (Palo Alto, CA: Harper Business, 1995).

186. At this time at Stanford, one still did not earn a bachelor's degree in electrical engineering, but a degree in engineering, even though the major course of study might have been in electrical engineering.

187. SC160/II/2/7, W. R. Hewlett to FET, n.d., but summer 1935.

188. SC160/II/2/8, W. R. Hewlett to FET, n.d., but early November 1935.

189. F. E. Terman, "Multirange Rectifier Instrument Having the Same Scale Graduation Field For All Ranges," *Proceedings, IRE* 23 (March 1935): 234–40.

190. SC160/II/2/8, FET to W. R. Hewlett, November 7, 1935.

191. SC160/II/4/3, FET to J. F. Maxwell, July 17, 1936.

192. Terman is slightly inaccurate here, but was nevertheless very proud of his student-athletes. Packard was an outstanding athlete. He was on the freshman basketball team and, as a sophomore, a center on the varsity basketball team (in a lean year for the team). He was on the track team in his freshman and junior years when world record holder (880 yards) Ben Eastman was captain and "Dink" Templeton was coach. He played football all four years. In his junior and senior years, Packard played second-string end but scored impressive touchdowns. In Packard's senior year, outstanding football players included guard Alf Brandin (later Stanford's business manager), Robert "Bobby" Grayson at fullback, Robert "Bones" Hamilton at right halfback, and James "Monk" Moscrip, ahead of Packard at left end. The Stanford team went 8–1–1 that year in the regular season, and lost to Columbia in the Rose Bowl on January 1, 1934. Bill Hewlett was keen on sports, although not as gifted (or physically as large) as Packard; he made the junior varsity football team in his junior year. Sources: *Stanford 1931 Quad*, vol. 38: 233; *Stanford 1932 Quad*, vol. 39: 248, 251; *Stanford 1933 Quad*, vol. 40: 227, 245, 265; *Stanford 1934 Quad*, vol. 41: 64, 73, 213. Packard, *HP Way*, 13.

193. General Electric conducted its own in-house technical education system, including a three-year Advanced Engineering Program. It was possible for a young bright employee with no college education to rise to a high position in the company and in the engineering profession, assisted by such education. A prominent example is Charles Concordia, member of the National Academy of Engineering and awarded the 1999 IEEE Medal of Honor; see Gadi Kaplan, "Charles Concordia," *IEEE Spectrum* 36, no. 6 (June 1999): 28–33.

194. SC160/II/3/11, FET to B. M. Oliver, July 2, 1937.

195. SC160/II/2/8, FET to W. R. Hewlett, November 7, 1935; SC160/II/4/3, FET to "Committee on Graduate Study," February 11, 1937.

196. SC160/II/3/11, FET to B. M. Oliver, June 2, 1938.

197. Hewlett-Packard Company, David Packard Collection, W. R. Hewlett to David Packard, May 21, 1938. Packard had been recently engaged to Lucile Salter.

198. F. E. Terman, R. R. Buss, W. R. Hewlett, and F. C. Cahill, "Some Applications of Negative Feedback with Particular Reference to Laboratory Equipment," *Proceedings, Institute of Radio Engineers* 27, no. 10 (October 1939): 649–55. Hewlett subsequently published a second well-received paper with Terman.

199. SC160/II/4/10, R. Sink to FET, July 27, 1938.

200. SC160/II/3/7, FET to C. V. Litton, June 29, 1938.

201. SC160/XIII/1/23, FET to H. Hoover Jr., October 5, 1932.

202. SC160/II/2/13, FET to R. L. Wilbur, July 5, 1939.

203. Packard, *HP Way*, 40–45.

204. SC160/II/1/8, FET to G. W. Dunlap, January 3, 1940. Robert Sink thus was probably the first HP employee, after Bill Hewlett, David Packard, and Lucile Packard.

205. Frances V. Rummell and Adelaide Paine, "He Searches For 'Steeples' of Talent," *Reader's Digest* (December 1962).

206. SC165/I/9/5, H. F. Elliott to FET, January 31, 1941.

207. *Terman Interview*, 199–200; Packard, *HP Way*, 52.

208. SC160/XIII/1/23, H. Hoover Jr. to FET, August 7, 1921; Hoover Jr. Correspondence with FET, various letters 1927–29 about their interest in ham radio and station 6XH; SC160/XI/1/9, FET to H. W. Dickow, August 25, 1967.

209. SC160/II/4/3, FET to J. F. Maxwell, July 17, 1936.

210. *Terman Interview*, 34–35. The interviewer confuses Stanford amateur radio station, 6XH, later licensed as W6YX, with the Stanford student broadcast station KSU (1947–49), later KZSU (1949–present). KSU/KZSU was first carrier current AM (1947–64) and then FM (1964–present). C. S. Gillmor, "Stanford Sadie and the Early Years of KZSU Radio Broadcasting," *Sandstone & Tile* 23, no. 1 (winter 1999): 11–20.

211. SC160/X/4/10, FET to C. G. Benjamin, April 5, 1935.

212. SC160/II/3/4, B. M. Oliver to FET, May 31, 1938.

213. Author interview with Oswald G. Villard Jr., 1998.

214. Author interviews with Oswald G. Villard Jr., 1998, and with Robert A. Helliwell, 1998.

CHAPTER THREE. BUILDING RADIO AND ELECTRONICS

1. Among his predecessors in this were Elihu Thomson, George Westinghouse, Alexander Graham Bell, Nikola Tesla, Michael I. Pupin, and Robert A. Millikan.

2. SC165/I/2/22, typewritten press release, May 29, 1931.

3. SC64B/81/2, R. E. Swain to R. L. Wilbur, December 8, 1930.

4. SC64B/81/2, R. E. Swain to R. L. Wilbur, April 13, 1931.

5. SC64B/81/2, R. E. Wilbur to R. E. Swain, April 20, 1931.

6. SC165/I/6/21, T. J. Hoover to R. L. Wilbur, April 17, 1925.

7. SC64A/123/2, T. J. Hoover to R. E. Swain, April 22, 1931.

8. SC64B/81/3, R. E. Swain to R. L. Wilbur, April 30, 1931. Edward Bowles of MIT, who knew Guillemin well during the 1920s and 1930s, later said he was a brilliant man and a wonderful teacher. Edward Bowles interviews by Arthur Norberg, Bancroft Library.

9. SC165/I/2/22, H. J. Ryan to T. J. Hoover, May 5, 1931.

10. Ibid.

11. This section utilizes SC64A/123/2, several documents and memos from T. J. Hoover, H. J. Ryan, and the Executive Committee, School of Engineering, April 21 to May 12, 1931.

12. SC64B/81/3, R. E. Swain to R. L. Wilbur, May 1, 1931.

13. SC64B/81/2, R. L. Wilbur to R. E. Swain, May 4, 1931.

14. SC64A/123/2, T. J. Hoover to R. E. Swain, May 12, 1931. Hoover's Executive Committee was the dean and the heads of the engineering departments plus the Military Science and Tactics Department: himself (as dean, and head of mining), Harris Ryan (electrical engineering), J. C. Lounsbury Fish (chemical engineering), Arthur B. Domonoske (mechanical engineering), and Donald C. Cubbison (military science).

15. SC64A/123/2, R. E. Swain to R. L. Wilbur, May 12, 1931; SC64B/81/3, R. E. Swain to R. L. Wilbur, May 14, 1931.

16. *Terman Interview*, 3. SC64B/81/3, R. E. Swain to F. W. Peek Jr., June 11, 1931.

17. SC64A/123/1, FET to R. E. Swain, July 14, 1931.

18. SC64A/123/2, H. J. Ryan to T. J. Hoover, July 10, 1931.

19. SC64A/123/2, H. J. Ryan to T. J. Hoover, August 11, 1931.

20. SC64A/123/2, T. J. Hoover to R. E. Swain, July 31, 1931.

21. SC64B/81/3, R. E. Swain to R. L. Wilbur, October 2, 1931.
22. SC64B/81/3, R. E. Swain to R. L. Wilbur, January 15, 1932.
23. SC64B/81/4, R. E. Swain to R. L. Wilbur, May 17, 1932.
24. SC64B/81/3, Results of Second Ballot for Elections, May 9, 1932.
25. SC64B/81/3, R. L. Wilbur to R. E. Swain, May 24, 1932.
26. SC160/XI/1/14, C. F. Elwell, "Autobiography" (manuscript), 1958.
27. Early in his career, Fred Terman hired Mrs. Burnice Bourquin as a part-time secretary to type his papers and book manuscripts. In the early 1930s, she became department secretary, but the department could only afford to pay her half-time. Author interview with Burnice Bourquin, 1998. SCM2, Burnice Bourquin manuscript, 1982.
28. Author interview with Robert R. Buss, 1998.
29. SC160/VIII/3/6, FET Convocation Speech, May 31, 1965.
30. Davis and Nilan, *Stanford Album*, 217–18, 224.
31. SC160/XIII/1/30, T. J. Hoover to R. L. Wilbur, January 10, 1936.
32. Morris (BA '11, Stanford) moved up through the ranks to become chief engineer and general manager of the Pasadena Water Department. He was the designer and builder of the Morris Dam (1934).
33. SC160/II/3/8, T. McLean to FET, November 26, 1937.
34. SC64A/181/13, FET to S. B. Morris, January 15, 1937; SC165/I/9/5, S. B. Morris to R. L. Wilbur, February 11, 1939.
35. SC64A/181/13, FET to S. B. Morris, January 15, 1937. Copy to R. L. Wilbur. SC64A/181/13, FET to H. Diederichs, March 16, 1937. Copy to R. L. Wilbur.
36. SC160/II/3/1, S. C. Hollister to FET, March 22 and May 5, 1938; and FET to S. C. Hollister, April 27 and [May] 1938.
37. SC64A/181/13, R. L. Wilbur to FET, May 21, 1937.
38. SC160/XIII/1/24, General C. McK. Saltzman to FET, February 1, 1930; R. Beach to FET, April 3, 1930; FET to R. Beach, March 22, 1930; J. M. Bryant to FET May 13, 1930; and FET to J. M. Bryant, June 18, 1930. SC160/XIII/1/30, H. J. Ryan, draft of Report to President Wilbur for Budget Recommendations for 1930–31.
39. SC160/II/1/3, FET to S. B. Morris, April 10, 1937.
40. As an example, SC160/II/4/11, FET to E. L. Chaffee of Harvard, January 14, 1937.
41. SC160/II/1/3, several letters of recommendation for K. Spangenberg.
42. SC64A/181/13, S. B. Morris to R. L. Wilbur, April 13, 1937; and R. L. Wilbur to K. Spangenberg, April 23, 1937.
43. SC165/I/2/24, S. B. Morris to FET, typescript copy intended for *Stanford Illustrated Review*, January 11, 1939.
44. SC165/I/2/24, S. B. Morris to R. L. Wilbur, December 30, 1941.
45. SC165/I/9/5, FET to S. B. Morris, September 10, 1941.
46. Bartholomew, Brinegar, and Nilan, *Chronology*, 33.
47. *Terman Interview*, 22–23.
48. SC160/II/3/9, FET to S. B. Morris, April 29, and May 10, 12, and 13, 1937; and S. B. Morris to FET, May 28, 1937.
49. SC160/II/3/9, Terman report, n.d. but December 1937; and S. B. Morris to P. H. Davis, December 23, 1937.
50. SC160/II/3/1, FET to S. C. Hollister, March 17 and April 27, 1938.
51. SC160/II/3/9, P. H. Davis to R. E. Swain, November 16, 1938.
52. *Terman Interview*, 25.
53. SC64A/181/13, R. L. Wilbur to I. M. Redeker, October 8, 1936.

54. SC160/II/1/3, FET to H. E. True, secretary to President Wilbur, September 26, 1938.

55. SC64A/Old Box 101, FET to H. E. True, September 26, 1938.

56. *Terman Interview*, 23–26. John Woodyard later became a professor at Berkeley. Two Berkeley undergraduates, Edward Ginzton and Joseph Pettit, made special contributions to Stanford: Ginzton became a professor of applied physics and electrical engineering at Stanford, director of the Hansen Labs, and first director of the Stanford Linear Accelerator Project as well as chairman of Varian Associates. Pettit, who worked directly with Terman in radio direction finding for his PhD dissertation, would cap a career on the Stanford faculty as dean of engineering at Stanford and later served as president of Georgia Tech. David Packard's contributions to Stanford are legendary.

57. SC160/II/3/1, FET to E. R. Hilgard, August 17, 1938.

58. SC160/II/4/17, FET to R. L. Wilbur, December 16, 1940.

59. SC160/II/9/6, n.d. sheets, Folder "Misc. Research and Studies 1937–47."

60. W. W. Hansen and J. R. Woodyard, 1938; W. W. Hansen and L. M. Hollingsworth, 1939. Terman and Hansen secured a patent for work related to this.

61. Author interview with O. G. Villard Jr., 1999.

62. SC160/II/1/3, handwritten tables, n.d., but 1939.

63. SC165/I/2/24, copy of special magazine *Stanford on the Job in Electrical Engineering*, published by Stanford University, February 1941. A typewritten document based on statistics in the Stanford *Register* books differs slightly, giving thirty-four total graduate electrical engineering students in 1939–40 and forty-one students in 1940–41. SC165/I/3/3, "Engineering Registration at Stanford 1925–1945."

64. SC160/II/1/3, FET to S. B. Morris, September 14, 1939.

65. SC160/II/1/3, S. B. Morris to R. L. Wilbur, September 18, 1939.

66. SC126/1/6, W. W. Hansen to D. L. Webster, December 17, 1937; SC126/3/24, W. W. Hansen to T. C. McFarland, April 25, 1947; SC126/2/17, W. W. Hansen to C. V. Taylor, October 24, 1940.

67. SC126/1/6, W. W. Hansen to C. V. Taylor, October 24, 1940.

68. SC165/I/6/51, materials on "Committee on Research," 1925–41.

69. SC126/2/15, W. W. Hansen to D. L. Webster, January 18, 1940.

70. SC126/4/35, "Statement of William W. Hansen," n.d., but after 1939. Edward L. Ginzton, "The $100 Idea," *IEEE Spectrum* 12, no. 2 (February 1975): 30–39, dates the statement as from 1949. David Webster wrote comments on the pages of Hansen's text in 1949.

71. SC160/II/2/10, FET to M. M. Boring, December 1, 1937.

72. Ginzton, "$100 Idea," 69.

73. SC160/II/3/1, H. Hoover Jr. to FET, May 18, 1937; and FET to H. Hoover Jr., May 24, 1937.

74. SC160/II/3/9, S. B. Morris to W. W. Wetzel, September 1, 1938.

75. SC160/II/1/3, sheets in FET's handwriting, n.d., but fall 1939.

76. SC160/II/4/3, FET to M. M. Boring, January 29, 1934.

77. SC160/II/4/10, E. Schoenfeld to FET, November 19, 1937.

78. SC160/II/3/8, FET to T. H. Morgan, March 23, 1938.

79. SC160/II/2/10, FET to E. L. Ginzton, April 28 and May 6, 1937; and E. L. Ginzton to FET, May 6, 1937.

80. *Transactions, AIEE*, 56 (October 1937): 1320.

81. SC160/II/2/2, FET to R. A. Deller, April 27, 1939.

82. SC160/II/2, Folders 3 and 4, for years 1931–33.
83. SC165/I/3/6, S. B. Morris to R. L. Wilbur, October 8, 1936.
84. SC165/I/3/6, T. J. Hoover to C. L. Wilson (ECPD) (draft), June 6, 1936.
85. SC165/I/3/7, G. M. Butler to S. B. Morris, May 7, 1937.
86. SC165/I/3/7, memo of Dean S. B. Morris, June 8, 1937.
87. SC160/II/3/9, W. B. Kindy and FET to S. B. Morris, April 15 and 26, 1937.
88. Ibid.
89. SC165/I/3/7, A. B. Parsons to R. L. Wilbur, October 6, 1937; and G. M. Butler to S. B. Morris, November 8, 1937; SC160/II/2/3, G. M. Butler to S. B. Morris, April 18, 1940.
90. SC165/I/3/7, K. T. Compton to R. L. Wilbur, December 4, 1937.
91. SC165/I/2/24, W. McDuffie to FET, August 5, 1938.
92. SC160/II/2/3, G. M. Butler to S. B. Morris, April 15 and 29, 1940.
93. SC165/I/3/8, "Summary of Recommended Electrical Engineering Curriculum," n.s., n.d., but FET to S. B. Morris, January 1940.
94. SC160/II/2/3, FET to S. B. Morris, October 22, 1940.
95. SC165/I/3/8, A. A. Potter to B. M. Woods, March 5, 1940.
96. SC165/I/3/8, S. B. Morris to R. L. Wilbur, March 6, 1940.
97. SC165/I/3/9, FET to C. L. Wilson (ECPD), December 9, 1948.
98. SC165/I/3/9, A. I. Levorsen to C. L. Wilson, January 14, 1949.
99. SC165/I/3/9, contains the 1949 correspondence involving Stanford and ECPD.
100. SC160/II/4/17, R. L. Wilbur to [Faculty] Members of Academic Council, November 5, 1937.
101. SC160/II, Boxes 10–12, "ITT Invention Disclosures, 1936–42."
102. SC38/18, Folder "President's Office–Business Office," D. L. Webster to R. L. Wilbur, December 7, 1937.
103. Henry E. Lowood, "History of Science and Engineering at Stanford" (unpublished paper, courtesy of Roxanne Nilan, 1989).
104. SC160/II/4/17, R. L. Wilbur to FET, December 15, 1937.
105. SC160/II/1/4, FET to E. L. Bowles, January 13 and 28, 1938.
106. Stanford archives, 1103. Stanford Business Manager's Reports in Annual Report of the President of Stanford University. Terman was replaced on the committee by Ed Ginzton. On this and the establishment of four area panels, see 1103/4. Annual Report for 1955–56.
107. Lowood, "History of Science."
108. Stanford Guide Memo: 75, June 6, 1962, "Patent Policy for Sponsored Research"; Guide Memo: 75, December 15, 1970, "Patents"; Niels J. Riemers to Patricia J. Black, April 23, 1970. Documents courtesy of Katherine Ku, director, Stanford Office of Technology Licensing.
109. Niels J. Riemers to author, July 23, 2002.
110. SC64A/181/13, FET to R. L. Wilbur, October 30, 1936.
111. SC165/I/6/51, FET to D. L. Webster, October 13, 1937.
112. Carnegie Institution of Washington, *Year Book No. 38* (1939): 87–88.
113. *Terman Interview*, 36–37.
114. Packard, *HP Way*, 34.
115. SC165/I/6/23, S. B. Morris to R. L. Wilbur, January 18, 1938.
116. Gillmor, "Stanford Sadie and the Early Years of KZSU Radio Broadcasting."
117. SC64A, Old Box 101, Folder "Electrical Engineering," FET to J. S. Thompson; J. S. Thompson to FET, January 13 and 23, 1939; and A. J. Pahl to FET, February 1, 1939.

118. SC165/I/5/35, H. H. Skilling to S. B. Morris, November 22, 1938; FET to S. B. Morris, November 29, 1938; S. B. Morris to FET, December 6, 1938; S. B. Morris to P. M. Downing, July 11, 1939; memo of Dean S. B. Morris, October 30, 1941; S. B. Morris to R. L. Wilbur, November 26, 1941; and R. L. Wilbur to FET, November 27, 1941.

119. See Peter Galison, Bruce Hevly, and Rebecca Lowen, "Controlling the Monster: Stanford and the Growth of Physics Research, 1935–1962," in *Big Science: The Growth of Large-Scale Research*, ed. P. Galison and B. Hevly), 46–77 (Palo Alto, CA: Stanford University Press, 1992).

120. Felix Bloch, "William Webster Hansen," *Biographical Memoirs, National Academy of Sciences* 27 (1952): 121–37; Charles Süsskind, "William Webster Hansen," *Dictionary of Scientific Biography*, ed. Charles C. Gillispie, vol. 6 (1972): 104–5.

121. Paul Kirkpatrick, "David Locke Webster," *Biographical Memoirs, National Academy of Sciences* 53 (1982): 121–37; Bruce Hevly, "David Locke Webster," *Dictionary of Scientific Biography*, ed. Frederic L. Holmes, 18, supp. 2 (1990): 984–86.

122. SC126/4/35, "Statement of William W. Hansen," n.d.

123. William W. Hansen and J. G. Beckerley, "Radiation from an Antenna over a Plane Earth of Arbitrary Characteristics," *Journal of Applied Physics* 7 (1936): 220; William W. Hansen and J. G. Beckerley, "Concerning New Methods of Calculating Radiation Resistance, Either with or without Ground," *Proceedings, Institute of Radio Engineers* 24 (1936): 1594.

124. William W. Hansen and J. R. Woodyard, "A New Principle in Directional Antenna Design," *Proceedings, Institute of Radio Engineers* 26, no. 3 (March 1938): 333–45.

125. SC126/1/8, W. W. Hansen to G. H. Gallineau, June 7, 1938.

126. SC126/1/5, W. W. Hansen to Comptroller H. Jackson, May 24, 1937; SC126/4/35, "Statement of William W. Hansen," n.d.

127. SC126/1/3. W. W. Hansen to N. S. Frohman, October 30, 1936.

128. SC126/1/4, memo of W. W. Hansen, January 22, 1937.

129. M508, Russell H. Varian Papers, Box 1.

130. Dorothy Varian, *The Inventor and the Pilot* (Palo Alto, CA: Pacific Books, 1983), 152–53, 180–81.

131. Ibid., 180–87.

132. Edward L. Ginzton, *Times to Remember: The Life of Edward L. Ginzton* (Berkeley, CA: Blackberry Creek Press, 1995), 74.

133. M508, Box 1, F. E. Terman typescript remarks, "Events Associated With the Invention of the Klystron Tube," n.d., but possibly in 1959, as memorial for R. H. Varian.

134. Ginzton, *Times to Remember*, 30–39.

135. SC126/1/5, W. W. Hansen to G. Duvall, October 13, 1937.

136. SC126/1/6, H. Willis (Sperry) to J. H. Jackson, December 9, 1937.

137. SC165/I/8/14, agreement, signed February 19, 1938. Sperry was the least financially healthy of the lot, having obtained much of its earnings by the mid-1930s from selling an obsolete gun-ranging device to the Soviet government.

138. SC165/I/8/14, E. E. Agreement with ISEC, signed December 13, 1938.

139. John R. Woodyard interviews by Arthur L. Norberg, 1980, the Bancroft Library, 39.

140. SC126/1, Folders 12–14.

141. Author interview with Walter G. Vincenti, 1999.

142. Ginzton, *Times to Remember*, 38.

143. SC126/1/10, D. L. Webster to W. W. Hansen, January 19, 1939; *Boston Evening Herald*, February 28, 1939.

144. SC126/1/12, D. L. Webster to W. W. Hansen, July 10, 1939; W. W. Hansen to D. L. Webster, July 12, 1939; and R. H. Varian to W. W. Hansen, n.d., but July 1939.

145. *Terman Interview*, 39–40.

146. Derek J. de Solla Price, *Little Science, Big Science, . . . and Beyond* (New York: Columbia University Press, 1986).

147. SC126/1, Folder 8, W. W. Hansen to L. M. Applegate, June 2, 1938; and Folder 9, November 8 and December 13, 1938.

148. SC131D/1, Folder "Klystron Job Upstairs," D. L. Webster, typed memo of October 13, 1939.

149. SC131D/1, Folder "1938 and 1939," outline of D. L. Webster talk to Palo Alto Junior Chamber of Commerce, September 25, 1939.

150. SC126/1/7, D. L. Webster to J. H. Jackson, March 12, 1938.

151. SC131D/1, Folder "Klystron Job Upstairs," memo of D. L. Webster, April 27, 1938.

152. W. W. Hansen, as quoted in Ginzton, *Times to Remember*, 39.

153. SC131D/1, Folder "DLW 1939–42," memos of D. L. Webster, November 22 and December 15, 1939; and D. L. Webster to R. L. Wilbur, December 15, 1939.

154. SC131D/1, Folder "Klystron Job Upstairs," Sperry officials to D. L. Webster, February 27 and June 20, 1940; and D. L. Webster to Sperry, July 2, 1940.

155. *Terman Interview*, 37–38.

156. Varian, *Inventor and Pilot*, 213.

157. SC126/1/12, I. I. Rabi to W. W. Hansen, June 17, 1939; and P. M. Morse to W. W. Hansen, May 29, 1939.

158. SC126/12/17, P. H. Davis to W. W. Hansen, October 11, 1940.

159. In a related press interview, Terman noted that klystrons of ten centimeters wavelength were in production as of October 1940. SC131D/1, Folder "Klystron Job Upstairs," *Palo Alto Times*, October 20, 1940; unidentified San Francisco paper, October 20, 1940; invitations from Stanford Associates.

160. *Terman Interview*, 40.

161. SC126/1/9, W. W. Hansen to J. H. Jackson, September 8, 1938.

162. SC126/2/15, W. W. Hansen to H. H. Willis, February 20, 1940.

163. Ginzton, *Times to Remember*, 67.

164. Ibid., 67–68.

165. SC131D/1, Folder "Klystron Job Upstairs," *San Francisco Chronicle*, October 25, 1940.

166. Ginzton, *Times to Remember*, 77.

167. Materials concerning the history of the AIEE and the IRE in this section benefit from A. Michel McMahon, *The Making of a Profession: A Century of Electrical Engineering in America* (New York: IEEE Press, 1984).

168. McMahon, *Making of a Profession*, ch. 4.

169. Ibid., 175–77. Thorstein Veblen, *The Instinct of Workmanship, and the State of the Industrial Arts* (1918; rpt., New York: Viking Press, 1946).

170. SC160/IV/9/18, FET to W. F. Grimes; and FET to C. B. Jolliffe, September 16, 1936.

171. SC160/IV/10/2.

172. McMahon, *Making of a Profession*, 190–93.

173. SC160/IV/9/18, A. L. Albert to FET, October 16, 1936; and W. F. Grimes to FET, October 20, 1936.

174. William W. Hansen, "A Type of Electrical Resonator," *Journal of Applied Physics* 9 (October 1938): 654–63.
175. SC160/IV/8/1, list of IRE San Francisco section meetings, 1934–35.
176. SC160/IV/8/2, FET to W. W. Lindsay Jr., March 10, 1937.
177. SC160/IV/8/3, A. L. Albert to FET, March 22, 1939, for example.
178. SC160/IV/8/2, FET to C. M. Jansky, December 31, 1937, for example.
179. SC160/IV/8/2, L. C. F. Horle to FET, January 14, 1938.
180. SC160/IV/8/2, FET to A. F. Murray, January 21, 1938.
181. SC160/IV/8/2, W. N. Eldred to H. P. Westman, September 28, 1938.
182. SC160/IV/10/5, FET to E. W. Engstrom, January 19, 1939.
183. SC160/IV/12/6.
184. Ibid.
185. SC160/IV/8/2, W. W. Lindsay to FET, October 12, 1938; S. W. Gilfillan to H. P. Westman, September 29, 1938; and FET to H. P. Westman, October 14, 1938.
186. SC160/IV/11/13, FET to H. P. Westman, December 28, 1938.
187. SC160/IV/8/3, H. P. Westman to FET, November 8, 1939.
188. SC160/IV/11/6, R. A. Heising to FET, January 8, 1940.
189. SC160/IV/8/3, FET to H. P. Westman, January 19, 1940.
190. SC160/IV/11/7, minutes of IRE Board of Directors, November 5, 1941.
191. SC160/IV/13/13, FET to H. P. Westman, September 8 and 23, 1938.
192. SC160/IV/8/4, L. J. Black to FET, March 25, 1941.
193. McMahon, *Making of a Profession*, 171–72.
194. SC160/IV/12/5, FET to M. Eastham, April 1, 1940.
195. SC160/IV/12/5, M. Eastham to FET, April 10, 1940.
196. SC160/IV/12/5, H. P. Westman to FET, April 8, 1940.
197. SC160/IV/8/4, J. R. Martin to FET, March 21, 1941.
198. SC160/IV/8/4, H. M. Pratt to FET, October 22, 1942.
199. SC160/IV/14/13, H. M. Turner to FET, December 28, 1940.
200. SC160/IV/12/5, H. M. Pratt to FET, April 10, 1940.
201. SC160/IV/12/5, FET to H. M. Pratt, April 15, 1940; and W. N. Eldred to H. M. Pratt, April 19, 1940.
202. SC160/IV/12/5, V. M. Graham to FET, August 16, 1940.
203. SC160/IV/12/5, H. M. Pratt to FET, August 21, 1940.
204. SC160/IV/11/10, IRE Election Circular and Ballot, August 15, 1940.
205. SC160/IV/14/13, H. P. Westman to IRE Board of Directors, vote tally sheet, October 29, 1940.
206. SC160/IV/14/10, FET to W. N. Eldred, January 4, 1941.
207. SC160/IV/8/4, FET to W. M. Smith, September 10, 1941; H. J. Reich to FET, October 6, 1941; and FET to A. N. Goldsmith, October 7, 1941.
208. F. E. Terman, R. R. Buss, W. R. Hewlett, and F. Cahill, "Some Applications of Negative Feedback with Particular Reference to Laboratory Equipment," *Proceedings, Institute of Radio Engineers* 27, no. 10 (October 1939): 649–55.
209. Sc160/IV/14/12, FET to H. M. Pratt, May 2, 1941.
210. SC160/IV/11/7.
211. SC160/IV/11/7, minutes of IRE Board of Directors, March 7, 1941.
212. SC160/IV/13/10.
213. SC160/IV/11/7, memo to IRE Board Members, R. A. Heising, October 1, 1941.
214. SC160/IV/11/8, R. A. Heising report to IRE Board of Directors, January 6, 1942.

215. SC160/IV/9/7, IRE Annual Financial Reports.

216. SC160/IV/11/7, minutes of IRE Board of Directors, March 18 and April 2, 1941.

217. SC160/IV/8/4, FET to A. F. Van Dyck, October 8, 1941.

218. SC160/IV/14/12, FET to H. M. Pratt, May 2, 1941.

219. SC160/IV/14/13, FET memo, May 5, 1980.

220. SC160/IV/8/5, H. M. Pratt to FET, October 22, 1941; SC160/IV/11/7, FET to IRE Board Members, October 3, 1941.

221. SC160/IV/8/4, FET to A. N. Goldsmith, October 11, 1941.

222. SC160/IV/8/5, H. M. Pratt to FET, June 19, 1942; SC160/IV/14/12, H. M. Pratt to FET, August 14, 1941.

223. SC160/IV/8/5, H. M. Pratt to FET, December 3, 1942.

224. SC160/IV/11/8 and 12/1, numerous documents concerning RTPB and Baker.

225. SC160/IV/8/9, FET to B. E. Shackelford, August 8, 1946.

226. SC160/IV/11/7, minutes of IRE Board of Directors, text of FET speech, June 24, 1941.

227. SC160/IV/14/13, "Report of Retiring President Frederick Emmons Terman," January 1942. Also summarized in F. E. Terman, "The Institute Moves Ahead in 1941," *Proceedings, Institute of Radio Engineers* 29, no. 12 (December 1941): 656–57.

228. SC160/IV/8/5, A. N. Goldsmith to FET, March 4, 1942.

229. SC38/18, Folder "President's Office–Business Office," LMT to R. L. Wilbur, May 24, 1939.

230. SC38/18, Folder "Faculty Committee on Selection of a President 1939–42," L. W. Cutler to LMT, July 24, 1939.

231. SC64A, Old Box 153/4, L. W. Cutler to J. P. Mitchell, August 17, 1939.

232. SC64A, Old Box 153/4, J. P. Mitchell to H. Hoover Jr., August 22, 1939; see also SC38/18, Folder "Faculty Committee on Selection of a President 1939–42."

233. SC64A, Old Box 152/1, E. B. Wilson to LMT, November 8, 1939.

234. SC64A, Old Box 153/3.

235. SC64A, Old Box 152/4.

236. SC64A, Old Box 153/1.

237. SC38/18, Folder "Faculty Committee on Selection of a President 1939–42," LMT to C. V. Taylor, May 7, 1941.

238. SC64A, Old Box 152/1.

239. SC64A, Old Box 153/4, J. P. Mitchell to H. Hoover Jr., August 20, 1940.

240. SC126/2/17, W. W. Hansen to H. Hoover Jr., October 21, 1940; and W. W. Hansen to C. V. Taylor, October 24, 1940.

241. SC151/39/3, F. Bloch to C. V. Taylor, October 23, 1940; C. V. Litton to C. V. Taylor, October 28, 1940; and H. F. Elliott to Judge Sloss, March 10, 1941. A year later D. L. Webster sent a disparaging letter about Terman to C. V. Taylor, dated November 8, 1941.

242. SC38/18, Folder "Faculty Committee on Selection of a President 1939–42," J. P. Mitchell to LMT; and LMT to J. P. Mitchell, November 7, 1940.

243. SC151/39/3, L. W. Cutler to I. S. Lillick, April 1, 1941; and I. S. Lillick to L. W. Cutler, April 5, 1941.

244. SC64B/83, Folder, FET and R. L. Wilbur to H. Hoover Jr., April 16, 1941.

245. SC38/18, Folder "Faculty Committee on Selection of a President 1939–42," LMT to C. V. Taylor, September 29, 1941; and LMT to G. S. Ford, March 18, 1941.

246. Frank A. Medeiros, "The Sterling Years at Stanford: A Study in the Dynamics of

Institutional Change" (unpublished PhD dissertation, Stanford University, 1979); Edwin Kiester Jr., *Donald Tresidder: Stanford's Overlooked Treasure* (Stanford, CA: Stanford Historical Society, 1992).

247. Minton, *Lewis M. Terman*, 201–4; *Stanford Daily*, October 2, 1941.

248. *New York Times*, October 3, 1941, 5; LMT to his colleagues, September 24, 1941, "Stanford University—HH Poll of Faculty," in Post Presidential subject file, Herbert Hoover Papers, Hoover Institution Archives; and FET "Memorandum, February 22, 1980," all cited by George Nash, *Herbert Hoover and Stanford University* (Stanford, CA: Hoover Institution Press, 1988), 115–17. (Nash discusses the implications of this debate with Stanford's faculty in detail.) See also, Minton, *Lewis M. Terman*, 204.

249. See Zachary, *Endless Frontier*, chs. 5–6.

250. SC165/I/5/25, W. L. Everitt to FET, October 11, 1940; and FET to W. L. Everitt, October 30, 1940.

251. SC165/I/9/5, FET to S. B. Morris, February 1, 1941. Pettit and Terman eventually shared a patent for a similar device.

252. SC165/I/9/5, S. B. Morris to FET, March 12, 1941.

253. SC165/I/5/9, FET to S. B. Morris, n.d., but ca. March 16, 1941.

254. SC165/I/9/5, S. B. Morris to FET, December 31, 1940.

255. SC165/I/8/25, S. B. Morris to C. Derleth Jr. (Berkeley), May 2, 1941.

256. SC165/I/3/21, S. B. Morris Announcement to Engineering Students, December 11, 1941.

CHAPTER FOUR. THE RADIO WAR

1. Wilbur, *Memoirs*, 573–74; Templeton Peck, "Paul C. Edwards: from Newsman to Trustees' President," *Sandstone & Tile* 11, no. 1 (fall 1986): 2–11, provides a useful sketch of the impact of the Stanford Associates and Edwards.

2. SC64B/83, Folder "F. E. Terman," R. L. Wilbur to H. Hoover Jr., April 16, 1941.

3. SC38/18, Folder "Pick of the Crop Committee."

4. SC160/XIII/1/19, program and guest list for Tresidder meetings.

5. Alvin Eurich, Stanford University Oral History Project interview, 1987, as quoted by Edwin Kiester, *Tresidder*, 38–39.

6. SC160/XIII/1/19, newspaper clipping announcing Terman's election as president of the IRE, November 7, 1940.

7. Zachary, *Endless Frontier*.

8. Kiester, *Tresidder*, 41–42.

9. UA V 728.95.1, Box 9, Folder "RRL Jamming-Alvarez," Harvard University Archives.

10. "Harvard and Radio Countermeasures," *Harvard Alumni Bulletin* 48, no. 6 (December 8, 1945).

11. "Institute News and Radio Notes," *Proceedings, Institute of Radio Engineers* (December 1941): 656.

12. SC160/IV/11/7, minutes of IRE Board of Directors, 1941.

13. SC160/XII/3, FET to SWT, September 11 and November 12, 1941.

14. Henry E. Guerlac, *Radar in World War II* (New York: Tomash Publishers/American Institute of Physics, 1987), 1:5.

15. De Forest, "Recent Developments"; Fuller, "Continuous Waves."

16. E. V. Appleton and M. A. F. Barnett, "Local Reflections of Wireless Waves from the Upper Atmosphere," *Nature* 115 (1925): 333–34.

17. G. Breit and M. A. Tuve, "A Radio Method for Estimating the Height of the Conducting Layer," *Nature* 116 (1925): 357.

18. Guerlac, *Radar in World War II*, 1:53.

19. Louis Brown, *A Radar History of World War II: Technical and Military Imperatives* (Bristol, Eng.: Institute of Physics Publishers, 1999).

20. C. S. Gillmor, "Wilhelm Altar, Edward Appleton, and the Magneto-Ionic Theory," 395–440.

21. Watt quoted in Guerlac, *Radar in World War II*, 1:129.

22. B. T. Neale, "CH—the First Operational Radar," in *Radar Development to 1945*, ed. Russell Burns, 132–50 (London: Peter Peregrinus Ltd., 1988).

23. Allan A. Needell, *Science, Cold War and the American State: Lloyd V. Berkner and the Balance of Professional Ideals* (Amsterdam: Harwood Academic Publishers, 2000).

24. C. S. Gillmor, "Lloyd Viel Berkner," in *Dictionary of Scientific Biography*, ed. Charles C. Gillispie, 17: 73–75 (New York: Charles Scribner's Sons, 1990).

25. SC165/I/6/51, FET to D. L. Webster, October 13, 1937.

26. SC165/I/2/21, FET to Comptroller A. E. Roth, August 5, 1929.

27. UA V 728.95.1, Box 20, FET to O. G. Villard Jr., March 16, 1942, Harvard University Archives.

28. Interservice Radio Propagation Laboratory (1944).

29. Arthur E. Thiessen, IRE Retiring Presidential Speech, in *History of the General Radio Company* (West Concord, MA: General Radio Company, 1965).

30. FET to A. Price, November 3, 1980, Association of Old Crows.

31. SC160/XII/3/2, manuscript of FET telegram, December 29, 1941; SC126/2/20, January 5, 1942; and W. W. Hansen telegram, January 5, 1942.

32. Luis Alvarez, "Alfred Lee Loomis, 1887–1975," *Biographical Memoirs, National Academy of Science* 51 (1980): 324. For a colorful if somewhat exaggerated account of Loomis's contributions, see also Jennet Conant, *Tuxedo Park: A Wall Street Tycoon and the Secret Palace of Science That Changed the Course of World War II* (New York: Simon and Schuster, 2002).

33. SC126/2, Folders 11–20. Bryant et al., *Rad Lab: Oral Histories* (for example, see interviews with Kenneth T. Bainbridge, Robert L. Kyhl, Ernest C. Pollard, Robert V. Pound, and Norman F. Ramsey).

34. SC165/I/9/5, draft of telegram, FET to S. M. Morris, January 5, 1942.

35. SC160/I/4/1, S. M. Morris to FET, January 12, 1942.

36. SC160/I/4/2, FET notes "Jan. 15."

37. SC160/I/4/2, K. T. Compton to FET, February 16, 1942. Terman's official appointment letter from Vannevar Bush, head of OSRD, was dated March 26, 1942.

38. Document reproduced in Alfred Price, *The History of U.S. Electronic Warfare*, Volume 1: *The Years of Innovation—Beginnings to 1946* (Alexandria, VA: Association of Old Crows, 1984), 269.

39. Luis Alvarez to O. G. Villard Jr., October 11, 1980, Association of Old Crows.

40. *Terman Interview*, 53.

41. SC160/IV/14/13, FET, May 5, 1980.

42. SC160/IV/14/13, FET, IRE Retiring Presidential Speech, January 1942.

43. *Terman Interview*, 55.

44. SC160/II/3/14, D. B. Sinclair to FET, April 8, 1934.

45. SC160/XII/3/6, SWT to FET, January 5 and 11, 1942; and FET to SWT, telegram, January 5, 1942.

46. UA V 728.95.1, Box 2, Folder, "Army Signal Corps: General" W. R. Hewlett to FET, April 1, 1942, Harvard University Archives; author's interview with Louise Hewlett "Hewie" Nixon, sister of William R. Hewlett, 2000.

47. *Terman Interview*, 52.

48. SC160/I/4/1, A. L. Loomis to FET, January 27 and 31, 1942; FET to A. L. Loomis and to K. T. Compton, January 31, 1942; and K. T. Compton to FET, January 31, 1942.

49. UA V 728.95.2, Box 2, File "Nov. 1945," Harvard University Archives. List compiled by O. G. Villard Jr.

50. UA V 728.95.1, Box 1, notes of FET Meeting with [Ralph] Bown, January 1942, Harvard University Archives.

51. *Terman Interview*, 65–66.

52. SC160/VIII/4/7, FET notes "Origins of RRL: 30th Anniversary Dinner 4/10/75."

53. UA V 728.95.1, Box 1, FET notes of meeting with Frank D. Lewis, February 12, 1942, Harvard University Archives.

54. UA V 728.95.1, Box 1, Folder "Intelligence Reports," February 17, 1942, Harvard University Archives.

55. UA V 728.95.1, Box 1, FET notes on visits to the Bell Labs, March 5, 1942, Harvard University Archives.

56. UA V 728.95.1, Box 1, typed notes of "Deloraine Conference March 19, 1942," Harvard University Archives.

57. Cockburn, "The Radio War," in Burns, *Radar Development to 1945*, 330–56, 341.

58. UA V 728.95.1, Box 1, Folder "Memorandum on RCM Personnel Situation 2/27/42," Harvard University Archives.

59. Winfield W. Salisbury File, Association of Old Crows.

60. Richard C. Raymond File, Association of Old Crows.

61. Donald B. Sinclair File, Association of Old Crows.

62. UA V 728.95.1, Box 11, N. McL. Sage to Rad Lab, RRL and MIT Administrators, March 20, 1942, Harvard University Archives.

63. UA V 728.95.2, Box 2, O. G. Villard Jr. to Henry Guerlac, December 6, 1945, Harvard University Archives.

64. UA V 728.95.1, Box 16, Folder "Technical Notes: General," entry of March 26, 1942, Harvard University Archives.

65. SC160/XII/3/1.

66. SC160/XII/3/10, FET to LMT, March 8, 1942.

67. SC160/XII/3/1.

68. SC160/XII/4/3, SWT to Anna B. Terman (ABT), n.d., but May 1942, and May 8, 1942.

69. SC160/XII/4/3, SWT to ABT, October 1, 1942.

70. SC160/XII/4/3, SWT to ABT, June 18, 1942.

71. O. G. Villard Jr. File: O. G. Villard to A. J. Morin, June 25, 1980, Association of Old Crows.

72. SC160/I/1/3, list for tour, February 1, 1944. (Tour postponed to February 4: Donald B. Tresidder telegram to FET, February 1, 1944.)

73. SC160/XII/3/6, SWT to FET, April 21, [1944].

74. SC160/XII/4/3, SWT to ABT, July 9, 1944.

75. SC160/XII/4/3, SWT to ABT, April 8 and 13, 1942.

76. SC160/XII/4/3, SWT to ABT; and SWT to LMT, April 14, 1942.

77. This section benefits from UA V 728.95.1, Boxes 3, 4, and 5, a collection of materials and notes from the English trip of FET.

78. SC160/XII/4/10, FET to SWT, April 19, 1942.

79. UA V 728.95.1, Box 1, "Plans for RCM Project," n.d., but probably discussed in March and early April, 1942, Harvard University Archives.

80. Ibid.

81. SC160/I/4/9.

82. Cockburn, in Burns, *Radar Development to 1945*, 341.

83. R. V. Jones, *Most Secret War* (London: Hamish Hamilton, 1978).

84. UA V 728.95.1, Box 4, minutes of meeting of May 15, 1942, and lists therewith, Harvard University Archives.

85. SC160/XII/3/10, FET to LMT; and FET to ABT, June 1, 1942.

86. SC160/XII/4/3, SWT to ABT, June 18, 1942.

87. UA V 728.95.1, Box 5, Folder "FET Trip to England," Harvard University Archives.

88. UA V 728.95.1, Box 16, Harvard University Archives.

89. UA V 728.95.2, Box 5, Folder "Staff Meeting Minutes FET," Harvard University Archives.

90. C. S. Gillmor, "Early History of Upper Atmospheric Physics Research in Antarctica," in *Upper Atmosphere Research in Antarctica*, ed. L. J. Lanzerotti and C. G. Park, Antarctic Research Series, 29: 236–62 (Washington DC: American Geophysical Union, 1978).

91. UA V 728.95.1, Box 4, "German Radar," July 14, 1942, Harvard University Archives.

92. UA V 728.95.1, Box 12, FET to B. Archambault, July 17, 1942, Harvard University Archives.

93. UA V 728.95.1, Box 15, "Radio Research Laboratory," n.d., but comments within suggest mid-July 1942, Harvard University Archives.

94. UA V 728.95.1, Box 12, F. D. Lewis to D. B. Langmuir, July 20, 1942, Harvard University Archives.

95. SC160/I/1/13, FET to D. B. Tresidder, August 5, 1942; and D. B. Tresidder to FET, August 12, 1942.

96. SC160/XII/4/2, FWT to ABT, April 15, 1942; SC160/XII/4/3, SWT to ABT, May 8, 1942.

97. SC160/XII/3/10, FET to LMT, July 10, 1942.

98. SC160/XII/4/2, FWT to ABT; and FET to LMT, June 5, 1945.

99. HUG 300, files: William Henry Claflin II, Nathaniel Preston Breed, Harvard University Archives.

100. UA V 728.95.1, Box 5, Folder "Field Station—ABL," FET to J. N. Dyer, June 6, 1944, Harvard University Archives.

101. UA V 728.95.1, Box 7, J. V. L. Hogan to V. Bush, March 2, 1944; V. Bush to H. H. Bundy, March 3, 1944; and FET to B. Archambault (London), April 4, 1944, Harvard University Archives.

102. SC160/XII/3/10, FET to ABT, March 23, 1942.

103. SC160/XII/4/3, SWT to ABT; and FET to LMT, September 23, 1942.

104. SC160/XII/4/3, SWT to ABT, October 1, 1942.

105. SC160/XII/4/2, T. C. "Bo" Terman (TCT) to ABT, October 5, 1942.
106. SC160/XII/4/3, SWT to ABT, October 14, 1942.
107. SC160/XII/4/2, Lewis M. Terman II (LMTII) to LMT, June 17, 1942; and TCT to LMT, June 22, 1942.
108. SC160/XII/4/2, TCT to LMT, November 27, 1942; SC160/XII/4/3, SWT to ABT, November 29, 1942; Minton, *Lewis M. Terman*, 214–15.
109. SC160/XII/3/10, FET to LMT, December 26, 1942.
110. SC160/XII/3/10, FET to ABT, February 23 and March 23, 1943.
111. SC160/XII/4/4, LMT to FET, March 11, 1942.
112. SC160/XII/4/2, SWT to ABT, May 6, 1944, and January 21, 1945.
113. SC160/XII/4/3, SWT to ABT, August 1, 1943.
114. SC160/XII/3/10, FET to LMT, June 24, 1943.
115. SC160/XII/4/4, ABT to FET; and ABT to SWT, August 11, 1943.
116. SC160/XII/4/4, ABT to FET; and FET to SWT, August 11, 1943; and LMT to FET, October 15, 1943; SC160/XII/4/5, ABT to FET, October 26, [1943].
117. Minton, *Lewis M. Terman*, 254.
118. SC160/XII/3/10, FET to ABT, June 9, 1944; and FET to LMT, June 5, 1945; SC160/XII/4/2, Frederick W. Terman (FWT) to ABT; and FWT to LMT, June 30, 1944.
119. SC160/XII/3/9, LMTII to SWT, July 8, 1944; SC160/XII/4/3, SWT to ABT, August 15, 1944.
120. SC160/XII/3/9, ABT to TCT, October 18, 1944; SC160/XII/4/2, TCT to LMT, October 23, 1944; SC/XII/4/3, SWT to ABT, August 21, 1945.
121. SC160/XII/4/3, SWT to LMT, December 5 and March 23, 1942; SC160/XII/4/3, SWT to ABT, April 20, 1943.
122. SC160/XII/3/10, FET to ABT, May 1, 1943; FET to LMT, June 24, 1943; SC160/XII/4/2, FWT to LMT; and FWT to ABT, June 30 and September 30, 1943; LMTII to LMT; and LMTII to ABT, "Sept." 1943; TCT to LMT, October 23, 1944; SC160/XII/4/3, SWT to ABT, August 1, 1943.
123. UA V 728.95.1, Box 4, John Dyer memo to FET, October 8, 1942, Harvard University Archives.
124. UA V 728.95.2, Box 5, unsigned diaries (of N. P. Breed), Harvard University Archives.
125. SC0900, FET interview by Raymond Henle, January 17, 1970, 42.
126. UA V 728.95.2, Box 5, N. P. Breed diary entry, June 19, 1942, Harvard University Archives.
127. UA V 728.95.2, Box 5, N. P. Breed diary entries, July 8, 1942, and May 24, 1943, Harvard University Archives.
128. Bainbridge Bunting, *Harvard: An Architectural History* (Cambridge, MA: Harvard University Press, 1985).
129. HUF 726.2, "Radio Research Lab: Memos, Forms, Notices," Harvard University Archives.
130. UA V 728.95.1, Box 2, Folder "Breed," E. D. Brooks Jr. to N. P. Breed, November 22, 1943, Harvard University Archives.
131. UA V 728.95.2, Box 5, N. P. Breed diary entry, December 13, 1943, Harvard University Archives.
132. SC160/XIII/1/21, FET to K. Sax, January 22, 1965.
133. SC160/I/4/7.

134. SC160/I/4/13, E. Mudge to FET, June 30, 1945.

135. UA V 728.95.1, Box 3, "Business Report 4: Florosa," June 1944, Harvard University Archives.

136. UA V 728.95.1, Box 3, F. C. Cahill to FET, November 24, 1943, Harvard University Archives.

137. UA V 728.95.3, materials on these are contained in eleven Boxes titled "Records containing Field Stations and Branch Laboratories, 1942–1946," Harvard University Archives, and in American British Laboratory Division of Division 15 of the NDRC, *Administrative History of the American British Laboratory of Division 15 of the NDRC*, n.d., but 1946.

138. UA V 728.95.1, Box 15, "Report on Visit to the D. T. M. on September 25 and 26, 1942," Dick Raymond, Harvard University Archives.

139. UA V 728.95.1, Box 20, O. G. Villard Jr. to FET, January 29, 1944, Harvard University Archives.

140. UA V 728.95.2, Box 3, "NDRC Division 15, Committee Minutes, September 23, 1943," Harvard University Archives.

141. Gillmor, "Early History of Upper Atmospheric Physics Research in Antarctica."

142. UA V 728.95.4, Box 1, Folder 117, H. F. Elliott to FET, July 28, 1943; UA V 728.95.4, Box 1, H. F. Elliott to FET, October 29, 1943; and FET to staff, October 12, 1943, Harvard University Archives; and Vincent Lane File, Association of Old Crows.

143. UA V 728.95.4, Box 1, H. F. Elliott to FET, October 29, 1943; and FET to staff, October 12, 1943, Harvard University Archives.

144. UA V 728.95.4, Box 1, "Report from Florosa, November 17, 1943"; and numerous following reports in Box 1 concerning Window, Chaff, and Rope, including Fred L. Whipple's diary report, February 23, 1944, and "Wide Wing Window Conference," June 7, 1944, at OSRD, London, Harvard University Archives.

145. SC160/I/3/4, Stanley Kaisel, September 1945.

146. SC160/I/3/13, FET to J. F. Shelley, January 12, 1953; and FET to A. P. Rowe, June 11, 1962.

147. References for this section include A. Price, *History of U.S. Electronic Warfare*, 30, 45, 77–78, 82–83, 104–5, 174; IEEE interview of William Rambo, 1994; author's interviews with Rambo, 1998, and with Villard, 1999.

148. UA V 728.95.1, Box 1, FET to J. N. Dyer, April 19, 1944, Harvard University Archives.

149. Author interview with William Rambo, 1999; and William Rambo File, Association of Old Crows.

150. SC160/II/1/8, M. Eastham to FET, September 28, 1939; Association of Old Crows, D15, John Chase, "Report on the incident resulting in the death of Wallace B. Caulfield Jr.," January 3, 1945; Lt. Col. Walter E. Lotz, December 31, 1944 (photocopies of originals in SC160).

151. UA V 728.95.1, Box 1, K. T. Compton to FET, February 16, 1942; K. T. Compton to F. D. Lewis, February 28, 1942, Harvard University Archives.

152. Price, *History of U.S. Electronic Warfare*, 24.

153. UA V 728.95.1, Box 11, C. G. Suits to FET, May 21, 1943, Harvard University Archives.

154. SC303/I/9/1, FET to F. Bloch, January 7, 1943.

155. UA V 728.95.1, Box 3, Folders 1–2, "RRL Business Reports," Harvard University Archives.

156. SC160/I/1/11, FET to H. H. Skilling, February 24, 1945.

157. C. G. Suits interview by McMahon, IEEE; and C. G. Suits File, Association of Old Crows.

158. UA V 728.95.1, Box 12, B. Archambault to FET, August 4, 1942, Harvard University Archives.

159. UA V 728.95.1, Box 16, FET to V. Bush, March 21, 1942, Harvard University Archives.

160. UA V 728.95.1, Box 11, C. G. Suits to I. Stewart, April 19, 1943, Harvard University Archives.

161. UA V 728.95.2, Box 4, FET memo, May 31, 1943, Harvard University Archives.

162. UA V 728.95.1, Box 11, FET to I. Stewart (OSRD), September 21 and October 19, 1942, Harvard University Archives.

163. UA V 728.95.1, Box 12, FET to K. T. Compton, August 16, 1943, Harvard University Archives.

164. UA V 728.95.2, Box 4, FET memo, August 19, 1943, Harvard University Archives.

165. UA V 728.95.2, Box 5, minutes of technical meeting, June 9, 1942, Harvard University Archives.

166. UA V 728.95.1, Box 12, transcript of telephone conversation between R. W. Larson and FET, May 23, 1944, Harvard University Archives.

167. Although exhausted from much work, Villard left for England, but only after Terman gave him a weeklong vacation. UA V 728.95.1, Box 20, FET to O. G. Villard Sr., June 9, 1944, Harvard University Archives.

168. UA V 728.95.1, Box 12, notes of FET conversation with W. Claflin, May 26, 1944, Harvard University Archives.

169. UA V 728.95.1, Box 12, FET to W. H. Claflin, July 19, 1943; W. H. Claflin to FET, July 20, 1943, Harvard University Archives.

170. UA V 728.95.1, Box 12, A. E. Cullum to FET, November 15, 1943, Harvard University Archives.

171. C. G. Suits file, Suits interview with AOC History Committee, ca. 1980, Association of Old Crows.

172. C. G. Suits interview by McMahon, IEEE; C. G. Suits file, Association of Old Crows.

173. UA V 728.95.1, Box 16, Frederick E. Terman and Warren D. White, "Notes on Power Required for Noise Jamming. May 31, 1943" (eleven pages, five figures, and one table), Harvard University Archives.

174. RG 227, OSRD, Directors Subject Correspondence, Countermeasures RCM, R. Bown to A. L. Loomis, September 9, 1942, National Archives.

175. RG 227, OSRD, Directors Org. Correspondence Division 15; John H. Teeter to Director's Office; "Rough Draft" memo, October 31, 1943, National Archives.

176. RG 227, OSRD, Directors Subject Correspondence, Countermeasures, RCM; J. V. L. Hogan to V. Bush, November 18, 1943, National Archives.

177. D11 File, J. V. L. Hogan to V. Bush, January 8, 1944, Association of Old Crows. Hogan sent a copy also to Terman at RRL. (Original in Stanford University Archives, SC160.)

178. This section utilizes SC160/I/2/1; *Terman Interview*; and *Administrative Report of the American British Laboratory of Division 15 of the NDRC*.

179. SC160/I/2/1, file of letters 1943–44 regarding ABL-15, between and among FET, Peter Goldmark, C. Guy Suits, John Dyer, Paul W. Kesten, and others.

180. This section utilizes SC160/I/4/3, FET Statement, September 24, 1945; *Administrative History of the Radio Research Laboratory*; *Administrative History of the American British Laboratory of Division 15 of the NDRC*; and Price, *History of U.S. Electronic Warfare*, 1984.

181. Needell, *Science, Cold War and the American State*, 91.

182. (U.S.) Radio Research Laboratory, 1947.

183. SC160/I/3/2.

184. SC160/I/3/14, T. S. Kuhn Entry, September 1945.

185. SC160/XII/4/5, LMT to FET, September 25, 1944.

186. SC160/XII/3/9, FWT to SWT, May 6, 1945.

187. SC160/XII/3/6, SWT to FET, April 21 [1944]; SC160/XII/4/2, FWT to ABT; and FWT to LMT, June 30, 1944; SC160/XII/4/2, FWT to SWT, September 24, 1944; SC160/XII/4/2, TCT to LMT, October 23, 1944; SC/XII/4/3, SWT to ABT, February 17, 1944; SC160/XII/3/10, FET to LMT, June 5, 1945; SC160/XII/4/2, FWT to ABT; and FWT to LMT, June 5, 1945.

188. SC160/XII/4/3, SWT to ABT, August 21, 1945.

189. SC160/XII/4/3, SWT to ABT, [September] and September 19, 1945.

190. SC160/XII/4/4, ABT to SWT, February 16, 1943; and ABT to FET, February 16, 1943.

191. SC160/XII/4/2, SWT to ABT, May 6, 1945.

192. SC165/I/10/9, FET to E. A. Yunker; and E. A. Yunker to FET, May 14 and 28, and June 14, 1946.

CHAPTER FIVE. JUMP-STARTING ENGINEERING AT STANFORD

1. SC151/27/2, FET to D. B. Tresidder, January 8, 1947; FET to A. C. Eurich, April 11, 1947; SC151/27/2, FET to A. C. Eurich, September 13, 1946.

2. SC160/I/1/2, P. H. Davis to FET, August 9, 1943.

3. SC160/I/1/2, FET to P. H. Davis, August 23, 1943.

4. SC160/I/1/2, FET to P. H. Davis, December 29, 1943.

5. SC160/I/1/2, P. H. Davis to FET, January 3, 1944.

6. SC160/I/1/2, FET telegram to P. H. Davis, January 7, 1944.

7. SC160/I/1/2, P. H. Davis to FET, February 29, 1944.

8. SC160/I/1/4, A. C. Eurich to FET, January 20, 1944.

9. SC151/26/6, A. C. Eurich to H. T. Heald, September 28, 1944.

10. He based these comments on notes he took in a conference with Alvin Eurich, December 20, 1944. SC151/15/20, Eldridge T. Spencer, "Progress Report February 28, 1945."

11. SC160/I/1/2, Stanford report (Davis), "A Proposal to Organize the Stanford Resources for Public Service," August 24, 1942.

12. SC160/I/1/2, numerous letters between FET and P. H. Davis; SC0900, Stanford Oral History Project interviews with Paul Hanna and John W. Dodds.

13. SC151/40/15, Donald Tresidder speech, "Reconversion at Stanford," June 15, 1946; and Kiester, *Tresidder*, 50.

14. Kiester, *Tresidder*, 51.

15. SC151/28/9, D. B. Tresidder to P. Hanna, November 11, 1943; minutes and notes of Tresidder's meeting with military representatives for ASTP Program, November 19, 1943.

16. *Stanford Alumni Review* 45, no. 1 (October 1943): 9.

17. *Stanford Alumni Review* 44, no. 8 (May 1943): 11.

18. SC165/I/2/24, Electrical Engineering Department report, "Need for Expanded Facilities," n.d., but fall 1942.

19. *Stanford Alumni Review* 43, no. 8 (May 1942): 14–15.

20. SC160/I/1/2, FET to P. H. Davis, June 1, 1942; SC160/I/1/8, K. Spangenberg to FET, March 17 and 23, 1942; SC160/I/1/9, O. G. Villard Jr. to J. H. Dellinger, March 9, 1942; and O. G. Villard Jr. to FET, March 21, 1942.

21. *Stanford Alumni Review* 45, no. 6 (March 1944): 5.

22. Kiester, *Tresidder*, 66.

23. SC151/16/17, A. C. Eurich to D. Swim, February 24, 1948.

24. SC151/40/15, D. B. Tresidder speech, June 15, 1946; and Tresidder, "Next Ten Years," speech drafted for the Stanford Academic Council, 1947, but not delivered. Kiester, *Tresidder*, 72–74.

25. SC151/27/1, J. B. Conant to FET, February 11, 1946; and FET to D. B. Tresidder, February 21, 1946.

26. SC151/8/1, clipping from *Palo Alto Times*, September 19, 1945.

27. Nash, *Herbert Hoover and Stanford University*, 93–94, 96.

28. 0900, Stanford Oral History Project interviews with John Dodds, Paul Hanna, and Paul Davis.

29. 0900, Stanford Oral History Project interview with John Dodds.

30. Kiester, *Tresidder*, 60–63.

31. 0900, Stanford Oral History Project interviews with Paul Davis, Paul Hanna, and David S. Jacobson. SC170/1/5, P. H. Davis to President Tresidder and Board of Trustees, January 15, 1946.

32. SC151/27/1, FET to A. C. Eurich, March 21, 1946; and D. B. Tresidder to FET, March 25, 1946.

33. SC151/37/4, notes for Dr. Tresidder from "Stephens," April 11, 1946.

34. SC151/37/5, D. B. Tresidder to D. J. Russell, March 12, 1947. Paul Hanna later claimed that he knew the identities of three of the postcard writers, but at the time he had had insufficient proof. See 0900, Stanford Oral History Project interview with Paul Hanna. Kiester, *Tresidder*, 76–77.

35. SC151/37/5, "Faculty Responses to Anonymous Attack on Tresidder" (1946–47).

36. SC151/26/6, S. B. Morris to D. B. Tresidder, October 5, 1944.

37. SC151/26/6, FET to D. B. Tresidder, October 30, 1944.

38. SC151/26/6, D. B. Tresidder to FET, December 1, 1944.

39. SC151/26/6, L. B. Reynolds to D. B. Tresidder, December 4, 1944.

40. SC151/26/6, Stanford publicity release, December 25, 1944; *Palo Alto Times*, December 25, 1944.

41. Author interview with former engineering dean William Kays, 1999.

42. SC165/I/9/6, FET to H. H. Skilling, December 27, 1944.

43. SC160/I/1/2, FET to P. H. Davis, December 29, 1943.

44. SC151/27/1, FET to A. C. Eurich, September 13, 1946.

45. SC151/27/1, FET to D. B. Tresidder, January 9, 1946; SC151/27/1, FET to A. C. Eurich, July 26, 1946. In his later post as provost, Terman maintained a "fighting fund" to attract and keep exceptional faculty members.

46. SC151/27/1, FET and H. H. Skilling to D. B. Tresidder, January 10, 1946.

47. SC151/27/1, FET to D. B. Tresidder, August 5, 1946.

48. SC151/27/1, D. B. Tresidder to Board of Trustees, January 16, 1946; H. D. Winbigler to A. C. Eurich, February 12, 1946; and FET to A. E. Eurich, March 6, 1946.

49. SC151/27/1, FET to D. B. Tresidder, June 14, 1946.

50. SC151/27/1, FET to A. C. Eurich, March 21 and May 16, 1946; FET to D. B. Tresidder, April 17 and May 22, 1946; D. B. Tresidder to FET, April 4 and May 29, 1946; FET to J. E. Laurance, June 1, 1946; R. D. Conrad to FET, June 7, 1946; and O. C. Maier to Office of the President, Stanford, January 11, 1946.

51. SC151/27/2, FET to E. R. Piore, August 15, 1947.

52. SC151/27/1, J. E. Laurance to FET, April 23, 1946 (copy).

53. SC151/27/7, E. Grant to General L. C. Craigie, April 20, 1946.

54. SC151/27/1, FET to A. C. Eurich, May 16, 1946; and FET to D. B. Tresidder, May 22, 1946.

55. SC151/27/1, D. B. Tresidder to FET, May 29, 1946.

56. SC151/27/1, FET to D. B. Tresidder and relevant faculty, May 31, 1946.

57. SC151/4/1, F. Mosteller to FET, July 15, 1946.

58. SC151/27/3, FET to A. C. Eurich, February 13, 1948.

59. SC151/27/2, FET to D. B. Tresidder, May 29, 1947.

60. SC151/27/1, FET to D. B. Tresidder, June 5, 1946.

61. SC151/27/2, FET to D. B. Tresidder, June 3, 1947.

62. SC165/I/3/2, minutes of School of Engineering faculty, October 14, 1946.

63. SC151/27/1, FET to D. B. Tresidder, February 24, 1947.

64. SC151/27/3, FET minutes of Engineering Executive Committee, February 17, 1948.

65. As witnessed by this author in spring 1959 in Ralph J. Smith's electronics course.

66. From 10:30 until noon Monday through Saturday and 2:15–3:00 in the afternoons Monday through Friday. SC165/I/3/2, School of Engineering Faculty Office Hours Schedule, October 9, 1946.

67. SC165/I/9/6, H. H. Skilling to FET, October 4 and November 2, 1945; and FET to H. H. Skilling, October 10 and 15, 1945.

68. SC151/27/7, H. H. Skilling to D. B. Tresidder, July 18, 1945; and D. B. Tresidder to H. H. Skilling, copy to FET, July 27, 1945; SC151/27/8, L. B. Reynolds to D. B. Tresidder, March 12, 1947.

69. Two of the three men had BS degrees. SC151/28/4, L. Jacobsen to D. B. Tresidder, July 31 and December 31, 1946.

70. SC151/28/3, S. B. Morris to D. B. Tresidder, August 4, 1944; S. B. Morris to A. E. Raymond, August 9, 1944; and A. E. Raymond to S. B. Morris, August 21, 1944.

71. SC151/28/3, E. G. Reid to D. B. Tresidder, February 3, 1945.

72. SC151/28/3, E. G. Reid to R. M. Hazen, April 17, 1945.

73. Author interview with Walter G. Vincenti, 2000.

74. SC151/27/2, FET to D. B. Tresidder, May 31, 1947.

75. SC151/28/4, L. Jacobsen to D. B. Tresidder, February 20, 1946; and FET to D. B. Tresidder, February 21, 1946.

76. SC151/27/2, FET to A. C. Eurich, October 29, 1946.

77. SC151/24/2, A. I. Leverson to D. B. Tresidder, April 2, 1945; D. B. Tresidder to H. Hoover Jr., February 6, 1945. *Stanford Alumni Review* 48, no. 4 (January 1947): 3 and 49; no. 6 (March 1948): 16.

78. SC151/24/2, A. C. Waters to D. B. Tresidder, January 20, 1945; and A. C. Waters

to H. Hoots, December 26, 1944. A. C. Waters, a former Stanford geology professor and senior geologist for the U.S. Geological Survey, believed that Levorsen and Tresidder could do much for Stanford geology.

79. SC151/24/2, A. I. Levorsen to C. H. Beal, March 13, 1946. Beal was a petroleum geologist and vice president of Tidewater Oil Company.

80. SC151/28/9, F. G. Tickell to D. B. Tresidder, May 15, 1946, with copies to Vice President Eurich and Dean Terman.

81. SC151/27/1, FET to A. C. Eurich, June 1, 1946.

82. SC151/27/1, A. C. Eurich to FET, June 17, 1946.

83. SC151/27/2, FET to D. B. Tresidder, April 25, 1947.

84. Ibid.

85. Author interview with Otto J. M. Smith, 2000.

86. For other accounts of this development see Ginzton, "The $100 Idea"; Galison, Hevly, and Lowen, "Controlling the Monster"; Ginzton, *Times to Remember*; and Leslie, *Cold War and American Science*, ch. 6.

87. *San Francisco Chronicle*, October 25, 1940.

88. All but Chodorow had been together at Stanford before the war. Ginzton, *Times to Remember*, 92; Varian, *Inventor and Pilot*, 230–31.

89. M708, Varian Associates Oral History Project, Edward Ginzton interview by Sharon Mercer, 1990.

90. SC160/I/1/6, FET to W. W. Hansen, September 27, 1945.

91. SC160/I/1/7, W. W. Hansen to P. Kirkpatrick, November 6, 1942.

92. SC160/I/1/2, P. H. Davis to FET, January 18, 1943.

93. SC126/4/40, F. Bloch to W. W. Hansen, November 9, 1941; F. Bloch to W. W. Hansen, December 30, 1942; F. Bloch to W. W. Hansen, January 14, 1943; W. W. Hansen to F. Bloch, February 3, 1943; F. Bloch to W. W. Hansen, February 14, 1943; F. Bloch to FET, February 19, 1943; and F. Bloch to W. W. Hansen, March 24, 1943 and subsequent similar letters. SC303/I/1/1, F. Bloch to D. L. Webster, March 23, 1943, copies to physics faculty.

94. SC126/4/40, W. W. Hansen to F. Bloch, November 5, 1942.

95. SC126/4/40, D. L. Webster to P. Kirkpatrick, January 9, 1943, copies to R. L. Wilbur and all physics faculty; SC303/I/9/17, D. L. Webster to P. Kirkpatrick, April 8, 1943, copy to F. Bloch.

96. SC160/I/1/2, FET to P. H. Davis, June 1, 1943.

97. SC160/I/1/2, P. H. Davis to FET, June 9, 1943.

98. SC160/I/1/2, P. H. Davis to FET, June 24, 1943.

99. SC160/I/1/2, P. H. Davis to FET, August 9, 1943.

100. SC160/I/1/8, W. W. Hansen to D. B. Tresidder, November 17, 1943.

101. SC160/I/8, D. B. Tresidder to W. W. Hansen, December 21, 1943.

102. SC160/I/1/8, W. W. Hansen to D. B. Tresidder, (first draft) September 27, 1944; SC126/4/40, F. Bloch to W. W. Hansen, comments on draft, September 29, 1944; FET to W. W. Hansen, Comments on Draft, October 2, 1944; and W. W. Hansen to D. B. Tresidder, report, October 5, 1944.

103. SC160/I/1/13, FET to D. B. Tresidder, October 17, 1944.

104. SC160/I/1/13, FET to D. B. Tresidder, December 22, 1944; SC126/4/41, W. W. Hansen to D. B. Tresidder, December 27, 1944; and D. B. Tresidder to W. W. Hansen, January 16, 1945.

105. SC151/25/1, D. L. Webster to D. B. Tresidder (Telegram), February 14, 1945.

106. SC126/4/41, P. Kirkpatrick to W. W. Hansen, March 11, 1945; SC151/25/1, D. L. Webster to P. Kirkpatrick (copy), February 22, 1945.

107. SC151/25/1, D. L. Webster to D. B. Tresidder (Telegram), January 29, 1945; D. L. Webster to P. Kirkpatrick, January 30, 1945; P. Kirkpatrick to A. C. Eurich, February 7, 1945; H. H. Skilling to FET, February 19, 1945; and D. B. Tresidder to A. Ellett, March 1, 1945.

108. SC151/15/5, E. T. Spencer to President's Office, September 4, 1945. A year later, Hansen was still agitating for modifications to the Physics Department spaces. SC151/15/17, W. W. Hansen to D. J. Tresidder, June 12, 1946.

109. Stanford Kroopf, MD, Hansen's physician, in personal remarks to the author, 2000.

110. SC160/I/1/11, H. H. Skilling to FET, October 13, 1944; SC151/13/10, memo from L. C. Owen to A. C. Eurich, January 4, 1945.

111. SC160/I/1/11, H. H. Skilling to FET, May 22, 1944.

112. M708, Varian Associates Oral History Project interview with Marvin Chodorow, by Sharon Mercer, December 1989; author interview with Marvin Chodorow, 1998. Ginzton, *Times to Remember*, 94.

113. SC126/2/23, OSRD: Administrative Circular 2.03 (Revision 1), April 15, 1946.

114. SC165/I/9/43, J. H. Van Vleck to FET, May 1, 1946.

115. SC126/3/26, "Proposed Development of a Billion Volt Linear Electron Accelerator," Microwave Laboratory, Department of Physics, Stanford University, March 1, 1948; W. W. Hansen to A. C. Eurich, March 23, 1948. *Stanford Alumni Review* 50, no. 2 (October 1948): 5–6.

116. Ginzton, *Times to Remember*, 117.

117. SC126/2/21, W. W. Hansen to Palo Alto, California Draft Board, September 17, 1943. SC126/3/24, USAEC form submitted by Hansen, n.d., but 1947. Kroopf remarks to author, 2000.

118. Kroopf remarks to author, 2000.

119. SC126, W. W. Hansen papers.

120. SC126/3/27 and 28, letters therein. Tragically, his wife Betsy died a few months later. Their only child, born with intestinal abnormalities (Hansen had designed special apparatus for the child), had died as a baby in late 1947.

121. *Palo Alto Times*, May 23, 1949.

122. M708, Varian Associates Oral History Project, Chodorow interview.

123. Ginzton, *Times to Remember*, 1995, 100–121.

124. SC126/2/23, R. H. Varian to P. Hunter, November 15, 1946.

125. Ginzton, *Times to Remember*, 1995, 95, 122–23. (Schiff's wife Frances and Ginzton's wife Artemas were cousins and had roomed together as students at Berkeley.)

126. M708, Varian Associates Oral History Project, Chodorow interview.

127. M708, Varian Associates Oral History Project, Ginzton interview; H. Myrl Stearns interview by Sharon Mercer, 1989.

128. M708, Varian Associates Oral History Project, Ginzton interview.

129. M708, Varian Associates Oral History Project, Theodore Moreno interview by Sharon Mercer, 1989.

130. Russell H. Varian, "Recent Developments in Klystrons," *Electronics* (April 1952).

131. M508, Russell H. Varian Papers, Box 1.

132. Ginzton, *Times to Remember*, 96–98.

133. M708, Varian Associates Oral History Project, Ginzton interview. See also Henry E. Lowood, "From Steeples of Excellence to Silicon Valley," *Stanford Campus Report* (March 9, 1988): 11–13.

134. SC160/I/1/11, H. H. Skilling to FET, June 26, 1944.

135. Weldon B. Gibson, *SRI: The Founding Years* (Los Altos, CA: Publishing Services Center, 1982), 5–17.

136. SC160/I/1/11, H. H. Skilling to FET, June 26, 1944.

137. SC160/I/1/12, K. Spangenberg to FET, October 28, 1944.

138. SC151/17/19, H. T. Heald to A. McBean (copy), January 28, 1946.

139. Gibson, *SRI: The Founding Years*, 26–30, 68.

140. Author interview with Stephen W. Miller and William McGuigan, 2000.

141. *Stanford Illustrated Review* 48, no. 2 (November 1946): 5.

142. SC151/17/19. SRI moved its headquarters to Building 100 at Stanford Village on May 26, 1947.

143. SC151/17/18, D. B. Tresidder memos of telephone conversation with William Talbot, November 19 and December 9 and 17, 1947.

144. Gibson, *SRI: The Founding Years*, 110–12.

145. Several months after Talbot's dismissal, one of his deputies, Carston Steffens, spoke to President Tresidder about Talbot's attitude and concluded to make every effort to develop contacts at the university. SC151/17/18, D. B. Tresidder memo of conversation with Dr. [Carston] Steffens, December 5, 1947.

146. SC151/17/19, A. E. Brandin to A. C. Eurich, October 25, 1946. There were plans for SRI to move into another building within a year of its founding. SC126/2/23, W. W. Hansen, memo of conversation with T. A. Spragens, August 28, 1946.

147. Gibson, *SRI: The Founding Years*, 87. SC151/17/18, SRI Accounts Receivable, August 1, 1948; "Active and New Projects," as of August 1, 1948.

148. Gibson, *SRI: The Founding Years*, 110.

149. SC151/27/1, FET to D. B. Tresidder, report, January 15, 1946, plus documents, including ACM(47509) cf, A6–4(b) from Rear Admiral A. C. Miles, USN.

150. SC151/17/18, W. F. Talbot to M. A. Garbell, April 28, 1947.

151. Gibson, *SRI: The Founding Years*, 110.

152. SC151/27/1, F. T. Letchfield to I. S. Lillick, ca. September 1945; I. S. Lillick to D. Tresidder, September 5, 1945; and D. S. Jacobson to I. S. Lillick, September 11, 1945.

153. *Stanford Alumni Review* 45, no. 5 (February 1944): 19.

154. SC151/27/4, material included with H. D. Winbigler report to D. B. Tresidder, March 28, 1946.

155. SC151/17/18, M. A. Garbell to A. C. Eurich, February 14, 1948.

156. Author interview with Walter Vincenti, 2000.

157. Terman is reported to have said that he knew nothing of Talbot's wind tunnel proposal. SC151/17/18.

158. SC151/27/5, FET to A. C. Eurich, July 1948; FET to H. L. Dryden, July 29, 1948; and A. C. Eurich to H. L. Dryden, July 30, 1948. Author interview with Vincenti, 2000.

159. SC170/2/6, P. C. Edwards to W. Sterling, December 18, 1948.

160. SC151/16/7, A. C. Eurich to D. Swim, February 24, 1948. *Stanford Alumni Review* 49, no. 7 (April 1948): 7–8.

161. SC151/17/18, FET to J. Hobson, January 28, 1948.

162. SC151/17/18, T. C. Poulter to H. Heald and Armour Research Foundation Executive Committee, February 2, 1948.

163. SC151/17/18, J. Hobson to A. C. Eurich, May 4 and 20, 1948. Eurich arranged for a summer meeting of Hobson with Terman, Leighton, and Levorsen.

164. This section benefits from the studies of Harvey M. Sapolsky, *Science and the Navy: The History of the Office of Naval Research* (Princeton, NJ: Princeton University Press, 1990); Bruce W. Hevly, *Basic Research Within a Military Context: The Naval Research Laboratory and the Foundations of extreme Ultraviolet and X-ray Astronomy, 1923–1960* (unpublished PhD dissertation, Johns Hopkins University, 1987); and Julius A. Furer, *Administration of the Navy Department in World War II* (Washington DC: Department of the Navy, 1959).

165. S. W. Miller, memo to author, 1999.

166. Sapolsky, *Science and the Navy*, ch. 2. A government committee, chaired by Charles E. Wilson of General Electric, set to work. Vannevar Bush pushed for a national research foundation. Frank Jewett, president of the National Academy of Sciences, wanted the NAS to have the leading role in fostering American research. Karl T. Compton headed a short-lived Research Board for National Security (RBNS). (RBNS died a quick death in late 1945.) They all were opposed to populist West Virginia Senator Harley M. Kilgore's proposal, drafted in 1943, for a single giant government science bureau. Bush's plan for a national science agency was submitted to President Harry S. Truman in July 1945 as the celebrated report *Science: The Endless Frontier*. It was not until 1950 that the National Science Foundation was established with ONR chief scientist Alan Waterman as first NSF Director. The NSF in the end was a combination of Bush's and Kilgore's plans.

167. Admiral Bowen, when director of the Naval Research Laboratory (NRL), had received the only unsatisfactory report of his navy career for refusing to follow the secretary of the navy's order to cooperate with civilian researchers on radar. Sapolsky, *Science and the Navy*, ch. 2.

168. Caltech, for example, had 2,500 employees engaged in rocket research for the army, navy, and NACA by late 1943. SC160/I/1/8, S. B. Morris to FET, December 18, 1943.

169. Sapolsky, *Science and the Navy*, ch. 3.

170. Ibid.

171. Author interview with Ralph Krause, 2000.

172. Charles J. Maisel and Teva W. Jones, *The History of SRI: The First Fifteen Years* (privately published, 1961).

173. SC151/17/18, J. Hobson to A. C. Eurich, May 23, 1948.

174. *Stanford Alumni Review* 48, no. 4 (January 1947): 4–5.

175. Project manager William Rand later became director of the SRI Physical Science Division, and Carston Steffans, director of the Chemistry and Chemical Engineering Department, within the Physical Science Division. S. W. Miller, memo to author, 1999.

176. SC151/27/3, O. G. Villard Jr. to FET, July 10, 1948; FET to A. C. Eurich, July 14, 1948; and A. C. Eurich to FET, July 19, 1948.

177. Kiester, *Tresidder*, 110–12.

178. Ibid., 122.

179. SC170/2/6, P. C. Edwards to P. H. Davis, June 29, 1948.

180. SC170/4, notebook of Paul C. Edwards, "Confidential."

181. SC170/4, notebook, P. Fuller Jr. to A. C. Eurich, February 19, 1948.

182. SC216/B21/1, Executive Committee of Faculty to members of the Academic Council, February 27, 1948.

183. SC216/B21/1, Faculty Presidential Search Advisory Committee to members of the Academic Council, May 17, 1948.

184. SC160/III/78/8, "Academic Council Election–April 1948."

185. SC160/III/78/8, FET memo, May 14, 1980.

186. SC160/III/78/8, "On the Qualifications of a President for Stanford," n.d., but summer 1948, signed by the seven-person committee, F. E. Terman, chairman.

187. SC170/4, notebook, Frank F. Walker to Board of Trustees, July 28, 1948.

188. SC160/III/78/8, FET memo, May 14, 1980.

189. SC160/III/78/8, I. S. Lillick to FET, July 15, 1948.

190. SC160/III/78/8, FET to E. E. Robinson, July 12, 1948.

191. SC160/III/78/8, FET notes, n.d., but summer 1948.

192. Ibid.

193. SC170/4, notebook, I. S. Lillick to Board of Trustees, August 3, 1948.

194. SC170/4, notebook, P. C. Edwards to I. S. Lillick, July 29, 1948.

195. SC170/4, notebook, I. S. Lillick to Trustee Committee, June 28, 1948. Chandler was replaced by C. H. Danforth. SC170/4, notebook, E. E. Robinson to I. S. Lillick, July 17, 1948.

196. 0900, Oral History Project interviews with John W. Dodds, Alvin C. Eurich, Paul Hanna, and David S. Jacobson.

197. The faculty committee submitted a "first list" with seven names: Fred Terman; Detlev W. Bronk, biophysicist, then at Pennsylvania; Theodore Blegen, graduate dean at Minnesota; Leonard Carmichael, president of Tufts; William C. De Vane, dean of Yale College; Reuben Gilbert Gustavson, chancellor of Nebraska; and Philip C. Jessup, law professor at Columbia. The faculty "second list" consisted of fifteen names, including Wallace Sterling. Two names were on the first lists of both faculty and alumni: Terman and Jessup; and six names were on the second lists of both faculty and alumni: Charles W. Cole, president of Amherst; Erwin Nathaniel Griswold; Carl B. Spaeth of Stanford; William V. Houston; William A. Noyes Jr.; and Wallace Sterling. Herbert Hoover vetoed Terman, Jessup, Bronk, Gustavson, Griswold, Spaeth, Houston, and Noyes.

198. SC170/2/6, P. C. Edwards to P. H. Davis, June 29, 1948.

199. SC170/4, notebook, Paul Edwards penciled notes of lists of August 24 and September 22, 1948, with Hoover's vetoes indicated.

200. SC170/4, notebook.

201. Ibid.

202. 0900/Davis, Paul H., Stanford Oral History Project interviews conducted 1979 and 1980 by Frederic O. Glover and Paul A. Hanna.

203. 0900/Jacobson, David S., Stanford Oral History Project interviews conducted October 4 and 10, 1978, by Frederic O. Glover and George H. Knoles.

204. 0900/Dodds, John W., Stanford Oral History Project interview conducted February 27, 1981, by Frederic O. Glover and Paul R. Hanna.

205. 0900/Hanna, Paul A., Stanford Oral History Project interview conducted by Rebecca Lowen, March 26, 1986.

206. 0900/Eurich, Alvin C., Stanford Oral History Project interviews conducted 1980 by Frederic O. Glover.

207. Nash, *Herbert Hoover and Stanford University*, 123.

208. SC170/I/9.

209. SC170/4, notebook, H. Hoover Jr. to S. G. Mudd, May 3, 1948; and further letters in August; Ray Lyman Wilbur, n.d., but summer 1948.

210. SC170/4, notebook, E. E. Robinson to I. S. Lillick, October 13, 1948; I. S. Lillick to Board Committee, October 14, 1948.

211. SC170/4, notebook, Sterling dossier; *Stanford Alumni Review* 50, no. 4 (December 1948): 6.

212. SC170/1/9, S. G. Mudd to P. C. Edwards, September 28, 1948.

213. SC170/1/9, S. G. Mudd to P. C. Edwards, November 11, 1948.

214. SC170/2/6, P. C. Edwards to G. Dorsey, September 12, 1949.

215. SC170/1/3, L. A. DuBridge to P. C. Edwards, December 20, 1948.

216. *Stanford Alumni Review* 50, no. 4 (December 1948): 5–6.

217. *Stanford Daily*, November 22, 1948; *Stanford Alumni Review* 50, no. 4 (December 1948): 3–10.

218. *Stanford Alumni Review* 50, no. 4 (December 1948): 6.

219. SC170/2/6, P. C. Edwards to W. Sterling, December 18, 1948.

220. SC170/2/6, P. C. Edwards to W. Sterling, December 6, 1948.

221. SC160/III/78/8, FET Notes, n.d., but summer 1948.

CHAPTER SIX. FROM BUILDING A DISCIPLINE TO BUILDING A UNIVERSITY

1. SC165/IV/4/1, FET, "School of Engineering," 1946–47 file.

2. SC216/39/24, W. Sterling to FET, April 28, 1953; and FET to W. Sterling, April 13, 1953.

3. SC165/IV/4/1, FET reports, "School of Engineering," 1945–46, 1946–47, and 1947–48 files.

4. Stanford archives, 1103/1, FET report, "School of Engineering," November 1949, 2.

5. Young Fred stayed on for an MS in electrical engineering in 1950 and then went east for further graduate study. Middle son Terence received his BS in physics from Stanford in 1952, before going elsewhere for graduate work in physics, while Lewis, the youngest, received a BS from Stanford in 1956 in physics, remained for his MS, and received his PhD in electrical engineering in 1961. Sources: Stanford University Registers; author interview with Lewis M. Terman II, 2000.

6. SC165/I/3/3.

7. SC165/I/3/29, FET to General Electric Education Fund, December 21, 1949.

8. SC165/III/3/14, H. H. Skilling to W. Sterling, January 2, 1951.

9. SC216/15/4, FET to W. Sterling, August 2, 1951; and L. F. McGhie to W. Sterling, July 23, 1951, and October 4, 1954.

10. SC165/III/4/1, FET to W. Sterling, January 2, 1952.

11. SC165/III/3/14, FET to W. Sterling, January 3, 1950.

12. SC165/I/3/28, FET to A. S. Fitzgerald, August 14, 1947.

13. SC216/38/36, E. H. Breed to FET, October 30, 1948; and H. H. Skilling to A. C. Eurich, November 1, 1948; SC216/38/37, FET to W. Sterling, December 29, 1949.

14. SC165/III/3/10, FET to C. H. Faust, January 3, 1949.

15. SC165/IV/1/2, FET, "President's Report 1952–1953," October 1953.

16. SC165/III/4/4, FET to W. Sterling, December 31, 1953.

17. SC165/III/3/14, FET to W. Sterling, January 2, 1951.

18. Between 1954 and 1958, at Stanford, course enrollments in engineering increased 58 percent for undergraduate and 100 percent for graduate courses.

19. SC165/III/4/6, FET to W. Sterling, December 30, 1954.
20. SC165/III/4/14, FET to W. Sterling, December 31, 1953.
21. SC216/39/24, E. Hilgard to W. Sterling, November 11, 1952.
22. SC160/I/1/11, FET to H. H. Skilling, September 28, 1945.
23. SC216/39/24, FET to E. Hilgard, October 13, 1952.
24. SC165/IV/1/2, FET, "President's Report 1954–1955" and "1955–1956."
25. SC165/III/4/10, A. H. Bowker to FET, December 14, 1956.
26. SC216/39/28, FET to W. Sterling, January 4, 1957.
27. John G. Linvill notes, July 24, 1997, "Goals and Features of Stanford Engineering," communicated to author.
28. Documents concerning the early history of the ERL and AEL buildings are in SC165/I/1/17 and SC216/18/10.
29. See Leslie, *Cold War and American Science*, ch. 2.
30. SC165/I/1/17, FET, "Memorandum on War Defense Program in Electronics," n.d., but July 1950.
31. SC165/I/1/17, FET, "Appendix—History of the Applied Electronics Program and the Financing of the Electronics Laboratories," n.d., but ca. January 1956.
32. SC165/I/1/17, FET to K. M. Cuthbertson, July 7, 1958. During the period 1951–60, he noted, the portions of the ERL and AEL buildings amortized from general funds amounted to 12.8 percent of electronics research contract overhead.
33. In 1962, he became associate dean of engineering. William Rambo interview by A. Michel McMahon, November 27, 1984. Frederick E. Terman Associates Collection, Institution of Electrical Engineers. Transcript is available online at http://engine.ieee.org/history_center/oral_histories/transcripts/rambo47.html.
34. William Rambo interview by A. Michel McMahon.
35. SC165/I/1/17, FET, "Space Requirements of School of Engineering for Period 1956–1961," n.d., but ca. January 1956. Terman assured the board of trustees that local industry funds could match 50–50 any university appropriations for further construction.
36. SC216/39/24, correspondence, FET and S. W. Gilfillan, December 1952 to March 1953.
37. SC216/39/24, FET to S. W. Gilfillan, January 7, 1953.
38. SC165/III/4/6, FET to W. Sterling, December 30, 1954; author interview with John G. Linvill, 1998.
39. SC216/38/43, FET to W. Shockley, September 20, 1955.
40. Author interviews with William E. Spicer, 2000; author's conversation with Emmy Lanning (Mrs. William) Shockley, 2000.
41. William Spicer believes that Shockley hired men whose creativity would have been missed in elite places such as Bell Labs. Spicer also credits Emmy Lanning Shockley, a gifted psychiatric nurse and teacher, with helping Shockley choose Robert Noyce and others for the Shockley firm. Author interviews with William E. Spicer, 2000. For a history of this period, see Michael Riordan and Lillian Hoddeson, *Crystal Fire: The Birth of the Information Age* (New York: W. W. Norton, 1997); and Ward Winslow, *The Making of Silicon Valley: A One-Hundred Year Renaissance* (Santa Clara, CA: Santa Clara Valley Historical Association, 1995).
42. John G. Linvill, notes, July 24, 1997, "Goals and Features of Stanford Engineering," communicated to author.
43. *Terman Interview*, 131–32.
44. Ibid., 122.

45. SC165/IV/1/3, FET, "President's Report, 1956–1957."

46. Stephen P. Timoshenko, born in the Ukraine in 1878 and educated in Russia, was a prolific writer and legendary teacher, and already a treasure when he came to Stanford in 1936. From the midnineteenth century to the 1930s, Russia had been the world leader in the field of engineering mechanics (Pafnuty L. Chebyshev, Andrei A. Markov, Aleksandr M. Lyapunov, and others developed mathematical techniques in Russian railroad and shipping design).

47. SC165/IV/1/2, FET, "President's Report 1955–1956" and "1957–1958."

48. See Leslie, *Cold War and American Science*, ch. 4.

49. SC216/17/19, D. Carlson to F. O. Glover, February 16, 1955.

50. SC216/39/29, "Recent Activities in the Department of Aeronautics and Astronautics of Stanford University," n.d., but 1963.

51. SC216/38/25, W. Sterling to E. E. Sechler, February 28, 1957.

52. SC216/38/25, FET letter appointing committee, April 11, 1956.

53. SC216/38/26, J. Pettit to W. Sterling, January 12, 1960.

54. SC216/39/25, J. Pettit to FET and Advisory Board, January 13, 1959.

55. SC216/B5/3.

56. SC216/39/29, "Recent Activities in the Department of Aeronautics and Astronautics of Stanford University," n.d., but 1963. The department also reported that in 1963 thirteen aircraft and avionics companies made annual contributions of $5,000 to $10,000 to it.

57. Stanford archives, 1103/1, Annual Report of Dean of Engineering, 1949, 7–8.

58. SC216/B5/1, School of Engineering Booklet, 1959.

59. SC165/III/4/4, FET to W. Sterling, December 31, 1953.

60. SC216/39/5, E. L. Grant to W. Sterling, May 3, 1955; Trustees minutes, June 16, 1955; SC216/39/6, FET to W. Sterling, December 30, 1954.

61. Stanford archives, 1103/3, Industrial Engineering—Departmental Report to the President," September 30, 1955, 2.

62. SC165/IV/1/2, FET, "President's Report 1955–1956."

63. This section benefits from MSS 96/33C, interviews by Harriet Nathan, "Albert H. Bowker, Sixth Chancellor, University of California, Berkeley, 1971–1980; Statistician, and National Leader in the Policies and Politics of Higher Education," 1995, Bancroft Library; from author's interviews with Bowker, 1999, 2000, 2001, 2002. See also Ingrid Olkin, "A Conversation with Albert H. Bowker," *Statistical Science* 2, no. 4 (1987): 472–83; Halsey Royden, "A History of Mathematics at Stanford," in *A Century of Mathematics in America*, ed. Peter Duren, pt. 2, 237–76 (Providence, RI: American Mathematical Society, 1989); and Donald E. Knuth, "George Forsythe and the Development of Computer Science," *Communications of the ACM* 15, no. 8 (August 1972): 721–26; and from SC98, George E. Forsythe Papers, and SC216/6, Folders 39–43, Statistics Department, SUL.

64. Lowen, *Creating the Cold War University*, ch. 4.

65. Royden, "History of Mathematics at Stanford," pt. 2, 265.

66. SC216/6/39, copies of letters between R. L. Wilbur and J. B. Canning, January and February 1934.

67. SC216/B24/2, "Committee on Instruction in Statistics."

68. Zachary, *Endless Frontier*, ch. 14.

69. Bowker interview, Bancroft Library transcript, 126–27.

70. This group had perhaps the greatest concentration of statisticians and mathematical economists ever gathered together—Churchill Eisenhart, Milton Friedman, Abraham

Girschick, Harold Hotelling, Frederick Mosteller, Herbert Solomon, George Stigler, Abraham Wald, W. Allen Wallis, Jack Wolfowitz, and numerous others, and young graduate student Albert H. Bowker, who had recently graduated from MIT. On the SRG, see W. Allen Wallis, *Journal of the American Statistical Association*, June 1980.

71. SC216/B24/2, H. Working to A. C. Eurich, November 15, 1945.

72. SC216/B24/2, various letters from 1943–46, between and among Donald Tresidder, George Pólya, Holbrook Working, Alvin Eurich, Eugene Grant, and W. Allen Wallis.

73. SC216/B24/2, H. Working to J. H. Willits (Rockefeller), March 26, 1946; H. Working to D. B. Tresidder, March 28, 1946; and H. Working and E. L. Grant to Office of Research and Invention (U.S. Navy), March 11, 1946.

74. SC216/B24/2, H. Working to J. H. Curtiss, November 17, 1945.

75. SC216/49/6, A. Wallis to W. Sterling, August 30; and A. Wallis to D. Whitaker, September 24, 1954. Wallis later assisted the Ford Foundation in advising on Stanford's self-study of the behavioral sciences and subsequent Ford grants to Stanford.

76. SC216/A31/3, Concerning Patrick Suppes: P. H. Rhinelander to R. J. Wert, July 13, 1960.

77. Royden, "History of Mathematics at Stanford," 267–68.

78. SC216/13/13, D. I. McFadden to W. Sterling, July 16, 1952, concerning July 15 meeting of FET, Bowker, Herriot, Peterson, and others.

79. SC216/13/17, G. J. Lieberman to FET, January 9, 1956.

80. Stanford archives, 1103/3, FET, "President's Report 1955–1956, School of Engineering."

81. Author interview with William F. Miller, 2000.

82. Author interview with Gene F. Franklin, 2001.

83. Author interview with Albert H. Bowker, 2001.

84. Tradition at Stanford dictates that students compose acronyms or nicknames for campus buildings: "MemAud," for the Memorial Auditorium; "MemChu," for Memorial Church; "FloMo" for the Florence Moore Women's dormitory; or "HooTow" for Hoover Tower. Thus, CroMem.

85. SC216/48/11, E. T. Spencer was appointed director of planning on January 19, 1945.

86. SC216/57/1, "Director of Planning."

87. SC151/6/1, Lewis Mumford, March 10, 1944, "Memorandum on General Education Plan for Stanford University"; SC151/15/8, Lewis Mumford to E. T. Spencer, March 6, 1947.

88. Bartholomew, Brinegar, and Nilan, *Chronology*, 70, 74; Leland W. Cutler, *America Is Good to a Country Boy* (Stanford, CA: Stanford University Press, 1954), 69; Kiester, *Tresidder*, 75–76.

89. SC165/I/2/3,4,5.

90. SC165/IV/1/2, FET, "President's Report 1953–1954," October 1954.

91. SC165/I/2/5, FET speech at dedication of Crothers Memorial Hall, November 12, 1955.

92. SC165/I/2/3, G. E. Crothers to FET, January 8, 1954; and FET to G. E. Crothers, January 20, 1954.

93. SC165/I/2/3, FET to G. E. Crothers, November 20, 1953.

94. SC165/I/2/3, FET to G. E. Crothers, August 17, 1953.

95. SC216/13/37–38, FET to G. E. Crothers, October 21, 1955, and March 17, 1956.

96. McAndrews, "Birthplace of Silicon Valley," 5. For a concise history of the emergence of land-use planning at Stanford between 1944 and 1965, see Rosemary McAndrews, "The Birthplace of Silicon Valley: A History of Land Development at Stanford University," *Sandstone & Tile* 19, nos. 1–2 (spring 1995): 3–11. (McAndrews was director of Stanford Shopping Center.)

97. SC216/30/25, collection of board of trustees' minutes.

98. April 30, 1950. SC216/48/8, minutes of Trustee committees, March 29, 1951. Within three years, Varian had leased sixteen and a half acres. Author interview with Alf Brandin, 1998.

99. SC216/30/24, M. M. Doyle to W. P. Fuller Jr., October 25, 1945.

100. SC216/30/24.

101. SC216/30/24, Hitchcock and Chamberlain to W. Sterling, April 30, 1953.

102. SC216/48/8, E. E. Hutchison, "Report on Land Use Survey of Stanford University Properties—San Mateo and Santa Clara County, California," June 5, 1951.

103. SC216/23/21, interim report, Stanford Master Plan, August 15, 1953. McAndrews, "Birthplace of Silicon Valley," 7.

104. SC216/30/24, F. O. Glover to W. Sterling, January 8, 1952.

105. Stanford archives, 1103/3, Annual Report to President, Business Manager, 1953–54. Stanford archives, 1103/3, Annual Report to President, Business Manager, 1954–55.

106. Stanford archives, 1103/2, Annual Report to the President, Business Manager, 1951–52; and Stanford archives, 1103/2, Annual Report to the President, Business Manager, 1953–54.

107. SC216/48/8, Lewis Mumford, "Memorandum on Planning," February 20, 1947.

108. SC216/48/11, Trustee George Morell, notes, February 14, 1955.

109. Stanford archives, 1103/2, "President's Report 1951–52."

110. SC216/23/21, "Master Plan for the Stanford Lands," June 1, 1954. Terman's subcommittee portion of the overall report was completed on May 13, 1954.

111. SC216/1.2/11–2, V. Twitty to M. F. Johnson, June 3, 1954.

112. SC216/1.2/11–1, R. W. Holm to FET, May 28, 1956; and FET to R. W. Holm, May 30, 1956; SC216/23/20, K. Cuthbertson to A. E. Brandin, June 25, 1956.

113. SC216/A32/24, collection of trustees' minutes, September 19, 1956, 21; SC216/30/A18, Land and Building Development Advisory Committee, October 23, 1956.

114. McAndrews, "Birthplace of Silicon Valley," 10.

115. Author interview with William Kays, 1998.

116. Author interview with Alf Brandin, 1998.

117. SC165/I/4/23, A. E. Brandin to D. Sarnoff, November 24, 1954.

118. *Industrial and Housing Review* (Los Altos, CA), September 1956.

119. SC165/I/4/23, *Industrial and Housing Review*, September 1956. Brandin's theory of lawns is described in McAndrews, "Birthplace of Silicon Valley," 11.

120. 1103/4, Annual Report to the President, Business Manager, 1956–57.

121. Hugh Enochs, "Electronics Research Community Develops Around Stanford Laboratories," *The Tall Tree* 1, no. 9 (May 1958): 3.

122. SC216/14/12, J. L. Shepard to T. Ford, September 28, 1960; and FET to J. L. Shepard, October 3, 1960.

123. For recent assessments of the Industrial Park, see Lowood, "From Steeples of Excellence to Silicon Valley"; and Michael I. Luger and Harvey A. Goldstein, *Technology in*

the Garden: Research Parks and Regional Economic Development (Chapel Hill: University of North Carolina Press, 1991), ch. 7.

124. Leslie, *Cold War and American Science*, ch. 2; Michael Riordan and Lillian Hoddeson, "The Moses of Silicon Valley," *Physics Today* (December 1997): 42–47.

125. Don Hoefner, "Silicon Valley—U.S.A.," *Electronic News* (January 11, 18, and 25, 1971). Hoefner credits the name to Ralph Vaerst, president of Ion Equipment at that time; *San Jose Mercury-News* (June 28, 1981).

126. Morgan, *Electronics in the West*; Arthur Norberg, "The Origins of the Electronics Industry on the Pacific Coast," *Proceedings of the IEEE* 64, no. 9 (September 1976): 1314–22; Lowood, "From Steeples of Excellence to Silicon Valley"; Timothy J. Sturgeon, "How Silicon Valley Came to Be," in *Understanding Silicon Valley: The Anatomy of an Entrepreneurial Region*, ed. Martin Kenny, 15–47 (Stanford, CA: Stanford University Press, 2000); and Christophe Lécuyer, *Making Silicon Valley: Engineering Culture, Innovation, and Industrial Growth, 1930–1970* (unpublished PhD dissertation, Stanford University, 2000).

127. William R. Hewlett to William C. Reynolds, December 16, 1991 (copy courtesy of Professor Reynolds).

128. James F. Gibbons, "The Role of Stanford University," in *The Silicon Valley Edge*, ed. Chong-Moon Lee, William F. Miller, Marguerite Gong Hancock, and Henry S. Rowen, 215 (Stanford, CA: Stanford University Press, 2000).

129. Brooks and Arbuckle in *Session on Wally*, 58.

130. SC216/1.3/16–2, F. O. Koenig to W. Sterling, August 14, 1951; L. Owens to W. Sterling, April 6, 1952; and D. Whitaker to W. Sterling, May 12, 1952.

131. SC216/1.3/15, 16.2, W. Sterling to R. C. Swain, July 6 and August 30; and D. Whitaker to W. Sterling, May 12, 1952; SC216/1.3/16.2, H. S. Loring to D. Whitaker, September 11; and W. Sterling to D. Whitaker, September 22, 1952; SC216/1.3/17.2, H. S. Loring to D. Whitaker, December 11, 1952; SC216/1.3/18, J. M. Luck to W. Cutting, April 5, 1954.

132. Ken Cuthbertson states that Sterling "resisted the idea of vice-presidents. That was hard for him to swallow. A provost he could understand" (*Session on Wally*, 58).

133. SC216/1.1/9, D. Whitaker to C. Faust, June 10, 1949; and C. Faust to W. Sterling, June 13, 1949.

134. *Stanford Review* (March 1952). Whitaker also served briefly as acting vice president, 1948–49, for Al Eurich.

135. Don Carlson remembers, "Wally would never have used a job description. . . . If he saw the man he wanted, he would hire him and by God, he would describe his own job" (Carlson in *Session on Wally*, 41).

136. SC216/3.1/1–1, T. A. Bailey to D. M. Whitaker, July 9, 1953.

137. SC216/3.1/1–7, T. A. Bailey to D. M. Whitaker, February 5, 1952.

138. Stanford archives, 1103/3, History Department Report to President, 1953–54.

139. Stanford archives, 1103/3, Graduate Division Report to President, 1953.

140. SC216/34/14, W. Sterling to D. Whitaker, July 28, 1953; and D. Whitaker to W. Sterling, "May '54."

141. SC216/A15/22, R. Faulkner to W. Sterling, December 22, 1954.

142. SC216/1.1/10, Department Report to President, 1955; SC216/1.2/11.4 and 11.5, S. A. Waksman to E. Tatum, April 30, 1953, V. Twitty to W. Sterling, January 22, 1953.

143. SC216/5/33 and 34, J. T. Watkins IV, Political Science Department Budget Report, December 27, 1956; and P. H. Rhinelander to FET, April 15, 1957.

144. SC216/3.1/2.3, T. A. Bailey to D. M. Whitaker, February 4, 1955.

145. 0900/F. O. Glover interview by Roxanne Nilan, Harry Press, and Don Carlson, 1993, Session Two, 15.

146. Glover and Wert replaced presidential assistant Tom Spragens, originally hired by Don Tresidder. Bob Beyers, "Ken Cuthbertson: Stanford's Financial Architect," *Sandstone & Tile* 24, nos. 2–3 (spring/summer 2000): 16. SC415, accn. 93–061, Sterling unpublished "Memoirs," 13.

147. SC216/34/14, D. Whitaker to W. Sterling, "May '54"; SC216/34/15, W. Sterling to D. W. Bronk, June 17, 1955.

148. SC216/39/26, W. Sterling to E. E. Sechler, July 25, 1955.

149. SC415, accn. 93–061, 14.

150. Tapes 1:15, F. E. Terman, Uncommon Man Award Dinner, December 7, 1978.

151. SC216/39/26, FET to W. Sterling, August 3, 1955. Terman thought both Pettit and young William Kays had administrative potential. Both succeeded Terman to the deanship. SC216/39/15, FET to W. Sterling, January 3, 1956.

152. SC160/VIII/2/1, FET notes of talk to Stanford AAUP Chapter, April 8, 1957.

153. As observed by the author while an undergraduate at Stanford, 1956–60.

154. Bartholomew, Brinegar, and Nilan, *Chronology of Stanford*, 81, 85; Gillmor, "Stanford Sadie and the Early Years of KSZU Radio Broadcasting."

155. SC216/A34/15.

156. Stanford archives, 1103/3, R. K. Snyder to FET, Admissions Report, 1955–56.

157. Stanford archives, 1103/3, R. K. Snyder to FET, Admissions Report, 1955–56; President's Report, 1955–56. Entering freshmen in fall 1956 were told at a welcoming event that half of the class entering five years before would not have gained admittance in 1956, as witnessed by the author.

158. SC36/2, "H&S Administration, '52–'53," typescript of press release, April 23, 1948.

159. Faust was acting president January 1 to March 30, 1949. SC170/2/6, P. C. Edwards to W. Sterling, December 6, 1948.

160. SC216/17/5, J. W. Dodds to W. Sterling, January 28, 1956.

161. SC216/A39/7, F. O. Glover to W. Sterling, October 24, 1955.

162. Author interview with Bliss Carnochan, March 15, 2001.

163. SC36/4, "A—General," November 1, 1956, "Procedures on Senior Academic Appointments," memo from W. C. Steere, R. Faulkner, A. H. Bowker, and P. H. Rhinelander to W. Sterling and F. Terman; SC216/A15/24, P. H. Rhinelander to W. Sterling, January 7, 1957.

164. SC36/5, "Provost's Office," FET to P. H. Rhinelander, February 28, 1958.

165. SC36/5, "Provost's Office," R. Faulkner to FET, December 10, 1956.

166. SC216/A12/34, contains McCord's reports on individual departments; and William M. McCord, "School of Humanities and Sciences—Final Report, Faculty Survey," forty-six pages, April 1, 1959.

167. *Session on Wally*, 61–62.

168. Ibid.

169. Ibid., 33, 46. Stanford President Gerhard Casper remarked to the author, in 1999, that he felt that one very significant thing about Sterling was that he had the confidence to appoint a very strong man (Terman) as second in command.

170. *Session on Wally*, 58. 0900/Glover, Oral History Project interview, 1993, Session One, 17.

171. 0900/Glover, Oral History Project interview, Session One, 17; Session Three, 17; *Session on Wally*, 58–59. Glover attributes the idea of picking Corson to Ken Cuthbertson, who had himself worked for McKinsey and Company as a management consultant.

172. SC216/49, Folders 17–19.

173. SC216/A9/16, copy of "Draft #2" of the Corson report.

174. SC216/C8/9, John J. Corson, "Strengthening the Top Organization of Stanford University," 1958.

175. SC216/A9/14, W. Sterling to Academic Council, April 4, 1958.

176. Cuthbertson in *Session on Wally*, 59.

177. SC216/A9/14, W. Sterling to J. J. Corson, June 12, 1958; SC216/A9/14, J. J. Corson to W. Sterling, June 16, 1958.

178. SC216/A9/14, minutes of Dean's Council, May 6, 1958.

179. Author interview with E. H. Brooks, 1999; and with Albert H. Bowker, 2001.

180. SC216/A38/4, W. Sterling to W. C. Steere, November 18, 1958. Sterling thought about making Bowker graduate dean *and* associate provost since he was so valuable to Terman, but finally decided graduate dean was sufficient.

181. *Session on Wally*, 57.

182. Ibid., 63–65.

183. SC415, accn. 93–061/1/1, Wallace Sterling's unpublished memoirs, "The Sterling Presidency 1949–1968," 45–46. Brooks in *Session on Wally*, 54.

184. SC216/A9/14, J. Goheen to W. Sterling, June 2, 1958; SC216/C8/9, H. Royden to P. H. Rhinelander, April 8, 1958.

185. "In Memorium: H. Donald Winbigler," *Sandstone & Tile* 24, nos. 2–3 (spring/summer 2000): 25.

186. SC216/A9/14, L. Tarshis to W. Sterling, October 21, 1958.

187. SC216/C8/9, FET to J. J. Corson, March 12, 1958.

188. SC165/III/4/10, FET, "School of Engineering Needs for 1958–59," n.d., but written in 1957–58.

189. SC36/5, "Provost's Office," FET to department heads, humanities and sciences, September 14, 1959.

190. *Session on Wally*, 46; 0900/Glover, Oral History Project interview, 1993, Session Three, 2.

191. SC165/III/4/10, FET, "School of Engineering Needs for 1958–59," n.d. but written in 1957–58.

192. *Chicago Tribune*, May 26, 1957.

193. SC165/IV/1/3, FET, "President's Report 1956–1957."

194. SC165/III/4/8, FET to W. Sterling, January 3, 1956.

195. SC36/5, "General H&S," W. Sterling to P. H. Rhinelander, June 24, 1957.

196. *Stanford Daily*, October 7, 1977.

197. Robert H. Moulton Jr., "Fear and Loathing on the Electron Trail," *Sandstone & Tile* 25, no. 1 (winter 2001): 3–4.

CHAPTER SEVEN. RAISING STEEPLES AT STANFORD

1. *Newsweek* (February 20, 1961), Education section.

2. SC216/A12/34, W. M. McCord to P. H. Rhinelander, Preliminary Report on Physics Department, August 4, 1958.

3. SC36/5, "Provost's Office," FET to department heads, humanities and sciences, September 14, 1959.

4. Hugh Davis Graham and Nancy Diamond, *The Rise of American Research Universities: Elites and Challenges in the Postwar Era* (Baltimore, MD: Johns Hopkins University Press, 1997), 6–7.

5. SC160/VIII/3/2, FET speech, "Higher Education and the Federal Government," May 16, 1963; SC216/13/23, "U.S. Contracts and Grants, Year ended August 31, 1960—Ten Year Comparison of Government Research."

6. SC216/48/13, W. Sterling memo, "Medical School," June 22, 1953.

7. Stanford archives, 1103/3, "Committee on Cancer Research," "Medical School Dean's Report, 1953–54"; 1103/4, Radiology Department Report, 1955–56; Bartholomew, Brinegar, and Nilan, *Chronology*, 76.

8. SC216/48/14, minutes of Trustees' Committee on the Medical School, December 8, 1953.

9. SC216/A23/7, W. Sterling, transcript of dedication remarks, September 18, 1959.

10. See John L. Wilson, *Stanford University School of Medicine and the Predecessor Schools: An Historical Perspective* (Stanford, CA: Lane Medical Library, 1999; electronically published at http://eLane.stanford.edu/wilson/home.html).

11. Abraham Flexner, *Medical Education in the United States and Canada* (Boston, MA: Merrymount Press, 1910).

12. Nash, *Herbert Hoover and Stanford University*, 35–45, passim; Wilbur, *Memoirs*, 178–79.

13. SC216/61/35, D. B. Tresidder to A. Gregg, November 15, 1944.

14. SC216/61/35, A. Gregg to D. B. Tresidder, November 1944, with copy of Gregg letter to anonymous, February 24, 1942.

15. SC216/61/35, excerpts from Stanford Historical Materials and from trustees' minutes; SC216/61/39, W. Sterling to L. R. Chandler, December 17, 1951.

16. SC216/61/39, L. R. Chandler to W. Sterling, January 28, 1952.

17. SC216/62/1, W. Sterling to Stanford Trustees, June 22, 1953. Sterling's thoughts also were strongly influenced by what he had learned as a member of the Commission on Financing Higher Education.

18. SC216/61/44, H. M. Weeks to W. Sterling, August 6, 1953. Stanford had eighteen hundred living medical alumni, half of whom practiced in the San Francisco Bay Area; all but three hundred lived in California.

19. SC216/61/44, "Medical School Plans," August 7, 1953.

20. SC216/61/2, R. V. Lee to W. Sterling, August 25, 1954.

21. SC216/48/14, Stanford University news release, November 18, 1953.

22. SC216/A12/10, W. Cutting to W. Sterling, August 30, 1955.

23. SC216/61/44, D. M. Whitaker to medical faculty, August 10, 1953.

24. "Good soldier," in the view of Sterling and Glover, as remembered by Glover in 0900/Glover, Oral History Project interview (1993), Session Two, 21.

25. Wilson, *Stanford University School of Medicine*, ch. 37.

26. SC359/31, "Stanford 57," "Schedule for Arthur Kornberg's Visit," and note from Alway to A. Kornberg, n.d., but June 1957.

27. 0900/Glover, Oral History Project interview (1993), Session Two, 20.

28. SC216/62/5, F. O. Glover to W. Sterling, October 31, 1956.

29. SC359/25/1, Stanford Medical School Progress Report for February 1959.

30. SC170/1/5, F. O. Glover to P. Edwards, June 29, 1960.

31. Wilson, *Stanford University School of Medicine*, 1999, ch. 37. The center was dedicated September 17–18, 1959.

32. *Wall Street Journal*, "Cash for Colleges," December 6, 1961.

33. SC216/A32/20, F. O. Glover to R. J. Wert, October 20, 1961.

34. Stanford University, *Stanford's Minimum Financial Needs in the Years Ahead* (October 10, 1959).

35. *Session on Wally*, 59.

36. This section benefits from author interview with Robert H. Moulton Jr., 2001; and from Moulton, "Fear and Loathing on the Electron Trail," *Sandstone & Tile* 25, no. 1 (winter 2001): 3–13.

37. Bob Beyers, "Ken Cuthbertson: Stanford's Financial Architect," *Sandstone & Tile* 24, nos. 2–3 (spring/summer 2000): 14–21.

38. SC216/B24/2, R. H. Moulton Jr. to W. Sterling, March 26, 1959.

39. Kenneth M. Cuthbertson, "Long-Range Financial Planning," in *Long-Range Planning in Higher Education*, ed. Owen A. Knorr, 67 (Boulder, CO: Western Interstate Commission for Higher Education, 1965).

40. SC160/VIII/2/3, FET, "Stanford's Academic Goals and Academic Needs," Board of Trustees' speech, October 10, 1959. Also in *Stanford's Minimum Financial Needs in the Years Ahead* (October 10, 1959).

41. SC216/A33/12, Trustee minutes, Development Steering Committee, for example, October 14 and November 17, 1959; and T. P. Pike to J. B. Black, September 21, 1960.

42. SC216/23/16, R. J. Wert, "Brief Outline of Suggested Academic Needs of Stanford's Schools," March 26, 1960.

43. SC415, accn. 93–061/1/1, Wallace Sterling, "The Sterling Presidency 1949–1968," 50–51.

44. 0900/Glover, Oral History Project interview (1993), Session Two, 19.

45. Cuthbertson, "Long Range Financial Planning," 67.

46. SC216/A18/17, David S. Jacobson, memo to files, July 28, 1960. 0900/Glover, Oral History Project interview (1993), Session Three, 18.

47. SC216/A22/4, "The Case for Stanford," text of Wallace Sterling address announcing PACE, April 18, 1961. Bartholomew, Brinegar, and Nilan, *Chronology*, 84.

48. SC36/1, "Ford Proposal," W. Sterling to staff, September 24, 1960.

49. Beyers, "Ken Cuthbertson," 16–18; Medeiros, *Sterling Years*, 184–85.

50. Medeiros, *Sterling Years*, 196–97; SC36/1, "Ford Proposal."

51. Beyers, "Ken Cuthbertson."

52. SC216/14/12, K. M. Cuthbertson to development staff, August 15, 1961. 0900/John Wendell Dodds interview, 15–16.

53. Stanford *Faculty Staff Newsletter* 8, no. 12 (April 6, 1965); Cuthbertson, quoted by Beyer, "Ken Cuthbertson," 18; SC415, accn. 93–061/1/1, Sterling, "Sterling Presidency, 1949–1968," 51–52.

54. Stanford *Faculty Staff Newsletter* 6, no. 7 (January 3, 1962).

55. SC160/III/62/2, provost meeting minutes, October 9 and December 10, 1962.

56. SC216/A12/38, Interim Report on the Ford Foundation Special Program in Education Grant to Stanford University, January 13, 1964.

57. SC216/A32/27, Wallace Sterling, Annual Report to the Trustees, June 1963.

58. SC160/XIV/13, Folders 16 and 20, PACE Campaign, 1962, 1963.

59. SC160/III/63, Folders 5–6.

60. SC216/B5/31, J. W. Dodds to Sterling, September 14, 1962; and W. Sterling to J.

W. Dodds, September 18, 1962. SC216/B7/13, F. O. Glover to W. Sterling, October 14, 1963; SC415, accn. 93–061/1/1, Sterling, "Sterling Presidency, 1949–1968," 53.

61. 0900/Glover, Oral History Project interview (1993), Session Three, 3.

62. Clark Kerr, as quoted in *Los Angeles Times*, October 13, 1963, from a series of articles by Irving S. Bengelsdorf, October 13–16, 1963. See also Clark Kerr, *The Uses of the University* (Cambridge, MA: Harvard University Press, 1963).

63. SC216/B3/3, H. S. Kaplan to W. Sterling, June 10, 1963.

64. SLAC is a national laboratory for high-energy physics and synchrotron-radiation research operated by Stanford University on behalf of the U.S. Department of Energy. Celebrating its twenty-fifth anniversary in 2002, SLAC logs in a resident staff of about twelve hundred, with an additional three thousand scientists visiting annually. Thousands of published papers and reports have come from research at SLAC's various facilities. To date, five physicists (Richard Taylor, Henry Kendall, Jerome Friedman, Burton Richter, and Martin Perl) have been awarded the Nobel Prize for work done there.

65. Very useful for this section is Edward L. Ginzton, "An Informal History of SLAC—Part One: Early Accelerator Work at Stanford," *SLAC Beamline*, special issue, no. 2 (April 1983). See also W. K. H. Panofsky, "An Informal History of SLAC—Part Two: The Evolution of SLAC and its Program," *SLAC Beamline*, special issue, no. 3 (May 1983); W. K. H. Panofsky, "Big Physics and Small Physics at Stanford," *Sandstone & Tile* 14, no. 3 (summer 1990): 1–7; Leslie, *Cold War and American Science*, ch. 6; Galison, Hevly, and Lowen, "Controlling the Monster," and Panofsky, "SLAC and Big Science," both in Galison and Hevly, *Big Science*. For a history of the project in its first years, also see Richard B. Neal, ed., *The Stanford Two-Mile Accelerator* (New York: W. A. Benjamin, Inc., 1968).

66. SC 220/14, E. Ginzton to E. Hilgard, April 20, 1953, as quoted in Galison, Hevly, and Lowen, "Controlling the Monster," 63.

67. Ginzton, "An Informal History of SLAC—Part One," 10–11. Ginzton credits Hofstadter with being the first to suggest the idea of a very long accelerator.

68. SC216/30/26, memos to W. Sterling from E. L. Ginzton, R. Hofstadter, W. K. H. Panofsky, and L. I. Schiff, October 8 and 26, 1954.

69. SC216/30/26, Sterling's notes on Accelerator Plans, n.d., but late 1954.

70. Ginzton, "Informal History of SLAC—Part One," 11.

71. Ibid., 13.

72. 0900/Glover, Oral History Project interview, Session Two, 25.

73. 1103/4, annual reports, W. W. Hansen Laboratories of Physics, 1956–57.

74. See Moulton, "Fear and Loathing."

75. Ginzton, *Times to Remember*, 141–42; M708, H. Myrl Stearns interviews by Sharon Mercer, 1989, 47–49.

76. Moulton, "Fear and Loathing," 12.

77. The Mark III accelerator had been constructed by one professor, twenty graduate students, and about thirty-five mechanical and electrical technicians. Ginzton, "Informal History of SLAC—Part One," 9.

78. Moulton, "Fear and Loathing," 8.

79. Ibid., 13.

80. This pun derives from Leslie, *Cold War and American Science*, 181.

81. SC216/A32/27, Wallace Sterling, Annual Report to Trustees, June 1963.

82. SC216/B5/21, A. H. Bowker, memo to files, October 10, 1960.

83. Author conversation with Eugene Rickensrud, 2001.

84. SC216/B3/9, S. Drell, W. K. H. Panofsky, and D. Ritson to A. H. Bowker, December 7, 1962.

85. SC303/I/1/12, and I/8/13, L. I. Schiff to F. Bloch, October 11 and November 2, 1954; F. Bloch to L. I. Schiff, December 5, 1954; and F. Bloch to R. Hofstadter, December 8, 1954.

86. Felix Bloch interview by Charles Weiner, American Institute of Physics, 1968 (transcript in Stanford University Archives 0900), 41. Bloch's relationships with Varian Associates and with William Hansen's brother James also became very rocky over patent royalty disagreements. M708, H. Myrl Stearns interview; p. 49; M708 Martin Packard interview, n.p.

87. SC216/B3/9, "Policy Statement Recommended by the Advisory Board," July 11, 1961.

88. Albert H. Bowker interviews, by Harriet Nathan, 1991, 144–45, Bancroft Library.

89. SC216/B5/21, A. H. Bowker to FET, October 13, 1960.

90. Galison, Hevly, and Lowen, "Controlling the Monster," 73.

91. SC216/B3/9, A. H. Bowker to S. Raffel, chairman, [Faculty] Advisory Board, February 15, 1963.

92. Ibid.

93. Panofsky, "SLAC and Big Science," 135; Stanford *Faculty-Staff Newsletter* 7, no. 10 (February 12, 1963); SC160/III/45/10, A. H. Bowker to FET, October 13, 1960. Reference to Bloch is in SC216/B5/21, A. H. Bowker to FET, October 13, 1960.

94. For examples see the following letters to Wallace Sterling, in SC216/B3/3: "Letter Signed by Eleven Members of the Mathematics Department," March 13, 1963; H. S. Kaplan, June 10, 1963; A. Kornberg and W. S. Johnson, September 1, 1965; H. Taube, September 2, 1965; and P. J. Flory, September 2 and 28, 1965.

95. SC216/B7/8, A. E. Brandin to Office of the President, August 27, 1958.

96. SC160/III/45/10, A. H. Bowker to FET, October 13, 1960.

97. SC98/13/5, G. E. Forsythe to FET (Draft), December 6, 1963; G. E. Forsythe to W. K. H. Panofsky, January 14, 1964; SC98/13/5, G. E. Forsythe to FET (Draft), December 6, 1963.

98. SC98/13/5, and SC98/15/6, 7. Correspondence between FET, G. E. Forsythe, W. K. H. Panofsky, H. Heffner and others, 1963–65, Concerning the Search for a Head of the SLAC Computing Effort, and the Offer to William F. Miller of a Joint SLAC/Computer Science Department Position. Also, SC160/VIII/4/7, FET speech to Bohemian Club Dinner, May 6, 1977.

99. SC160/III/63/1, G. E. Forsythe to V. K. Whitaker, July 29, 1964. See also SC98/2, Folders 19 and 38a, Concerning Formation of Computer Science Department.

100. SC98/15/7, G. E. Forsythe to M. L. Minsky, February 13, 1964.

101. SC160/III/63/1, H. Royden to FET, October 26, 1964.

102. SC216/B3/9, L. I. Schiff to H. Royden, May 26, 1964.

103. Some years after Terman's retirement, Miller was appointed provost.

104. SC216/B3/9, W. Sterling (Draft #3) "General Policies," February 1, 1963.

105. John Walsh, "SLAC: Stanford-AEC Accelerator is Coming Along on Schedule, but Creating Some High Tension," *Science* 143 (March 27, 1964): 1419–21.

106. SC216/B3/9, W. E. Meyerhof to Physics Graduate Students, February 10, 1964; and FET to W. Sterling, March 20, 1964; SC216/B3/9, W. Sterling to FET, March 27, 1964.

107. SC216/B3/9, A. H. Bowker to S. Raffel, February 15, 1963.

108. Richard P. Feynman, Robert B. Leighton, and Matthew Sands, *The Feynman Lectures on Physics*, 3 vols. (Redwood City, CA: Addison-Wesley, 1963–65).

109. SC216/B3/9, Associate Provost H. Heffner to W. Sterling, April 6, 1965.

110. SC216/B3/9, W. Sterling to V. K. Whitaker, July 30, 1965.

111. SC216/B3/9, V. K. Whitaker to W. Sterling, September 28, 1965.

112. SC216/B3/9, Folder "SLAC-Physics Dept. Relationship 1963–66."

113. SC36/5, "Provost's Office," FET to department heads, humanities and sciences, September 14, 1959.

114. *Session on Wally*, 46.

115. SC160/VIII/4/6, FET notes for talk to Stanford Fellows, February 27, 1974.

116. J. Pearce Mitchell, *Stanford University, 1916–1941*, 78.

117. SC216/1.2/11–4, pamphlet "Biology at Stanford," n.d., but 1953.

118. SC216/1.3/2.1, Clifford Grobstein, "Stanford Biology and the Future," December 19, 1963.

119. SC160/III/4/7, FET notes, "Meeting with Biology Department," December 2, 1955; and author interview with David D. Perkins, 2001.

120. SC216/1.3/12–1, Wallace Sterling notes for remarks to Board of Trustees, December 18, 1963; and J. P. Thurber Jr. to R. J. Wert, December 17, 1963.

121. SC216/1.2/11–1, V. Twitty to W. Sterling, January 10; and J. M. Luck to W. Sterling, March 12, 1956.

122. SC160/III/4/6, "Biochemistry," FET notes, n.d., but February 1956; and W. Sterling to FET, n.d., but February 1956.

123. SC160/III/4/11, FET to W. Steere, December 1955; and FET notes concerning Douglas Whitaker and Ed Tatum, February 5, 1957.

124. SC160/III/4/7, V. Twitty to FET, September 18, 1956.

125. SC160/III/4/7, V. Twitty to W. Steere, October 22, 1956; W. Steere to V. Twitty, November 8, 1956; V. Twitty to P. H. Rhinelander, November 26 and December 26, 1956; and FET notes, November 27, 1956.

126. SC160/III4/6, letters and notes, spring and summer of 1957.

127. *San Francisco Chronicle*, August 20, 1957.

128. SC359/24, D. R. Schwarz to A. Kornberg, October 8, 1957.

129. SC359/24, A. Kornberg to B. Wood Jr., September 23, 1958.

130. SC359/24, A. Kornberg to R. Alway, April 9, 1958.

131. SC186/1/11.

132. SC186/25/1, R. Alway to A. Kornberg, n.d., but early January 1959.

133. SC359/25/1, A. Kornberg to H. S. Kaplan, February 3, 1959.

134. *Bulletin*, Stanford University School of Medicine, 1959–60, entry for biochemistry.

135. SC160/III/4/6, R. Alway to FET, May 7, 1957; SC359/25/1, H. S. Loring to A. Kornberg, February 16, 1959; and A. Kornberg to R. Alway, February 19, 1959.

136. SC359/29/1,2, R. Alway to A. Kornberg; and A. Kornberg to R. Alway, October 20 and December 1, 1959.

137. SC359/24, H. S. Gutowsky to D. Kornberg, September 22, 1958; D. Kornberg to H. S. Gutowsky, October 23, 1958.

138. SC359/32, D. Kornberg to R. Alway, November 4, 1963.

139. SC359/31, R. K. Snyder to A. Kornberg December 15, 1964; and A. Kornberg to R. K. Snyder, December 23, 1964; Stanford archives, 1103/3, R. K. Snyder to FET, Dean of Admissions Report, 1955–56.

140. SC359/24, A. Kornberg to J. Lederberg, September 8, 1958.

141. SC359/24, H. Kaplan to A. Kornberg, January 2, 1958; SC359/31, R. Alway to J. Lederberg, July 1, 1958.

142. SC186/1/13, FET to J. Lederberg, February 20, 1959.

143. SC359/23/10.

144. SC/36/5, "Provost's Office," FET to P. H. Rhinelander, February 28, 1958.

145. SC160/III/4/8, letters and notes, January to June 1957, V. Twitty, P. H. Rhinelander, FET.

146. Charles Yanofsky, "Advancing Our Knowledge in Biochemistry, Genetics, and Microbiology Through Studies on Tryptophan Metabolism," *Annual Reviews in Biochemistry* 70 (2000): 11–12; author interview with Charles Yanofsky, 2001.

147. SC160/III/4/8, C. Grobstein to V. Twitty, January 30, 1957.

148. SC160/III/4/8, C. Grobstein to V. Twitty, June 25, 1957.

149. SC160/III/4/9, V. Twitty to FET, January 30, 1961; SC160/III/4/10, V. Twitty to Biology Faculty, May 27, 1963; H. Royden to FET, May 28, 1963; and V. Twitty to FET, June 14, 1963.

150. SC160/III/4/8, V. Twitty to P. H. Rhinelander, June 9, 1961.

151. SC160/III/4/9, R. D. Owen to W. Sterling, June 6, 1962; and FET to R. R. Sears, June 11, 1962.

152. SC160/III/4/8, "Department of Biological Sciences," n.d., but fall 1960. For a description of the older Biology Department, see J. Perry Baumberger, "A History of Biology at Stanford University," *Bios* 25, no. 3 (October 1954): 123–47.

153. SC160/III/4/II, FET to F. O. Glover, memo, ca. June 27, 1965.

154. SC160/III/4/7, V. Twitty to P. H. Rhinelander, February 14, 1958.

155. SC160/III/4/7, P. H. Rhinelander to V. Twitty, February 25, 1958.

156. E. O. Wilson, *Naturalist* (New York: Island Press, 1994): 201–2.

157. SC160/III/4/7, P. H. Rhinelander to FET, May 8, 1958.

158. SC160/III/4/7, C. Michener to V. Twitty, June 5, 1958.

159. SC160/III/4/7, V. Twitty to P. H. Rhinelander, December 9, 1958; and P. H. Rhinelander to FET, January 19, 1959.

160. Paul R. Ehrlich, *The Population Bomb* (New York: Ballantine, 1968).

161. SC160/III/4/9, V. Twitty to P. H. Rhinelander, May 3, 1961.

162. Author interview with Virginia Walbot, 2000.

163. M. L. Goldberger, B. A. Mahler, and P. Ebert Flattau, *Research-doctorate Programs in the United States: Continuity and Change*, Committee for the Study of Research-Doctorate Programs in the United States. National Academy Press, Washington DC (1995). See Appendix, Table N-3 (401), "Selected Characteristics of Research-Doctorate Programs in Ecology, Evolution, and Behavior, where Stanford was tied with University of Chicago for first place in ratings for 'Reputation.'"

164. SC160/III/4/8, V. Twitty to P. H. Rhinelander, October 4, 1960; FET note to P. H. Rhinelander, fall 1960; and FET letters to Visiting Committee, fall 1960. Four eminent biologists visited Stanford, December 7–16, 1960: Ernst Mayr of the Harvard Museum of Comparative Zoology; David Keck, head of the National Science Foundation's Division of Systematic Biology; Lincoln Constance, a botanist and dean of Berkeley's Humanities and Sciences; and Carl Hubbs, an ichthyologist from Scripps Institute of Oceanography, La Jolla.

165. SC216/1.2/11–1, R. W. Holm to FET, May 28, 1956; SC216/1.2/11–1, FET to R. W. Holm, May 30, 1956; SC216/23/20, K. Cuthbertson to A. Brandin, June 25, 1956.

166. SC36/2, Folder "Natural History Museum," L. R. Blinks to R. J. Wert, December 12, 1951; and R. L. Bolin to R. J. Wert, December 12, 1951.

167. Timby, "Dudley Herbarium," 3.

168. See Lowen, *Creating the Cold War University*; Timby, "Dudley Herbarium." Lowen suggests that Donald Kennedy, acting department head in 1965, was pressured by Terman, but Kennedy contends that this was not so, that Stanford's Biology Department was not a museum, and that a more appropriate location for the collections was found at the California Academy of Sciences where the combined collections of several institutions are more efficiently cared for and utilized. Author interview with Donald Kennedy, 2000.

169. Author interview with Ehrlich, 2001, and correspondence with Raven, August 19 and 20, 2002.

170. SC160/III/4/8, G. S. Myers to FET, December 15, 1960; V. Twitty to FET, December 19, 1960; and FET to V. Twitty, January 9, 1961.

171. SC160/III/4/9, R. W. Holm to V. Twitty, January 10, 1962.

172. SC160/III/4/10, A. H. Bowker to provost staff, regarding visit of Ford Foundation executive Paul B. Pearson, December 26, 1962.

173. SC160/III/32/2, D. Mazia to L. Blinks, December 13, 1958; L. Blinks to D. Mazia, December 19, 1958; and FET's notes to L. Blinks, December 1958.

174. Lawrence R. Blinks, "Hooked on Biology: A Memoir of 50 Years at Stanford," *Sandstone & Tile* 16, no. 4 (fall 1992): 18. The contemporary records do not substantiate some of Blinks's recollections.

175. SC160/III/32/2, A. H. Bowker to FET, April 6, 1959; and L. Blinks to FET, June 25 and July 3 and 4, 1959.

176. SC160/III/32/2, FET notes of conversations with R. Revelle and G. Beadle, July 1960; FET to H. J. Carlson of NSF, July 21, 1960; and FET notes of conversation with John Wilson of NSF, November 2, 1960. SC160/III/4/7, FET to M. Travis, March 17, 1959.

177. SC160/III/32/1, L. Blinks to FET, November 8, 1960; V. Twitty to P. H. Rhinelander, November 10, 1960; and P. H. Rhinelander to FET, November 10, 1960.

178. SC160/III/21/1, R. Bolin to FET, October 27, 1960; SC160/III/32/2, A. T. Waterman (NSF) to W. Sterling, April 14, 1961; C. W. Tarr to A. H. Bowker, May 23, 1961; FET notes, July 2, 1961; and J. P. Thurber Jr. to FET, October 25, 1961. Blinks, "Hooked on Biology," 18.

179. Blinks, "Hooked on Biology," 18.

180. 0900/Glover, Oral History Project interview (1993), Session Four, 33–34.

181. Blinks, "Hooked on Biology," 18.

182. SC160/III/4/8, V. Twitty to P. H. Rhinelander and FET, January 4, 1960.

183. David Epel, "Stanford by the Sea: A Brief History of Hopkins Marine Station," *Sandstone & Tile* 16, no. 4 (fall 1992): 9.

184. 1103/3, F. V. L. Pindar to FET, "W. W. Hansen Laboratories—President's Report," December 13, 1955.

185. SC317/I/5.

186. D. W. Dupen, "History and Development," in *The Stanford Two-Mile Accelerator*, ed. Richard B. Neal, 31–32. SC216/18/16, Annual Report to President, "Summary of Experience with Six MEV Linear Accelerator," Henry Kaplan, January 29, 1957. Stanford archives, 1103/4, Annual Report, W. W. Hansen Laboratories, 1956–57.

187. SC303/I/6/4, L. I. Schiff to E. Ginzton, April 28, 1957. Stanford archives, 1103/4, Annual Report, W. W. Hansen Laboratories, 1956–57.

188. SC359/32, A. Kornberg to T. R. Howell, September 28, 1964.

189. Author interview with David Perkins, 2001.

190. SC160/III/4/11, W. Sterling to R. R. Sears, June 15, 1965.

191. Not surprisingly, biologist George S. Myers wrote a bitter letter and complained about the imbalance within the committee, unfairly favoring the fields of molecular biology and biochemistry. SC160/III/4/11, G. S. Myers to W. Sterling, June 26, 1965.

192. SC160/III/4/11, FET to F. O. Glover, June 1965; and FET to R. R. Sears, August 27, 1965.

193. Timby, "Dudley Herbarium," 13.

194. Allan M. Cartter, *An Assessment of Quality in Graduate Education* (Washington DC: American Council on Education, 1966).

195. SC186//9/12, J. Lederberg, memo to file, September 6, 1976.

196. Hutchinson, *Department of Chemistry*, 18–19.

197. Stanford archives, 1103/1a, Annual Report to President, Business Manager, 1949–50.

198. Stanford archives, 1103/2, Annual Report to President, Business Manager, 1951–52.

199. For a concise history of the "Old Chem" building, see Karen Bartholomew and Claude Brinegar, "Old Chemistry: One of Jane Stanford's Noble Buildings," *Sandstone & Tile* 23, no. 1 (winter 1999): 3–10.

200. Stanford archives, 1103/1, "Departmental Projection Reports," Department of Chemistry, December 5, 1949.

201. Swain (Stanford BA, chemistry, '28) and son of Robert E. Swain (head of chemistry and acting university president) maintained a keen interest in the Chemistry Department and served as an influential advisor. SC216/1.3/15, W. Sterling to R. C. Swain, July 6, 1951.

202. Hutchinson, *Department of Chemistry*, 16–17.

203. SC216/1.3/19–2, J. M. Luck to W. Cutting, August 13, 1954.

204. SC216/1.3/18, J. M. Luck to W. Cutting, April 5, 1954. SC216/1.3/19–1, J. M. Luck to G. S. Parks, January 25, 1955.

205. SC36/2, Chemistry, 1953; Report of J. S. Walton visit of December 3–4, 1952; George S. Parks memo, September 25, 1953.

206. SC216/1.3/19–1, R. R. Paxton to D. Whitaker, September 13 and 22, 1954. SC216/1.3/9–1, R. R. Paxton to G. S. Parks, January 20, 1955; and G. S. Parks to D. Whitaker, January 27, 1955.

207. SC216/1.3/19–1, D. Whitaker to W. Sterling, May 10, 1955.

208. SC216/A12/17, G. S. Parks to President's Office, "Memorandum on Plans," December 20, 1955.

209. Hutchinson, *Department of Chemistry*, 17.

210. SC216/1.3/19–1, D. S. Jacobson to D. Whitaker, October 20, 1954.

211. SC216/1.3/19–1, R. C. Swain to D. Whitaker, December 6, 1954.

212. SC216/1.3/19–1, D. Whitaker to W. Sterling (copy to Fred Terman), July 26, 1955.

213. SC216/1.3/20, FET memo to committee members, April 3, 1956.

214. SC216/1.3/20, FET to R. Adams, May 31, 1956.

215. Hutchinson, *Department of Chemistry*, 29.

216. SC216/1.3/20, W. Sterling to E. Hutchinson, January 10 and April 4, 1956.

217. Wilson's son, Kenneth G. Wilson at Cornell, won the Nobel Prize in Physics in 1982.

218. SC160/III4/11, FET to R. R. Sears, August 27, 1965.

219. Libby won the Nobel Prize in Chemistry in 1960.

220. SC216/1.4/21.4, FET memos to W. Sterling, n.d., but early fall 1957.

221. SC216/1.4/21.4, W. Sterling to W. F. Libby, November 19, 1957.

222. SC216/1.4/21.4, W. F. Libby to W. Sterling, January 23, 1958.

223. SC415, accn. 93–061/1/1, Sterling, "Sterling Presidency, 1949–1968," 36–37.

224. SC216/A12/34, W. M. McCord to P. H. Rhinelander, October 15, 1958.

225. SC160/III/4/11, FET to R. R. Sears, August 27, 1965.

226. William S. Johnson, *A Fifty-Year Love Affair with Organic Chemistry* (Washington DC: American Chemical Society, 1998), 83–85.

227. Carl Djerassi, *The Pill, Pygmy Chimps, and Degas' Horse: The Autobiography of Carl Djerassi* (New York: Basic Books, 1992), 66–67, 102–4.

228. Ibid., 95–96, 100, 154–58.

229. SC216/1.4/21.4, "Chemistry Department Program," memo from FET to President's Office as preparation for Board of Trustees' action on March 19, 1959.

230. SC216/1.4/21.4, W. Sterling to W. S. Johnson, April 7, 1959; and W. Sterling to W. S. Johnson, telegram, April 15, 1959.

231. SC216/B3/17, R. C. Swain to W. Sterling, May 22, 1959.

232. SC160/III/10/4, W. S. Johnson to FET, May 25, 1959; E. Hutchinson to W. S. Johnson, June 2, 1959; FET to W. S. Johnson, June 9, 1959; W. S. Johnson to E. Hutchinson, June 17, 1959; and C. Noller to W. S. Johnson, July 8, 1959.

233. SC160/III/10/4, S. Weissman to FET, July 17, 1959; FET to W. S. Johnson, August 24, 1959; W. S. Johnson to S. Weissman, October 7, 1959; and W. S. Johnson to FET, November 4, 1959.

234. Bruno H. Zimm to author, August 12, 2001.

235. SC216/21.3, E. Hutchinson to W. Sterling, May 13, 1960.

236. Johnson, *Fifty-Year Love Affair*, 91–92; author interview with Henry Taube, 2001.

237. Bartholomew, Brinegar, and Nilan, *Chronology*, 154.

238. SC359/32, H. M. McConnell to W. S. Johnson, April 17, 1962.

239. SC216/1.4/21–2, FET to J. Stauffer, March 21, 1962.

240. Author interview with Harden M. McConnell, 2001.

241. SC216/1.4/21–1, W. S. Johnson to P. J. Flory, August 4, 1964.

242. SC165/I/1, Folder 24. The three Stauffer buildings were for General Chemistry (dedicated, 1961), Physical Chemistry (1964), and Chemical Engineering (1966). SC359/31, "Stanford Correspondence 1961–66," report by Richard H. Eastman, "The General Chemistry Program at Stanford," August 6, 1964.

243. SC359/31, Folder "Freshman Chemistry Teaching"; A. Kornberg to W. S. Johnson, August 19, 1964; and W. S. Johnson to A. Kornberg, August 26, 1964.

244. Author interview with Henry Taube, 2001.

245. See Appendix D, "Stanford in the Ratings."

246. SC 359/32, F. H. Harrington to K. P. Link, March 24, 1964.

247. Faculty appointments often were made one or two years before the member took up residence on campus. Hutchinson, *Department of Chemistry*, 44–45. Bartholomew, Brinegar, and Nilan, *Chronology*, 153–57.

248. SC216/B5/1, staff paper, prepared by Dean J. M. Pettit, D. M. Mason, and others, n.d., but fall 1960.

249. Hutchinson, *Department of Chemistry*, 33; and SC160/VIII/4/6, Folder "Chemistry."

250. SC160/VIII/3/2, FET, "Higher Education and the Federal Government," May 16, 1963.

251. Johnson, *Fifty-Year Love Affair with Organic Chemistry*, 84.

252. SC530, Introductory Materials to Johnson Papers.

253. SC160/III/7/14, FET to W. S. Johnson, July 14, 1970; and W. S. Johnson to FET, July 21, 1970.

254. Mitchell, *Stanford University*, 82, 85–86.

255. SC36/5, "Provost's Office," FET to department heads, humanities and sciences, September 14, 1959.

256. SC160/VIII/4/6, FET notes for talk to Stanford Fellows, February 27, 1974.

257. Robert Hoopes and Hubert Marshall, eds., *The Undergraduate in the University: Stanford Study of Undergraduate Education, 1954–56* (Stanford, CA: Stanford University Press, 1957), 39–41.

258. SC36/3, Folders "H&S," Budget 1952–53 and Budget 1954–55.

259. SC36/3, Folder "H&S," Budget 1955–56.

260. Hoopes and Marshall, *Undergraduate in the University*, 39–41.

261. SC36/4, Folder "Development," 1961.

262. Author interview with Robert Rosenzweig, 1998.

263. SC160/III/60/5, FET to D. Whitaker, February 29, 1956; and FET notes on Whitaker conversation, summer 1955. The political science faculty member arguing to Whitaker for abolishing the department was Anthony Sokol.

264. SC216/A12/34, W. M. McCord to P. H. Rhinelander, September 21, 1958. According to Stanford commencement programs, the Political Science Department for the period 1954–58 awarded a total of twelve PhD degrees compared to forty-one in history and fifty in English. For the period 1964–68, the figures were, respectively, twenty-eight, fifty-five, and seventy-one for the three departments. A 1957 study ranked the department generally thirteenth out of twenty-five in the survey, but few on its faculty were considered productive scholars.

265. Gabriel A. Almond, "Political Science: The History of the Discipline," in *A New Handbook of Political Science*, ed. Robert E. Goodin and Hans-Dieter Klingemann, ch. 2 (Oxford: Oxford University Press, 1996).

266. SC216/A12/41, E. R. Hilgard and D. M. Whitaker to Faculty Committee, July 19, 1951; and Associated Report of the Committee, n.d.

267. SC216/A15/22, R. Faulkner to D. M. Whitaker, December 21, 1953.

268. SC160/III/4/1, "The Stanford Survey of the Behavioral Sciences, 1953–54, Report of the Visiting Committee, September 1954." The committee was Charles J. Hitch, economist, Rand Corporation; Carl I. Hovland, psychologist, Yale; Paul F. Lazarsfeld, sociologist, Columbia; Donald McKay, historian, Harvard; Peter H. Odegard, political scientist, Berkeley; and Stanley A. Weigal, attorney in San Francisco. See also "Report of the Executive Committee and Staff, July 1954," Stanford's in-house committee of Wallace Sterling, Provost Douglas Whitaker, Graduate Dean William Steere, Acting Humanities and Sciences Dean Ray Faulkner, plus four faculty; with the assistance of twenty-six Stanford faculty as an advisory committee. SC36/1, Ford: Behavioral Sciences Survey, Political Science Report by Peter H. Odegard, March 17, 1954.

269. SC216/5/37, FET to J. T. Watkins IV, November 7, 1956.

270. SC216/5/37, J. T. Watkins IV to P. H. Rhinelander, February 25, 1958.

271. Mulford Q. Sibley and Philip E. Jacob, *Conscription of Conscience: The American*

State and the Conscientious Objector, 1940–1947 (Ithaca, NY: Cornell University Press, 1952).

272. SC216/5/37, FET notes on conversations with University of Minnesota faculty, including on April 30, 1958, Associate Graduate Dean John G. Darley (psychologist), Henry Riecken (sociologist), and, on April 28, 1958, Bryce Crawford (chemist).

273. SC216/5/37, Philip H. Rhinelander memos to files, February 27 and 28, 1958.

274. It is clear from Hartz's letter that no detailed offer from Stanford had yet come his way, but he responded that he would give serious thought to any specific proposal. SC216/5/37, L. Hartz to P. H. Rhinelander, March 3, 1958.

275. SC216/5/37, P. H. Rhinelander to A. H. Bowker, March 7, 1958.

276. SC216/5/37, P. H. Rhinelander to J. T. Watkins IV, March 18; and P. H. Rhinelander to FET, March 18, 1958.

277. SC216/5/34, P. H. Rhinelander to FET, April 15, 1957.

278. SC216/5/35, P. H. Rhinelander to FET, March 21; FET to W. Sterling, March 21, 1958; W. Sterling to J. T. Watkins IV, March 26, 1958; and J. T. Watkins IV to W. Sterling, March 31, 1958.

279. SC216/5/37, P. H. Rhinelander to FET, March 27, 1958.

280. SC216/5/37, A. H. Bowker memo, March 27, 1958.

281. SC216/5/37, A. H. Bowker memo, April 10, 1958.

282. SC216/5/37, P. H. Rhinelander to FET, April 15; J. Goheen to P. H. Rhinelander, April 21, 1958; and A. H. Bowker to FET, n.d., but ca. April 15, 1958.

283. SC216/5/37, FET notes of telephone conversation with P. H. Rhinelander, April 10, 1958.

284. SC216/5/37, T. A. Bailey to P. H. Rhinelander, April 30, 1958.

285. SC216/5/37, FET "Sibley—Report from Minnesota," April 30, 1958.

286. SC216/5/37, P. H. Rhinelander memo, December 27, 1957.

287. SC216/5/35, FET notes on conversation with Sterling, May 2, 1958.

288. SC216/5/37, P. H. Rhinelander to W. Sterling, May 5, 1958.

289. SC216/A12/34, W. H. McCord to P. H. Rhinelander, September 26, 1958.

290. SC216/5/35, W. Sterling to M. L. Godfrey Jr., May 27, 1959.

291. Lowen, *Creating the Cold War University*, 215–18.

292. Ibid., 218–19.

293. Author interviews with Sanford Dornbusch, 1997; with Heinz Eulau, 2001; and with Robert Rosenzweig, 1998.

294. Author interview with Robert Rosenzweig, 1998.

295. Sears learned this after detective work during the fall of 1961 by his assistants Sanford Dornbusch and Patrick Suppes. SC216/A15/26, R. R. Sears to FET, January 9, 1962.

296. See G. Robert Hamrdla, "Four Decades of Stanford Overseas Studies," *Sandstone & Tile* 24, nos. 2–3 (spring/summer 2000): 8–13.

297. SC216/5/38, R. A. Horn to W. Sterling, February 28, 1963. A colleague told Eulau that upon learning of Sears's thoughts of possibly appointing Eulau, Watkins slumped into a chair and groaned. Author interview with Heinz Eulau, 2001.

298. SC216/A15/26, R. R. Sears to FET, March 20, 1963.

299. SC160/III/62/3, provost minutes, April 12, 1963.

300. SC160/III/62/1, minutes of provost staff meeting, May 29, 1962.

301. SC160/3/45/2, R. R. Sears to R. J. Wert, January 27, 1963.

302. Author interview with Robert Rosenzweig, 1998. Rosensweig also served as asso-

ciate provost and, later, vice president of public affairs at Stanford, and was president of the Association of American Universities.

303. Gabriel Abraham Almond and Sidney Verba, *The Civic Culture: Political Attitudes and Democracy in Five Nations* (Princeton, NJ: Princeton University Press, 1963).

304. Author interviews with Almond, 2001; with Eulau, 2001; and with Triska, 2001.

305. Author interview and conversation with Gabriel A. Almond, 2001; and Almond letter to author of July 5, 2001.

306. SC160/III/78/4, R. R. Sears to FET, October 28, 1964; and FET memo, January 29, 1965. Author interview with Gabriel A. Almond, 2001.

307. See Chapter 8, below.

308. 0900/Robert R. Sears interview by Frederic O. Glover, October 27 and December 1, 1982. 0900/Virgil K. Whitaker interview by Eleanor Bark and Harvey Hall, May 24, 1982.

309. Mitchell, *Stanford University*, 82, 85.

310. SC36/4, Folder "ACLS."

311. Author conversation with Lawrence Ryan, 1999.

312. SC410, accn. 93–104, Box 1, minutes of English Department Executive Committee, 1951–58. For a view of English in 1961, see SC36/4 "Development Office," "The Department of English, Past Present and Future," n.d., but early 1961.

313. Author interview with Bliss Carnochan, 2001. See also Carnochan, "English at Stanford, 1891–2000: A Brief History," *Sandstone & Tile* 26, no. 1 (winter/spring 2002): 3–15.

314. Author interview with Walter F. W. Lohnes, 1999.

315. SC359/29/2, correspondence regarding "Stanford Today" Panel on November 29, 1961, featuring Herbert Packer, Arthur Kornberg, Philip H. Rhinelander, Leonard I. Schiff, Hugh H. Skilling, and Robert J. Wert. See *Stanford Today* no. 7 (spring 1962).

316. SC160/VIII/3/2, FET, "Higher Education and the Federal Government," May 16, 1963.

317. SC36/4, "Development," February 28, 1961, "Humanities Council—Report on the Next Ten Years."

318. SC216/A16/1, "Humanities Council—Stanford University—Preliminary Report for Discussion," May 12, 1960.

319. SC216/B5/30, "Humanities Council—Report on the Next Ten Years," received February 17, 1961.

320. SC216/B5/31, "The Status of the Humanities at Stanford," April 1962.

321. SC36/2, "H&S Administration '52–'53," R. Faulkner to D. M. Whitaker, December 19, 1952.

322. SC160/III/62/2, "Faculty Salaries, 1962–63."

323. For example, see SC160/III/62/2, provost's staff meeting agenda, September 18, 1962; SC160/III/62/3, R. R. Sears to FET, February 18, 1963; SC160/III/62/4, FET to deans and heads of departments, January 15, 1964. SC216/A32/27, Annual Report to the Trustees, Wallace Sterling, June 1963.

324. SC216/B5/30, "Research Funds for the Humanities," Albert H. Bowker, October 31, 1961.

325. George H. Knoles, "History of Western Civilization at Stanford," *The Stanford Historian* (published by the History Department of Stanford University) 6 (April 1980): 8–15.

326. 1103/3, History Department Annual Report to the President, 1954–55.

327. SC216/A12/23, H. Stuart Hughes, "Report to the President," March 5, 1956.

328. SC216/3.1/1–1, T. A. Bailey to D. M. Whitaker, July 9, 1953. For more on Bailey, see Alexander DeConde, "Thomas A. Bailey: Teacher, Scholar, Popularizer," *Pacific Historical Review* 56 (May 1987): 161–93.

329. SC36/1, Ford: Behavioral Sciences Survey, History Report by Donald C. McKay, March 21, 1954.

330. SC410, accn. 93–104, Box 1, minutes of English Department Executive Committee, 1951–58.

331. Hoopes and Marshall, *Undergraduate in the University*, 96.

332. SC36/1, "NDEA," A. H. Bowker to FET, December 2, 1958.

333. SC216/3.1/4–5, FET to T. A. Bailey, August 11, 1959.

334. SC160/III/61/3, A. H. Bowker to P. H. Rhinelander, August 29, 1960.

335. SC216/3.1/1.5, T. A. Bailey to W. Sterling, February 13, 1952.

336. SC216/3.1/2–1, T. A. Bailey to W. Sterling, June 17, 1955.

337. SC216/3.1/3–3, T. A. Bailey to W. Sterling, January 3, 1957.

338. SC216/3.1/3–3, T. A. Bailey to P. H. Rhinelander, January 3, 1957.

339. SC216/3.1/4–5, G. Wright to R. J. Wert; and T. A. Bailey to FET, February 23, 1960.

340. SC216/3.1/4–5, FET to W. Sterling (and staff), n.d.

341. SC216/3.1/4–5, FET to T. A. Bailey, March 11; and T. A. Bailey to FET, March 14, 1960.

342. 0900/Thomas A. Bailey interview by Frederic O. Glover, July 8, 1978; SC415, accn. 93–061/1/1, W. Sterling, "Sterling Presidency, 1949–1968," 38–39.

343. SC216/3.1/4–3, T. A. Bailey to FET, April 28, 1960.

344. SC216/3.1/4–4, P. H. Rhinelander to R. J. Wert, April 27, 1960.

345. SC216/3.1/4–4, T. A. Bailey to FET; and FET to W. Sterling, April 28, 1960.

346. SC216/3.1/4–4, G. Wright to D. M. Potter, April 29, 1960.

347. Carl N. Degler, "David Potter," *American Historical Review* 76 (October 1971): 127–75.

348. SC216/3.1/4.2, T. A. Bailey to FET, November 1, 1960.

349. Author interview with Gordon Craig, 2001.

350. For a 1961 view of the History Department, see SC36/4 "Development Office," Gordon Wright, "The Department of History at Stanford University," February 8, 1961.

351. SC160/III/62/2, Gordon Wright to FET, June 15; and Otis Pease to FET, May 9, 1962.

352. SC36/4, "Development Office," report by Gordon Wright, "The Department of History at Stanford University," February 8, 1961.

353. Lyman went on to become provost in 1967, succeeding Terman, and then became Stanford's seventh president in 1970.

354. *San Jose Mercury-News*, February 21, 1965, article on Terman by Bob Lindsay; and author interview with E. Howard Brooks, 1999.

355. SC160/III/83, folders 1–12.

356. 0900/Robert R. Sears interview by Frederic O. Glover, October 27 and December 1, 1982; author interview with Robert Rosenzweig, 1998.

357. *Stanford Daily Magazine*, special section on retirees, November 22, 1967, interview with Lillian Owen. Lillian had graduated with her BA in Economics at Stanford in Fred's class of '20 and had served in the President's Office for forty-four years.

358. SC216/A12/24, P. H. Rhinelander to W. Sterling, May 21, 1957.

359. SC216/A12/24, "Draft #1, May 29, 1957, [Sterling] to Terman."

360. SC216/39/27, FET to W. Sterling, December 30, 1954.

361. SC216/A16/1, W. Sterling to P. H. Rhinelander, December 8, 1958; and P. H. Rhinelander to W. Sterling, December 7, 1959.

362. SC216/A16/1, P. H. Rhinelander to FET, December 8; F. O. Glover to W. Sterling, December 15; K. Cuthbertson to P. H. Rhinelander December 15 and 18; and P. H. Rhinelander to K. Cuthbertson, December 21, 1959. Cuthbertson felt that Rhinelander misunderstood, or ignored, certain financial figures.

363. SC216/23/16, Robert J. Wert, "Brief Outline of Suggested Academic Needs of Stanford's Schools," March 26, 1960.

364. SC36/1, "Ford Proposal," P. H. Rhinelander to R. Faulkner, February 9, 1960. Draft of letter to FET, and Faulkner's response.

365. SC216/A16/1, P. H. Rhinelander to W. Sterling, March 1 and 2, 1960.

366. SC36/4, "Development Office," Sanford Dornbusch to all humanities and sciences faculty, March 9, 1960.

367. SC216/A16/1, "Record of Interview" by Robert J. Wert, June 2, 1960.

368. SC216/A16/1, P. H. Rhinelander to R. J. Wert, January 24, 1961.

369. SC36/4, "Development," K. M. Cuthbertson to P. H. Rhinelander, December 22, 1960.

370. SC36/4, "Development," S. Dornbusch to P. H. Rhinelander, January 10, 1961.

371. SC36/4, "Development," J. W. Dodds, to P. H. Rhinelander, March 13, 1961.

372. SC216/A16/1, P. H. Rhinelander to K. M. Cuthbertson June 7 and July 7; and K. M. Cuthbertson to P. H. Rhinelander, June 12, 1961.

373. SC216/A16/1, P. H. Rhinelander to FET, July 10, 1961; SC216/A39/8, P. H. Rhinelander to FET, June 19, 1961.

374. SC216/A39/8, P. H. Rhinelander to W. Sterling, July 10, 1961.

375. SC216/A16/1, FET to P. H. Rhinelander, July 10, 1961.

376. SC216/A39/8, P. H. Rhinelander to W. Sterling, July 10, 1961.

377. SC216/A39/8, P. H. Rhinelander to W. Sterling, July 24, 1961; SC216/A39/8, *Stanford Summer Weekly*, August 3, 1961.

378. SC216/A39/8, W. E. Meyerhof to W. Sterling, August 3, 1961.

379. SC216/A39/8, L. Tarshis to W. Sterling, August 4, 1961.

380. SC216/A39/8, W. Sterling to P. H. Rhinelander, August 8, 1961.

381. SC216/A39/8, W. Sterling to S. Drell, August 18, 1961.

382. SC216/A39/8, W. Sterling to P. H. Rhinelander, August 29, 1961.

383. Author conversation with Lawrence Ryan, 1999.

384. Author interview with Albert H. Bowker, 2001; and with Bliss Carnochan, 2001. Sears's lieutenants would be John Dodds of humanities, "Sandy" Dornbusch of sociology, Patrick Suppes of philosophy, and Leonard Schiff of physics.

385. SC216/A16/1, R. R. Sears to provost office, July 11, 1962.

386. SC36/5, "General H&S," W. Sterling to P. H. Rhinelander, June 24, 1957.

387. Author interview with Sanford Dornbusch, 1997.

388. 0900/Glover Oral History Project interview (1993), Session Two, 18.

389. Ibid.

390. Author interview with Robert Rosenzweig, 1998.

391. Personal communication, Esther M. Lederberg, January 26, 1999. Author interview with Albert Hastorf, 1998.

392. Author interview with E. Howard Brooks, 1999. Personal communication, Cassius L. Kirk Jr. to author, January 12, 2001.

393. Author interview with Burnice Bourquin, 1998, and Bourquin remembrance, SCM 2, "Frederick Emmons Terman, 1900–1982." Helen Liddle Leppert, Terman's secretary while dean of engineering, has similar memories. Author interviews with Helen Liddle Leppert, 1998; and with Elizabeth Patton, 1999. Mrs. Patton also recalls him being addressed as "Dr. Terman" by the secretarial staff but otherwise as being called "FET" or "Dr. T."

394. Author interview with Laurence A. Manning, 1999; and interview with O. G. Villard Jr., 1998.

395. 0900/Alf E. Brandin interview by Robert de Roos, 1989, 25.

396. Author interview with E. Howard Brooks, 1999; see also McAndrews, "Birthplace of Silicon Valley."

397. 0900/Alf E. Brandin interview by Robert de Roos, 1989, 51–52.

398. Author conversation with John W. Harbaugh, 2001.

399. Author interview with Ronald Hilton, 1999; author conversation with Eric Hutchinson, 1998.

400. 0900/Thomas A. Bailey interview by Frederic O. Glover, July 8, 1978, 33–34.

401. SC216/1.3/20, E. Hutchinson to W. Sterling, November 26, 1955, and March 25, 1956.

402. Gordon Craig, *Campus Report* (Stanford) 11, no. 40 (July 11, 1979): 4–5. Author interview with Craig, 2001.

403. Author interview with Robert Rosenzweig, 1998.

404. Author interviews with Albert Hastorf, 1998; with Moses Abramovitz, 1998; and with Donald Kennedy, 2000.

405. 0900/Glover Oral History Project interview (1993), Session Three, 2.

406. SC216/A16/1, FET to P. H. Rhinelander, July 10, 1961. Author interview with William R. Rambo, 1998.

407. Author interview with William Kays, 1998.

408. 0900/Virgil K. Whitaker interview by Eleanor Bark and Harvey Hall, 1982, 31, 44–45.

409. Author interview with William E. Spicer, 2000.

410. 0900/Virgil K. Whitaker interview by Eleanor Bark and Harvey Hall, 1982, 31, 44–45. Terman was, in fact, the first senior administrator to turn his close attention to the library, and he supported the recruiting of Rutherford "Rudy" Rogers, then deputy librarian at the Library of Congress. Author interview with Richard Lyman, 1998.

411. Some examples given to author in interviews with Alf Brandin, 1998; with E. Howard Brooks, 1999; and with Albert H. Bowker, 2001.

412. 0900/Glover Oral History Project interview (1993) Session Two, 16.

413. Author interviews with E. Howard Brooks, 1999; and with Richard W. Lyman, 1998.

414. Arbuckle in *Session on Wally*, 46; 0900/Glover, Oral History Project interview, Session Two, 18.

415. Sterling's "simple philosophy" was well articulated by Cuthbertson in *Session on Wally*, 66.

416. 0900/Paul Hanna interview by Rebecca Lowen, 1986. Emeritus Professor of German Walter F. W. Lohnes agreed that Stanford's rise during the 1960s was due in large part to Sterling and Terman. Author interview with Walter W. Lohnes, 1999.

417. Glover papers, W. Sterling to R. J. Wert, January 11, 1983 (courtesy of Cassius L. Kirk Jr.).

418. 0900/Glover, Oral History Project interview (1993), Session Three, 3.

419. Materials used for this section include: *Bohemian Club, History, Officers and Committees, Incorporation, Constitution, By-Laws and Rules, Former Officers, Members, In Memoriam* (San Francisco, January 20, 1960); *Bohemian Club, History, Officers and Committees, Former Members, In Memorium, House Rules, Grove Rules* (San Francisco, 1973); Nuel Pharr Davis, *Lawrence and Oppenheimer* (New York: Simon and Schuster, 1968), 69–70; G. William Domhoff, *The Bohemian Grove and Other Retreats: A Study in Ruling-Class Cohesiveness* (New York: Harper and Row, 1974); Robert Thomas Legge, MD, *History of the Sons of Toil Camp—Bohemian Grove, 1905–58*, typescript (Monte Rio, CA: November 1958), copy courtesy of Harold Hyde; John Van der Zee, *The Greatest Men's Party on Earth: Inside the Bohemian Grove* (New York: Harcourt Brace Jovanovich, Inc., 1974); Harvey E. White, *The History of Sons of Toil from 1959*, typescript (n.d., copy courtesy of Harold Hyde); author interviews with Albert H. Bowker, 1999; with Ronald Bracewell, 1998; with Alf Brandin, 1998; with Harold Hyde, 1999; and with David Ridgway, 1999; and Stanford Oral History Project interviews with Paul Davis, 1979 and 1980, and with Alvin Eurich, 1980.

420. SC64B/6, R. L. Wilbur to V. Bush, May 1, 1939.

421. SC160/I/14, F. F. Walker to FET, July 6, 1945; SC160/I/14, F. F. Walker to FET, July 31, 1945.

422. SC160/I/14, M. Price to FET, August 7, 1945; and FET to F. F. Walker, draft of letter of September 24, 1945; SC160/I/14, FET to F. F. Walker, September 24, 1945.

423. SC160/III/63/5. See, for example FET's calendar for 1961–62.

424. 0900/Terman, Frederick E., Oral History Project interview by Raymond Henle, January 1970. Author interview with Alf Brandin, 1998.

425. Davis, *Lawrence and Oppenheimer*, 69–70; Van der Zee, *Greatest Men's Party*, 115–16.

426. Van der Zee, *Greatest Men's Party*, 119–21.

427. Author interview with Alf Brandin, 1998; 0900/Glover, Oral History Project interview (1993), Session Three, 31; remarks of W. Sterling. Stanford Associates' Uncommon Man Award Dinner for Frederick E. Terman, December 7, 1978 (Stanford University Special Collections audiotape).

428. SC160/VIII/3/6, FET, convocation response, May 31, 1965.

429. SC216/A32/8, F. O. Glover to G. K. Walker, quoting Sterling, July 16, 1965.

430. SC216/A32/8, P. Allen to B. Bliven, May 12, 1965.

431. Medeiros, *Sterling Years*, 201.

432. 0900/Glover, Oral History Project interview (1993), Session Two, 18; Session Three, 3. E. Howard Brooks, Virgil Whitaker, and Associate Provost for Research Hubert Heffner took over many of the duties while Sterling recuperated and reconsidered the provost's position. Author interview with E. Howard Brooks, 1999.

433. SC216/A39, Folders 21–22. SC216/A39/21, Wallace Sterling notes for Faculty Advisory Board, December 14, 1965.

434. SC216/A39/24, FET to W. Sterling, August 3, 1965.

435. SC216/A39/22, W. Sterling to D. Hornig, August 22 and 23, 1966.

436. SC216/A39/24, D. B. Truman to W. Sterling, September 1, 1966.

437. SC216/A39/24, W. Sterling to D. B. Truman, September 7, 1966.

438. 0900/Thomas A. Bailey interview by Frederic O. Glover, July 8, 1978.

439. 0900/Glover, Oral History Project interview (1993), Session Three, 19–20; Session Four, 30; Session Five, 23–25.

440. Author interview with Richard Lyman, 1998, and conversation, 2001.

CHAPTER EIGHT. "IF I HAD MY LIFE TO LIVE OVER AGAIN, I WOULD PLAY THE SAME RECORD"

1. SC160/XIV/1/5, FET to H. F. Olson, December 22, 1966.

2. SC160/XIV/5/4, FET to C. H. Green, November 7, 1977.

3. Terman's notes for the two talks are in SC160/VIII/4/1. Since at least the mid-1950s, Electrical Engineering Department Head Hugh Skilling had offered an annual seminar for prospective teachers of engineering. Skilling invited some of Stanford's better teachers among the engineering faculty to speak and share ideas, including Terman, Ralph J. Smith, and David F. Tuttle. This author took Skilling's seminar in 1960.

4. In connection with ideas developed in his teaching seminar, Skilling subsequently published a short book on teaching that summarized the teaching philosophies of Terman and other Stanford faculty. Hugh Hildreth Skilling, *Do You Teach? Views on College Teaching* (New York: Holt, Rinehart and Winston, 1969).

5. For the "Community of Scholars" description, see F. E. Terman, "Engineering Growth and the Community," *Journal of Engineering Education* 55 (February 1965): x, xiii; and an extended version in John Whinnery, ed., *The World of Engineering*, ch. 11 (New York: McGraw-Hill, 1965).

6. SC160/VIII3/6, FET to D. R. Hauser, July 26, 1965; and D. R. Hauser to FET, September 13, 1965; notes for "Governing the University," August 22, 1965.

7. SC160/VIII3/7, E. F. Hollings to FET, October 25, 1967. (Hollings later wrote Fred thanking him for support of his stance.)

8. SC160/VIII/3/8, typescript of FET speech, "The Development of an Engineering College Program," May 18, 1968.

9. F. E. Terman, "The Development of an Engineering College Program," *Journal of Engineering Education* 58 (May 1968): 1053–55. In 1971, Terman was dubbed the pioneering author of "quantitative studies of efficiencies of engineering schools," while the most useful measure of efficiency for such studies was Terman's "instruction cost index." R. D. Shelton and J. C. Prabhakar, "Efficiency Ratios for Engineering Schools," *Proceedings, Institute of Electrical and Electronics Engineers* 59, no. 6 (June 1971): 843–48.

10. SC160/VIII/4/2, FET speech notes, April 29, 1970.

11. Frances V. Rummell and Adelaine Paine, "He Searches for Steeples of Talent," *Reader's Digest* (December 1962).

12. IEEE *Grid* (April 1966): 9–10.

13. Gene Bylinsky, "California's Great Breeding Ground for Industry," *Fortune*, June 1974.

14. SC160/VIII/3/6, FET typescript of talk, "Community Dinner Speech," November 3, 1965; published in *Palo Alto Chamber News* 19, no. 9 (November 1965).

15. SC160/III/64/1, final report submitted November 1967.

16. SC160/III/64, Folders 2–12.

17. Allan Cartter, *An Assessment of Quality in Graduate Education* (Washington DC: American Council on Education, 1966).

18. SC160/III/64/4, R. W. Lyman to FET, October 31, 1967; R. F. Bacchetti to FET,

June 18, 1969; E. H. Brooks to Deans of Stanford's Schools, April 15, 1969; L. Tarshis to H. Royden, April 25, 1969; Brooks to K. Pitzer, May 20, 1969; and R. W. Lyman to FET, September 29, 1969.

19. *Stanford Daily*, November 17, 1969.

20. SC160/XIV/5/6, FET to R. Nilan and M. Coesfeld, March 28, 1979.

21. SC160/III/64/11, "A Study of Faculty Retirement at Stanford," n.d., but October 1966.

22. SC160/III/64/12; SC160/XIV/1/4, correspondence between TIAA-CREF executive George R. Harrison and FET.

23. SC160/III/64/12, V. A. Anderson to FET, April 19, 1967.

24. SC160/III/64/12, Provost R. W. Lyman, notice to retired faculty, August 18, 1967. *Minimum* retirement income for emeriti full professors was subsequently set at:

Years of Service	*Single*	*Married*
10	$2,400	$3,000
20	$4,200	$4,800
30	$5,400	$6,000

25. SC160/XIV/2/3, FET to R. W. Lyman, August 26, 1968.

26. Bartholomew, Brinegar, and Nilan, *Chronology*, 100.

27. SC160/III/66/2, E. H. Brooks to FET, November 24, 1969.

28. SC160/III/66/7, F. E. Terman, "A Study of General Fund Ceiling as Applied to the Graduate School of Business," February 16, 1970, revised March 10, 1970.

29. SC160/III/66/4, W. G. Knopf to FET, February 23, 1970.

30. SC160/III/66/2, E. H. Brooks to K. S. Pitzer, March 6, 1970, and subsequent correspondence.

31. SC160/III/66/3.

32. SC160/III/66/4, W. G. Knopf to FET, February 23, 1970.

33. SC160/III/66/6, FET notes on conversation with Carl Janke, May 1, 1970.

34. SC160/III/67/2, F. E. Terman, "Application of General Fund Ceiling Operation to Stanford Law School and Stanford Graduate School of Business—A Comparative Study," Draft, ca. July 1, 1970.

35. SC160/III/67/1, FET memo, April 28, 1977.

36. SC160/III/67/3, FET note, April 28, 1977.

37. SC160/XIV/2/7, FET to J. W. Gardner, May 2, 1969.

38. SC160/XIV/3/3, FET to R. W. Lyman, September 29, 1970.

39. Author interview with William F. Miller, 2000.

40. SC160/XIV/3/7, FET to W. F. Miller, August 31, 1971.

41. Trustees Wally Sterling and Dick Guggenhime cochaired the campaign. Bartholomew, Brinegar, and Nilan, *Chronology*, 108.

42. SC160/XIV/1/1, FET to P. H. Davis, September 27, 1965.

43. Some of the schools and states for whom Terman consulted were: Ohio, 1964; Delaware, 1965; Southern Methodist, 1965 and after; New Jersey, 1965 and after; Colorado, 1966–67 and 1970; California, 1967–68; Lehigh University, Pennsylvania, 1967; Tufts University, Massachusetts, 1968; University of Rochester, New York, 1969; New York State Regents, 1968–69; Polytechnic Institute of Brooklyn, 1969; New York University, 1969; University of Missouri (Rolla), 1970; Marquette University, Wisconsin, 1970; University of Bridgeport, Connecticut, 1970; Florida State Regents, 1971; Texas Christian University Research Foundation, 1971–77; Massachusetts, 1972; Utah, 1973; Oregon, 1973; Tulane University, Louisiana, 1974; and John F. Kennedy University,

California, 1975–76. Terman turned down several requests per year to consult at additional schools.

44. F. E. Terman, "Scientific and Engineering Manpower in a Highly Competitive World," *Stanford Review* (May–June 1963): 16–22; F. E. Terman, "Supply of Scientific and Engineering Manpower: Surplus or Shortage?" *Science* (July 30, 1971): 399–405 (a shorter version appeared as "Changing Needs for PhDs," *IEEE Spectrum* [January 1972]: 79–81).

45. SC160/VII, Boxes 1 and 2. Kenneth D. Roose and Charles J. Andersen, *A Rating of Graduate Programs* (Washington DC: American Council on Education, 1970).

46. SC160/VII/2/3, J. W. Hicks to FET, August 21, 1968.

47. The record of this series of exchanges in 1968–69 is in SC160/VII/2/3.

48. SC160/XIII/1/16, FET notes, May 20, 1980.

49. *Dallas Times-Herald*, July 11, 1965.

50. SC160/XIII/1/16, FET to T. L. Martin Jr., May 13, 1970; and FET to J. D. King, November 8, 1972.

51. SC160/XIV/1/2, FET to L. Griffis, November 23, 1965.

52. SC160/XIV/2/4, FET to E. Jonsson, October 11, 1968.

53. SC160/XIV/5/6, FET notes, June 12, 1980.

54. SC160/X/2/17, FET report, "Graduate Center for Science and Technology in New Jersey—The Dimensions of the University," prepared for Industry Committee for a Graduate Center for Science and Technology in New Jersey, October 15, 1965, forty-six pages; and the final version, "Institute for Science and Technology in New Jersey—The Dimensions of the University," June 15, 1966, fifty-nine pages.

55. SC160/VIII/3/7, FET remarks, October 6, 1966.

56. SC160/XIV/2/4, FET to E. Jonsson, October 11, 1968.

57. SC160/XIV/1/3, FET to W. Ayres, March 4, 1966.

58. SC160/XIV/4/4, FET to T. L. Martin Jr., June 20, 1973.

59. SC160/XIII/1/16, T. L. Martin Jr. to FET, August 2, 1973.

60. SC160/XIV/4/4, FET to M. Shepherd, June 21, 1973.

61. SC160/XIV/4/6, FET to W. M. Tate, March 21, 1974.

62. SC160/XIII/1/16, FET to K. Willenbrock, January 6, 1978; SC160/XIII/1/16, FET notes, May 20, 1980.

63. SC160/XIII/1/20.

64. SC160/XIV/2/6, FET to C. Bowen, February 28, 1969. The MIT Press wanted to publish the report as a separate monograph, but Fred felt that it would be better to include additional states and problem situations.

65. SC160/VIII/4/1, FET speech, "Plans, Programs, and Problems," delivered at Westminster College, Fulton, Missouri, December 2, 1969.

66. SC160/XIII/1/5, CCHE, minutes of Committee on Educational Programs, May 20, 1968. The CCHE, a state advisory with representatives from public and private institutions, was created with the state's educational master plan of 1959.

67. Unattributed material in the following section is from F. E. Terman, "A Study of Engineering Education in California," assisted by R. Hind and L. F. McGhie, March 1968.

68. SC160/XIV/2/4, FET to O. A. Knorr, September 21, 1968.

69. SC160/XIV/2/4, FET to O. A. Knorr, September 24, 1968.

70. SC160/XIV2/4, FET to O. A. Knorr, September 23, 1968; SC160/XIII/1/5, C. Hitch to O. A. Knorr, September 5, 1968.

71. SC160/XIV/2/4, FET to O. A. Knorr, September 24, 1968.

72. SC160/XIV/2/4, FET to F. McGhie and R. Hind, October 15, 1968.

73. SC160/XIII/1/5, CCHE, Committee on Educational Programs, October 7, 1968. "Suggested Resolution—Engineering Education in California," with FET annotations of final amendments and alterations of the Resolution as voted.

74. *San Francisco Chronicle*, October 9, 1968.

75. *San Francisco Chronicle*, November 1, 1973.

76. SC160/VIII/3/8, FET talk to New York State Regents, December 20, 1968; SC160/X/2/22, report, "Engineer Education in New York," F. E. Terman, assisted by Glenn E. Reeling, Albany, New York, March 1969.

77. SC160/X/2/23, report, "The Polytechnic Institute of Brooklyn," F. E. Terman, Albany, New York, March 1969; SC160/VIII/4/6, G. Bugliarello to FET, October 16, 1974.

78. *St. Petersburg Times* (Florida), October 14 and 15, and November 20, 1971.

79. SC160/XIV/3/6, FET to R. Uhrig, May 14, 1971; and FET to W. Long, May 14, 1971.

80. SC160/XIV/3/6, FET to R. Uhrig, May 14, 1971.

81. SC160/XIV/3/7, FET to R. Uhrig, August 13 and 16, 1971.

82. SC160/VI/3/2, FET notes, IDA meeting, April 5, 1956.

83. SC160/VI/3/1, E. L. Cochrane to W. Sterling, June 29, 1955; and W. Sterling to E. L. Cochrane, July 19, 1955.

84. SC160/VI/3/2, W. Sterling to J. McCormack Jr., March 29, 1956.

85. SC160/VI/3/2, FET notes, IDA meeting, April 5, 1956.

86. Author interview with Susie Rathman Zaremba, 2000.

87. SC160/VI/3/7, J. McCormack Jr. to IDA Trustees, memo, June 3, 1958.

88. SC160/VI/4/2, FET to IDA Trustees, June 29 and ff.; and Approval by IDA Board, September 21 and 22, 1959.

89. *Resistance* 1, nos. 1–2 (March 9 and April 4, 1967).

90. A detailed summary of these events between 1965 and 1973 can be found in Bartholomew, Brinegar, and Nilan, *Chronology*, 89–109.

91. SC160/XIV/1/7, FET to A. M. Minton, May 31, 1967.

92. SC160/VI/6/1, FET interview with Michael Morton, Bob Beyers in attendance, November 18, 1967; *Stanford Daily*, November 22, 1967.

93. University of Chicago *Record* 2, no. 2 (February 16, 1968). *Stanford Daily*, March 6, 1968.

94. *Los Angeles Times*, March 15, 1968; *Science*, 160 (May 17, 1968): 744–48.

95. SC160/VI/7, Folders 3–4. Stanford Trustees' Resolution, May 16, 1968; IDA Public Statement, June 4, 1968.

96. SC160/XIV/5/6, FET notes, "Institute for Defense Analyses," 9, n.d.

97. The renamed SRI International agreed to pay one percent of its gross sales annually to Stanford until total payment of $25 million was reached, thereafter SRI would pay 0.5 percent of its gross sales annually.

98. SC160/XIV/3/1, FET to J. Hawkinson, February 2, 1970.

99. *Palo Alto Times*, May 1 and 2, 1970. Bartholomew, Brinegar, and Nilan, *Chronology*, 101–2.

100. SC160/XIV/3, Folders 3–4, FET to A. Rydell, July 20, 1970; and FET to H. Rohrer, December 22, 1970.

101. John Walsh, in David Riesman and Verne A. Stadtman, eds., *Academic Transformation: 17 Institutions Under Pressure*, 303–22 (New York: McGraw-Hill, 1973).

102. SC160/XIV/2/6, FET to B. Dysart, March 21, 1969.

103. *Palo Alto Times*, December 6, 1972.

104. F. E. Terman, *Education in Engineering and Science in the U.S.S.R.*, prepared for U.S. Office of Education Mission, December 3–29, 1965 (131 pages).

105. SC160/VIII, Boxes 2 and 3.

106. SC160/VIII/3/8. The keynote speech was on June 24, 1968. His other talks were delivered on June 25 and July 8, 1968.

107. *China Post* (Taipei), July 7, 1968.

108. SC160/X/3/8, "Trends in Engineering Education in the United States," talk delivered in Taiwan, June 1972; *China Post* (Taipei), July 18, 1972.

109. SC160/X/3/7, F. E. Terman, "Changing Needs for PhDs," *IEEE Spectrum* (January 1972): 79–81.

110. SC160/VI/20/7, Hyung-Sup Choi (Minister of Science and Technology, Republic of Korea), "Adapting a Developing Country to the Development of Adaptive Technologies," talk given in Honolulu, Hawaii (Copy) October 4–6, 1972.

111. SC160/XIV/3/4, FET to C. S. Bell Jr., October 27, 1970.

112. SC160/X/3/3, Donald L. Benedict, Kun Mo Chung, Franklin A. Long, Thomas L. Martin, and Chairman Frederick E. Terman, "Survey Report on the Establishment of the Korea Advanced Institute of Science," prepared for USAID (copy), December 1970.

113. *KAIS* (Seoul, Korea: Korea Advanced Institute of Science, 1971).

114. Author's correspondence with Sang Soo Lee, June 27, 2000.

115. SC160/XIV/3/6, FET to S. S. Lee, June 17, 1971.

116. SC160/XIV/3/9, FET to S. S. Lee, January 4, 1972.

117. SC160/XIV/4/1, FET to W. G. Ireson, August 11, 1972.

118. SC160/XIV/4/1, FET to W. G. Ireson, August 14, 1972. Other Stanford faculty, including electrical engineers Malcolm McWhorter and James Gibbons, helped on certain KAIS tasks. SC160/XIV/4/3, FET to M. McWhorter, August 3, 1973.

119. SC160/VII4/4, FET speech, "Role of Advanced Graduate Training in Industrial Development," September 1, 1972.

120. SC160/XIV/4/2, FET to N. A. Hall, December 6, 1972.

121. SC160/XIV/4/5, FET to F. A. Long, November 1, 1973.

122. SC160/XIV/4/5, FET to F. A. Long, October 25, 1973.

123. SC160/VIII/4/6, FET notes, talk to KAIS faculty, November 20, 1974.

124. *Policy and Strategy for Science and Technology* (Ministry of Science and Technology, Republic of Korea, 1975).

125. SC160/VI/20/7, F. A. Long to FET, January 29, 1979.

126. Author's correspondence with Haeng Ung Park, June 13, 2000.

127. Author's correspondence with Sang Soo Lee, June 27, 2000.

128. *Chosun Ilbo* (Seoul, Korea), December 11, 1975; *San Jose Mercury-News*, December 26, 1975.

129. SC160/XIV/2/7, FET to J. V. N. Granger, June 13, 1969.

130. SC160/XIV/3/3, FET to R. Barker, September 4, 1970.

131. SC160/XIV/3/6, FET to H. J. Volk, April 21, 1971. Electrical Engineering Professor Ralph J. Smith chaired a faculty and staff investing group called the "Farmer's Investment Club," and Fred spoke to them on banking and investing for retirement. SC160/VIII/3/8, R. J. Smith to FET, April 18, 1968.

132. Author communication from David Leeson, 1999; author interview with Donald Hammond, 2000.

133. SC160/XIV/2/9, FET to T. T. Holme, November 15, 1969; and FET to T. L. Martin Jr., November 29, 1969.

134. Author communication from David Leeson, 1999; author interview with Donald Hammond, 2000. Some wished that he would have given up his attendance earlier.

135. David Packard as quoted in *San Mateo Times*, July 15, 1965; in *Palo Alto Times*, June 6, 1965; and in *Stanford Engineering News* 52 (July 1965).

136. SC160/XIV/3/1, FET to R. Young, January 14, 1970.

137. This section utilizes especially SC160/V/6/9 through V/8.

138. Terman was proud of these files and specifically remarked on them to an archivist during the archiving of his papers at Stanford. Author correspondence with Roxanne Nilan, 2002.

139. SC160/V/6/10, FET to H. G. Laun, February 9 and August 4, 1949.

140. SC160/V/6/12, FET to H. G. Laun, March 11, 1952.

141. SC160/V/6/13, FET to H. G. Laun, December 15, 1953.

142. SC160/V/6/11, H. G. Laun to FET, March 1 and 21, 1950.

143. *Barron's*, June 13, 1955.

144. SC160/V/6/12, FET to H. Garland, September 26, 1952.

145. SC160/V/6/16, W. H. Cooley to FET, September 18, 1959; and FET to W. H. Cooley, October 6, 1959.

146. SC160/V/7/3, Technology Fund, Inc., *Annual Report* (Chicago, IL, 1968).

147. SC160/V/7/4, J. Hawkinson to FET, September 15, 1978.

148. SC160/V/7/4, D. E. Noble to FET, January 11, 1978.

149. Terman's Sigma Xi records are found in SC160/XIV/5/6, in SC160/IV, Boxes 19–26, and in occasional letters throughout his papers, especially in SC160/XIV, Boxes 1–5.

150. SC160/IV/20/8.

151. Terman's ASEE activities for 1946–77 are recorded in SC160/IV, Boxes 2–4. Letters concerning ASEE affairs are scattered throughout his correspondence, and during his retirement in SC160/XIV, Boxes 1–5.

152. SC160/IV/2, Folders 6–7. On Ray Lyman Wilbur, see Chapter 1, above.

153. SC160/IV/4/1.

154. SC160/IV/3/6.

155. SC160/VIII/4/1, FET notes of ASEE remarks, June 24, 1969. His cribbed outline sheet lists many other examples, however, of his success stories: "getting 'Pitch' Johnson into Harvard Business School, Charles Rajnus, Turk, Hicks."

156. SC160/XIV/5/6, FET to M. Williams, March 22, 1979.

157. *Palo Alto Times*, June 23, 1971.

158. SC160/XIV/2/8, FET to N. Hall, July 11, 1969.

159. Terman's IEEE records are found in SC160/IV: Box 1, for the AIEE; Boxes 8–16 for the IRE; and Boxes 5–7 for the IEEE. Terman's correspondence concerning the IEEE during his retirement years is located throughout his papers, and particularly in SC160/XIV, Boxes 1–5.

160. SC160/IV/5/9, FET to D. Fink, April 8, 1969; D. Fink to FET, April 16, 1969; H. Pratt to FET, June 26, 1969; and FET to H. Pratt, July 10, 1969.

161. SC160/IV/5/9, FET to W. R. Crone, May 13, 1970.

162. SC160/XIV/4/3, FET to C. C. Gillispie, January 3, 1973.

163. SC160/IV/5/9, W. R. Crone to FET, November 19, 1970; and FET to W. R. Crone, December 2, 1970.

164. References concerning IEEE History Committee not specifically indicated are taken from SC160/IV, Boxes 5–6.

165. *Frederick Emmons Terman, interviews by Arthur L. Norberg, Charles Süsskind, and Roger Hahn, 1975*. Transcript, a joint project of Bancroft Oral History Project on the History of Science and Technology and [the] Stanford Oral History Project, 1984.

166. SC160/XIV/4/2, FET to A. H. Bowker, November 7, 1972.

167. SC160/XIV/4, Folder 7, FET to L. M. Clement, June 10, 1974; and FET to J. Ryder, May 28, 1974; and Folder 8, FET to Mrs. A. Stevens, October 17, 1974; *Palo Alto Times*, May 8, 1973.

168. Author correspondence with Roxanne Nilan, 2002.

169. SC160/XIV/5/4, FET to C. H. Green, November 7, 1977. Author interviews with William Spicer, July 2000. The McCullough building has since been renovated and the interior office numbers changed.

170. First Sandra (Tervol) Dyer, and then Donna Soderberg.

171. SC160/XIV/1/5, FET to W. R. Gould, December 22, 1966.

172. SC160/XIV/1/6, FET to G. T Beauchamp, April 28, 1967.

173. SC160/XIV/1/7, FET to J. E. Jonsson, August 7, 1967.

174. SC160/XIV/1/8, FET to G. Reid, September 15, 1967.

175. Author interview with Susie Rathman Zaremba, 2000.

176. SC160/XIV/2/1, FET to V. Bush, April 19, 1968.

177. SC160/XIV/2/2, FET to California Department of Motor Vehicles (DMV), May 28, 1968.

178. SC160/XIV/3/9, FET to California DMV, April 5, 1972; SC160/XIV/5/1, FET to N. Finch, November 18, 1975; author interview with Susie Rathman Zaremba, 2000.

179. SC318, Stanford Alumni Association, Box 1, Folder, "1920 Committee Work."

180. Author interview with Esther M. Lederberg, 2000.

181. Professor Walcutt went on to publish another book on reading instruction in 1961.

182. SC160/XIV/XIV/1/4, FET to J. Kelly, March 27, 1966.

183. Author conversation with Terence C. Terman, 2000.

184. SC160/XIV/2/5, FET to "Winnie" (Mrs. Faurest Davis), December 31, 1968.

185. SC160/XIV/2/7, FET to W. F. Cavier, June 9, 1969; FET to J. F. Coales, June 13, 1969; and FET to E. C. Cook, June 13, 1969.

186. SC160/XIV/2/8, FET to E. Privateer, August 29, 1969.

187. SC160/XIV/3/2, FET to R. W. Husband, June 19, 1970; SC160/XIV/3/3, FET to W. P. Cavier, August 10, 1970; SC160/XIII/1/26, FET to H. Terman Mosher, November 28, 1969; SC160/XIV/3/4, FET to H. White, December 15, 1970.

188. SC160/XIV/3/2, FET to R. W. Husband, June 19, 1970.

189. SC160/XIV/3/3, FET to F. R. Pagnotti, July 23, 1970.

190. SC160/XIV/3/6, FET to *Electronics* magazine, May 26, 1971; SC160/XIV/3/7, FET to J. B. Cary, September 24, 1971.

191. SC160/XIV/2/7, FET to F. Riddle, June 16, 1969.

192. SC160/XIV/1/2, FET to J. E. Greene, October 1, 1965.

193. SC160/XIV/3/7, FET to C. R. Wade, July 14, 1971.

194. SC160/XIV/3/9, FET to C. R. Wade, March 3, 1972.

195. SC160/XIV/4/5, FET to K. J. Bowman, September 17, 1973.

196. SC160/XIV/4/3, FET to D. L. Caldwell, March 9, 1973. Milton Saier had been Sibyl's physician for a number of years but then he retired.

197. SC160/XIV/4/4, FET to K. Terman, June 22, 1973; SC160/XIV/4/5, FET to California Medicare, October 16, 1973. When Lee retired, he turned over his longtime

patients and friends Fred and Sibyl to the care of Dr. Walter Bortz. Author interview with Walter Bortz, M.D., July 2000.

198. SC160/XIV/4/6, FET to H. White, April 5, 1974.

199. SC160/XIV/4/8, FET to "Whom It May Concern," September 25, 1974.

200. SC160/XIV/4/5, SWT to "Elizabeth," December 14, 1973.

201. SC160/XIV/4/7, typed list, "FET Trip Aug. 18–21" (1974); and FET to P. Terman, August 2, 1974; SC160/XIV/4/8, SWT to Medicare, December 18, 1974.

202. SC160/XIV/4/9, FET to H. Gross, April 30, 1975; and FET to R. Summers, March 4, 1975.

203. SC160/XIV/5/1, FET to "Ruth," December 31, 1975.

204. SC160/XIV/5/1, FET to A. Spilhaus, July 11, 1975; and FET to F. Muhs, July 23, 1975.

205. SC160/XIV/5/1, FET to Finch, Sauers, Player, and King, July 25, 1975; and FET to Lois P. Reed, July 25, 1975.

206. SC160/XIV/5/1, FET to B. D. Napier, August 18, 1975.

207. SC160/XIV/5/4, FET to Mrs. F. Davis, June 24, 1977; and FET to L. and B. Terman, June 24, 1977.

208. SC160/XIV/5/5, FET to C. Walcutt, August 29, 1978; and FET to O. G. Villard Jr., December 19, 1978.

209. In this section, various statements are from author's interviews with Mrs. Thomas E. Marr, Marci Smith, Susie Rathman Zaremba, and Hewlett Lee, MD.

210. Author interview with Arthur Fong, 1999.

211. SC160/XIV/8/2, P. H. Davis to FET, August 12, 1975; and FET to P. H. Davis, January 11, 1967.

212. Author interviews with Marci Smith, and with Susie Rathman Zaremba, 2000; SC160/XIV/5/5, FET to Blue Shield of California, September 15, 1978.

213. SC160/XIV/5, Folder 6, FET to Blue Shield of California, February 7, 1979; Folder 7, prescription list for July 1980. SC160/XIV/4/8, FET to R. Lee, December 16, 1974.

214. SC160/XIV/4/8, FET to "Whom It May Concern" (at Foothill College, Los Altos, California), September 25, 1974.

215. SC160/XIV/5/4, FET to J. Baxter, September 15, 1977.

216. SC160/XIV/5/6, FET to J. Baxter, January 22, 1979.

217. SC160/XIV/5/5, FET to D. R. Goddard, October 17, 1978; and FET to O. G. Villard Jr., 1998.

218. SC160/XIV/5/6, FET memo, "1/22/79."

219. SC160/XIV/5/7, FET to Blue Shield of California, May 19, 1980.

220. SC160/XIV/5/7, FET to C. and I. Green, April 23, 1980.

221. Mudge in her later years became very active in supporting nuclear power for electrical utility use. Author interview with Eva Fenn Reynolds, 2000.

222. SC160/XIV/5/7, FET to E. Mudge, February 15, 1980.

223. *San Jose Mercury-News*, June 7, 1979.

224. *Stanford Chaparral*, February 12, 1975, 4.

225. SC160/XIV/11/10.

226. Stanford *Daily*, October 7, 1977.

227. SC160/VIII/4/7, FET—"Stanford's Growth to Greatness," original typescript of talk, December 7, 1978.

228. SC160/XIV/5/7, D. Soderberg to E. Gloystein, May 29, 1980.

229. Author interview with Susie Rathman Zaremba, 2000; SC160/XIV/5/5, FET to E. Samuels, November 8, 1978.

230. Lee, then in his mideighties, was a founder of the Palo Alto Clinic and one of the area's most influential physicians. He had retired in 1960 from the clinic, although he had kept many favorite patients, like the Termans, well into the 1970s.

231. Details in the latter part of this paragraph are taken from SC160/XIV/5/8.

232. *San Francisco Chronicle*, December 21, 1982; *Peninsula Times Tribune* (Palo Alto), December 21, 1982; *Stanford Daily*, January 3 and 4, 1983.

233. Lewis M. Terman II, correspondence with the author, June 20, 2000.

234. SC160/XIV/1/3.

235. SC160/XIV/2/2, FET to Watkins-Johnson Company, May 7, 1968; SC160/XIV/1/6, FET to J. Granger, March 28, 1967.

236. *Palo Alto Times*, March 3, 1973.

237. SC160/XIV/1/4, FET to K. M. Cuthbertson, May 6, 1966.

238. SC160/XIV/1/4, FET and SWT to Stanford Board of Trustees, July 11, 1966.

239. Author interview with Laura Breyfogle, Stanford School of Engineering, 2000.

240. Frederic O. Glover, "Fred Terman's Paper Trail: A Goldmine of Scientific Research" (with the assistance of Roxanne Nilan), *Stanford Observer* (April 1979): 5, from *Stanford Historical Society Newsletter* (winter 1979): 10–13; author's correspondence with Roxanne Nilan, 2002.

EPILOGUE. BUILDING, MOMENTUM, WAVES, AND NETWORKS

1. E. Howard Brooks, Terman's assistant, was vice provost at Stanford from 1965 to 1971, and then was provost of the Claremont Colleges of California. Don Carlson was assistant to the president from 1945 to 1961, and then became director of university relations at Stanford. Ken Cuthbertson, as vice president for finance and development, went on to manage the highly successful Campaign for Stanford during the 1970s and later served as president of the James Irvine Foundation (*Session on Wally*, 73).

2. For a good review of the literature, see Stuart W. Leslie and Robert H. Kargon, "Selling Silicon Valley: Frederick Terman's Model for Regional Advantage," *Business History Review* 70 (winter 1996): 435–572. This quote is from page 467. See also Tony Taylor, "High-Technology Industry and the Development of Science Parks," *Built Environment* 9, no. 1 (1984): 72–78; Michael I. Luger and Harvey A. Goldstein, *Technology in the Garden: Research Parks and Regional Economic Development* (Chapel Hill: University of North Carolina Press, 1991); Anna Lee Saxenian, *Regional Advantage: Culture and Competition in Silicon Valley and Route 128* (Cambridge, MA: Harvard University Press, 1994); and Roger G. Noll, ed., *Challenges to Research Institutions* (Washington DC: Brookings Institution Press, 1998).

3. E. J. Malecki and P. Nijkamp, "Technology and Regional Development: Some Thoughts on Policy," *Environment and Planning C: Government and Policy* 6, no. 4 (1988): 383–99.

4. Leslie and Kargon, "Selling Silicon Valley," 469–71.

5. Leslie, *Cold War and American Science*; Lowen, *Creating the Cold War University*.

6. Lowen, *Creating the Cold War University*; Sara Timby, "The Dudley Herbarium: Including a Case Study of Terman's Restructuring of the Biology Department," *Sandstone & Tile* 22, no. 4 (fall 1998): 3–15.

7. See Appendix D for ranking data.

APPENDIX C

1. UA V 728.95.2, Box 2, File "Nov. 1945." List compiled by O. G. Villard Jr.

APPENDIX D

1. *A Study of the Graduate Schools of America* (1925) ranked University of Chicago first; when Stanford ranked lower than expected on two national surveys in 1935, and significantly lower than Berkeley, university officials feared fund-raising among alumni might ensue. Bartholomew, Brinegar, and Nilan, *Chronology*, 56, 63.

2. Bob Beyers, comment to author, 2001.

3. *Chicago Tribune*, May 26, 1957.

4. Keniston studied only twenty-five universities, including Stanford, belonging to the Association of American Universities (Hayward Keniston, *Graduate Study in the Arts and Sciences at the University of Pennsylvania* [Philadelphia: University of Pennsylvania Press, 1959]).

5. Cartter used large panels of experts in measuring more than twenty-nine academic disciplines (Allan M. Cartter, *An Assessment of Quality in Graduate Education* [Washington DC: American Council on Education, 1966]).

6. Kenneth D. Roose and Charles J. Andersen, *A Rating of Graduate Programs* (Washington DC: American Council on Education, 1970).

7. Cartter, *Assessment of Quality*, 107.

8. SC160/III/60/13, W. C. Steere to P. H. Rhinelander, March 3, 1958.

9. SC160/VIII/4/6; SC160/XIV/11/7, FET to R. Lyman, November 21, 1969.

10. SC216/A12/38, Interim Report on the Ford Foundation Special Program in Education Grant to Stanford University, January 13, 1964.

11. SC160/III/60/15, FET to R. D. Mackenzie (draft unsent), November 20, 1960.

12. *Session on Wally*, 66.

Bibliography

ARCHIVAL MATERIALS

Association of Old Crows, Alexandria, VA. Letters, transcripts of oral interviews, and other documents collected regarding the history of electronic countermeasures.

Bancroft Library, University of California, Berkeley.

Bowker, Albert H. Interviews by Harriet Nathan, 1991–ca. 1995. Banc MSS 96/33C.

Bowles, Edward L. Interviews by Arthur L. Norberg, May 6, 1977 (in process).

Fuller, Leonard Franklin. Interviews by Arthur L. Norberg and O. G. Villard Jr. 1973–75. Banc MSS 77/105C.

McCullough, Jack A. Interview by Arthur L. Norberg, April 15, 1974 (in process).

Terman, Frederick Emmons. Interviews by Arthur L. Norberg, Charles Süsskind, and Roger Hahn, 1975. Transcript, 1984, Bancroft Oral History Project on the History of Science and Technology and Stanford Oral History Project, 1984. Banc MSS 87/165C (also at Stanford). (Abbreviated in text as *Terman Interview*.)

Woodyard John R. "Cyclotron and Klystron Development." Banc MSS 84/18C.

Woodyard, John R. Interviews by Arthur L. Norberg, 1980. Banc MSS 84/18C.

Harvard University Archives.

Nathaniel Preston Breed Papers. HUG 300.

William Henry Claflin II Papers. HUG 300.

Arthur Edwin Kennelly Papers. HUG 1479.

Radio Research Laboratory Records. UAV 728.95.1 to .4.

Radio Research Laboratory. Misc. Records of Director Frederick E. Terman, 1942–46. UAV 728.95.2.

Radio Research Laboratory. Records containing Field Stations and Branch Laboratories, 1942–46. UAV 728.95.3.

Radio Research Laboratory. Memos, Forms, Notices. HUF 726.

Hewlett-Packard Company Archives, Palo Alto, CA. David Packard Collection.

Hoover Institution Archives (Stanford University). Herbert Hoover Papers. Post-Presidential subject file, "Stanford University—HH Poll of Faculty."

Institute of Electrical and Electronic Engineers. Frederick E. Terman Associates. Collection (also available at http://engine.ieee.org/history_center/oral_histories)

Massachusetts Institute of Technology, Institute Archives and Special Collections.
Bush, Vannevar. Papers. MC78.
Jackson, Dugald C. Papers. MC5.
Kennelly, Arthur Edwin. Papers. MC328.
Massachusetts Institute of Technology, Office of the Registrar, transcript, Frederick E. Terman, 1924.
Palo Alto (CA) High School, transcript, Frederick E. Terman, 1916. Access courtesy of Patricia Terman.
Princeton University Archives.
Carmen, A. P. Files.
Perrine, F. A. C. Files.
Stanford University. Department of Special Collections and University Archives.
Bailey, Thomas A. Interview. Stanford Oral History Project. 0900/Bailey.
Bloch, Felix. Interview by Charles Weiner, American Institute of Physics, 1968 (copy in 0900/Bloch).
Bloch, Felix. Papers. SC303.
Bourquin, Burnice. "Frederick Emmons Terman, 1900–1982." SCM2.
Brandin, Alf E. Interview by Robert de Roos, 1989. 0900/Brandin.
Davis, Paul H. Interview, 1979 and 1980. Stanford Oral History Project. 0900/Davis.
Dodds, John Wendell. Interview by Frederic O. Glover and Paul R. Hanna, 1983. Stanford Oral History Project. 0900/Dodds.
Edwards, Paul C. Papers. SC170.
Elwell, Cyril Frank. Papers. M0049 (photos in BP, Box 6, Folders 7, 8).
Elwell, Cyril Frank. *Radiotelegraph and Telephone Pioneer, 1908–1958, Inception of the Electronic Era*. Unpublished manuscript, 1958. Cyril Elwell Papers, M0049, Box 1 (also in Terman Papers, SC160/XI/1/14).
Engineering, School of. Records. SC 165.
Engineering, School of. Miscellaneous. Archives #3111.
English, Department of. Records. SC410, accn. 93–104.
Eurich, Alvin C. Interview, 1980. Stanford Oral History Project. 0900/Eurich.
Forsythe, George E. Papers. SC98.
Glover, Frederic O. Interview, 1993. Stanford Oral History Project. 0900/Glover.
Hanna, Paul. Interview by Rebecca Lowen, 1986. 0900/Hanna.
Hansen, W. W. Papers. SC4, SC126.
Humanities and Sciences, School of. Records. SC36.
Johnson, William S. Papers. SC530.
Kaplan, Henry. Papers. SC317.
Kornberg, Arthur. Papers. SC359.
Lederberg, Joshua. Papers. SC186.
Marx, Guido H. Papers. SC129.
Schiff, Leonard I. Papers. SC220.
Sears, Robert R. Interview. Stanford Oral History Project. 0900/Sears.
Stanford Alumni Association. Files. SC318.
Sterling, J. E. Wallace. Papers. SC216.
Sterling, J. E. Wallace. Papers. SC415, accn. 93–061.
Sterling, J. E. W. Remarks at Stanford Associates' Uncommon Man Award Dinner for Frederick E. Terman, December 7, 1978.

Terman, Frederick E. Oral history interview by Raymond Henle, Hoover Institution, January 1970. 0900/Terman/1970.

Terman, Frederick E. Papers. SC160.

Terman, Lewis Madison. Papers. SC38.

Tresidder, Donald B. Papers. SC151.

Varian, Russell H. and Sigurd. Papers. M508.

Varian Associates Oral History Collection. Interviews by Sharon Mercer, 1989, with Marvin Chodorow, Edward Ginzton, Theodore Moreno, Martin Packard, and H. Myrl Stearns. M708.

Webster, David Locke. Papers. SC131D.

Whitaker, Virgil K. Interview by Eleanor Bark and Harvey Hall, 1982. Stanford Oral History Project. 0900/Whitaker.

Wilbur, Ray Lyman. Papers. SC64.

Stanford University, Registrar's Office, transcript, Frederick E. Terman, 1922. Access courtesy of Patricia Terman.

U.S. National Archives. Office of Scientific Research and Development. Record Group 227.

Author's collection.

Niels J. Riemers letter to C. S. Gillmor, July 23, 2002.

Curtis G. Benjamin letter to William Kaufmann, April 26, 1982.

Louis Brown letter to C. S. Gillmor, July 19, 1999.

R. Hanbury-Brown letter to R. N. Bracewell, July 22, 1999.

William Kaufmann letter to C. S. Gillmor, n.d. (August 2001).

Stephen W. Miller memo to C. S. Gillmor, n.d. (February 1999).

Niels J. Riemers (Stanford Office of Technology Licensing) letter to Patricia J. Black, April 23, 1970.

INTERVIEWS CONDUCTED BY AND IN THE COLLECTION OF THE AUTHOR

Moses Abramovitz, conversation, 1998.
Gabriel A. Almond, 2001, and letter, 2001.
Robert Beyers, 2001.
Henry G. Booker, 1973, 1981.
Walter Bortz, 2000.
Burnice Bourquin, 1998.
Albert H. Bowker, 1999, 2000, 2001, 2002.
Ronald N. Bracewell, 1998.
Alf E. Brandin, 1998.
Laura L. Breyfogle, 2000.
E. Howard Brooks, 1999.
Louis Brown, 1999.
Robert R. Buss, 1998.
W. Bliss Carnochan, 2001.
Donald J. Carpenter, 1998, 1999.
Marvin Chodorow, 1997.
Sanford Dornbusch, 1997.
John N. Dyer, 1975.
Mrs. T. L. Eckersley, 1976.
Paul R. Ehrlich, 2001.
Heinz Eulau, 2001.
Arthur Fong, 1999.
Gene F. Franklin, 2001.
Donald Hammond, 2000.
John W. Harbaugh, conversation, 2001.
Albert Hasdorf, 1998.
Robert A. Helliwell, 1997, 1998, 1999.
Ronald Hilton, 1999.
E. O. Hulburt, 1974.
Eric Hutchinson, conversation, 1998.
Harold Hyde, 1999.
Payton Jordan, 1999.

William Kaufmann, letter, August 2001.
William M. Kays, 1998, 1999.
Donald Kennedy, 2000.
Cassius L. Kirk Jr., 2000, and personal communication, 2001.
Ralph Krause, 2000.
Stanford Kroopf, 2000.
Esther M. Lederberg, 2000, and conversation, 1999.
Hewlett Lee, 2000.
Sang Soo Lee, correspondence, 2000.
David Leeson, 1999.
Helen Liddle Leppert, 1998.
John G. Linvill, 1998, and document provided of 1997.
Walter F. W. Lohnes, 1999.
Richard W. Lyman, 1998, and conversation, 2001.
Laurence A. and Dallas Manning, 1998, 1999, and document provided 1998.
Mrs. Thomas E. Marr, 2000.
Harden M. McConnell, 2001.
William McGuigan, 2000.
Stephen W. Miller, 2000, memorandum, February 1999.
William F. Miller, 2000.
Robert W. Moulton, 2001.
Roxanne Nilan, 2002.
Louise Hewlett Nixon, 2000.
Haeng Ung Park, correspondence, 2000.
Elizabeth Patton, 1999.
David D. Perkins, 2001.
Byron and Nelle Phillips, 1998.
William R. Rambo, 1998.
Peter Raven, correspondence, 2002.
Eva Fenn Reynolds, 2000.
William C. Reynolds, conversation, 2001.
Eugene Rickensrud, conversation, 2001.
David Ridgway, 1999.
Robert Rosenzweig, 1998.
Lawrence V. Ryan, 1999.
Martin Ryle, 1976.
Emmy Lanning Shockley, conversation, 2000.
Marci Smith, 2000.
Otto J. M. Smith, 2000.
Robert Soderman, 1998.
William E. Spicer, 2000.
Henry Taube, 2001.
Lewis M. Terman II, 2000, and correspondence, 2000.
Terence C. Terman, 1998, 1999, 2000.
Merle A. Tuve, 1974.
Lyman P. Van Slyke, 2001.
Oswald G. Villard Jr., 1997, 1998, 1999.
Walter G. Vincenti, 1999, 2000.
Virginia Walbot, 2000.
Charles Yanofsky, 2001.
Susie Rathman Zaremba, 2000.
Bruno H. Zimm, correspondence, 2001.
Stanford Research Institute: retired engineering and contract staff members' group discussion, 2000, included Morse Cavender, William E. Evans, Charles F. Hilly Jr., Fred Kamphoefner, William McGuigan, Stephen W. Miller, Donald Nielson, Jerre D. Noe, and Donald R. Scheuch.

PUBLISHED MATERIALS

A Session on Wally: Transcription of an Oral History about J. E. Wallace Sterling. Stanford Oral History Project, 1985. Portions appeared in *Stanford Magazine* (winter 1985).
Agnew, Harold M., and Raemer E. Schreiber. "Norris E. Bradbury." In *Bibliographical Memoirs, National Academy of Sciences*, vol. 75, 58–69. Washington DC: National Academy Press, 1998.
Allison, David Kite. *New Eye for the Navy: The Origin of Radar at the Naval Research Laboratory*. NRL Report 8466. Washington DC: Naval Research Laboratory, September 29, 1981.
Almond, Gabriel A. "Political Science: The History of the Discipline." In *A New Hand-*

book of Political Science, ed. Robert E. Goodin and Hans-Dieter Klingemann, ch. 2. New York: Oxford University Press, 1996.

Almond, Gabriel A., and Sidney Verba. *The Civic Culture: Political Attitudes and Democracy in Five Nations*. Princeton, NJ: Princeton University Press, 1963.

Alvarez, Luis. "Alfred Lee Loomis, 1887–1975." *Biographical Memoirs, National Academy of Science* 51 (1980): 309–41.

Andreopoulos, Spyros, ed. "Stanford University Medical Center: 25 years of Discovery." *Stanford Medicine* (fall 1984).

Appleton, E. V., and M. A. F. Barnett. "Local Reflections of Wireless Waves from the Upper Atmosphere." *Nature* 115 (1925): 333–34.

Atlas of the City of Boston. Philadelphia, PA: G. W. Bromley and Co., 1928.

Barron's Magazine, June 13, 1955.

Bartholomew, Karen. "Frederic O. Glover: Exceptional Stanford Man." *Sandstone & Tile* 18, no. 1 (winter 1994): 3–19.

Bartholomew, Karen, and Claude Brinegar. "Old Chemistry: One of Jane Stanford's Noble Buildings." *Sandstone & Tile* 23, no. 1 (winter 1999): 3–10.

Bartholomew, Karen, Claude Brinegar, and Roxanne Nilan. *A Chronology of Stanford University and its Founders, 1824–2000*. Stanford, CA: Stanford Historical Society, 2001.

Bartholomew, Karen, and Roxanne Nilan. "Stanford Observed" (Centennial Supplement to the *Stanford Observer*). Stanford University News Service, June 1991.

Baseball-Reference.com.

Baumberger, J. Perry. "A History of Biology at Stanford University." *Bios* 25, no. 3 (October 1954): 123–47.

Baxter, James Phinney. *Scientists Against Time*. Boston: Little, Brown and Company, 1946.

Benedict, Donald L., Kun Mo Chung, Franklin A. Long, Thomas L. Martin, and Frederick E. Terman. "Survey Report on the Establishment of the Korea Advanced Institute of Science." Prepared for USAID. December 1970.

Beyerchen, Alan. "On Strategic Goals as Perceptual Filters: Interwar Responses to the Military Potential of Radar in Germany, the UK and the US." No. 15 in *Tracking the History of Radar*, ed. Oskar Blumtritt, Hartmut Petzold, and William Aspray. New York: Institute of Electrical and Electronic Engineers, 1994.

Beyers, Bob. "Ken Cuthbertson: Stanford's Financial Architect." *Sandstone & Tile* 23, nos. 2–3 (spring/summer 2000): 14–21.

"Biographical Sketch of Melville Eastham." General Radio Company, May 25, 1944. (Copy courtesy of Henry Hall.)

Birdsall, Paul. "Neutrality and Economic Pressures, 1914–1917." *Science and Society* 3 (spring 1939): 217–28.

Blinks, Lawrence R. "Hooked on Biology: A Memoir of 50 Years at Stanford." *Sandstone & Tile* 16, no. 4 (fall 1992): 15–18.

Bliven, Bruce. "The Innocent Decade." In *Stanford Mosaic: Reminiscences of the First Seventy-Five Years at Stanford University*, ed. Edith R. Mirrielees. Stanford, CA: Stanford University Press, 1962.

Bloch, Felix. "William Webster Hansen." *Biographical Memoirs, National Academy of Sciences* 27 (1952): 121–37.

Blumtritt, Oskar, Hartmut Petzold, and William Aspray, eds. *Tracking the History of Radar*. New York: Institute of Electrical and Electronic Engineers, 1994.

Bohemian Club. *History, Officers and Committees, Former Members, In Memoriam, House Rules, Grove Rules*. San Francisco: November 1973.

———. *History, Officers and Committees, Incorporation, Constitution, By-Laws and Rules, Former Officers, Members, In Memoriam*. San Francisco: January 20, 1960.

Boston Evening Herald, February 28, 1939.

Bowen, E. G. *Radar Days*. Bristol, Eng.: Adam Hilger, 1987.

Bowker, Albert. "Quality and Quantity in Higher Education." *Journal of the American Statistical Association* (March 1965): 1–15.

Bradbury, N. E. "Electron Attachment and Negative Ion Formation in Oxygen and Oxygen Mixtures." *Physical Review* 44 (December 1933): 883.

———. "Fundamental Mechanisms in the Ionosphere." *Journal of Applied Physics* 8, no. 11 (November 1937): 709–17.

———. "Ionization, Negative-Ion Formation, and Recombination in the Ionosphere." *Journal of Geophysical Research* 43 (March 1938): 55–66.

Bradbury, N. E., and W. T. Sumerlin. "Night-Sky Light and Nocturnal E-layer Ionization." *Journal of Geophysical Research* 45, no. 1 (March 1940): 19–24.

Breit, G., and M. A. Tuve. "A Radio Method for Estimating the Height of the Conducting Layer." *Nature* 116 (1925): 357.

Brewster-Raph, composers. "Big Boy Jess of the Western Air Express." 1929.

Brown, Hugh Alexander. *Radio Frequency Electrical Measurements*. New York: McGraw-Hill, 1931.

Brown, Louis. "An Annotated Bibliography of Radar History." No. 19 in *Tracking the History of Radar*, ed. Oskar Blumtritt, Hartmut Petzold, and William Aspray. New York: Institute of Electrical and Electronic Engineers, 1994.

———. *A Radar History of World War II: Technical and Military Imperatives*. Bristol, Eng.: Institute of Physics Publishers, 1999.

———. "Significant Effects of Radar on the Second World War." No. 6 in *Tracking the History of Radar*, ed. Oskar Blumtritt, Hartmut Petzold, and William Aspray. New York: Institute of Electrical and Electronic Engineers, 1994.

Bryant, John H. "Generations of Radar." No. 1 in *Tracking the History of Radar*, ed. Oskar Blumtritt, Hartmut Petzold, and William Aspray. New York: Institute of Electrical and Electronic Engineers, 1994.

Bryant, John H., William Aspray, Andrew Goldstein, and Frederik Nebeker, eds. *Rad Lab: Oral Histories Documenting the World War II Activities of the MIT Radiation Laboratory*. New Brunswick, NJ: Center for History of Electrical Engineering, Institution of Electrical and Electronic Engineers, 1993.

Buderi, Robert. *The Invention that Changed the World*. New York: Touchstone, 1997.

Bunting, Bainbridge. *Harvard: An Architectural History*. Ed. Margaret Henderson Floyd. Cambridge, MA: Harvard University Press, 1985.

Burchard, John. *QED: MIT in World War II*. New York: John Wiley and Sons, 1948.

Burns, Russell, ed. *Radar Development to 1945*. London: Peter Peregrinus Ltd., 1988.

Bush, Vannevar. "Arthur E. Kennelly." *Biographical Memoirs, National Academy of Sciences* 22 (1941): 83–119.

———. *Pieces of the Action*. New York: William Morrow, 1970.

Bush, Vannevar, and R. D. Booth. "Power System Transients." *Transactions, American Institute of Electrical Engineers* 44 (1925): 80–97, and Discussion, 97–103.

Bylinsky, Gene. "California's Great Breeding Ground for Industry." *Fortune*, June 1974.

Callick, E. B. *Metres to Microwaves: British Development of Active Components for Radar Systems 1937 to 1944*. London: Peter Peregrinus Ltd., 1990.

Carnegie Institution of Washington. *Year Book No. 38* (1939): 87–88.

Carnochan, Bliss. "English at Stanford, 1891–2000: A Brief History." *Sandstone & Tile* 26, no. 1 (winter/spring 2002): 3–15.

Cartter, Allan M. *An Assessment of Quality in Graduate Education*. Washington DC: American Council on Education, 1966.

Chamber News (Palo Alto, California) 19, no. 9 (November 1965).

Chicago Tribune, May 26, 1957.

China Post (Taipei, Taiwan), July 7, 1968, and July 18, 1972.

Chosun Ilbo (Seoul, Korea), December 11, 1975.

Chubb, L. W. "The Crest Voltmeter." *Transactions, American Institute of Electrical Engineers* 36 (1916): 109–16.

Clark, Birge. *An Architect Grows Up in Palo Alto*. Palo Alto, CA: Palo Alto Historical Association files, Palo Alto City Library, 1982.

Clark, J. Cameron, and Harris J. Ryan. "Spark Gap Discharge Voltages at High Frequencies." *Transactions, American Institute of Electrical Engineers* 33 (1914): 973–87.

Clark, Philip C., and Charles E. Miller. "The High-Voltage Wattmeter." *Transactions, American Institute of Electrical Engineers* 43 (1924): 1124–29.

Cockburn, Robert. "The Radio War." *Institution of Electrical Engineers* 132 (part A) no. 6 (October 1985): 423–34.

Conant, Jennet. *Tuxedo Park: A Wall Street Tycoon and the Secret Palace of Science that Changed the Course of World War II*. New York: Simon and Schuster, 2002.

Craig, Gordon. *Campus Report* (Stanford University, Palo Alto, CA) 11, no. 40 (July 11, 1979): 4–5.

Crouch, Kenneth W. "Students' Army Training Corps." *Stanford 1920 Quad* 26 (1919): 84–89.

Cuthbertson, Kenneth M. "Long-Range Financial Planning." In *Long-Range Planning in Higher Education*, ed. Owen A. Knorr. Boulder, CO: Western Interstate Commission for Higher Education, 1965.

Cutler, Leland W. *America Is Good to a Country Boy*. Stanford, CA: Stanford University Press, 1954.

Daily Palo Alto (title changed to *Stanford Daily* in 1926), Stanford University.

Daily Palo Alto Times (title changed to *Palo Alto Times* in 1938), Palo Alto, CA.

Dallas Times Herald, July 11, 1965.

Davis, Margo, and Roxanne Nilan. *The Stanford Album: A Photographic History, 1885–1945*. Stanford, CA: Stanford University Press, 1989.

Davis, Nuel Pharr. *Lawrence and Oppenheimer*. New York: Simon and Schuster, 1968.

Davis, Tenney L., and H. M. Goodwin. *A History of the Departments of Chemistry and Physics at the M.I.T., 1865–1933*. Cambridge, MA: MIT Press, 1933.

DeConde, Alexander. "Thomas A. Bailey: Teacher, Scholar, Popularizer." *Pacific Historical Review* 56 (May 1987): 161–93.

De Forest, Lee. "Recent Developments in the Work of the Federal Telegraph Company." *Proceedings, Institute of Radio Engineers* 1 (1913): 37–51.

De Maria, Michelangelo, Mario Grilli, and Fabio Sebastiani, eds. *The Restructuring of Physical Sciences in Europe and the United States, 1945–1960*. Singapore: World Scientific, 1989.

Degler, Carl N. "David Potter." *American Historical Review* 76 (October 1971): 127–75.

Deighton, Len. *Battle of Britain*. New York: Coward, McCann and Geoghegan, 1980 (first American edition).

Devereux, Tony. "Strategic Aspects of Radar at Sea." No. 8 in *Tracking the History of Radar*, ed. Oskar Blumtritt, Hartmut Petzold, and William Aspray. New York: Institute of Electrical and Electronic Engineers, 1994.

Djerassi, Carl. *The Pill, Pygmy Chimps, and Degas' Horse: The Autobiography of Carl Djerassi*. New York: Basic Books, 1992.

———. *Steroids Made it Possible*. Washington DC: American Chemical Society, 1990.

Domhoff, G. William. *The Bohemian Grove and Other Retreats: A Study in Ruling-Class Cohesiveness*. New York: Harper and Row, 1974.

Dupen, Douglas W. "History and Development." In *The Stanford Two-Mile Accelerator*, ed. Richard Neal, 27–38. New York: W. A. Benjamin, 1968.

Ehrlich, Paul R. *The Population Bomb*. New York: Ballantine, 1968.

Elliott, Orrin Leslie. *Stanford University: The First Twenty-Five Years*. Stanford, CA: Stanford University Press, 1937.

Elwell, Cyril F. *Der Poulsen-Lichtbogengenerator*. Trans. A. Semm and F. Gerth. Berlin: Springer, 1926. (There is a 1923 English edition that this author has not seen.)

Enochs, Hugh. "Electronics Research Community Develops Around Stanford Laboratories." *The Tall Tree* (Palo Alto, CA) 1, no. 9 (May 1958).

Epel, David. "Stanford by the Sea: A Brief History of Hopkins Marine Station." *Sandstone & Tile* 16, no. 4 (fall 1992): 3–11.

Feynman, Richard P., Robert B. Leighton, and Matthew Sands. *The Feynman Lectures on Physics*. 3 vols. Redwood City, CA: Addison-Wesley, 1963–65.

Flexner, Abraham. *Medical Education in the United States and Canada*. Boston, MA: Merrymount Press, 1910.

Forman, Paul. "Behind Quantum Electronics: National Security as Basis for Physical Research in the United States, 1940–1960." *Historical Studies in the Physical and Biological Sciences* 18 (1987): 149–229.

Franklin, William Suddards, Barry MacNutt, and Rollin L. Charles. *An Elementary Treatise on Calculus*. South Bethlehem, PA: The authors, 1913.

Franklin, William Suddards, and Frederick Emmons Terman. *Transmission Line Theory, and Some Related Topics*. Lancaster, PA: Franklin and Charles, 1926.

Fuller, L. F. "Continuous Waves in Long-distance Radio-telegraphy." *Transactions, American Institute of Electrical Engineers* 34 (1915): 809–27.

Furer, Julius A. *Adminstration of the Navy Department in World War II*. Washington DC: Department of the Navy, 1959.

Galison, Peter, and Bruce Hevly, eds. *Big Science: The Growth of Large-Scale Research*. Stanford, CA: Stanford University Press, 1992.

Galison, Peter, Bruce Hevly, and Rebecca Lowen, "Controlling the Monster: Stanford and the Growth of Physics Research, 1935–1962." In *Big Science: The Growth of Large-Scale Research*, ed. Peter Galison and Bruce Hevly, 46–77. Stanford, CA: Stanford University Press, 1992.

Gebhard, Louis A. *Evolution of Naval Radio-Electronics and Contributions of the Naval Research Laboratory*. NRL Report 8,300. Washington DC: Naval Research Laboratory, 1979.

Geiger, Roger L. *Research and Relevant Knowledge: American Research Universities Since World War II*. New York: Oxford University Press, 1993.

Gibbons, James F. "The Role of Stanford University." In *The Silicon Valley Edge*, ed. Chong-Moon Lee, William F. Miller, Marguerite Gong Hancock, and Henry S. Rowen. Stanford, CA: Stanford University Press, 2000.

Gibson, Weldon B. *SRI: The Founding Years*. Los Altos, CA: Public Services Center, 1982.

———. *SRI: The Take-Off Days*. Los Altos, CA: Public Services Center, 1986.

Gillmor, C. Stewart. "The Big Story: Gregory Breit, Merle Tuve and Ionospheric Physics at the Carnegie Institution of Washington." *History of Geophysics* 5 (1994): 133–41.

———. "Early History of Upper Atmospheric Physics Research in Antarctica." In *Upper Atmosphere Research in Antarctica*, ed. L. J. Lanzerotti and C. G. Park, Antarctic Research Series, 29: 236–62. Washington DC: American Geophysical Union, 1978.

———. "Federal Funding and Knowledge Growth in Ionospheric Physics." *Social Studies of Science* 16 (1986): 105–33.

———. "The History of the Term 'Ionosphere.'" *Nature* 262, no. 5,567 (July 29, 1976): 347–48.

———. "Ionospheric and Radio Physics in Australian Science Since the Early Days." In *International Science and National Scientific Identity*, ed. R. W. Home and S. G. Kohlstedt, 181–204. Netherlands: Kluwer, 1991.

———. "Lloyd Viel Berkner." In *Dictionary of Scientific Biography*, ed. Charles C. Gillispie, 17: 73–75. New York: Charles Scribner's Sons, 1990.

———. "Stanford Sadie and the Early Years of KZSU Radio Broadcasting." *Sandstone & Tile* 23, no. 1 (winter 1999): 11–20.

———. "Threshold to Space: Early Studies of the Ionosphere." In *Space Science Comes of Age*, ed. Paul A. Hanle and Von Del Chamberlain, 101–14. Washington DC: Smithsonian Institution Press, 1981.

———. "Wilhelm Altar, Edward Appleton, and the Magneto-Ionic Theory." *Proceedings, American Philosophical Society* 126, no. 5 (1982): 395–440.

Gilpin, Robert. *American Scientists and Nuclear Weapons Policy*. Princeton, NJ: Princeton University Press, 1962.

Ginzton, Edward L. "An Informal History of SLAC—Part One: Early Accelerator Work at Stanford." *SLAC BEAM LINE* (Stanford, CA). Special issue no. 2 (April 1983).

———. "The $100 Idea." *IEEE Spectrum* 12, no. 2 (February 1975): 30–39.

———. *Times to Remember: The Life of Edward L. Ginzton*. Berkeley, CA: Blackberry Creek Press, 1995.

Glover, Frederic O. "Fred Terman's Paper Trail: A Goldmine of Scientific Research." *Stanford Historical Society Newsletter* (winter 1979): 10–13. A shorter version appeared in *Stanford Observer* (April 1979): 5.

Goldberger, M. L., B. A. Maher, and P. Ebert Flattau. *Research-Doctorate Programs in the United States: Continuity and Change*. Committee for the Study of Research-Doctorate Programs in the United States. Washington, DC: National Academy Press, 1995.

Goldstein, Andrew. "Some Unpublished U.S. Sources for Radar History." No. 18 in *Tracking the History of Radar*, ed. Oskar Blumtritt, Hartmut Petzold, and William Aspray. New York: Institute of Electrical and Electronic Engineers, 1994.

Goodin, Robert E., and Hans-Dieter Klingemann, eds. "The Discipline." In *A New Handbook of Political Science*, ed. R. E. Goodin and H.-D. Klingemann, 101–14. New York: Oxford University Press, 1996.

———. *A New Handbook of Political Science*. New York: Oxford University Press, 1996.

Graham, Hugh Davis, and Nancy Diamond. *The Rise of American Research Universities: Elites and Challenges in the Postwar Era*. Baltimore, MD: Johns Hopkins University Press, 1997.

Greenberg, Daniel S. *The Politics of Pure Science*. New York: New American Library, 1967.

———. *Science* 160 (May 17, 1968): 744–48.

Guerlac, Henry E. *Radar in World War II*. 2 vols. New York: Tomash Publishers and American Institute of Physics, 1987. (Edited and condensed version of original 1947 unpublished report in three volumes.)

Hamrdla, G. Robert. "Four Decades of Stanford Overseas Studies." *Sandstone & Tile* 24, nos. 2–3 (spring/summer 2000): 8–13.

Hansen, William W. "A Type of Electrical Resonator." *Journal of Applied Physics* 9 (October 1938): 654–63.

Hansen, William W., and J. G. Beckerley. "Concerning New Methods of Calculating Radiation Resistance, Either With or Without Ground." *Proceedings, Institute of Radio Engineers* 24 (1936): 1594.

———. "Radiation from an Antenna Over a Plane Earth of Arbitrary Characteristics." *Journal of Applied Physics* 7 (1936): 220.

Hansen, William W., and L. M. Hollingsworth. "Design of 'Flat-Shooting' Antenna Arrays." *Proceedings, Institute of Radio Engineers* 27, no. 2 (February 1939): 137–43.

Hansen, William W., and J. R. Woodyard. "A New Principle in Directional Antenna Design." *Proceedings, Institute of Radio Engineers* 26, no. 3 (March 1938): 333–45.

"Harvard and Radio Countermeasures." *Harvard Alumni Bulletin* 48, no. 6 (December 8, 1945).

Hevly, Bruce W. *Basic Research Within a Military Context: The Naval Research Laboratory and the Foundations of Extreme Ultraviolet and X-ray Astronomy, 1923–1960*. PhD dissertation, Johns Hopkins University, 1987.

———. "David Locke Webster." *Dictionary of Scientific Biography*, ed. Charles C. Gillispie, 18: 984–86. New York: Charles Scribner's Sons, 1990.

H. J. Ryan, Edison Medallist, 1925. New York: AIEE, 1925.

Hoefner, Don. "Silicon Valley—U.S.A." *Electronic News* (January 11, 18, and 25, 1971).

Hoopes, Robert, and Hubert Marshall, eds. *The Undergraduate in the University, Stanford Study of Undergraduate Education, 1954–56*. Stanford, CA: Stanford University, 1957.

Hoover, Theodore J. "Training the Engineers of Tomorrow." *Stanford Illustrated Review* (May 1926).

Hund, August. *High-Frequency Measurements*. New York: McGraw-Hill, 1933.

———. *Hochfrequenzmesstechnik*. Berlin: J. Springer, 1922.

Hutchinson, Eric. *The Department of Chemistry, Stanford University, 1891–1976: A Brief Account of the First Eighty-Five Years*. Stanford, CA: Stanford University, Dept. of Chemistry, 1977.

IEEE Grid (San Francisco, CA) (April 1966), 9–10.

Industrial and Housing Review (Los Altos, CA), September 1956.

Institute for Defense Analyses. *Annual Report*. Arlington, VA: IDA, 1957.

Johnson, William S. *A Fifty-Year Love Affair with Organic Chemistry*. Washington DC: American Chemical Society, 1998.

Jones, R. V. *Most Secret War*. London: Hamish Hamilton, 1978.

KAIS. Seoul, Korea: Korea Advanced Institute of Science, 1971.

Kaiser, Walter. "The Development of Electron Tubes and of Radar Technology: The

Relationship of Science and Technology." No. 12 in *Tracking the History of Radar*, ed. Oskar Blumtritt, Hartmut Petzold, and William Aspray. New York: Institute of Electrical and Electronic Engineers, 1994.

Karapetoff, Vladimir. *The Electric Circuit*. New York: McGraw-Hill, 1912.

———. *Electrical Engineering Laboratory Notes*. Ithaca, NY: Cornell University, 1906.

———. *Elementary Electrical Testing*. New York: John Wiley and Sons, 1913.

———. *Engineering Applications of Higher Mathematics*. 5 vols. New York: John Wiley and Sons, 1912–16.

———. *Experimental Electrical Engineering*. 2 vols. 3rd ed. New York: John Wiley and Sons, 1922–27.

———. *The Magnetic Circuit*. New York: McGraw-Hill, 1911.

Kaplan, Gadi. "Charles Concordia." *IEEE Spectrum* 36, no. 6 (June 1999): 28–33.

Keniston, Hayward. *Graduate Study in the Arts and Sciences at the University of Pennsylvania*. Philadelphia: University of Pennsylvania Press, 1959.

Kennelly, Arthur Edwin. *The Application of Hyperbolic Functions to Electrical Engineering Problems*. London: University Press, 1912.

———. *Artificial Electric Lines*. New York: McGraw-Hill, 1917.

———. *Chart Atlas of Complex Hyperbolic and Circular Functions*. Cambridge, MA: Harvard University Press, 1913.

———. *Tables of Complex Hyperbolic and Circular Functions*. Cambridge, MA: Harvard University Press, 1913.

Kenny, Martin, ed. *Understanding Silicon Valley: The Anatomy of an Entrepreneurial Region*. Stanford, CA: Stanford University Press, 2000.

Kern, Ulrich. "Review Concerning the History of German Radar Technology up to 1945." No. 9 in *Tracking the History of Radar*, ed. Oskar Blumtritt, Hartmut Petzold, and William Aspray. New York: Institute of Electrical and Electronic Engineers, 1994.

Kerr, Clark. *The Uses of the University*. Cambridge, MA: Harvard University Press, 1963.

Kiester, Edwin, Jr. *Donald Tresidder: Stanford's Overloooked Treasure*. Stanford, CA: Stanford Historical Society, 1992.

Kingsley, F. A., ed. *The Applications of Radar and Other Electronic Systems in the Royal Navy in World War 2*. London: Macmillan, 1995.

Kirkpatrick, Paul. "David Locke Webster." *Biographical Memoirs, National Academy of Sciences* 53 (1982): 121–37.

Kneitel, Tom. *Radio Station Treasury, 1900–1946*. Commack, NY: CRB Research, 1986.

Knoles, George H. "History of Western Civilization at Stanford." *The Stanford Historian* (Stanford University) 6 (April 1980): 8–15.

———. "The Stanford History Department: An Historical Sketch, 1891–1971." Unpublished paper, 1997. (Copy courtesy of Roxanne Nilan.)

Knuth, Donald E. "George Forsythe and the Development of Computer Science." *Communications of the ACM* 15, no. 8 (August 1972): 721–26.

Kummritz, Herbert. "On the Development of Radar Technologies in Germany up to 1945." No. 2 in *Tracking the History of Radar*, ed. Oskar Blumtritt, Hartmut Petzold, and William Aspray. New York: Institute of Electrical and Electronic Engineers, 1994.

Lécuyer, Christophe. *Making Silicon Valley: Engineering Culture, Innovation, and Industrial Growth, 1930–1970*. PhD dissertation, Stanford University, 2000.

Legge, Robert Thomas, M.D. *History of the Sons of Toil Camp—Bohemian Grove, 1905–58*. Typescript, Monte Rio, CA, November 1958. (Copy courtesy of Harold Hyde.)

Leslie, Stuart W. *The Cold War and American Science: The Military-Industrial-Academic Complex at MIT and Stanford*. New York: Columbia University Press, 1993.

Leslie, Stuart W., and Robert H. Kargon. "Selling Silicon Valley: Frederick Terman's Model for Regional Advantage." *Business History Review* 70 (winter 1996): 435–572.

Liebendorfer, Don E. *The Color of Life Is Red*. Stanford, CA: Stanford University, Dept. of Athletics, 1972.

Link, Arthur S., William B. Catton, and William M. Leary Jr. *American Epoch*. New York: Alfred A. Knopf, 1967.

Los Angeles Times, October 13–16, 1963.

Lowen, Rebecca S. *Creating the Cold War University: The Transformation of Stanford*. Berkeley and Los Angeles: University of California Press, 1997.

Lowood, Henry E. "From Steeples of Excellence to Silicon Valley." *Campus Report* (Stanford University, Palo Alto, CA) (March 9, 1988): 11–13.

———. *From Steeples of Excellence to Silicon Valley: The Story of Varian Associates and Stanford Industrial Park*. Palo Alto, CA: Varian Associates, 1988.

———. "History of Science and Engineering at Stanford." Unpublished manuscript, 1989. (Copy courtesy of Roxanne Nilan.)

Luger, Michael I., and Harvey A. Goldstein. *Technology in the Garden: Research Parks and Regional Economic Development*. Chapel Hill: University of North Carolina Press, 1991.

Madrono (Palo Alto High School), 1916–17.

Malecki, E. J., and P. Nijkamp. "Technology and Regional Development: Some Thoughts on Policy." *Environment and Planning C: Government and Policy* 6, no. 4 (1988): 383–99.

Maisel, Charles J., and Teva W. Jones. *The History of SRI: The First Fifteen Years*. Menlo Park, CA: Privately published, 1961.

McAndrews, Rosemary. "The Birthplace of Silicon Valley: A History of Land Development at Stanford University." *Sandstone & Tile* 19, nos. 1–2 (spring 1995): 3–11.

McMahon, A. Michel. *The Making of a Profession: A Century of Electrical Engineering in America*. New York: IEEE Press, 1984.

Massachusetts Institute of Technology (MIT). *Catalog*.

MIT. *Courses of Study*.

MIT. *Directory*.

MIT. *Graduation Exercises*.

MIT. *President's Report*.

MIT. *Yearbook*.

MIT. "Twenty-Five Year Report, Class of 1924." Ed. Henry B. Kane, 1949.

Medeiros, Frank. A. "The Sterling Years at Stanford." *Sandstone & Tile* 9, no. 4 (summer 1985): 3–11.

———. "The Sterling Years at Stanford: A Study in the Dynamics of Institutional Change." PhD dissertation, Stanford University, 1979.

Minton, Henry L. *Lewis M. Terman: Pioneer in Psychological Testing*. New York: New York University Press, 1988.

Mirrielees, Edith R. *Fifty Years of Phi Beta Kappa at Stanford, 1891–1941*. Stanford, CA: Stanford University Press, n.d.

Mitchell, J. Pearce. *Stanford University, 1916–1941*. Stanford, CA: Stanford University Press, 1958.

Moffat, Shannon. "Stanford's Power Line Research Pioneers." *Sandstone & Tile* 12, no. 1 (fall 1987): 3–7.
Morecroft, John Harold. *Electron Tubes and Their Application*. New York: John Wiley and Sons, 1933.
———. *Experimental Radio Engineering*. New York: John Wiley and Sons, 1931.
———. *Principles of Radio Communication*. New York: John Wiley and Sons, 1933.
Morgan, Alfred P. *Wireless Telegraph Construction for Amateurs*. New York: D. Van Nostrand Co., 1910.
Morgan, Jane. *Electronics in the West: The First Fifty Years*. Palo Alto, CA: National Press Books, 1967.
Moullin, Eric Balliol. *The Theory and Practice of Radio Frequency Measurement*. London: Charles Griffin and Co., 1926.
Moulton, Robert. "Fear and Loathing on the Electron Trail." *Sandstone & Tile* 25, no. 1 (winter 2001): 3–13.
Nakagawa, Yasuzo. *Japanese Radar and Related Weapons of World War II*. Ed. Louis Brown, John H. Bryant, and Naohiko Koizumi. Laguna Hills, CA: Aegean Park Press, 1997.
Nalder, R. F. H. *The Royal Corps of Signals: A History of its Antecedents and Development (circa 1800–1955)*. London: Royal Signals Institution, 1958.
Nash, George H. *Herbert Hoover and Stanford University*. Stanford, CA: Hoover Institution Press, 1988.
Neal, Richard B., ed. *The Stanford Two-Mile Accelerator*. New York: W. A. Benjamin, 1968.
Neale, B. T. "CH—the First Operational Radar." In *Radar Development to 1945*, ed. Russell Burns, 132–50. London: Peter Peregrinus Ltd., 1988.
Needell, Allan A. *Science, Cold War and the American State: Lloyd V. Berkner and the Balance of Professional Ideals*. Amsterdam: Harwood Academic Publishers, 2000.
New Republic, May 2, 1960.
Newsweek, February 20, 1961.
Noll, Roger G., ed. *Challenges to Research Institutions*. Washington DC: Brookings Institution Press, 1998.
Norberg, Arthur L. "The Origins of the Electronics Industry on the Pacific Coast." *Proceedings of the IEEE* 64, no. 9 (September 1976): 1314–22.
Norberg, Arthur L., and Robert W. Seidel. "The Contexts for the Development of Radar: A Comparison of Efforts in the United States and the United Kingdom in the 1930s." No. 11 in *Tracking the History of Radar*, ed. Oskar Blumtritt, Hartmut Petzold, and William Aspray. New York: Institute of Electrical and Electronic Engineers, 1994.
Olkin, Ingrid. "A Conversation with Albert H. Bowker." *Statistical Science* 2, no. 4 (1987): 472–83.
Packard, David. *The HP Way: How Bill Hewlett and I Built Our Company*. New York: Harper Business, 1995.
Palo Alto Times (Palo Alto, CA), October 20, 1940; December 25, 1944; September 19, 1945; May 23, 1949, and various issues.
Panofsky, W. K. H. "An Informal History of SLAC—Part Two: The Evolution of SLAC and Its Program." *SLAC BEAM LINE* (Stanford, CA), special issue no. 3 (May 1983).
———. "SLAC and Big Science: Stanford University." In *Big Science: The Growth of Large-Scale Research*, ed. Peter Galison and Bruce Hevly. Stanford, CA: Stanford University Press, 1992.

Peninsula Times Tribune (Palo Alto, CA), December 21, 1982.
Perrine, Frederic Auten Combs. *Conductors for Electrical Distribution*. New York: D. Van Nostrand Company, 1903.
———. *Municipal Monopolies*. Rev. ed. New York: T. Y. Crowell and Company, ca. 1899.
———. *Power Plants of the Pacific Coast*. New York: New York Electrical Society, 1902.
Policy and Strategy for Science and Technology. Ministry of Science and Technology, Republic of Korea, 1975.
Price, Alfred. *The History of U.S. Electronic Warfare, Volume 1: The Years of Innovation—Beginnings to 1946*. Alexandria, VA: Association of Old Crows, 1984.
———. *Instruments of Darkness*. 1967; rpt., London: Granada Publishing, 1979.
Price, Derek J. de Solla. *Little Science, Big Science, . . . and Beyond*. New York: Columbia University Press, 1986.
Ramsey, Rolla Roy. "Experimental Radio." Ann Arbor, MI: Edwards Brothers, 1922. (Mimeographed.)
———. *The Fundamentals of Radio*. Bloomington, IL: Ramsey Publishing Co., 1929.
Republic of Korea, Ministry of Science and Technology. *Policy and Strategy for Science and Technology*. 1975.
Resistance (Stanford, CA [?]) 1, nos. 1–2 (March 9 and April 4, 1967).
Riordan, Michael, and Lillian Hoddeson. *Crystal Fire: The Birth of the Information Age*. New York: W. W. Norton, 1997.
———. "The Moses of Silicon Valley." *Physics Today* (December 1997): 42–47.
Roose, Kenneth D., and Charles J. Andersen. *A Rating of Graduate Programs*. Washington DC: American Council on Education, 1970.
Rowe, A. P. *One Story of Radar*. Cambridge: Cambridge University Press, 1948.
Royden, Halsey. "A History of Mathematics at Stanford." In *A Century of Mathematics in America*, ed. Peter Duren, pt. 2, 237–76. Providence, RI: American Mathematical Society, 1989.
Rummell, Frances V., and Adelaide Paine. "He Searches For 'Steeples' of Talent." *Reader's Digest* (December 1962).
Ryan, Harris J. "The Conductivity of the Atmosphere at High Voltages." *Transactions, American Institute of Electrical Engineers* 23 (1904): 101–34, and Discussion, 135–45 and 168–70.
San Francisco Call, May 9, 1929.
San Francisco Chronicle, October 25, 1940, August 20, 1957, December 21, 1982.
San Jose Mercury-News, February 21, 1965, June 28, 1981, and other issues.
San Mateo (California) Times, July 15, 1965.
Sapolsky, Harvey M. *Science and the Navy: The History of the Office of Naval Research*. Princeton, NJ: Princeton University Press, 1990.
Saxenian, Anna Lee. *Regional Advantage: Culture and Competition in Silicon Valley and Route 128*. Cambridge, MA: Harvard University Press, 1994.
Science and Invention, June 1924.
Seagoe, May V. *Terman and the Gifted*. Los Altos, CA: William Kaufmann, 1975.
Sharp, C. H., and E. D. Doyle. "Crest Voltmeters." *Transactions, American Institute of Electrical Engineers* 36 (1916): 99–107.
Shelton, R. D., and J. C. Prabhakar. "Efficiency Ratios for Engineering Schools." *Proceedings, Institute of Electrical and Electronics Engineers* 59, no. 6 (June 1971): 843–48.

Sibley, Mulford Q., and Philip E. Jacob. *Conscription of Conscience: The American State and the Conscientious Objector, 1940–1947*. Ithaca, NY: Cornell University Press, 1952.

Skilling, Hugh Hildreth. *Do You Teach? Views on College Teaching*. New York: Holt, Rinehart and Winston, 1969. (Second edition published as *Teaching Engineering, Sciences, Mathematics: Guidance by Distinguished Teachers*. Huntington, NY: R. E. Krieger Publishing Co., 1976.)

———. *Electric Transmission Lines*. New York: McGraw-Hill, 1951.

———. *Fundamentals of Electric Waves*. New York: John Wiley and Sons, 1942.

———. *Transient Electric Currents*. New York: London, McGraw-Hill, 1937.

Stanford Alumni Review.

Stanford Alumnus, 1914.

[Stanford] Campus Report.

Stanford Chaparral. February 12, 1975.

Stanford Daily. Various issues, but especially October 2, 1941, November 22, 1948, issues of March and April 1960.

Stanford Daily Magazine, special issue, November 22, 1967.

Stanford Engineering News 52 (July 1965).

Stanford Faculty Staff Newsletter (renamed *Campus Report* in 1968).

Stanford Historical Society Newsletter (winter 1979): 10–13.

Stanford Illustrated Review, February 20, 1917.

Stanford Quad.

Stanford Summer Weekly. August 3, 1961.

Stanford Today no. 7 (spring 1962).

Stanford University. *Annual Register*.

Stanford University. *Commencement, Order of Exercises*.

Stanford University. Guide Memo 75 (June 6, 1962), "Patent Policy for Sponsored Research"; Guide Memo 75 (December 15, 1970), "Patents."

Stanford University. *President's Reports*.

Stanford University. Stanford-Cal Track Meet Program, May 3, 1919 (courtesy of Lloyd McGovern).

Stanford University, School of Medicine. *Bulletin, 1959–60*.

St. Petersburg Times (Florida). October 14 and 15, and November 20, 1971.

Sturgeon, Timothy J. "How Silicon Valley Came to Be." In *Understanding Silicon Valley: The Anatomy of an Entrepreneurial Region*, ed. Martin Kenny, 15–47. Stanford, CA: Stanford University Press, 2000.

Sullivan, Mark. *Our Times: The United States, 1900–1925*. 6 vols. New York: Charles Scribner's Sons, 1926–35.

"Superpower Transmission [session]." Papers. *Transactions, American Institute of Electrical Engineers* 43 (February 1924): 1–103.

Süsskind, Charles. "William Webster Hansen." *Dictionary of Scientific Biography*, ed. Charles C. Gillispie, 6: 104–5. New York: Charles Scribner's Sons, 1990.

Taylor, Tony. "High-Technology Industry and the Development of Science Parks." *Built Environment* 9, no. 1 (1984): 72–78.

Terman, Frederick E. *Administrative History of the Radio Research Laboratory*. Assisted by Oswald G. Villard Jr. Contract OEMsr-411, Radio Research Laboratory, Harvard University, Office of Scientific Research and Development, National Defense Research Committee, Division of Radio Coordination (15). March 21, 1946.

Terman, Frederick Emmons. *Characteristics and Stability of Transmission Systems*. ScD dissertation, MIT, 1924.
———. "The Circle Diagram of a Transmission Network." *Transactions, American Institute of Electrical Engineers* 45 (1926): 1081–92.
———. "Commentary" on "Superpower Transmission" papers. *Transactions, American Institute of Electrical Engineers* 43 (1924): 84–85.
———. "The Development of an Engineering College Program." *Journal of Engineering Education* 58 (May 1968): 1053–55.
———. *Education in Engineering and Science in the U.S.S.R.* Prepared for U.S. Office of Education Mission, December 3–29, 1965 (131 pages).
———. "The Electrical Engineering Research Situation in the American Universities." *Science* 65, no. 1,686 (April 22, 1927): 385–88.
———. "Engineering Growth and the Community." *Journal of Engineering Education* 55 (February 1965): x, xiii. (An extended version appears in *The World of Engineering*, ed. John Whinnery, ch. 11. New York: McGraw-Hill, 1965.)
———. "Feedback Amplifier Design." *Electronics* (January 1937): 12–15, 50.
———. "The Institute Moves Ahead in 1941." *Proceedings, Institute of Radio Engineers* 29, no. 12 (December 1941): 656–57.
———. "The Measurement of Transients." *Transactions, American Institute of Electrical Engineers* 42 (February 1923): 389–93, and Discussion, 393–94.
———. *Measurements in Radio Engineering*. New York: McGraw-Hill, 1935.
———. "Multirange Rectifier Instrument Having the Same Scale Graduation Field for All Ranges." *Proceedings, Institute of Radio Engineers* 23, no. 3 (March 1935): 234–40.
———. *Radio Engineering*. New York: McGraw-Hill, 1932.
———. *Radio Engineer's Handbook*. New York: McGraw-Hill, 1943.
———. "Resonant Lines in Radio Circuits." *Electrical Engineering* 53 (1934): 1046–53.
———. "Scientific and Engineering Manpower in a Highly Competitive World." *Stanford Review* (May–June 1963): 16–22.
———. "Supply of Scientific and Engineering Manpower: Surplus or Shortage?" *Science* (July 30, 1971): 399–405. (A shorter version appeared as "Changing Needs for PhD's," *IEEE Spectrum* [January 1972]: 79–81.)
———. "William Frederick Durand." *Biographical Memoirs, National Academy of Sciences* 48 (1976): 153–93.
Terman, Frederick E., R. R. Buss, W. R. Hewlett, and F. C. Cahill. "Some Applications of Negative Feedback with Particular Reference to Laboratory Equipment." *Proceedings, Institute of Radio Engineers* 27, no. 10 (October 1939): 649–55.
Terman, Frederick E., assisted by Robert Arthur Helliwell and others. *Electronic and Radio Engineering*. New York: McGraw-Hill, 1955.
Terman, Frederick E., and F. W. MacDonald. *Fundamentals of Radio*. New York: McGraw-Hill, 1938.
Terman, Frederick E., and Joseph Mayo Pettit. *Electronic Measurements*. New York: McGraw-Hill, 1952.
Terman, Lewis M. "Genius and Stupidity: A Study of Some of the Intellectual Processes of Seven 'Bright' and Seven 'Stupid' Boys." *Pedagogical Seminary* 13 (1906): 303–73.
———. "Trails to Psychology." In *A History of Psychology in Autobiography*, ed. Carl Murchison, 2: 297–331. Worcester, MA: Clark University Press, 1932.
Terman, Sibyl. Interview in *Link* (Stanford ERL Bulletin), December 1955.

Terman, Sibyl, and Charles Child Walcutt. *Reading: Chaos and Cure*. New York: McGraw-Hill, 1958.

Thiessen, Arthur E. *History of the General Radio Company*. West Concord, MA: General Radio Company, 1965.

Thompson, George Raynor, and Dixie R. Harris. *The Signal Corps: The Outcome (Mid-1943 Through 1945)*. Washington DC: Office of the Chief of Military History, 1966. (In the series *United States Army in World War II, The Technical Services*.)

Thompson, George Raynor, Dixie R. Harris, Pauline M. Oakes, and Dulany Terrett. *The Signal Corps: The Test (December 1941 to July 1943)*. Washington DC: Office of the Chief of Military History, 1957. (In the series *United States Army in World War II, The Technical Services*.)

Timby, Sara. "The Dudley Herbarium: Including a Case Study of Terman's Restructuring of the Biology Department." *Sandstone & Tile* 22, no. 4 (fall 1998): 3–15.

U.S. Department of the Navy, Bureau of Equipment. *List of Wireless Telegraph Stations of the World*. Washington DC: U.S. Government Printing Office, 1909.

U.S. National Bureau of Standards. Interservice Radio Propagation Laboratory. "International Radio Propagation Conference, Held Under Auspices of Wave Propagation Committee, Combined Communications Board." Washington DC: National Bureau of Standards, April 1944. (Mimeographed government report.)

U.S. National Defense Research Commission. American British Laboratory of Division 15. *Administrative Report of the American British Laboratory of Division 15 of the NDRC*. Contract OEMsr-1045. Cambridge, MA: Harvard University, n.d. (ca. 1946).

[U.S.] Radio Research Laboratory (Harvard University). *Very High-Frequency Techniques*, ed. Herbert J. Reich, Louise S. McDowell, et al., with foreward by F. E. Terman. 2 vols. New York: McGraw-Hill, 1947.

U.S. War Production Board. "History of the Radio and Radar Division of the War Production Board and Predecessor Agencies, 1940–1945." Washington DC: War Production Board, November 1, 1945. (Typescript.)

University of Chicago *Record* 2, no. 2 (February 16, 1968).

Van der Bijl, Hendrik J. *The Thermionic Vacuum Tube and Its Applications*. New York: McGraw-Hill, 1920.

Van der Zee, John. *The Greatest Men's Party on Earth: Inside the Bohemian Grove*. New York: Harcourt, Brace, Jovanovich Inc., 1974.

Varian, Dorothy. *The Inventor and the Pilot*. Palo Alto, CA: Pacific Books, 1983.

Veblen, Thorstein. *The Instinct of Workmanship, and the State of the Industrial Arts*. 1918, rpt., New York: Viking Press, 1946.

Villard, O. G., Jr. "Frederick Emmons Terman, 1900–1982." *Biographical Memoirs, National Academy of Sciences* 74 (1998): 308–31.

Walcutt, Charles Child. *Tomorrow's Illiterates: The State of Reading Instruction Today*. Introduction by Jacques Barzun. Boston: Little, Brown, 1961.

Walcutt, Sibyl. "An Attempt to Provide a Basis for Grading and Classifying Red-Green Color Blindness." Unpublished master's thesis, Stanford University, 1928.

Wall Street Journal, December 6, 1961.

Wallis, W. Allen. "The Statistical Research Group, 1942–1945." *Journal of the American Statistical Association* 75, no. 370 (June 1980): 320–30.

Walsh, John. "SLAC: Stanford-AEC Accelerator is Coming Along on Schedule, But Creating Some High Tension." *Science* 143 (March 27, 1964): 1419–21.

———. "Stanford's Search for Solutions." In *Academic Transformation: 17 Institutions Under Pressure*, ed. David Riesman and Verne A. Stadtman, 303–22. New York: McGraw-Hill, 1973.

Wang, Jessica. *American Science in an Age of Anxiety: Scientists, Anticommunism and the Cold War*. Chapel Hill: University of North Carolina Press, 1999.

Watson-Watt, Robert. *Three Steps to Victory*. London: Odhams Press Ltd., 1957. (Revised in 1959 as *The Pulse of Radar*.)

White, Harvey E. *The History of Sons of Toil From 1959*. Typescript, n.d. (Copy courtesy of Harold Hyde.)

Whitehead, J. B., and M. W. Pullen. "The Corona Voltmeter." *Transactions, American Institute of Electrical Engineers* 36 (1916): 809–33, and Discussion, 834–43.

Wiener, Norbert. *Cybernetics, or Control and Communications in the Animal and the Machine*. 2nd ed. Cambridge, MA: MIT Press, 1961.

Wilbur, Ray Lyman. *The Memoirs of Ray Lyman Wilbur, 1875–1949*. Ed. Edgar Eugene Robinson and Paul Carroll Edwards. Stanford, CA: Stanford University Press, 1960.

Wildes, Karl L., and Nilo A. Lindgren. *A Century of Electrical Engineering and Computer Science at MIT, 1882–1982*. Cambridge, MA: MIT Press, 1985.

Wilson, E. O. *The Naturalist*. New York: Island Press, 1994.

Wilson, John L. *Stanford University School of Medicine and the Predecessor Schools: An Historical Perspective*. Stanford, CA: Stanford Medical School, Lane Medical Library, 1999. Electronically published as http://eLane.stanford.edu/wilson/home.html.

Winslow, Ward. *The Making of Silicon Valley: A One-Hundred Year Renaissance*. Santa Clara, CA: The Association, 1995.

———. *Palo Alto: A Centennial History*. Palo Alto, CA: Palo Alto Historical Association, 1993.

———. "Tall Trees: The Palo Alto Stanford Connection." *Sandstone & Tile* 18, no. 2 (spring 1994): 3–12.

Wood, Dallas E., and Norris E. James. *History of Palo Alto*. Palo Alto, CA: A. H. Cawston, 1939.

Work, William R. "Notes on the Measurement of High Voltage." *Transactions, American Institute of Electrical Engineers* 36 (1916): 119–27, and Discussion, 127–46.

Yanofsky, Charles. "Advancing Our Knowledge in Biochemistry, Genetics, and Microbiology Through Studies on Tryptophan Metabolism." *Annual Reviews in Biochemistry* 70 (2000): 1–37.

Zachary, G. Pascal. *Endless Frontier: Vannevar Bush, Engineer of the American Century*. New York: Free Press, 1997.

Index

Frederick Emmons Terman is abbreviated as FET; Stanford University is abbreviated as SU.